MAURICE GEE
Life and Work

MAURICE GEE
Life and Work

Rachel Barrowman

Victoria University Press

TE WHARE WĀNANGA O TE ŪPOKO O TE IKA A MĀUI
VICTORIA
UNIVERSITY OF WELLINGTON

VICTORIA UNIVERSITY PRESS
Victoria University of Wellington
PO Box 600 Wellington
vup.victoria.ac.nz

First published 2015
Reprinted 2015

National Library of New Zealand Cataloguing-in-Publication Data

Barrowman, Rachel, 1963-
Maurice Gee : life and work / Rachel Barrowman.
Includes bibliographical references.
ISBN 978-0-86473-992-6
1. Gee Maurice. 2. Gee, Maurice—Criticism and interpretation.
3. Authors, New Zealand—20th century—Biography. I. Title.
NZ823.2—dc 23

Index by Tordis Flath

This book was researched and written with the support of the Creative New Zealand Michael King Writers' Fellowship.
It is published with the support of a grant from Creative New Zealand.

creative nz
Arts Council of New Zealand Toi Aotearoa

Printed in China by 1010 Printing International

Contents

List of Illustrations

(Unless otherwise indicated, photographs are from the collection of Maurice and Margareta Gee)

After page 184:

After page 368:

At home at Cleveland Terrace, Nelson
Charles Brasch
Kevin Jowsey (Ireland), Tony Stones and Robin Dudding
Moss Gee and Jim Baxter
Moss Gee, Maurie Shadbolt, Dave Walsh and Kevin Jowsey
Nigel Cook
Julie Cook
At Nigel and Julie's
Smiling for Marti Friedlander
Hera Smith
With Hera and Nigel
Len and Nigel
1964 Robert Burns Fellow
With Margaretha Hickman
The new Napier city librarian
New home owners and parents-to-be
Book covers: *The Big Season*, *A Special Flower*, *Plumb*, *Meg*, *Under the Mountain*, *Going West*, *The Scornful Moon*
Family portrait
At the Tomb of Agamemnon
Digging out the septic tank
Writing, Cleveland Terrace
Moments of Invention, with Greg O'Brien
Emily, Nigel, Abi
Menton-bound
At San Gimignano
With Larry Parr on the set of *Fracture*
Auckland Writers and Readers Festival

A Life in Writing; A Writing Life

All the best murders happen in Loomis.[1]

Maurice Gee once described himself as 'a New-Zealandy sort of writer living in a New-Zealandy sort of place . . . writing New-Zealandy sort of books'.[2] It is that 'New Zealanderness', to use C.K. Stead's term, its intense and particular familiarity, that gives Gee's work its essential, central place in New Zealand literary culture: widely read, loved and awarded. His novels have won him many literary prizes. They have examined the domestic lives and drawn the landscapes of New Zealand's provincial towns and middle-class suburbs with, in another critic's words, 'the fidelity of a Balzac'.[3] Yet it is far from a comfortable familiarity. Maurice Gee's fictional New Zealand is a dark place, where murders happen, suicides and drownings, where families hurt and self-destruct, where there is violence and cruelty and evil. The term New Zealandy he took from the Australian novelist Patrick White, who referred to a certain, 'New Zealandy' kind of murder and recognised a 'despair and confusion under the simple, uncomplicated New Zealand surface'.[4] This is Gee's territory.

It has frequently been remarked that it is a curious thing: that such a quiet, reserved, unassuming—ordinary—man as Gee should write such dark and troubling stories. 'The man in the grey cardy', a late profile of him was affectionately titled, encapsulating Gee's abiding impression of gentle ordinariness.[5] Where does the darkness come from?

It is curious too that a man whose instincts tend to privacy should produce novels which both contain and examine self-revelation. More than many writers, more perhaps than most, Gee has written his life into his fiction. He has done so directly—in his *Plumb* trilogy, which draws extensively on his family history, and remains the core of his literary achievement, especially—and in smaller, subtle and allusive ways: in stories, names and places, words and images, in an increasingly rich and familiar symbolic and metaphoric repertoire.

Across his extensive output—seventeen adult novels, thirteen novels for children, a short story collection, and screenplays for television and film, written over more than 50 years—Gee's fictional landscape has drawn from a very particular, personal place.

Looking for the traces of the life in the fiction is at one level an easy game. It gains an added dimension in the case of a writer whose novels most characteristically take biography or autobiography as their frame and the single consciousness as their point of view; whose principal themes include the workings of memory and telling, and the processes of self-knowing—which include concealment and evasion.

Maurice Gee's place in New Zealand's literary history is both large and difficult to define, solid and diffuse. *Plumb*, instantly recognised in 1978 as a classic, and the *Plumb* trilogy established his enduring central position; and somehow set him apart from his contemporaries. From the outset, when he began writing and publishing in the 1950s, while closely connected with the young writers of his own generation, his affinities with his seniors, Sargeson and Brasch, seemed stronger. *Plumb* was only his fifth novel, though published when he was 47. Through three more decades of changing literary fashions, he would go on quietly and steadily doing his own thing—'mov[ing] about in my middle class suburbs', seeking out 'evidence of disorder, passion, of the primitive thing'.[6]

The place from which that fiction arises, and which it inscribes, is both a geographical and an emotional one. He was to end where he began.

1

Beginnings

At Falls Park the boy watched a man dive into the creek and break his neck. It was a Thursday afternoon, a week before Christmas 1940; summer. He was nine years old, barefoot down at the swimming hole with his brothers and their friend Minnie, along with a bunch of other local boys. They watched the man bouncing on his toes at the end of the spring board, showing off to the two young women sitting in their bathing costumes on a blanket by the side of the pool. They had been watching, covertly, for some time, hoping to see something they shouldn't: a bit of cuddling, sex. It did not occur to them—until it was too late—that the man was going to dive. They knew that the pool was a tidal pool, the brackish, green-brown water rising and falling several feet with the Waitematā tide, and that the tide was low that afternoon and the water below the diving board only three feet deep. A boy could still dive, launching himself into a bellyflop as far out as he could. They ran down the bank yelling out to him to stop, 'Don't dive! Don't dive!', but he was already in the air, executing a neat, high pike.

He surfaced face down, his head flopping loosely from side to side. Minnie was the first into the water, and called out to the two women, 'Quick, he is drowning!', for they seemed to think their friend was only skylarking. Another boy ran to fetch the police. When Constable Wakelin arrived he found the two women supporting the man in the water at the bottom of the diving board steps. They pulled him out onto the bank and laid him on the level ground. There was a gash on his head, and a lump, as big as a boy's fist, on the back of his neck.

The constable went to call the doctor. The other boys hared off, home to tell their story. But the girl pleaded with him not to leave, and he was left alone there, the nine-year-old boy, with the kneeling, crying girl and the dying man. That is how he remembers it.

This is Maurice Gee's affective place; here is where his imagination begins, and returns: 'an eely creek', 'an inland creek', 'slow and deep and green'.[1] When he was about three years old he nearly drowned in this creek, one day when his mother was out walking with her three sons and turned to see him floating past under the water, eyes open, tiny fists clenched across his chest, and ran along the bank until she could reach in and pull him out. That is his first creek story.

The creek flowed through the township of Henderson, 12 miles north-west of Auckland: in 1940 a small rural town surrounded by orchards and vineyards. He spent his boyhood, and most of the first 25 years of his life here. His family, however, did not have roots here. His father, Len Gee, was born and brought up in Christchurch, as his own father had been; and like his father, and his father before him, had become a carpenter by trade. Maurice Gee's great-grandfather, Alfred Gee, from the east Midlands town of Northampton, came to New Zealand in 1874, aged 24, with his wife, also 24, Alice Theresa Flynn. She was a Londoner, born in Woolwich, and their marriage was registered in the Poplar district of east London in February 1874, three and a half weeks before they sailed on the *Northampton*, their passages paid by the colonial government under the Vogel assisted immigration scheme.

The Gee family story is a typical one of colonial migration. The great wave of immigration to New Zealand in the nineteenth century came in the 1870s under the Vogel scheme, through which the colonial treasurer, Julius Vogel, sought to rescue the colony from economic depression by borrowing overseas to finance public works and large-scale immigration. At its peak, in 1874, 38,000 new migrants arrived, after the passages, initially subsidised, were made free. The majority of the Vogel immigrants were from Britain and Ireland, many from the Home counties and south Midlands (although Northamptonshire was not, in fact, well represented). They were mostly young, and were domestic servants, agricultural or general labourers, or craftsmen such as carpenters, like the Gees. Also on board the *Northampton*, which reached Lyttelton harbour on 6 June 1874 (after an unusually fast passage), were Alfred's older brother, William, and his wife and young family. Alfred and William's father, George Gee, had been a Northampton carpenter too.

Alfred and Alice Gee lived for the rest of their lives in the working-class suburb of Sydenham in south Christchurch, moving three or four times but never far. Little about their lives is recorded. By the 1890s Alfred was in business with his brother in Linwood as Gee

Bros. The first of Alice and Alfred's two surviving sons, Henry William—known as Harry (and as Pater to his grandsons)—was born in July 1876. In October 1901 he married Ellen, or Helen, Celia Davidson, the daughter of James Davidson, a mine manager, and his wife, Sarah Jane White, at her brother's house in St Albans. The Davidson family had come to Christchurch from Victoria, Australia, when Helen was a year old. Her father's occupation suggests a degree of class difference between the Davidsons and the Gees, although she was working as a domestic servant in Linwood when she married, while her brother William was a saddler. Certainly, the family later understood that Harry Gee had married 'above himself'.

Harry and Helen Gee set up home at 10 Beckenham Street in the suburb of Beckenham, a few streets away from Alfred and Alice, and there they stayed for twenty years, before moving around 1920 out to the seaside suburb of New Brighton. Leonard William, their second son, was born in Beckenham on 22 April 1906, three years after Alfred and followed by sisters Rona, in 1909, and eight years later Kathleen.

Len attended Christchurch Technical High School, until leaving early to be apprenticed to his father. For reasons unknown—although the economic depression of the early 1920s may have been one—the family left Christchurch a few years after having moved to New Brighton and went up north to the Bay of Plenty: by 1924 they were living in Spring Street, Tauranga. Tauranga was a port town and the commercial centre of a predominantly dairy farming district. It was an isolated district in the early 1920s still, with the East Coast main trunk railway line not completed until 1928 and roading poor, but with substantial roading and bridging work under way by the middle of the decade. For the next three or four years Len and his father worked together as building contractors throughout the Bay of Plenty. He was to tell his sons that the two of them built most of the wooden bridges between Katikati and Te Puke.

Maurice Gee grew up listening to stories. The stories his father told were about hard work and hard times—heroic stories, of a kind; but the ones his sons loved best were his boxing stories. As a young man Len Gee was a champion amateur boxer, a rising and popular local star, 'noted as an excellent sport, and a game fighter, win or lose' in the *Bay of Plenty Times* report of the Bay of Plenty Boxing Association's tournament in May 1926, under the headline 'Victory for Gee'. His win, in what had been anticipated as the star bout of the evening but disappointed by being over in the second round, added 'another to his list of successes, and there is every indication', the paper predicted, 'that this young amateur has a very promising future in the ring'.[2]

Boxing was in its golden age in the 1920s: the era of the million-dollar gate and of star fighters like Jack Dempsey ('The Manassa Mauler'), Gene Tunney and George Charpentier ('The Orchid Man'), and in New Zealand as elsewhere of huge popular support. The newspapers—like the young Gee boys—relished the details of both amateur and professional fights. Len Gee's local successes took him four times to the provincial championships in the Auckland Town Hall, the first time in July 1924, at the age of eighteen: competing as a lightweight, he won his first fight, described by the reporter for the *Auckland Star* as 'a well-intentioned mixture of wrestling, quadrille-dancing, and boxing', using 'a straight left with telling effect' to have his opponent on the mat in the middle of the second round, but lost his next.[3] The following year he was again beaten in the eliminating rounds, by Jack Bishara (a name his sons would hear), 'a rugged but clever fighter from Taumarunui'; it was a close fight, however, and Gee was 'roundly applauded on leaving, while a section of the crowd indulged in counting-out tactics'.[4] In 1926 he competed in the national championships in the Municipal Theatre in Napier, at which the 70-plus entries that year marked 'a record as far as the fistic art in the Dominion is concerned', but was beaten in the preliminary light-heavyweight round.[5]

He made it through to the provincial semi-finals the following year and again in 1928, when the tournament took place two days before Tom Heeney from Poverty Bay met Gene Tunney at New York's Yankee Stadium, the only time a New Zealand-born boxer would challenge for the world heavyweight title. Back in Tauranga, this was Len Gee's last fight (at this level at least) and a punishing one. Fighting with an injured right hand, he 'gave the better display of boxing' in the first round but was unable to maintain his stamina against a 'fast hard-hitting opponent . . . The final round was torrid, and crowded with incident, both boxers hitting hard to head and body. Forsyth's jolts to the point distressed the Tauranga lad, who gamely boxed back until a fast right swing put him down'. Up again on the eighth count, 'his defence was gone', however, 'and another right swing flush to the jaw put him on his back. Pluckily he got to his feet near the end of the count, the crowd cheering him for his grit', before the referee stopped the fight. He received 'an enthusiastic ovation' before collapsing on his way to his corner, and 'it was several minutes before he could leave the ring'.[6]

What his sons heard was that their father gave up boxing on his doctor's instructions after a particularly bruising fight. Perhaps it was this one. But perhaps, too, his giving up boxing around this time had something to do with the fact that he was to get married early the following year.

Lyndahl Chapple, the girl he had fallen in love with, was from a very different sort of family from the Gees. It was a family she believed—and encouraged her sons to believe—was 'special'. In common with the Gees, however, the Chapples had moved to Tauranga from Christchurch in the mid-1920s; although as far as is known it was in the Bay of Plenty not Christchurch—though both had spent their teenage years there—that Len and Lyndahl met.

Her mother told a romantic story of how she and Lyndahl's father met. It was at a church picnic in Ballarat that James Henry George Chapple first set eyes on Florence Eugenie Gough, 'a demure young girl cutting sandwhiches [sic] and making tea for the elders . . . in the tent'. Enchanted, he found out where she lived: a notice in the window advertised French and music lessons, and he applied to learn the piano in the hope of seeing her again. There came a day when Mrs Gough had to go out of a sudden, and left her daughter to take the lesson. Or was it possible, her granddaughter later speculated, that Mary Gough, having sized him up as 'a decent young man with prospects, pulled on her gloves with a purpose' and left the two to become acquainted on the double piano stool?[7]

Florence's parents, Mary Froomes, an innkeeper's daughter, and Henry Gough, a plumber—who had looked so handsome in his 'brown corduroy jacket'[8] when he came on a job for her father—emigrated after their marriage (possibly in Gloucestershire) to Victoria, Australia. Florence, born in Ballarat in January 1870, was the seventh of eight children, but grew up a lonely child, with her three sisters some years older.

James Chapple had grown up an only child among women. Born in Rockhampton, Queensland, in 1865, he was the first-born son of William Sandy Chapple, a butcher, and his wife, Elizabeth Bancroft, who were from Somerset and Manchester respectively and had emigrated to Australia two or three years before. When his son was twenty months old William Chapple drowned, and a second son born four months later died in infancy. Elizabeth took James back to England, to her brother-in-law Walter Chapple's house in Ashcott in Somerset, where he was raised by his two maiden aunts and educated at the private girls' school they ran, while his mother went away to America. He was sixteen or so and apprenticed as a plumber when she came back to reclaim him (against the wishes of his aunts) and took him back to Australia.

Faith, not music, was the foundation of Florence and James Chapple's long and devoted marriage. Both were members of the Salvation Army when they met, and they were married, on 27 August 1890, at the army barracks in 'Coalopolis' (Newcastle), New South Wales, she wearing a white sash over her lieutenant's uniform blue dress (her bridesmaid a crimson one), he in the captain's red, yellow and blue.[9] Over the next few years the couple served in New South Wales, South Australia and Victoria, before being appointed to Invercargill, in the cold far south of New Zealand, in 1893. James arrived at Bluff in January on the *Mawhera*, Florence two months later on the *Tarawera* with the first two of, eventually, fifteen children—nine daughters (one dying in infancy) and six sons—rather too many, thought Florence's very proper mother (surely a clergyman should have known better?). Their itinerant life of service to the church continued while the family grew. Between 1893 and 1898 they were at Invercargill, Ōamaru, Dunedin, Gore, Blenheim, Ashburton and, finally, Christchurch, where James Chapple was briefly editor of the army newspaper the *War Cry* before leaving the Salvation Army to begin training for the Presbyterian ministry.

The Presbyterian church sent Chapple as a home missionary to Kūmara, a West Coast goldmining town with four churches and fifteen hotels and a six-bedroomed manse whose weatherboards rotted in the endemic West Coast rain and hot sun: it was the church's practice, Florence was sure, to send the home missionaries to 'hard difficult places to see what they were made of'.[10] She bore two children there, and two more in Eltham, Taranaki, where they spent a further probationary year before James Chapple was ordained in 1903 as a minister in the Presbyterian church at St Andrews in Canterbury, 10 miles north of Timaru.

It was not too many years before James Chapple's increasingly radical political and wayward doctrinal views began to test the tolerance of the Presbyterian church hierarchy. He joined the recently formed New Zealand Socialist Party around 1905, and expressed from the pulpit his support for the interests of the working man. He became a subscribing member of the Rationalist Press Association of London, and read widely, his intellectual interests encompassing Marxism, Darwinism and eugenics. About 1907 the Timaru presbytery made its first, unsuccessful attempt to have him removed; his congregation voted overwhelmingly to stand by him. This was also the year that, in Timaru on 7 May, Harriet Lyndahl, the Chapples' twelfth child and eighth daughter, was born: she was named Harriet after one of the Ashcott aunts, but was always to be known as Lyndahl (a misspelling of Lyndall, the heroine of Olive Schreiner's novel *The Story of an African Farm*).

Three years later the church fathers' concern at James Chapple's heterodoxy came to a head when he helped to organise and chaired a public meeting in Timaru addressed by the visiting English Rationalist Joseph McCabe. Called to account for himself and for having 'given utterance to some disquieting statements' before a public meeting of the presbytery on 13 September 1910, he read a statement—printed in full in the *Timaru Herald* and the *Lyttelton Times*—which argued that 'the new truth of evolution' was consistent with a true and useful religion and a belief in God, and succeeded in forcing the presbytery to ask for his resignation.[11] He gave it to them then and there.

Cast out by his church, he was appointed librarian at the Timaru Public Library (the church fathers might not have wanted him, but he was clearly not wholly in public disfavour), while he found his spiritual place with the more tolerant Unitarians, co-founding the Timaru Unitarian Society and giving lectures under its auspices, from 1912 in the church hall built for him by a benefactor.

The Chapples spent six years in Timaru, living in at least three different houses. One they named Glastonbury after the abbey near Ashcott where, according to legend, King Arthur and Guinevere were buried. But the largest and best, and the house Lyndahl remembered, was the one they called Holleon, after the two eldest sons, Leonard and Hollis: a ten-bedroomed house (which later burned down) on Wai-iti Road in Highfield, with a large cherry orchard, a conservatory and a rose garden. It was 'a funny house', Lyndahl later wrote, just as her father was 'a funny sort of Minister'; 'We don't always have interesting things to eat but we have interesting pictures on the walls and a big bronze statue in the hall and our Father's study is full of valuable books.'[12] She grew to be a romantic, bookish, sensitive, sometimes solitary child, nicknamed by her older sister Dora 'Saint Lyndahl'—'a dreamy sort of kid, at a loss in a large family, happiest when left alone to dream on, and read romantic stories and live out fantasies'; close to her mother, who was the emotional centre of the family.[13] Father was a distant and slightly austere figure, taking his meals in his study each night while he prepared his lectures and sermons, and doubly remote because of increasing deafness.

When war broke out in 1914 he preached pacifism, and in July 1915 took Florence and thirteen of their fourteen children to non-aligned America. Leonard, the eldest son, stayed behind, having signed on for military service, to his parents' bitter disappointment. 'Population of California is increasing', the *San Francisco Chronicle* headed a collage photograph of the handsome and smiling Chapple family when they arrived, names and ages all noted, from 23-year-old Dora to three-and-a-half-year-old Aynsley: 'Never was a family of thirteen healthier youngsters seen than those of Rev. and Mrs. Chapple. Several of them are crowned with a thatch of fiery red hair, and all, boys and girls alike, are sturdy.'[14] (The red hair James Chapple had inherited from his mother; Sandy, his father's middle name, had been his paternal grandmother's name.) He expected to buy a farm, the paper reported, and engage in church work. But instead he bought a house in Thousand Oaks, Berkeley, where the younger children attended Oxford Elementary School.

The older Chapple siblings thrived in exotic California, but seven-year-old Lyndahl and her closest brother, Maurice (Dick), aged five, pined with homesickness and grew thin, like 'two trees which didn't transplant', their mother said.[15] They were part of the reason the family returned to New Zealand at the end of 1916, five months before the United States entered the war. Not all of them went back. Along with Hollis, three of the girls stayed behind: Bernice, Mercy, who was married a week before the family sailed, and Jean; while Dora returned to America three months later to marry her fiancé. Their departure was found as newsworthy as their arrival and another photograph appeared of the Reverend Chapple, who had 'arrived . . . practically a political exile from the little British island, after years of fighting against imperialism, inveighing against military training and spreading anti-war doctrine of Socialism and internationalism', and his assembled smiling family as they embarked on the *Sonoma* for Sydney in November.[16]

He continued to do so back in New Zealand, where the family settled in Christchurch—in Chrystal Street, Shirley, a slightly more genteel suburb than Sydenham where the Gees lived—until May 1918, when he was charged in the Christchurch Magistrates' Court on two counts of having 'uttered sedition' in Greymouth during a lecture tour of the West Coast. He was sentenced to eleven months in gaol.[17] The children remembered their mother weeping often—in the kitchen so they would not see her—during that bitter, hard and lonely year.

On his release Chapple continued to serve as a minister in the Unitarian church in Christchurch, and wrote two books—*The Divine Need of the Rebel* and *A Rebel's Vision Splendid*; he travelled to England for their publication there in 1924—until he retired from active ministry in 1925 and the family moved to Tauranga, to a house in Cameron Road they named Dove Cottage.

The 'rebel parson'[18] and his devoted disciple and wife; the flight to America; heresy, trial and imprisonment: these were some of the stories Maurice Gee's mother told her sons.

When Len Gee was courting Lyndahl Chapple she was living in Te Puke, probably with her brother Kingsley (the third son), a schoolteacher, and his wife, Winifred, and was working as a teacher aide at the country school where Kingsley was in sole charge. On the banks of the Kaituna River one day, as she watched her class of children laughing and swimming, she rejected the proposal of a young reverend, despite the offer of his mother's genuine pearls as an inducement. For she was 'bewitched', in love already with 'the young boxer/carpenter with the jet-black hair and widow's peak and pale blue eyes'.[19] They were married (by the same reverend) in the Tauranga Baptist church on 16 February 1929.

Their first child was born five and a half months later, in Auckland ('To think,' Lyndahl would write in less happy times, 'we married for love—or was it because we had to?')[20] and was named Aynsley Emerson, after the youngest Chapple sibling and the great American transcendentalist Ralph Waldo Emerson. These were Depression years and the young couple moved about in search of work. They boarded for a time with Kingsley and Winifred in Te Puke. At one point they were living in a tiny tin shack at Ngā Motu beach at New Plymouth in Taranaki, where Len was on relief work, until they could no longer pay the rent and fled under moonlight with the baby

Aynsley wrapped in a blanket and caught a free ride from a friendly service car driver to Auckland. Such at least is the story as Lyndahl later told it.

They were back in the Bay of Plenty when their second son, Maurice Gough, was born on 22 August 1931, in Whakatāne. As a boy he would be grateful that he had been given family names: Maurice after his mother's favourite brother (who was always known, however, as Dick), Gough from his maternal grandmother. (None of these names came from the Gees.) His younger brother, who was born in Auckland in January 1933, was named Gareth Carlyle after the knight of the Round Table and the Scottish philosopher and friend of Emerson, Thomas Carlyle. Nicknames were necessary. Aynsley, because there was an uncle Aynsley, was known as Junior; Maurice to family and friends was, and remained, Moss; Gary (Gareth only to his grandmother) became Gus, much to his mother's annoyance. This name was, according to Aynsley, bestowed by Irish Mrs Flynn across the road, when one day the two-year-old, dressed only in his nappies, wandered down to the front of the section and across the gravel road, over a ditch and through the long grass up to her door: 'My goodness, and who are you?' she exclaimed, 'My, what a gus you are!', in an Irish reference to his intrepid nature.[21]

By this time they were living in Henderson, where they had moved about 1932, probably because it was where Lyndahl's parents now were.

Henderson: town, creek, kitchen. This is where story begins.

2

Creek and Kitchen

Henderson lay between two streams, the Opanuku Stream and the Oratia Stream, which flow down from the Waitākere ranges, converging just below the town, out to the Waitematā harbour. The land they cross was known in the nineteenth century as 'the Whau', then a gently undulating, scrub-covered terrain of mānuka and fern: 'a barren waste of thousands of acres of dun-brown, fern-clad land', according to one 1880s observer. Travelling through 40 years earlier, the missionary William Colenso had complained that he couldn't find any trees tall enough to supply poles for his tent.[1] Henderson began, nevertheless, as a timber mill settlement, known as Henderson's Mill, founded in the late 1840s by Thomas Henderson, an entrepreneurial Scot who arrived in Auckland in 1841 and quickly saw the potential to exploit the densely wooded ranges to the north and west of the city by erecting a sawmill at the head of the tidal waters of what became known as Henderson's Creek. Logs were floated downstream as far as the mill, and the cut timber transported by raft out to the sea. (His other business interests included the Circular Saw shipping line.) The mill ceased operation in the late 1860s, by which time the firm of Henderson and Macfarlane had processed and exported an estimated 45 million super feet of kauri.

The modern township of Henderson was surveyed and the first sections sold in 1881, after the railway line from Auckland went through—advertised to 'Farmers, investors and others desirous of securing a comfortable homestead within easy distance of the City'.[2] By the early twentieth century the area was established as an orcharding and market-gardening district and already 'noted for its manufacture of New Zealand wines'.[3] The original mill workers had been joined, as well as by farm workers and some brickmakers, by Dalmatian gum diggers, who, when the gum was exhausted, acquired smallholdings of land which they planted with fruit, vegetables and grapes. The first wine in the district was made in 1902 by Stipan Yelich, who named his vineyard Pleasant Valley. A Lebanese immigrant, Assid Corban, destined to become the largest winemaker in the district, planted his first grapes the same year and sold his first wine—a coarse red—from his Mt Lebanon Vineyard in 1909. By the end of the 1930s there were some twenty vineyards in and around Henderson, almost all of them owned by Dalmatian families.

The Gee family lived at first in a tiny shack in View Road, of which his older brother would retain some memory but Maurice only in story: of their mother cooking outside over a fire in a hollow dug into a bank with a sheet of corrugated iron over the top for shelter. Then they moved to a little two-bedroom house in Henry Street, by the creek. His first memory attaches to this house: a memory of his brother coming back from the letterbox proudly carrying a package containing a jersey knitted for him by his grandmother Gee in Christchurch. By late 1935 they had moved again, across the creek and a few streets away to Newington Road, into the house in which he would spend the rest of his childhood. A part of him never left. Number 52[4] sat above the road on the high side of the street on a sloping, quarter-acre section, with a view out to the blue, bush-clad Waitākeres, 'a crooked line on the sky'[5] to the west. At the back the porch opened onto the kitchen, with table and chairs, worn brown lino, black wood range set into an alcove (an electric stove came some years later), a Philco radio 'shaped like a church doorway'[6] on a shelf. To the right of the kitchen was a match-lined scullery and a bathroom. A meat safe hung in the porch, low enough for Grandpa Chapple, who was only about five foot four, to walk into one day and badly cut his head. A wash house, with its copper and wooden tubs, opened off to one side. The 'dunny' was up a short path out the back, 'hidden by a scrawny growth of willow and eleagnus'.[7] It was too small a house to have a hallway. The two bedrooms opened off the living room. The three boys slept in one, Moss and Gus in one bed, 'a tangle of skinny arms and legs'.[8] Later their father closed in the front porch at the north end of the living room and Aynsley slept here. Soft, coloured light continued to shine through the rose-patterned stained-glass window in the original front wall into the living room, off to the side of which Len also built an alcove.

> If you live in one place all through your childhood that place grows around you like a skin and it can never be put off. It also gets deep into your mind, into the darkest recesses . . .

> It's where those most important things happened—not the best or worst things necessarily, though possibly those, but the original happenings that make the mark on us we can never erase. It's where we learn to see, to name, and suspect the thing behind the thing.[9]

Seventy years later he could still name and locate all the families in this street. Their stories had leaked into his fiction. Opposite, on the corner of Newington and View roads his friend Murray Scanlon lived, an only child (in a street with a conspicuous number of one-child families) whose father drank poison when his son was eleven. There was an empty paddock next door in which a couple of retired draught horses grazed; beyond them old Ben Hart, whose wife sat on the porch each day wearing a lace cap. Behind the Harts was an abandoned orchard, its gnarled trees draped, tent-like, with honeysuckle. Beyond another empty section through which a small stream flowed were the 'wild Catholic Flynns',[10] a family of all boys and a reputedly drunken and violent father (he would beat his four sons with tomato stakes). After the Flynns left John Kaye lived here, whose mother belonged to the School of Radiant Living, a peculiar complex of Jungian-influenced beliefs based on holistic psychological, spiritual and physical health, and with a strong emphasis on diet: when her son had a birthday party his friends were offered, to their dismay, nuts and raisins instead of cake. Next door to them lived Evans Scott, the Henderson chemist; he kept dozens of budgerigars in a large aviary by his front fence, and made enormous kites.

Directly opposite the Gees were the Greenoughs (they pronounced it Green-oh). Gordon was a lonely only child and tagged along with the Gee brothers. His father Stan was the signalman at the Henderson railway station, and grew flowers and made wreaths, 'inventing' new flowers by wiring the stamen of one to the petals of another—to the disapproval of Lyndahl, who liked all things to be as Nature meant. There were three or four more railway houses on this side before the street came to a dead end, beyond which lay farm paddocks and then the Great North Road.

Next door to the Gees lay two empty, ti-tree scrub sections, the nearer one of which Len Gee bought in 1944, converting the shed on it into a carpentry workshop and letting Stan Greenough use part of it to grow flowers.[11] On the other side lived the Pinkneys, who thought themselves 'too good' for the Gees. Mrs Pinkney was the daughter of Ben Hart. They grew orchids, kept their side of the hedge neatly clipped, and sewed canvas goods for a living after Lionel Pinckney retired. A childless couple, they disapproved of the three rowdy Gee boys. Further along from them were the Harveys: Mrs Harvey was renowned for reciting comic monologues at parties. (Probably the Pinkneys disapproved of her too.)

Through the macrocarpas at the back of the Gee section was the Holy Cross convent and school (opened in 1932). From a hiding place in the school pine grove the boys spied on the nuns walking two by two along the path between the convent and the church, strange, sinister and threatening in their black and their wimples, their crosses and beads. They had been taught perhaps—or thought they had been—that nuns and Catholics need not be respected. One day Moss and Junior broke into the school and ransacked the classroom, tipping over the inkwells, tearing up books and pictures and putting drawing pins on the chairs, while Gus, too small to climb in the window, sat outside and pulled the plants out of the garden: a minor act of schoolboy vandalism. They were found out: the local constable (Constable Norton, himself a Catholic) came to Newington Road and gave them a stern, but slightly amused, talking to. (Their father whipped their legs with a willow stick.)

From the corner of Newington Road and across View Road, a 15-minute walk along Millbrook Road, beside the creek, took one to Peacehaven, where the Chapples lived. When they left Tauranga for Auckland at the end of 1929, James and Florence Chapple had lived in Mt Eden for two years, then briefly in Mt Albert, before moving out to Henderson about 1931 or 32. The reverend had not quite retired. During the 1930s he wrote articles for a radical newspaper, the *Eden Gazette*, and lectured for the Unitarian church and at the Rationalist Association hall, 'mov[ing] steadily to the Left', in his own words,[12] until he withdrew from active ministry in the early years of the Second World War for fear that his support for the Soviet Union would be damaging to the church. As a small boy Maurice was taken to hear him speak once. He would remember only a small, bald man shouting from the stage and the audience laughing; at him not with him, he thought, being too young to understand. But a sense of the power of the man's oratory remained.

The place the family called Peacehaven consisted of perhaps six acres on a hillside. A driveway wound left off Millbrook Road up to a modest weatherboard bungalow—'a pretty little, rather quaint place', in Florence's description.[13] To the side lay fruit trees, a rose garden and lawns, and a ti-tree summer house (built by uncle Dick). Behind a vegetable garden at the back, paddocks ran up to a pine grove. There was an orchard, and a small stream crossed by a brick bridge, a tributary of the Oratia Stream. Lyndahl visited almost daily, taking her sons with her at weekends. To them Peacehaven was a place of wonder. When he saw them coming their grandfather retreated to his study (so it seemed to them), where he stayed—quite deaf now, communicating with the world, when he chose to, by notes or with the aid of a bakelite ear trumpet—while their mother talked with her mother in the kitchen, and they roamed free outside: running in the orchard or playing by the creek. Grandma Chapple, who always had a biscuit for them or a slice of bread, was the centre of their Peacehaven world. Very occasionally they were allowed to go into their grandfather's study, and stroke the belly of the bronze buddha, which held incense sticks (while Grandpa Chapple perfumed the room with his asthma cigarettes). But he was also to be encountered sometimes in the garden, tending his roses, feeding sparrows or reading in the summer house, in his grey suit and tennis shoes and panama hat. He fished with his grandsons in the little stream with bent pins on the ends of pieces of cotton.

The creek of Maurice Gee's childhood, memory and imagination was not Henderson Creek, strictly speaking, but the Oratia Stream, the mile and a half of it which stretched from just upstream of the derelict log dam opposite Peacehaven to Falls Park: 'a chain of deep slow pools of a muddy green linked by yellow-white rapids'.[14] The dam was part of the remains of a blacksmith's factory where heel and toe plates had once been made;[15] across the other side was a pit, too deep and black to see the bottom of, and the remains of a shed and a water race: a spooky place. (Here is where he would bury his first body.) Just upstream was the pool which held his first creek memory: of his father swimming across with the boys, one by one, clinging to his back 'like . . . tiny animal[s]'.[16] In the pool below the dam they searched for eels. Below this was a waterfall, shallow and climbable, then a hundred yards of knee-deep slippery rocks to where the Peacehaven stream flowed in, passing through a muddy culvert under Millbrook Road. From here the creek lay sunken between high, densely grown banks, overhung with willow trees whose roots made 'squishy mats' of red fibre,[17] to the set of rapids where, aged three, Maurice fell in and his mother rescued him.

These flowed into the long deep pool where the boys mostly swam.

But the pool where they spent most of their creek time lay a few hundred yards further down, beyond the View Road bridge and at the foot of the draught horse paddock they would cut through from Newington Road. This one was too deep and dark and slow-moving for swimming. Here they fished for tiny crayfish and tommy cods and silver bellies—baby sprats which flashed deep down where 'the water darkened from green to black as the bottom fell away';[18] and Moss and Junior one day launched tin canoes, made from sheets of corrugated iron bent into shape, a piece of wood at each end for stern and prow, sealed with pitch, and headed off downstream—to Falls Park, and beyond into the brown, salty, tidal water of Henderson Creek, past a dead pig with eels feeding on its bloated body, through the mangroves and mud and 'smell of salt and rot and ripeness',[19] out to the Waitematā harbour, where they abandoned their canoes and made their way on foot, in the gathering dark now, thigh deep through the muddy water then through the town back home. This was an epic journey. He was to recreate it four times in fiction.

School was over on the Great North Road. The quickest way to get there would have been across the farm paddocks at the end of Newington Road, but instead they went the long way round, through the town and back up the hill. Across Newington Road they passed the draught horses in their paddock, and could cut through Ben Hart's orchard and a swamp which drained into the creek. A suspension bridge crossed the creek by the Henry Street house they had once lived in. Moss preferred to go by the road. When he first started school, when they reached the brick jam factory he would stop and look back across the creek and wave to his mother standing on the porch, then duck behind a hedge and back out and wave again, then once more: three times, religiously, every morning, anchoring himself in the safe knowledge of mum and home against the larger world beyond. (Junior, embarrassed, kept on walking.)

The main part of Henderson township was ranged along Station Road. There was not much to it in the 1930s. Across the road from the railway station was the concrete town hall, where, from 1931, the pictures were shown on Saturday nights (*Tarzan*, *The Three Stooges*). There was a blacksmith's, where the boys could lean in the doorway and watch the blacksmith beating out red-hot horseshoes; a chemist and a hairdresser's; P.C. Holborow, 'Family Butcher';[20] a billiard room; Norcross's general store; two more grocers and a post office. On the corner of Station Road and Great North Road was the wooden two-storey Central Hotel—originally the Oratia Hotel, then the Falls—which had operated as a boarding house since the district had gone dry in 1909. The proprietor, Anna Ozich, was the wife of the local land agent (and taxi-driver), Steve Ozich, who was to make good in the building boom after the war; working for him, Len Gee did too.

Henderson School was 300 yards back up the Great North Road. It had a roll of 226 when Maurice Gee started in the third term of 1936, a 'Fairy', as the newest entrants were known, in the two-roomed stucco infants' block up behind the main school. His lasting memories of his earliest years at school were of humiliation. When Miss Sutton sent him home—a half-hour walk each way—to fetch the regulation handkerchief he had forgotten, he sat outside the classroom and counted to a hundred while his late-arriving friend Roy Dally tore his in two; Miss Sutton was not fooled and called him a liar. Miss Woolf, whose perfumed, powdered cheek the children were invited to kiss when they went out at the end of each day, accused him of taking a bite out of her apple because his crooked teeth, she claimed, matched the mark on the fruit. There was injustice in the world, he learned already. But school life improved. He raced through his *Milly-Molly-Mandy* readers; was quick on the sports field, and playing in the school football team by his standard-six year; was made school bell-ringer in standard two (a responsible job requiring the ability to tell the time).

His best friendship of these years he made in battle, after a stand-up fight in the bike shed. Harry Smith lived in the little house in Henry Street where the Gees once had. Together they made a 'two-man purity squad', patrolling the playground for bad language and improper behaviour.[21] For Maurice had absorbed from his mother (although his brothers had not) a virtuous, prissy puritanism. Years later he would look back on himself at this time as 'one of the most horrible little prigs nature and nurture ever turned out'.[22] He was the boy who refused to spy on the girls in the changing shed at Falls Park, and took a lead in beating up Fatty Walker who did. And who left the Boy Scouts in his Tenderfoot year when he discovered that they were not as 'pure in word, thought and deed' as they were meant to be (upset by a display of typical schoolboy scatological humour). (His mother, though, had never been happy about his joining in the first place, disapproving of the movement's militarism.)

During his first years at Henderson School his father was on the school committee. Len Gee built the bicycle shed, and in 1942 the school library—a cupboard in the standard-six classroom, for which the children had to ask for the key—after a library fund was established in 1940 (and some of it diverted to the sports fund). His mother made the posters for the annual children's fancy dress ball in the Town Hall, at which Maurice appeared on stage one year as the king counting out his money in his counting house—dressed in his pyjamas, at the teacher's insistence, another episode of humiliation, and his first and only acting experience. Lyndahl was a talented artist: as a girl she had won a drawing prize at Christchurch Girls' High School and attended evening classes at the art school.

There was an annual school picnic too, held at Titirangi beach or nearer by at Tui Glen, a 13-acre pleasure park on the eastern bank of the Oratia Stream downstream from Falls Park: 'A Charming and Picturesque Beauty Spot, Pleasure Resort, and Camping Park'[23] which had opened in 1924, and was New Zealand's first registered motor camp. It had birds and 'curious animals' and '40 DIFFERENT AMUSEMENTS', including a pirate ship, a Fairy Dell, and donkey rides free for children.

The three brothers were very different. 'Our youngest child is our wit; our middle boy is our scholar and our eldest son is our "handiest",' Lyndahl characterised them.[24] Neither Junior nor Gus were academically minded, despite those literary names. Aynsley was even-tempered, practical (he was to go into apprenticeship with his father when he left school), softly spoken—as they all were—but still a boy's boy, the leader of the gang by virtue of being at least six months older than the other boys in his year (he did not start school until he was nearly six). Gus was a tearaway, a 'tiger of a kid',[25] small and fast and quick-witted: when he was young Lyndahl dressed him in red so she could easily keep sight of him out the kitchen window. He loved to pick fights but had an inflated idea of his own toughness, and relied on his older brother Moss to get him out of trouble. As teenagers, Moss was his hero: tough, right-minded, straight-talking, good at everything he did. They were closest, the younger two, in age and in sibling friendship.

Maurice was the closest to their mother, but all three idolised their father. He 'could punch harder, lift heavier things, build better houses, than anyone else's dad'.[26] To them he was invincible. When he took them on jobs they sat on the floor punching nails into the floorboards with a hammer and punch while he perched high above them on a scaffold or atop a newly framed wall, seeming giant and magical against the sky. When he sharpened chisels in his workshop on an emery wheel 'white sparks streamed up his arm'.[27] He wrestled with them on the lawn, and taught them how to box, showing them the deadly combination of straight left, right cross. 'Your arms are too short,' he told Maurice when he took on Ernie Lisk, who lived on the other side of the scrub section next door and was four or five years older (and had a violent and erratic temper following a head injury suffered in a bike accident). They loved listening to their father's stories: of the first-round knockouts, the blood on the gloves; of how he dived all day from the Tauranga wharf to bring up, piece by piece, a load of jarrah fallen from a barge, then knocked out Jack Bishara in the town hall that night. Their mother told them of the row of cups, belts and medals that had once sat on the mantelpiece but were sold in the Depression (there were only two now); and of how, hating relief work, he would get on his bicycle every morning with his toolkit slung over the handlebars and ride after the trucks leaving the timber yard in hope of a day's work. He was a tough guy, but he was also easy-going, happy-go-lucky, fun: he made life 'full of unexpected things and wildly comic and delightful things'.[28] He won the nail driving contest at the Labour Party picnic at the Henderson Domain or Tui Glen; while their mother won the ladies' 50-yard dash.

Lyndahl had absorbed and stayed true to the political values of her parents: socialist, humanist, anti-war. She was active in the Labour Party, at one time president of the local women's branch and a delegate to the national conference. Accompanying their mother on her visits to the home of a local party official—a long walk through town, past Corban's winery and up Sturges Road—where they waited outside while she talked party business was not nearly as much fun for her sons as visiting Peacehaven. She regarded Michael Joseph Savage, the first Labour prime minister, whose kindly bespectacled face hung framed on the wall of so many working-class New Zealand households in the 1930s (although not, as far as the three boys recalled, at Newington Road), 'almost as a saviour';[29] she never, to the end of her life, relinquished her belief in the goodness of 'Uncle Joe' Stalin.

Political engagement was the inheritance of her father, whose religion was fierce, activist and intellectual. Her mother's was a softer thing. Florence Chapple's young religious belief became in her later years—in the words of her eldest daughter—'more a matter of right living and right loving than a matter of creed. She lived from her heart'.[30] She was gentle, soft-hearted and loving, especially of her children and her grandchildren, and sentimental—'a Chapple failing', she thought (yet 'not a failing, that is not the right word').[31] Lyndahl was all of those things. Florence was also very conventional, an old-fashioned old lady of her time who regarded 'drink smoking & swearing' as a 'trinity of evil'[32] and disapproved of women wearing trousers as much as she hated greed, hypocrisy and war. Lyndahl was not. Increasingly her spiritual inquiring moved beyond and in other directions from her parents', although she always followed, in her own intellectual adventures, her father's lead. In the 1940s she was reading Jung and *Cosmic Consciousness* (given to her by her father), and the teachings of the Oxford Group. She studied Krishnamurti and attended meetings. She believed in Beauty and Truth, and she sought to instil in her sons a sense of the wonder of the natural world, a capacity of wonder at 'the true mystery' and 'the little and the large miracles' of life. 'To point out the miracles of nature from the minute to the milky way is practically the only religious training I give them', she wrote after they had watched together the life cycle of a monarch butterfly one day. 'I hope my boys take their shoes off coming home to-day', she also recorded; 'there is health in bare feet. I believe in known and unknown currents from the earth being good medicine for young and old alike.'[33] She was, her son later observed, 'a few steps off from the centre of . . . the basic earthiness of life'.[34]

The Chapple family loomed large in the Gee lives in part because of the stories Lyndahl told about them: about the brave and uncompromising reverend who defied authority and injustice and war and went to gaol (although not about the 'stark and dark'[35] days that followed); of her girlhood. These were fireside stories, told in front of the kitchen range in the evenings while work socks steamed on the drying rack and stew and doughboy bubbled on the stove, and by the living room fireplace in the winter; bedtime stories in the little single bedroom at night. '[H]ow my sons love to encourage me to remember!'[36] They loved to hear, over and over, about the thirteen Chapple children going off to America: of how their mother hid her dolls' tea set beneath the willows by the river for her return; of them sailing from Wellington harbour in thick fog on a winter's night, with a large tin of fancy biscuits given to Florence by a parishioner; about her brothers dropping paper pellets into the captain's soup through a hatch in the deck above. And about California, where snakes hid under the leaves in the gutters and houses had swimming pools, and they swapped their brown bread and honey sandwiches at lunchtime for the more exotic fare (grapes, ice cream) of their classmates. She told stories with artistry and passion, and she made—unwittingly, perhaps—the Chapples out to be special, a family not like—and better than—others; just as she made the Depression into a magical time, when a young couple fled from a smoky tin shack at moonlight beside a sea navy blue and a beach bone-white.

Their father had a different view. 'Bloody Chapples', he would say, though not uncharitably. But he was no romanticiser.

The Chapples also loomed large because of their proximity. As well as the grandparents at Peacehaven, there were uncles and aunts nearby. The walk along Millbrook Road took them past the small orchard of Hollis (known as Holl), who had stayed in California in 1916 and travelled much before returning to New Zealand (with a marked American accent he would retain all his life). In the 1930s he drew cartoons for the Labour paper the *Maoriland Worker* and the Communist Party's *Workers' Weekly*, and painted. The two youngest Chapples, still in their twenties, were living at Peacehaven in these years, helping out with the garden and orchard: Dick, and Aynsley for a time until he left for America again in the mid or late 1930s (his plans to go into teaching having been thwarted by the closure of the teachers' colleges in the Depression). An aunt, Joyce, one year younger than Lyndahl, lived over on Great North Road with her husband Phil Reanney—a great mate of Len's—and their son. They were regularly round at Newington Road on Friday nights, with quantities of 'Dally' wine. Although 'a different kind of girl altogether'—in their mother's words—a 'good-time girl', fond of poker and sherry and crème-de-menthe, Joyce and Lyndahl were close.[37] Flo, one of the older sisters, and her husband were not far away. Another Chapple uncle, Geoffrey, and his wife lived in Henderson as well. Christmases were most often spent with Chapples at Peacehaven.

The extended Gee family, by comparison, was largely absent—except for the time Harry Gee came to stay. One of the aunts, Kay (Kathleen), also stayed for a month or so, while she trained before going overseas as an army nurse; she later lived in Australia and became a devotee of Indian guru Sathya Sai Baba. Uncle Alf and his family, who lived in Gisborne (he was clerk of works at the hospital there), they saw seldom. Harry—Pater—lived at Newington Road for about a year. He moved to Auckland after his wife (whom her grandsons never met) died in 1938, and for a time lived at the Central Hotel. At Newington Road he slept in the sunporch that had been Aynsley's room, keeping the small house awake with his snoring. He brought with him his gentle, faithful kelpie dog Kep, whom the boys loved: when Kep died while he was with them they buried him on the section next door and poured a concrete slab on top of his grave. Harry, though, was 'a tough old bugger', with a vicious tongue. He believed in giving boys regular hidings, and when he threatened to do so Lyndahl sheltered her sons out of his way behind her. He stayed in Auckland, working for some years with Len, buying a shed further along Newington Road in which he lived for a time, before moving to Glen Eden, until his death in 1956. In his later years he took up photography and became the bane of the local photographic society. He invented things, such as a machine for making concrete blocks which languished, never quite working, in his backyard. The Gees might not have thought of themselves as special, but they were interesting in their own way.

It was, in memory and myth, a happy, outdoor childhood: wrestling on the back lawn; firing BB guns and shanghais; making night-time raids on the neighbouring orchards, abetted by Lyndahl who blacked out the pale faces of the small bands of orchard-raiders with charcoal; going barefoot, stubbing toes in the gravel; above all, mucking about down at the creek, eeling, fishing, swimming, exploring.

The creek held danger and threat; was a place where, on a sunny afternoon on 1940, a boy might see a man die. It also held excitement, mystery and adventure. The war which began in September 1939 brought these things too. Just as last time, only one Chapple—Dick—went away to war. Len did not go, but as a carpenter was manpowered to build shelters and gun emplacements at Whenuapai airport. (Not going to the war was a lasting blow to his self-esteem.) Next door the Pinckneys' sewing machines hummed busily, stitching knapsacks and tents. At school the children grew vegetables for the war effort in the school garden and saluted the flag every Wednesday morning. When the Japanese took Singapore early in 1942, slit trenches were dug in the wattle grove: in the first air raid drill the infants managed to evacuate their classrooms in two minutes, the lower school in one, which the school committee found 'very satisfactory'.[38] When the Americans came—nearly 3000 servicemen to camps in Auckland for 'rest and recreation' between June 1942 and February 1944—they came out to Henderson in their Jeeps, in their smart blue (Navy), green (Army) or olive (Marine) uniforms, to buy flagons of Dally wine. In the playground the boys traded trophies: gum, candy and empty cigarette packets (Camels, Chesterfields and Lucky Strikes). Their gangs became Army, Navy and Air Force. At home in the evenings Junior, Moss and Gus gathered round the Philco radio to listen in to *The Air Adventures of Jimmie Allen*, teenage Spitfire pilot, and his sidekick Speed Robinson. The Americans were young, well-spoken, well-dressed, and had money. Aunt Joyce, like many New Zealand women whose husbands were away at war, became very friendly with some of them. Two in particular—Bob and Red—Lyndahl befriended and were frequent visitors to Newington Road. She enjoyed their talk; the boys their jokes and gifts and dashing.

With the Japanese advance into the Pacific the threat of war became real, and fear was palpable. But death did not come too close to Newington Road. One cousin (Hollis's son Max) was killed in the last weeks of the war; they knew no one else who lost a close relative or friend. A nearer death was that of the school headmaster, W.H. Stevenson, near the beginning of Maurice's final year, 1944. The whole school was gathered in the grounds for the announcement, then the children told they had the rest of the day off. With a whoop of delight the boys headed down to Falls Park.

3

Swamp

The creek days came to an end when he left Henderson School. He lost touch too with the friends of his primary school years—even Harry Smith, after a time, although they continued to play tennis together for a few years, joining the Holy Cross tennis club so they could use the courts through the Gees' back hedge: Maurice became club champion.

Peacehaven was no more, as well. The Chapples had sold the Millbrook Road property about 1940, moving to Mt Albert for a few years, then back to Henderson, but to Lincoln Road, over the other side of Great North Road. And in 1948, when Maurice was in his lower-sixth-form year, his family moved from Newington Road to Tirimoana Road, up near the Te Atatū corner. (The Greenoughs bought their Newington Road house: Gordon was to live there for the rest of his life.)

There were no regrets about this move. Number 63 Tirimoana Road was a newish, modern, flat-roofed house, open and sunny, with a large outdoor patio. It was a huge step up from Newington Road. There were three bedrooms, of which Gus and Aynsley shared one while Maurice had his own, because he needed to study. Outside his bedroom window a large, heavy-bearing fig tree produced the finest figs ever tasted. They acquired their first fridge. The house was set at the back of a sloping corner section; the living room window gave a view across mangroves to the harbour and Rangitoto. Behind it two paddocks—five acres or more—stretched down to a tributary of the Whau creek. Len built a large joinery workshop here, and in the postwar years began building up a successful business: one of his first jobs was a new presbytery for the Holy Cross church. He built houses for clients and on spec, and as contractor for Steve Ozich built two blocks of shops on the Great North Road, as the centre of town shifted around the corner from Station Road. (The Henderson of Maurice's childhood was disappearing already.)

It was about a mile and a half from Newington Road to Tirimoana Road. He could easily still have walked down to the creek, but he no longer wanted to.

He had expected when he left primary school to go to Mt Albert Grammar, as Aynsley had done. Instead he went to a new school, Avondale Technical High School; Gus started a year behind him. Avondale was five train stops from Henderson station, one before Mt Albert. From Tirimoana Road they went from Te Atatū corner by bus—a more sedate journey. The train was ruled by the Seddon Tech and Mt Albert boys: fortifications were constructed from seat stuffing; insults (and more) flung; bags dropped out of windows a mile from the station. There were a few who sat quietly reading.

Avondale Technical High School had been built in 1943 as an American naval hospital, with the intention from the outset that when the American forces left the main buildings would be converted into a secondary school. The process of conversion was not yet complete when the foundation pupils arrived on 6 February 1945, and made their way between the assembly hall and their classrooms 'over slippery floors, round machinery, over timber, rubble, flex, boxes, concrete ditches and mounds of earth'.[1] The din of sanding machines and concrete mixers and drifting clouds of dust through which they sat their entrance tests and posed for the school photo would go on for three months. Murals by James Turkington which adorned the hall walls, depicting ten 'scenes of New Zealand life and industry', were still being painted when the first assembly was held, the artist at work high above them on scaffolding (he put down his brush during the prayers). At the hall entrance the Renaissance scholar held in one hand the scroll of knowledge, the world in the other, while the tree of life burst into leaf behind him and New Zealand fern fronds unfurled at his feet.[2]

The modern, near-new buildings were long and low and light-filled, with acres of glass and corridors which seemed to go on for miles; and a wondrously large gymnasium in which the boys were introduced to the new game of American basketball. Laying out of the sports grounds did not start until the second year: in April the whole school spent a day advancing slowly in long lines picking up twelve lorry-loads of stones in preparation for the sowing of five and a quarter acres of football fields. The school was modern in other ways too. It had a Māori motto: Kohia ngā taikaka—seek the heartwood, meaning strive for the best in life. And it was coeducational; although, whether by rule or human nature, the girls sat on one side of the classroom and the boys on the other. They had separate playgrounds.

The first-year intake was entirely of third formers, which meant that for all of his secondary school years Maurice was in the senior form. In hindsight he would wonder if this imparted a democratic spirit or just 'made us big-headed and arrogant'.[3] A downside was that when they reached the sixth form the foundation-year pupils were not allowed to benefit from the recently introduced accrediting system for university entrance but all had to sit the examinations, because the school had to establish its academic standards. From the school they felt a burden of expectation.

As a technical high school it was divided into three streams: general, commercial and industrial. When it changed its name in 1947 to Avondale College it was an indication of where its ambitions lay. Maurice went into 3A General, the top academic class. Their form teacher, Bill—Froggy—Martin, was a teacher of the old-school kind, formal and disciplinarian, but a good one, who believed that literature was to be enjoyed not just studied and introduced his senior pupils to things outside the curriculum: the poetry of T.S. Eliot and Dylan Thomas, the plays of Ibsen. He was Maurice's English teacher for three years.

From having been top of his class at primary school, by the end of his first year he found himself—to his distress—near the bottom. He was put into 4 Science and General the following year, but with a warning that this was a second chance. Academically he was not to distinguish himself until his senior years. In sport, however, he did so from the start. He played cricket in his first year, and won first, second or third places in the athletic sports (the 100 yards or hurdles—he was fast) and swimming. He boxed for a time too, perhaps at the encouragement of his father, and well enough to fight in the tournament final in his fifth-form year. In Aynsley's recollection—or rather fancy—he gave this sport up abruptly one day, mid-fight, with his opponent against the ropes with blood pouring from a cut above his eye; one punch would have taken the boy down. It was not in his nature.

It was rugby that was his real sporting talent and passion (a passion that had begun when his uncle Dick took him to Eden Park to see Auckland play Taranaki when he was six or seven). He played in the grade teams in his first two years at Avondale and vice-captained the third-grade team in 1947; made the First XV in the lower sixth form and was vice-captain in 1949. He also played for the Waitemata Rugby Football Club, along with Gus. On Saturdays they played for school in the morning and Waitematā in the afternoon, travelling to the latter matches with their team mates on the back of a truck, announcing their arrival with 'Ra! ra! ra! Here we are! WAI-TE-MA-TA!' He played wing three-quarter for school and second five-eighth for Waitematā (Gus, small and nimble, was a hooker.) Twice he made the Auckland reps, playing one game against Kaipara in the seventh grade (scoring two tries), though in the fourth grade chosen only as a reserve. He loved the game: the team aspect, the physical activity, the contest, the winning, running with the ball. He was good at it and proud of his skill. For the rest of his life he would remember games played, tried scored, and the injuries—a badly dislocated elbow (Avondale College versus Thames Valley High), a broken finger, a permanently stiffened finger joint and bad ankle. Gus, who idolised him in this as in most things, would be bitterly disappointed when he gave the sport up.

Outwardly he was a regular guy: good at sport, quite good at school work. Inside, things were different. At thirteen, 'puberty hit me like sledgehammer'.[4] So it does many thirteen-year-olds but for Maurice his sufferings were worse—and were in large part responsible for his poor academic performance that first year. 'Swampy' is the word he would eventually come up with to describe his adolescence.[5]

The prissy puritanism in the service of which he and his friend Harry had patrolled the Henderson School playground had not been just a passing, childish phase. He had taken in deeply his mother's belief in 'the holiness of the affections and the purity of the body', what he would later term her 'twisted puritanism': her elevation of the intellectual and spiritual and 'withdrawal from physical things'.[6] This is what he referred to when he described her as being 'a few steps off from the centre of . . . the basic earthiness of life'. It was not something he was taught; he 'absorbed [his] mother's puritan attitudes out of the air'. 'It made my growing up difficult.'[7]

In practical terms what it meant was that he and his brothers were taught nothing helpful about sex: 'love was beautiful and that I would find out about the other things when I was ready'.[8] '[T]he study of the propagation of any specie [sic] is my method of teaching them sex', Lyndahl wrote after observing with them one day the birth of a calf:

> I drew their attention away from propagation to the product and left them admiring the new-born velvet calf. It is my belief that in explaining sex to children one should be as spontaneous and detail indifferent as the child. . . . And always it is wise to admit ignorance as to the true mystery of life which has us all baffled. This is where sex training steps over to religious training. The mystery of life is God's secret.[9]

This is as she herself had grown up to believe. In an unpublished autobiographical story—written when she was 'a young mother of three adolescent sons'—her narrator, teenage Margot, ignorant of and fearful of sex, is taken aside by the boarder living with her family, an older young woman (who is based to some extent on her beloved oldest sister, Dora). Physical union, Margot is told,

> should be as natural and beautiful as day merging into night if your love and his is purehearted; the way of it is not important—now; but your mental attitude will be; remember always—God ordained it so—love and union between man and woman is His loveliest miracle—unless the loveliest be the child of that union—but remember the spirit must not be abased to the flesh nor the flesh abased to the spirit . . .

Margot will remember this 'moment of wisdom; she would fight all ugliness with this beauty she now felt'.[10]

Maurice internalised this lesson in a way his brothers did not. While they found out about the facts of life in the ways boys normally did, he 'simply didn't believe that sexual intercourse took place':[11] he refused to believe that people did that, and was prepared to challenge to a fist fight a boy who insisted that his parents obviously had. But then puberty showed him otherwise, and plunged him into an adolescent torment of confusion, shame, guilt and humiliation; into a lonely, dark and miserable time.

It was not just an intellectual problem, this conflict between belief and evidence, the mind and the body. Its physical manifestation was a condition one of his fictional characters would diagnose (not quite correctly) as priapism. That is not something rare, perhaps, among teenage boys, but in his case it was—emotionally certainly, and he believed physically as well—extreme. There were times he couldn't leave the classroom until everyone else had left, and did so with his schoolbag held in front of him; when he would stay on the bus or train to the end of the line and then come back. He only had to think about a girl to be afflicted. He never had girlfriends during his secondary school years, never appeared to show any interest, although there were plenty of girls who wished he would, for he was good-looking, sporty and smart. But he never asked the girls to dance at the Henderson dances or the Oratia Fruitgrowers' Ball; he was one of the boys drinking beer out in the carpark. He told no one about his suffering, not his brothers, not his parents. His brothers, he believed, just thought him 'a weirdo' (he did too).[12] But there would be references to it, often oblique or passing, throughout his fiction: in the story of the boy who hangs himself from a rafter in his father's barn when 'given for the first time his body's evidence that generation requires a physical act'; and the 'shy boy . . . who whispered and blushed and furtively smoothed the front of his shorts', and later hangs himself in the family garage; a headmaster who warns his boys that sex obsession leads to madness and suicide; in a succession of male characters who have been damaged by their adolescence: most explicitly Raymond Sole in *Sole Survivor*, whose uncle Alfred it is who gives his nephew's 'trouble' a name—'Priapism. . . . And sex in the head.' Alfred makes comparatively light of Raymond's affliction ('Pretty usual with boys').[13] For Maurice it was a dark private pain that he was to carry with him well beyond his teenage years.

He did not become a writer because of this, but it had a good deal to do with the kind of writer he became.

Rugby—being good at something normal—anchored him through these years, through the 'biological swamps, psychic recesses'[14] of his adolescence. Being good at sport was also useful if one was a bookish boy who preferred above all else to be reading.

He had not been a particularly precocious reader in his primary school years. A Robin Hood collection displaced a *Chums* annual found by his father on a job as his first favourite book, the first that 'really thrilled me', with its '[s]tory, heroic action, comradeship',[15] and right-doing—robbing the rich to give to the poor. Like his brothers and his friends he was an avid reader of the British boys' weekly *The Champion*: of the adventures of Rockfist Rogan, the 'boxing daredevil of the skies', ace RAF pilot and boxing champion, and the detective Colwyn Dane. By his teens he was into the swashbuckling adventures and historical romances of Rafael Sabatini, Rider Haggard and Jeffrey Farnol; Baroness Orzcy's Scarlet Pimpernel; R.M. Ballantyne; Conan Doyle; and above all Westerns, especially

Zane Grey. At fourteen, in competition with a school friend he read between 20 and 30 Zane Grey novels—or was it really 45?—in six months, inhabiting the landscape of purple sage, dry gulch and endless range, alongside 'the sweat-stained man on the dusty horse, galloping into the badlands with the posse at his heels'.[16] Here he learned—in hindsight, at least—that we are all alone, that we each make our own destiny, and we lose what we most desire. These were the first books that 'had a mind-toughening quality'.[17]

From Zane Grey he moved on to Dickens; from the dust-swept, sun-scorched badlands of the American West to the dark interiors and grubby streets of nineteenth-century London. Dickens was a fortuitous discovery. When he was fifteen or sixteen, in his fifth-form or lower-sixth year, perhaps at the suggestion of his mother, he played a game of draughts each Sunday afternoon with Ben Hart, the retired orchardist who lived over the other side of Newington Road, a little round old man with rheumy eyes and shaky hands whose wife served them tea and cake in a dark, lace-curtained living room cluttered with china and knick-knacks, and books. One day Ben Hart gave him *The Adventures of Oliver Twist* to take away; by chapter two he was captivated. He read his way through the entire Dickens œuvre—well, perhaps not everything, not *The Uncommercial Traveller*, but all the great novels at least—in a year, in editions with tiny print and the original Phiz and Cruikshank illustrations. He discovered from Dickens that one could create, and enter, an entire fictional world, a complex, 'huge and violent and tragic and heroic and comic and swarming world of the imagination', and of emotions he could connect with his own. He 'stood in the tumbril with Sidney Carton, spelt win-der for Wackford Squeers, and stared in horror at the yellow puddle that had been Mr Krook'.[18] Later he would see that it was a moral world, in which good confronted evil and human nature tested the limits of human possibility; and would know that Dickens was 'a wounded being who worked off his pain in his fiction'.[19]

Dickens was just the beginning of a Victorian binge. He read Thackeray, the Brontës, Eliot and Hardy (these he found at school); and poetry—Keats and Shelley, Whitman, Wordsworth, and Browning, his favourite—even, eventually, *The Ring and the Book*. He had his grandfather's Browning, whose favourite Browning was too. He read big, bad Victorian epic poems like *The Light of Asia*; and all the major Shakespeare plays in a single, thick volume. Dickens, however, remained 'the great reading experience of my life': 'I'd be different if I hadn't read Dickens'.[20] Zane Grey had been an escape from the things he had 'to get away from'; Dickens saved him.[21]

When he came to start writing himself, among his earliest efforts would be a poem based on Dick Swiveller from *The Old Curiosity Shop*.

To write was nothing unusual in Maurice Gee's family—his Chapple family. This was a family who named, and so gave stories to, their houses: Holleon, Dove Cottage, Peacehaven (which the minister also called Journey's End, from a John Davidson poem). His grandfather had lived by the power of the word: preaching, lecturing, writing, reading—'he was always reading,' Florence wrote, 'it was his life.'[22] An aunt, Dora, was a poet. She published a dozen volumes, along with some children's books, under her first married name of Dora Hagemeyer (the name as glamorous as her being a poet to her nephew), mostly in California, where she lived for many years in the bohemian township of Carmel-by-the-Sea,[23] but two in New Zealand: *Sonnets and Other Songs* (Harry Tombs, 1940, with a foreword by C.A. Marris) and the *Secret Parables* (Pegasus, 1955). Her verses appeared occasionally in the literary pages of the local press. She was, wrote a reviewer of *Sonnets and Other Songs* in the *Auckland Star*, and comparing her slightly unfavourably with Eileen Duggan, 'mostly occupied with the beauty of Nature, which she sees with eyes of tremulous ecstasy'.[24] Her brother Leonard, who had returned to teaching after his service in the First World War, became an historian and 'well-known . . . literatteur'[25] in Wanganui, of which he wrote a centennial history, and a collector of antiquarian books; he compiled the 1938 supplement to the bibliography of the Hocken Library.

And there was Lyndahl, who not only told stories but wrote them too. As a girl she had begun to write, or tried to write, poetry, like her sister Dora. Twenty years later, as a young mother, the 'invitingly clean pages' of a spare school exercise book left lying around by her oldest son prompted her to start again.[26] In the late 1930s and early 40s she had some short stories and poems published in the left-wing journal *Woman To-day* and the *Mirror*, and two or three poems in the *New Zealand Herald*; some too in the *Carmel Pine Cone* (arranged by Dora). Her *Woman To-day* contributions were politically themed: calls to arms to young women to use their influence to prevent the coming war, and a story, 'Mother's Holiday', about a young mother's experience giving birth in hospital to her fifth child. The two stories accepted by the monthly 'home journal' the *Mirror* in 1941 were more domestic. In one, a farming wife deals with the unexpected arrival home of her youngest son with a baby but no wife: maternal love wins out over her initial moral recoil. In 'The Parting of the Ways'—a Kaituna River story—two schoolboys and best friends, Tou Tou, a Māori boy, and Carlyle, spend what they don't realise will be their last ever day together playing hooky down by the river.[27] Always her writing stayed close to her own life. An unpublished story written in the 1930s drew on her experience living at Ngā Motu during the Depression: 'Tiger Town' is a seaside settlement, a place of 'green water, grey rain and black sand', where a young woman spends a 'wind driven winter' with her brother, who is on relief, and is courted by a rich, golf-playing businessman and a rough Irishman and thief.[28]

She wrote when she could, usually in the evenings—using a rubber ring from a jam jar for an eraser when she found that her sons had 'taken their rubbers to school'.[29] They would find her at night writing at the kitchen table, with her feet in the range during the winter for the last of the warmth. Then Len built her a writing desk, inlaid with a design incorporating the Southern Cross, to go in the sunny alcove he had built on to the living room. He might not have understood her urge to write—he did not read books himself—but he supported it as best he could.

In 1940 a story in verse for children, *Mihi and the Last of the Moas*, was broadcast on Lady Gay's Young New Zealand's Radio Journal. It was the tale of a Māori boy accidentally abandoned by his tribe, who is cared for by the creatures of the forest and befriended by the lonely, last living moa, who takes him away to live with him in his underground cave, from which, when he becomes ill, Mihi rescues him by building a raft and rowing him out through a 'long secret tunnel' into the sun (was it written after Moss and Junior's epic canoe journey down Henderson Creek to the Waitematā harbour?): 'a charming fantasy . . . prettily told', one reviewer found.[30] Three years later she arranged for its publication by Oswald-Sealy, illustrating it herself with half-a-dozen delicate watercolours and pen-and-ink drawings.[31] The *New Zealand Herald* was complimentary—'beautifully told . . . Young readers will love' it—in a column which, in a review of Charles Marris's *Best New Zealand Poems of 1943*, also admired Dora Hagemeyer's 'lovely lilting lines'.[32] To her disappointment, however, the *New Zealand Listener* books page accorded it just a single sentence in its acknowledgement of books received: 'The printers have done their work well'; though this was perhaps not as hurtful as her brother Kingsley's dismissal of it as mere doggerel.[33] It delighted her sons, however, who could recite whole verses.

In 1946 she submitted another illustrated children's story, a short novel, to Reeds this time, more ambitiously—the firm was one of the two significant local publishers of children's literature—but despite finding it 'a most unusual and well written book' they turned it down reluctantly, citing an increasingly competitive international market since the war, although they asked to keep the manuscript, with 'a series of fairly inexpensive books', along the lines of Whitcombe and Tombs 'Storytime' books, they were contemplating in mind.[34] (The story, 'Tane and George', never published, was set on a backblocks sheep station during the Depression and featured a six-year-old boy named Tane Carlyle Emerson Gough and his Māori friend, George.)

But she did not want only to write for children. Her proudest achievement was having a story included in the anthology *Speaking for Ourselves* (1945), edited by Frank Sargeson and published by Denis Glover's Caxton Press. This was to be accepted in the front ranks of New Zealand literature, among serious writers. The anthology contained work by, among others, Maurice Duggan, Roderick Finlayson, A.P. Gaskell, G.R. Gilbert, Greville Texidor and Sargeson himself. Lyndahl Chapple Gee's story, 'Double Unit' (one of several she submitted), was a wartime story about two married women whose husbands are away at war, 'Mrs. Gladson, a blonde bleached to a dazzling point, and dark Mrs. Dunbar', with a son each the same age and living in adjacent, mirror-image semi-detached flats: 'Millie was fond of saying that the Government architects, when planning double units, simply drew half a plan in ink and doubled it over while still wet.'[35] In a matching reversal of expectations it is Millie Gladson's husband, whose wife dallies with handsome American servicemen while he is away, who is faithful and self-righteous Mrs Dunbar's who returns home with a secret. The story is rather schematic but distinguished by its sharp observation and tone. Sargeson found it 'refreshingly honest & high-spirited',[36] and he continued to be supportive of her writing. A 'short novel' which she submitted to Caxton in 1947 but was turned down was, he told her, 'far & away ahead of most of what gets into print', while consoling her that novellas were especially difficult to sell.[37]

Over the next few years she sent a number of contributions to

Landfall, the new quarterly founded by Charles Brasch in 1947, which quickly established itself as the country's serious literary journal and arbiter of cultural taste, the place to be published. The first, which she sent with her first subscription in June 1948, was a memoir of her father (who died in 1947); another a story 'about the sad lot of a woman'.[38] They were all returned.

Sargeson told her that her stories showed a rare 'sincerity & genuineness' but that she 'somehow lack[ed] the technical cleverness to put it across'.[39] What she lacked, as the wife of a carpenter and mother of three young sons, was the time and space to develop that skill. She knew this, knew that her talent was sacrificed—if not unwillingly—for her family. Her frustrated ambition to become a writer, a real writer, was a cause (although not the only one) of her at times deep unhappiness. She became embittered by a sense of lost opportunity. She had wanted a life of the mind and had only to some extent found it in her reading, in political meetings, in discussions with like-minded friends—among them interesting and unusual friends of father's, like the homosexual couple John Watson, a talented amateur pianist, and Jim Leaney who visited Newington Road often, John amazing her sons with his virtuoso performances, of Sibelius's *Finlandia* and Manuel de Falla's *Ritual Fire Dance*, of Mendelssohn perhaps or Godowsky (while Jim did because he smelled of eau-de-cologne). And Muriel Parker, a fervent Jungian and acolyte of James Chapple, who with her brother Jack bought Peacehaven when the Chapples left.

Len was not interested in these things. His two best friends were the local bookies (Bob Norcross and Alan Place); his great enthusiasm was racing. It was his ambition, which he would eventually realise in the 1950s, to own a racehorse (he had two, the first a filly, Little Beauty, and a few years later a hurdler called My Sun). He was ambitious to succeed in his business too, and as he began to do so after the war he would work long and late into the night at the kitchen table, poring over plans and specifications. He became stressed and short-tempered, and 'we . . . lost him for a while'.[40] He aspired and began to mix in successful business circles, and hosted memorable parties at Tirimoana Road, but these were not Lyndahl's people. She could not be the businessman's wife, and dress and perm her hair and wear make-up in the appropriate way. She had always hated what she termed 'cake talk', the domestic conversation of housewives. She was aware that he was attractive to these women—'when he smiles there is a touch of the satyr about him; I know that women like his smile'.[41] When he was being ardently pursued by the wife of a client for whom he was building a new factory—Frances Wilkinson was the woman's name: she would invite him in for a cup of tea, then disappear and re-emerge from the bedroom wearing only a petticoat under her dressing gown—she mischievously insisted that he put a pound to win on a horse named Frances racing in the Auckland Cup. (It won, but Len always insisted that the 'affair' went no further than the woman's overtures and his amused embarrassment.)

'She married the wrong man and he married the wrong woman', was how her son later saw it; though it was a good enough marriage in so far as marriages of that time were expected to be.[42] They loved and supported each other but they were two very different people, and these were difficult years.

Lyndahl's unhappiness may also have had a deeper source. Her sons when growing up were aware of her sadness, of times when she cried and could do nothing. There was a prolonged period, lasting perhaps some months, just before or in the early years of the war of what would later have been termed a 'nervous breakdown', during which she took the three boys on holiday to Piha, and there befriended a young nurse who helped them get back to Auckland when she could not manage (to find poor Len with a week's worth of unwashed dishes in the sink). As a child she had suffered from periods of blackness which may have been depression, which she later wrote about—or rather, a semi-fictionalised version of her young self wrote about: times when she cried easily and books and music made her sad and she 'hat[ed] everybody and everything', and her mother told her that she had 'a little black dog on my back'.[43] It was a tendency her mother also recognised in herself: 'We are both inclined to be a bit melancholy', Florence wrote in a diary when she was in her eighties. 'It seems at times we have a <u>dual personality</u>. The good & the bad seems to be in our natures . . . I've been charged with being a melancholy sort of person, one who looked on the <u>dark</u> side, but I think it's <u>dual</u> personality. I try hard to be bright & cheerful, but I feel <u>sometimes</u> that this world is a very <u>pathetic</u> place, so many things are <u>wrong</u>.'[44]

It was the opinion of Lyndahl's close friends the Parkers that she was deeply affected too by her father's death in April 1947; that she was changed by it. This was not something of which Maurice was particularly aware, however; but he had preoccupations of his own.

*

When he started to write himself he began, as his mother had, with poetry: imitations of Wordsworth, in which 'Nature had a capital N, and . . . the movement was away from the flesh towards the spirit': 'Ever sad suspended just below the brink' is a line he would remember.[45] His first published literary effort was a poem in the Avondale College magazine, *Taikaka*, in his final year. Entitled 'Ngauruhoe', this was one of the Wordsworthian ones: '. . . boulders coughed and flung/ From the mountain's smouldering sulphurous lung/ Where generates such breath as makes men pale' and 'The silent sweeps of snow and ice impart/ Upon the scene a grandeur calm and stern'.[46] It was written after a weekend tramp he went on with his upper-sixth English teacher, Maurice Hutchinson, and another teacher to the Mangatepopo River in Tongariro National Park, not a school tramping trip as such but a reconnaissance of the area by the three of them for possible future ones. Hutchinson, as well as a keen alpine tramper, was one of his memorably good college teachers; even if he refused to believe the sixteen-year-old had read all of Dickens.

His first literary success, however, could be counted the Temperance essay prize he had won at primary school, with a story about an old man who gets drunk and is run over by a motor car. Taken into town to collect his prize, he disappointed the woman behind the counter at the Presbyterian Book Room by choosing a book about the Crusades with a medieval knight in armour on its cover rather than the one on Methodist missionaries she suggested. (This was a few years before the afternoon a boy came running down the train carriage after school yelling to him and Gus, 'Your father's been killed! Your father's been killed!'—after Len, driving home from a work site, had been hit side-on by a train on a level crossing on Henderson Valley Road, ending up alive, in fact, but pinned beneath his truck several hundred yards down the track and spending a few days in hospital.)

He did not stay long a poet, and would never go back to it. It is significant that it was the dramatic poetry of Browning, among the Victorians, that as a reader he liked best.

It was only in his last two years at Avondale College that he began to do conspicuously well. Nineteen forty-eight—his lower-sixth-form year—was a short year, the school not opening until April due to the polio epidemic that swept the country from north to south between the end of 1947 and July 1949 (claiming 77 lives). For those first two months they had correspondence lessons, and for English a list of books to read: he was probably the only student in his class who read them all. (Like Maurice Hutchinson, Froggy Martin didn't believe him.) He was appointed an assistant prefect, and at the end of the year came first in his class in history and second in English. In 1949 he was a prefect, as well as vice-captain of the First XV. He was the only prefect who was still only a corporal in the school cadets, having taken a pacifist stance in keeping with his family background, rather than, he would later admit, considered opinion. Perhaps to avoid embarrassment the school allowed him to sit out cadet drill in the prefects' room with a book. He was on the magazine committee and the library committee, in the latter capacity writing the notes for *Taikaka*, and noting, among the other innovations in the library this year, that a 'large portrait of Dickens now occupies a prominent position', the first of what was hoped to be a gallery of portraits of famous authors.[47] It is tempting to think that this had been his initiative.

At prize-giving he collected one of two 'special prizes', having come first in history and second in English, again (it irked him that he was unable to beat John Titheridge, the son of the headmaster, to first place in English), and second in French. Oddly, these were the only subjects he took this year—the latter, despite knowing that he had no particular aptitude for languages, only because he understood that he would need a foreign language to do an MA in English at university, which was his plan.

4

Albert Park

When Maurice Gee walked out of the gates of Avondale College at the end of 1949, just as when he left Henderson School he left his schoolmates as well as the school behind. He had made no enduring friendships there. Fourteen foundation-year pupils made up the college's first upper-sixth form, whose photograph appeared in the 1949 *Taikaka*; apart from at his university graduation, he saw none of the other thirteen again. The difficulties of his adolescence had something to do with this detachment and reserve, but he would always be by nature a solitary person.

At Auckland University College he enrolled in English, history, French and education: the first two because he wanted to, French because it was required, and education to fill up his degree. Although, if he hadn't already decided to become a teacher, no other career suggested itself to him. (And Chapples had been teachers: Leonard and Kingsley, and Aynsley would have, while Dora and Lyndahl had both taught before they married.) In his third year he added philosophy I. He worked hard at university, determined to get a good degree, and took no part in social or any organised form of extracurricular activity. And English (also history) was a good department, with some notably fine teachers, including the professor, Sydney Musgrove, and J.C. Reid, an exceptional lecturer to first-year students: hugely learned, articulate and lively. There were writers on the staff, too: M.K. Joseph, and poet Allen Curnow who joined the department in 1951. A.R.D. Fairburn, appointed at Elam School of Fine Arts the same year, sometimes lectured in English. (The critic E.H. McCormick, on the other hand, author of the foundational *Letters and Art in New Zealand* (1940), as a lecturer was execrable: hesitant and halting.)[1] He did a mediocre undergraduate degree, averaging Bs (English and history) and Cs. His studies did, however, introduce him to areas of English literature he had not yet discovered, for all the riches and obscurities of his grandfather's library: to *Beowulf* and

Chaucer, the Metaphysical poets and *The Faerie Queene*.

He made three important friendships at university. Two of them were with ex-Avondale College boys, but they had been a year behind him and he had not known them well there, although both had also been on the magazine committee in 1949. Maurice Shadbolt started university the same year as he did, going straight from the sixth form. He was a part-time student, and a desultory one, while working variously as a proofreader on the *New Zealand Herald*, a builder's labourer and in the coolstores, and gave up his studies after two or three years. His Avondale College classmate (and Gus's) Carl Freeman enrolled in an unfocused BA in 1951 and dropped out within a few months, the next year going to teachers' college. Kevin Jowsey—later Kevin Ireland—who lived in Takapuna on the North Shore and met Gee through Maurice Shadbolt, also started in 1951. Like the other two he never completed his degree, being much too busy with other—more exciting, more fun, more imperative—things.

These three—Kevin, Carl and Maurie (Maurice Shadbolt was Maurie; Maurice Gee was Moss)—became passionately engaged in political activity, and in the wider bohemian scene around downtown Auckland (drinking at the Queen's Ferry, coffee at Somervell's, cheap Chinese food at the Golden Dragon). Nineteen fifty-one was the year of the waterfront dispute, a 151-day lockout of striking watersiders by shipowners encouraged and backed by the right-wing, red-baiting National government which had ousted Labour from power at the 1949 general election. It was the largest and most bitter industrial confrontation in the country's history, and more than an industrial conflict: an ideological battle waged against the background of intensifying Cold War. In 1950 Shadbolt had (by his own account) commandeered the university Labour Club, which renamed itself the Socialist Club—a misnomer still for they liked to think of themselves as far to the left of socialist. Students on the whole were a conservative lot; some signed on as strikebreakers on the wharves during the lockout, some as special constables on the campus. Shadbolt and his Socialist Club comrades, who included Jowsey and Freeman, organised a protest meeting against the government's punitive emergency regulations and leafleted lecture theatres with broadsheets of Jack London's 1903 anti-strike-breaking polemic *The Scab*. The three also frequented the Young People's Club, a kind of junior Communist Party, and Shadbolt tried to join the party itself (but the local secretary thought a student was more useful to them as an accomplice and sympathiser than as a card-carrying member). He fancied himself as a spy in the *Herald* copy room.

It was natural that these three should join the struggle on the left. Carl Freeman was from a Jewish and Marxist family. Kevin Jowsey's father was a former insurance agent and a radical who had gone to work as a seagull—a casual labourer—on the wharves, joined the Waterside Workers' Union and was out on strike. Shadbolt's father, a Post and Telegraph worker, along with an uncle had become a member of the Communist Party in the early 1930s back in Huntly, where Shadbolt had grown up.

Maurice Gee, with his own socialist family credentials, ignored it all, to his subsequent consternation. He kept his head down in the library, and the tumult of 1951 passed him by.

Shadbolt and Jowsey were also, or soon would be, aspiring writers. At lunchtimes the two Maurices would meet in Albert Park by the fountain to eat their sandwiches, earnestly discuss literature and read each other poems. 'There were flower beds, Moreton Bay fig trees, and a statue of Queen Victoria enclosing us on three sides. Sunny hours after morning lectures; girl students all about us in their summer frocks: we could not avoid writing about it.' These two poet-lovers are Jack Skeat and Rex Petley in the novel *Going West*.[2] And one of them Gee, writing poems to the person he didn't want to be (Hopkins-like poems—he liked his sprung rhythm; Shadbolt's were heavily influenced by T.S. Eliot)—so he would later recall it.[3] Yet he had moved on from poetry by now. He had a larger ambition: he was writing a novel.

This was not just any novel, but a novel that would change the world: a pacifist novel that was going to make war impossible for all time. He wrote it during his first year at university. It featured a young man, Mr Graham, who always dressed in black and went about making pacifist speeches, and spent a lot of time explaining to a young boy (out in Henderson) why war was evil. He was to go into a conscientious objectors' camp, if the writer had got him that far. He had done several chapters before he abandoned it. It was a typical expression of a young man's idealism. More particularly, of course, it was an expression—a literary instead of an activist expression—of this young man's Chapple inheritance: of his grandfather's, and mother's, pacifism and idealism and crusading activism and of having grown up imbued with a belief 'in Man, in Perfectability' and 'that one can be sure of Right and Wrong and find a Way'.[4]

It was written too in the aftermath of two world wars and the gathering shadow of another. New Zealand troops were already in Korea. In late 1949 compulsory military training had been introduced under an act under which all males became liable for military service on reaching the age of eighteen: fourteen weeks' full-time training, three years' part-time service and six years in the army reserves. It had been approved in principle by the Labour Party's annual conference in May that year—to the dismay of many on the left and to the party's cost at the election—and in a referendum in August. That was the month Maurice Gee turned eighteen. In fact he never did his. When he went down to the Henderson Post Office to register he asked for the form to fill out to register as a conscientious objector. They didn't have that one and told him to come back in a week or so. He didn't, and no one called.

He had discovered with that first attempt that didacticism and conviction were not enough. His second novel, which he wrote during his second or third year, was also a novel of ideas, but it had character, and plot—murder and guilt and redemption. It was about a young man named Kirkstone (perhaps David, perhaps Rob) who lives with his widowed mother, a young man 'afflicted with pride and "purity" and secret lust', 'mother-fixated and a bit in love with death', and the battle waged by three men for his soul.[5] Goodall is a righteous, moral, church-going man who regularly visits his mother. Horner is a life-lover and hedonist, 'natural man': he first encounters Horner sitting under a tree fern by the side of a road beside a stream (Millbrook Road, the Oratia Stream) drinking from a bottle of beer, or maybe a flagon of wine. Crassin represented all that is dark and nasty: a dirty little, lascivious, rich, miserly and sadistic man who lives in a filthy house infested with blow flies which he kills by throwing darts at them and pinning them to the wall.

One thing Gee had learnt by now, from Dickens, was the importance of names. Graham had been simply the kind of name he thought, unimaginatively, a black-clad young pacifist might have; while Horner referred to cornucopias, not lust—a meaning of 'horny' he was not familiar with then. (Maurice, he would later discover, means Moorish or dark.)

When the vile Crassin makes a proposal of marriage to his mother Kirkstone kills him, and disposes of the body in the deep pit beside the dam upstream from Peacehaven. Wracked with remorse, he contemplates suicide. The moonlight shining through his bedroom window casts the shadow of the rope he has tied to a rafter as a dark noose across his pillow—or is it a halo? Goodall, to whom he confesses, urges him to give himself up to the police, but it is Horner who wins his soul, persuading him that he is young, he has his life to live; the body has not been found, no one need ever know. (In the end he gets the girl too.)

He finished this novel, and got his sister-in-law Margaret, Aynsley's wife, who worked as a secretary, to type it for him. And sometime in the future he discarded it, along with his first attempt. And although he would retain in his memory this much of its plot (and heavy-handed symbolism), he would not remember its title. Yet he had been so pleased and excited by what he was doing that his fingers would twitch in anticipation; so worried that he might lose, by some act of god, what he had written that he would recite it to himself chapter by chapter at night. If his first novel had been a product of his grandfather's intellectual inheritance (or burden), this one expressed his mother's intellectual and emotional one. Clearly it was an attempt to exorcise his adolescent demons. It didn't work.

He was the only one of the three boys still at home now. Aynsley had been apprenticed to and then began working for his father when he left school. He got married in 1952 (to a girl he met at a ballroom dancing class; Maurice was their best man), and a year or so later they moved into a house he built on a section Len had given them in Te Atatū; he was to do the same for Gus. Meanwhile, his father effectively financed Maurice's university studies, although he had the usual holiday jobs: as a labourer for a brickie working for his father; at the city markets, cracking open crates, bagging wheat, and still-flapping chickens after someone else had wrung their necks; at Corbans vineyard picking grapes and in the winery. Gus had gone from school into the bank in Henderson (the newly opened branch of the Bank of New Zealand that Len had built) and moved into the bank flat.

At home he talked a lot with his mother: about what they were reading, perhaps about what he was writing. A university friend was shocked when Gee told him that he had given her *Ulysses* to read. Lyndahl was unhappy in these years and often unwell, her depression and disappointment compounded by a prolonged and difficult menopause, alleviated by barbiturates which left her for periods unfocused and drowsy. She was still trying to write—she and Moss both—mostly autobiographical or semi-autobiographical material. A long story entitled 'The Change', narrated by a ten-year-old and then nineteen-year-old girl called Lynda, was a close account of her own childhood and family (their names, too, subtly changed) in Timaru, Christchurch and California. She was encouraging her mother to write too. In 1953 she gave Florence a notebook and asked her to write down her memories of her childhood and life as a young wife and mother when her own children were growing up. This Florence found difficult to do, but she tried, sitting at Lincoln Road looking out on a lawn and rock garden and bird bath—'I notice a bit out of plumb with age . . . I'm a bit out of plumb myself'.[6] She was on her eighties now. Mostly, as well as railing against Winston Churchill and the evils of a greedy and selfish world, she wrote an occasional diary of family events and comings and goings: visits, holidays, graduations (Maurice's), birthdays (her own always with a cake with all 84 or 85 or 86 candles), Len losing half a finger in a circular saw (in August 1956).

She was fond of Len—'a fine man' and 'good [and] kind'[7]—but she worried about Lyndahl, with whom she felt a particular affinity. They made a pact that they 'would only talk about things that make for happiness'.[8] As well as the others of her children nearby whom she regularly saw—Dick and his wife (who lived next door), Hollis, Joyce, and Bernice (who was at Whangaparāoa) and Florence (less frequently, on visits from Waikato)—the youngest, Aynsley, another favourite, made extended, much anticipated Christmas trips home through the 1950s, staying for a few months each time. He now ran an antique store in Salinas (The Spinning Wheel), and he and Lyndahl spent much time cruising antique shops and auction sales together.

Of her grandchildren, Maurice was a special favourite, because he had always since a boy been so kind. 'He is "tall, dark & handsome" but a very quiet, modest man', who 'likes nothing better than to be left alone reading'.[9] He brought her books he thought she might like; for Christmas in 1955 she gave him T.S. Eliot's *Collected Poems* (though one can be sure that either Lyndahl or he himself suggested it).

Maurice led his social life still out in Henderson: playing rugby for Waitemata, 'tagging along' (as he later recognised it) with his younger brother to pubs and parties, dances, the Fruitgrowers' Ball, or on the occasional overnight jaunt out of town—to Orewa one time, for example, where they had to walk to Silverdale and back for beer. Gus's bank flat was a regular venue for impromptu and after-football drinking. It was a completely separate life from his university one, and his writing one.

His third life was his hidden one: his private pain and shame and anxiety—worrying about his continuing inability to relate to girls, wondering how could he be, when would he be, normal? He did not become suicidal, but he thought about it at least once with more than literary interest. It was one of the duties of the junior bank clerks to take turns sleeping on the premises at weekends: a loaded revolver was kept in the dressing table drawer. This constituted bank security. Twice a year they were taken down to the creek to practise firing at a target pinned to a tree. A few times Maurice filled in for Gus when his brother couldn't do his shift. He took the gun out of the drawer one night and thought about how easy it would be, how this would be one solution to his trouble. As Raymond Sole would imagine himself (melodramatically) 'going down to the wharves and tumbling off like a shot man, sinking into the clean cold, not coming up'.[10]

He was too busy at university in his honours year to do any writing; certainly not a novel. He struggled particularly with Old and Middle English, taught by the fearsome Elizabeth Sheppard, and was disappointed to graduate (be 'crowned', as his grandmother playfully put it)[11] on 7 May 1954—his mother's birthday—with second-class honours. He had applied for an Education Department bursary and in 1954 enrolled for the one-year graduate course at Auckland Teachers' College, simply because teaching seemed the kind of job one would do if one really wanted to write. For the third time he took a principled stand on the basis of his Chapple family beliefs and refused to sign the oath of allegiance to the queen that teachers were required to take. He was told to go away and think about it for a week and they never called him back.

Uncommitted to teaching, he loafed his way through the year, to the extent that he was called into the principal's office and told off for absenteeism, but graduated nevertheless. The hard part was going out on section: four two-week blocks of practical classroom experience. His first, uneventful one was at his old school, Avondale College. At his second, at the new Henderson High School, he faced two intimidatingly keen, bright boys in the front row of the fifth-form English class who were later to become a professor of English at

Auckland University and a vice-chancellor.[12] At the last, at Mt Albert Grammar, he encountered the notorious Butch Brown, who, when Gee meekly commented after giving a lesson that perhaps his voice was a little monotonous, thundered back 'monotonous as hell!'

The one he enjoyed was his country section, which he did at Waihī in the winter term. He stayed in a boarding house there, and in the classroom was evaluated by Ken (Stinger) Rae, who had been his French teacher at Avondale College and coach of the First XV and was now lecturing at teachers' college. It was his first extended time away from home apart from family holidays, almost. In May he had gone on a road trip with Gus and two of Gus's friends to Wellington, shortly before Gus left Henderson for Kaikohe where he had been transferred by the bank. In a rented Humber 10 they drove via Hawke's Bay, staying with Uncle Alf in Gisborne en route. It was his first visit to a city which was to play a very important part in his life; although of this one he would remember little, only the coast and fishing for crayfish and paua.

With teachers' college not claiming very much of his attention he had time to go back to writing. Although pleased with his novel he had not done anything with it—not tried to get it published, nor sought any advice, although perhaps he gave it to his mother to read. He had learned, though, that this—to write—was what he most wanted to do; but also that his ambition had overreached his ability. And so he went back to the beginning and began writing short stories, and, as starting-out New Zealand writers normally did, sending them to literary magazines. Later, he would look back on this as the beginning of his apprenticeship. Carpentry is a metaphor he would frequently invoke to describe both the process and quality of his fiction—the acquired, practical craft of fitting things together—liking to see this as the Gee influence on his writing as a balance to the more obvious Chapple one.

Ambitious as he was, though, he sent his stories from the first to *Landfall*, and not, for example, to the weekly *New Zealand Listener* or to one of the tiny handful of 'little magazines' that were emerging now in challenge to *Landfall*. He sent five stories to Charles Brasch in the course of this year. All of them were returned.

The first two, sent back in February, he probably wrote over the summer holidays. 'Saturday Afternoon' survives only in Brasch's note of it as featuring drinking and playing poker on the lawn, a girl missing and one of the searchers wandering endlessly on into the bush. The other, 'While the Flag was Flying', although it did not suit Brasch, would be published (re-titled 'While the Flag was Up') elsewhere a few years later. It is a bitter and sad little suburban story about a man driving with his wife to view the progress on the new house they are having built. As is the custom when the roof has gone on—and the flag of the title has been hoisted by the builders to signal the fact—he has bought beer to drink with them. He is a timid, self-conscious man for whom drinking beer with the tradesmen is painfully out of character: this is his attempt to be 'one of the boys', as his needling wife sarcastically reminds him. He hoists the crate of bottles manfully onto his shoulder and into the car, and practises in his mind's eye drinking in just the right way, the neck resting against the top lip, the beer flowing down over the tongue; and one day, even, doing so with coarse abandonment like 'the fat Maori at the cricket . . . with a beard of foam and beer-stained shirt and a shining hissing bottle. One day he would try it like that. One day he just wouldn't give a damn.'[13] When they get to the house, though, the roof is on but the flag is not up. To his wife's mingled satisfaction and relief he drives surreptitiously away.

His third offering was rejected by Brasch in March as 'a very plain tale of very little interest'.[14] It could have been another story of alienation, discomfort and envy which Gee would remember writing about this time, one concerning 'a rather screwed up young man' at a rugby match enviously admiring his neighbour noisily drinking beer and shouting at the players—like Gee/Raymond Sole at university, 'filled with envy of those easy boys who sat in the cafeteria, who walked in the cloisters and the park, holding girls by the hand'.[15]

'Talk of Eric', returned by Brasch in August, was evidently a more complex effort, which he found clumsy and unskilful 'but . . .?', indicating promise. Set on a vineyard, it contained a 'story within a story' told by the vineyard owner about 'a concealed murder by a henpecked little man who frames pictures of babies cut from magazines till his wife becomes pregnant by her lover & he murders him (off)'.[16] (Gee retained no recollection of this story; perhaps he heard this sinister scenario or something like it during his holiday vineyard job, although the henpecked husband and his strange, obsessive hobby are certainly his.) 'Facade', however, Brasch found 'a decided advance',[17] and was another story Gee eventually published. This drew on his Waihī experience: the story takes place in a boarding house. The landlady, Mrs Saunders, takes pride in her establishment, in her relations with her boarders, in her hearty breakfasts (porridge, which will make regular appearances in Gee's fiction) and especially her 'historic' room, the dining room, furnished with dark embossed wallpaper, embroidered homilies and Maxfield Parrish prints: 'the best room, the most perfect room'. Her husband, meanwhile, is a chronic asthmatic who spends most of his time in bed, coughing (an error, Gee would later realise: asthmatics do not cough so much as wheeze). But periodically, to take down her 'too big' pride, she retrieves from its hiding place and re-reads a letter that a boarder once wrote and she illicitly opened and kept, a cruel letter which describes 'Mine Hostess' as 'a little round hair-netted woman with a red face that has a religious sort of shininess', whose husband 'looks quelled and washes the dishes', and the boarding house as having been 'built right after the Flood', her special room a reliquary of Victoriana.[18]

The boarding house is a fairly accurate description of the one Gee stayed in in Waihī—the landlady, the boarders, the invalid husband, the dining room with its Maxfield Parrishes and pride-of-place *Soldiers of the Queen*. In the fiction the boarder who wrote the offending letter was a young schoolteacher 'with green, red-rimmed eyes' (ever since, schoolteachers had 'made her nervous'); as is the new boarder whose 'eyes were large and frightened behind thick glasses, and [who] had fat lips that made him look helpless' (that face (though not its frightened and helpless expression) is Maurice Shadbolt's).[19] Gee might have written a letter like that home, and the story as a sort of apology[20]—for its sympathy lies with the landlady rather than with the smart, sarcastic young man who mocks her so easily. But a shift in perspective at the end to that of the bedridden husband shifts the focus from that conflict of values to a sense of a claustrophobic, constricted marriage. Unhappy marriages, and a desire for escape, are conspicuous in these stories.

Brasch may have rejected all five, but he had been encouraging nevertheless. He saw what Gee believed: that he could—should—be a writer.

5

Paeroa

Gee spent the first two months of 1955 at home in Henderson with his mind more on writing than on a teaching career. By the time he got around to applying, half-heartedly, for jobs the pickings were slim. In fact he applied for only one, at Kelston High School, unsuccessfully even though, or perhaps because, the principal had been one of his teachers at Avondale College: he was also a passionate cricket man and he gave the job—so Gee surmised—to the rival candidate who would make a better coach for the school teams.

When a late vacancy came up at Paeroa District High School, however, it appealed for a number of reasons. He had enjoyed his time in Waihī, which lay just through the rugged Karangahape Gorge from Paeroa; and it would be good too to get his country service—required of all teachers if they were to advance beyond a certain level—out of the way early. In addition, he knew that one of his friends at teachers' college, Stan Nield, who was a Paeroa local, had taken a job there.

Paeroa was a go-ahead provincial town with a population of a little less than 3000—roughly the same as Waihī—on the banks of a flood-prone river, originally a landing place for the miners heading for the Ohinemuri goldfield which opened in the 1870s. Now it was primarily a service centre for a dairy-farming district—with a small amount of manufacturing, including the commercial bottling of mineral water from a nearby warm spring—and the county seat, and solidly National in its political temper. Its business district stretched four or five blocks along the main street. The school, across the river, as a district high school comprised both a primary and a secondary department, the former located across town except for forms one and two, known as the Junior School, which were housed in two prefabs behind the secondary block. It was a happy school despite the palpable tension that existed between the heads of the two departments: George Gubbins, principal of the school but head of the primary department, and thus seldom seen; and Rex—Shorty—Heward, the secondary head and resentful second-in-command. He was a white-haired, red-faced, irascible (and very short) man who strode briskly about the grounds with his academic gown and smoke from his pipe billowing theatrically behind him, and much liked (with a degree of affectionate derision) by his staff.

Insofar as the job ever would be, Paeroa was Gee's happiest teaching experience. Not that he actually enjoyed it. He was given third-form English and social studies; also commercial practice, although he had never had a bank account and didn't know how to write a cheque: the trick, he learned, was to stay one lesson ahead of the class. Phys ed was easier: taking the class outside and setting them to run around the football field. He also coached rugby. Arriving a month into the first term had the advantage that he was spared inspection, which he dreaded. Always, though, what he found the most difficult about teaching was keeping classroom discipline. On the two or three occasions he had to administer corporal punishment—a strap across the hand—it made him feel physically sick.

He found the staff congenial in general but he became best mates with Stan Nield. They made an unlikely pair. Stan was a rough, loud-mouthed, hard-drinking type, who played representative rugby for Thames Valley. Gee had given up rugby after university, and had spent his teachers' college year playing golf with his brother Aynsley on Saturdays at Huapai. (Aynsley and Margaret were by this time sharemilking on a farm Len had bought at Waimauku, the beginning of a restless period of property speculation and planned semi-retirement on Len's part; a not very successful attempt to break away from his father on Aynsley's.) In Paeroa Gee took up rugby again, playing for Paeroa Old Boys with Stan. The club was a relatively new one, founded (by the school maths teacher) five years before, and 1955 was the first year it was admitted to senior status, controversially and against the opposition of the two existing Paeroa teams, West and Netherton, making this a keenly watched season.

At school the two competed in flirting with one of the attractive younger (though married) woman teachers, Norma Wishnowsky, who flirted innocently back. Almost every day after school they went straight down to Fathers Hotel—'the family hotel' of the four in town—to drink beer, and got up to 'foolish things': behaviour neither appropriate nor becoming to a teacher in a conservative small town, as Gubbins was forced to remind them.[1] Most of the school staff were older and married; they were 'two wild guys out on their own'.[2] As he told Maurie Shadbolt, he was 'catching up on the fun I missed at University'.[3]

And finally he had left home; though not really. His parents visited more than once: in March 1955, just after he'd gone down, with his uncle Aynsley. He went back home for the school holidays and every few weekends. (It was only 80 miles by road.)

For his first few weeks in Paeroa he stayed with a couple who had a daughter in one of his classes, but that (and the character of his fellow boarder) made this less than ideal, and so he accepted an offer of board from Bruce Seaton, one of the Junior School teachers, and his wife, Mary, who rented a house in Railway Street towards the west end of town. Bruce had been teaching for only a few years, and the couple had a one-year-old daughter. They all got on well together. The Seatons found their guest quiet, thoughtful, mature for his years (except when he was with Stan), serious-minded but with a quiet sense of humour they appreciated. He made no secret of the fact that he was interested in writing. Not that he had time to do much, if any, what with teaching, rugby and gadding about with Stan.

Midway through this year he had his first story published, in the Auckland University students' association literary annual *Kiwi*. He had probably written it the previous year, when the bulk of the 1955 issue of the magazine was compiled: like most things printed by Bob Lowry's Pilgrim Press it was rather late coming out. 'In at the Death' has similarities with 'Facade' in its claustrophobic atmosphere, and another bedridden husband. But here he mined his family history. Lying on his deathbed is Whitakker, a retired reverend, courageous and idealistic still as in his missionary days, but without the strength to fend off the attentions of Crassin, a frightened Catholic he long ago befriended and helped to find the right path but who now torments him with his lingering fear of death and the afterlife: a coarse, ugly man with 'horse-brown teeth', tobacco breath and 'long white gums'.[4] In the living room sit waiting Whitakker's distressed wife and their son Donald, who quotes Browning ('Prospice') to be one up on the uneducated Crassin.

The reverend clearly recalls James Chapple; Crassin—the name recycled from Gee's unpublished second novel—is based on a friend and acolyte of his grandfather's (Frank ('Bluey') Morrow in real life) who will reappear in more realised form in Gee's fiction. Outside there are pines, a bridge, a creek. Whitakker has first encountered

Crassin—much as Kirkstone had Horner—sheltering beside a muddy road under a tree. Gee, however, is not wholly unsympathetic to this Crassin, who has been damaged by his religious upbringing. Crassin, in various forms, is to come back many times: as, Gee would later remark, 'one of the vehicles I travel in away from that Puritan territory I lived in as a boy'.[5]

The other characters are similarly drawn with a mixture of dislike and sympathy. Mother is sharp and weary, with 'bone-thin hands' which make 'swift fussy motions in the air', 'waxen ear-lobes', and yellow nails exposing 'rose-pink strips of scalp', her face prone to drawing into 'the severe yellow look that father called lemonish' (she is not Florence Chapple), but genuinely loving and protective of her husband. He, meanwhile, cruelly recalls her ladies' bridge meetings as 'a place where there was really sickness and dying'.[6] Donald is a meek character (Gee's Donalds are always meek), but at the anxious urging of his mother he finally brings himself to throw Crassin out.

Of more moment than seeing his first story in print, though, was having already, by the time it came out, had another accepted by *Landfall*. Gee had sent 'Holiday Harvest' to Charles Brasch early in 1955, so most likely had written it in those summer months after teachers' college finished (when he was not applying for jobs). Brasch responded at the end of March—apologetically, having finally got it back from a reader he had sent it to—enthusiastic about printing the story but making some editorial suggestions: including deleting two opening paragraphs, clarifying an ambiguity in the final scene (which Gee did not see, but attended to nevertheless) and a few other minor revisions, such as removing a 'woolly-footed' horse. Brasch was an astute and careful editor, and this the beginning of a warm and mutually respectful editor–author relationship. Gee worked on the story at home in Henderson over Easter—having, he told Brasch, neither the time nor his typewriter in Paeroa—following all of Brasch's suggestions, including supplying a new title, 'The Widow'.

'The Widow' was another story about a death. It takes place on a run-down coastal farm very like one Moss and Gus holidayed on one Christmas near Leigh. Phil Welch, whose point of view frames the story, is a young city office worker (and former boxer whose career was ended by a broken hand) spending two summer weeks on his uncle Herb and aunt Mae's farm, as he used to do regularly as a boy. He is shocked at how changed he finds them since he was last there five years ago. Mae, who always enjoyed a tipple, has become a sad alcoholic (a recognisable enough portrait of Gee's own sherry-drinking aunt Joyce to cause offence: a first lesson in the perils of putting family into fiction). She seems so much older, too: her hair 'whitish-yellow, the colour of old men's moustaches', her skin 'loose and uncontrolled', her words 'carrying ragged scraps of memory', 'broken and pointless'. Uncle Herb, once a 'cheerful aimless wanderer', is, Mae tells him, losing his mind, has become anxious, 'dreamy and unreal'. And his cousin Selly, too, has somehow turned 'grumping and surly and his face full of mean lines'.[7] He needs to know how they got this way.

He learns that Herb feels responsible for a man's death: he got his quiet, hard-working sharemilker Bill Carson drunk one night out by the log bridge and the man fell from the bridge and drowned—Gee's first fictional drowning. The bridge is a Henderson bridge, a broad, moss-covered log with a wire for a handrail which crossed a deep gorgey stretch of the Opanuku Stream between the back of the Henderson Domain and the blackberry patch at the foot of the Sturges Road farm of Bill Cameron, one of Lyndahl's Labour Party friends. Now Herb obsessively watches the man's widow as she comes and goes daily with the milk can. Phil, needing to understand more, befriends and becomes obsessed with her in turn, and only when she describes for him how she managed to drag her husband's body from the stream, and he can fix a mental image of it in his mind, can he let her and the story go.

The final, short scene, with which Brasch struggled, has Herb tricking Phil into a drinking bout at the bridge, and remains slightly mysterious, although Gee meant no ambiguity—as to what Herb intends and has done—as Brasch read it. (It was, he agreed, the weakest scene in the story but not an important one and 'I can't explain it more fully'.)[8]

In *Kiwi* he had signed himself 'M.G. Gee', because everyone used initials then, but this seemed a little, undignified name. Here he signed himself Maurice Gee, which had more resonance. With this story, and its publication in *Landfall*—in the September 1955 issue—he really felt he had made a start.

Gee left the Seatons' towards the end of 1955. Mary had become pregnant and then miscarried, and having a boarder, albeit a congenial one, was an extra burden they could do without. For the rest of his time in Paeroa he lived at Heysham House, a boarding house on the main street of town. It was better known to the locals as Passeys' after the previous owners, Eve and Bill Passey, who had sold it only recently to the present proprietor, Olga Featherstone; there was a Mr Featherstone too but he was seldom around. It was a large old villa with room for about half-a-dozen boarders, half a block beyond the bridge at the eastern end of town, not far from the school. As Heysham House it had a reputation as a slightly disreputable establishment: not the sort of place for a teacher to be living, as Olga had tried to persuade Gee. The boarders were all single men. His fellow residents included a loud-mouthed bully and tax evader named Errol, and a bank robber, Jack West, also known as the Tank Man, who had done time and was arrested again while Gee was there. Two old men slept in lean-to shacks out the back. Various transients came through; one shared his room for a while, until (after the man urinated out the bedroom window one night) Gee persuaded Olga that he was happy to pay the extra board to have it to himself. There were two other teachers, but they soon left.

Olga cooked and everyone ate together in the kitchen except on Fridays, her night off, when she came home from the pub with a large packet of fish and chips for whoever was there. Moving to Heysham House, Gee would later say, was 'one of the luckiest things' that ever happened to him.[9] This was real, gritty life, away from home, away from family, among a different kind of people. He felt freed up; grown up.

He lost his virginity here, in somewhat sordid circumstances befitting the location: drunk, in one of the front bedrooms, with a young woman whose name and face he would not remember. She was a friend of the landlady's sister, both of them passing through Heysham House one weekend. It was an unmemorable but momentous occasion. At last. He was 24.

He also enjoyed a brief flirtatious romance while in Paeroa, the previous year, with one of the senior girls at the school, whose parents were friends of the Seatons. He was attracted by her liveliness, intelligence and maturity—a sassy, self-conscious maturity ('Haste thee nymph and bring with thee jest and youthful jollity', from Milton's 'L'Allegro', was her character sketch in the class notes in the 1955 school magazine).[10] She was flattered by the attentions of this older man—younger, better looking and more interesting than most teachers, quietly spoken and gentle compared with the local boys. And hugely impressed too that he had told his students that he was not going to be a teacher for very long because he was going to be a writer. They went to the pictures a few times; there was some kissing and cuddling in the park. The 'affair' lasted a few months.

Both of these experiences would find their way into his fiction.

In March 1956 he had a letter from Maurice Shadbolt, the first he had heard from him for four or five years. They had last seen each other, Moss thought, just before a stage two exam. Since abandoning his studies Maurie had spent several months in Hāwera working as a cadet reporter on the *Taranaki Daily News*, and had got married, to a fellow journalist he met there, Gill Heming. They were now in Wellington where he had a job with the National Film Unit, and was writing. He had had his first story published, in the *New Zealand Listener*, in the same month as Gee—a small story narrated by a young man very much like its author, a failed university student who aspires to write and is spending his last summer working holiday sharkfishing on the Kaipara harbour to earn his passage to England, and debating with the fishermen (hard-bitten, salty types) why life isn't enough for him here: a subject which exercised young writers in the 1950s as much as it had in the 1920s and 30s.[11]

He and Kevin, he told Moss, had a publishing plan: an anthology of new, previously unpublished writing by writers under the age of 30—a kind of *Speaking for Ourselves* for their time. Oxford University Press's *New Zealand Short Stories* (1953) in its World's Classics series (nominally edited by Dan Davin but in fact selected by E.H. McCormick and Frank Sargeson) had included many of the writers from Sargeson's 1945 anthology. This would showcase the new wave. In Auckland, Jowsey—who had drifted out of university into a year in the public service and then a series of part-time jobs—was handling the practical matters. In the middle of March he delivered advertising copy to the monthly *Here & Now* ('We're committed now', he told Maurie) calling for submissions to be sent to The Editors, Young NZ Writing by 31 July, and had received a quote from Bob Lowry, of £70–80 for a 70–80-page volume in a print run of 250–300.[12] The third member of their 'joint Auckland–Wellington committee' was Ross Fraser, a twenty-year-old yet-to-be-published writer and artist.

Meanwhile, their friend John Yelash—who harboured incipient criminal tendencies as well as literary aspirations—had another scheme: to solicit half-a-dozen short (say, 1000-word) stories, get a public typist to cut stencils cheaply, run off 500 copies and sell them in pubs and bookshops for a bob each—'something of the style of Overland', the recently founded Australian 'realist' literary magazine: 'call it something like "Mate" which is perhaps a bit studied but will be one in the eye for the mystics', Kevin reported to Maurie.[13] Yelash was from out Henderson way, part of the extended family that included the pioneering winemaker who established the original Pleasant Valley vineyard (though his father was a gum-digger-turned-farmer), had gone to Avondale College and played rugby for Waitematā, but Gee didn't remember him.

He was, Gee replied to Shadbolt, 'having too good a time' in Paeroa to be getting much serious writing done, and had written only two stories since 'The Widow', both of which had been rejected.[14] One he had sent in January to *Numbers*, a small but provocative Wellington-based quarterly established two years earlier by poets Louis Johnson, James K. Baxter and Charles Doyle, to upset the established cultural order with work distinguished by its 'experimental nature or forthrightness'—its first issue in homage to 'the spirit of Dada'.[15] They finally sent his story back (it 'wasn't clear they said'; nor, most likely, 'experimental' enough)[16] eight months later. The other he had sent around the same time to Brasch, who had responded both promptly and with enthusiasm—'What an interesting story—what a good idea! . . . The story so well deserves working on'—and some suggestions. Gee sent him a new version two months later, but Brasch still was not convinced that it 'comes off' and suggested that he put it aside for a while to come back to later: 'What you've attempted in this story is peculiarly difficult, I fancy'. The story, entitled 'The Separation', was never published (although elements of it would re-surface in a much later one). It involved adultery, and included a 'dream or "imagining"' sequence in which a preacher appeared: perhaps he was trying something experimental here.[17]

Two unpublished stories: it was not much to show for six months' work. So, he told Shadbolt, he had decided to resign from teaching from the end of the term. He had enough money saved, he thought, to support himself for a year, and was 'going to settle down at home and write myself silly'.[18]

He finished teaching at the end of June (well before the end of the second term, in fact) and, back in Henderson, launched straight into serious work. His head was 'full of bright ideas for a short novel' and material for four stories, all of which he hoped to complete by

Christmas: 'I feel that if I don't carry out this programme of work I shall have missed my chance'. He was painfully aware of his friend's apparent industriousness. Shadbolt was also working on a novel (he said), had had five short stories published now and was thinking of putting together a collection, all while being married and holding down a full-time job. Immediately, however, he set about revising a long (16,000-word) story, one he would continue to work on over the next six months, and two others—one of them 'The Separation'—which he sent off during July for the 'young writers collection'.[19]

What his father thought of him giving up his career to sit at home writing he didn't ask.

At weekends he went into town to drink at the Queen's Ferry or the Occidental next door in Vulcan Lane, as he had done in the first few months of 1955 before he went down to Paeroa, and to some extent during his teachers' college year, but it was in this second half of 1956, and the following summer, that he was most part of the literary–bohemian Queen's Ferry scene. The tiny pub, also known as The Hole in The Wall, was as it had been for years the favoured drinking place of journalists, writers—those of an earlier generation such as Sargeson still frequenting it on occasion—and 'the newer types on the fringes of Art': 'the city's young bohemians and hobobohemians . . . aspiring poets and painters, university dropouts, political activists . . . and one or two whose ambition it was to make a name in crime'.[20] His drinking companions included Jowsey and Shadbolt (when he was up from Wellington) and Carl Freeman, back in 1956 after a year or two in London; and Robin Dudding, a twenty-year-old journalist on the *Auckland Star* from Hastings, who also became a good friend. So did Ian Middleton, who worked across the road in the mail room of the *New Zealand Herald* (even though he was beginning to go blind as his older, writer brother Ted already had). There were two young English artists: Tony Stones, painter, sculptor and sometime waiter at the Macambo coffee bar, and Michael Illingworth; architects of the modernist Group circle; and flamboyant German political refugee, left-wing iconoclast and landscape gardener Odo Strewe.

He went along too, sometimes, to the literary parties, at Tony and his wife Cushla Stones' place in Freeman's Bay, for example, or Strewe's 'butterfly house' out in Titirangi. The latter were to become almost as legendary as those hosted in Epsom by Bob Lowry: the house, designed by the Group Architects, was so-named for its avant-garde roof-line; a banana palm grew up through the living room. Strewe's wife Jocelyn served garlic bread (equally exotic). They were smaller parties than Lowry's but tended to be more raucous.

But while he was around this scene, Gee was neither a regular nor a conspicuous presence. He was a quiet participant, to the side rather than at the centre, a watcher and listener rather than a talker, a drinker but not a heavy one: he was never the maker of that kind of story. Jowsey, later, would see him at this time as serious, self-possessed, quietly and determinedly getting on with his writing while the rest of them were still to some extent striking a pose. Equally it was the case that social conversation was something he did not find easy. Whether this was because of 'some sort of emotional constriction or just mental poverty', he remarked to his mother, he didn't know.[21]

Kevin and Maurie's publishing venture was not going well. Ambitious as such projects always are, they had intended it to be 'a comprehensive publication with as many contributors as possible rather than an anthology of the work of a few', to represent 'the recent upsurge in creative writing by writers in their early twenties' and to 'accurately reflect trends for the future in New Zealand writing'; while also to attract a wide audience with an 'editorial emphasis . . . heavily in favour of readability'.[22] They advertised in three consecutive issues of *Here & Now*, in *Arena*, in bookshop windows and in the main daily newspapers. By mid-July Kevin was despairing. They had received 'hundreds of contributions' from dozens of contributors—by the closing date, 80 short stories and 175 poems from 75 writers—'of which NOT ONE is worthy of the printing', he reported to Maurie. 'God alone knows where the next generation of Masons, Fairburns, Glovers, Baxters is coming from. . . . One thing that certainly stands out is that there's no Shakespeare hidden, unnoticed in the heart of the Urewera country . . . Jesus, Maurie there's some awful stuff been pouring in—and I don't mean just bad writing, but diseased.'

Still, he thought, 'out of yourself, Gee, Stead and the other two editors and a couple of others perhaps, we'll get enough to call it a representation, even if it has to be half a book by the Editors!'[23] True enough, the shortlist that was shaping up by September consisted largely of contributions by themselves and people they knew. Ideally they would include both of Gee's stories—'The Separation' was their first choice and his—but there was the question of cost: another 4000 Gee words meant another £10. Lowry had suggested printing the volume in 8-point type to save space. Jowsey in fact had more invested in the project than just ambition, having paid Lowry £100 of his own money in advance when Lowry—inspired printer but incompetent businessman—was 'down on the beam ends'.[24]

There was the problem of a title, too: it was a pity, Kevin remarked to Maurie, that *Speaking for Ourselves* had already been used. By October their co-editor had come up with 'Chapter and Verse'.

They were showing likely material as it came in to Frank Sargeson, who was fully supportive of the venture. Of the flock of young writers to whom Sargeson served as a willing mentor in these years (which were for his own writing worryingly unproductive ones), Jowsey—a near neighbour—was one whose friendship and lively, youthful company he valued especially. Jowsey had met Sargeson for the first time in January this year, and he was to spend the summer of 1956–57 living in the army hut in Sargeson's back garden recently vacated by Janet Frame. He was writing poetry, and had his first poem published in the *New Zealand Listener* in November.

He and Yelash, meanwhile, had by the middle of the year assembled the copy, and had a cover sketch by Tony Stones, for the more imaginatively titled *Mate*,[25] which was developing into something a little different from Yelash's original conception. It would not, however, be out in print (Lowry had offered to do this one for free) for another year.

In Henderson, Gee too was becoming despondent. He had a story published in September in *Arena*, a magazine of longer standing and less militant editorial purpose than *Numbers*, and loyally appreciated by a wide range of writers as a useful outlet for work not substantial enough or suitable for *Landfall*—a story 'so small that I almost overlooked it myself'.[26] The author's note inserted by the editor confused him with his mother. It was a slight but disturbing sketch of a couple trapped in a bitter and unhappy marriage, very like the relationships depicted in 'Facade' and 'While the Flag was Up'. The husband spends his evenings sitting by a fireless stove working at a somewhat obscure hobby which seems to consist of drawing in outline and filling in pastel-coloured circles and letters, while he and and his wife engage in resentful, competitive, hurtful conversation. Both are disappointed and lonely; the author's sympathy moves between the two.[27] He had had something else rejected by the *Listener*. 'I've made a real mess of this full time writing business', he wrote to Maurie in

October, in a longish letter in which he unburdened himself of his self-doubts: 'Of course it's a little early to be so depressed, but if I can read the signs right I was only meant to be a Sunday afternoon writer.' Although, perhaps writing was like golf, he thought: one had to expect to get much worse before getting better. He had, he felt, 'a weakness for the airy-fairy poetic phrase—a residue of immaturity in me I think. Result is something that sounds all right, but doesn't mean much. Then again, I'm finding it increasingly difficult to write anything in a straight forward way. Simple narrative is almost an impossibility. I find things turning back and twisting off to the side etc, which would be all very well if there was some purpose in it. Whole truth is I lack control & direction'—two things he believed his friend did have.

On the other hand, he might be being a little hard on himself: he was reading Thomas Mann at this time ('really marvellous . . . He uses "whitely" three or four times?'). Really he was, he suspected, just lazy, and 'annoyed with myself—but quite determined to go on to better things. You see up to now I have not been prepared to work hard enough. I wanted things to come easily—with the result that I've been getting what I deserve, shoddy writing. At the same time there are certain things I want to say—I'm not just writing for its own sake. So that really, if I want to preserve my self respect I'll have to take myself in hand, and work.'[28]

In November he sent off two competition entries. One was a revised version of the story rejected by *Numbers* back in January, and which he entered for a competition being run by Noel Hoggard in *Arena*. The prize was two guineas. Gee's entry (one of 30) was a Paeroa story inspired by an experience the Seatons had had when they first moved to Paeroa and were living on the rural outskirts of town, when a dog, frightened by a storm, hid itself under the kitchen stove and could not be persuaded out. In the story the owner of the house is a lonely, middle-aged woman, regarded as an eccentric in the town, who seeks love and 'a new beginning' from Joe, a rough quarry worker who knocked on her door two years before looking for a place to stay. When she asks him to help her entice the dog (driven there by the noise of the quarry blasting) out from under the stove he fetches a pig dog which he sets on the terrified animal, which it kills, leaving her to ask which is worse: loneliness, or sharing her life with a person who could do such a thing, a man of 'his smallness, his dullness, his mind that was twisted from life'.[29] '[L]ight and simple', Gee described

'The Quarry' to Shadbolt. It won him his second literary prize, and first press notice.[30]

Landfall's tenth-anniversary prose award, announced in the December 1955 issue, required something more ambitious: especially given Brasch's accompanying editorial lamenting the quality of current New Zealand prose (compared with the poetry), which 'exude[d] a tired smell of orthodoxy, a dull, spiritless, conforming sameness', and reminding of 'the yearlong steady application, the sheer labour, patient and untiring, which prose writers have to learn' while their craft also demanded 'ripeness of form and perfection of language in its kind no less than poetry does'.[31] (Gee certainly read this.) Two awards were offered, for fiction and non-fiction, of a handsome £25 each. The story Gee sent was a revision of the long one he had sat down to work on when he first got home in July, and which he may have had in mind when he commented to Shadbolt about the elusiveness of straightforward narrative: 'a queer sort of story . . . queer in construction I mean', with the title 'From Now On', which Brasch had rejected in September, having found it '[a] long flat dreary story seen through the eyes of the 5 people concerned . . . none of them interesting.'[32] With a dreary title too, he might have said: when it was published a year later it was as 'In a Sleeping Face'.

The setting is Piha, where Lyndahl had taken her sons on holiday when she was unwell: the characters are at a seaside hotel; they take the scenic bush track to the falls (Piha's Kitekite Falls), two plummeting cascades separated by a 'quiet and green and deep pool'.[33] In five sections (one in the form of a diary, another a confessional letter) the same situation is seen from their separate points of view. ('Don't ask me why I'm doing it like that', Gee remarked to Shadbolt, '—I know there are simpler ways.')[34] Bernard Lambourne, retired, takes a nosy, but compassionate, interest in his fellow guests. Over breakfast (porridge) he observes the newest arrival, a young woman who is always 'so gloomy', and wonders what 'mystery' lies behind this: a tragic love affair, perhaps.[35] (There is a slightly unpleasant aspect of the voyeur about him.) She, Hilda, is concerned about and befriends Alice Matthews, a woman suffering from an incipient emotional breakdown who is taking a holiday with her young son (her husband was too busy to come) on her doctor's advice. The son, Graham, is a 'weedy', 'pale effeminate child'—she 'wouldn't have been surprised to learn that [he] had been fed from birth on linseed and nuts', Hilda observes—and yet, she believes, has 'strength of a sort, a kind of inborn selfishness that would see him through', just as Bernard discerns in his eye 'a gleam of cunning' at times.

The physically meek boy is not his creator, but there is a good deal of Lyndahl in his mother, in her unhappy marriage, and in the oppressive, mutually dependent mother–son relationship which both of these observers find unsettling and is the story's centre. Alice feels abandoned by her husband, who has become consumed by his work (a menswear business) and making money, and drinks too much whisky sometimes at his club. She clings to her son out of fear of losing him too: is constantly fearful, telling him not to stand too close to the edge of the falls, to be careful of the sharp cutty grass—which brings a memory: of 'a tiny friendly busy child, red-ribboned pigtails swinging as she played—and games that end with bleeding fingers. Always it was the same. Imagination or memory? She couldn't tell. But she felt that the mind didn't lie with these pictures: they held all sorts of reality, truths she hadn't the strength to find in any other way.'[36]

Graham yearns to break free from a mother who always holds his hand, and who tells him 'now you say after me the world is full of God's beautiful things and I'll only see the beautiful things'.[37] Meanwhile, his father (whose off-stage voice, in a letter to a colleague, is the least convincing in the story) feels unappreciated, sexually frustrated, unsympathetic to his wife's emotional state and resentful of what he sees her doing to their son. Hilda's unhappy story is an abortion forced on her by her fiancé and the disillusionment of her dreams of husband 'and home and baby and at last quietness and love . . . the life that was cool and ordinary and real'. By the end of the holiday she knows she no longer wants the kind of marriage, 'dull and proper', that Alice and John Matthews' promises ('nothing ever lasts when you've made it perfect', Alice tells her).[38]

Graham's escape, in the end, is fleeting but triumphant. When he finds himself for a moment unobserved (as Hilda goes to the aid of his mother when her equilibrium finally collapses; she will escort the two home a week early) he makes a dash for the beach; perhaps he'll even make it to the blowhole. The theme of the story, Gee told Shadbolt, was 'one I feel quite strongly about'.[39]

Shadbolt was the joint winner of the competition (which attracted a disappointing 25 entries in total—in part, Brasch was sure, because of 'the sheer difficulty of breaking new ground to write imaginatively about life in this country')[40] with 'Play the Fife Lowly', a story about people like himself: young bohemian types at a party. Gee's, further revised, was accepted by *Landfall* in May the following year, not by Brasch but by acting editor W.H. Oliver (in Brasch's absence on one of his regular cultural sabbaticals overseas). He may have felt that his friend's writing had control and direction and a confidence that his did not, but it was also predictable, the kind of stories one expected from a young writer of their age and at that stage. Gee's were different. Shadbolt's first *Landfall* story, which had appeared in the issue after Gee's, was a small story about a country girl going to her first dance.[41] In 'The Widow' the New Year's Eve dance Phil goes to with his cousin Selly and his fiancée (based on one Moss and Gus went to at Leigh) is one scene in a much more complex, fully realised, more interesting story.

Gee did not apply for the State Literary Fund's new Scholarship in Letters, worth £500, being offered for the first time for 1957. Maurie and Gill had alerted him to it. Shadbolt did; but it went, as Gee thought it would, to an older, established writer (E.H. McCormick). He didn't have the confidence yet, he told them, 'to go chasing after things like that'. And besides, he had 'no "project" in mind other than drifting around the country writing the odd story—there's not really £500 worth of effort in that'.[42] Unlike Maurie, he was making no plans, immediate at least, to go to England. The Shadbolts planned to get away in the middle of next year; as had Kevin until he gave the first boat fare he saved to Bob Lowry. Gee had no further destination in mind than Wellington, where he had a standing invitation from Maurie and Gill to stay.

6

Wellington

Forty years later Maurice Shadbolt wrote a highly romanticised account of how Gee got to Wellington. He and Kevin, he recorded, sought him out in Henderson one summer night, got him drunk and 'kidnapped him'. Hitchhiking south a few days later, the two Maurices 'whittled lines as we waited for rides on dusty roadsides. When a car came we travelled on, past the farms, hills and forests of our unlettered land'—sharing family histories and 'looking for stories to make sense of our lives'.[1]

It's not quite how Gee remembered it. For one thing, he had been thinking about going down to Wellington for some months; though some persuasion did help. It's true that there was a night not long before Christmas when Kevin and Maurie came out to visit him at Tirimoana Road, bringing beer, and someone got drunk. Perhaps it was that night he read them the draft of a story—about a young boy spying on the nuns walking past from his hiding place amongst the pine trees—which they clearly thought was no good and he discarded. A few days after Christmas he and Shadbolt hitchhiked south, going 'a roundabout way through Taranaki' (like Rex Petley),[2] staying with a friend of Maurie's in Hāwera and making it to Wellington the next day.

Maurie and Gill lived in a small cottage at the southern end of The Terrace—number 370a, a few houses before The Terrace turned the corner into Abel Smith Street. That first night Jim Baxter turned up after tea, and talked for three or four hours in his eloquent, 'brilliant fashion'; Gee, exhausted from the journey, fell asleep.[3] His second, and more significant, encounter a few days later, on the steps of the main Post Office, was with Nigel Cook, who was not a writer, though fancying for a time that he might be and a close friend of Frank Sargeson's.[4] Cook and his girlfriend, Julie Tangney, lived near the Shadbolts in Ghuznee Street and were friends of theirs. They became Gee's closest and most supportive Wellington friends, taking the place of the Shadbolts when the latter left for Europe in June. Gill 'and Julie between them, or rather together,' he wrote later to Maurie, 'a composite figure, me dear old Wellington Mum'.[5]

To his mother he wrote soon after he arrived, reassuring her: 'I think I'll get to like Wellington quite well. I know the main streets and the bookshops already, and that at least is a beginning.' He was 'well-fed comfortable and busy—so please don't worry'. 'P.S.', he added, 'Wellington is a nice place but not as good as Paeroa.'[6] In fact, Wellington—his Wellington of the 1950s—became another magic place: not as powerfully or as darkly complex as Henderson, but a 'magical territory'[7] of its own. 'At last my life has started', said Jack Skeat.[8]

He stayed for a month at the Shadbolts', sleeping on the sofa, 'wide-eyed with wonder at the life he wrongly imagined we lived', Maurie told Frank Sargeson, as they took him out and introduced him to the city and their friends: 'I don't think he realised we were just entertaining him, taking him to meet people, and so on.'[9] Dinner with Louis Johnson and his wife was another early literary encounter to leave him feeling inadequate in the presence of 'fluent' and 'clever' conversationalists: 'I have nothing to say when I'm with people like that', he wrote afterwards to Lyndahl.[10]

It was early on too that he was taken by the Shadbolts to a party at the studio of drama teacher and producer, and German-Jewish refugee, Maria Dronke on Lambton Quay, along with Meg Anderson, a nineteen-year-old aspiring actress about whom Gill had recently written an article for the *Evening Post*, as his 'date'. She was beautiful, and he was entranced. Unfortunately for him, it was at this party that she first saw the equally beautiful Alistair Campbell, 'propped on an elbow drinking a beer' across the other side of the room, looking 'grim and cynical', and there with his pregnant wife and fellow poet Fleur Adcock. Gee had met them already at their house in Tinakori Road where they lived with their young son, taken there by Maurie. While Fleur left the party to go home early, the others walked through town to the Shadbolts', where they had coffee and talked long and late, Alistair aloof but observing Meg intently while Gee 'seemed more tangibly friendly'. Within a very short time she and Alistair were a couple. Everyone there that night had been shocked by what they saw going on; except Gee, who remained unaware, and wondered why his phone calls and shy attempts subsequently to ask Meg out were met with friendly but repeated excuses until Gill put him right. His passion, however, did not die easily. Campbell would later remember him 'quivering with desire' for Meg.[11]

Wellington was full of writers, poets especially. 'Their example and their company turned my life about,' he would later recall: 'that larger than life way of responding to the world, of making a place in it, of answering back, of condemning nonsense and making sense'.[12] Back then he was merely thrilled and tongue-tied. Along with Baxter, Johnson and Campbell, he got to know to varying degrees others associated with the teachers' college and the so-called 'Wellington group': Anton Vogt, Barry Mitcalfe, Peter Bland; Charles Doyle the following year. He met the older, more gentle Noel Hoggard, editor of *Arena*, a quiet civil servant when not producing his magazine on his private printing press in his shed out at Pukerua Bay. Kevin was around too for some of 1957, living in a flat halfway along The Terrace, before he headed back to Auckland where he worked for several months for Odo Strewe landscape gardening. By the end of this year he was no longer Kevin Jowsey but Kevin Ireland, having changed his name by deed poll as a statement of a new—literary—identity (although the choice of Ireland was accidental).

There were others on the literary fringe. John Yelash was about, dangerous and disreputable, self-created in a way Gee found admirable (though most people did not), with his affected plummy English accent and ambition, as he told Gee one night, to make his name not in letters but as New Zealand's 'king of crime'; though meanwhile his short stories, *Forty Thousand Beers Ago*, came out that year from the Pilgrim Press. And Brian Bell, another well-known reprobate (though not a criminal one) around town, sometime poet (a potential contributor to 'Chapter and Verse') and author of an occasional satirical *Broadsheet*, number one of which appeared in January the following year, composed in a coffee shop and run off on the teachers' college duplicator.

It was Bell possibly who first took Gee round to a house at the bottom of Everton Terrace where five young women, all university students, flatted together. All of them were friendly, but one in particular 'really sparkled'.[13] Angela Sears was in the final year of an English degree, and passionate about literature (secretary of the university Literary Society) though she didn't write seriously herself. She was attractive, vivacious, 'very intelligent, extremely friendly' and he, again, 'seriously smitten'.[14] It was another unrequited passion. Her fondness of and admiration for him were flattering, no doubt, but she was seriously and enduringly in love with someone else (although the man in question—Tom Garland—was away in England at this time). She and Moss became very close friends but she would not be fully aware until much later of how much he suffered on her account. In his notebook from this time (a Croxley li-flat, bought from the Henderson Book Shop), in which he wrote down literary quotes and references and ideas and try-outs for stories, there is this: 'Loss of pride in this affair with A. I keep going back for the little of herself she gives me.—the beggar accepting crumbs under the rich man's table.'[15]

Angela introduced Gee to another circle, separate from but overlapping with the literary crowd, of mostly occasional and former students. At its centre, and the centre of everything he was involved in, was Ron Polson, loud, gregarious, often outrageous, a witty raconteur, assiduous womaniser and sexual provocateur, and with a fine singing voice: he was wont to perform impromptu at the parties he very often organised (later he would have a career as a jazz singer in Australia). His flatmate, Ben Goffman, was quieter and a closer friend of Angela's and Gee's: a Cockney raised in an east London orphanage who wrote a bit of poetry and attached himself to the university literary crowd. They had a flat in Terrace Gardens, a pathway leading into a bushy gully halfway down Allenby Terrace; which was not a terrace at all but a precipitous flight of steps which plunged from The Terrace (right where Kevin's flat was), 'past the windows of half-furnished rooms, past rotting aerial ways into kitchens',[16] down to Willis Street. There were lots of parties there, and at Everton Terrace.

Geographically Gee's Wellington was a thin slice, from the south end of Willis Street and The Terrace to the northern reaches of Lambton Quay and Tinakori Road. After a month at the Shadbolts he found himself a bedsit in Grant Road, Thorndon, hard up against Tinakori Hill. It was one half of a lean-to at the back of the landlady's house, with another man in the room next door and a tiny shared kitchen, bathroom and toilet block further along. It was pretty substandard, however not for long. When the Shadbolts left in June Nigel and Julie moved into their Terrace cottage and offered their Ghuznee Street place to Gee, to his delight.

Number 112a Ghuznee Street had been just a shed when Nigel

(who was taking night classes with the aim of going to architecture school) took it over from two students and rebuilt it into a 'bachelor pad' of great charm: everyone who lived or went there thought so. It was just around the corner from Willis Street heading up towards The Terrace, at the back of a yard next to the two-storeyed brick doctor's residence on the corner, and flanked by the high brick walls of the buildings on either side. A high fence hid it from view of the street. There were two rooms, one up, one down: downstairs a small kitchen stove and sink, and a table screened by a shelving unit from an open staircase leading to a hole in the ceiling; upstairs there was a shower box, a desk between the two windows and a bed built in across the end of the room against a blood-red-painted wall; when he stretched out lying down he touched both walls. Coir matting was on the floor. The toilet was outside out the back. It was known by everyone as 'the bach'. Gee lived there for the best part of a year and a half; Raymond Sole and Gordon Ferry (*Blindsight*) would live there too. It was, he would years later say, his favourite of all the places he had ever lived in.[17]

There were always people round, visiting, sometimes sleeping downstairs on the floor: Goffman and other friends from the Polson crowd; and Dick Packer, a well-known and volatile pseudo-literary character who carried a large unfinished manuscript about with him (in which everyone assumed they appeared) and fancied himself as New Zealand's Rimbaud;[18] Baxter regularly (School Publications where he and Alistair Campbell both worked was on the Willis/Ghuznee Street corner); Yelash and Bell—who was so pleased with himself for coining the term Curnoid upstairs there one night, in reference to the Auckland poets, that he wrote, signed and dated it on the wall; two or three of Baxter's alcoholic friends to whom Gee lent too much money (making the mistake once of giving one of them his key: he took all the money he could find); one night a cross-dressing Wairarapa farmer who tagged along with the group after pub-closing time, disappeared back to his hotel for a while as they sat crammed around the little table sharing a meal, and returned wearing a pink blouse with short puffed sleeves—he had listened to them talking and thought they wouldn't mind.

It was through Nigel Cook also that he found one of the best jobs he ever had, as a hospital porter at Wellington Hospital in Newtown (where Nigel was, or had been, working too). He had this job for most of the year, and loved it: wheeling patients to the wards in chairs or on trolleys; collecting dirty laundry, delivering meals; taking used instruments to the autoclave and warm specimen dishes to pathology; helping the nurses change oxygen bottles and turn patients who were too heavy. And the morgue run, with a trolley with 'a lid like those dishes where you carry in the roast', helping the nurse transfer the body onto the morgue table, arrange the jelly-like limbs and bind tight the jaw. Down in the ambulance basement, where trolleys waited in a 'bleak windy corridor' ('Ordinary trolleys, Cardiac trolley with raised head, Phillips trolleys for fractures'), Mac the attendant—'bitter of face, tiny sharp eyes'—fed the sparrows that nested in the pipes and concrete beams.[19] He enjoyed the backchat with the nurses, speeding the trolleys along the corridors and round corners (once nearly colliding with the hospital matron, who was stern and not amused), and the time spent sitting around on benches outside the receptionist's office waiting for new patients to come in. It was experience he stored for future use, making notes in his notebook. Rex Petley would have this job (and put it into poetry); Gordon Ferry too.

Hospital portering was a full-time job with regular hours. Social—and literary—life went on in the pub, at parties, and in the coffee bars which had appeared quite suddenly in New Zealand's cities in the mid-1950s: establishments serving real coffee made on imported espresso machines and furnished in European-modern style, where one could sit and talk, or, on one's own, read or write if one had nothing else to do, for as long as one liked. Pubs closed at six; the chicest of the coffee shops stayed open all night. '[U]nknown in New Zealand . . . little more than two years ago', the *Listener* observed in 1958, today 'they are as much a part of the local scene as the T.A.B.—and almost as ubiquitous', with their characteristic decor of 'concealed or subdued lighting, pot-plants and foam-rubber or cane upholstery', and 'the atmospheric gimmick—the fishnet curtaining, the low-wattage electric bulb, the tropical fish-tank, the contemporary print', and exotic names.[20] Gee went most often to the Picasso, which was the closest to him, upstairs just round the corner on Willis Street; or to the Man Friday in Dixon Street, where there were 'black footmarks painted on the wall';[21] and the Casa Fontana on Victoria Street, 'The Pioneer of Coffee Houses', whose 'Il Paradiso Room' it boasted as 'Wellington's only salad bar' and where a jazz band played on Sunday nights; [22] to the Ca D'Oro perhaps on Lambton Quay around the corner from Willis Street; La Scala in Panama Street further down;

or the Symposium in Vivian Street, whose name expressed its owner's aspirations for it to become a literary salon.

The hotel they drank at was the St George, halfway down Willis Street at the bottom of Allenby Terrace; less often The Grand further down (occasionally the Waterloo near the Railway Station). Baxter was regularly there, drinking sarsaparilla, not beer, having joined Alcoholics Anonymous. Yet it was not Baxter's sobriety that his friends were all talking about this year but his conversion to Catholicism (he was baptised into the church in January 1958). Gee, unlike others, was not worried about the effect this might have on his poetry, as he tried to explain to Maurie: 'I don't see it as a surrender. I think it's just a shift to a new position from which he can conduct a different kind of exploration.' What Baxter wanted, Gee guessed, was 'something that would transcend his own intelligence, something that would give him at least periods of rest from his own insights. . . . I don't think that is withdrawal or defeat. . . . I'm sure the emphasis is still going to be firmly fixed on what Jim sees more clearly than anyone else I know—that is, the sufferings of individual people. I'm quite excited about what we may get.' (But, he hesitated, '[h]e's too complex for me to understand.')[23] It was a thoughtful and generous response to something the literary fraternity was having difficulty understanding.

As always Gee was a quiet, observant presence. At the Shadbolts on The Terrace on Sunday nights when a group would gather regularly for a meal, and the men would talk loudly about their writing, Moss wouldn't. In the back bar of the George he was conspicuous only by the Waitematā Rugby Football Club blazer he always wore, unfazed by the gentle ribbing it attracted. He wore it not as any sort of statement or affectation but simply because it was a perfectly good blazer; he was not nor would he ever be at all appearance- or fashion-conscious. Eventually he passed it on to Carl Freeman, who continued to wear it for several years after he had unstitched the WRFC badge from the breast pocket.

A 'scrape' he, Kevin and John Yelash 'got into with the police' one night—and of which he gave a slightly exaggerated account to Maurie—was uncharacteristic. Leaving a party, very drunk, and passing the open door of a flat on The Terrace, they helped themselves to food they saw lying on the table and to several items from the kitchen cupboards, including an electric kettle. The next morning, alarmed by what they had done and worried that the robbery would be reported, they disposed of the loot down a rubbish chute in the Dixon Street flats and decided that it would be wise to leave town for a while.[24] Gee went to Paeroa for a few days and stayed with the Seatons, and told them—proudly, Bruce thought—that he had been getting himself into 'some pretty shaky sort of situations' in Wellington and had had to get out. (He seemed to be collecting experience, was Bruce's impression—of life 'in the raw'.)[25] The robbery was not, in the event, reported and the police were never involved.

This criminal escapade, however, did not compare with some of the other things Yelash was getting up to. Later that year he took off down south on a road trip with his girlfriend, Diana Fussell, the young and love-struck daughter of the governor of the Reserve Bank of New Zealand (she had been Robin Dudding's girlfriend, until the day Gee witnessed the more magnetic Yelash 'steal' her from under Bob's nose), forging cheques in her name along the way. Eventually they were caught, and Yelash charged on two counts of forgery and sentenced to a year in gaol.[26] Before they left they had stayed with Gee at Ghuznee Street for a few nights, and he had been with them to (a very uncomfortable) dinner at the Fussell house in the posh part of the posh suburb of Karori. Her father later came round to the bach to find out from Gee where they were (he didn't know). Gee took a less dim view of Yelash than many did, and he visited him in Wi Tako prison; and resented, he told Maurie, that just because 'I defend John now and then I'm accused of being under his influence'.[27]

And yet, for all the bohemian romance and occasional drama, the fun of fast-cornering trolleys down hospital corridors, and the overall thrill of being in Wellington, he was not happy. This was not apparent to most of his friends—although Baxter, he felt, saw it. He was unhappy because he was lonely; because he didn't have a girl and he didn't know how to get one. He had long talks with Julie about his relationship troubles: about his unrequited longings for Meg and for Angela. She was both worried for him and puzzled by the intensity of his pain—wondering how real, let alone realistic, it was, feeling that his depth of suffering seemed out of proportion to its cause.

At weekends he would often wander the streets alone, looking for someone to talk to. One day he followed a young couple walking hand-in-hand along Willis Street and Lambton Quay who were demonstrably in love, 'in a world complete and timeless', and envied them; and returned home thinking of Dylan Thomas ('In my craft or sullen art'), Kierkegaard and Thomas Mann's Tonio Kröger, and consoling himself that after all he was a writer and that was not for him[28]—like Thomas's poet who writes of 'lovers, their arms/ Round the griefs of ages/ Who pay no praise or wages/ Nor heed my craft or art'. He wrote a story about it. In his notebook there are long quotations from Camus (*The Myth of Sisyphus* and *The Fall*); Lionel Trilling ('Art and Neurosis' (1945), including 'disease and mutilation are available to us all—life provides them with prodigal generosity. What marks the artist is his power to shape the material of pain we all have'); from Kierkegaard and Herbert Read (on 'The Creative Nature of Humanism'). He transcribed a passage from Alfred Hayes' 1954 novel *In Love*, in which a man sitting in a Manhattan bar recounts to the young woman on the bar stool next to him the story of a past love affair:

> [. . .] I appear to be someone who apparently knows where he's going, assured, confident of myself, and aware of what, reasonably, to expect when he arrives, although I could hardly, if now you insisted on pressing me, describe for you that secret destination.
>
> But there is one. There must be one. We must behave, mustn't we, as though there is one, cultivating that air of moving purposely somewhere, carrying with us that faint preoccupation of some appointment to be kept, that appearance of having a terminal . . . But the truth is, isn't it, that all our purposefulness is slightly bogus, we haven't any appointment at all, there isn't a place where we're really expected or hoped for, and that nobody's really waiting, nobody at all, and perhaps there never was [. . .]
>
> [. . .] I tell myself that there isn't, and hasn't ever been, a place at all, thinking that to be, not disillusioned, but just the opposite of illusioned, is a sort of improvement, when it probably isn't; and with this sense, that's hard to describe, of permanent loss; of having somewhere committed an error of a kind or a mistake of a kind that can never be rectified, of having made a gesture of a sort that can never be retracted.[29]

Writing to Maurice Shadbolt the following year, he adopted a certain existentialist swagger in describing how he had lately 'been alternately calm and depressed—depressed because I can't even begin to see my future, calm when I realise it doesn't really matter—good or bad something will happen'.[30]

Reading Camus and identifying with Tonio Kröger were typical of a young man with literary interests in the 1950s. But he did not feel typical; and his problems were not typical. He thought he was odd, that he was not normal. At the heart of his inability to engage romantically with women was his adolescent torment and the ongoing problem of sexual performance (something he did not talk with Julie about). But there was something else too, larger than this 'trouble', and more personal than existentialist alienation. Writing to his mother two years later he tried to explain his sense of himself as being somehow not part of real life:

> I can't have real worries—I'm not equipped for them. I'm a spectator more than an actor—all my own problems & feelings seem fake—definitely unimportant. It's a queer position to be in—not entirely a pleasant one, but not one I'd change. It makes life very easy—you're sort of insulated against real pain. And it's valuable—its law seems to be that everything you haven't got in the area where experience is <u>immediate</u> or <u>actual</u> you have <u>permanently</u>, to hold & look at. As long as you're not soured.[31]

What Julie thought she recognised was a position of detached observation. 'I've always had myself watching me,' Jack Skeat will write.[32]

It was not proving a very productive writing year, 1957; at least not as productive as he had intended. He had arrived in Wellington full of determination. 'I feel that I should plan my days, allot time more strictly, discipline myself down here just to force myself to work, get into the habit of producing,' he told his mother in his first letter home, after having spent five hours writing that day.[33] He launched immediately into revising his story 'In a Sleeping Face' to try again with *Landfall*; and then into a novel—based on his Paeroa boarding house experience—but this seems to have ground to a halt by the middle of the year. He had completed only two stories, he told Maurie at the end of December, since the Shadbolts left in June. After his 'flight to the bush' (as he romantically described his few days in Paeroa) he had been descended on by people wanting a place to stay (including two of Baxter's alcoholics) and '[a]part from this I drank too much, went to too many parties, and spent too much time and money in coffee shops.'[34]

At the end of the year, to his subsequent regret, he resigned from his hospital job to spend a decent summer holiday in Auckland, hitchhiking up with Gay Jackson, one of the girls from the Everton

Terrace flat. They made it up in one day. He spent a quiet four months at home in Henderson; pleasantly so, he told Maurie, after the 'hectic second half' of the previous year 'with all its entanglements, financial, emotional, social, alcoholic, very nearly legal'. He used the time to get on with his writing, revising and typing all of his short stories to date. By the end of March he had fifteen, published and unpublished, twelve of which he wanted to see if he could get published as a collection: he thought he'd ask Louis Johnson, who ran the small Capricorn Press, in the first instance. The latest was 'a 6000 word effort about the love of a young Wellington bohemian for a varsity girl'—'trespassing a bit on your preserves', he apologised to Maurie. In his notes for this story the girl is a university actress (part Meg, part Angela), the young bohemian a student from a country town who, after passing four units in his first year, in his second is drawn into a 'bohemian boozing . . . semi crim world', trying 'to find & express a meaning', and consequently loses the girl. After a night 'on the grog' (involving robbery and arson and stashing stolen goods in 'a flat full of girls . . . but only one is pretty'), and wandering disconsolately around the empty streets and crowded coffee shops, he goes home and takes out of the wardrobe the charcoal grey suit the girl had made him buy, thinking of cutting it up or burning it, but instead decides he'll try to sell it and carry on: 'His is the world of no rewards.'[35] 'I see it', he explained to Maurie, 'as the story of a person fighting his way out [of] two constricting sets of social generalisations to a position from which he will be able to create his own standards, a lonely position, and a hard one to hold. If you'll allow me to be pompous for a moment, it's a story in which I reject the attitudes struck by bohemians as even more dangerous than the values accepted [by] the middle class.'[36] Here is Tonio Kröger again—'standing between two worlds . . . at home in neither'.

He went into town to the Queen's Ferry on Fridays, but otherwise saw few people. Kevin was around, before he headed down south with Mike Illingworth to go tobacco-picking, then got a job as a guide at Waitomo Caves to earn another passage fare to England (keeping himself occupied during the winter writing 'a picaresque novel' for fun and reading Jack Kerouac's *On the Road*).[37] And Carl Freeman had turned up just before Christmas from a period of teaching up north, seeming 'rather lost' and 'unnerved too at finding so many people gone or married'; Bob Dudding and Tony Stones were the most recent among the latter.[38] If this accentuated Gee's own awareness of his solitary state, however, it was not something he wrote to Maurie about.

The person he saw most in these days was Barry Crump, an itinerant bushman and deer culler with a gift with words (and women), whom Kevin Ireland was subsequently to be instrumental in transforming from a teller of yarns into a writer of stories: 'A wonderful character', Gee described him to Maurie, 'The original wild man from the bush . . . [and] a genuine comic talent.' For his part, Crump, Gee reported, thought Gee was 'hopelessly neurotic and am destined for a padded cell. Considers it his duty to tell me home truths . . . He thinks I treat women with too much consideration—should haul off and belt them he says'.[39] A few months later it would be Gee giving Barry advice about women.

It was probably in these months too that he met for the first time Frank Sargeson, nervously, visiting him in his asbestos cottage on a jungly quarter-acre section in Takapuna with Nigel Cook. Sargeson already knew of Gee, of course, through his mother, and also no doubt through the likes of Ireland and Shadbolt; and had already seen that he possessed a talent of a different order from the latter's.

He went back to Wellington after Easter, in late April, moved back into the Ghuznee Street bach and got a job as a postie. It was meant to be a job that would allow him plenty of time in the afternoons for writing. In reality he found that he was so tired by the end of his run that he couldn't do any writing at all. He had the Aro Valley run, which took him from the top block of Abel Smith Street and southern stretch of The Terrace (delivering the Cooks' mail—Nigel and Julie were married now too) across to Aro Street and up as far as Adams and Semeloff Terraces, the latter a rough flight of a hundred or so steps, up and around Durham Street and Mortimer Terrace and back down to the little branch Post Office on the corner of Aro and Epuni. It was made more strenuous by the fact that the experienced postie charged with showing him the run (a fit and efficient Dutchman, Gee would remember) neglected to tell him about the parcel drops along the way, so that he carried all of the day's mail in his bag until someone else tipped him off. But he enjoyed the physical demands of the job, and enjoyed the 'running in'—sorting the mail into bundles down at the central Post Office before heading out—although he never became very fast at this. It was also in the sorting room and over morning tea that he got to socialise with his fellow posties, who included two poets who became friends, Gordon Challis and John Boyd.

He forged a closer and enduring friendship this year with Ray Grover, whom he met at the Cooks very soon after he came back down. Grover was working on his first novel and as a gas meter reader (an even better job for a writer than being a postie, he reckoned, because he could get through his run (at a run) in two or three hours). Later he was to live in the Ghuznee Street bach for a few years, after Carl Freeman to whom Gee passed it on. Carl, meanwhile, turned up in Wellington later in 1958 (after walking out of another teaching job), and while working for a time at the *Evening Post*, a few doors down the road from the George, would walk up to Ghuznee Street to have lunch most days with Moss, stopping at a Hungarian delicatessen on the way for rolls and beetroot and cream cheese.

Crump was in Wellington now too, and a regular visitor to the bach with his new girlfriend, Jean Watson. Gee had already met Jean, in fact, several years before, in entirely different circumstances: she had been the shy nurse aide with whom he had discussed D.H. Lawrence when he was in Auckland Hospital having a pin inserted in a finger after detaching a tendon during a rugby game. One day she and Barry came round to Ghuznee Street and told him solemnly that '[s]omething terrible's happened': they were in love, which was terrible because Crump was married. Whatever Gee said to them in reply, he would hope, in retrospect, that he was not as 'prissy and pompous' as he appeared in Watson's 1965 novel *Stand in the Rain.*[40] There, over coffee at the Red Slipper (the Picasso) round the corner, David/Gee advises Sarah and Abungus (a name Crump, obscurely, used for himself at this time: Abungus Barrington-Wank) that they should wait and not see each other for a week, and then write to each other 'and see exactly how you feel then'.[41] Watson's novel, as well as being a portrait of the beginning of her and Crump's marriage, is an evocative picture of Gee's 1950s Wellington: of the Man Friday 'thick and droopy with the smell of smoke and sweat and sensuality' as a band played loudly at 2am; parties in flats 'somewhere among the Terrace gardens where little bridges and high board fences lead to old-fashioned front doors, up narrow stairs, dingily carpeted and pervaded by a faint smell of gas'; of wandering lonely after midnight looking in the windows of shops and coffee bars on 'those nights when there doesn't seem to be anyone around'.[42]

Gee was now becoming entangled in a romance of his own: in a real relationship this time, not just an unrequited or imagined infatuation. He first saw (but did not meet) Hera Smith early in 1957, one night when he was down at Queen's Wharf with Ron Polson, Ross O'Rourke and some others. Nigel Cook was there too, seeing off Julie on the *Wanganella* to Sydney. The attractive young Māori woman leaning against the railing next to her, the two of them smiling down and waving, was Polson's girlfriend. She was a nurse and was going to Sydney to look for work. (Gee would later believe, wrongly, that she was going for the unspoken reason many single young women travelled to Sydney at this time.) They were away for some months (spending several weeks working on a sheep station in Queensland). When Hera came back, some time after Julie, she stayed with Julie and Nigel on The Terrace and it was here that Gee met her.

She had been brought up in Rotorua, at Ōhinemutu: her mother, Lydia, was Ngāti Whakaue and Te Whakatōhea, her father 'a little drunken white South African' (a laundryman by trade when Hera was born) whom Gee met only once.[43] Eventually Lydia walked out on him with her two youngest children and fled to Wellington, and Hera followed her when she was sixteen. She put herself through nursing training and when Gee met her was sister-in-charge of outpatients at Wellington Hospital—the youngest nurse ever to be made a full ward sister, so he was told. She was 26, just a few months younger than him. They began a relationship that would last—turbulently, often unhappily—for seven years.

She was very beautiful—the kind of woman a man liked to be seen with, as Ray Grover would later remark[44]—vibrant, intelligent, and they had absolutely nothing in common. She liked popular music and dancing; he knew nothing about the former and couldn't dance. She had no interest in books. She had had a hard upbringing, and she was subject to and suffered from a deep-seated and endemic racism of the time of which he was scarcely then aware. She was also self-possessed and determined and very strong-willed—the strongest-minded person he had ever met, he would later say—and, it would become increasingly apparent, slightly unstable. From the outset it was a difficult relationship, and an uneven one: one in which Hera made all the decisions.

At some point during 1958 the Cooks moved from The Terrace to a large, old, run-down rooming house in Glenmore Street in Thorndon which they had bought with a deposit paid by Hera. She had applied for a job at a United Nations hospital in Indonesia (where she had worked for a few months) and her plan was that her mother, who was then back in Rotorua, would come down to Wellington and live at Glenmore Street where Julie and Nigel could look after her when Hera went away. In fact Hera did not go to Indonesia, and Lydia had no desire to be looked after and instead found a place on her own to live (in Cottleville Terrace not far away). Gee spent a lot of time at 88 Glenmore Street, helping Nigel and Julie do the place up—re-piling and painting—and for meals, often with Hera, often with Carl Freeman and Ray Grover and Angela Sears, but not at the same time. Angela, who had been in Auckland at teachers' college for most of this year and was surprised when she got back to find that he and Hera were together, gained the impression that he deliberately kept Hera apart from her (and from his other friends too, perhaps) because he felt Hera would not like it otherwise. He was, both she and Ray perceived, very nervous about the relationship. But happy.

After five months as a postie he resigned from his job, for a second time, to stay home and write. He handed in his notice in late September. He wanted to get back to the novel he had started but not touched since the middle of last year. He had sent an application in for the Literary Fund Scholarship in Letters (for which he was to be shortlisted: one of four out of seventeen applicants). He had sent his short stories away to the Pegasus Press in Christchurch, who had turned them down (but they would be interested in seeing a novel, they said), and to Blackwood Paul, who had given them to a reader for another opinion and from whom he had not yet heard back; Gee was not hopeful. How did London publishers react to work from 'young unknowns from south sea islands?' he inquired of Maurice Shadbolt: 'Have you submitted anything yet?'[45]

Meanwhile he had sent two stories away to Bob Dudding, who was editing—with Dave Walsh, a mutual friend and at this time fire-watcher—the second issue of *Mate* ('in effect, a new venture', Dudding described it to Brasch).[46] He had also been gathering up—or endeavouring to—contributions from other Wellington writers for them. 'Sorry about the soup on one of the stories', he apologised of his own.[47] One was 'The Separation', from the still-languishing young writers' anthology 'Chapter and Verse'. This had been turned down for a Literary Fund grant and was consequently having to be drastically reduced in size—down to eleven writers (from sixteen as advertised in *Here & Now* in October 1957, as due 'Shortly from THE PILGRIM PRESS').[48] The pages were already set up in type, but this was as close to publication as it would get. The other was 'A Girl in Blue', which was, like the novel he was working on, a Paeroa story. It described the last day of the year at a provincial high school and last day in the job for young teacher Arthur Wylde. The girl in blue is Mary, a fifth-former with a 'crush' on him, which 'he knew must be sticky and formless' but he is flattered nevertheless, and 'found himself thinking of her too often'; and also the girl at Paeroa District High School, brown-eyed, brown-haired, physically mature ('the uniform fitted like a tailored dress') and conscious of her charms (the women teachers observe disapprovingly).[49] On that final day, when she comes to bid him a tearful farewell, he kisses her.

Other Paeroa teachers, if they read the story, would have recognised themselves: Stan in Jack, Shorty Heward in McKinlay, Norma Wishnowski as Mrs Warnock, head of English John Jensen as the genial, poetry-writing Peter. It was published in *Mate* in November, alongside, amongst other things, Barry Crump's first published story, 'A Good Keen Man'. He had also submitted his earlier story 'While the Flag was Up' in May for this year's *Arena* competition: it was jointly highly commended with one by Maurice Shadbolt and published in the Summer 1958–59 issue.

He had met Charles Brasch for the first time in June this year when the latter was in Wellington on a visit—over coffee at Roy Parsons' newly opened bookshop on Lambton Quay. (Recording his impressions in his diary, Brasch described Gee's 'remarkably feeling, understanding expression . . . the gentle wisdom in his look seemed to tell me at once a good deal about his stories'.)[50] Writing to Brasch in July, he told him that there was 'quite a little prose ferment going on' up there—'something worth while will come of it I'm sure'.[51] Three months later, to Maurice Shadbolt in London (who had moved since he last wrote from Byron House in Ealing to Shelley Court, Chelsea: 'a step down according to critical opinion in the fifties', Gee noted)[52] he reported on the wider literary scene. There was a lot happening. There were new little magazines: *Mate*, of course, the first, Jowsey/Yelash-edited number of which had come out in September the previous year, including work by Frank Sargeson, R.A.K. Mason and A.R.D. Fairburn, and—more indicative of its intent to support new writers—the first published work of Janet Frame, and its cover sketch by Tony Stones of a cloth-capped man sitting at a chessboard. And *Image*, from Auckland, of which there had been three issues so far. (As Brasch too had noted in the June *Landfall*: 'New magazines have been erupting in the last few months almost as fast as artificial satellites'.)[53] He had read Sylvia Ashton-Warner's debut novel *Spinster*, which had reached the New Zealand shops at the end of July, on Shadbolt's recommendation and been impressed ('makes me wonder how many people a[re] sitting at home quietly writing while I waste my time just thinking about it'),[54] but not yet Ian Cross's *The God Boy*, which had also just appeared locally after having been published to acclaim in America in 1957. (He didn't, however, fancy the look of M.K. Joseph's *I'll Soldier No More*.) It was apparent to everyone looking, not just the habitués of the Man Friday and the George, that there was an efflorescence of fiction going on. These three novels, in one year, had followed Janet Frame's *Owls Do Cry* in 1957 and Maurice Duggan's short story collection *Immanuel's Land* the year before. In 1959 would come *A Gap in the Spectrum* by Marilyn Duckworth—sister of Fleur Adcock—whom Gee would get to know. He first encountered her in the window of Modern Books in Manners Street as the younger-than-him and lovely author on the dust jacket of this, her first novel, published in London by Hutchinson: he was deeply jealous.

In December, his collection having been returned to him by Blackwood Paul (and having 'temporarily given up the idea of publishing that way'), he sent a story to Charles Brasch which was to be his own small contribution to this late 50s literary flowering. Brasch accepted it straight away: 'a striking story . . . it seems both denser and more economical than any earlier story of yours I've read'. Titled 'The Losers', it was a horse-racing story. 'I take it the lingo is authentic at every point?' Brasch queried. 'I'm in no position to check it.'[55] But Gee, while he may never have been to the races, knew at second-hand his father's racing world. The shocking and brutal climactic scene, in which a horse is deliberately mutilated for the insurance pay-out, was a story told to him by Len's ex-jockey trainer, George Carmont. Frank Sargeson when he read the story recognised that it was, having his own entrée into this world (his live-in friend Harry was a racing man): 'devastatingly authentic,' he described it to Kevin Ireland, and (though not perfect) 'very surely written at a level he has never previously achieved to my knowledge. In fact, a milestone story.'[56]

It was technically a more complex story than his previous ones, with a larger cast of characters—albeit within a self-contained, and precisely drawn, world: of ambition, disappointment and desperation, corrupt owners, complicit trainers and compliant jockeys, of a carefully protected hierarchy of money and power, of racing-lounge smells of 'lino and hops, vinegar and disinfectant'[57]—and with a shifting narrative point of view managed more subtly than the structured artifice of 'In a Sleeping Face'. Brasch identified an emerging distinction of Gee's fictional style when he complimented him on 'the way in which you make everyone talk to him or herself only in trying to communicate to someone else'.[58] It is the women who are the most self-aware and critically observant, specifically Mrs Betham, wife of the essentially decent but ambitious owner Lew, and Connie, fiancée of the desperate, losing ex-jockey Stan Philpott, whose conversation is reminiscent of the connection made between Alice Matthews and Hilda in 'In a Sleeping Face'. The story also brought Gee his 'first letter of appreciation', from Alan Horsman, the professor of English at the University of Otago: it was 'much the best thing of its kind that has appeared for a long time—in interest, in intensity and in authentic New Zealand flavour'.[59] Gee knew himself that it marked something significant: 'I'm beginning to find my material now', he told Maurie, '—I hope I don't get too distorted a view of it.'[60] It would become his best known and most anthologised.

7

Nigel

Gee revised 'The Losers' in Auckland in January, having gone up at the end of the year to spend another extended Christmas holiday at home. He was not back in Wellington, and the bach, before late February.

By now Hera was pregnant. It was not an accident. She wanted a child, and both she and Moss had discussed the subject with Julie Cook—who did not encourage the idea, having disapproved from the beginning of a relationship she thought would only bring them both harm: Moss especially, she feared, as the most vulnerable. They were not talking about a long-term future together. When it happened Gee was delighted. Later he would come to believe that he had simply been chosen as a suitable father for the baby Hera had always wanted to have. (He had not been sure either, that past year, if she had not also still been seeing something of Ron Polson.)

When the pregnancy began to show they left Wellington—probably some time in March—and went to Dunedin. This was Hera's decision.[1] They stayed briefly in a place in High Street before moving to a bedsit in a rooming house in Clyde Street, down near the university and the Leith. Hera found a job nursing at Port Chalmers. The best Gee could do was one with Commercial Cleaners, cleaning shops and offices, and, mostly, windows. An enduring memory would be standing in the freezing wind that blew along Princes and George streets in winter washing windows with cold water and the torn-up old shirts and underwear the company provided as rags.

He knew no one in Dunedin; or virtually no one. He was up a ladder in his cleaner's uniform one day when Charles Brasch, walking past, discovered he was, clandestinely, down there. He went several times to lunch or dinner at Brasch's house in Heriot Row over the next few months. Brasch liked the quiet, modest writer as much as he admired his work, describing him—in another of the deft pen portraits he recorded in his journal of people who interested him—as 'slight with pale skin & thin dark hair, quiet, diffident, with his sad self-deprecating smile', and 'shyly & rather sadly humorous'. He was so modest, he wrote after Gee had been for dinner one evening in June, that 'last night he almost apologized for not caring for music', so unforthcoming that 'he always seems to me to lack vitality or else his vitality is deeply hidden'; but he found him 'gentle, warm-hearted, very observant'. He did not let on why he was in Dunedin but Brasch surmised 'that it was to be with a friend or lover'.[2] He told no one, in fact—telling Maurice Shadbolt, for example, three months after he got there simply that he was 'having a few months in Dunedin'.[3]

At least once he went along to one of the occasional meetings of a writers' group of which Brasch had been one of the instigators, on this evening at poet Alan Roddick's house: among those present were Fleur Adcock and Brian Bell, who, however, he made a point of avoiding while he was in Dunedin (like most people he was wary of Bell). Another literary friend from Queen's Ferry days who was down there for a spell and of whom he was fonder, Don Terris, he saw once or twice. But otherwise he was leading a very uneventful life, he told his mother, seeing very few people and never going to pubs: 'I'm forgetting what beer tastes like'. Dunedin, he informed her, was 'a dull little city' in which he would never live if he could help it.[4]

He had promised Robin Dudding that he would scout around for subscribers and contributors to *Mate*, and blamed his lack of success on his monkish life: 'It's no bullshit Bob, I really don't see anyone and don't go out'.[5] Dudding had sent two dozen copies of the second issue to him in Wellington, a dozen of which Gee had passed on to Anton Vogt at the teachers' college and the rest left behind with Carl Freeman at the bach. Dudding posted a package of flyers for number three, which came out in July, which Gee pinned up around the university. He didn't have the personality, however, to make a literary agent. Nor did he have any new stories of his own to offer Dudding; and only one old one that 'I'd care to see in print at present', and sent up in July, doubting though that it was 'lively enough' for *Mate*: 'It's just about an old woman in a boarding house—sounds familiar doesn't it—and nothing much happens.'[6] This was 'Facade', the Waihī boarding house story which Brasch had rejected in 1954, but Dudding accepted for *Mate* 4, which came out in February the next year.

He was proud, however, to find a new writer for Brasch. One of his fellow window-cleaners was a young Scotsman, Alex Guyan, who had emigrated as a teenager from Aberdeen and who, Gee discovered, wrote, but had neither published nor ever submitted anything, nor met an actual writer before. Gee took him round to see the *Landfall* editor, who liked Guyan immensely and published the first of several stories by him in his September issue. Brasch in turn introduced Gee to Ian Cross, author of *The God Boy*, who was in Dunedin as the inaugural holder of the Robert Burns Fellowship at the University of Otago, which Brasch had anonymously endowed—New Zealand's first literary fellowship. Gee found he got on well with him, but suspected that he was too nice to be a writer—'too amiable to view life in what I think is the correct way', he commented to Gill Shadbolt: 'I don't think he's been able to steady his gaze on some of its less pleasant parts.'[7] Cross was working on his second novel and pleasing the fellowship committee by being 'throughout the year a model of consistent effort, six days a week' (setting a precedent some of his successors would find difficult to match).[8]

What Gee was doing with the time he had left over from window-cleaning was typing (on his mother's typewriter, or rather the one they shared) the final draft of his as-yet-untitled novel. He had finished it by mid-August. It was, he told his mother in his self-deprecating way, 'lively enough' (unlike his letters, he felt) 'tho' not very intelligent'.[9] Finding a title was only his first problem. Where did he send it? he asked Maurice Shadbolt in London. He thought perhaps Secker and Warburg or Victor Gollancz; or would it be better to give it to an agent? Ian Cross had offered to write to his. And 'how does one do a ms up? And how does one address it so that it does get itself read?'[10] He readily accepted Gill's suggestion that he post it over to them to look at first and then pass on to a publisher 'if you think its worth sending on'. He wanted, he said, a frank opinion: 'I'm a little more mature, I hope, in my feelings about my writing—I know it's not the end of the world if this novel is not publishable. There is enough in it that's good to encourage me to try again'; but confessed a paragraph later to 'a spot of hypocrisy . . . The fact is I want to believe it's publishable but can't quite bring myself to believe it is. So, like all writers, I'll have to be told.' He thought Gollancz might be the best bet.[11]

He knew by now that Maurie's own book of short stories had been accepted by Gollancz—the first publisher he had sent it to—for a £75 advance. 'Of course I was immediately envious as buggery'.[12] It was tentatively titled—'I blush', Shadbolt had confessed to Brasch—

'The New Zealanders', and was due out in October.[13] During August he put in an application for the Literary Fund Scholarship in Letters again, enclosing a carbon of his novel, but without great confidence—not only out of modesty, for he knew that Maurie was applying too. Nor did he feel ready to go for the Burns, despite Cross telling him he should and that 'a few short stories and a bit of promise' were enough.[14] He was more hopeful of the inaugural Katherine Mansfield Memorial Award, entries for which were also due at the end of that month, and for which he entered 'The Losers', which had appeared in *Landfall* in June, along with 'In a Sleeping Face'. The award, established by the New Zealand Women Writers' Society and funded by the Bank of New Zealand, carried a prize of 50 guineas in each of two categories, short story and essay; the judge this year for the short story category was Victoria University senior lecturer Joan Stevens. It seemed that the late 50s was seeing a burgeoning of literary funding to match the efflorescence of literary production, with this award, the Scholarship in Letters, and the Literary Fund's £100 Award for Achievement introduced the following year (going that first year to Janet Frame for *Owls Do Cry*), and the Burns. Everyone was wondering who was applying for what.

The following month what everyone was talking about was the Writers' Conference held in Wellington at the university in the first week of September. It was the first such event since 1951. Literary funding was one of the topics addressed in a programme which focused almost exclusively on the politics and infrastructure of writing, rather than on writing itself: 'There was the same attitude toward writing as a fit subject for discussion that I'd expect a League of Mothers to hold toward sex', Ian Cross remarked in a candid report in *Landfall*.[15] By almost universal agreement the conference was a disappointing affair, with '[l]ittle good talk from the floor', Brasch reported to a friend, a 'disgraceful schoolmasterish lecture' from director of broadcasting J.H.E. Schroder, which ended in 'almost a brawl', and a conspicuous absence of younger writers.[16] Maurice Gee was one who was not there.

In the last week of August he and Hera left Dunedin and went to Melbourne. He expected to be there about two months, he told Gill and Maurie, and then, he hoped, go on to England. 'I want to break the patterns of [my life] again,' he had written to Maurie the month before, as when he had hitchhiked down to Wellington three years earlier: 'my life really began to move at that point'.[17] This suggests a degree of control, or at least volition and purpose, that belied the lack of control he really had; and, if not dishonesty, some disingenuousness about what was going on. The decision to go to Melbourne had been Hera's, again. She did not want anyone—any welfare authorities—interfering with her and her child. To be an unmarried mother carried a heavy stigma in the 1950s; to be a young Māori unmarried mother even more so. What Moss thought about the plan is not clear—nor does it appear to have been to him. They flew from Whenuapai airport on the morning of the 24th, only passing through Auckland and not going out to see his parents: he had warned his mother that he did not think he'd be able to get home before he left. He appears to have told them no more about his plans and his situation than he had Maurie, to his mother's consternation. Unexpectedly, Len came out to the airport to see him off, and as he was leaving and as Gee was boarding the plane caught sight of Hera; but not, it appears, noticing that she was pregnant.

They spent two nights in a hotel in Elizabeth Street while Moss went out looking for a flat, finding one in Studley Park Road in Kew, an area which, he told his mother, was 'sort of Remuera'. The place was not cheap but that would not matter if it was only for a month or so. Two weeks later they moved to somewhere less grand half a mile away in Fellows Street, without a view of the park and river and with a shared kitchen down the hall, but 'more homely' and with 'a brand new little infra-red cooker in the room'. Don't worry, he reassured Lyndahl, writing two days after they arrived, '[e]verything is well under control'.[18]

The baby, a boy, was born at Royal Women's Hospital on 1 September. They named him Nigel, after Nigel Cook. (The Cooks' baby, a girl, born a few months earlier, was named Hera.)

The letters Gee wrote to his mother in these two months were full of reassurance and the—slightly muted—pleasure of new parenthood. He was 'happy and well and enjoying this spell of domesticity. It's hard work being a father but fairly rewarding—and I'm really keen on Nigel': he was 'a nice little chap . . . dark haired and olive-skinned', vigorous ('a great kicker') and strong competition for the 'T.V. maniacs' next door, whose set blared with 'gunshots & indian war whoops till midnight'. He couldn't quite work out the colour of his eyes: they 'sometimes seem brown, sometimes blue, sometimes my colour' (green). Hera was happy. Exactly when he told his mother about Hera and the pregnancy is not clear, but he asked her, writing two weeks after Nigel was born, to keep it quiet, and in particular not tell Len: 'one day perhaps you can, but not at present'. He didn't mind if she said something to Gus if she felt the need to talk to someone, '[b]ut I don't really want people knowing.'[19] It was Hera who had decreed secrecy.

To 'keep [his] hand in' he had started writing a story, based on an incident at Henderson High School involving a Chapple cousin and aunt that had become a small local scandal. He asked his mother to send him the newspaper cuttings. Along with these she sent copies of the *8 O'clock News*, the weekly sports section of the *Auckland Star*, so he could keep up with the rugby; and the news that Len's horse My Sun had won a race (the only win he would ever have). Before he left Dunedin he had sent his novel—which now had a title, 'The Petition'—to his mother for her to post to the Shadbolts in London; and immediately started worrying whether he had packaged it up well enough and if it should have gone airmail and in what condition it had arrived. Gill received it by mid-September (Maurie was then away in eastern Europe) and responded enthusiastically, sending it once she had read it to Victor Gollancz, who, she told him, would undoubtedly want to publish it.

Maurie and Gill were by now making plans to come home. They had never intended to stay away indefinitely, and their decision to leave before the end of the year had been precipitated by Gill becoming pregnant. Gee congratulated her on 'your expected "blessed event"' when he wrote about the novel in September: 'I know how pleased you'll both be—paternity will be a valuable experience for Maurie as well as being personally satisfying I suppose.'[20] There was nothing in any of his letters to them about Hera and Nigel. Instead he wrote about his plans to come on to England. He knew as little about how to travel as he had about how to submit a manuscript, and wanted Maurie to find out how Kevin, who had arrived in London that northern spring, had gone over: 'send instructions in detail. I've no clues'. He had been told the cheapest way to go was on a Greek boat to Athens: the Italian ones cost over a hundred Australian pounds, and he wouldn't have much money; 'washtubs with shirt for sail, I wouldn't mind so long as I eventually arrived'.[21] If he got the Mansfield award he might get there before the end of the year, but it was more likely to be the next. That would mean spending four, unwelcome months in Melbourne, but he would use the time, he told Gill, to work on getting a collection of stories together.

In the meantime he found himself a job, as a clerk at soap manufacturers Kitchen and Lever at Port Melbourne, processing orders and invoices for Persil, Surf and Solvol: 'the dullest most arid & useless occupation imaginable,' he described it to Maurie, 'but a wonderfully valuable experience I feel'. To both Shadbolt and Brasch he explained his ulterior purpose as being in the role of a 'spy'. Perhaps more to the point was his remark to his mother that 'I think the people I work with find me an odd fish.' (Nor was it a job he did particularly well: his worst mistake was sending a wagon-load of Persil to Queensland instead of Western Australia.) He was earning £A17.14 (£NZ14) a week—not enough, unfortunately, to save a boat fare by Christmas—at the end of each day returning from his clerking to 'a nice bright but definitely clerkish suburb'.[22]

By late October he had heard that he had not won the Mansfield prize (Maurice Duggan had). He was disappointed not only because he was still pleased with 'The Losers' but because he had been counting on the prize to get to England: had 'persuaded myself that I had the money in my pocket'.[23] Instead he was now pinning his hopes on the Literary Fund scholarship; although, he told his mother, 'I feel they will give the money to Maurice Shadbolt'. Or if not the scholarship perhaps a grant of a few hundred pounds like they had given Maurie the previous year. He had been considering applying for the Burns Fellowship, he told her, but 'I've got a step on the way and feel I'd be stepping right back over it to come home now'. The Burns he could save for later. He wrote to his mother of his frustration: he wanted to be writing, not selling soap; 'should be writing—schoolteaching, window cleaning, clerking, are all a waste of time'.[24]

Nigel, he told her in the same letter, was nearly eight weeks old, 'fat and healthy & very very hungry'. His skin was not olive but darker: 'a slight duskiness'. His eyes, he had decided, were 'the colour of leaf mould', 'brown & yet not-brown, sort of shading towards grey'. Hera knitted constantly.[25]

'Soon is the time of quickening', he remarked to Gill Shadbolt in a letter written possibly the same day, '—it should be fascinating.'[26]

Two weeks later he and Hera, or rather Hera, decided to give Nigel up for adoption. It was Maurice who took him to Royal Women's Hospital to hand over to the almoner; half an hour later his new parents—a professional couple, Gee was pleased, and slightly embarrassed to be pleased, to know—would come and take him away. In his letters to Lyndahl the decision had been a mutual, though hard, one. In his memory it was Hera's and he was taken completely by surprise. This was the baby she had wanted. They had known all along that they were not going to stay together as a family, which was itself a cause of distress to his mother—and to some extent to him too, now. He had gone to Melbourne to be with Hera for the birth, and then he would go his own way. But he had written to his mother, in that late-October letter in which he had discussed his plans for writing and the scholarship and London, also of 'the desire to keep Nigel somehow, and the knowledge that it can't be done'.

It was also in this letter that he had spoken about his inability to 'have real worries', and tried to explain his feeling of dissociation from real life and experience, of being 'insulated against real pain'.

Gary and his wife, Ngaire (they had been married in September 1956), offered to have Nigel with them for a time. They were living next door to Len and Lyndahl, on a section Len had bought for them, and had their own baby boy just a few months older than Nigel. His mother was keeping an eye out for possible jobs in Auckland for Moss. But they couldn't leave Nigel with Gus and Ngaire for too long, he reminded her, 'and when the time came to take him we wouldn't be in any better position to make a home for him than we are now'. Once again he asked her to be discreet, and not let Len worry: 'I'm all right—for some curious reason I seem to travel safely thro' all these upsets & events.'[27] But he was not happy about the situation, and Hera seemed distressed. Within a week she was having second thoughts. There was a trial period before the adoption became final: they had 30 days to decide.

He had been reading Dante's *Inferno* while all this was going on: 'It's just a chronicle of misery & pain', he told his mother. Perhaps he would try *Paradise* next.[28]

Hera found a nursing job and moved into the nurses' home, while Gee looked for somewhere else for himself to live. He found a room in Carlton, but the landlady would not allow female visitors (to his outrage, while Hera was merely amused), so moved after a night to the Bella Vista Private Hotel in Parliament Place, near the Fitzroy Gardens: 'an awful bloody barn cum brothel cum prison', he described it to Maurie,[29] but it was closer to his work than Kew and Hera was working at St Andrews Hospital nearby. They saw each other a lot. A welcome distraction from the tedium of his job, and worry about Nigel and Hera and his future, was spending a Saturday at the Royal Melbourne golf course in the third week of November watching the Canada Cup (soon to be renamed the World Cup), the first big international golfing tournament to be hosted in Australia. It was worth enduring the 30,000-strong crowd and 94°F (over 32°C) heat, he wrote to Lyndahl, to see the world's greatest golfers play.

By now Hera was thinking seriously of claiming Nigel back. (Gee would later wonder if she hadn't in fact been intending to do so all along.) She still aspired to work overseas, and was planning now to go to New Guinea to nurse for two or three years: Nigel would live with the Cooks in Wellington while she was away and she would send most of her salary over to them. If this came to pass they would take Nigel back to New Zealand for Christmas and leave him with the Cooks in mid-January (Julie and Nigel had yet to say what they thought of this scheme). Gee's plan was to then go back up to Auckland 'and have another intensive writing spell' there, and then, if he got the scholarship or a grant, go to England. 'A lot depends on the Lit. Fund'.[30]

They flew back to Auckland—all three of them—on 7 December 1959, on the first Lockheed Electra to fly out of Essenden airport. The *Aotearoa* was the flagship of the three new turboprop Electras TEAL introduced into its trans-Tasman and Pacific fleet, replacing the old Solent flying boats, that month, cutting the trans-Tasman flight time by an hour and three-quarters. ('No quiver, no shake', the advertisements declared: 'Step aboard the Electra and prepare for a new air travel experience.' The four Auckland 'press women' who were also on board as guests for the inaugural Auckland–Melbourne run had just had time for a few hours' shopping before the return journey.)[31]

They stayed for five or six weeks at Tirimoana Road, having a family Christmas with the Gees, to Lyndahl and Len's delight: they liked Hera, and adored Nigel. Just before Christmas Gee sent Charles Brasch, at his request, a photograph of himself for the 'portrait gallery' of writers Brasch was planning for the next *Landfall*. It was one taken by his parents' next-door neighbour, Marti Friedlander, a newly arrived immigrant from London whose first photographs published in New Zealand had appeared in the September 1959 issue, and marked the beginning of a long and highly regarded career. Gee was her first portrait.[32] He sat at his mother's dining table, wearing a plain flannel shirt, looking directly into the camera—young, expectant, and slightly worried. Over the page Maurice Shadbolt posed on the Embankment in London, cigarette in hand, leaning on the low concrete wall looking pensively out over the Thames (self-conscious in another way).

Gee had written to Brasch two days after he returned, explaining that he had got no further on his travels than Melbourne because he didn't have enough money to go on, and confessing that he had neglected to follow up any of the introductions Brasch had given him other than to call on Stephen Murray-Smith, the editor of *Overland*, on his last day (and only because Shadbolt had especially asked him to, to let him know when he himself would be passing through). His time in Melbourne, he told Brasch, he looked on as 'a lost weekend', though a valuable one for the undercover research he had been able to do at Kitchen and Lever: 'I now have a fair command of sales and office jargon, a knowledge of office routine, and understand the importance of "pleasing the boss"', who was 'a figure who deserves a story . . . a bald mean-spirited little sales-chart worshipper . . . [who] can't help being a little larger than life size'. 'Now I've returned from the underworld', he told him, 'and can resume my normal life'.[33]

He had returned to a letter from the Literary Fund advising him that he had not been awarded the scholarship (Shadbolt had; Gee had come a close second) but that they were giving him £200 instead. This would at least get him on his way—England was still his plan—and time to work some more on his novel, which, he was prepared to admit to Brasch if not to Shadbolt, 'I really feel . . . deserves to be published'.[34] He had heard before he left Melbourne that Gollancz had rejected it, about which he was disappointed 'but not dismayed'.[35] Gollancz editor Hilary Rubinstein had written regretfully to Gill Shadbolt, after an initial, encouraging phone call, that while at first glance he had been impressed by the 'vigour' of the writing he found problems with the plotting and with the 'over-emotionalism' of some of the major scenes.[36] Brasch told Gee not to be worried about Gollancz, who were 'not all that good as publishers', and congratulated him heartily on the Literary Fund grant: it seemed 'exactly right' to him that Maurice Duggan should have got the Burns this year, Shadbolt the scholarship and Gee a substantial grant.[37]

Shadbolt had then sent the novel to Florence James, an independent agent and reader lately for Constable and now for the all-women agency of Richmond, Towers and Benson, with whom he had signed up. James, New Zealand-born and Australian-educated (and co-author of the controversial 1951 novel *Come in Spinner*), had worked as a literary agent in England for some twenty years and been a valuable talent scout for Australian and New Zealand writers. She was not entirely convinced by 'The Petition', however. The novel described a town a lot like Paeroa, and a young man a little like Gee, the star player in the town's top rugby team, as he struggles to rebel against the expectations of his family—his rugby-coach father, emotionally demanding mother and self-righteous schoolteacher brother—and the conservative, narrow-minded values of a provincial New Zealand town. It contained 'some brilliant writing', James thought, 'cool, incisive and unsentimental', but had technical flaws. The chapters read like separate scenes or short stories, so that 'one doesn't get the sweep of a continuous and developing story', and the reader did not become engaged with the central character and his problems until the last 50 pages: until then '[h]e stumbles along and one just stands off and watches him.' The final chapter, however, was 'a fine piece of writing', and the author had 'a lively natural talent, an unusual gift for getting below the sentimental shallows of his characters and something worthwhile to say'.[38]

Gee received her comments before Christmas. He had enough confidence in himself to describe them to Brasch as 'sound in parts but rather unintelligent in others', feeling that she had 'overlooked some of the obvious weaknesses of the book' and criticised things he remained satisfied with. (And to write to her directly thanking her but telling her that he did not entirely agree.)[39] Ursula Winant at Richmond, Towers and Benson, to whom she had sent it to look at nonetheless, had decided not to handle it, however.

Maurie and Gill arrived back in New Zealand at the beginning of January, having left 'The Petition' behind in London with Michael Illingworth—who had been over there for several months—at Gee's request. *The New Zealanders* had preceded them, in the bookshops locally before its UK publication date in late October; as had news of its reception there. Shadbolt had enclosed copies of and quoted at length from the 'excellent' British reviews, including one in the *Times Literary Supplement*, in his letters to his friends. It had been chosen as a Book Society recommendation for 1959, featured in the *Bookman*, and one of the stories published in the *New Yorker* in October. It had sold 3300 copies by January—'which must be something of a record for a book that is both a "first" and a volume of short stories!', Gollancz told him—the first edition selling out in a month. Whitcombe and Tombs had taken only 500 for New Zealand, to Shadbolt's justified disgust; Modern Books' twelve copies were gone in a day.[40]

The local critical response was less positive. Gee's initial comments to his mother, when he read the copy she sent over to him in November (it had not reached the Melbourne bookshops yet), expressed what would remain consistent themes in the critical assessment of Shadbolt's work: 'His [book], I'm afraid, has not impressed me. There's a faint phoniness about it all, a faint flavour of literariness in the relationships of his characters, and I'm afraid he's not really sensitive to language—doesn't seem to have an intimate relationship with words.' He liked some of the stories, those that were 'solid and unpretentious', but others were 'amateurish', '[h]is language is terribly imprecise at times and his dialogue theatrical'. There was 'better writing' in his own book, he thought, than this.[41]

Shadbolt had not been helped by the exaggerated blurb which covered the front and back covers of the book, hailing him as 'a remarkable new voice from the Antipodes' who 'is likely to become one of the most widely acclaimed writers of the present time', which even Gee confessed made him resistant. Even his detractors, however, found the review by Ian Hamilton which appeared in *Mate* in February unnecessarily harsh—Brasch, for example, describing it as a 'rank concoction of envy and spite', and telling Shadbolt so.[42] It led to an acrimonious exchange of letters and falling out between Shadbolt and Dudding (the acrimony largely on Shadbolt's side) when Shadbolt, before he had read the review but on the basis of what Dudding had told him about it, interpreted it—wrongly, Dudding felt—as a personal attack, and withdrew the 5000-word essay he had submitted for the next issue. This was intended to be the first of a series in *Mate* of 'credo' articles, 'statements of faith—literary, political, philosophical, and above all contemporary, and concerned with New Zealand', which had in fact been Shadbolt's suggestion, and now did not eventuate.[43] Gee had been on the list of potential contributors in mind; as he had been one of the several people Dudding had approached to review *The New Zealanders* who had turned him down ('To be fair,' Dudding told Shadbolt, 'Mos [sic] I talked to only late in the piece, but I was pretty sure he would not take it on, an opinion which he confirmed in no uncertain terms').[44]

The Hamilton review, and the muted response to his homecoming generally, in the wake of his self-promoting efforts and overseas reviews fuelled an enduring, and often intemperate, resentment and bitterness from Shadbolt towards the local literary establishment, and quickness to take offence. On the other side there was an exasperation with Shadbolt—with his erratic talent, his undisciplined writing and his brash self-confidence—which contrasted with the quiet expectation that people such as Brasch, Frank Sargeson and Dudding had of Gee.

In mid-January Gee went down to Wellington—on his own—and moved into the Ghuznee Street bach once again. He was planning to be there 'for a few months at least' (the Cooks had a room for him but he had found it too small).[45] He went out to see the Shadbolts (having apparently missed them in Auckland), who were living not in the downstairs flat at Glenmore Street that Nigel and Julie had made ready for their return but at Eric Schwimmer's place at Te Marua, north of Upper Hutt, which they had been offered for the year: an army hut and a small A-frame on either side of a stream.[46] (Gill lived in the hut while Maurie had the A-frame, where he was working on a novel in which he was 'trying to see NZ as a whole . . . reconciling the large vision of the pioneers, for example, with the suburban mentality': he was not afraid of the big themes.)[47] Hera and Nigel stayed in Auckland, where Hera at some point found a house to rent in Avondale. She spent a lot of time in the first half of this year helping to nurse Florence Chapple, who was 90 now and suffering from advanced Alzheimer's disease, until her death in May.

In March he brought Nigel down to Wellington and they moved into the Cooks' downstairs flat. Here he spent the next two–three months looking after not one baby but two: Nigel and the Cooks' Hera while Julie went off to work. It was a miserable time: an endless round of scraping and washing nappies in a cold, grotty washhouse. Wellington was 'the city I hope to live in finally', he had told Maurie a year before, but this was not the Wellington he remembered.[48] At least the house was across the road from the Wellington Botanic Garden, a good place for wheeling babies. But full-time childminding did not leave him time for writing. He had sent a short story collection to Blackwood Paul again, and had an idea for, if no time to get started on, a new one, based on a story he had been told about a group of middle-aged people savagely beating a teddy boy. He waited for news of the fate of his novel. Mike Illingworth had sent it to Hutchinson for consideration for their New Authors imprint, and when they returned it, to MacGibbon and Kee.

By June he was back in Auckland and had a passage booked on a boat sailing on 19 July; Carl Freeman was going then too. He planned to work on the novel again in London if MacGibbon and Kee turned it down—as they did, returning it to Illingworth in July. His Literary Fund grant had been awarded, on the basis of his scholarship application, 'to assist him in writing a novel, in the promotion of a collection of short stories and to travel overseas in connection with these projects', and he dutifully informed the committee in May of his departure 'in the latter part' of the year.[49] In Auckland he sat down to some hard work on the stories, hoping to have a revised version of his collection ready by the end of the month; he had eight stories selected.

'By now you must be an experienced nappy-changer, bottle-heater etc', he wrote early in June to Maurie, of the news that the Shadbolts' baby had been born in May: 'Congratulations to you—hope the joys of fatherhood are all they're supposed to be. . . . While this great event has been taking place in your life my life has been running on quietly.'[50]

By early July he had cancelled his booking and put back his departure until the end of the year. 'Why does Maurice Gee not push off, I wonder?' Brasch remarked to Shadbolt. 'Perhaps personal ties here; it's clear he wants to go, or one side of him does.'[51] Brasch was not the only one who was beginning to wonder if he ever would. His reasons are unclear, but confusion and uncertainty—emotional as well as practical—concerning his relationship with Hera and with Nigel, and over Nigel's future were part of this picture. He told Brasch simply, obliquely, that 'several things came up that demanded my presence here'.[52] He still intended to go. That is, unless he got the Burns, for which he put in an application in September, in which case he would put off the trip for another year. His projected programme of work if he did was to revise 'The Petition' and work on a new novel 'with [a] racing background'.[53]

He took a job relieving at Avondale College for the third term, beginning in mid-September, teaching English and social studies, and finding the experience no more gratifying than he had in Paeroa; less so, in fact. He had been given, he told Brasch, 'some very low forms—genuine reluctant learners and slow learners', some of whom 'can barely read and write'. The day after he started he sent Brasch a story from the collection that had now been returned to him by Pauls, which he did not think was 'quite such a lump of pudding' as Pauls' reader did (the word used had been 'shapeless'). The reader had also told him that he did 'not have a healthy mind' and failed 'to "affirm" life', which Brasch was pleased to hear. 'Cherish your unhealthy mind', he told Gee. 'Don't let any publisher's reader persuade you to be purified. A publisher's reader can afford to be a spotless Buchmanite, perhaps, but writers belong to the Fall and are born under Original Sin.' He didn't like the story—entitled 'Three Women'—however. The narrator 'lacks colour and flavour . . . and diffuses his colourlessness over the people and the action, so that everything goes flat and loose'; and did Gee really care about his characters? It was not a story he cared to publish after 'The Losers', in which part of Gee's achievement had been that the reader—this most demanding one at least—was made to care about all of them. Gee, while agreeing that they were 'a rather mousy lot', still felt the story had promise, however, and he was to go back to it: it was to develop a few years later into his second novel.[54]

He had nothing else to offer Brasch. Teaching he was finding too demanding to have any energy left over for new writing, and the story he had just sent Robin Dudding he had felt was not substantial enough for *Landfall*. Brasch, when he read 'Schooldays', disagreed. 'What a good story of yours in Mate!' he wrote to congratulate him, 'it brings something fresh to the book of N.Z. stories.'[55] This was the story Gee had been writing in Melbourne. The incident that had inspired it concerned a school classmate of his young cousin Geoff Chapple—son of Geoffrey, the tenth of the Chapple siblings (who had died young, at 44)—and his mother Dawn: a group of school prefects had forcibly cut the boy's unruly long (in the story red) hair, and Dawn Chapple, enraged and offended, had confronted the principal. The boy in the story, Trevor Jones, is clever and independent-minded, like his mother; his longstanding enemy, the ringleader prefect, 'a tall lithe crew-cut boy', champion athlete and scholarship hope, handsome and popular with the girls. The school headmaster wears a clipped moustache and a military bearing (Alfred Woolcott, the principal of Henderson High, had been a major during the war) and runs his school accordingly; its too-quiet corridors and too-polite pupils remind Mrs Jones of a hospital or the army: 'Most schools had something of St Trinian's about them', but this one feels almost sinister.[56]

He had been so incensed by the hair-cutting episode, Gee had told his mother, that he wanted to write the story 'savagely, but I must be delicate about it', demonstrate rather than describe the 'smallness of mind' it exposed, as Brasch appreciated, complimenting him on its 'light touch . . . and the oblique attack on conformity is splendid'. Dudding described it as 'a vicious little story'.[57] But what equally distinguishes 'Schooldays', and the confrontation between Mrs Jones and the principal, as well as the obvious clash of values is the subtle sexual interplay Gee depicts between Trevor's mother, who is young and attractive, and the principal and prefect, as she becomes aware of and gently exploits the former's undisguised lustful gaze at her breasts each time she shifts in her chair, and the seventeen-year-old boy's emerging, arrogant but self-conscious sexuality.

'Do you still think of going to England?' Brasch had asked him.[58] But by the time he wrote this letter Gee had already gone. When he next wrote to Brasch it was from on board the *Castel Felice*, nine days out of Auckland off the islands of Indonesia in the Java Sea.

8

London

The *Castel Felice* ('Happy Castle') sailed from Auckland on the afternoon of 3 January. The family were there at Princes Wharf to see him off: Len and Lyndahl, Gus and Ngaire, and Hera with Nigel. He was going to work on his novel and get it published, and then move on to what came next. He was going to experience London, then come back and get on with his writing career. And he was going to put an end, finally, to the relationship with Hera. Some of these things would prove easier to achieve than others.

The *Castel Felice* was an ageing ship that had been serving the Australian migrant and tourist trade since the war, tired and cramped still after several refits but popular with young travellers for her affordable fares and Italian style. (Sitmar was an Italian line; the ship's crew were all Italians.) He shared an eight-berth cabin with three Englishmen, a Scotsman, a Dutchman and two other New Zealanders (but not Carl, who had gone in July without him). He did not make lasting friendships with any of them, though he enjoyed the company of two, Peter and Frank, a friendly, boozy, middle-aged Scot and Englishman (or vice versa), with whom he made his shore trips and who were 'a lot of fun in a rough and ready sort of way'.[1] His table was relaxed and friendly, if a little dull; decent Italian wine at five or six shillings a bottle, though, was a revelation. He did not take part in any of the organised recreational activities on board: concerts by the ship's band twice a day, a dance and pictures every night, classical concerts on tape, deck games, Italian lessons. Instead he spent most of his time on the journey writing—in the beer garden because his cabin was too stuffy—and was pleased to find himself writing better and more than ever before: two or three pages a day. He was working on the story he had had the idea for in Wellington the previous year, about the violent attack on a teddy boy, and had it finished just before they reached Colombo, then set about revising his collection. Maurie had no doubt told him that Florence James, writing to him in July, had suggested that if 'a N.Z. publisher is interested in a collection of short stories by Maurice Gee, we might be able to arrange a simultaneous Eng. edition here—no promises of course, but it's worth trying.'[2]

'Writing is the only justification I have for leaving Nigel', he wrote to his mother in his first letter home. 'One thing I become more and more determined about is getting back inside a year':

> I'm beginning to realize what having him has meant to me—I don't mean my pride in him or love of him. I think because I've got him in my life I'm much less restless and discontented than I used to be. I'm not looking for something all the time the way I used to be. I've fewer and fewer worries of a personal sort—fewer trivial concerns. I care only about the writing, which I feel is for Nigel almost as much as for me. I feel much older and more of a real person than I was two years ago.

Missing Nigel, wanting to get back and be a father to him before too long, became a constant refrain in his letters home. 'There are hundreds of kids on the boat', he told her, 'but none like him.'[3]

The journey itself did not become interesting until they reached Indonesia, where they passed massive coral reefs and little rugged, jungle-covered islands, porpoises and sharks. He went ashore, with Peter and Frank, at Singapore, where they had an overnight stop-over, and hired bicycle rickshaws to go into the poorer parts of the city, 'drove through the most picturesque and sordid streets I've ever seen' and ate at a Chinese market at midnight;[4] and the Scotsman was disgusted that his companions refused to put on ties so that they could go into the bar at Raffles. In Colombo—where he ate a bad curry which laid him low for several days—he found the poverty even more striking. He did not go ashore at Suez or Aden, saving his money, and so missed the pyramids; the Red Sea, though, was a wonder, surrounded by sandy wastes of desert on either side.

By the time they reached Naples, where they were allowed ashore for only half a day, he had finished revising all of his stories for typing, and was feeling pleased with himself for having got three times as much work done on board as he had thought he would.

They reached Southampton in early February. He took the train to Waterloo, where he was met by Kevin Ireland, and they took the Underground to Victoria Station where Carl was waiting. He spent his first night in London with Carl wandering around Soho. He had arrived on the cusp of 'Swinging London'—that was a year or two away yet—but Soho had long been the city's bohemian heart, with its cosmopolitan nightlife, its clubs, brothels, Italian restaurants and coffee bars. Going back on his own the next day, he found it 'full of barrow boys etc':[5] another, working-class London. Two years before in Ghuznee Street he had listened to Carl and Ray Grover one night reminiscing about 'the Mandrake Club, the Gyre and Gymble, the French, Ironfoot Jack, streetgirls etc', as if Soho was London and leaving him feeling that he 'must go', but had remarked to Maurie a few days later: 'I daresay it's just Wellington's stale old bohemia on a larger scale. If so I can do without it.'[6] Now he found it his favourite part of the city, 'sleazy and sordid but full of life', along with Chelsea (if that was a little 'phony').[7]

He stayed for a few nights with Carl in Pimlico before moving to a room Carl and Kevin had found for him in Ebury Street in Belgravia, a 'desirable' address, he informed his mother (surely with irony), just down the road from Buckingham Palace.[8] (He would not have appreciated, given his lack of affinity with music, that it was also where Mozart had written his first symphony at the age of eight.) At 64 Ebury Street he had a tiny room up four flights of stairs, with just a bed, a shared bathroom and a cooking alcove by the door. His landlord was a friendly old Hungarian, Mr Hoogly (as pronounced; a refugee from the 1956 uprising). On day two he went with Kevin to see Peggy Ashcroft in *The Duchess of Malfi* in a Royal Shakespeare Company performance at the Aldwych Theatre, and was 'fairly bowled' (as Kevin was too), and decided he 'must go at least once a week'.[9] If London was not yet swinging, the theatre was. Since 1955 the young actors of the English Stage Company—Joan Plowright, Alan Bates, Glenda Jackson—had been performing the new English and contemporary overseas drama at the Royal Court Theatre: it was here, with the kitchen-sink drama of British theatre's New Wave (specifically, in reference to John Osborne's 1956 *Look Back in Anger*), that the term Angry Young Men originated, identifying the cultural zeitgeist of the time. And *The Duchess of Malfi* had inaugurated the Royal Shakespeare Company's first London season.

Dinner last night at Kevin and Donna's, he reported to Lyndahl in his first London letter home (he took a bottle of Italian wine from the ship), after which they spent the evening in a pub with a 'very gay' bunch of Kevin and Donna's friends: 'imagine that, Sunday night in a pub, women as well as men'. Don't worry, he again reassured her (as he had done when he went to Wellington), 'I'm sure I'll be happy here for a while. Rest assured that I'll look after myself—eat well etc—and do you know it's no colder than Auckland, not so far anyway.'[10]

'I don't get emotional in London,' the letter continued, 'at the sight of Westminster Abbey etc, I don't feel I've come Home. N.Z. is definitely Home for me', London a 'semi foreign country'.

This generation of New Zealand writers travelled to England with a less complicated, more sceptical, or at least more relaxed view than their predecessors had of the 'colonial problem', of the relationship between home and Home; with more modest expectations of the transformative power of London (in the cultural sense, at least). For the most part they went, like Gee and Shadbolt, to see what it was like and then go home, confident about where, and what, that was. England, Ireland remarked to Shadbolt not long before Gee arrived, 'just shakes a bit of the dust off you and not much else'; Moss was 'such a kiwi too, but he may get out of a bit of his mustiness I guess'.[11]

Kevin hated England, or the English at least, so he professed to Frank Sargeson: 'such strange, mixed-up people', '[t]hey have a melancholia of continental proportions, and a capacity for folly that makes them really believe they're human'; and 'the parties are dull, the class system cut and dries everyone into a handful of categories, there's nothing that you want to smell or taste or touch—no vitality'.[12] He had arrived in London in the spring of 1959 knowing no one and with nowhere to stay, and had wandered into Soho with the idea of finding a friend from Auckland and Wellington bohemian days, John Kasmin, and duly found him at Victor Musgrave's Gallery One in D'Arblay Street. Kasmin arranged a bed and job as a handyman for him at the gallery.

It is odd that Gee never met Kasmin, who had been John Kaye when his family arrived in Auckland from London in the mid-1950s, but was calling himself Kasmin—a made-up name (though some derivation from his family's original Polish name of Kosminsky)—by the time he had a poem published in the 1955 *Kiwi* in which Gee's first published story appeared; he had one later on the shortlist for 'Chapter and Verse'. In Wellington in the second half of the 50s he had shared a flat with Ireland for a time. He was a Yelash-like character without the criminal tendencies, but with a reputation for being always on the make; self-made, flamboyant and always immaculately dressed in beret and velvet jacket and tie. (Like an earlier, more eccentric Polish/New Zealand poet, Geoffrey Potocki de Montalk,[13] he also liked to go about in a cape and pretend to be a Polish count.) In London he had married the niece of Ben Nicolson and was at the beginning of a very successful and wealthy career as an art dealer: his clients would include David Hockney, whom he gave his first solo exhibition in 1964. The Kasmin Gallery which he opened in New Bond Street in 1963 became one of the fashionable locations of the London scene of the 1960s (famous equally for its exhibitions, its minimalist interior and its social style).[14]

Ireland, meanwhile, abandoned London after three or four months (leaving his Gallery One spot to Mike Illingworth) and went to Bulgaria, where he rendezvoused with Maurie (who was travelling in Europe on a journalism assignment), found occasional work as a translator, fell in love, and returned to London in the summer of 1960 with his Bulgarian wife, Donna. When Gee arrived he was living in the basement flat of Kasmin's house in Ifield Road, from which Kasmin was running his newly established dealership on the ground floor while looking for gallery space, and had a job as night doorman-cum-caretaker at a posh private hotel a mile away in Ebury Street, just down the road from Gee. When he had been out at night Moss would knock on the basement door on his way home—often after midnight—and Kevin would make them ham sandwiches and tea in the hotel kitchen and they would talk for a few hours, about books, writing, women, carrying on the same conversations they had had in Auckland and Wellington. He was getting to know Kevin properly now, and found him 'excellent company'.[15] They had a regular quiet drink together at a pub on Sunday nights. Gee's drink in London was Guinness: 'a sort of cross between beer and stout', he explained to his mother.[16]

Kevin introduced him to football. The Chelsea football ground was just along the road, and Fulham's not far away, but the real thrill was to trek across London to White Hart Lane to see the magical Tottenham Hotspur play. This was the season of the great Danny Blanchflower team: 1961 the year Spurs became the first team to win both the FA Cup and the First Division. They went together regularly.

It was Carl who got him along to political demonstrations. He went to a few anti-apartheid demonstrations, and heard the soapbox orators at Hyde Park corner, but the big issue of the day was nuclear disarmament. In 1961–62 the recently formed CND was at the height of its popular support and activism, conducting a campaign of mass civil disobedience which attracted, conspicuously, actors, writers, middle-class students and left-wing intellectuals. Tens of thousands went on the annual three-day march at Easter between the British atomic energy research facility at Aldermaston in Berkshire and Trafalgar Square. Three years earlier he had lamented to Maurie about the problem of finding 'a worth while job' ('apart from writing') or something meaningful to believe in: 'the Causes exist all right but they're not bloody simple enough. I can't get a good strong hold of one' (sounding more like Jimmy Porter in *Look Back in Anger* than a Chapple).[17] London galvanised him, as Kevin observed to Shadbolt, made him 'more militant and aware'; though he would never become as passionate as Carl, who was actively organising the local New Zealanders and Australians to the cause ('with some people, Carl for instance,' Gee commented to his mother, 'the thing almost becomes a neurosis').[18]

He nearly went, but didn't, on this year's Aldermaston march, the largest ever, with 100,000 people at its climax in Trafalgar Square. But he was there on 18 February, only a week or so after he arrived, when Bertrand Russell led a two-and-a-half-hour sit-down of some 5000 outside the Ministry of Defence in Whitehall. On 29 April he and Carl were among the more than 800 arrested when the police—3000 of them—stopped 2500 marchers on the way from Trafalgar Square to Parliament Square, at the Cenotaph. The marchers sat down and ignored three warnings to leave. Carl was forcibly thrown into the paddy wagon; Gee went quietly. At Bow Street station—one of several the protestors were taken to, there were so many of them—they were allowed to make a public statement if they wished to, were fined £1 and let go. (John Neville and Vanessa Redgrave, among the handful who refused to pay the fine, were bailed in time to appear in a matinée performance of *The Lady from the Sea* at the Queen's Theatre.)[19] 'they ate through the sitters systematically, like an army of locusts', Gee reported to his mother. 'It was all very British, particularly the court proceedings—very polite.' She would have read about it in the *New Zealand Herald*.[20]

He was at the third major CND rally this year too, on 17 September, Battle of Britain day, when 1300 protestors were arrested (though not Gee)—less politely this time, the police's heavy-handed tactics causing 'quite a fuss'—after a seven-hour sit-down. Up to 17,000 had marched.[21]

He was loving London. 'I'm seeing my first real plays, first real paintings', he wrote to Charles Brasch a week or two after he arrived. 'And I've marched down Whitehall in the wake of Bertrand Russell. But I don't feel I've come Home. . . . I'm enjoying myself tremendously but I'm grateful to N.Z. in my future.'[22]

In one sense he hadn't really left home at all. He counted it a stroke of luck to fall in with a convivial group of New Zealanders who shared a house in Cheyne Gardens in Chelsea. Neil Perrett was a doctor from the North Shore who really wanted to be an artist.[23] (He had been in the same class as Kevin Ireland at Takapuna Grammar, though they had no memory of each other there.) His glamorous Australian wife, Antoinette, earned good money as a model, and defied Gee's prejudices by being both tall, thin and beautiful and one of the 'most delightful' women he had ever met.[24] Their tight-knit London circle included Neil's younger, quieter brother Tony, also a doctor, and their older brother Hugh, an engineer; another doctor, Colin Crawford; and Tom Soper, a serious, bookish Southlander with whom Gee became good friends. Upstairs four young women flatted, one of whom Soper was to marry. There were lots of parties and casual dinners at Cheyne Gardens. Carl and Kevin were usually there. The 'Chelsea Colony', Kevin called it.[25] Gee made no English friends (though many acquaintances) while he was in London at all.

He saw a bit of Angela Sears too, who had gone over in 1959 and was studying at the London School of Economics, and sharing a flat in Swiss Cottage with Helen Pavitt, one of the Everton Terrace girls. A trip to Angela's home town of St Albyns in Hertfordshire was one of only three he made out of London (along with a Continental tour) the whole time he was there.

But what he was there for was to write—enough and well enough to 'establish a claim to one of the bigger literary awards',[26] the Literary Fund scholarship or the Burns. He hoped to get a part-time job for three months while he revised his novel, and then perhaps teach: he made enquiries soon after he got there and found that he could earn enough money supply teaching (hateful though the prospect might be) to be able to have several weeks on the Continent and then take an 'unorthodox' route—overland as far as Asia, perhaps—home. (He was planning his return journey as soon as he arrived.)

Half of 'The Petition' needed complete rewriting, he decided. He was 'itching to get to work'.[27] Firstly though he typed the new story he had written on board the boat, on an old typewriter borrowed from Kevin but which was so worn out he quickly decided he'd have to get his own. Not long after he arrived he received a letter from New Authors Limited asking him to submit work for a short story anthology. New Authors had been established by Hutchinson in 1957 to publish 'first books only by writers from the British Commonwealth, South Africa, and the Irish Republic', in 'an attempt to reconcile the frustrations of the new writer who has a clear talent . . . with the harsh economic climate of publishing as it is today'.[28] Marilyn Duckworth's *A Gap in the Spectrum* (along with her second novel) had been published under this imprint. The short story volume, announced in September 1960, was the first of a planned annual series. Their approach to Gee came about through Karl Stead—who, six years before at Auckland University College, had been Gee's first editor as the co-editor of the 1955 *Kiwi*, and had just taken up a lectureship there. His own story 'A Race Apart' had been the first selected for the anthology. Hutchinson at the same time had also been looking for a New Zealand 'correspondent' who could identify new authors and manuscripts for them, offering £25 to anyone who put them on to a manuscript which was subsequently published, an offer Charles Brasch in the first instance turned down (a little offended),[29] and Frank Sargeson too, but Stead took up. It was he who suggested they look at Maurice Gee.

He sent them three stories: 'The Losers'; the new one, titled 'The Eleventh Holiday', with which he was pleased ('very taut'); and 'Three Women', about which he was less confident.[30] New Authors had also expressed interest in seeing a novel. By the middle of March he had four chapters of 'The Petition' revised.

He started teaching on 13 March at Walworth School, a comprehensive school in Lambeth in south London—'which is I'm told <u>real</u> London'.[31] Supply teaching paid well—£15 a week—and he would be able to save enough, he thought, by the end of July when the job finished to then go travelling. He stayed there for only eight days. The school was nice enough, but the kids were tougher than he was used to. He started at Nelson School, in the same area, on the 23rd. This was worse. 'I've never met such thoroughly rough unpleasant kids, never had such a bad time in the classroom', he wrote to his mother after two days. He found his class so uncontrollable that he had to resort to physically manhandling them, 'was actually on the point of knocking one of them down—I had my fist up to do it'. A few days later he did, fearing he'd given the boy a black eye. This position was supposed to be for three months but the headmaster was happy for him to look for something else.[32]

To add to his classroom difficuties he ran into bureaucratic ones with the Ministry of Education. He had had a letter sent from the New Zealand Department of Education detailing his teaching qualifications and experience ('This teacher's conduct, character and ability as a teacher have been satisfactory', was the comment), but the ministry in London insisted on verification of his undergraduate degree from the University of Auckland as well before it would recognise them. This meant that he was not being paid. He had already borrowed money from Carl to get him through to his first pay day, and asked his mother to send him £10 so he could repay him (she sent him £15), and had to do so again early in April (this time she sent £20). Late that month he was informed by the ministry's Teachers Branch that he had been provisionally recognised as a qualified teacher, subject to verification of his BA, but he was still receiving only part of his pay; and to make matters worse being taxed at the emergency rate of 30%. He did not start receiving his full pay (and have his tax status changed to the visitors' no tax rate) until some time in May.[33]

But at least his third classroom experience was a pleasant and easy one: at Rosedale Primary School in West Dulwich (also south London but a nicer south) for the second half of April, after he had spent the two-week Easter holiday working on his novel. By the end of those two weeks he had completely revised 'The Petition', which he had still to type; but was still not happy with it.

He heard just before April that New Authors wanted two stories, 'The Losers' and 'The Eleventh Holiday'. One of the readers was Rosamond Lehmann, who, he was told, thought his stories the best in the book.[34] The anthology would come out in September. The other contributors, along with Stead, were Maurice Duggan (with four stories) and a recent winner of the *Observer* short story competition, Diana Athill.

The new story he had described to his mother as similar to 'The Losers' in style. Like 'The Losers' it was an ensemble piece with a shifting narrative point of view, and also like 'The Losers' it culminated in a sudden, brutal act of violence. Thematically however it developed on from 'Schooldays', as a study of bigotry and small-mindedness (and, less overtly, sexual transgression), but a more complex one. At the Mayall Cottage Resort a group of middle-aged, middle-class couples are taking their annual summer holiday, as they have been doing together for years. The discovery this year that a new motor camp has opened at the other end of the beach is disturbing at first, but 'a vision of the place overrun by Teddy boys', in their ducktails and tight black jeans, seems to be unfounded; only a little noise disturbs them. The group's various backgrounds and characters, and subtle distinctions of status and gradations of prejudice, are succinctly drawn. There is a Queen Street barber, full of professional bonhomie; the owner of a small electrical repair shop in the outer suburbs (always a little diffident at first in the presence of his professional betters); a dairy farmer from the Hauraki plains; an insurance valuer—Remuera, Rotary and RSA man. (All are here with their wives but this story focuses on the men.)

The interesting one of them in Brian Hughes, sales manager for a large soap-making company (the Kitchen and Lever man has found his story), younger than the others but deferred to because of his social success, although a man of 'unpredictable moods and opinions'; in an unhappy marriage (a marriage that wasn't planned, 'But things can happen suddenly . . . people get tangled up': there is a little of Len Gee in him too), but devoted to his pretty sixteen-year-old daughter Cheryl—the only one of the couples' children to still join her parents on holiday—as she is to him. While the resort owner fuels the group's prejudices with exaggerated stories of sexual debauchery and all-night drinking down at the motor camp, she makes friends with a boy staying there. Frank Milich, his name is: 'not only a bodgie but a Dalmatian. It was suddenly plain in the smallness of his eyes and the prominent bones in his face.' He makes things worse for himself by beating one of the men at tennis.[35]

When Hughes suspects (wrongly) that Frank has raped his daughter it is he who, at the New Year's Eve dance at the Parau Hall, leads the boy's savage beating. The obvious point is the clash of generations and values, and the corrosive effect of bigotry and smug narrowmindedness. But there is something more interesting, and sinister, here than an outburst of male violence sparked by prejudice and pride. It is in the question—an implicit hint—of whether the 'shocking secret'[36] Hughes has betrayed to himself by his act relates not to the violence he has shown himself capable of but to the nature of his relationship with his daughter.

On 5 April Gee had lunch with Raleigh Trevelyan, editor at Hutchinson, to sign his contract, and also discuss his novel. This he hoped to have ready by the end of July, when he would finish teaching and go on his travels. He was planning to have two months in Spain: the popular and affordable choice then of holidaying Britons and New Zealanders, and especially penniless writers and artists. After that he would start for home. Towards the end of April he booked a passage on a boat leaving at the end of October, and paid the deposit two weeks later.

He was missing Nigel 'more and more not less and less', he wrote to his mother. 'I feel he really must have a father again by Xmas. . . . I think I'd feel terribly lost, the way Carl Freeman does, if it wasn't for him . . . Nigel, and writing, frees me from the sense of futility that seems to grip so many people, especially those of my age, today. All this', he continued, 'is an explanation of what will look like a premature return'.[37] She was sending him regular news and photographs of Nigel, and Hera wrote occasionally too. She was now enrolled in a radiography course at Auckland Hospital and had hired someone to look after Nigel during the day. At first this was a young Māori nurse from the hospital, who turned out to be something of a fantasist and a habitual liar, however, and left after a few weeks when Hera became suspicious of her stories; Len didn't trust her either and had been keeping a close eye on things at Roberton Road. In her place, to everyone's reassurance, Hera had got in a nurse she had trained with in Wellington and whom Gee knew and liked.

Through May and June he worked on the novel when he could—deciding that the first four chapters needed complete rewriting again—while teaching. He had two weeks at Tower Bridge Primary School, his favourite of all the London schools he taught at; ten days at Victory Primary School, near the Elephant and Castle; and the second half of June at English Martyrs, a Catholic primary school in Tower Hamlets in the East End, where the pupils he found tough and dull. (Either he or the authorities appear to have decided that he was better suited to primary teaching.) He finished revising at the end of May, just as his New Authors story proofs arrived, and when he had sent these back began typing the novel.

He was also reconsidering his homeward travel plans, again: he was thinking of cancelling his October booking (the Panama route was boring, he had been told) and once more of taking an overland route, possibly via Norway where Carl Freeman now was, working on a coastal steamer (this part of the plan quickly fell through).

He finished at the English Martyrs at the end of June, leaving him two weeks to finish the novel before his planned departure date for Spain, now in mid-July: 'typing just as hard as I can', he told Lyndahl, getting through fifteen to twenty pages a day. He felt, now, that he had 'lost any sense of purpose' he had about being in London, although he was still 'quite' enjoying it: 'It's an interesting interlude, but no more.' He would turn 30 in Spain, he reminded her: 'that's a milestone. I must decide what I want to be soon. I really don't feel I've got the talent to write as well as I want to, so soon I may set my sights on something else and become a hobbyist—I could still turn out a story now and then. But I'll never be a schoolteacher.'[38] It was a harsh self-criticism (apart from the last part) after he had had his stories accepted for London publication and an invitation to submit a novel. But along with Gee's conviction that he wanted to and should be a writer, he had a clear idea of the kind of writer that must be: he set himself high standards. It was his dissatisfaction with his novel, in particular, that had put him in this frame of mind. He delivered it to Hutchinson on 14 July—20,000 words shorter, 'about the length of a Graham Greene novel'—'[b]ut I'm not happy with it—it's the work of an amateur.'[39] Three days later he left for Spain.

He travelled with Kevin and Donna, for a while at least, taking a 9am train to Folkstone from Victoria Station. They did not stop in Paris but got straight on the overnight train to Barcelona. Donna got a couchette while Moss and Kevin sat up and attracted the derisive looks of their fellow passengers by sharing a baguette and cheese and a bottle of wine, pretending to be French. From Barcelona they went immediately to Tarragona, where Kevin and Donna were intending to stay for a few weeks. He spent three days with them (it had been going to be a week: he found Donna difficult, and they may well not have appreciated having a third party along), and discovered real Mediterranean food—his first bouillabaisse, and another memorable fish meal with Kevin at a restaurant on the beach. Then he set off on his own. 'I hope to just drift,' he had written jauntily to his mother, 'down as far as Valencia and Alicante—and perhaps get over to the Balearic Islands if my money holds . . . I'll live in cheap hotels and inns, and just travel by bus or train from town to town, seeing bull fights, drinking wine, doing a spot of writing here and there, sun bathing etc.' He should be able to manage on £6 a week, which would take him to the end of August. 'I'll be perfectly safe,' he assured her, 'perfectly happy—travel gives you plenty of confidence.'[40]

In fact he didn't like travelling on his own at all, finding it lonely and hard, and he hated bullfights. He travelled quickly, spending a night or at most three in each place. Besides (he told his mother) he didn't enjoy lounging around on beaches. He was interested in cities and people.[41] He didn't do any writing. From Tarragona he went south to Valencia, where he saw his first bullfight and was impressed enough by the spectacle of it to want to go again. From there he took a bus to Alicante, through 'fantastic country, stone mountains like dragons teeth and red-earth valleys . . . there's a wonderful feeling of primitiveness about it . . . and a sense of violence', and steeply terraced olive orchards and vineyards ('I've really gone for olives—I don't know how I'll live without them in N.Z.'). He spent two or three days in Alicante, which he found very touristy though 'lovely' (it was the high season, too). Almeria, by contrast, on the far south-west coast, where he spent one night was 'a rather grubby little city' but 'more honest'. From there he went to Malaga, where he saw his second bullfight, and was convinced that it was 'a disgusting, sadistic business'. Malaga though he liked.[42] There were lots of kids in Spain who looked just like Nigel, he wrote to Lyndahl.

By now his money was beginning to run out and he realised he'd have to cut short his trip, and abandoned hopes of getting to Tangiers or the Balearic Islands. (It looked like he was going to turn 30 in London after all.) In Granada he admired the Moorish architecture of the Alhambra but remained unaware that he was also in the city of Lorca. Then he headed back north to Madrid, where he stayed for three or four days, spending most of them in the Prado, enjoying Velazquez and Breughel, but above all the dark, violent, strange works of Goya—especially *The Third of May 1808*, Goya's frightening painting of the execution of Spanish revolutionaries by French soldiers.

He left Spain on 10 August, spending a few days in Paris on the way back, most of the time lying on his hotel bed with a pounding headache.

He had given up his Ebury Street room when he left London, and spent the first three weeks after he got back staying at the Perretts' before moving to a place with Tom Soper in Ladbroke Grove: a third-floor flat in a semi-detached in Bassett Road. The neighbourhood was 'working class and coloured', a little raffish and exotic as the Notting Hill area was increasingly becoming in the early 1960s; the street a nice one lined with overarching plane trees, like 'a green cave'.[43] A friendly Blake expert across the hall, Deirdre, invited them in occasionally for a drink.

Post-Spain, he entered into a prolonged period of torpor: 'immobile', Ireland reported to Shadbolt in October, '—not writing, not working, not travelling' (and starting to complain about the weather—'Every day he asks: "Does it really get any colder than this?"')[44] Jobs, he told his mother, were hard to get. A vague plan to go to the south of France for the grape harvest with Carl came to nothing. His next trip out of London was a weekend punting on the Cam with Angela and some of her friends. He awaited news of his novel, went to the football, slept a lot.

By mid-September he had had encouraging news. The publisher had read 'The Petition' and 'likes it very much' and readers' reports were favourable. He was to meet with the publisher on the 13th. If it was accepted, he told Lyndahl—which he thought likely—he would consider staying on in London for another six months. At the end of the month it was with Hutchinson's literary editor for a final decision and he thought it had 'a fifty fifty chance'.[45] Ireland passed the news on to Sargeson with more confidence than Gee himself was prepared to express: a certainty, he thought, 'and as much as one knows one shouldn't trust good signs, there is a definite promise of inevitability about Maurice himself.'[46]

Meanwhile, *New Authors Short Story 1* came out on 18 September: 'quite attractive' he thought, 'though the cover is rather dull' (in fact a quite striking, but restrained modernist one, in brown, black and white imprinted in red with a vaguely Māori design). He was 'fairly happy with it'.[47] There were only two short, but good, reviews over the next couple of months, in the *Guardian* and the *Observer* (Shadbolt reassured him that it was normal for reviews of short stories, as opposed to novels, to be slow). New Zealand reviews did not appear until after the book reached the shops there in November. The *New Zealand Herald* reviewer thought Gee's stories were 'the least polished but most powerful' in the book, and remarked that 'his grip on character and dialogue, his fascination with violence and conflict and his creative vigour seem to mark him out as a potential novelist', an opinion with which A.E. Horsman—already a fan of

'The Losers'—agreed in his *Landfall* review in March the following year, where he described that story as 'a rich novella' and Gee as 'perhaps essentially a novelist' in his interest in the group more than the individual (comparing him in this to Maurice Duggan)—in 'the extensive exploration of a tract of social life', but achieved through his skilful handling of multiple viewpoints and engagement of the reader's interest in the parts of the whole (Brasch's point too). He didn't like 'The Eleventh Holiday' quite so much, however.[48] (It was Shadbolt who got it wrong when he told Ireland he thought Gee was 'primarily a short-story writer'.)[49]

Gee heard that his novel had been accepted in the first week of October. It was to come out next year. He wrote home to his mother straightaway: 'wonderful news . . . It's the way I've always wanted to repay all the help I've had from you and Dad.' He was getting '£100 plus royalties', he told her (presumably £100 as an advance on royalties). He had given it a new title, 'The Big Season': 'a footballing title', he explained.[50] He had an author photo taken a few weeks later, by Tower Bridge by the Thames.

He was sure now that he would stay in London until the following spring, but then would definitely be going home. He had put in an application for the Literary Fund Scholarship in Letters (thinking of the Burns for 1963). He had a new novel in mind already, with 'a suburban and racecourse setting. I want to carry some of the ideas of The Losers a bit further' (this he had had in mind, in fact, since before he left New Zealand and had applied then for the Burns).[51] London, he had found, did not provide him with material for stories, as he (apologetically) told Brasch: 'when I think of writing my mind automatically goes back to New Zealand', and to novels.[52] This would never change.

He started teaching again in late October or early November, needing to earn his boat fare home, at Kennington school in Lambeth, near the Kennington Oval. This was an all-boys' secondary modern, predominantly West Indian, and his hardest job yet. Secondary moderns took mostly those who had failed their Eleven Plus exam. The class he had was at mixed levels of ability and language, and 'a nasty bunch'.[53] One challenged him to a fight. 'Aren't kids awful?' he wrote to Bob Dudding (who had been a teacher himself briefly before he took over the editorship of *Mate*): 'Why do we have them?'[54] But he found that teaching 'snapped me out of a lethargy that had sat heavily on me since I came back from Spain'.[55] That and, perhaps, the acceptance of his novel. It was with the printer in early November (after legal advice had been sought as to whether some references to the police were libellous), with a publication date of 28 May, and Hutchinson wanted an option on his next two.

At the beginning of November, when Tom Soper got married, he moved in briefly with Carl in Maida Vale, then back to the Perretts'. As he was leaving Maida Vale, he left his suitcase on the porch while he went off to find a taxi, and his suitcase was stolen. It had in it most of his clothes, his books and papers, including manuscripts of two stories he had no copy of, and his author copies and reviews of *New Authors Short Story*; and a mohair rug his mother had sent him. He was enjoying the novelty of the London winter nonetheless, he told her—although in fact London was experiencing an unusually dry and mild November: a month later he was feeling 'colder than I was cleaning windows in Dunedin's winter', he admitted to Brasch.[56]

His parents had moved themselves now too, to Torbay on the North Shore, after an abortive plan to move to Titirangi. This was the beginning of an unsettled and still unhappy period for them. Len had now sold his business, and they moved five or six times over the next few years. Lyndahl had continued to be unwell, spending some time in hospital, and Gee was worrying about her drinking. More than her mother's, the unexpected death of her sister Joyce—at 49 from a stroke—a few years earlier had deeply affected her.

Yet another plan was forming in his mind for the journey home. He now hoped to persuade Hera to come to London with Nigel when her radiography course finished, and they would travel back together 'in a leisurely fashion' in April or May.[57] Gee's uncertainty and endless changes of plan about when and how he would make his way home were matched by his confusion of motives about why: for Nigel? to try again with Hera? And to write. Some of all of those things. He had come to London in part to end things with Hera, to leave behind the confusion and unhappiness that relationship meant. He had arrived, Kevin Ireland would later remark, 'very lacerated', nervy, jumpy and depressed: 'he was in a state'.[58] There were two or three desultory affairs in London, desultory precisely because he was not free of Hera. And through each of them his 'trouble', his sexual problem, persisted. Finally, in desperation he sought advice from Neil Perrett, who prescribed a drug (it appears to have been potensin),[59] and when that made no difference referred him to Maudsley, the psychiatric hospital in Denmark Hill where Janet Frame had been treated a few years before: an institution with a high reputation for its progressive and humane care and the calibre of its staff. Gee had three sessions of psychotherapy there, talking about it all: his childhood, his family, his tormented adolescence. The doctor, Alwyn Lishman, was a young (the same age as him), recently appointed registrar who was to go on to a distinguished career as the pioneer of the field of neuropsychiatry. Gee found his manner aloof. He didn't prescribe anything; there was no miracle cure.

Hera in the end was not so keen on his travel plan.

By the beginning of December he had moved again, to a room not far from his old Ebury Street one, from which he could look across a mile of rooftops to the towers of Westminster. He was feeling now that he had 'sort of come to the end of London', and had a tentative booking on a ship leaving on 28 May—the day his novel was due to come out. With thoughts of leaving in mind, he described to his mother the things about it he liked best: the Battersea power station, his favourite London building, 'a monster of a building, ugly and beautiful'; but most of all the river, which he crossed at Vauxhall Bridge each morning and night, 'a small excitement for me every time': 'a fat, greasy, strong river, really alive, with swirling tides and noise and scum, not just a pretty stream like the Seine in Paris', and full of activity, 'small tugs towing as many as four huge flat lighters . . . coal boats for the power station'. 'I feel happy every time I cross it.'[60] But he was sure that he was leaving. By the middle of December he had heard that he had been awarded the Literary Fund scholarship.

He finished teaching just before Christmas, which he spent at Cheyne Gardens with Carl and Kevin and the Perrett crowd having a feast of turkey and duck and wine. On New Year's Eve it snowed all day, leaving grey slush underfoot but three inches of snow still on the roofs and trees the next day. He celebrated with his friends in a 'real London pub with singing and a piano' on Fulham Road. On New Year's Day he started work on a new novel—'or rather, a short novel', the first of two he had ideas for and hoped Hutchinson might be persuaded to publish together in one volume. This was not, in fact, the 'suburban and racecourse' one he had mentioned to his mother in October, but one based on the story 'Three Women', though 'much changed'.[61]

With the scholarship money coming he didn't have to worry about teaching, at least for a while, and was ambitious to get 'some really intensive work done'.[62] A few weeks after New Year he left his room in Victoria, after a misunderstanding with his landlady (he had found her very pleasant and friendly; in retrospect he would wonder if he had misread her intentions), and moved back to the Perretts for a week, then to a new place in Fulham Road, a hundred yards from Kevin and ten minutes' walk from Cheyne Gardens. Here he had a 'big room with easy chairs, a good bed, table, and a writing desk', it was warm and private and 'fairly cheap'.[63] He would stay until he left London. Not far away on the King's Road was an old-fashioned restaurant, the Cosy Caf, with long communal tables and cubicles seating five or six down the sides and two-course meals for three shillings, and where the waitress called everyone 'love': a bit of old, working-class Chelsea. He went there often with Kevin, and always ordered steak and kidney pudding and golden pudding. This, and 'real English pubs' where whole families went together on Sunday nights, rather than the young, fashionable bohemianism that was soon ushering in the Swinging Sixties, was the London Gee liked.

Ensconced in his cosy room at 443 Fulham Road, he got down to serious work on the new novel, writing mornings and afternoons, living as frugally as he could so he could keep doing so for as long as possible. He was still getting to the theatre, though—including *The Fire Raisers* by Max Frisch, a dark comedy of Nazism and communism, directed by Lindsay Anderson at the Royal Court Theatre in its English première—and to foreign films; and made one more excursion out of London, to Henley-on-Thames. The novel was going well, he thought. 'I know I always get enthusiastic about new work, but this does seem as good as anything I've done yet', he told his mother.[64] Back home, news of his London and Literary Fund success had made it into the press, courtesy of Gill Shadbolt, who was working for *New Zealand Truth*. 'News of the impending return to New Zealand of Maurice Gee', she wrote, came after the award of the Scholarship in Letters 'to enable this talented young New Zealand visitor to continue writing short stories and to work on a second novel'; she noted the publication of *New Authors Short Story* and the acceptance of his novel. 'During the 18 months he was been been abroad', she reported, not quite accurately, he 'has taught in schools in London's East End and has travelled widely on the Continent.'[65] It was, Gee must surely have been relieved, not quite the fanfare that had preceded Maurie's return. (For his part, Shadbolt wondered why Gee was coming back at all: he would make better use of the scholarship money, he had remarked to Ireland, in Spain where he could live for a year in Formentera or Ibiza 'and still have his return fare to NZ left over'.)[66]

He had asked his mother to send over £150 of the scholarship money (£500) when it arrived. When it appeared by mid-February that the Literary Fund was holding it for him until he got back he had to ask his parents for help. Lyndahl had already been sending occasional small sums even when he didn't ask (as she had done when he was in Melbourne), and £100 in June to cover his (then) plans for getting home. Gee's money troubles, however, were not all other people's fault. He had been 'wildly optimistic', he admitted, to come away with so little (£45) 'and thinking I was going to be able to have a good time and finance myself home again as well', and London was expensive. Even seasoned hands like Kevin Ireland found it 'bloody tough'. And Gee, Ireland complained to Dudding, was 'absolutely the most financially incompetent person I've ever struck—makes me feel like Morgan. . . . Moss can't face a diet of tea and buns. Donna and I try to sling a feed into him on a Sunday to give him a start for the week, but it doesn't seem to make much difference.'[67]

With Hera definitely not coming now, he was rethinking those plans yet again. He thought he'd go overland as far as Colombo (with Carl as far as Israel) and get a boat to Sydney from there. The £150 he had asked his mother to send, along with whatever he received from Hutchinson by way of an advance, 'should see me home comfortably'. Instead, he made a last-minute booking in the third week of January on a ship sailing on 1 March.

His last week in London was spent in a panic over money and his fare; and checking the final proofs of his novel. It snowed as well: the temperature didn't rise above –3° on the 26th. When the money from home hadn't arrived by the 27th and he was being threatened with the forfeit of his whole fare (£160), he sent an urgent cable to Auckland asking his parents to pay the travel agent, Thomas Cook, £100 sterling immediately and have them urgently telegraph their head office in London. The cheque from his parents arrived that same afternoon.

He left London in a state of emotional turmoil of another kind as well—not unlike that in which he had arrived. Not long before, he had met and become romantically involved with a young woman, of whom he would remember only that her name was Rosemary. He imagined that he was in love—as he tended to do—and told her he was coming back, to her. And yet he had thought he was, or might be, going home to Hera. Kevin Ireland, watching, thought this was all just posturing and histrionics, that his 'agony of supposed love' was a novelist's flourish, a dramatic exit, and he wrote Gee a stern letter telling him so.[68] To Shadbolt he wrote a week after Gee had gone:

> Poor old Maurice Gough Gee is on the high seas at this moment not knowing what he wants to do or where he wants to be. He has a wonderful way of turning what you or I would call having a good time into high personal tragedy—tragedy that to anyone else appears more like high comedy. If there is a heaven for the misunderstood then M.G.G. will be right in the front row of the choir.

Still, he thought London had done Moss good, 'given him a peace of the spirit . . . a privacy, and an opportunity to sling off those late adolescent traits that cripple kiwis into middle age': 'Worth the trip for the sexual and political education alone'. He had 'never seen anyone change quite so much in so short a time'.[69]

Gee's later view of the influence of London was more muted. 'It opened me up a little. Helped me grow up. I had to grow up before I could write. I left it late. London helped but London wasn't the important thing.'[70]

9

The Big Season

He sailed home on the *Southern Cross*, a newer ship (she had made her maiden voyage in 1955) and more comfortable than the *Castel Felice.* He had a two-berth cabin this time (and one above the water-line), sharing it with a young Australian who aspired to be a professional dancer. They did not become friends; the Australian was off having his own fun. He did read Gee's proof copy of *The Big Season*, and told him he didn't like it much. When he found that he was sharing his table with an elderly couple Gee asked if he could be moved and was given a place instead at the chief engineer's, in the company of four friendly young Australian women, with one of whom he carried on an innocent flirtation (she was on her way home to get married). They spent much of their time on the voyage in each other's company, playing a lot of deck golf with the engineer.

He had fun on this journey, though he was missing London already, he wrote to his mother as they were 'chugging along towards Panama' in mid-March: 'There's so much there that no other place I've lived has to offer. And there's so much of England and the Continent I didn't see. It's obvious that I'll have to go back one day.'[1] It would be in twenty years.

The *Southern Cross* took the east–west route, through the Panama Canal. He went ashore, with the Australian girls, at Trinidad, where he found Port of Spain 'hot, smelly and dirty' and spent the evening in 'a rather sleazy little club' watching limbo dancing and bottle dancing, drinking rum and Coke; at Curaçao, 'a lovely little city, one of those baked, rusty, dusty, places';[2] and Panama City for a few hours only on the 15th. In Tahiti he had a late St Patrick's Day celebration at Quinn's Bar with Sean Cooke, an Irishman with whom he had also become friendly, who was emigrating to New Zealand with his wife Frieda. They made an agreement to meet up again next St Patrick's Day at the Queen's Ferry, an appointment Gee would miss (he was not in Auckland then). He made no attempt to stay in touch with Cooke subsequently, but Cooke kept in touch with him, ringing him every year on St Patrick's Day almost without fail (he was still doing so four decades later).

In Tahiti he also posted a letter to Rosemary, telling her he would not be coming back to London after all.

He did no writing on the *Southern Cross*, but he would later write a story based on a shipboard experience, when he had found himself holding hands one night with a lonely fellow passenger. It was an innocent gesture on the young man's part, a consoling one on Gee's. In his story the central character, Jack, is a teacher on his way to London. He holds himself aloof from the other passengers, disliking the 'disturbing intensity' of the groups into which they form themselves, preferring to spend his time alone on deck reading Stendahl (*The Red and the Black* in one version of the story, *The Charterhouse of Parma* in another), while they in turn think him a 'snob or misfit'; but when he begins to regret this in his growing loneliness he occasionally has a drink with four young men he calls 'the wolfpack', footballers he once played against who huddle in the bar around 'a miniature city of beer cans', their conversation limited to lewd talk about sex, and who 'roamed the ship in a baying knot, scrummed against groups of girls, tossed wisecracks back and forth like footballs'. (There had been gangs of young Australians like this on the *Southern Cross*, Gee would remember, running riot all over the ship.) He also spends some time with Dennis, a university student and would-be actor, liking him but amused by his cocky naïveté—he is going to London with £20 and no plans, looking forward to the challenge of 'a kind of pioneering in reverse'—and affectations. Dennis refers to the Stendahl by its French title (he himself has brought along Proust) and drinks campari and soda, not beer. (In London in the 1960s campari was the 'right drink' that the right set drank at cocktail parties.)[3] He is, as the footballers surmise, 'a pansy': he is also going to London to leave behind the family that has disowned him. (Jack's limited experience of homosexuals includes Ted and Malcolm, piano-playing, eau-de-cologne-wearing friends of his 'cranky, neighbour-shocking mother'.) When the very drunken footballers take over the ship's concert one night with an impromptu striptease and seize upon Dennis—ripping off his green monogrammed shirt—Jack seeks the terrified, near-hysterical young man out on the darkest stretch of the deck where he has fled. Here, it is Dennis who grasps Jack's hand; the latter is pleased with himself for not, although almost, pulling away.

Gee worked hard on this story—it went through several drafts and changes of title—but it was never published.[4]

The *Southern Cross* docked at Wellington in the early morning of 4 April. He went straight to the Literary Fund to see about his scholarship money. (It had been sent to his parents' address on 2 March.) He spent two or three days in Wellington, staying with the Cooks, who were now in Oriental Terrace, and catching up with other friends, including Gill and Maurie, who had recently moved to Fairview Crescent after spending most of the previous year living in Nigel and Julie's downstairs Glenmore Street flat. Shadbolt reported to Ireland that Moss was 'looking fit but very confused', but wondered if he was going back to Auckland too soon and shouldn't stay in Wellington longer, to 'avoid emotional complications . . . over his boy'.[5] He also called in on Ray Grover at the Alexander Turnbull Library, where Ray was now working, on his first day straight off the boat, carrying a model outrigger canoe he had bought for Nigel in Tahiti or Fiji.[6] But Shadbolt did see the change in him, feeling—hoping—that 'in its usual perverse way, Europe may have given Moss the grip on things here which he needed.' Not until he was back down there a few months later, though, did they have 'several long yarns (the first real yarns since he got back)'.[7]

In Auckland he was met by Len, who drove him straight to Avondale to see Nigel (two-and-a-half now). He spent most of the rest of this year in Auckland, living with Hera and Nigel, evidently trying to make the relationship work. He thought he and Hera 'might get married', he told Maurie when he was down in Wellington for a visit mid-year.[8] They were at Roberton Road until May, then in a place in Matata Street in Blockhouse Bay. He also appears to have spent some time at his parents' house in Torbay, where Len and Lyndahl had bought a house in Beach Road, on the southern headland looking across to the north (it would have become a very valuable real estate investment if Len had not sold it within a year). With Hera working, Gee was childminding. He was still trying (or at least hoping) to get some writing done too. He had the Literary Fund scholarship after all, it was what he was supposed to be doing: working on the 'short novel' he had begun in London on New Year's Day. He was later to describe it as 'a domestic tragedy about the wrong people marrying each other'.[9]

The Big Season—dedicated to his parents—came out in London at the end of May and was in the shops in New Zealand by mid-July. 'As you know the book's fallen a bit flat', Gee wrote to Maurie in September, '—combination of poor dust cover, inept reviewing etc—you see I'm blaming everything but the writing'.[10] One, sympathetic, reviewer's comment that '[b]y and large, it's had a perplexed dismal reception' was only a slight exaggeration.[11] The reviews in the daily press were mixed, with the unfavourable ones outweighing the favourable. But this reviewer, under the heading 'Fine NZ novel deserves better reception', could not 'imagine a better New Zealand novel appearing this year—and perhaps for quite a long time to come. . . . You can put this book on the top shelf beside Cross, Ballantyne, Ashton-Warner and Janet Frame'. D.G.B. in the *Otago Daily Times* judged it 'a success for which his stories in the volume "New Authors' Short Story" had encouraged readers to hope', while the same city's *Evening Star* found it 'a surprisingly good first novel', and the *Bay of Plenty Times* 'vigorous', 'exciting' and 'colourful' reading, its plot 'woven with skill and dexterity' and Gee 'a writer of great honesty and power'. In the *Rotorua Daily Post*, Fiona Kidman, a 22-year-old librarian who was just starting to write herself, described the author as 'an obviously brilliant young New Zealander with an unerring eye for detail and a sharp ear for dialogue', though there were some 'raw edges', she thought, and the novel's 'sordidness' was occasionally gratuitous.[12]

The Big Season was not a Bildungsroman, but it had quite a lot of Gee in it. Its setting, a small town called Wainui, is undisguisedly Paeroa: a flood-prone provincial town with 'shops and churches, domain and river, race-course and hills'.[13] It opens with the central character, Rob Andrews, as a ten-year-old down at the river with his friend Arthur fishing for whitebait, and spying on the Jenkins boarding house: a bad place, his parents have warned him, where 'the wrong sort of people' live.[14] (Other childhood escapades include building tin canoes and raiding the Catholic school.) The boarding house is a close and fond recreation of Heysham House; in their spying one night the two boys watch a drunk man peeing out the open kitchen window. Now, in the novel's real time, Rob is 21 and beginning to question the values of a town where respectability and rugby rule. He is a star back who also reads John Steinbeck and Graham Greene (even if he didn't like the Greene). After a chance encounter in the Norton Hotel one night he is drawn in by the semi-underworld of the boarding house, in particular the trio of Bill Walters, a charismatic safe-breaker just out of gaol (Heysham House's Jack West, the Tank Man), his wife Mary, and Arnie, their gentle, homosexual friend. When he was ten Rob's father had told him that 'there were two sorts of people, the good and the bad, and the good couldn't touch the bad without starting to go bad themselves'; now, as then, Bill Walters seems to him 'something between a sinister pirate and Robin Hood'.[15]

The pig-shooting expedition into the Ureweras that Rob goes on with Bill and Arnie, for which he forsakes an important rugby game (Wainui versus North Coast for the Federated Farmers' Cup) and his chance of selection for the union reps, is based on one Gee had made with two fellow teachers' college students in 1954. He had taken his notebook and recorded a Gothic description of the landscape and the derelict farm which is now where Bill Walters' father lives—an old man Gee will later describe as one of his Crassin incarnations (who had first appeared in his second unpublished novel), a mean, dirty, violent, malicious old man.[16] On the shoot, pigs root silently in the ti-tree and fern scrub 'like eels in a creek'.[17]

Rob's rebellion against Wainui's small-town culture, encapsulated by his small businessman father and schoolteaching brother and their conventional, intolerant minds, is the central and simple narrative here. The more complex relationship, and the harder for him to find his way free of, is with his mother, who 'made her capacity for love an excuse for demanding it'—to whom he sometimes 'listened with fear as she talked: every fond word she gave him showed her belief that they were knotted together for the rest of their lives. But it was not true. He belonged to himself.' He hears her 'using him, working inside his knowledge of her'. She is thought 'strange' by the rest of Wainui not only for being uninterested in rugby but because she reads poetry; but knows that he will, and thinks that he should, leave.[18]

Gee would later describe *The Big Season* as 'the typical young man's novel—a symbolic act of rebellion', 'that novel full of easy scorn so many of us write first time up'.[19] He is not Rob—he was not rebelling in Paeroa in the way Rob is against Wainui—but Paeroa had been for him a liberation.

There is a girl too, of course, to whom Rob becomes engaged: Carol Duncan. She has been away from Wainui, having a finishing school education in Auckland and Hawke's Bay and a year at university; but she reads romances, not poetry or Graham Greene. Her (not Rob's) move to consummate their relationship, in a car under the trees at Rugby Park after a movie (*The House of Wax*) on the night Rob has planned to break off their engagement, comes undone as soon as she undoes his top fly button. 'His physical reaction had been too excited, too sudden.' At the boarding house later that night he confides his problem to Mary, who responds sympathetically and matter-of-factly (as Alfred Plumb will to Raymond Sole)—'You got yourself all screwed up, I'd say, and as soon as she touched you you went off like an alarm clock. That sort of thing happens'—then loses his virginity to her.[20] Bill's discovery of this precipitates his leaving for Auckland and a risky bank job; he is arrested after his friends' frantic search for him alerts the police, and is beaten up in the holding cells. The petition of the novel's original title is the one Rob, guilt-tormented twice over, writes, calling for an official inquiry, and takes around at the big final match of the season: United against Railways for the shield (played in a swamp of mud which covers the field like 'steaming porridge'; the white and green jerseys of the United team are similar to Paeroa Old Boys', the wide black-and-red hoops of Railways' to Waitemata's).[21] His mother signs it; his father grinds it under his heel. But Rob has made his decision already. In the novel's final scene he drives off in a Ford Prefect with Arnie, headed for Auckland, reading in a backward glance the gold-lettered words on his father's shop window: *Wainui Shoe Shoppe. Ray Andrews and Rob.*

The 'sordidness' was all too much for some. Gee, wrote H.M. Marshall in the *Southland Times*, 'must have decided that he would outmodernize the modernists in vulgarity, crudeness and—well there's no need to go into details'. The novel was entirely unredeemed by 'lightness, levity or wit', or likeable characters (except perhaps Mrs Andrews); Rob disappoints his girlfriend, who is too good for him, and 'let[s] down his football team for the big match—to go pigshooting. Surely Gee knows that no New Zealander would do that.' The *Southland Daily News* described the novel as 'a study in decline, a preparation for decay', featuring small, ordinary people, and 'most disconcertingly wanting in what can only be called innocence', and thus lacking the charm or grace 'that innocence brings in its train'—for 'what moving or saddening fall from grace can there . . . be when the young man, unable to draw back, moves closer and closer to dubious or scruffy people?'[22]

This was not only the opinion in the deep south. The *New Zealand Herald* review—the first to appear, along with the *Auckland Star*'s—completely missed the point, describing the novel as a 'frank, unrestrained yet vital', 'compelling' story of a young man 'whose adolescence is influenced in the wrong direction', as he is swayed towards 'undesirable companionships and finding himself involved in the seamy side of life, so much so that he finally gives up football, at which he shines, betrays the trust of his family and neglects his fiancee': it 'gives a true picture of a section of modern youth starting out with all the advantages in the world only to clutch at the wrong straw swaying the wrong way in the wind'—a review Shadbolt described to Kevin Ireland as 'a bloody scream!'[23] (Robert Goodman in the *Star*, meanwhile, alone among the reviewers was offended not by the content, of what he thought was 'an unusually interesting novel', but by its 'disregard for style'.)[24]

Such reviews need not, perhaps, be taken seriously. The substantial ones, though, were more disappointing. In the *New Zealand Listener* David Hall, while praising its 'heartening authenticity' and finding it 'an oddly attractive novel', was not convinced by Rob, 'a fumbling lover and a depressive' who he could not believe would give up the only thing he was good at, football, for 'a dubious motivation'. Similarly, Winston Rhodes, professor of English at the University of Canterbury, in the quarterly public affairs review *Comment* the following year found Rob 'a hero without any real cause', and Wainui's 'spiritual poverty' and 'mental dullness' all-too-pervading for Gee's acknowledged energy, anger ('more strident than incisive') and craftsmanship to shape into a 'satisfying' novel. But it was the *Landfall* review—in the December 1962 issue—that was the harshest. Its author was Rhodes' junior colleague R.A. Copland. While also recognising Gee's craftsmanship—the organisation, economy and authenticity, and his 'flair, too little exercised, for irony of situation'—it was 'a pity', he wrote, 'that these abilities have been misspent in an attempt to reconcile two literary conventions, to produce as it were an Angry Young Man Alone', lacking both the 'brute hardiness and peril' of the latter and 'the bitter, derisive and comic play of an educated and lively intellect'. The 'greatest weakness in the novel' was 'the author's grave approbation of a hero whose exploits are as preposterous and bungling as any modern Quixote's' and who has 'an inner life about as complex and interesting as a St Bernard's'. The denizens of the Jenkins boarding house he described as 'a shrunken epileptic of homosexual tendency', a 'misunderstood and maltreated' professional burglar and his 'muscular, middle-aged moll'.[25] Reviewers are entitled to dislike or be disappointed by the book they are reviewing, but in its tone this was cruel. It caused

Shadbolt, characteristically, to stop buying *Landfall* and to instruct his publisher to stop sending copies of his own books for review, and to write a vitriolic letter to the editor explaining why: a letter he did not in fact send until several months later, for Brasch's information. But this of course was not all about Gee: the review was only the latest incitement of Shadbolt's growing dissatisfaction with *Landfall*, the letter one more volley against a literary community he had described to Kevin Ireland a year before as 'a bitter collection of freaks and frustrates'.[26] (The novel itself he told Ireland he thought was 'solid and tenacious (like Moss himself)'.)[27]

Gee told Brasch that he had found the review 'a little upsetting', and that while he was aware that the book had shortcomings he did not feel it was quite as bad as that. But 'most of the points made were fair', he conceded, 'and one or two possibly helpful. After all, if I can't do better I should stop writing'. Brasch had already let him know his personal opinion, which was that while he was 'very interested in' the novel he 'could not help feeling that you had not detached yourself sufficiently from the material to get it well into focus', which was typically astute for someone who knew Gee only as well as he did.[28] As for the review, it is possible that he had not commissioned it himself, for he was in England when *The Big Season* came out.

By December 1962 Gee's domestic situation had changed, and he was not going to be doing any writing for a while. It was Hera who suggested—or decided—that they should move to Rotorua, to live in the house her mother owned there. This was a falling-down, two-bedroomed, bungalow-style house on Koutu Road—number 96—about a mile around the lakeshore from Ōhinemutu and the Ngāti Whakaue meeting house, Tamatekapua. The area was known simply as 'the pā'. It was entirely Māori: Gee was the only Pākehā in Koutu Road. This was Hera's home ground.

They went down some time lateish in the year, Hera at first just to introduce him—establish his credentials—while he spent some weeks there on his own working on the house, which was barely liveable, helped by two of Hera's cousins, Lamby (Morrison) and Bunky. By the third week of December he had installed a flush toilet and shower—digging out the hole for the septic tank, a soak hole and drains, then demolishing the outside dunny and filling in the longdrop, all that on his own—and had been back to Auckland to bring Nigel down from Torbay in time for Christmas. 'I've got all my books up', he wrote to Lyndahl, 'so I feel at home here.'[29] There were fourteen there over Christmas, including Hera and her mother, her siblings and their families, a demanding test of the new facilities while they were still being built. He spent the next two or three months renovating the house: relining and repainting inside, removing one wall; building on a back porch; replacing the roof (knocking out two front teeth in the process) and rotting weatherboards; painting the exterior (that was Lamby's job). Len came down for a while to help with the interior work. As a builder's son Gee had, and was proud of his, practical know-how, but he was no carpenter. By the end of May he had pretty much finished working on the grounds: putting up a garage and digging out and concreting a new driveway.

He was in a foreign place. 'There seems to be a tradition of giving to neighbours', he remarked to his mother, '—smoked trout, eel; crayfish, wild pork, mussels, pipi etc', lots of sharing.[30] There had been no Māori in Henderson. He was never to feel fully at home here. Nor, however, did he have anything to do with the other Rotorua, the tourist-city Rotorua of ritzy hotels and dance halls and nightlife—a Rotorua that, while not Auckland or Wellington, was a little more cosmopolitan than other small cities or provincial towns. Yet he never felt properly accepted down at the pā. 'I often feel I've missed something in Rotorua', he wrote to Maurie later in the year, with the prospect of leaving it. 'I've lived for a year in a Maori community—Koutu—without really getting in touch with it.'[31] Partly, he felt, the people never fully welcomed him. Partly it was that he didn't really try, did not take some necessary, final step. As he has frankly admitted since, 'I wasn't terribly interested in things Māori.'[32] They would never be material for his fiction.

He found friendly and got on well enough, though, with people on an individual level, like Bunky and Lamby, and the two middle-aged sisters who lived next door, on a large macrocarpa-surrounded section, with their more distant brother: he was Haane Manahi, a Māori Battalion veteran who had won a Distinguished Conduct Medal for his action in Tunisia in 1943, and would later be awarded a posthumous Victoria Cross. The exception was Hera's mother, who was living alternately in Wellington (Hera going down several times with Nigel to visit her) and Rotorua through much of this year; and whom he had always liked and had a good relationship with until one day she all of a sudden started to hate him, and didn't stop. Lydia and Hera fought constantly and loudly, and he made the mistake one time of taking Hera's side in an argument. 'I've never been hated before', he wrote to his mother. 'It's an uncomfortable experience.'[33] He would vividly remember standing on a table painting the living room ceiling one day while Lydia shook the table beneath him screaming 'Get this Pākehā out of my house!' But she was ill this year, too, with lung cancer, spending some time in hospital in Wellington before she came back to Rotorua finally in September or October.

By mid-March he had started a job, not the one he had hoped to get at the Māori Affairs Department but at the Rotorua office of the Department of Health, filing dental-benefit records. It was the most boring job he would ever have: it 'makes me feel ashamed of himself', he told his mother. '[M]y office girl's job', he described it to Maurie—in a letter written in his lunch hour on green public service minute sheet paper—made bearable only by the presence of a woman in the office who lent him the *New Statesman* and had bought three copies of *The Big Season*. 'For the rest it's giggles & clothes & babies & shops & football.'[34] It was a necessary evil, however, because with Hera not working, the financial situation was precarious. Winning £100 in the Golden Kiwi lottery was only a temporary boon. For a while they had in a boarder, a young bank clerk, while Gee bought a Golden Kiwi ticket every payday now.

He was making escape plans. To Brasch in March he mentioned that he might be in Wellington in the second half of the year. At some point during the first half of the year he wrote to Kevin Ireland to ask his advice about going back to London, with Hera and Nigel. Kevin thought he shouldn't. For one thing, New Zealand was a much better place to bring a boy up in. And, more importantly, what work would he do? 'You must remember what teaching was like here: the Hell it tore out of you.' If he was to teach, he'd be better off doing so back home. And then there was the weather, he reminded him: the 'murdering winters and summerless summers'. But 'if you really are determined to chuck it all up and come over here', he suggested he train as a librarian first (an idea Gee had already had). 'But, whatever you do Moss,' Kevin wrote, 'ride your luck a bit. You've got it; you can take chances.'[35] By the time he got this letter that was not at all how Gee was feeling.

Ireland's own circumstances had markedly improved since his friend had left. He had a new, well-paying job as a proofreader on *The Times* (with Carl Freeman). And back home his first book of poems had just come out. Bob Lowry had been going to publish this, until Dudding finally wrested the manuscript off him when nothing had happened for over a year, intending to do it himself: 'Delighted to be number one author of R.N. Dudding, Publishers', Ireland wrote thanking him for the offer.[36] Since neither of them had any money, the plan was to raise it from their friends: Gee among others pledged £5. In the event, however, Ireland's *Face to Face: twenty-four poems* was published by the Pegasus Press. (Dudding was having enough of a struggle keeping *Mate* alive.)[37] Shadbolt, meanwhile, had his second collection of stories out this year, from Eyre and Spottiswoode in London, and was in Dunedin as the Burns Fellow. New Zealand publishing, he remarked to Ireland in June, 'has boomed'[38]—and he appeared to be right. The *Auckland Star* in an editorial at the start of New Zealand Book Week in October noted the 'unprecedented volume' there had been the previous year, and while most of it had no literary pretensions, it was true, authorship and publishing were 'cumulative processes' and 'a community in which authorship is no longer regarded as an unprofitable eccentricity is readier to support serious writers': a 'steady stream' of locally published first novels was beginning to appear, and authors 'are seeing the first glimmering of a competitive market for their work and of a public interest in broader themes than the introspective recollections of childhood and adolescence that made up the bulk of creative writing in New Zealand during the early post-war years'.[39] Among the books worthy of notice this year was Bill Pearson's novel *Coal Flat*, a semi-autobiographical study of life and the pressures of social conformity in a small West Coast coal-mining town: long in gestation through the 1950s and published five years after it was completed, it was 'the richest and strongest work of its kind yet to appear in New Zealand', Brasch would describe it the following year, in a *Landfall* note in which he observed that fiction—as well as art—'is visibly coalescing at last into a body of work' (though he was still waiting for 'one clear sharp masterpiece, however short, of whatever kind—poetry, fiction, music, painting, sculpture. Assuming one had the gift to recognise it, of course').[40] But it was the phenomenal sales of Barry Crump's that the *Star* editorial mentioned.

In 1963, though, Brasch was not feeling quite so upbeat, for he was finding 'a shocking dearth' of publishable stories, as he complained to Dan Davin over at Oxford University Press; and it was no doubt partly for this reason, as well as his lack of enthusiasm for *The Big*

Season, that he regretted that Gee had apparently 'deserted to the novel, not wisely I suspect, though it may be too soon to judge'.[41]

In June Gee took Nigel to Auckland for a holiday, not at Torbay but Kumeū where Len and Lyndahl now were: Len's latest investment was a small farm there. And he appears to have been thinking of staying up there himself for the remainder of the year, or for some time at least. Writing to his mother a week before they went up he mentioned wanting to 'start on a new job soon after getting up there, so I hope that airport one is still available. I don't know what it is exactly, but anything will do.' Then next year he would probably enrol in the Library School diploma course in Wellington. He hoped he would be able to get some writing done at their place too: 'My fingers itch sometimes to get at it again.'[42]

Instead he was back in Rotorua, and the dental records office, within a month. 'Circumstances have closed on us again like a bloody Iron Maiden', he wrote to Maurie. He was referring to the situation with Hera's mother, whom Hera was now nursing at Koutu Road. 'There's little chance of us getting out of here now before the end of the year', and even then if he left Hera would probably stay behind. 'It's a bastard of a situation, but one which Hera at least would never have any peace of conscience about if she walked out on.'[43] He was stuck there; stuck in his 'office girl's job'; unable to write. 'Letter from Moss', Shadbolt reported to Ireland, 'Desperate, moody. He's in another terrible situation. . . . still with Hera and his son; marriage seems as far off as ever though Hera calls herself "Mrs Gee." . . . Hera's mother is dying of lung cancer. The family is all around. You can guess the rest. A situation like that might yet send Moss round the bend.' Write to him, he urged.[44]

But he and Hera and Nigel were 'fairly happy together', Gee told Shadbolt, '—so there is a bright side. I'm doing <u>something</u> constructive at least.'[45]

What was not working—still—was his sex life. His difficulties had persisted throughout his relationship with Hera; in retrospect he would concede that she had as much to put up with from him as he did from her. They were troubling him enough that when he had written to Kevin about the idea of going back to London *en famille* he had also asked him to ask Neil Perrett about the drug Perrett had prescribed, or perhaps another. ('The name of the drug is POTENSON', Ireland had written on the bottom of his reply.) He also wrote to Alwyn Lishman, the doctor he had seen at Maudsley, who sent a kind letter back: 'I was pleased to hear from you and learn that in some ways things are going better, but sorry that this particular problem continues. I certainly think it would be worth your while to see a Doctor in New Zealand', he advised. As for drug treatment, however, he had had little experience of the use of drugs for this kind of problem, and suggested that Gee have his own doctor write to him directly.[46] But Gee did not consult anyone here.

In September Hera started working, as supervising night sister at Rotorua Hospital. This meant that the financial situation, at least, was 'more or less under control', and should enable them to clear their debts on the house by Christmas, he hoped.[47] But until then he remained trapped, in a place he didn't what to be, doing a job that was 'driving me nuts'.[48] 'I get bouts of deep depression at my inability to write in my present circumstances', he wrote to Shadbolt at the end of August. 'Well Maurie, I'll finish now,' he ended this letter, 'I'm kind of ballsed up—with life's petty frustrations & can't put two thoughts together.'[49]

He saw his hope of rescue now in the Burns Fellowship, for which he applied in the first week of September, feeling that he was 'really allowing myself to hope too much': 'I want it very badly, so keep your fingers crossed', he wrote to his mother after he'd posted off his application, '—I wouldn't even object to a prayer'. To Shadbolt he remarked 'this may be a last chance'.[50] He heard that he'd got it at the end of the month. '[C]uriously I'm not really exalted', he replied to a congratulatory telegram from Maurie, '—just bloody determined to use the year well. . . . Still, . . . I'm feeling alive again, literary-wise, for the first time in over a year.'[51] The local newspaper ran an article he thought was 'a bit silly', he told his mother. It described him as 'a Rotorua clerk', who 'said today the fellowship would enable him to attempt his "most ambitious novel"'; but he wasn't saying what it was about.[52] At the office he had 'a busy morning . . .—people offering to be the hero of my next book, and telling me about things happening in their street that would make Peyton Place seem anaemic. They seem genuinely pleased anyhow.' (Had he been expecting derision? Perhaps just disinterest.)[53]

Winning the Burns more than made up for not winning the Hubert Church award, which was given annually by the New Zealand centre of PEN for the best work of prose each year, and worth £100. He had thought either he (for *The Big Season*) or M.K. Joseph would get it—but 'it went to Barry Crump!', he exclaimed to Lyndahl. 'This makes serious writing a joke.'[54] This was for Crump's third book of deer-culling and yarn-spinning and rough-country life. The first two, *A Good Keen Man* and *Hang On a Minute Mate*, had between them sold 100,000 copies by October 1962, a publishing phenomenon in New Zealand which his publishers Reeds had marked with the release of single-volume edition. By October 1963 Crump's total sales were nearing 150,000. *The Big Season* in its first year had sold 3100. 'They'—Hutchinson—'seem satisfied', Gee remarked to Shadbolt, 'but I think it's bloody poor.' (*New Authors Short Story*, he also told him, had lost Hutchinson money, selling only 1300—not that short story collections were expected to sell well.)[55] But Hutchinson, he had now heard, were doing a paperback later this year, for which he might get £100 or £150. 'I like to earn money from writing', he told his mother, '—it gives me confidence.'[56] It came out as an Arrow paperback in 1964, described on the front cover as a 'raw, uninhibited story of a boy's growing up in a rugby mad New Zealand town', and on the back, in a review quote from the *Reynolds News*, as a 'Racy and salty novel . . . about a man's rebellion against the clean-limbed, rugger-club values of New Zealand suburban life. It has a freshness and honesty that gives me high hopes for Mr Gee.' (If there had been other British reviews, Gee appears not to have seen them.)[57]

He was disillusioned with Hutchinson, however, and had decided he would go through an agent from now on. If he ever got his new book finished, he told Shadbolt, he would see if Richmond, Towers and Benson were interested. He had just received, in July 1963, the first money—£40—he had had from Hutchinson since his £100 advance the previous year. 'I don't think Hutchinson's are dishonest, but I'm sure I could get better terms from them.' He had also just discovered that the royalty he was getting on overseas (meaning New Zealand) sales was not on the published price (in England 16/-) but on 8/-: 'I think you warned me of this sort of thing once'.[58] A reduced 'export' royalty was in fact the norm at this time (and Shadbolt and other writers were waging a campaign directed at Whitcombe and Tombs about the reduced royalty they were paying on joint UK/New Zealand publications).

Less disappointing than not winning the Hubert Church award, but mainly because he hadn't been expecting to, was not winning the 100-guinea Katherine Mansfield short story prize (for which he had probably entered 'The Eleventh Holiday'), the result of which was announced in late October. Shadbolt did, with one of the stories in his new collection, *Summer Fires and Winter Country.* In this, Gee had told his mother when he read it in August, there were two good stories and some poor ones. To Shadbolt, writing the same day, he was more enthusiastic, of course. Those two stories were '"definitive" . . . they make a complete authoritative statement about life in N.Z.', they were 'stories that will live for a long time—I firmly believe that'. His writing, Gee told him, had maturity, strength and true feeling: 'By maturity I mean it looks unwaveringly at the painful facts of loneliness & lost illusion, lost innocence. By strengths I think perhaps I mean body, concreteness, sense of place—I get this from very little N.Z. writing. . . . In your stories place has been assimilated until it is organically part of a whole—part of the life of the story.' This was something he felt he could not do: 'I have very little sense of place, & I cannot put people in a setting without too much effort . . . "Setting" here is the giveaway word'.[59] (He was wrong: place is something he would do very well.)

He had started this letter with an apology for not having written to Shadbolt sooner: 'not laziness, believe me, but a sense of the futility of "carrying on" about works of art, finished products. A thing is, the reading of it with enjoyment & an enlarging of sympathy is the only act of praise it needs. Words after the event, from me at least, always seem to muddy & obscure what was fresh.'[60] Reading was one thing he had managed to do a lot of this otherwise wasted year, at least. It included, along with Shadbolt, Patrick White's *Riders in the Chariot*, which he had loved and recommended to his mother, although writing of a very different style from his own (Brasch had read it already and had loved it too); *A House for Mr Biswas* by V.S. Naipaul ('marvellous'); and *Catch-22*.[61]

He planned to go down and take up the fellowship as early as he could, in the first week of January; perhaps even earlier if it was allowed. Until then he would keep working at the Health Department until mid-December. Hera had agreed to go down for the year as well, or at least part of it; and was now in a position to. Her mother died in Rotorua Hospital on 21 November. Gee, ironically, was the last person by her bedside before she died. She seemed to have accepted him at the end, calling him now her 'son'. Her tangi was held over two days—Nigel Cook came up for it, in place of Julie—and she was buried on Ngongotahā mountain on the 23rd. It was in the bar of the Rotorua Hotel afterwards with Nigel and some others that Gee heard the news of the Kennedy assassination.

10

Burns Fellow

Before the end of 1963 Hera had changed her mind and decided she wouldn't go down to Dunedin after all. Gee could hardly have blamed her: she had a good job and a house in Rotorua, and their relationship was far from secure. But he felt let down. He went to Dunedin, therefore, to take up his Burns Fellowship 'in a bit of a state'[1]—unhappy, hurt, confused, wondering at the mess he was making of his life—and he stayed that way for much of the year. He was still hoping Hera and Nigel might come down and join him later. They did go, but for a two-week holiday only.

He travelled down, as he had planned, in the first week of January. He went straight to the university registrar's office, then across the road to the University Bookshop, and then around the corner to the Captain Cook, that favourite drinking place of students and Burns Fellows. At the Cook he got talking to artist Don Binney and his wife, Judith, the daughter of Gee's old English professor at Auckland, Sydney Musgrove. When they discovered how miserable he was at the hotel the university had put him up in they offered him a sleeping bag and the floor of their flat. How he missed his porridge, is what Judith Binney would remember of his stay.[2]

He had hoped, indeed expected, that he would be able to rent the university house the Shadbolts had had, a three-bedroom house in Union Street a stone's throw from the campus (still in anticipation of Nigel and Hera being there too), but the university had another use for this now and had booked him a hotel while he looked for something else. He found a small flat in Queen Street, ten minutes' walk from the university: a bedsit built onto the back of the landlord and landlady's house, comprising a bedroom, a small living room with kitchenette and a shower. The toilet was across the concrete yard at the back, a drawback in the Dunedin winter, but the place was comfortable enough, and cheap enough (£3 10s), for him to stay there the whole year.[3]

He wrote reassuringly to his mother (as he always did) three days after he arrived, sounding happy and optimistic. 'I think I'm going to like it all right'. The English Department, an old two-storey house in Leith Street (formerly the home of one of the founding professors), was 'wonderfully quiet and restful', and he had 'a cosy little room' at the top of the stairs. 'I think I'll be able to get plenty of work done.'[4]

He had been worrying even before he sent his application about what expectations there might be of him—not of his writing but to contribute to the work of the department, as Burns Fellows were 'requested' but not required to do: with some lecturing or tutorial work, or a course of public lectures, or at least by being available to talk to students.[5] The idea terrified him. He had asked around and found that none of the previous fellows had refused. Maurie advised him not to mention the subject in his application, but he felt he 'ought to be frank'. Whether or not he was, there had been 'a rather ominous sentence' in the letter he received from the university registrar when he was awarded the fellowship referring to 'arrangements for the work I may be carrying out in [the] Dept'.[6] Earlyish in the year he turned down an invitation to talk to the English Association from Margaret Dalziel, who was acting head of the department this year (in Professor Horsman's absence on sabbatical overseas): 'Very courageous of me', he told Shadbolt, for as he would know Margaret Dalziel was 'not easy to say no to. Future Burns Fellows may thank me. I'm setting a precedent of strict silence.'[7] They left him alone after that.

The other price of a fellowship which carried, he discovered, 'quite a load of prestige'[8] was the attention of the press. The *Otago Daily Times* when it announced the award of the fellowship in October had described him, quoting the Burns selection committee, as an author of 'great promise . . . whose short stories have been for some time attracting attention for the vividness and pungency with which they evoke and comment upon certain areas of New Zealand life' and whose first novel had 'made quite a stir'.[9] The paper ran another piece on him a week after he arrived, in which he explained that he would be spending the first six months of the fellowship 'completing—or, as he put it yesterday, "repairing"—his second novel', of which he already had a first draft: 'a quiet little story', although his main task now was 'to take a bit of the talking out and put more action into it . . . a novel should make its points through demonstration rather than explanation'. After that he hoped 'to embark on a more ambitious novel for which he has already started collecting material'.[10]

He submitted also at some stage to a radio interview, with 'a young man whose questions I could not understand'.[11] But an interview with the student newspaper *Critic* early in March was the first time he had spoken publicly in more general terms about his writing, and himself. He regretted it afterwards; although he had hardly been loquacious. To the inevitable question about what it meant to be 'a New Zealand writer' he answered matter-of-factly that he wrote about New Zealanders because he knew them: it was natural that if a person lived in one country for 25 or 30 years, that country is 'going to be his fundamental background as a writer'. He 'absolutely' thought of himself as a New Zealand writer but he did not try consciously to be one. He gave the predictable, worthy answer to the question of what writing should aim to do: 'enlarge the understanding and the sympathies', but not point morals or seek to 'improve'; the 'primary aim . . . is exploration'. Asked what he thought was most disturbing about New Zealand society, he replied—as readers of his latest stories or *The Big Season* would have expected—'intolerance, a readiness to destroy what can't be understood'. He defined himself as politically a socialist (a real one, not the watered-down Labour Party kind) and philosophically a humanist: 'I'm interested in man. I'm not interested in anything that transcends him.' He had 'never found it necessary to examine' the question of religious faith; 'It has never been relevant to my personal life or to my work.'

He wrote, he said, '[b]ecause I have a few ideas about the way people behave'—though not, he might have admitted, himself. Asked about his current novel he replied: 'Reduced to its most simple terms it is the examination of a marriage that should never have been made.'[12]

He did not take much part in the informal life of the English Department either, let alone the formal one—such as engaging in conversation, although Dennis McEldowney, a regular visitor to the department for morning or afternoon tea (from Knox College where he was librarian), may have been overstating it when he wrote in his diary towards the end of the year, in his wry way: 'The current Burns Fellow, Maurice Gee, comes down, drinks his tea in a corner, speaks to no one, and no one speaks to him.' But he 'ventured to this afternoon and found him friendly'. It was partly, this apparent aloofness, shyness he thought, 'but partly, as he said, deliberately isolating himself for the sake of work'.[13] This was not quite honest on Gee's part. A few years later when he was asked to contribute to a *Landfall* symposium on the Burns, for which he submitted a short (and he would subsequently think churlish) piece, he wrote in his longer and more personal first draft about feeling uncomfortable in the academic environment, implying more than his fear of students and audiences: of a 'sense of fraud, (which, in self defence I often turned into contempt,) at being associated with an institution I was not equipped to function within. Shit!'[14]

He was also, more simply, not very happy.

He was not, however, leading 'a cloistered life', as he assured his mother (though nor 'a wild one').[15] He saw a lot of Charles Brasch—possibly on the first day he was there, for Brasch's *Landfall* office was upstairs from the University Bookshop, and for dinner at Heriot Row a number of times during the year. A few weeks after he arrived this was with the Shadbolts, just before they left town, and Margaret Dalziel: a farewell and welcome dinner in one. 'The Shadbolts have gone, Maurice Gee is here,' Brasch reported afterwards to Frank Sargeson, 'with his gentle sad face', but 'a little more confidence now, both outward and inward'.[16] Brasch found Gee intriguing, as he had in 1959, and sympathetic:

> M.G.'s strangely unguarded face expresses so openly & without reserve his feeling from moment to moment—warmth, concern, pain, pleasure—extraordinary in its delicacy & vulnerability: a tenderly beautiful face of small fine features; & his voice belongs with it, quiet, low & yet light, with little carrying power. He's lightly built, with small bones, but strong, decidedly a man's man among other things, a footballer & boxer.
>
> [He] responds to everything as an artist: very striking in comparison with Maurice Shadbolt, who is only half an artist, & very little one in his habitual responses. M.G. is perhaps unaware of being one, & might never call himself one, would certainly conceal rather than press it on you; but I notice it now each time I see him.[17]

They shared a temperament, as well as literary judgement: thoughtful, watchful, reserved. (Dinner with just Charles and Moss, a mutual friend would observe, could be a long evening: one made a point of inviting someone else as well.)[18]

He also went to dinners at Rodney Kennedy's, Brasch's artist and drama-producer friend, in High Street (these tended to be wilder), one a dinner party held for a touring troupe of Shakespearean actors from Sydney (whom Gee may have gone with Brasch to see performing scenes from *Macbeth* at the museum in April);[19] and at the home of John Griffin, manager of the University Bookshop, and his wife, Nan. He also met early in the year and had a long talk with Richmond, Towers' reader Florence James, who was in New Zealand visiting family. (Shadbolt had given her his address.)

But the closest friendship he made this year was with Michael Noonan. Noonan worked at the University Bookshop, and was on the staff of *Critic* (it was he who interviewed Gee) and also editor of this year's Otago University *Review*. They became drinking companions at the Captain Cook, having a few beers together once a week or fortnight. Noonan had made something of a name for himself with the highly successful 'Beyond the Fringe'-style revue he, Michael Neill (brother of Sam) and Gee's old Dunedin friend Alex Guyan had put on the previous year, and was deeply involved with theatrical things. He was writing his script for this year's capping concert in May on the theme of the Beatles, who were to make their week-long 1964 tour of New Zealand the following month (they performed two, riotous shows in Dunedin on the 26th). When he described this to Moss one day he was astounded when the latter interrupted to ask, 'What are the Beatles?' Gee may have been meeting some younger people, as he told his mother, but he was not exactly in touch with what was going on.

It had taken him a few weeks to settle down, but by the beginning of February he was diligently at work in his room in the English Department; for four or five hours a day, at least. The 'really good thing that's happened down here', he wrote to his mother, 'is that I've started to write again', and it was going well enough for him to think he'd be able to send the novel off to Hutchinson in early May. 'I feel better about my work at this moment than I have in years.' She would like this one, he thought: 'It's chiefly about women', and the writing 'much more controlled' than in *The Big Season*.[20] He started typing the final draft at the beginning of March, and sent it to Florence James and to Hutchinson in mid-April—though after 'a very bad last few days with it' when it 'seemed horribly bad'. It still seemed 'barely good enough for publication', he told her after he'd posted it off, its 'one serious flaw . . . a false intensity of tone. The characters are too often hysterical—life isn't lived on this plane of feeling.'[21] He had decided too, however, that there was the prospect of a play in it (influence of Noonan, no doubt), which he would go on to next. And he had had an idea for a short story, the first for three years.

The shadow over all this—and over his whole Burns year—was his unresolved relationship with Hera. That and missing Nigel, and worrying about the unsettled life Nigel was having; and his awareness that he had 'off-loaded quite a large part of my life on to him—which is, as a matter of fact, not very good for either of us'.[22] But most of all he and Hera.

Nigel spent much of this year living not in Rotorua but in Auckland with Len and Lyndahl, who had moved again, at the beginning of the year to Takapuna on the North Shore, where they had a beachfront section on Hurstmere Road. The burden of this on his mother was another worry, but they enjoyed having him. Nigel and Len, in particular, became very close. (Gee would later describe his father as the father to Nigel he had never been.)

In March Hera and Nigel went down for a holiday. The three of them went by bus to Queenstown for a few days—which Hera evidently enjoyed more than Maurice ('Moss can admire views of lakes & mountains for about 1/2 hour and then it becomes rather boring', she wrote to Lyndahl and Len from Dunedin)—and stayed for a night in Gore on the way back with an ex-patient she had met in 1959. They were invited to dinner one night at Brasch's ('He's a homosexual', she told them, '—there seems to be quite a number down this way'), before Gee flew back with them to Wellington, then back on his own to Dunedin.[23] He was still hoping at this stage that Hera would come down to live in the winter. As a statement of faith, or hope, in them staying together he had enrolled in an adult education Māori language course, starting in April; he went, however, only to the first lecture (it was harder than he expected). (Hera herself had not grown up speaking Māori, because her father didn't speak it, but had started to learn.) He referred to Hera as his 'wife', Brasch noted, even though they were not married.[24]

In the May university holidays he made a much-looked-forward-to trip north—the first of three and perhaps four he made during the year (one of these times turning down an invitation from Brasch to holiday with him at Paradise, near Glenorchy at the head of Lake Wakatipu, where Brasch had friends)—going firstly to Rotorua and then to Auckland for a few days. Nigel was just starting kindergarten, at St Anne's School for Girls and Boys (mostly girls), a private school just along the beach at Takapuna. He had as well a few weeks' tuition with Winifred Chapple, wife of Lyndahl's snobbish schoolteacher brother Kingsley, a now retired infant mistress and living just a few hundred yards along the beach.

Back in Dunedin, Gee got back to work on the play adaptation of the novel, which he had started before he left 'just as an exercise in a new form'.[25] He had this finished by the end of June, leaving him free to go on with the planned new novel. (The play, however, he decided to shelve a few weeks later because it was 'no good', now or some time later handing it to Michael Noonan to do what he liked with—which in the end was nothing, although there had been some talk of publishing it.)[26] In Auckland in May he had collected some research material he needed for the novel. This included a memoir by his aunt Dora Hagemeyer about her father, and a piece of semi-autobiographical writing by his mother about her girlhood in Timaru and Christchurch: probably 'The Change' which Lyndahl had written in 1954–55, or possibly 'The Meek', written several years earlier. Hers was better than Dora's, he told her: she wrote 'more physically, with more immediacy . . . Timaru and Christchurch came alive for me'. Brasch, to whom he gave it, also admired it, although finding it unsuitable for *Landfall*, and 'wondered why you hadn't kept going' (as Gee did too).[27]

What he had in mind for it himself is not clear; he may not have quite known. He told her when he first read it that, while he liked it, he was 'not sure' that he could use it for a novel—'perhaps one day, but I [can't] quite see my way to it yet'.[28] The new novel, of which he had written twenty pages by the middle of July, centred on a 'well-to-do' family living in Takapuna: a middle-aged couple, their son and daughter, and the husband's elderly mother, in poor health. He was using her material 'quite extensively', he told his mother now, for the 'old lady', who was the novel's narrator: it was 'very backward-looking', and would be 'looser in form' and 'more discursive' than 'Three Women'. 'I'm feeling quite enthusiastic about it. . . . I didn't think I had another novel in me'.[29]

In the three chapters that survive of this novel, Harriet Brabrook, in her mid-sixties, is convalescing at her son and daughter-in-law's Takapuna beachfront home. She grew up in Timaru, in a large family; moved to Auckland—to Newington Road—after her marriage. Her son Keith (whom she appears not to like very much) is a successful used-car salesman: ambitious, materialistic, pig-headed; he owns a Jaguar, and a racehorse too, whose ex-jockey trainer fancies Keith's wife. But she remembers when he was a timid, insecure eight-year-old who had to stop each day on his way to school by the jam factory 'half a mile away across the valley where the creek ran', and see his mother standing on the front porch and wave to her, then duck behind the eleagnus hedge and back out again, and again, three times. The granddaughter Adrienne is a university student rehearsing a part in *Look Back in Anger*. It offends her younger brother Michael that she prances about the house in the mornings in her shortie pyjamas; while it offends Harriet that there is no porridge for breakfast ('I've had porridge every morning of my life since I was a little girl'. She is distressed too by the antagonism she perceives between Adrienne and Michael, and the cruelty in the latter). The novel, as far as Gee got with it, appears to draw on the ideas for a 'suburban and racecourse' one he had had in mind in London in 1961, and on his mother's writing.[30]

Possibly there had been another idea in his mind for Lyndahl's manuscript too. His mother's and grandfather's close Henderson friend Muriel Parker, writing to him in December 1963, had remarked, 'To write about him [his grandfather], you will have to train, as he did.' She wrote to congratulate him on getting the Burns, and also complimented him on *The Big Season*. A friend to whom she had recommended it had also been impressed: it was clear that Gee 'feels deeply the existence of evil, and its power to hurt & destroy. I should say he has himself suffered a deep personal hurt which has initiated him into the agony of personal, mental suffering. . . . He overdraws the dark side . . . simply because he has not yet seen the other side, for himself.' Muriel's letter went on to discourse at length on and recommend he read Jung, particularly *Memories, Dream, Reflections* (just published): 'It should open the door into your grandfather's world for you, and cause you to see that you are already in it! . . . You don't know what lies in your psyche. Dreams are the revealer. . . . you've got to let it all come out into consciousness, the evil, and the good, & watch them, unflinchingly.'[31] He and his grandfather, she believed, were of a kind.

Whether he read Jung or not, one thing he did read along these lines in 1964 was *Black Ship to Hell* (1962) by Brigid Brophy, a fictionalised psychological treatise which he described to his mother as 'a Freudian analysis of man's destructive and self destructive impulses—it also contains a very convincing analysis of and attack on religion which it sees as basically immoral in the sense that it denies a creative response to life. Just my cup of tea'.[32]

*

Something had happened up north in May that had shaken him. 'I'm still very confused about everything that happened', he had written to his mother in his first letter after he got back, '—I think I've made all sorts of silly mistakes, but I'll give myself a month to consider things before doing anything about it'. He was pleased Hera had rung her. This remains obscure. He had been (fairly) optimistic earlier in the year about the relationship getting back on track; something appears to have happened to derail it yet again. '[O]f course I still don't know what is going to happen', he wrote in early July, just back from another visit, regarding Nigel, anxious about his parents having to have him for so long.[33]

Towards the middle of the year he had become involved in a relationship with a student in Dunedin. She was young, in her first or second year at medical school, smart, and well connected—the daughter of academics and sister of Miss Otago. They had a relaxed affair for two or three months. It petered out because of his continuing attachment to and confusion over Hera.

In August he fell into a state of deep depression which lasted some weeks, perhaps longer. A remark to his mother at the end of July, 'Dunedin gets me down a bit—I'm not geared to the sort of bachelor life I have to lead here', and to Shadbolt the same day, 'frankly, I've had enough of Dunedin', were the first signs.[34] The end of that relationship, and the apparent hopelessness, the mess, of his relationship with Hera precipitated it. He was deeply lonely. (The Dunedin winter probably didn't help either; it snowed a lot that year.)

Gee was not the first Burns Fellow to have an unhappy year. The first, Ian Cross, for all his conscientiousness left early, as soon as he could, though it is hardly surprising he found the Otago English Department dull and petty after his only previous university experience, studying journalism at Harvard four years before, and the city empty and lonely.[35] Maurice Shadbolt suffered a crisis of confidence midway through his year. He had gone down planning to write several short stories, work on the draft of 'a long novel covering forty years of New Zealand life' (the novel he had started in Te Marua in 1960), which he expected would take him four years, revise another novel and collaborate on a short pictorial volume. He abandoned the 'big book' after six months and produced something different entirely (while that creative crisis, confided to James K. Baxter, provided the impetus for the latter's *Pig Island Letters* written that year).[36] Poet

R.A.K. Mason, the 1962 fellow, had lapsed into a deep trough of depression in the winter which saw him suicidal and committed to Dunedin Hospital for psychiatric care.

Gee's was not that bad (and he was not a manic depressive as Mason was), but his experience suggests that he was suffering from clinical depression. He could not get out of bed, for days on end, until four o'clock in the afternoon, when he might go in to the English Department, or just straight to the Captain Cook, then home again and back to bed, and repeat the process the next day. No one in the English Department appeared to notice his absence; perhaps, he thought, they assumed he was upstairs in his room working all this time. Nor did his landlord, pottering about outside the bedsit in the garden, know he was in there behind the drawn curtains. To Brasch, when he went to dinner in September, he expressed doubts and gloom about his writing: 'he feels that his fund of ideas or inventiveness may be drying up; once he saw things clearly & plans for fiction presented themselves to him readily; now all is confusion, & nothing comes to him'.[37]

How he got out of this state he doesn't know. He sought no help or treatment.

News of the acceptance of his novel may have helped. It was waiting for him when he got back to Dunedin from another trip north in the first part of September (perhaps for Nigel's birthday).[38] Hutchinson would publish the novel subject to 'some expansion and "reslanting"—whatever that may be', he informed his mother, though he agreed once he got started that it was a good idea: it had been, as he put it to Maurie, 'a bit on [the] sudden side'.[39] He got to work on it within a week, confident enough to feel that it had 'the makings of an interesting small novel' and 'a satisfactory piece of work for the Burns year'; though not confident enough not to tell both Brasch and his mother that he felt he was 'no longer . . . geared to novel writing' and would go back to short stories in the future—an idea Brasch encouraged ('I fancy', Brasch recorded, 'he now sees that "The Losers" is a much better piece of work than The Big Season').[40]

He grew increasingly positive as the work progressed. 'I'm . . . quite enjoying myself', he told Maurie in October; his mother, 'I feel I'm writing as well as ever before'.[41] He was, he explained, trying to 'slow it down a little—give the characters, who are a rather emotionally unstable bunch a few periods of calm between their crises', although the pace was 'still very fast and the tone still rather hysterical'.[42] He felt good enough about it to be persuaded to give an excerpt (the first ten pages) to Michael Noonan to publish in the university literary *Review* (to his subsequent regret).[43]

The change of season was helping to lift his spirits too: Dunedin was 'very pleasant' in October, and he was 'much happier' than he had been in the first part of the year.[44]

He sent it away in November, with the usual mixed feelings: 'parts very good I think, other parts rather sentimental, rather hysterical, some a bit overwritten and others underwritten'.[45] Its working title was still 'Three Women'; it was the publisher's editor who would provide a new one, *A Special Flower*. How far through with the novel he had been when he took up the Burns Fellowship is not clear. The revisions he made at Hutchinson's request included adding a third section to the two-part draft he had submitted in April. It was still comparatively short, fewer than 200 pages, and was intense and unhappy.

The genesis (of the original short story), he would later record, was a remark made to him by a friend who worked with the elderly that as people approached death they often felt a need to forgive their enemies, along with a domestic situation a group of people he knew were caught up in (although who the people were he would not remember).[46] The character around whom the story pivots is not one of the three women but a 46-year-old bank accountant named, ironically, Donald Pinnock. The irony is that Pinnock was the name of the boy who challenged Gee to a fight at his last school in London. Donald Pinnock is a meek, placid man, a bachelor who lives with his mother, seemingly happy with his small quiet life, tending his roses, seeking his vicarious excitement at the pictures. His prim, watchful mother conducts her life (and his) by the rule of 'moderation in all things', the distrust of extravagance and strong feeling she learned in her Methodist childhood having been reinforced by her marriage to the strictly Rationalist, staunchly socialist (now long dead) Arthur, as a father a strict disciplinarian. Donald, a late and dangerously premature baby, had been 'a delicate small boy, old-fashioned and serious . . . prim even at seven or eight', as 'a youth bringing complaints and confessions of failure to his mother, but always appeased, always calmed, by her love'.[47] His father didn't like him. His mother has turned her devoted admiration for her husband into a suffocating devotion to her adult son (like Alice Matthews and Mrs Andrews, a mother who loves her son too much).

Jean is Donald's older, married sister, eight years his senior, and once a girl who worshipped 'pure feelings' and fantasy until fear of life turned her bitter and severe; her dentist husband Peter is perpetually cowed. When he was two she saved Donald from drowning: running along the creek bank to pull him out when 'she saw him below her, floating below the surface of the water. He was on his back, with his fists tightly clenched on his chest. His mouth was pinched shut, and his eyes were staring up with a grave expression she later believed was of trust' (the first creek story). Thereafter she believed herself to be his guardian angel.[48]

Donald, as Gee would later say, is 'a man crippled by his upbringing',[49] but not too crippled to take his chance of escape by marrying Coralie Marsh, a breezy, blowsy, good-time girl twenty years his younger whom he meets one night at the pictures (Bob Hope in *A Bachelor in Paradise*). When they move in after their marriage to the Pinnock family home in Kohimarama a battle begins between the two Mrs Pinnocks for Donald's salvation. (Coralie replaces his starched-collar shirts with buttoned-down collars and narrow ties, a stylish new suit and suede shoes; his mother puts his old shirts back in his drawer.) His mother abhors Coralie's vulgarity and carnality: her 'thighs and stomach standing hard and slippery under her tight olive-green dress like rocks in creek-water'. On their wedding day, 'for the twentieth time that morning, she wiped Coralie out in a traffic accident on her way to the registry office'; when they toast the marriage with her invalid's port '[s]he pledged herself to work for its dissolution'.[50] (Moderation does not extend to animosity.) She is horrified by Coralie's working-class parents, 'grotesque and ignorant people'; by her railwayman father with two fingers missing from one hand (why didn't he cover its ugliness with a glove?).[51]

It doesn't need Mrs Pinnock to derail the marriage. What drives Coralie to disillusionment and into an affair with the virile rugby player Morrie Giltrap (no irony here)—famous for his strength at lock and an All Black hopeful (the antithesis of Donald with 'his skinny hands and sad face')[52]—is not just the stifling propriety of the Pinnock household ('churchy', she describes it) and her failure to 'remake' Donald but above all his sexual inadequacy. Her hopes that her pity towards him would turn into love 'had turned to contempt. His ineptness, his shame and guilt and physical inadequacy, now caused revulsion in her.' Of course when he had told her about his childhood—about the 'quiet, studious child, nervous of his father, but otherwise not lacking spirit; a child who read more books than was usual and stayed indoors more (with his mother, she guessed), but who also managed to do the normal things: climb trees, play by creeks, crawl through culverts, etc'—'Coralie noticed Donald's story stopped short of the time of his adolescence. Of course, she thought, adolescence—that would be when his real troubles started, when he got screwed up about sex.' In the letter he writes her after she leaves he calls her his 'daylight' escape, unlike the others that had been 'so crippled, so dark and nasty' (later, his sister finds pornographic photographs in his room).[53]

Coralie's desertion and his inability to take action (when he tries to confront Morrie Giltrap he is paralysed by his timidity and fear) cause Donald to at first lose his sense of self, and then face what it is. 'He was impotent. He was weak. He was cowardly. He was sick beyond cure with frustration and accumulated defeat. Facts of his life. He passed and repassed them.' He would always be 'the coward bent on proving his courage', never Wyatt Earp.[54] It is, finally, Coralie's request that he collude in a staged adultery (his) so that she can get a quick divorce that forces him to the only act he is capable of—driving his car off the northern motorway into a creek.

The forgiveness in the novel is Mrs Pinnock's, when, in the short, third section, reverting to the Methodism of her upbringing in her failing health she accepts Coralie, now pregnant and abandoned by Morrie Giltrap, into her home for the final month of her term; they become unlikely friends (to the dismay of Jean, who has moved in now too). But this is a minor theme and (as Gee recognised) the least successful.[55] The larger point is the self-knowledge Coralie and Jean—like Donald—come to in accepting their part in his suicide. Jean's is small—recognising what she is, her lifeless life, but, like Donald, unable to change. Coralie, whose guilt is greater, achieves more, as she admits her true, selfish reasons for marrying Donald ('fear of never finding a husband, bitterness at her plain looks'),[56] reconciles herself with the Pinnocks and plans her new life. (Jean and Coralie were the names of one of Gee's Chapple aunts—one of the ones who behind stayed in California, which is perhaps why he was comfortable giving them her names.)

It is a disturbing, often tense, creepy novel. It is not surprising the publisher asked for a third part, which focuses on the, albeit prickly and partial, understanding reached between and by the three women. Not that many people would like it though.

In October Gee gave an upbeat interview to the *Otago Daily Times*, which was written up under the headline '"Satisfying year" for Burns Fellow' and accompanied by a photograph of him looking serious at his typewriter. He had completed (almost) his second major novel, which he described as telling 'a story of an extroverted young girl who marries into an overcivilised family, and the conflict that ensues', and as better than *The Big Season* ('It has more control and a better use of language; the prose is not so amateurish, and the characters appear more rounded'), and had three chapters written of a new one which had 'exciting prospects'. Its completion would be some time away, however. As to future writing, he did not think he would have much time for it. At the end of his fellowship he was going to 'rejoin his wife and young son in Auckland, where he hopes to find employment with a publishing firm'.[57]

Nigel was by this time back in Rotorua with Hera and going to school. 'I'm missing him very much, and spend a large part of my time trying to work out a way for the three of us to be together next year', Gee had written to his mother earlier in October.[58] By now, getting back together with Hera seems to have been the agreed plan. He was not sure about library school anymore, and had started looking—'casting round in some desperation', he wrote to Shadbolt—for a job in Auckland. Publishing 'seems to me one of the few jobs I'd be competent to do, and interested in': he had already written to Blackwood and Janet Paul, and wondered if it was worthwhile trying Whitcombe and Tombs. He asked Robin Dudding if he knew of anything going too.[59] He was 'quite sure now' that Auckland was where he wanted to live. The job for which he told his mother he would be coming up for an interview in December may have been one he said he'd been offered but was 'rather commercial', or it may have been one with Pauls.[60]

In November he took driving lessons and sat for his license, with the intention that he and Hera would buy a car after Christmas. He also found time, while trying to get the novel finished, to go to Christchurch for a weekend with Noonan and some others—they travelled up in a rented van—to see a visiting Sydney theatre company production of *Who's Afraid of Virginia Woolf?* (which he had read in preparation).[61] He posted the novel away in the last week of November, and a few days later got on the train to go north.

He left town without saying goodbye to anyone in the English Department, Brasch recorded in his journal, not even telling anyone he was going—although he wrote later (and may have told Brasch if the latter had not been away). Margaret Dalziel 'not unnaturally is rather disgusted', and Brasch too thought it 'extremely bad manners, & strangely ungrateful too, not really excusable in Maurice who was well brought up'. ('And yet I suppose it is all part of his self-effacingness', he concluded.)[62]

Later Gee was to look back on his Burns year as 'encapsulated', a year out of time.[63]

11

Ballsed Up

Publishing, it turned out, was not one of the few jobs Gee was competent to do.

He took the train, ferry and bus home to Rotorua, then presumably went up to Auckland for the job interview he had mentioned to his mother in the second week of December, but was back at Koutu Road at Christmas. In January he started working at Pauls. He had been interviewed for this not in Auckland but at the home of Blackwood and Janet Paul in Hamilton, travelling down from Auckland by train and back with them (and their four daughters) by car the same day. The Pauls' publishing business was in a phase of expansion. Its list, a mix of fiction and non-fiction, had more than doubled in the five years to 1964, and the imprint changed that year from Paul's Book Arcade (the name of the original, family owned Hamilton bookshop) to Blackwood and Janet Paul. The editorial department was in offices upstairs from the Ernst Plischke-designed Auckland shop in High Street, where editor Phoebe Meikle presided over a staff of two.

He was 'most unhappy there', as he later confided to Charles Brasch.[1] Years later Meikle would tell him he had been 'terrible'.[2] He did not think he had been that bad, but he knew very soon that it wasn't going to work out. He was not quick enough, did not have the 'mental nimbleness', as he put it to Brasch, to be a publisher's editor—was 'a bit dreamy', and inclined to spend too long dithering over which was the right word.[3] Most of the time he was reading and assessing manuscripts. Here his problem was formulating critical judgements. Almost all of the manuscripts were bad but he could never explain *why* they were bad. This should not have surprised him, as someone who, as Brasch had noted a year earlier, 'will not write criticism, shies away at the mere suggestion of reviewing'.[4] He counted as his one success finding a major chronological error in the page proofs of the autobiography of popular novelist Mary Scott. When Maurice Shadbolt saw him at the end of January—meeting him for a beer with Tom Soper, who was over from London—he was, Shadbolt reported to Kevin Ireland, 'apparently determined not to last long'.[5] It cannot have been more than a month.

He was especially sorry that it had been in the last month of Blackwood Paul's life, knowing that he was causing Paul added worry when he was sick with the cancer with which he had been diagnosed just months earlier; immensely grateful for the kindness with which Paul reacted to the news that he was leaving already. (Paul died on 16 February.)

And so he found himself back in Rotorua, looking for a job. With a sense of déjà vu, perhaps. He asked about his old job but it was not available; nor it seemed was anything else. He would even consider teaching, he wrote to his mother around July; and by now was 'almost decided' on library school again for next year.[6] Hera, however, was still working at the hospital, so at least there was some money coming in, and with Nigel at school he was able to get on with writing: sorting out his stories for a collection, and working on two new ones. He also checked and sent back mid-year the proofs of his novel, with 'a fair number of changes'.[7] He was getting a lot of reading time too: for, amongst other things, Patrick White's newly published first short story collection *The Burnt Ones* and Saul Bellow's *Herzog*, and a biography of Freud.

On the domestic front, though, things were not good. He and Hera were not living now 'as man and wife', and he was aware that there had been, and still were, other men. It did not seem like they were getting back together. When Shadbolt visited him in the middle of the year—coming across from the King Country where he was on a reconnaissance with the thought of going back to his half-written historical novel—he found him deeply unhappy. He and Nigel, he also observed, recounting the visit to Kevin Ireland, were 'very attached to each other, and I hope the future doesn't have too much pain for Moss on this account'.[8] Other visitors too found him clearly unhappy: Ray Grover and Ross O'Rourke, for example, passing through on their way to Auckland. Another time Grover stayed at Koutu Road for a couple of nights, and felt his friend's discomfort and pain when a man came round in the evening and Hera went off with him.[9]

In particular, Hera had developed over the past year and more what Gee would later describe as 'a strange friendship' with the elderly medical superintendent of Rotorua Hospital, Eric Bridgman.[10] What the precise nature of this relationship was he was never sure: only that Bridgman was, as he perceived it, infatuated with Hera. He did not assume—as Shadbolt did—that it was an affair. Eric Bridgman was in his late sixties and had been superintendent of Rotorua Hospital since 1939. He was especially well liked and respected by the local Māori, and had been awarded an OBE for the work he had done for Māori health in Rotorua and Maketū and in the Ureweras after the war. He was a sociable and genial man who liked good food and fine things and entertaining, a 'hunting and fishing' man, who enjoyed the company of women but never married: 'Bridgie' to his friends, 'Pukeora' to the Māori after the hill on which the hospital stood.[11]

He had first met Hera when she began working at the hospital in September 1963, and started to become close to and supportive of her after her mother was admitted the following month. Through 1964 he had visited her daily for an hour in the late afternoon, and shopped for her weekly. (Hera's sister Grace and her children were also living at Koutu Road that year when Gee was in Dunedin.) He was also keeping her supplied with whisky and barbiturates, a dangerous and addictive combination which was fuelling a growing dependency.

Gee liked him well enough, while Bridgman, he felt, tolerated him and thought him a wastrel—as he did. Bridgman would later remark that Gee 'spent most of his time writing and did not often leave the house'.[12] He and Hera frequently visited Bridgman together at his house up on the hill behind the hospital, where he had a private hot spring, and a large collection of black velvet paintings by Edgar Leeteg of which he was very proud, acquired on the biennial trips he had made to Tahiti since the war, many from the artist himself whom he had known well. (He later gave them, along with a large collection of Henri Bouvier painted carved shells, to the Rotorua Museum.)[13] Len and Lyndahl would also be invited up to the doctor's on their visits to Rotorua, and liked him enough to have him convalesce with them the following year when he went to Auckland for a cataract operation.

Shadbolt was taken up to see the Leetegs too, as he later described in the rather over-heated account he gave of his visit in his memoir: 'My eyes flickered toward Moss. He sat impassively in a corner of the room. I had the feeling that he wished to hide his head in his hands. The paintings suggested the nature of the relationship between the doctor and Sarah [Hera].'[14]

It was clear by August at least that Hera and Gee's relationship had completely broken down, and a decision was made that at the end of the year they would go their separate ways, at last. Apparently. 'What we will do (I mean Hera & I with our own lives) I don't know for certain yet', Gee wrote to his mother, probably in September; nor what would happen to Nigel. 'By one of those paradoxes, just as soon as we decide to break up we start getting on better. It's thoroughly confusing.' Even in mid-October he was 'wondering still if there's not some way for Hera & I to sort things out. Still,' he added, 'this is largely selfish'—meaning his regret at the prospect of losing Nigel—'the boy is well & happy and his parent's [sic] neuroses haven't begun to bother him yet.'[15] Yet things were tense. They didn't fight, though there was the time Hera locked him out of the house and he smashed a glass panel in the back door with a piece of firewood to get back in, and then ripped the phone from the wall when she tried to call the police. It was the closest he would ever come in his life to physical violence.[16] (Eric Bridgman came down to sort things out.)

An added strain in the second half of the year was having living with them for several months two school-age cousins of Hera's, named Thomas and Alberta, the children of a widower uncle in Maketū. He sent maintenance money for them to Eric Bridgman, who by now was handling Hera's financial affairs. Gee found them good kids, in hindsight, but they were mischievous and badly behaved.

In the August school holidays he took Nigel for a too-short visit to Takapuna, relishing the quiet break away but having to get Nigel back for his birthday on 1 September. A week later he started teaching at Sunset Intermediate School, having first applied unsuccessfully for a job at Rotorua Boys' High School, where an old Paeroa colleague, Cyril Peacocke, was now principal. He cycled the four miles there and back each day (not having bought a car). That he enjoyed. The teaching he hated, naturally: knew after a day, he wrote to his mother, that he was right not to be thinking of going back to teaching permanently. Discipline, as always, was his problem. He could not control his classroom, and was acutely aware of how easily the young woman teacher in the next-door room could hers. Her name was Leigh Barron and they became good friends over the course of the term. That (along with keeping fit) was the one good thing about the job.

In a repeat of his London experience, he also ran into some bother with the authorities, when his having inadvertently escaped inspection at Paeroa District High School caught up with him. He took the job only after telling the principal that he was not prepared to submit to an inspection. When the Education Board discovered this two months later they decided it meant he was not a certified teacher and should not be paid as one. He wrote an angry letter, pointing out that his credentials had been accepted in London as well as already by the Auckland and South Auckland boards, refusing to pay back any money and threatening to resign immediately if his salary was reduced.[17] Whatever transpired, however, he stuck it out until the end of the year.

He was leading, he wrote to his mother at the beginning of November, a dull and routine life: 'I go off to school, I come home, read, play with Nigel, mow the lawn etc. No crises, no excitements. I'm not sure whether to be bored or thankful—I'm something of both most of the time.'[18] But it was at least finite. It was seven weeks to the end of the term and he was counting the days. He had sent off his library school application in the middle of October (including references from Brasch and Ray Grover). He liked to think, he told Brasch, that he could discern a reason for his feeling that this was 'the right step for me to take' other than panic—that he was '34 & still not settled—if I couldn't I'd grit my teeth & stay in Rotorua', although what that reason was eluded him.[19]

He was also waiting for his novel to arrive: it should be out in London 'any day now' he thought in early October. 'Thinking about it alternately excites me and gives me a pain.'[20] It was in the shops in New Zealand in December, in time, as he had hoped, for the Christmas market. He didn't like the dust jacket—white with a loose sketch of a blonde Coralie in a bright pink jacket and yellow skirt in front of a Gothic-looking family portrait of the dour-faced Pinnocks—but was happier with the title now that 'The' had become 'A' special flower (Coralie, his full-blown, slightly over-ripe rose). Despite his having specifically asked Graham Nicol, his editor at Hutchinson, when he returned the page proofs to tell the printer that the word really was *bach*, on page 126 Morrie Giltrap's friends and the Pinnocks' neighbours, the Frasers, rented a beach on Waiheke Island.[21]

A Special Flower met with a limp response, and would sell fewer copies than *The Big Season* (2500).[22] Olive Johnson, in the small radical magazine *Dispute* (the November–December issue, co-edited by Maurice Shadbolt), hated it: 'Mr Gee's characters are so unpleasant that he can hardly have expected to give his readers any enjoyment', and unconvincing, 'a set of cardboard dummies with no possibilities beyond their demonstrated disagreeableness'; his style 'clumsy and graceless' and 'as flat as a New Zealand vowel'.[23] Not many people would have read this, unlike David Hall's in the *New Zealand Listener*, in February, which also found the Pinnocks in their vapidness hard to stomach, and yet having more 'depth' than Coralie, he thought, who in the end 'is discarded by life, the rose whose petals have dropped away'. There was 'a forlorn hopelessness' about the novel which reminded him of 'the sort of impasse of melancholy' reached by Stan and Amy Parker in Patrick White's *The Tree of Man*—a comparison Gee might have found flattering, at least. He also found a sort of praise for the writing, as 'spare, economical, curiously precise'.[24]

Hall had 'missed the point . . . obtusely', Brasch wrote to Gee, but 'good books survive bad reviews', he consoled him, and the *Landfall* reviewer disagreed. Brasch had written already to congratulate him after he had read the novel, over Christmas, for which Gee thanked him: his letter 'came at a time when I'd become aware that a number of people felt it was a poor performance—so it was most heartening'.[25] This surprised Brasch. Yes, the people were 'dreadfully unattractive', but, he had remarked to another friend as soon as he finished it, 'I think it's scrupulously truthful, and it lets one hope'.[26]

The *Landfall* review was out not until June and was by Dennis McEldowney. His opening observation, that in this novel Gee 'shows even better than he has before his ability to make whole and credible, if deliberately unattractive, people. This is his chief business as a novelist',[27] was Brasch's appreciation too. To his close friend Margaret Scott, when she told him she had read only 'The Losers' and had not liked it because it was about '[s]uch dreary people', Brasch had replied:

> To me it seems the greatest achievement of works of art to redeem the ordinary, the shopworn, the lifeless, to make dust and dry bones live, whether with words, themes, people. M.G's new novel does this more strikingly than his story, & he carries one with him so that in the end the people seem worth writing about; & this while their dreariness continues to be plain enough. The impulse to do this, the gift that enables M.G. to do it, seem to me rare and precious. I see him as a purer artist than any other writer of fiction since Sargeson—unless I must except Janet Frame. He is raising the dead.

> Which is what every artist does in one way or other; he does it more directly & less pretentiously than most.[28]

In *Landfall* McEldowney had high praise for Gee's ability to make his readers (good readers) both dislike and like his characters. Donald Pinnock 'though a dispensable catalyst, has genuine power in his diffidence and his smouldering aspiration, his desire to act'. But it is Coralie he finds most complex and interesting, and sympathetic. Other readers and critics would find the contrasts of character, and thus author's purpose, in the novel too simple and plainly stated. McEldowney argued that Gee's attitude towards the aesthetic and moral discomfort his characters provoke in his readers—his choice of 'spontaneous, exuberant, instinctive behaviour over restrained and conditioned behaviour, of living over non-living'—is not so straightforward or simply expressed: 'his coldness in investing a character like Coralie with a quite horrifying callousness is a coldness not directed so much (though no doubt partly) at common notions of right and wrong, as at his own instinctive preference. That is, it is an exploration rather than a judgment' (as Gee of course believed a novel should be).[29]

McEldowney took a summer holiday in Central Otago around the time he was writing this review, and in a hotel in Queenstown recorded in his diary: 'At our table a ravaged woman and her as yet far from ravaged but highly enamelled daughter from Invercargill, whose conversation with a Scotsman at our table—every sentence with a double meaning—makes me feel like one of Maurice Gee's rigid unheroes.'[30] As well as the authenticity of his characters, he also admired in his review the subtlety of Gee's creation of place—how 'although his New Zealand is typical and vivid—his parties, rugby games, beaches, directly and physically experienced—New Zealand is an element in his characters, rather than his characters an element in New Zealand'. 'Technically', he observed, 'he has become very accomplished indeed.' The novel is constructed through five alternating narrative viewpoints in discrete, named sections, similar to the short story 'In a Sleeping Face' but here overlaid with a more complex, carefully managed time structure—handled, as McEldowney commented, 'so confidently, even nonchalantly'.[31]

The greater control in his writing Gee recognised himself is also evident in precise tactile images and visual descriptions: the shattered glass of his father's photograph over which Donald treads 'knives of glass that broke with gritty reluctance'; when coming into the living room on Donald and Coralie's confrontation Mrs Pinnock's 'woken face, knotted hand, even her blunt yellow toenails, expressed determination'.[32] Capturing character and motive in small physical detail and so few words is something he would become increasingly good at.

Janet Frame—who was the 1965 Burns Fellow—was less impressed, in brief notes on the novel which were possibly written as a reader's report. The style she described as 'humdrum' (while at the same time appreciating a 'pleasant lack of hysteria'): 'Fallacy that a book about ordinary people must be written in dull way?' The novel's main strength she thought was its sharply observed characters, and 'strong sense of pathos, helplessness'—but need it 'have been written at all?' Still, she found it 'enjoyable to read'; 'a pleasant change to have no river-bathing, at least no scenery descriptions'.[33]

A Special Flower had come out at the end of something of a bumper year for New Zealand fiction. Other novels published that year included Jean Watson's understated, under-appreciated *Stand in the Rain*; Janet Frame's fourth novel, and a significant development of her theme and subject, *The Adaptable Man*; Frank Sargeson's *Memoirs of a Peon*; and Maurice Shadbolt's Burns year novel, *Among the Cinders*. Gee was not the only one to feel hurt by his reviews (the *Landfall* one excepted). *Memoirs of a Peon* followed Sargeson's *Collected Stories* published in 1964 (in New Zealand by Blackwood and Janet Paul) and *Wrestling with the Angel*, his plays, from Caxton earlier in 1965, together signalling the end of a decade-long and anxious creative drought for him. *Memoirs of a Peon* was not his first novel, but it also marked the emergence of a new fictional style compared with that of his laconic, sardonic short stories, one many people would not like. He had had trouble finding a publisher for it and it had very mixed reviews.

Shadbolt's *Among the Cinders*, meanwhile, which came out early in the year, had received 'some tough notices' in London, as Sargeson noted,[34] and at best lukewarm ones at home. Much of the novel recounted the picaresque adventures of its Holden Caulfield-like hero, teenage Nick Flinders, with his hard-bitten, cantankerous, salt-of-the-backblocks grandfather Hubert—including a pig-hunting expedition in the Ureweras. Shadbolt would say a few years later that it had been written as 'a playful pastiche of some New Zealand writing',[35] but it was not reviewed as such, but just as a not very good novel. It was obviously so only in the set-piece party scene at the end in which several easily identifiable local literary figures appeared, including Ian Cross, Barry Crump and James K. Baxter, and '[t]his Shadbolt character', who turns out to be the novel's ghost narrator: a literary joke most critics particularly didn't like and one described as 'a backhanded form of self-advertisement'.[36] ('[I]t does seem odd', Kevin Ireland wrote privately to Sargeson, 'that one so young should bear so many grudges'.)[37] The most cutting portrait was that of C.K. Stead—with whom Shadbolt shared an enmity dating back to 1955—as the poetry-writing university lecturer Derek. Stead would reply to this years later with his young New Zealand writer in London, Dick Flinders, in moustache and 'darkly horn-rimmed glasses'—photographed on the back flap of his first collection of short stories, *The South Sea Islanders*, smoking his pipe on the Embankment—in his 2001 novel *The Secret History of Modernism*.[38]

Maurice Gee was not at the party.

The issue of *Landfall* in which Dennis McEldowney's review of *A Special Flower* appeared also had a new short story by Gee, with a rare *Landfall* typo in the first line (a Nuie Islander). It was one of two he had written first drafts of in Rotorua in 1965, before he started teaching, and sent to Brasch on 1 February, apologising: he would have liked to have had something better to offer, 'but at the moment I'm afraid I have no strong involvement with anything I do. I've suffered a kind of loss of direction in writing, and with it almost a loss of language, I feel. But I do things like these stories to keep in training against the time when I'll see my way again.'[39] One was his shipboard story 'Holding Hands'. This was the story he had had his 'one lone little idea for'[40] in Dunedin two years before: Brasch recognised the echo of the Hagley Park murder, the killing of a homosexual man in Christchurch's Hagley Park in January 1964 by a group of youths out one night to 'bash a queer', for which all six were acquitted, controversially, of manslaughter. (Being set upon by 'a gang of thugs' is 'one of my worst nightmares', which causes Dennis to flee in terror from the drunken footballers.)[41]

'Holding Hands' Brasch was not impressed by: it was loose and Dennis 'rather type-cast'. The other story, though, was 'beautifully done, well-knit, sustained, convincing all through'. If this was how he kept in training 'you have nothing to fear in the long run', he assured Gee: 'you write as a writer born, with sureness and ease'.[42]

'The Champion' featured bad-tempered, competitive, bigoted and misogynistic Eric Wilbraham, the semi-retired owner of a service station. He had once been a champion amateur boxer, before he sold his cups, medals and the two plated belts he won at the 1926 national championships 'for a tenner' in the Depression. Now he has a 'flabby chest and belly shaped like a melon' and hypertension. He is long since out of love with his wife, Joyce (no one had warned him about 'the "change of life"'). But now it is she who is the champion—at croquet, a game he regards with contempt ('as simple as tiddly-winks'). Wilbraham is a character who will become familiar: 'a sick bad-tempered old man', as he recognises himself in a rare moment of insight. In the story's final scene, driving home after watching his wife play in the quarter- and semi-finals, he finds himself in a slow queue of traffic behind her red Mini Minor 'putting along at thirty', and in a sudden rush of contest and revenge knows that '[h]e must beat her home', passing car after car in the face of heavy oncoming traffic, fancying that the blaring horns are applauding him on.[43]

Brasch asked for one change to the story and suggested another. The first was that Gee change the name of Eric Wilbraham's son-in-law and service station manager Harry Scott 'if not wedded to it', as it was the name of a very close friend who had died six years earlier climbing on Mt Cook. (He became Harry King.) The second was a change to the ending, which Gee made in part, and making, as Brasch recognised, the better judgement. He removed an anticipatory phrase as Brasch suggested on the last page, but did not add a new final paragraph, instead leaving the ending suggestively as it was: with Wilbraham pulling out to overtake the last car into an impossibly small gap 200 yards from home.[44]

By the end of the term at Sunset Intermediate Gee's friendship with his next-door teacher, Leigh, had deepened. She was an attractive, red-haired 20- or 21-year-old, very talkative, sharp and strong-minded, sometimes belligerently so, and they got on together extremely well, despite her Waikato farming upbringing and political views (she was a member of the Young Nationals). At the end of the year they took their two classes on a bus trip to Mt Maunganui, where they sat on Ocean Beach and talked for four hours while their charges ran wild. He took her to the hospital staff Christmas party, held at one of the big Rotorua hotels. Hera was there with Eric Bridgman. Hera by now was making plans of her own: it was definite that she and Gee were not staying together. It was when he took Leigh home that night that their friendship began to develop into something else.

After the school year finished he packed his things into a rental car and drove to Matamata to meet Leigh's parents, staying a night there before going on to Auckland. She told them she was breaking off her engagement to a doctor twenty years her senior, David Minnitt, to her parents' displeasure; they were not impressed by Maurice Gee. Leigh then took a planned summer holiday in Sydney. On her return Gee met her at the airport in a rented car, and took her out to meet his parents before they drove to Northland for a three- or four-day 'honeymoon'.

He had been accepted into library school by now, having gone up for an interview in Auckland late in November or in early December. He would go down to Wellington in mid-February. The plan was that Leigh would join him there.

12

Library School

Within three weeks Leigh had changed her mind and decided she was going to marry David Minnitt after all. She told Gee this by letter, to which he replied angrily and self-righteously, accusing her of choosing a safe life over the one she could have had with him. She did not respond. It was not, as it turned out, the safe choice at all. He was to meet Leigh again only twice, both by chance: in Wellington two years later; the second time in a bookshop in Nelson in the late 1970s, only a few years before her violent death at the hands of David Minnitt.

He went down to Wellington in mid-February 1966, two weeks before library school started on 1 March, and moved into a flat he had already found in Rossmore Crescent, a tiny street of half-a-dozen old villas at the northern end of Molesworth Street. It was not far from the Grant Road bedsit he had rented in 1957, and, while not as bad as that, was small and shabby and on first sight depressing: 'bare and tatty looking' with 'rather grubby walls and broken lino'.[1] There was one bedroom, a largish living room with kitchen adjoining, a bathroom and toilet. How he had thought Leigh would consent to live there with him he could not afterwards imagine. He borrowed furniture from friends and his mother sent down some curtains. Pat Soper, Tom's wife, offered to make him some too. The Sopers were living next door, having now moved out from London, and it was possibly through them, or Ray Grover, that he had found the place. With a few things in it he thought it might be all right.

Abandoned by Leigh, in a grotty flat, unenthusiastic about the year at library school ahead, a little lonely, he was '[a] bit depressed at times', he wrote to his mother with his usual reassuring understatement. He was missing people, and, '[f]unnily enough' he thought, 'Auckland as a place'. He didn't intend staying longer than a year, and would be back in Auckland, 'for good, I hope', after that. 'But all this I can cope with—seem to have left the really deep dark bad times behind. Touch wood.'[2] Whether he wrote this before or after he received Leigh's letter is not clear.

Either way, though, the city had lost its magic. His friends were almost all gone, and with them the late 50s literary-bohemian Wellington he had known. The Cooks were in Auckland, where Nigel was studying architecture, and the Shadbolts were up there now too, in Titirangi (where one of Nigel Cook's first projects was a writing room for Maurie). Carl and Kevin were still in London, as was Angela, although she would be back later this year; Ben Goffman was in Sydney. Baxter was in Dunedin on the Burns Fellowship.

The exception was Ray Grover, who was now assistant chief librarian at the Alexander Turnbull Library and had arranged for his friend two weeks' work in its manuscripts section before library school began, thinking (wrongly) that this was the branch of librarianship that would suit Gee best. Here Gee worked in a small room at the top of the stairs in the three-storey, brick former residence of the reclusive, cocaine-addicted merchant-bachelor Alexander Turnbull in Bowen Street, over the road from parliament, which still housed the main part of the library he had bequeathed to the nation in 1918.

The New Zealand Library School was housed in a more modest, old wooden house in Hobson Street, a few streets away from Rossmore Crescent: if nothing else his flat was conveniently located. He was doing the one-year graduate course that led to a diploma. Whatever explanation he had made (or tried to make) to Charles Brasch, he was doing it out of desperation. As he admitted to his mother, 'there are no real alternatives': he needed a job that would pay him after 'ten years bumming about' and two failed careers;[3] though as with teaching there was at least a family precedent, he might had been aware, in James Chapple's two-and-a-half years as public librarian in Timaru.

There were 28 students in the class. On day two Margaret Scott, Brasch's friend and the widow of Harry (who had nearly lent his name to Eric Wilbraham's downtrodden son-in-law), introduced herself to him. Brasch had told her to look out for Gee: 'slight, gentle-faced, quiet; photo of him in Lf 53'.[4] On approach, she reported, Gee 'was unexcited but friendly and we chatted about Lf & the Burns Fellowship & Jim's house'. She was living with her three young children in Jim and Jacquie Baxter's house in Ngaio, having moved up from Christchurch: for her too this had been a choice made out of necessity, the need for a career to support her family. When she then told Gee she had read *A Special Flower* 'and thought it impressively good' he 'looked faintly embarrassed'. But '[h]e stands out', she told Brasch, '—to me anyway—as the only person of real substance in that group of students and staff', 'intelligent, imaginative & warm'.[5] They became friends and allies not only by virtue of their mutual connection with Brasch but as two of the handful of older students in the class. Apart from Gee, one older man and two other women her age 'the rest of the 28', she remarked, 'are children'.[6]

They were friends in school only, though. 'We are very interdependent indeed in school, but outside school he goes his own compelling ways and I peel potatoes.'[7] Brasch saw them both when he was up in Wellington a week later, staying for a weekend with musician Fred and painter Eve Page at their house in Hobson Street: 'where you came once before to see me and Fred and Eve', he wrote to Gee (in 1958), and by coincidence next door to the library school.[8] ('How strange' too, he had earlier remarked, that Gee was going to Rossmore Crescent, where a 'very dear old friend of mine'—Valmai Moffett, a cellist in the National Orchestra—lived.)[9]

Gee found library school deeply and unrelentingly boring. He hated the year, and thought seriously more than once of tossing it in—talked out of it one time when he announced that he was doing so by the only person on the staff he found likeable and interesting, the erudite and drily humorous Polish senior lecturer Jerzy Podstolski (known to the students as Pod) who taught on reference materials. Even in the third term he was still wondering if 'I haven't made a mistake being a librarian'.[10] Scott was equally disenchanted. 'The lecturers', she informed Brasch, 'are startlingly bad—poverty of vocabulary, dreary hesitating delivery, inability to express concepts'.[11] Visiting lecturers—the infamously garrulous-when-drunk Denis Glover was one, ostensibly talking about printing—were no better.

Nor did he excel. When they received essays back at the end of the first term from Brian O'Neill, the school's director—they had both chosen as their topic 'The social effects of the invention and development of printing'—his was marked C 'with a caustic comment about "conventional banalities"'. Scott, to whom Brasch had recommended a book to read, got an A. Maurice 'is very depressed, can't swot for the exams, sleeps an awful lot, goes to the pictures', she informed Brasch. O'Neill, she reported two letters later, 'seems to have taken a scunner to Maurice and me, and has shown himself to have a prejudice against "literary" people', and they were both feeling 'angry and rather upset'.[12]

She was aware, though, of a restlessness and depression in Gee that came from somewhere other than boredom and bad grades. She would describe him in this year, a year later, as 'a quiet, reserved, not very happy person'.[13]

He had missed Nigel on his way down, to his regret, and went up to Rotorua a few weekends later, thinking it would be his last chance for a long time. Some time in March Hera and Nigel moved to Auckland, from where they would be leaving for Australia: for Hera this was intended to be a fresh start. Gee managed to get bookings, late, to go up at Easter, a week into April, and planned to go again a few weeks later and stay 'until Nigel goes off', although no one knew exactly when that would be.[14]

He didn't see Nigel go, in the end. Instead he wrote to his mother, back in Wellington 'after those rather upsetting two weeks', expressing sadness and resignation rather than upset; almost detachment, and concern for his parents' feelings more than his own: 'I'm sorry you and Dad had to go through that nasty scene—and sorry Nigel had to be dragged into it too. It's the sort of thing I've been putting up with for 7 years—so you see why it has to end. I think Nigel has a good chance of coming through it not too badly damaged', he continued, '—at least that's what I try to believe'. He thanked them for all they'd done, 'and now it's all over. . . . I'll try not to bring more trouble down on you. . . . Let me know if you should happen to see Nigel again—I won't be coming to see him off. There's a chance, if Hera's true to her word, that I won't ever see him again. I'll decide what to do about this when the fact's established. In the meantime, I refuse to worry.'[15]

The adult emotion, drama and sense of finality in all of this was not apparent to the seven-year-old boy, who went off quite happily, Lyndahl let Moss know, with a good crowd of people to wave him goodbye from the new Auckland airport at Māngere, and who would later retain no memory of the departure, or of what if anything he had been told.

They heard nothing from Hera for two months. She had left no address. The welfare authorities were in touch with Gee, however, about maintenance money, which he was happy to pay for Nigel, 'but I'll refuse to even consider paying anything for Hera', he told his mother.[16] Hera was asking for £5 a month; he offered 30/-, which the child welfare department seemed to think was enough although they normally asked for £2 14s regardless of the father's income. 'The fact that I've lived with Nigel so long baffles them a little—they are not sure of my rights', and they were 'rather disturbed' that he had been taken to Australia. A sixteen-page typed letter they had from Hera they considered entirely irrelevant to the case. (Gee had been advised by a friend of Ray Grover's and his, Bryn Jones, a former child welfare officer, to keep off the personal and focus on the money.)[17]

It was not until the end of June or early July that Hera sent a note to Len and Lyndahl from Sydney, giving them news of Nigel. She was nursing in North Sydney (at the end of this year working at the Spastic Hospital in Allambie Heights, which treated children with cerebral palsy) and boarding Nigel out with a family, which Gee was not pleased to hear: 'I don't like him being boarded, and never have, which Hera has always known'. He wondered, and worried, about whether she had the right to have him adopted without his permission. Welfare didn't think so. 'But she's so far away now, I've a feeling she could do much as she liked.'[18] He could only accept her assurances that he was with a good family and was happy, and if so hope that he could stay there for as long as Hera remained in Australia.

'I still miss him', he wrote to his mother two months later, 'and feel quite sick with it sometimes'.[19]

He spent the between-term break in August in Auckland—Ray came up for the second week and stayed with his parents in Takapuna as well—then it was back to the tedium of library school. Two weeks working in the university library this term was if anything even more boring than school. 'The library I get to will count for everything.' He hoped it would be Turnbull, which was 'by far the most interesting' in New Zealand.[20] At least in the course now they were doing bibliographies, which was more interesting than most of it. For his assignment he chose Bertolt Brecht, for no obvious reason, having never read Brecht let alone seen any of his plays performed. Perhaps, though, his own passing interest in theatre lay behind this. His adaptation of *A Special Flower*, with the title 'The Tin God', was being considered by the newly established Downstage Theatre. (It was Ray Grover not Gee who was responsible for this, however, and like the last time nothing came of it.)

As the school year went tediously and undemandingly on he could turn his mind to his writing. Once more he was revising and sorting his stories for the collection he still hoped to publish—he had 'enough to make quite a fat volume now'[21]—and he wrote a new one, having a first draft completed by the end of September. He may have been prompted by a letter from Bob Dudding in June, asking if he had anything for his last *Mate*: 'I'd like the last one to be a good one'.[22] Dudding needed something by return post, however, and Gee then had nothing new to offer. It was Dudding's last *Mate* because he was about to start working at the Caxton Press and take over the editorship of *Landfall*, from which Brasch was retiring after twenty years (the last seven thinking about a successor), as Gee probably already knew: Brasch had asked Margaret Scott to tell him a week earlier when he realised that the news had already reached Wellington. (The changeover was formally announced in Brasch's last, September issue, with the modesty and reticence characteristic of both men: a single sentence at the end of his Notes—'From the end of this year, *Landfall* will be edited by Robin Dudding.')

In June too the *Landfall* issue with Dennis McEldowney's admiring review of *A Special Flower* had appeared, and with Gee's story 'The Champion', for which he received a welcome £10. With the maintenance payments he was making for Nigel he was 'just scraping by' financially.[23] He would enter this story the following year for the Katherine Mansfield award, and come runner-up to Maurice Shadbolt, although the judge, Victoria University professor of English James Bertram, praised it highly as a 'vivid, fast-moving, very cleverly constructed action story in the tougher New Zealand manner Gee has made his own', and showing shrewd social judgement: 'a devastating criticism of life' and 'first-rate story of its kind'.[24]

The new story, which would be published by Dudding in September 1967, was a lesser effort, and one with the feel more of a *Mate* than a *Landfall* story. It was a Paeroa and Wellington story, incorporating elements from the much earlier, unpublished 'The Separation' which he had written in Paeroa, submitted to Brasch, for the young writers' anthology, and then to Dudding. In its later incarnation, 'Down in the World', Robin Wallace has come down to Wellington from Auckland with his friend Dick (a coarse, Crump-like character to the more sensitive Rob); they have taken a room in 'a run-down hotel—Railway or Commercial or Criterion' (the last two were Paeroa hotel names)—but actually, to Robin's surprise, called the Alhambra. From the window he watches a crowd emerge from a cinema onto the street below and imagines them inside moments before 'in a darkness green as creeks; floating, submerged in a dream'; the theatre is showing *Peter Pan*. The story describes their ensuing 'night of dirt and spying'[25] as the pair break into the flat of Rob's wife Jenny, from whom he is separated (they had married hastily in a registry office, four months after meeting at Takapuna's Mon Desir; it had lasted two years), with the plan to catch her in bed with her current lover and so establish grounds for divorce. The episode leaves him feeling at once sordid and painfully reminded of his sexual inadequacy. It is a short and comparatively slight story, and the only writing Gee would do in his library school year.

Way back in his mind there was still a half-formed idea of something much larger, something that would draw in some way on his family background. He had asked his mother once more for information: he was interested in anything, he said, that she could dredge up from old papers or memory,

> not just about Chapples, but about anything that happened before I was born—that is anything beyond the range of my memory. I don't know why I want it—the hoarding instinct possibly—the feeling that one day it might fit into a novel or story, or throw a bit of light that will help me understand how things were then and where we came from (in a restricted sense). So do keep at it if you can.

'This sort of material is really valuable,' he told her, writing again and thanking her for the notebook she was keeping for him, 'both as a starting point and to fill in the background'; also the early New Zealand material, 'all this is worth keeping an eye open for'.[26]

Gee's interest appears to have inspired Lyndahl to return to her own writing, in particular to the children's story 'Tane and George' which she had written in the 1940s and sent to Reeds. She was working on it again now and sent it in October to Blackwood and Janet Paul, but it was again turned down. It pleased Gee nevertheless that she was writing, not only because it seemed a sign of the improvement in her health. She had not been well for much of the past year—for much of the last fifteen years—and had spent time in hospital with what her sister Dora referred, writing to her in August, as her 'nerves',[27] an inadequate euphemism for the complex combination of her long, difficult menopause, frustrated marriage and literary aspirations, and family worries, not least now the welfare of Nigel.

He saw as well a bit of his youngest uncle, Aynsley Chapple, around this time, and perhaps he talked to him about the Chapple family history too. Aynsley was over from California on another of his extended family and antique-buying visits and they saw each other when Gee was again in Auckland during October, and twice in November and early December, for dinner and lunch and directions to the second-hand shops and auction market, when Aynsley passed through Wellington on his way south. (He was determined to come back to New Zealand to live eventually, Gee told his mother, though he never did.)

Gee was happier in Wellington in the later part of this year. He was growing fond of the city again: 'In many ways it's an impossible place, and I wouldn't want to be here too long, it's like living on an island. But it's got a charm Auckland lacks—just as Auckland has a vitality Wellington hasn't got.' They were having lovely spring weather, he told his mother; 'I feel cheerful and adolescent'. That the end of the year was in sight must also have helped lift his mood, and he thought he had perhaps 'scraped a pass mark' in the last lot of exams.[28] In mid-October he learned that he had a job at the Turnbull Library next year, as he had been hoping; had been invited to apply, in fact, and he would be getting the top salary in his scale (£1300).

Possibly too it was at this time that he had a relationship with a young woman in the library school class. It did not last long, was nothing more than a fling as he later saw it, although he also recognised it as a sign of his desperation at the time, after the failure and hurt of the relationship with Hera, his abandonment by Leigh, alone again in Wellington without a girl. Angela Sears was back in Wellington and by one of the small-world coincidences at which Wellington is so adept was living in the Wadestown house of an old friend of hers, Patricia (Pon) Paterson, a friend of Gee's now too, where his girlfriend was also flatting. With amused embarrassment—amusement on Angela's part, the embarrassment Gee's—they would pass each other in the kitchen in the mornings.

The library school year finished on 9 December, with graduation in the morning followed by lunch hosted by Margaret Scott for 35—the class and extras—at her house in Pitt Street in Wadestown (which she had recently bought with financial help from Brasch). 'Perhaps then I can get on with some writing', Gee had remarked to his mother a few days earlier, '—the <u>only</u> thing I do well!'[29] He had been planning already to spend a month or so in Auckland after the year finished even before the family learned in that first week of December that Hera was sending Nigel over for the holidays. Nigel flew directly from Sydney to Wellington a week and a half before Christmas. By a complicated arrangement Gee was to borrow Scott's car, in return for mowing her lawns, to pick him up from the plane, then take him back to her house for dinner before she drove them both back to catch their flight to Auckland. Nigel's flight arrived late however and they had only a rushed half-hour to eat. Maurice, Scott wrote—reporting on all this to Brasch—had been 'touchingly excited about the prospect of seeing Nigel after 6 months'. She was charmed by Nigel: 'The child is glorious looking: cochineal and cocoa, large shiny brown eyes, white teeth, impish grin—oh, quite breath-takingly handsome. Maurice trying desperately not to let his pleasure show.' He 'has masses of self-confidence and a strong streak of mischief. M. will be hard put to it to keep up.'[30]

Gee returned to Wellington on 29 January, to start work at the Turnbull the next day. He went back to his Rossmore Crescent flat, although there had been some uncertainty about this. Residents had been informed that the Ministry of Works wanted the property, which was in the path of the Wellington urban motorway which was halfway through construction, carving a trench through Thorndon and alongside The Terrace to Ghuznee Street. Rossmore Crescent was one of three of Gee's Wellington places that would eventually fall victim to this controversial, eighteen-year project, along with 3 Everton Terrace, Angela Sears' old flat, and, most sadly, the Ghuznee Street bach. The Sopers—now expecting—moved out from next door towards the end of the year. Gee planned to stay until the end of library school and then look for somewhere else. But the house, it turned out, was not needed quite yet, and flats, he found, especially ones so central, were expensive. Besides, he had come to like it. He had his books sent down from Auckland, and a picture of Rangitoto, and planned to get some curtains up and a few more bits of furniture 'to make my barn look like a home at last'.[31]

He found his first day at Turnbull 'interesting, if a bit confusing'.[32] His job was in cataloguing, which was not what he had wanted nor particularly liked (Margaret Scott had been offered the position in manuscripts where Grover had imagined Gee). But he enjoyed working at Turnbull more than he had feared he would: he had been, Scott had reported to Brasch, 'apprehensive & expects not to like it'.[33] But the days he found went by quickly and his colleagues—mostly women, as librarians then were—were friendly and easy: his immediate boss, Nancy Irvine, the head of cataloguing, 'a lovely woman . . . everybody loved Nancy'.[34]

The mid-1960s was an unnaturally turbulent and charged time in the normally quiet world of New Zealand libraries, in fact. In 1965 the National Library Act had been passed, creating a new National Library incorporating the Alexander Turnbull Library. This followed a long, emotional (and sometimes silly) public debate, with opponents of the act fearing that the special character of the Turnbull Library—of its rich research collection of New Zealand and Pacific books, manuscripts and pictures, its significant Milton collection and assorted other Old World bibliophilic treasures (a reflection of the collecting interests and budget of its creator)—would be lost. Debate continued, and would for decades to come, over the housing of the library, whether within or apart from the new institution. The following year, although uncontroversially, a new chief librarian of Turnbull was appointed: Graham Bagnall, previously head of the National Library Service. He took with him to his new job responsibility for national bibliographic control, and this was where Gee fitted in: preparing the monthly, cyclostyled lists for the national bibliography, and doing some work on the annual cumulation.

'The work itself', he explained to his mother, 'is a kind of discipline and requires a fair amount of mental agility, though not much imagination. So when I get home I feel like spreading myself'. He was working on his short stories in the evenings, and had 'written quite well since getting back', with only two left to revise before the collection would be ready again for typing.[35]

He had left Nigel at the end of January still in Takapuna with Len and Lyndahl. When Hera had sent Nigel over, there had been no arrangements made for his return, and when the Gees still had heard nothing from her as the school year started they began to wonder if she had abandoned him. Gary and Ngaire offered to have him with them in Taumarunui—where Gary was now managing a menswear shop—and he was enrolled at Taumarunui School where their own children (three now) were going. For the next two months Gee kept up an exhausting schedule of weekend visits, catching the overnight Limited after work on Friday, letting himself into the house at 2am, and taking the train back on Sunday night, arriving just in time to start work on Monday morning. Nigel 'seems to depend on the visits', he told his mother, but was increasingly unsettled by the uncertainty and his father's comings and goings. '[A]s for the future,' he wrote, 'it's a puzzle. I don't know what to do. The more time that goes by now the better I like it as it gives me a better chance of eventually being able to keep him with me.' He was thinking now about trying to gain custody. 'But of course, we'll get some brief note soon, saying, "Send him." She still has the law on her side in spite of her irresponsibility over the last two months. But I think now I would stand at least some chance'.[36]

In April he brought Nigel down to live with him in Wellington. Maurice was 'resigned, even happy, about it,' Margaret Scott reported on the situation to Brasch, 'though he doesn't really understand the stresses and strains it will entail. Still, he says it will do no harm to him as a person to have the complete responsibility of his son for a while'.[37] He enrolled him at Wadestown School, which was not too far away but, more to the point, was where Scott's own children went. They came to an arrangement whereby Gee would take Nigel to her house after breakfast and he would walk to school with her children, and go home with them after school to be looked after by her child-minder (Gee contributing £1 a week to her wages) until they both got home from the library at six. Scott was not convinced this was going to work—her children were not the same age, Nigel was a 'very exuberant' child, and her minder, 'Mrs Mac' (McManemin) in her sixties and 'not terribly patient or understanding'—but it seemed to go well enough until the end of the second term. She found Nigel, however, less charming and more troubled than she had before: a 'slightly disturbed' child, with a tendency to 'pocket things' at her house as well as at school, while Mrs Mac reported him by turns 'withdrawn and uncommunicative' and 'cheerful and defiant'.[38]

Gee was more positive. 'This is better than I expected', he wrote to his mother after a week or so—even if the television set Len had sent down wasn't working. Nigel was happy at school; while Gee was still able to get some work done in the evenings after he had cut Nigel's lunch and put him to bed. He had borrowed a bed for him, but it had been clear that the Rossmore Crescent flat was not going to be suitable for long. In May they moved to a house in Weld Street, at the edge of the green belt of Tinakori hill, only a hundred yards from Wadestown School and a few hundred from Margaret Scott's. It was an old, slightly run-down three-bedroomed villa with a harbour view, a friendly English landlord and rent at £8 10s a week. (He had been hoping that he might be able to rent the house next door to Scott's, which was administered by the Public Trust, but this was about to be put up for sale, she discovered. She may well have been relieved, for while she was happy to be a support for Gee he 'is inclined to lean a bit', she told Brasch, 'and is aware of it'.)[39]

Some time around now Nigel received a letter from Hera telling him that she was 'sending someone to Wellington to bring you back to Sydney soon': he would be living with a family in North Sydney, but she would be able to see him every day. 'Tell Daddy, you will return to N. Zealand for the school holidays, and of course—to Rotorua as well'.[40] It may have been this which prompted Gee to do something about getting custody. He went to see Mike Bungay, whose office was just around the corner from the Turnbull, but who was a criminal defence lawyer and referred him instead to Shirley Smith, who specialised in family law. She had a sole practice in a building not far up The Terrace. After first contacting Child Welfare and writing to Hera, she got court proceedings underway in July, and on 14 July an interim court order was granted making Nigel a ward of the court in Gee's custody at Weld Street.

By this time Hera was in Wellington, with her new partner, Maurice Walch (an electrician she had met in Sydney), and living in Holloway Road, a sunless street of poor housing in a narrow valley at the top of Aro Street. She had become by now a serious alcoholic, and a violent one, and unstable. Gee feared her snatching Nigel away; as Nigel, he had told his father, feared the uncertainty of going back to Sydney and 'who knows what'.[41] He would remember one day during this time taking Nigel by the hand and walking out of the house in Weld Street, followed by Maurice Walch down to the bus stop, taking a bus into the middle of town and then a taxi to Pon Paterson's house in Cecil Road, where he stayed for two or three days, knowing that Hera wouldn't find them there, sneaking back to Weld Street and peering in the windows to make sure she was gone before returning home (fearing what havoc she might meanwhile have wreaked). It is from this time too that Nigel's single memory of his parents together dates: of sitting on his father's shoulders while his mother and father physically grappled with each other in a violent argument—he didn't know if it was about him or not—a strange replay of Gee standing on the table at Koutu Road painting the ceiling with Lydia Smith violently shaking the table beneath him, only this scene is not comic.

At Shirley Smith's request that he provide an affidavit from 'someone in good standing, of some reputation, etc. in the University or writing worlds', Gee turned to Charles Brasch, hesitantly both because it was a more personal favour than he felt comfortable asking and because Brasch was away on holiday in England at this time. All that was required, he assured him, was a few lines attesting that 'I have a "literary reputation" however small . . .—although if you felt inclined to add that I am a person of good character it might help'.[42] Brasch replied promptly and willingly from the Isle of Skye: 'Your letter fell gratefully into this beautiful wilderness of bog and heather.' His statement, handwritten on the back of the aerogramme and sworn in Dunedin a few months later, described Gee as 'in my opinion one of the few most gifted of the middle generation of New Zealand prose writers. His stories, and more recently his two novels, show an innate artistic gift disciplined by long and careful practice'; he had known him personally for a number of years and had 'a very high regard for his character', he added.[43]

He had had so little news from home since he had been away, Brasch told Gee, 'N.Z. might almost have slipped into the sea'; did he have any new stories? Gee didn't, although his last, 'Down in the World', was about to be out in *Landfall*. But while all this was going on he did receive some good literary news in mid-October: that *A Special Flower*, ignored or disliked on its publication except by a discerning few, had won him the $200 Literary Fund Award for Achievement.

Shirley Smith, meanwhile, engaged a QC, G.C. Kent, to represent the case for permanent custody in court, while she made investigations and obtained affidavits. She spoke to Len and Lyndahl, to Nigel's teacher (Mrs Duncan, a modern-dressing, chain-smoking woman with rebellious children of her own), to Ray Grover, Angela Sears and Bryn Jones. Angela was recruited as Gee's 'housekeeper', which she wasn't but she lived nearby and was happy to be named by Gee as someone who would cook for him and give practical, womanly advice.[44] Margaret Scott made an affidavit testifying to the change she had seen in both Gee and Nigel since she had known them, and her confidence that he could give Nigel 'a serene, secure, warm, and enlightened upbringing'. She had not been confident of how Gee 'would wear under the increased responsibility, the decreased freedom, and the variety of complications' that bringing his son to live with him would mean, but on the contrary he not only coped 'but seemed to gain strength from doing so . . . . His tendency to be restless and discontented disappeared, his sense of humour was readier, and he saw his situation mainly in positive terms instead of (as in the year before) negative', while Nigel, 'fairly deeply disturbed' when he came to Wellington, Mrs McManemin now found 'very much improved' and she herself 'very much more responsive, less defensively withdrawn'.[45] A consultant psychiatrist, Anne Hall, interviewed Nigel at her Talavera Terrace rooms in early December, and Gee too. She described Nigel as a normal, friendly and relaxed eight-year-old who showed no signs of maladjustment despite the frequent upheavals he had been subjected to, but observed that he needed emotional stability. There was no reason, she stated, why a child of his age should necessarily live with his mother rather than his father (though preferably with both), if, as she was satisfied, the father 'has a very genuine love and concern for his son' and 'is prepared to guarantee a stable environment'.[46]

Hera produced only an affidavit from Eric Bridgman, in which he wrote of the excellence of her nursing skills and her solicitous care of her dying mother and of her son, and characterised Gee as, although he 'did his best', an 'inept' father and a layabout who did little or nothing around the (Koutu Road) house and was interested only in writing. Of Hera's decision towards the end of 1965 to make 'a fresh beginning' for herself and Nigel in Australia, he stated that '[s]he had the feeling that the applicant's parents were out to get Nigel for themselves as soon as he was old enough' (an ungenerous and hurtful accusation).[47]

At the end of November, however, both Smith and Kent were threatening to withdraw from the case over Gee's refusal to make an affidavit himself 'as to the matters which have caused you legitimate concern since the arrival of the respondent in Wellington': her unpredictable and sometimes violent behaviour, her drinking, and his fear that she would try to steal Nigel away.[48] As he would later explain this, he did not want their accusations and recriminations against each other to be heard in a courtroom and go on public record for Nigel possibly one day to read. The psychiatrist, Anne Hall, remarked on the 'absence of bitterness' he showed towards Hera; though he was certainly feeling anger and dismay. Reflecting years later, Gee would be adamant that, for the faults and failures of their relationship and what they put Nigel through, he and Hera were at least equally to blame. Over Nigel there was ego and desperation at play on both sides, a feeling that Nigel 'was mine'—of which the incident of them struggling with each other while he sat on his father's shoulders was a frightening illustration. But reticence and fairmindedness were not very helpful to his lawyers.

He did finally consent to appear in court, but 'didn't tell any of the totally disreputable stories'.[49] On 7 December another interim custody order was made by the Supreme Court, by which Hera was granted access to Nigel at 87 Weld Street on schooldays between 3 and 6 o'clock and custody every second weekend. For the forthcoming Christmas holidays, she would have him for the first half and Gee for the second.

13

The Lost Child

He had thought two years ago that he had left 'the really deep dark bad times' behind. He was wrong. In January Hera failed to bring Nigel back. She simply disappeared with him. Gee immediately contacted Shirley Smith, then went to Auckland. Hera had told him she was taking Nigel for his holiday up north to Tutukākā, on the coast out from Whāngārei, where her sister Grace and her husband, Dick Dorset, were living and ran a hotel. He borrowed his father's car and drove up there to find the house empty and Dorset, at the hotel, refusing to say anything. Julie Cook too swore she didn't know where Hera was; and didn't, although Gee, she thought, did not believe her.

Back in Wellington, Shirley Smith got in contact with solicitors in Whāngārei and Waipu, and set further court proceedings in motion—the issuing of warrants and orders and gathering of more affidavits, having further conversations with Julie, Margaret Scott, Nigel's teacher and Anne Hall. A permanent order for custody was made in the Supreme Court in March, although Hera had still not been found. In April she made enquiries with the wharf police. It seemed very likely that Hera had taken Nigel back to Australia.

Back home, and at work, there was nothing much Gee could do except wait, as he evidently felt when he asked Smith at the end of April to send him another bill for her services. Together the custody suit and search had cost him in legal fees so far just over $500 (which he was able to pay without borrowing thanks to another timely Golden Kiwi win, of, in his memory, $700). In May, Smith passed on to him Maurice Walch's address in Sydney, in Milsons Point; if Gee wrote to it he received no reply. He wrote to Ben Goffman, who was living in Mosman and who told him that he hadn't seen Hera for well over a year and had last spoken to her by phone in October; when he had tried to phone her now he was told she had left that address a year ago.

She had disappeared, and Nigel was gone.

'One was always inclined to admit defeat when facing Hera,' Gee would later comment; 'she was sort of a force of nature. . . . she just went and did things, and that was that.'[1] He had not admitted defeat; but he had other things to get on with, another life to lead.

He was in a new relationship, in its early, heady stages, and this one not a mere fling. Margaretha Hickman worked in the reference department at the Turnbull Library. He had first met her during his two-week 'internship' at the library at the beginning of 1966, when she had come bounding up the stairs one day and into his little room, full of bright energy, and introduced herself (he was reading letters of the nineteenth-century ornithologist Walter Buller at the time, he would remember). When he remarked some time later to Ray Grover how attractive he found her, however, Grover warned him off: she was already married, he told him, to Stuart Hickman, another librarian, and 'mad anarchist' by repute. She had started working at the Turnbull in 1963, and married a year later.

Maurice and Margaretha became good friends as well as colleagues at Turnbull during the following year: 'circled round each other' for a long time, mutually aware of 'some sort of electricity'.[2] It was at a Turnbull party towards the end of 1967 that they got together properly (though not yet publicly). The party was in Hataitai and afterwards they walked back together through the Mt Victoria tunnel to Margaretha's place in Footscray Avenue, at the top of Cuba Street, a nineteenth-century cottage she had shared with Stuart Hickman until midway through this year, when he had gone to Hamilton to take a job with the Country Library Service, neither of them sure whether or not they were staying together. She moved in with Gee at Weld Street some time in 1968. They had a holiday together at some point this year in Nelson, where Margaretha had spent four or five years of her girlhood, hiring a car and driving around the Nelson lakes and Golden Bay, stopping to see an old friend of hers in Māpua (the mother of her closest school friend). In a hotel somewhere Margaretha was refused service in the bar because the barman didn't believe she was over 21 (she was 28).

They thought they were keeping their relationship secret (for privacy and for the excitement of it as much as propriety); of course everyone at Turnbull knew.

There was the writing life, too, although a job, a new romance and a disappeared child were not leaving him time to actually do any. Halfway through 1968 he sent his short stories to his agents, Winant, Towers. He had been in correspondence with them the previous year about 'The Losers', which had been included in the second Oxford World's Classics *New Zealand Short Stories* volume, published in 1966 (edited by C.K. Stead), but for which he had not yet received his fee. They found that Oxford University Press had paid Hutchinson the permission fee of 20 guineas in May 1966 but that Hutchinson's royalty department had, instead of paying Gee his 10 guinea share as instructed, put it towards unearned royalties on *New Authors Short Stories 1*. This, as Hutchinson admitted, 'is obviously rather unfair as Maurice Gee only wrote a quarter of the book'.[3] His cheque arrived (for 10 guineas minus his share of the unearned advance minus 10 per cent) from Ursula Winant a few months later, along with £1 in royalties on *The Big Season* (there was nothing owing on *A Special Flower*).

When he thanked her he sent her a collection (as yet untitled) of ten stories to send on to Hutchinson, all previously published except for 'Holding Hands', and including the most recent, 'Down in the World'. (Those he had rejected were 'In at the Death', 'Evening at Home', 'A Girl in Blue' and 'While the Flag was Up'; all the *Landfall* stories were in.) He asked her if she would look at them first and see if she thought any could be placed in either American (in the first instance, because they paid better) or British magazines (on which she felt unable to advise); and also to ask Hutchinson 'how they feel about joint publication with N.Z. publishers. Their New Zealand agent is not interested in "highbrow books"—his description of mine—and as a result publicity, and, I suspect, distribution leave a lot to be desired. New Zealand publishers do better.' Caxton Press in Christchurch, for example, would be interested, their editor had already told him.[4]

Gee would no doubt have discussed this with Robin Dudding when the latter was in Wellington in March this year. He was with Dudding when he ran into Leigh Barron, now married and Leigh Minnitt. It was at the Peace, Power and Politics in Asia conference being held at the university, coinciding with a SEATO ministerial conference in the city, and she invited them back to lunch at her flat in Aro Valley (David was not there). She was bright and friendly, and talked passionately about politics, in which she had completely changed: no longer a Young National but intensely involved in the protest politics of the day. Gee, meanwhile, remained, as he had been in London but more so, a passive supporter of the causes he believed in, in these years of the anti-Vietnam war and 60s 'counter-culture' movements, going along to the occasional political meeting or demonstration. He had been at the lunchtime protest at parliament in October 1966 when Lyndon B. Johnson, on his 24-hour visit to New Zealand, arrived with Lady Bird for a state luncheon—the largest anti-war protest to that date, although dwarfed by the 200,000-strong crowd which cheered the motorcade in the rain as it progressed through the city to the airport.

Responding 'at long last' to Winant, Towers in October, Michael Dempsey at Hutchinson expressed interest, even enthusiasm, in publishing the stories, but 'does feel that it would be far wiser to publish a novel first'—on which Hutchinson had an option—'and then follow up with the stories'.[5] Was Gee working on a full-length novel, Ursula Winant wondered? Dempsey turned the stories down finally in December: 'only . . . because the present publishing climate seems to exclude short stories. He writes extremely well, often in a minor key which is often the most difficult to adopt and his stories are extremely well planned and he never gives into the temptation to sensationalise his form of violence.' Hutchinson were very keen to retain their option on his next novel; Winant disagreed.[6]

Michael Joseph also turned the stories down, and she sent them next, in February, to Cassells at Gee's suggestion. His only published piece of writing in 1968 was his short, slightly churlish contribution to *Landfall*'s Burns Fellowship symposium in the September issue (in which he bluntly stated that he would rather have just been given the money and allowed to stay at home).

At the end of January 1969 he resigned from the library to go and look for Nigel. Enquiries had continued. Len and Lyndahl had contacted, through their lawyer, the Department of External Affairs, who had in turn contacted the New Zealand High Commission in London, but, they learned just before Christmas, to no avail (a Sister H. Smith the commission thought might have been Hera was somebody else). About the same time Lyndahl heard from a woman with whom Nigel had lived in Northbridge on the Sydney North Shore, who was able to tell them that he had gone to Northbridge School; 'when he was with us he was always talking about you', she said, and about 'a Doctor in New Zealand'.[7]

He gave up the Weld Street house (Margaretha found a flat of her own in Oban Street) and went to Auckland. He borrowed his father's car again and drove to Waipu, where he had heard Grace was staying with her other sister, Joyce. He made a 'long, weary and completely abortive trip' by rental car to the Bay of Plenty, thinking that Eric Bridgman might be his best chance, only to find Bridgman was out of town; talked to everyone he could think of in Rotorua, Maketū, Matatā and Mount Maunganui 'and drew a dead lousy blank'. He spoke to Julie Cook again in Auckland. 'Everybody guesses she's no longer in N.Z.', he reported to Margaretha. 'What to do?'[8] He made a trip back to Wellington at the end of February to follow up a possible sighting by Pon Paterson of Nigel at a convent school in Lower Hutt, and went out to see Hera's brother Sonny in Wainuiomata. Returning via Rotorua—a 'hellish trip' by bus—he found Bridgman at home this time but denying any knowledge of Hera's whereabouts (he was still, however, managing the rental on the house in Koutu Road).[9]

By now he was making plans to go to Sydney, though with more resignation than hope. He flew over on 20 March. 'It's terribly expensive,' he wrote to Margaretha a few days before he left, 'but in a way I'm looking forward to it. This is apart from the search aspect of it—I've a kind of hollow feeling about that, that it's going to be fruitless, and then I really will have come to the end of the road. Seeing Sydney, if only for a few days, will be some sort of compensation.' He had budgeted for nine days but he hoped it would only take five or six; two or three if he met dead ends straight away. 'If there's a real lead though I might be heading for the outback. If there's a lead that points further afield than Australia I'll come back to N.Z. before going further.'[10] A list he had made of places he thought Hera might have gone included New Guinea, Singapore, Indonesia, Malaysia, Ceylon, India, Canada and the United States.

He booked into the Manhattan Hotel in King's Cross. 'Sydney is O.K. I like it', he wrote home—to Margaretha—the next night. 'It's a bloody madhouse of course, like a dozen Aucklands stuck together and tarted up. But it's got colour—brown and green where N.Z. cities are grey and green—and variety, and it's noisy and belligerent and friendly.' A 'week of this' though 'would be more than enough'; and his hotel had mosquitoes. King's Cross itself 'is like a miniature Soho and doesn't seem to do much for me. It's the harbour that makes this city.'[11]

On that first day he went to Northbridge School: 'felt quite upset seeing it and realising Nigel had been there for two terms'. His school records, they told him, had never been asked for. He went to the attorney-general's office to look for Maurice Walch's address in the register of justices of the peace (unaccountably, Walch, they had discovered, was a JP). The registrar of marriages agreed to conduct a search, after Gee showed them a court order, and found no record of a marriage between Hera and Walch. There was no deed poll registered for a Gee, Smith or Walch. The New Zealand High Commission were helpful and sympathetic, but they had no record at all of Hera and thought that her passport must have expired, which meant that she could not have gone further than Australia or its island territories, to his relief: this meant he would not 'have to go to the various Embassies'. At the Department of External Territories he was told to make a written request to the head office in Canberra. The Citizenship Branch 'were reluctant to divulge too but I find with some of these women if I just act helpless and sad they want to help. Anyhow this one disobeyed her boss and looked in the files for me', but found no record of Hera ever having applied for Australian citizenship. By the end of the day he had blisters and had to swap his leather shoes for a pair of jandals.[12]

The next day he rang Irene Tipene, president of the Māori Club in Sydney, who, the High Commission had told him, 'seems to know the movement of all Maoris in Sydney', but the last she had heard of Hera was in 1967.[13] He went out to Bondi where Tipene thought Hera's half-brother Mark Metekingi was but didn't find him. He also went to see Ben Goffman. After considerable difficulty he tracked down Maurice Walch. '[T]he poor little bugger was in a mess', he told Margaretha, his mother having died a few weeks before, and on his own. He was slightly hostile: 'I think I get the blame for her breaking up his romance.' He had not heard from Hera since the beginning of 1968 when she was in Northland and had been trying to find her himself. 'So I left him to his brooding and headed back to town.'[14]

He was back in Auckland in under a week. Now he did finally admit defeat. As well, he knew he needed to do something serious about his relationship with Margaretha, aware that he was in danger of losing it through his preoccupation with hunting for Nigel. 'I keep telling myself it's time I tried to integrate the business of Nigel into our life rather than trying to fit you into it', he had written to her before he left for Sydney. They were talking about a future together.

While he was off in Sydney or driving up and down country she waited, becoming despondent and unsure. 'It's simply a matter of getting present business finished,' he assured her, 'and then of settling into shape opposite one another.'[15] (There had been a pregnancy scare, as well.)

Evidently he saw himself too—or liked to—as a bit unconventional, a carefree, writer-bohemian type: he was more optimistic about their future: '[p]erhaps . . . because I'm more conditioned to a footloose way of life. I see how the woman in you wants something "solid", and I think there's a good chance for us to reach some solid state without sinking into suburbia.' She must be tolerant of 'my too easy acceptance of what comes up. It's my style of life'. There is something here, perhaps, of striking a pose. But there was not when he wrote about the cost of a lack of emotional stability: 'I know the destructiveness involved—a kind of loss of identity'.[16]

Back in Takapuna, he now wrote: 'I feel that just the act of going to Sydney has worked something out of my system and I'm readier now to come to terms with "us". . . . I hope it's over, and that Nigel/Maurice, whatever that may be and however it may alter as time goes by, is something we can integrate into Maurice/Margaretha (the order is incidental).' Yes, he told her, I can live at 44 Oban Street.[17]

14

In My Father's Den

Back in Wellington in April 1969, Gee moved in with Margaretha in Oban Street: still in Wadestown, but without a harbour view. This relationship was to endure.

She had been born Margaretha Garden in Sweden (in Uppsala), and come to New Zealand with her mother when she was nine months old. (Margaretha would eventually become Margareta because New Zealanders spelt the name as it was pronounced—and vice versa—and it became tiresome constantly correcting them.) Her mother, Greta, was Swedish; her father, Oscar Garden, was Scottish-born but had spent his late teens and early twenties in New Zealand. They both had stories to tell. In 1930 Oscar Garden had learned to fly, and bought a second-hand de Havilland Gipsy Moth which he named *Kia Ora*. On 16 October, with only rudimentary training and an 'A' license, and carrying half-a-dozen sandwiches and no hat (reported a local paper), he had left Croydon airfield outside London bound for Australia, aiming to accumulate enough flying hours for his commercial pilot's license; he landed, unknown and unannounced, eighteen days later at Wyndham in Western Australia. In these days of heroic aviation, it was the fourth solo flight between England and Australia and earned him the sobriquet 'The Sundowner of the Skies'.

Returning to England, he worked as a commercial pilot (and for a time for a flying circus) and was doing night-mail flights in Europe and Scandinavia when he met Greta Norlén, whom he married in 1937. She was seven months pregnant when Oscar returned to New Zealand in 1940 to take up a job with the national airline, TEAL, delivering its second Empire flying boat, the *Awarua*. Greta and their baby daughter came the following year, making a five-month wartime journey from Sweden overland and by steamer via Moscow, Baku, Iran and the Persian Gulf, and from there by air to Australia. Oscar piloted the *Awarua* for their final leg from Sydney to Auckland, where they were met by waiting reporters on 3 February: 'Airman's wife. Arrival in Auckland. Travelled by strange route', the *Auckland Star* headed its report, accompanied by a photograph of Greta and baby.[1]

Naturally, Gee would make fictional use of the Oscar Garden story. Margaretha, though, grew up with her mother and saw little of her father after they divorced in 1948. He had given up flying the year before (in dispute with TEAL) and spent the rest of his working life as a horticulturalist, growing tomatoes near Tauranga. Driving back through the Bay of Plenty to Auckland in February, Gee had gone out to Ōtumoetai to have a look at 'the Oscar Garden estates' but was disappointed to find 'no Gardens about. I was hoping to get a look at your Dad.'[2]

'You're the first person I've met who doesn't want to take me to bits and put me together again in a different shape,' he had written to her from Auckland, 'and that's why I can give you more than I've ever given any other woman. I can just act without intent'.[3] She was also the first woman with whom he was no longer tormented by his 'trouble'—with whom he finally felt 'normal'. Perhaps this was, partly at least, because he had got to know her over a period of time, rather than falling in love instantly, passionately and a little fancifully as he had done in the past whenever anyone had shown any interest. Or perhaps it was simply a matter of time, and he had at last outgrown his 'chronically prolonged adolescence'.[4] He turned 38 in 1969.

While Margaretha was still working at Turnbull, Gee found a part-time job across the road in the New Zealand Broadcasting Corporation library, working in the afternoons as a research librarian, hunting down information needed by broadcasters for their programmes, which he found diverting, undemanding and enjoyable. He also worked for a time this year in the mail sorting room at the Manners Street branch of the Post Office, again in the afternoon. In the mornings he wrote.

In Auckland, to keep himself busy when he was waiting for news and not driving around the country or off in Sydney searching for Nigel, he had written a new story, which he sent to Dudding for *Landfall* at the beginning of April. 'I think this is vintage Gee and I'm tickled pink to have it', Dudding replied.[5] It was very like 'The Champion'. It's 'about a lonely and bad-tempered old man,' he had described it to Margaretha when he was 6000 words through, though not as bad tempered as Eric Wilbraham and this was a gentler story:

Falls Park swimming pool and tea kiosk, late 1920s (looking a little more kempt than Gee would remember it from his boyhood a decade later)
Frank Morris photograph. Auckland Libraries West Research Centre, Frank Morris Collection, 2003.9

Helen Gee (Marmie)

Harry Gee (Pater)

James Chapple
Alexander Turnbull Library PAColl-3245-1-01

From left: the Reverends Jellie, Chapple and Hall outside the Unitarian Hall, Timaru

Aynsley and Florence Chapple, about 1930
'At fourteen he looked like Shelley: small head round as a ball and cluster of auburn curls.'
(*Plumb*, p.179)

James, Aynsley, Lyndahl and Florence Chapple, Peacehaven, on the eve of Aynsley's departure for America, 1930s

A young Lyndahl Chapple,
and (above right) in the mid-1930s

James and Florence Chapple at Lincoln Road

Len Gee (front) and friends, probably in Tauranga, 1926–27

Lyndahl and Len at Peacehaven

Lyndahl and Len at Tirimoana Road (top) and in the late 1960s

Len with his bookie mates Bob Norcross (left) and Alan Place

Lyndahl with Moss (left) and Gus at Newington Road, about 1934

First day of school, September 1936

In costume for the Henderson School fancy dress ball
'He sat at a table, wearing pyjamas, slippers, a dressing-gown and a cardboard crown pasted over with gold paper. He sorted florins and shillings into piles. "The king was in his counting house counting out his money," Gordon said.'
(*Blindsight*, p.156)

Father and sons, from left: Junior, Gus, Moss

Family picnic at Tui Glen, about 1940. From left: Christine and Dick Chapple, Len, Moss, Lyndahl, Gus, Joyce Reanney with baby Darryl, Junior

Lyndahl, Aynsley and Moss at Tirimoana Road, about 1950
Gary Gee

Moss (left) with his friend Harry Smith and Jimpy

Graduating from Auckland University College, May 1954, with Avondale College classmates Susan Waters and Brian Craven (right)

Waitemata Rugby Football Club 6th grade team, 1946, winners of the Australasian Battery Company Shield, third in the 6th grade championship. Moss back row, right; Gus middle row, left
Gary Gee

'I want to show him in the end making a positive response to his condition. It is possible'.[6] He is Cliff Poulson, a 67-year-old retired accountant who spends his idle time keeping a proprietary eye on the beach in front of his Takapuna house. 'No, my dear, you're not the pink-eyed blue-haired wife', Gee assured Margaretha. 'She's a nasty old thing who manages the junior staff at a chemists shop' (she doesn't get a name), and with whom Poulson has a prickly relationship.[7] When an agitated man and woman come to his door this day and ask him to call the police because there is a young couple '[p]erforming indecent acts' on the beach ('Like animals'), Poulson is scornful of their 'Baptist' outrage, but disturbed by his own reaction when he goes to see for himself. He knows he is a voyeur. 'God, he thought, here I am, sixty-seven, an old man troubled by dirty thoughts. Exactly where I was at sixteen. He knew that when he went back to his chair he would take out *The Carpetbaggers*.'[8] When he's not at the window or reading Harold Robbins, he reads about dinosaurs in the *Popular Encyclopaedia* (bought from a door-to-door salesman); or about the stars (he believes there is intelligent life out there, as did Oscar Garden). He is distanced from his wife, in a marriage which lacks both physical intimacy and understanding; and from his accountant son who is trying to persuade him to subdivide his large beachfront section and sell to property-developer friends. Poulson defies both his son and his wife by steadfastly refusing. His 'positive response' is not this, however, but his realisation that he is, and is happy enough being, old and alone.

The story, 'A Retired Life', was published in *Landfall* in June, and brought Gee an appreciative letter a few months later from Frank Sargeson: 'Just a word to say how much I enjoyed your knocking it off so surely sentence by sentence by sentence in Landfall', wrote Sargeson, and Karl Stead, he told him, thought it was 'probably the most positive thing you have written'. Gee responded in kind, telling Sargeson that he had just finished reading *Joy of the Worm*, his earthy and blackly comic latest novel, about a young man's intellectual and emotional tussle with his domineering, ecclesiastical father: 'this is the best New Zealand novel I've read. . . . I read it making exclamations of delight and with a kind of creeping in the guts.'[9] They shared, Sargeson and Gee, a mutual appreciation of the craftsmanship of writing. 'Let's agree always to leave out that word "best"', Sargeson responded. 'With me it's always whether a writer can write good sentences—if so interest entertainment and all the rest may well follow. It goes without saying I admire your own sentences—ear, eye what weight of thought feeling humour they are carrying. . . . I too try to provide civilized entertainment', he continued, one connoisseur to another, '—it seems too few have much notion what we are up to.'[10]

Gee was now working on a new novel himself, every evening reading what he had written that morning to Margaretha. Meanwhile, Dudding, having heard that Hutchinson had turned down his stories, was keen for Caxton to do them, 'despite the non-economic aspect of publication'.[11] He was planning a uniform series of short story volumes, of which Maurice Duggan's *O'Leary's Orchard*, due out later this year, was to be the first; Gee's collection he hoped would be the second. He was 'still fairly confident' in November when he asked Gee to send them back when he had done his revisions.[12]

But for the future he was planning with Margaretha—marriage perhaps, perhaps children—writing was not going to be enough. He needed a proper, paying job. In July he applied for the position of city librarian in Napier. He was interviewed twice. The town clerk and the chairman of the city council library committee came down to conduct a preliminary one, following which Gee was called up to Napier for what turned out to be more of an ordeal than he had anticipated. He had expected the formal interview there to be with the mayor and the library committee chairman, not the entire council. It did not help his composure either when in his office beforehand the mayor remarked that in his experience male librarians tended to be rather effeminate. Whether or not Gee found occasion to mention his rugby background, a half-hour's wait in the secretary's office later he was told that he had the job. He was formally offered it on 16 October, starting on 5 January on a salary of $3700.

In November he and Margaretha rented a cottage for two weeks in Kaiteriteri in Tasman Bay, for what they thought of as their 'honeymoon'. In December they gave up the Oban Street flat and spent a few weeks living in a bach owned by Margaretha's mother in Paekākāriki north of Wellington, where Gee was hoping to finish the first draft of his novel, before going up to Napier to start his new job—to start a new life.

And yet it was not all over yet, the disruptive and distressing influence of Hera in his life. Early in the new year his parents received a phone call from her—the first they or he had heard from Hera in two years—telling them that Nigel was dead: he had died of a tropical disease in Papua New Guinea. She said nothing more, and there was nothing they could do: they still had no idea where Hera was and so no way of contacting her. The shock, confusion and grief lasted a week, perhaps two or three; until Hera rang again to say that it was not true, Nigel was fine and they were coming to Auckland for a holiday. Why she had made that first call Gee would never know or understand. Perhaps she had been drunk. Perhaps the lie that Nigel was dead had seemed at some moment a way to keep her son with her forever.

For Lyndahl especially, the brief but profound shock of this compounded the greater one of the actual death of her eleven-year-old grandson Stephen, Aynsley and Margaret's boy (the third of four children), four months earlier. This had been a death of the hardest kind. He was a bright, sensitive boy struggling in an accelerated class in his first year at intermediate school, and threatened at the end of the second term with being put back. Something tipped his solitary anxiety and shame into the desperation that drove him to drink the weed killer in his parents' garden shed. For Lyndahl, devoted to her family and especially in these years her grandchildren, Stephen's death was a grief almost too much to bear, and precipitated a major breakdown (she 'seemed almost to lose her mind'),[13] from which she never fully recovered, and her decline in the last decade of her life into alcoholism.

It also made the Takapuna Beach house too painful to stay in. Aynsley and Margaret lived in Northcote (where Aynsley had a small joinery business) but Stephen had spent a lot of time there. She and Len sold the Hurstmere Road house not long afterwards and moved to a modern unit a few streets away (but not on the beach) in Gibbons Road.

When Gee saw Hera and Nigel in Auckland in February an arrangement was reached whereby Nigel would continue living with his mother but come over for holidays (the next in May this year). It was only at the end of this year that he learned—after the Social Security Department requested the information—that they had flown directly to Sydney from Wellington in January 1968 and had been living there ever since. They went back there now, Hera getting a job in a nursing home in Summer Hill and Nigel going to Summer Hill School.

In February Gee paid Shirley Smith a final bill of $25 (twice, because of a mislaid cheque), and the police were told that the case could be closed. 'At this point', she wrote to him—after reminding him about the cheque he had in fact already sent—'perhaps I may tell you that after you became my client, I bought a copy of "A Special Flower", not having done so before because of the reviews, and in my opinion, the reviewers were a crass lot who did not recognise a novel of subtle power and insight when they read it.'[14]

Arriving in Napier, Maurice and Margaretha stayed at the Arcadia Private Motel before moving to a house they had rented in Cameron Road on the south side of Bluff Hill, ten minutes' walk from the library in Tennyson Street in town. (Appropriately, they had moved to a city whose main streets were named after writers: Emerson, Carlyle, Dickens (of course), Milton, Thackeray, Browning.) Two weeks after he started the job Gee did an interview for the local paper in which he gave a romantic version of his literary career: explaining how, '[f]inding his interest in writing growing, he left his teaching career to "taste life"', and followed 'in the footsteps of other New Zealand literary figures, such as the poet James K. Baxter' by working as a postman, as well as a 'hospital porter, clerk and agricultural labourer' (that was working in the Corbans vineyard in the university holidays).[15] In March they bought a house—for $8000—in France Road, further up the hill with a view to Cape Kidnappers to the south: a desirable area of narrow streets winding through 'flowery gardens, ripening fruit, neatly numbered boxes', late-model cars and genteel houses.[16] Theirs was a small bungalow in need of some work (Len came down and helped with the carpentry, letting them know that it was not a good house and they should never have bought it). The following month Gee bought his first car, a 1952 Morris Oxford (black), 'as is where is' for $220.

In July they got married. Margaretha's divorce had finally come through on 10 June. (Angela Sears had been the witness at the initial separation hearing three years earlier: she had moved into the Footscray Avenue cottage next door to Margaretha's and was there to testify that Margaretha and Stuart were no longer co-habiting.) They had a registry office wedding in Hastings on 3 July, in 'a dingy little office with pipes crawling down the wall and a tourist photo of Rotorua' depicting dust-covered horses pulling a stagecoach, and the clerk as their only witness: 'It was a memorable ceremony . . . I thoroughly enjoyed it'.[17] Afterwards they went to a hotel for a buffet lunch, then Maurice took Margaretha home before going back to work. They had gone to Hastings and not to the Napier Registry Office because he had told the city council (or let them believe) when he took the job that they were already married.

By this time Margaretha was five months pregnant. A girl, Emily, was born at the Salvation Army Bethany Hospital on 7 November, with Gee not only present but actively participating throughout the labour and birth: it was so quick the doctor arrived after it was all over and one of the nurses also got there late. 'Maurice was marvellous,' Margaretha reported to her mother, 'he became quite authoritarian'—quite the opposite of what she expected—and 'so actively enjoyed the whole thing it makes up for anything I didn't find pleasurable'.[18] She had the Chapple red hair.

Nigel, in Takapuna for the summer school holidays, came down to stay for a week in January, with his cousin (Gary and Ngaire's son) Carl, an exhausting visit which Gee especially found 'very rugged'—having two eleven-year-old boys in the house along with a two-month-old baby—though Nigel proved confident and competent with her. It was only from him that they had learned at new year that he also had a ten-day-old baby brother, Brett, Hera and Maurice Walch's child. Len, when he had been in Sydney in November to check on Nigel, hadn't even noticed Hera was pregnant. With the benefit of his superior experience Nigel thought his father and Margaretha were 'a bit sissy' with Emily.[19]

Gee had had no experience of working in a public library when he applied for the Napier position (and bluffed his way through the interview), nor of administration: drawing up staff rosters and the like. He learned quickly enough on the job with the help of his very capable, sometimes exasperated deputy; and perhaps some tips from Margaretha who had been librarian in charge of the Taumarunui Public Library before she went to the Turnbull. He had a staff of thirteen, and it became apparent early on that it was an unhappy one, the source of the trouble, he surmised, being the children's librarian, and an antagonism of longstanding between her and some of the other women on the staff in particular; but she was pleasant enough to the new boss.

The part of the job he enjoyed most was the book selection and buying. He introduced himself straight away to the three or four local booksellers. While he was careful to share the business around, his favourite became Beattie and Forbes, on the ground floor of the Masonic Hotel. It had been opened just the year before by two brothers-in-law, Graham Beattie, who had been an accountant with the ANZ bank, and Barry Forbes. Beattie in particular became a good friend, one of the small circle of like-spirited—broadminded, book-reading, left-leaning—people they found in this conservative provincial town. They had been warned: 'Not that I think your job will be a niche, in the sense of a comfortable nest to feather', a librarian friend had remarked to Gee when he had written to congratulate him, 'The city fathers will take care of that. You'll have to compete with the dolphins'—at Marineland, Napier's main tourist attraction—'although among the most intelligent Napierites, they don't read yet, unfortunately.'[20]

Gee had arrived sporting a flamboyant Zapata moustache he had grown since his interview, as some sort of statement of identity, but he shaved it off after a few months: it seemed a little radical for Napier. He and Margaretha joined the Napier Film Society, and they developed a taste, as far as they could afford to, for the local wine. (Hawke's Bay, like Henderson, was a pioneering wine-making area: Marist missionaries had planted New Zealand's first grapes there to make altar and table wine in the 1850s.) At home Margaretha made yoghurt. But they never saw themselves staying in Napier in the long term. It was such a relief, Margaretha remarked to her mother every time she went down to visit her, 'to be able to get to Wellington and know the world still exists and that there really are people we can talk to'. She hated Napier's small-town formality, that 'even going to coffee with a person I knew well one was supposed to dress up'.[21] They made enough friends in Napier, but would never feel at home there.

An extracurricular task of the city librarian Gee had not expected was writing book reviews for the Napier *Daily Telegraph*. He no more liked book reviewing now than he had six years ago, and Margaretha did most of it. He took care of the 'Quick Flips': 50-word reviews of popular titles (selected from the library's new acquisitions when they ran out of review titles from the *Telegraph*). Chairing the local branch of the New Zealand Library Association was a less onerous duty. Only a month after he started he went down to Nelson for the association's annual conference. When he organised the local branch annual meeting in October the following year he invited the veteran, maverick Labour politician and writer John A. Lee to give the after-dinner speech: true to form, once started Lee did not stop talking until the hotel staff began flashing the lights. At a private party for him the night before he had subjected the twenty or thirty guests to an impromptu oratorical performance (no one else could get a word in) for almost as long.

A good part of Gee's first year as city librarian was taken up with organising the library's move to new premises, and this he found a highly enjoyable logistical challenge. The old premises, in the Market Reserve Building on Tennyson Street, were not only much too small, they were also on the building's second floor which meant that a significant proportion of library users—elderly people who could not manage the stairs—had to go out to the branch library in Taradale or catch the bus to Hastings. At the request of the city council Gee collaborated with a local architect to draw up plans for a new, purpose-built library, which the council then shelved because of the cost. Instead they decided on an interim move to the old Majestic Ballroom in Dalton Street. This had the drawback of being away from the main shopping street, and there were still three steps at the entrance (Margaretha wrote to the *Daily Telegraph* criticising the new library for the lack of ramp access on behalf of the elderly, the infirm and mothers with pushchairs), but it had more than twice the floor space. The original, 3000-foot ballroom, which now became the children's library, had become the supper room when Hastings modernist architect John Scott had added a 5000-foot dance hall in 1963. This became the adult library, and possessed, Gee wrote in an article on the new premises for *New Zealand Libraries*, 'one noteworthy aesthetic feature, a pitched timber ceiling rather like that of a Maori meeting house', enhancing the feeling of space above the (still, however, cramped) bookshelves below. The dark green walls were painted white, gold carpet laid over the dance floor, and a partition erected in front of the old stage for hanging pictures loaned from the Hawke's Bay Art Gallery and Museum. Overall, a 'comfortable and homely rather than a quiet or studious atmosphere has been achieved'.[22] Gee believed, as he told a meeting of the Napier branch of the National Council of Women the following year, that libraries should be lively, not deathly and forbiddingly silent places.[23]

The new library was formally opened by the mayor on 25 March 1971, after the entire staff had spent a long weekend moving in the 60,000 or so books. In the first two months, 466 new child and 347 new adult members joined. Over the first year issues rose 5.7 per cent;

and '[a]reas previously dead are attracting borrowers, for example the 800s' (literature).[24]

In the first half of that first year he had also managed to finish the new novel (it was a short one) he had not managed to in Paekākāriki in December. He send it to Faber and Faber—having withdrawn Hutchinson's option—because 'The Losers' had been included in a Faber anthology, *Best Racing and Chasing Stories 2*, edited by Dick Francis and John Welcome, published in 1969. They at least, therefore, knew who he was. He heard from Winant, Towers in December that they wanted to publish it, and were offering an advance of £150.

Faber were not, however, interested in his collected stories. Dudding still was, but preferably with the help of an English co-publisher. He had tried, without success, to interest MacGibbon and Kee and Jonathan Cape in Maurice Duggan's, which he had finally got out, as *New Zealand Short Stories: no. 1* in his projected Caxton series, in May 1970. He sent Gee's now to Jonathan Cape, but they would not consider them knowing that Faber had turned them down but still had a contract for his novel.

Before the page proofs of the novel arrived, in October 1971, he had another short story written to add to his collection. It was a Napier story in a subtle way: Susan Neeley is a bored young mother living with her husband and their three-year-old daughter with her parents-in-law in 'a dull town . . . full of dull people', 'frustrated pretending my interests don't go beyond babies and cooking. . . . We need ideas. We need them as much as we need food', she tells her father-in-law, Lloyd, explaining why they have decided to go back to the city. 'We're big city people. We need to be with our own kind.'[25] The story is really about Lloyd Neeley, though, like Cliff Poulson another ageing man facing the vacuum of his life—the realisation that 'we are all essentially lonely'[26]—or at least he is, but a bleaker one this time. He mulls over the suicide (by drowning) of his close—he thought—friend Jack Nash, trying to find a reason for it. 'Had Jack been a case of sex in the head?' (his bookshop 'had reeked of sex'); 'had there been a disease—heart?—cancer?' Or had he simply discovered the 'emptiness' of his life? The more Lloyd thinks about Jack, the more he realises he didn't really know him at all: 'A few tastes shared, a few interests. Habits in common'. Yet 'without Jack he was adrift, he had no friend, he had lost his habits'; and this was why he clung to his granddaughter, who is being taken from him too.

In symbolism that is perhaps too obvious, the hole in the window of the story's title is the one made by the burglar who breaks into Lloyd's jewellery store in the small hours of the morning; it appears to him as he surveys the damage 'like a black sun; an opening into nothing'. Later, back in bed 'he made his descent in a lurching way and stopped short of sleep in a place where everything was edgeless. Something threatened, something huge, but he could not see its shape.'[27]

Gee would have written this story before he saw Dudding at the Fiction Writers' Conference which was held at Massey University in Palmerston North at the end of August, afterwards giving Dudding a ride up to Hastings (his home town). His presence there was little noted. He arrived a day late (he had only decided to attend at the last minute, at Margaretha's persuasion). But nor had he missed much: the conference was an uneventful affair; V.S. Naipaul had cancelled. It was memorable for Gee because he was given the room, in the City Court student accommodation block, vacated early by the alcoholic novelist Ronald Hugh Morrieson from Hāwera, the author of under-appreciated Gothic tales of Taranaki's dark side (a different kind of tragic-comic vision of provincial New Zealand from the one Gee was creating): the room had not been cleaned and there was a large bloodstain on the pillowcase and a stash of empty beer bottles in the wardrobe.[28]

'Your story hasn't been lost in the mail has it?' Dudding wrote to him six or seven weeks later. Or perhaps, he thought, he was waiting for the announcement of the Katherine Mansfield Memorial Award in November, for which Gee had entered 'The Hole in the Window' (under the pseudonym 'Nigel Gough').[29] It did not win. He had also entered 'The Tin God' for the Rothmans Play of the Year Award in June, where it made the 'commended' list of fifteen—out of an 'astonishingly large' number of entries—and was not in the top three only, explained the judge and head of the Rothmans Cultural Foundation, Roy Hope (an experienced theatre professional), when he returned the script, because he 'found the theme slightly dated. It seemed that you were writing about something that happened about ten years ago' (as indeed he was).[30]

'The Hole in the Window' appeared in the December—100th—*Landfall*: on the facing page Dudding had placed a Tony Stones sketch of a bespectacled, late middle-aged-looking man holding a baby. 'Again a story rich in material—enough for a novel almost,' Brasch complimented it, 'and all set out in such brief space with excellent economy and clarity' (though not to Gee, he also expressed the view that it was 'not quite at his best').[31] Again too Sargeson was impressed and wrote to tell him so: 'I know the work that goes into the surface-clear sentences, and I'm not sure that in The Hole you haven't made them suggest more than ever before. Of course it's a problem—how many are going to get the pleasure that I do?'; to which Gee again replied in like spirit, congratulating Sargeson on 'The Drive', his autobiographical piece in the same issue. 'I think I've read everything you've published'. When he mentioned that he had called in to see Sargeson a few weeks before (he had been in Auckland to see Nigel, who was over again for the school holidays), but although the door was open his sign—the one that told visitors to go away—was up so he had done so, Sargeson replied, '[a] few people can always disregard my notice, you be one of them.'[32] They compared notes this time on the discipline of their craft. 'My compliments on the discipline of writing before breakfast', Sargeson replied to Gee's remark that he was 'writing fairly steadily before breakfast and in the weekends'. For himself, 'I find my mind won't begin to spin unless I drift into the day's work, and I'm in no drifting mood at 6 in the morning.'[33]

What Sargeson would not have appreciated was that he wrote before breakfast not by choice but necessity. Emily was a wakeful and very hungry baby, and when she woke for her second morning feed at 4am Gee would get up too and write for two or three hours before going to the library. It was a routine which worked well. He was on to a new novel now; and they were in a new house. He and Margaretha had sold 26 France Road in November, a little reluctantly (though it had taken them more than a year, and Len's help, to make the house comfortable) but wanting something bigger and on the flat. Margaretha became pregnant again around the same time. They moved to a two-storey, stucco, art deco-cum-Spanish mission-style house in Vigor Brown Street in Napier South, a prominent one in a neighbourhood of single-storey wooden bungalows—an ugly house, they thought, but the unexpectedly quick sale of France Road had forced their hand. It had a small section but large, light-filled rooms. He could walk home easily for lunch too.

While this was going on—house buying and selling and moving—he was also checking page proofs for Dudding and for Faber and Faber.

'Minor novel! I don't know; I enjoyed it immensely', Dudding wrote at the beginning of June after he had read the advance copy of the novel Gee had sent him.[34] *In My Father's Den*, the novel he had started in Wadestown and finished at France Road—and dedicated 'to Margaretha'—came out in Britain in July 1972 and was in New Zealand a month or so later, with another cover he did not like. It did, as one reviewer observed, make it look like a children's book, which it definitely was not. 'It is basically about domestic cannibalism', Gee had told the *Daily Telegraph* reporter who interviewed him when he arrived in Napier.[35] It went back, though, to childhood: to Henderson—Wadesville here—and its creek, and a boyhood burdened by puritanism and guilt. He had been here before, of course, but not with such sustained and deliberate focus. *In My Father's Den* is rich in the place, incidents, and the agonies of Gee's growing up.

It was also a thriller. The girl depicted (a little too young) on the cover, flowers in one hand and books in the other, is seventeen-year-old Celia Inverarity, who has been brutally murdered (strangled), her body hidden in a patch of scrub at Cascade Park, by the creek. Suspicion falls on Paul Prior, the English teacher with whom she has an out-of-school student–mentor relationship which teeters on the brink of being something else (recalling Gee's experience in Paeroa). He is Paul Emerson Prior, the novel's narrator, a Wadesville boy who has returned from several restless years overseas—teaching, travelling, sending back postcards of 'cathedrals, bullfights, vineyards, Gauguin nudes' (he makes the decision to come home while on holiday in Alicante in August 1962), flatting in Ladbroke Grove. The Wadesville he left was a small country town surrounded by orchards and vineyards, and cut through by a creek, 'green, mysterious, frightening, magic. I can travel down it in my mind, remembering each pool and mossy rock and fallen tree'; now it is an industrial suburb of Auckland, the creek 'a ditch of grey scummy water' polluted with factory waste, the Priors' orchard long since sold.[36] Here the novel is a paean to lost innocence. The murder of Celia, commentators readily noted, equated with Wadesville's demise ('Auckland grows, innocence goes', as one review was headed).[37]

Paul's happy childhood is Gee's: the teacher with powdery cheeks, the incriminating bite mark in her apple; orchard raids, Rationalists' picnics and Catholic Flynns; fishing for tommy cods and silver bellies. The day he and his best friend Charlie make canoes of corrugated tin and paddle all the way down the creek to the sea, wade home through the mangroves and mud at twilight 'was the happiest day of my life.

I keep it safe by formalizing it'.[38] It is Charlie who later steals Paul's first girlfriend, Joyce, from under his nose at the Fruitgrowers' Ball, and marries her. Celia is Joyce and Charlie's daughter.

The novel follows a double time sequence in alternating sections (building interplays of image and irony), as Paul seeks to discover who killed Celia by looking to his own past. The key is his mother. Mrs Prior was a 'grim and fundamental' Presbyterian, her 'vice was spirituality', twisted and dour: 'She knew her soul was of the common grey. Her life was a struggle to scrub it clean'; 'She did not wish to know about ugly things and had developed turning away to a code of conduct.'[39] She is Jean Pinnock and Alice Matthews; in ways a monstrous version of Lyndahl (but in important ways not: Mrs Prior burns books, and is unloving). Paul's brother Andrew is devoted to her, absorbs her teaching and masturbates at night in sin, guilt and shame—his adolescence was 'a kind of torture chamber where his human nature racked him and our mother stood Christ-like, with blessing and forgiveness, if he could only reach her'.[40] Paul gravitates to his lapsed-Presbyterian, Unitarian-leaning father—James Chapple not Len Gee: a 'scholar-hermit' and 'Rationalist *manqué*'—especially after he discovers his father's den, the 'poison-shed' in the garden where the weed killer and insecticides are kept, which his father has transformed into a secret, book-lined refuge. Here Paul discovers Rider Haggard, Rafael Sabatini, Conan Doyle; 'took Dickens at a gulp' at fourteen; moves on to the Victorians.

The birth and death of a 'mongoloid' third son and brother, John (he has Down's Syndrome), push each member of this family further into their own psychic withdrawal (towards or away from a Calvinist God). The den is Paul's first escape; his second his libertarian, bohemian, wanderlust years away, from which he returns to a solitary, bookish, aloof, watchful—in his own word, hollow—life, a life lived in 'cultivated detachment'.[41]

In a way *In My Father's Den* was another go at Gee's second apprentice novel—the troubled young man, a murder, a body stashed by the creek; an exorcism, or writing out, of childhood and adolescent demons. It is by writing, about both himself and Celia, that Paul seeks to 'find a shape. Shape might be understanding.' There is some of both Goodall and Horner (the saintly and the life-loving) competing in Paul; and Crassin as well as Goodall in Andrew. The adult Andrew is a money-coveting businessman: he owns a small furniture factory on the North Shore which makes overstuffed sofas 'like quilted sarcophagi, and pink porky chairs' (another kind of ugliness).[42] Initially Gee had intended to have Paul solve the murder on his own through his investigation of his and his brother's past, but this proved too difficult (or unlikely). It is his teenage nephew, Jonathan, Andrew's son, who finds the incriminating evidence and brings it to him. The boy has already confided in the uncle he admires his own secret, what troubles him and is worrying his mother by making him silent and withdrawn. 'Probably some worry at school', Paul reassures her; but Jonathan, he discovers, is burdened by his father's and the author's own problem ('Presbyterian dong-beater's guilt', as Paul puts it).

What Paul learns on his own is that he has never, in fact, escaped from his puritan past: all his life, '[e]verything took its tone from Mother.'[43]

The particular genesis of the novel was a murder Gee had read about, though not the murder itself (which was commonplace enough) but the action of the local townspeople in burning down the hedge where the girl's body was discovered: the ritualistic act of catharsis or revenge intrigued him. (In the novel, a lynch mob of 'mustered Rotarians' and 'angry Bowling Club men'[44] drag Paul from his bed in the middle of the night and force him to watch.) He started with *Crime and Punishment* in mind, and the idea of a duel between the narrator and a smart detective, but this he realised would detract from his primary interest in the damaged psychologies of Andrew and Paul.[45] His desire to write a crime story was also inspired by his avid reading at this time of Raymond Chandler and Ross Macdonald, masters of the 'hardboiled' and psychological thriller. What he liked about these writers in particular was not just their taut, pacy, dialogue-driven, *noir* style, as he was to explain to a journalist a few years later: 'the whole atmosphere of a Chandler book or a Macdonald book is something that immediately strikes a chord with me . . . if you like, a kind of *greyness* that sometimes comes down over my own writing . . . the kind of greyness that exists in Graham Greene's "entertainments", for example'. It was also—and this he related to his short stories being increasingly about lonely old men—that 'Chandler doesn't really believe any proper communication is possible. What I'm discovering is the belief that everybody is alone.'[46]

At just 166 pages, *In My Father's Den* was a tightly written, carefully crafted, and dark novel (grey is not really the word), like but very different from his last; sparser in language but richer in texture and structure. It fared better than *A Special Flower.* Not everyone appreciated the grafting together of a thriller and a psychological study of family and social dysfunction. 'The point is', concluded the Napier *Daily Telegraph*'s reviewer, 'that Gee conceived a big, heroic novel and theme and then either lacked the stamina and concentration to see it through or decided that what he really wanted was to write a thriller': it was 'highly readable and sometimes even compelling', but 'I am left with this strong feeling—that Gee could fill a fine novel with living characters and could also manage a pretty fair fast-pace thriller, if only he wouldn't try to do them both at the same time'.[47] But that seemed to be the minority view. In August it was number two in the fiction bestseller list, behind R.F. Delderfield's *To Serve Them All My Days*; the next month at number four, after Herman Wouk, Len Deighton and Jack Higgins (helped, Gee surmised, by one of his aunts buying five copies). Auckland bookseller Robert Goodman, reviewing it in the *Star*, thought it 'a novel of quite unusual merit' with 'a distinction rare in New Zealand fiction'. '[B]loody marvellous, all the way', Maurice Shadbolt wrote to congratulate him.[48]

It received a positive but fairly pedestrian review in *Landfall.* This had not, however, been commissioned by Dudding, who had been fired from Caxton and *Landfall* at the beginning of April, for reasons nobody in the literary world could fathom: Caxton's business manager Dinny Donovan's 'insanity' and the press's financial problems, Dudding decided.[49] When he gave Gee the news (still confidentially) he also sent him back his short stories. Having failed to persuade Caxton to let him take *Landfall* away with him, he now set up a journal of his own, with Charles Brasch's encouragement and financial help. ('Wicked as it is', Brasch, though perhaps rueful, had thought Dudding's sacking might be good thing.)[50] Word went out announcing the launch of *Islands. A New Zealand Quarterly of Arts & Letters* in July, with copy deadlines of the 21st and in September for Spring and Summer 1972 issues. 'Look forward to your best-ever story', Dudding wrote separately to Gee. 'Important that Moss Gee features in an early issue.'[51]

There was no Gee story in the first *Islands*, but there was a largely admiring review of *In My Father's Den*, meatier than *Landfall*'s, about which Dudding warned Gee in slight trepidation. It placed the novel within a New Zealand fiction Tradition which combined the archetypes of the odyssey and the Garden of Eden, but as a knowing and ironic contribution to it: that Paul Prior essentially *was* the tradition, in both rebelling against and remaining defined by his puritan past (and in his unlikeableness), was 'a profoundly depressing revelation contained in a beautifully true book'.[52] Its weakness, the reviewer felt, was Paul's self-consciousness as narrator and the lack of a consistent distance between his point of view and the author's. A 'good solid job—sensible and unpretentious', Gee commented. 'I agree with a lot and find my feelings about the book cleared a little by it . . . He's a good phrase-maker—wish I'd thought of some of them myself.' The one that would be picked up and quoted was the observation that '*In My Father's Den* ought to be the definitive novel of New Zealand puritanism'.[53] But Gee had not finished with puritanism yet.

15

A Glorious Morning, Comrade

By the time *In My Father's Den* was in the shops Gee had resigned from the Napier Public Library and was making preparations to move to Auckland.

Things had started to go wrong at the library towards the end of 1971, following local body elections and the appointment of a new chairman of the library committee. He had got on well with the previous chairman, Lloyd Duckworth, who ran an electrical repair shop, knew nothing about running libraries and was happy to let Gee get on with his job. The new chairman, Arthur Richards, was a retired collector of customs who knew nothing about libraries either, boasted that he didn't read books, but knew about balancing them, and was a meddler. He would come regularly into the library and run his finger along the shelves checking for dust, and look in the toilets to make sure there were enough toilet rolls. He kept a close eye on the noticeboard too in case there was dirt there as well.

These, though, were trivial things, however irksome Richards' fussing surveillance increasingly became to the librarian. At a special council meeting in December he presented a report enumerating his more serious concerns. He was not happy with the policy of not fining children for overdue books, with the 40 per cent rental discount for senior citizens, and with the holding of overdue 'amnesties'. Above all he was unhappy about the balance of free and rental books. Under New Zealand public libraries' free-and-rental system, light popular fiction for which there was a heavy demand was placed in a separate 'B' category for which a rental fee was charged. As far as Gee was concerned the purpose of the 'B' section—as he explained to the National Council of Women's meeting he addressed in May 1972—along with a legitimate one of providing entertainment, was primarily to act as a lure to get people into the library where they might be encouraged to borrow serious fiction and free non-fiction. Richards wanted the rental section enlarged and extended to include general interest and sporting books. Since the system had been brought in, he noted (replacing the old subscription one in 1965), rental revenue had remained stable while library membership had trebled: something was not right. The librarian's book selection came in for his criticism too.

The council in response launched an investigation into the running of the library. Letters flooded in to the *Daily Telegraph* and the *Hawke's Bay Herald-Tribune* expressing dismay at the pettiness of many of Richards' complaints, and alarm at the more disturbing underlying assumption that the library should be run on economic lines. The councillor needed to be reminded, wrote 'Reader', that 'a public library is a public amenity, not a book club run solely for the financial gain of the owner'; 'a welcome oasis' in what was 'a lovely city in many ways but hardly a hotbed of culture', contributed another; 'Although a regular user of the Napier Public Library I have seen no trace of the accumulation of filth that so upsets some of our house-proud councillors', commented a third.[1] When a recommendation was made by the library committee in March that the librarian should have sole discretion over the display of notices on the noticeboard, Richards publicly dissociated himself from it. The recommendation was rejected by the council.

By this time Gee was finding working under such conditions intolerable, and that it was turning him into a person he didn't like. Writing to his mother in February, he apologised for having been 'snappish': he was becoming irritable, he told her. 'I don't enjoy being short with people, not only because it insults and hurts them, but also because it seems to diminish me.'[2] A week away at Rotorua that month for the New Zealand Library Association conference and a few days at his aunt Winifred Chapple's bach at Lake Okareka came as a welcome break; as much for Margaretha who went up too, three months pregnant and still exhausted by Emily, fifteen months and 'a determined wench'.[3] At the end of February they escaped for a ten-day holiday at Māpua (staying with Margaretha's old friend there, Ivy Brett).

He was already on the look-out for another job. Auckland or Wellington were where they wanted, and were now very determined, to be (though even Dunedin, he told Charles Brasch, now appealed 'as one of the cities I'd like to live in').[4] An enticing vacancy at the National Library had come up inconveniently a week before they moved into the new house; he had toyed the following month with applying for one in Whāngārei, which would at least take them close to Auckland; tried unsuccessfully for another in Wellington in March. In May he accepted a position as assistant librarian at the School of Architecture library at the University of Auckland. Never mind that it meant taking a drop in salary. He resigned from the Napier Public Library on 15 May, giving the council four months' notice instead of the required three, intending to take up the new job in September, six or seven weeks after the new baby was due.

'In library matters librarians are almost always many years in advance of their controlling councils', he remarked to the National Council of Women a few weeks later, 'and a good deal of tension arises from this.'[5] There was more of it to come yet.

At the end of July, while he was serving out his notice, he was informed that the city council was firing two of the library's long-serving and most experienced part-time staff members: its only competent cataloguer, Beryl Bolton, and Pat Mooney, who had been in charge of the adult library since the deputy librarian had left in April. Gee was outraged, not only because his staff had been given notice without him being consulted. The ostensible reason for their dismissal was a new council policy of reducing numbers of part-time employees. He knew that it was really to make way for the appointment of the difficult and unpopular children's librarian to the position of deputy, in which she had been acting since April, and who had made this a condition of her accepting the job. Given the news on Friday, he spent the weekend composing a frankly worded report arguing that the dismissal of the two women would be not only unethical but demoralising to the rest of the staff, and cautioning the council against appointing the children's librarian as deputy because she had 'a temperament that . . . makes her entirely unfitted for the job of controlling staff'. He recommended too that his own position be re-advertised as soon as possible: they had interviewed only one applicant (a fellow library school graduate of 1966), but he had already been warned off by Gee and was happy not to be offered the job.

For good measure, he also gave his opinion on the deficiencies of the present library committee, in which, he stated, 'I no longer have confidence . . . to manage the affairs of the library intelligently and responsibly. In particular, I have no confidence in the Chairman.'[6] He had not been invited to a meeting of the committee, he noted, since May.

It was a report, Gee told his mother, 'that would either get [Mooney and Bolton] reinstated or me fired'. It got him fired. He handed it to the town clerk on Monday morning, and, lest it simply be put in a drawer and ignored, delivered copies that afternoon to the members of the library committee and any other councillors he could find in their shops and offices around town. He had been asked by the town clerk what his intentions were if the dismissals went ahead, and replied that he would reduce his notice period from four months to three and leave on 18 August. The next morning, following an urgent meeting of the council the night before, he was called back in and told that his terms had been accepted but that he was to be out of his office by the end of the day.[7]

'It's the year for getting sacked', he wrote a few days later to Robin Dudding—himself recently fired from Caxton—enclosing a newspaper clipping from the *Daily Telegraph* along with his subscription to *Islands*: 'I feel it's a compliment to be fired by N.C.C.'[8] He was neither surprised nor (or perhaps a little) disappointed that all but one of the councillors had voted against him. Richards had been on the council for many years and commanded a lot of support in the community for his 'sterling work in the cause of pensioner housing' (in the words of 'JUST A PHILISTINE' writing to the *Telegraph*); they called him 'The Pensioners' Friend'.[9]

The affair became a minor scandal. There was another flurry of letters to the newspapers, almost unanimously in support of Gee, and it made the television news, although he was making no further comment beyond having described the council's action to newspaper reporters as a 'stupid blunder'. The *Daily Telegraph* reported an 'emotional scene' as library staff burst into tears when Bolton and Mooney left.[10] The president and vice-president of the New Zealand Library Association went to Napier to investigate, meanwhile blacklisting the library to the extent of advising its members not to apply for the vacant librarian's position until they had done so. The Local Body Officers' Union also investigated (but found no case of wrongful dismissal to pursue). A group of concerned citizens headed by the local Presbyterian minister presented a submission to the city council about the future running of the library, supported by an editorial in the *Daily Telegraph* which observed that 'It certainly is a better library for the guidance of Mr Maurice Gee'; the council ignored them.[11]

Gee was happy to be out of it. '[A] valuable experience to have collected,' he summed up his last six months in Napier to Brasch, 'but not much fun to live through'.[12]

In the free time he now had before leaving for Auckland he wrote a story, getting a first draft finished by the first week of September. It was about a long-serving city councillor named Vincent Brown in a provincial city named Hardinge: he has just been re-elected for his ninth term by a margin of just 73 votes, and for the first time in 24 years is without a chairmanship, fobbed off instead with a seat on the library and special purposes committees—and 'if by any sad chance this should be your last term', suggests the mayor at the first meeting of the new council, perhaps a street named after him ('Vincent Brown Street. Think of it.'). Brown's *bête noire* is Olga Fulton, chair of the library committee, twenty years on the council and '[a]ll she'd done was fill the library up with arty books'. 'Reading was a luxury', Brown believes. He had argued against the change from subscription to free-and-rental and proudly claims not to have read a book since *The Cruel Sea*.[13] When a flasher begins exposing himself to schoolgirls at Olsen Park, he sees his chance to challenge her by leading a campaign to have the stand of pine trees in which the man lurks cut down (this too was based on a local incident which both amused and horrified Gee). In the course of this he learns that the former mayor, whom he had served for two terms as deputy and, he had thought, indispensible right-hand man—he had even held hopes of holding the mayoralty himself—had only regarded him as a lackey and a joke (had nicknamed him 'Little Brown').

The template is familiar. Brown's bleak but not unhappy understanding by the story's end is 'that possibilities once his, for adventure, for love, for a place in the minds of other people, were lost . . . He had done none of the things that once—fifty years ago—he had dreamed that he might do.'[14] (Familiar too is his discomfort—like Brian Hughes's in 'The Eleventh Holiday', perhaps, and Lloyd Neeley's—at what the idea of the flasher reveals to him about himself.)

The Vigor Brown Street house had sold (with difficulty) in July—for $10,900, just $250 more than the Gees had paid for it—and they were keeping an eye on the Auckland real estate pages, though not intending yet to buy, sending clippings up to Len and Lyndahl for properties in Takapuna and the North Shore, Green Bay and Kohimarama in the range of $12–15,000. Abigail, another red-haired daughter, was born at Bethany Hospital on 15 August, a late but again alarmingly precipitate arrival. Abigail (winning out after a week over Ursula) was an uncommon name for the time: the biblical Abigail, Gee explained to his mother, 'was one of the women David got his hands on by his usual cunning methods'. She looked, Margaretha told Greta, 'like a little miniature Oscar Garden'.[15]

With the $30 Lyndahl sent Gee for his 41st birthday the first thing they bought was a bottle of wine, Margaretha's first since her pregnancy. They celebrated his birthday, Margaretha and Abigail's arrival home from Bethany, and his novel with steak and chips and the wine.

They left Napier on 15 September—after having a celebratory lunch at the Mayfair a few days earlier—stopping for a night in Taupō en route (they had traded up by now from the Morris Oxford to an Austin Farina). 'We will be so pleased never to set eyes on Napier again', wrote Margaretha to her mother.[16] Len and Aynsley had conveniently just bought a house in Hororata Road in Takapuna as an investment property, and they rented this while they looked for something to buy, Gee taking the bus in each day to the architecture school library in Symonds Street.

The job, he very quickly realised, was a mistake. The librarian in charge, Christina Troup, had begun working at the university library in 1946 and was four years away from retiring, and she suffered from crippling and painful arthritis in her hands. The problem, however, was her inability to delegate. Gee's job was cataloguing. Each morning she would place half a dozen books from the shelf behind him on his desk for him to catalogue; he was to hand them to her when he had finished and she would select him six more. He felt 'like the boy around the place';[17] in Napier he had been in charge of a staff of thirteen. The books weren't interesting either. 'My job is so bloody boring', he wrote to Robin Dudding after six weeks, explaining why the story he had promised him defied finishing, 'I'm never mentally ready for writing fiction.'[18] In November he applied for a job at Ardmore Teachers' College in Pakuranga, but the current librarian then decided to reapply. (Meanwhile, the Wellington job he had been hoping to come up, at the teachers' college, finally did within a month of their leaving Napier.)

Whatever library he found himself in, though, it was not the life he wanted: working full-time and writing when he could in the evenings and weekends. 'Still dream of the part-time job, part-time writing combination in some quiet spot like Nelson or Titirangi', he told Dudding; 'we have a scheme . . .', he wrote to Charles Brasch a few weeks later, but was not saying any more 'or it will come to nothing'.[19]

He had finished (he thought) typing his new—Napier—novel at the end of July, a few days before he was fired from the public library. 'I don't expect to write a great novel ever, or even a very good one,' he wrote to his mother the month before, halfway through, 'but if I can turn out half a dozen well-made small novels I'll be satisfied. It's the only activity I have that gives me the sense of really working—of using myself properly as opposed to just earning a living. You will know the feeling, because you wanted to do it too.'[20]

It was to be another two years before he had this novel ready to send to Faber and Faber. However, it seemed that his short story collection was finally going to be published. He had been approached by Brasch, he told Dudding in October, about him having it for the imprint he and Janet Paul had just established together, Square & Circle. Where did Dudding's plan stand? Gee wondered; 'I regard you as having an option on the stories, but would like to see them move soon, they've been around so long.' It was Dudding in fact who had suggested that Brasch sound out Gee, and he was happy (philosophically) to resign his own interest, 'unless I win the Auckland Cup sweepstake'.[21]

Brasch and Paul had founded Square & Circle in 1971 to publish 'small things in which writer and artist collaborate; not just illustrated books', as Brasch explained to Frank Sargeson when he sent out feelers to possible writers in the middle of that year, starting modestly with two titles a year.[22] The first, as Stories and Drawings 1, was planned to be *The Loners*, Ted Middleton stories with drawings by Ralph Hotere. There followed the usual kinds of vicissitudes that beset small publishing ventures—financial difficulties, delays, Paul's unreliability, in Brasch's periodically exasperated view ('Square & Circle will come to nothing, I fear', he despaired in his journal in September after she had 'insisted' on taking a full-time job at the Turnbull Library at the end of the year),[23] an unexpected four-month visit by Brasch to England the next (where, however, he took the opportunity to try to interest London publishers, but without success)—and *The Loners* appeared in October 1972 as the second Square & Circle, preceded in April by Poems and Drawings 1, *The Elaboration* by Hotere and Bill Manhire—Manhire's first collection, although not his first book.

It was possibly that book, *Malady*—words (four) by Manhire with art work by Hotere, published by their own Amphedesma Press in 1970 to accompany a Hotere exhibition—that had inspired Brasch's concept for Square & Circle; that and perhaps the careful matchings of text and image Dudding had been doing in *Landfall*. For 1973 Brasch and Paul set their sights higher, wanting at least one title this year to be 'a book, not a pamphlet'. Paul was keen that it be a collection of essays by historian J.C. Beaglehole. Toss Woollaston's autobiography, *Sage Tea*, was another possibility, but it turned out not to be ready yet. Essays by James Bertram, stories by Roderick Finlayson and poems by Ian Wedde were also on the list.

Brasch's first preference was for Gee's stories: they 'would make a very strong collection and probably sell well'. He had just read *In My Father's Den* and it was 'very good', and it was to say this in the first instance that he wrote to Gee at the end of October: 'I greatly admired its economy, the ease of writing, its assurance; and kept feeling that here was a writer I could trust. Not so many writers give one that confidence.'[24] This was praise Gee was grateful to receive. 'I was very pleased to get your note', he wrote back, '—especially to know that you'd taken some pleasure from my grim little tale. There has been very little response reaching me from other readers—but one gets used to this. There seems to be a feeling about that it's bad manners to mention a person's writing to him.' 'Yes,' Brasch agreed, 'it's odd that even friends won't mention our work to us; it was the same with Lf and with my own books, I found. A foolish convention, discouraging to writers.'[25] As for his stories, he would be 'delighted' to let Square & Circle have them, he told Brasch, so long as Dudding was too (although he felt in good conscience that he should also let Brasch know that both Hutchinson and Faber had turned them down).

He sent them to Brasch in late January: ten, including 'all the published stories that seem worth reprinting to me', plus the new one, 'Right-hand Man', which he had finally got off to Dudding for *Islands* before Christmas. He had been intending to make a collection rather than a selection, he explained, 'but in fact it's both'; and he would be willing to discuss dropping some stories to make a smaller volume if necessary, though would 'be sorry to'. He had, after all, been working at and refining it for fifteen years. 'Sorry about the condition of the manuscript', he apologised; 'It has been handled too much.'[26]

Brasch was impressed all over again when he reread them, particularly by 'The Champion' 'in which the tone is so beautifully judged that form, language and content fit perfectly'. Janet Paul, however, had not read them all yet. When she did—on holiday on d'Urville Island in February—she was not at all sure. It was all too depressing, she found: 'the final flavour of the whole collection is one of the author's distaste for people: of dour observation of tedious, limited people. And I am left with a sad, flat feeling.' Most of the stories told her nothing she didn't already know about 'intolerance & prejudice & fear', and the violence done to the horse at the end of 'The Losers' was 'so unbearably graphic . . . almost sadistically inflicted on the reader' that 'I wouldn't want to read the story again—even in proof'. She thought again, though (and added a 'p.s.' before posting it: 'I was feeling pretty depressed when I wrote this letter').[27] It was a critical response Gee's work would continue to attract, however, and which would irk him: that it was depressing (he didn't think so) and sometimes violent (yes it was, but life was violent too).

As for an artist, Brasch had already asked Gee if there was anyone in particular he preferred. They didn't want to have Hotere again, although Gee would have been happy to: he had thought Hotere's drawings for *The Loners*—delicate, wonkily geometric line drawings, like a geomorphologist's field sketches—'superb'. He mentioned Pat Hanly, Michael Smither and Toss Woollaston, or any of the 'half dozen other painters I admire' (but did not name), only he was not familiar with their drawings. His stories were more suburban than Middleton's, he noted, so of these Hanly or Smither might suit them best.[28]

Gee was developing some interest in New Zealand art—and in classical music—since meeting Margaretha. He would later regret that when Peter McLeavey, whom he met a few times in Wellington during his library school year, invited him back one day to his flat on The Terrace where he had just set up his dealer-gallery in his front room to see the Woollastons he had there, he had declined. In Auckland in the first months of 1969 when he was on his hunt for Nigel he had spent some of his idle time going to galleries, sending the catalogues down to Margaretha: seeing, among other things, 'McCahon's McCahon' (works from the artist's private collection) at Mollers Gallery, on as part of the Auckland Festival, and hoping to get to the Don Binney show opening at Barry Lett Galleries in April, though 'I know I'll want to buy one so it will be very frustrating.'[29]

Brasch preferred somebody younger, Binney perhaps, or Philip Trusttum or Barry Cleavin, the latter two of whom Gee had not heard ('my three years in Napier put me out of touch with new people', he apologised), John Drawbridge possibly or 'Fomison—he especially', he said to Paul. She proposed Jeffrey Harris. He was 'very gifted, very prolific, and developing strongly', Brasch informed Gee, who had not heard of him either, only 23 but with three major solo exhibitions already; and was married to Paul's daughter Joanna (herself an artist, but Gee, as Brasch remarked to Paul, was 'not Joanna's meat').[30] Despite having seen none of Harris's work Gee told Brasch in March that he was happy for them to go ahead.

In the middle of March he and Margaretha moved into the house they had finally bought, a 50-year-old bungalow in Mewburn Avenue, Mt Eden. Finding something had been more difficult than they had expected: they had imagined having a leisurely look around, but anything good was sold 'literally . . . overnight' and it became quickly apparent that they weren't going to get the 'large modern mansion' they had in mind. By the beginning of November they had looked at nearly a hundred places. Prices on the North Shore—their first choice—were rising by $35 a day.[31] These were economically tough times: Britain had become a full member of the EEC in 1973, and it was the year of the first oil shock. The effects of both on the New Zealand economy were severe.

13 Mewburn Ave would turn out to be another in a succession of unsatisfactory houses: it got hardly any sun, the kitchen was 'awkward', and there were noisy neighbours. For now, 'in spite of its peculiar drawbacks', they were very pleased with it.[32] The purchase price was $17,000, of which they were borrowing $11,500. 'Mortgaged up to the epiglottis', Gee observed to Dudding in January just after the papers had been signed, writing to thank him for picking up errors in 'Right-hand Man' which Dudding was putting in the Autumn *Islands*. 'The only reason I want to write a Carpetbaggers', he told Dudding, 'is so I can dish some of the dirt money out to you to keep it [*Islands*] going. (Well, not the only reason—I'd like to be able to afford whisky with and without the e.)'[33] They could still afford to buy wine, though, including that August subscribing to an offer from west Auckland vineyard Nobilos for five dozen bottles of red—a dozen each of the next five vintages—with their own label. They chose the Private Bin Dry Red for $65 rather than the 'classical vinera variety' at $95 (cheap drinking wine, not cellar wine) and for the label, unimaginatively, 'Maurice & Margaretha Gee'.[34] It was not

one of the labels that was peeled off and kept, among those a 1962 Coonawarra Estate Cabernet on the back of which was inscribed 'My oldest bottle of wine to date'.

He didn't go out west any more; or seldom. Driving out to Huapai to collect their wine from Nobilos in June 1974 may have prompted him and Margaretha to take the train to Henderson the following month, Gee coming over all 'weepy and nostalgic', Margaretha told her mother.[35] But Henderson was no longer his Auckland (while in another sense, it always would be). He regularly went over to the North Shore, where Len, in his retirement, spent his days at the racetrack or drinking whisky and playing snooker at his club. Lyndahl was still unhappy; still drinking heavily, at home on her own or down at the Mon Desir; and still writing. In 1973 she sent Frank Sargeson another long autobiographical manuscript, to which he responded with genuine praise and gentle advice: 'You don't need me to say it again, but here it is—everything you write is worth anybody's while, and I can't for my life imagine there's a thing you need to learn except perhaps a few clear ideas about how to "organise."' Write slowly, he told her, 'finishing off each page before you go on to the next', then rereading, 'cutting amplifying re-arranging'.[36] She continued to write, sad, bitter poems and fragments of prose, in the modern 'unit-flat' from which she could still see from the upstairs windows the much-loved, low sprawling kauri house on the beach on Hurstmere Road, its 'wild shrubs and roses; tall cabbage trees; rotting verandah', until it was demolished some time in 1973.[37]

They had Nigel living with them from the middle of this year, after rescuing him from the life he had been living with his mother. Hera had returned from Sydney to live in Whakatāne where her sister Grace and Dick now were, running the Commercial Hotel, at the end of 1972 or early in 1973, with Nigel and her three-year-old son Brett. (Maurice Walch was not with them.) Nigel, thirteen now, was enrolled at Trident High School, a new school—like Avondale College in 1945—tough and predominantly Māori. He was tough himself but he took frequent beatings there. At home he looked after Brett, while Hera's drinking, her instability, her descent into alcohol-induced violence and poor health (physical and mental) continued. Periodically Grace or Dick would come and take her sons back to the hotel to stay for a while until Hera came to retrieve them. On other nights Nigel would pick Brett up and walk to the police station where they would be given a cell to sleep in for the night and taken home the next morning; the police came to know them well.

Probably Dick Dorset, or perhaps Grace, let the Gees know where Hera and Nigel were and what was going on. It was after a fight in which not only Hera and Grace but also Nigel was involved that Len got into his Holden Torana and drove down to Whakatāne to get him. At a family conference Hera was persuaded to let Nigel go. He lived with Len and Lyndahl in the townhouse in Gibbons Road for the remainder of his teenage years and his early twenties, attending Takapuna Grammar for three. His father took him along to enrol him on his first day, on which he was caned before the end of his first lesson after he turned around and thumped the boy behind him who had been quietly taunting him, 'Abo, Abo'. Takapuna Grammar was a whiter school than Trident High. Hera had returned to Sydney, where Nigel went regularly to visit her in his holidays, always dreading doing so.

It was only much later that Gee would learn something of the life he had had with her since they had disappeared there in 1968: the frequent moves; the fear that would descend on him when he saw her get out the sherry bottle, knowing that just two glasses would turn her into another person, not his loving, beautiful, smart, capable mother—like a switch being flipped; the flat filling up with her also-alcoholic friends; 'lots of crazy days and crazy nights'.[38]

Maurice and Nigel saw each other in Auckland, of course; but Nigel did not feel part of Maurice and Margaretha's life. They were two separate families, it seemed to him.

'Auckland okay, job still lousy', Gee wrote to Dudding on 20 May. He was appreciating Auckland 'for the people it allows us to see'—not that that was many. He had seen a bit of Maurice Shadbolt (four years separated now from Gill and in the process in 1973 of destroying his second marriage) and of Sargeson, and Bill Pearson once or twice. 'None of them see each other so I must be moving fairly cunningly', he wrote, perhaps (or possibly not fully) aware of the complicated, strained relationships that existed between these three in this period (the continuing enmity between Shadbolt and Sargeson going back to the 1950s; Shadbolt's towards Pearson for an uncomplimentary review of *The New Zealanders* in 1963; Sargeson's private, declared but unreturned romantic feelings for Pearson, and the latter's defensive, offended reaction).[39] Sargeson, a near neighbour in Takapuna, after the Gees moved to Mt Eden visited them several times at Mewburn Avenue, seemingly fascinated by the family, with Margaretha feeding Abigail. He was, Gee felt, always very interested in the detail of domestic life.[40]

'P.S. Monday. Brasch is dead', he added to this letter the next day. Brasch had died on that Sunday, from what he had described to Gee two weeks earlier as 'a stomach complaint called Hodgkins' Disease': cancer of the blood.[41] Few people had known that he was ill; fewer still how seriously. 'This hits me harder than Baxter's death' (which had happened in October the previous year), Gee told Dudding. 'I liked him best of the older writers', for his support and his courtesy and his generosity. He had become, he later said, his internal reader, 'took up residence in my head' and set the standard; he felt his death as 'a real bereavement'.[42] Dudding felt it as badly: 'I'm completely flattened', he replied five days later after a 'dismal depressing visit' to Dunedin for the funeral, a small, private one at which he was lonely and hated it. 'I feel I am without a tetherstone, a centrepoint, a point of reference or something.' Other than to Gee and Kevin Ireland he was 'refusing to write letters about it', he told the latter.[43]

Everything had stopped on Square & Circle for a month while Brasch had been in hospital in March. Three days before he died Paul had sent Gee two preliminary drawings by Jeffrey Harris for his opinion, both for 'The Widow' (the first story in the book; the first Brasch had published). The man (Phil), he responded, was 'excellent, his face has just the right combination of innocence and concern', but the aunt, Mae, he found 'too ravaged, and perhaps too fussily drawn. I see Mae as having a sort of ravaged prettiness, and if this is not in the story then I think the remnants of gaiety in her are. She's not as defeated as J.H. shows her—not the thirties, depression figure. It's booze, and a sort of openness and expectation that have done for her.' It was a personal history not a social one his story was meant to draw.

While he did not have 'unqualified liking' for the drawings, however, he was pleased with their overall impression 'of strength, and strong feeling', and for Harris to go ahead—if, that is, Paul still intended to go ahead with Square & Circle after Brasch's death.[44] She did, if she could.

He still needed a title, something he always had difficulty with, he had remarked to Brasch. Brasch suggested just 'Ten Stories' if Gee could think of nothing else, but he thought this was too plain and would rather find a collective title: 'The Childless Land', he wondered, from Dylan Thomas's 'Fern Hill', but perhaps its meaning there made it unsuitable. 'I guess it mustn't be The Losers & other stories, for various reasons', Dudding contributed when asked for help.[45] 'The Champion' was probably the best story, Gee thought (trusting Brasch's judgement); 'The Hole in the Window' the best title, but neither Brasch nor Paul liked this; 'Down in the World' the most apposite, but one of the weaker stories. His second choice was 'A Retired Life' (though he should perhaps have realised that from a publisher's point of view that was not a lot better than 'The Losers').

Then the manuscript went missing, to Gee's growing consternation. He did not have carbons of all of the stories, and had made revisions directly on the printed versions of several; the copies he had sent to Jeffrey Harris were his only other complete set. Paul had written to Brasch's lawyer and then to his literary executor about the original set in Brasch's possession; then to Stuart Strachan, archivist at the Hocken Library at the University of Otago where Brasch's papers had gone. It took Strachan two searches through the 23 boxes before he found the manuscript, and posted it to a defunct address for Blackwood and Janet Paul Ltd he had found in the Auckland phone book, from where it was sent to publishers Longman Paul, with whom there had been no connection since Pauls was sold to them in 1967. It made its way back to Paul in Wellington finally in October.

When the collection was eventually published it was with the title of the last story he wrote for it. He wrote the first draft of 'A Glorious Morning, Comrade' in his head on the tram going in to work one morning from Mt Eden: a short, sharp story featuring another bitter, cantankerous old man, Charles Pitt-Rimmer, retired lawyer, who makes a carefully planned escape one afternoon from the suffocating care of his two daughters, Mercy and Barb, champion bridge players and vegetarians who address him as 'daddums' and feed him avocado salad. It was another Hardinge story: Pitt-Rimmer takes the same walk down Bluff Hill as Gee had in the mornings to the library (and as Harry Pratt will in the next novel), although his escape is also an extended version of Mr Webb's along Takapuna beach pursued by his two spinster daughters in 'A Retired Life'. It is the most comic of Gee's portraits of bad- and sad-tempered old men. Pitt-Rimmer is almost likeable when, recaptured at the story's end, he writes on the last page of his library book: '*My daughters are keeping me prisoner. Help! I have not had a piece of meat for 20 years . . .*'.[46]

He didn't think it was worthy of *Islands*—'a trifle . . . knocked off in three nights, just as an exercise. It's got a sort of professional gloss and a few neat turns, but nothing more'—and sent it to Ian Cross, newly appointed editor at the *Listener*, where Dudding appreciated it when it came out in the 22 December issue: 'it's the sort of light relief I look for in our fiction every now and again'.[47]

16

Games of Choice

Friday 21 December 1973 was Gee's last day of work at the architecture library, a job that still had him feeling 'homicidal/suicidal by turns' after more than a year.[1] In October he had applied for the position of deputy librarian at the Auckland Teachers' College library, and he was to start in the new year. The job would have appealed not only as an escape, and because the librarian, whom he already knew, Roy Carroll, was young, energetic and friendly, but also because the appointee would be expected to be heavily involved in planning of the new joint library of the Auckland teachers' and secondary teachers' colleges which was scheduled for opening in April 1974, as part of a major redevelopment of the teachers' college campus. This was in Epsom, so the job was also closer to home.

He still had mixed feelings about Auckland: 'too big, too noisy etc., but there is plenty I like too—people, when they don't swarm too heavily, beaches, Mt Eden (a pleasant suburb) and the cosmopolitan feel that can be sampled now & then'.[2] But he and Margaretha didn't fancy bringing up their daughters, nor living themselves, in an asphalt jungle. Plans for a new Newton–Mt Roskill motorway which would cut a path through Mt Eden with the sacrifice of 400 houses were under public discussion in 1973; a Motorway Action Group had been formed.[3] (The job at Albany had appealed partly because it would be quiet out there.)

Nor were they finding they liked Auckland's climate—its 'damp heat and constant rain'.[4]

Over the next year the 'secret scheme'[5] of which he had written to Brasch evolved into what they came to call their 'five-year plan': when Abigail turned five—in 1977—Gee would give up full-time work and they would leave Auckland and move to Nelson 'or some similar place'.[6] With both the girls at school, Margaretha would be able to work, at least part- if not full-time. She had been doing some casual part-time work already, in the Boys' High School library in

Napier, and in Auckland at the Grafton branch of the Auckland Public Library and the local parents' centre. Now, she would go to work. Maurice would write.

Meanwhile, life in the suburban wasteland of Mt Eden went pleasantly and uneventfully on, until one morning at breakfast Emily asked why Abigail had two plates of porridge while she only had one. There were sometimes two Abigails too. The doctor reassured them that it was probably just tiredness, but a second opinion and a visit to an eye specialist a few months later confirmed that she had double vision, requiring an alarming-sounding (though for the surgeon straightforward) operation, and glasses thereafter. Otherwise, as Gee had told Dudding, 'Family thrives'.[7]

He did not feel part of a literary family in Auckland, not as he had in Wellington in the 1950s; but not isolated like he had been in Rotorua (lost, there) or in the provincial wasteland of Hawke's Bay. He was pleased when Bob and his family moved back to Auckland early in 1974, to live at Torbay. Dudding, mind you, was even less sociable by nature than Gee. A small party he held in August when Colin Crawford, one of the Cheyne Gardens expatriate circle of London days, was visiting was an exception; Cushla Stones, Jocelyn Strewe and Don Terris were among other old Auckland faces there.

At the end of 1973 when an Auckland branch of PEN was formed Gee had agreed to be the treasurer, with president Maurice Shadbolt and secretary Karl Stead. He had been involved in PEN before in Wellington when he had been elected onto the national executive in 1967, reluctantly. It was not something he enjoyed—he was not a committee man—but he was prepared to do his bit if asked.

PEN in 1973 had awarded *In My Father's Den* its Hubert Church award for the previous year—'a sort of mini Booker prize', Gee had explained to Faber, though minuscule better described the $200 prize money compared to the £21,000, recently established Booker. It was a pity too that the Literary Fund gave it no publicity, which might have helped sell copies.[8] In May 1974 he learned that it had also won him the Literary Fund's $500 Award for Achievement for 1973 (oddly, the novel having come out in 1972; and he only found out when he read it in the *New Zealand Herald*, the Literary Fund not sending him a letter until few days later). This was welcome recognition when he had been disappointed after all with the novel's popular reception. It had received positive reviews, it 'had the aspects of a thriller and it had violence. But it didn't seem to light the reading public', he would remark a few years later.[9]

He sent his new novel, *Games of Choice* (a good title, he thought, supplied by Margaretha), to Faber and Faber at the end of July—letting his agents Winant, Towers know not until a year or more later that he was now dealing directly with Faber—and received an enthusiastic response back in October, offering an advance of £200 and the usual terms. By the time he returned his signed contract a month later they were already copy-editing (no, he insisted, it was not necessary to explain 'bach'). They were not to send page proofs, however, until September the following year, with publication pencilled in for May the next.

Before then his short story collection, *A Glorious Morning, Comrade*, was published finally, in November 1975, not by Square & Circle but by Auckland University Press. Dudding had offered to approach the press's editor Dennis McEldowney on Gee's behalf late in 1973 when Square & Circle was seeming like a lost cause, but Gee had told him then that he wanted to see things through there 'as a sort of last salute to Charles' (although he agreed that the university press would be a better choice).[10] With the manuscript at last recovered and the drawings completed, Janet Paul applied in 1974 for a Literary Fund grant, requesting $1000 for a print run of 1000 (100 cloth-bound, the rest paper). The committee recommended a grant of $300, for which its new chairman, C.K. Stead, apologised, but they had so little money to give out this year, he explained, and $1000 represented a very large subsidy for what 'looked rather like a half-way point between ordinary publication and the circulation of a private edition'.[11] With the committee's encouragement she re-applied, this time for $700, but with the same result, which was not enough to enable her to publish without personal loss. It spelled the end of Square & Circle, which was formally wound up the following year.

Auckland University Press's own application to the Literary Fund (for $618.62), for a hardback and paperback edition but with no illustrations, was treated more favourably and McEldowney was at work on the manuscript in the new year: 'Not that Maurice Gee requires much copy-editing', he noted in his diary: 'A very meticulous writer with only an occasional blind spot, like "occured".' Meticulous himself, he was horrified when he discovered when he was collating the page proofs a few months later a mistake: the misspelt 'Nuie' in 'The Champion' ('*twice*') that had gone unnoticed, by Brasch, by Gee and now by himself, since the story's first appearance in *Landfall*—'a cautionary tale'.[12] For the cover Roger Horrocks of the English Department, newly on the press committee, suggested Ian Scott's *Bay Light* (1966), one of the artist's several Auckland suburban paintings from that year which combined his pop art style and surrealist eye—here placing the typical suburban weatherboard house improbably high above a wild west coast beach. The large (1.7 x 1.5 metre) painting was photographed propped up on concrete blocks outside Scott's Henderson house, with the wall of the house mirroring the weatherboards in the painting and his bare feet visible beneath it: '[a] glorious surrealistic effect', noted McEldowney. Gee, however (to his later regret), vetoed Wystan Curnow's suggestion that they use the photograph uncropped, worrying that 'it would mislead the reader into supposing his style was experimental'.[13]

The poor production values of the volume were only a small disappointment. He was just pleased to have it out at last.

He dedicated *A Glorious Morning, Comrade* to Nigel, 'The Losers' 'also for Lyndahl Gee'. It was to win him in June 1976 the $1000 fiction prize (jointly with Ted Middleton's *Selected Stories*) in the inaugural New Zealand Book Awards—inconveniently, McEldowney lamented, just when a surprise order from London for 100 copies had put the paperback out of print and with a reprint (of another 1000) not due for another month. Award notwithstanding—and largely admiring reviews ('gripping and troubling fables for our times', Kevin Cunningham described them in the Christchurch *Press*)—sales of this were 'not spectacular' (but of short stories they seldom were).[14]

A new story, 'Buried Treasure, Old Bones', which he entered, unsuccessfully yet again, for the Katherine Mansfield award and which was published in the Spring 1975 *Islands*—about a 42-year-old teacher drawn uncomfortably back into her memories by an encounter with an old primary school classmate; familiar territory, though there is no curmudgeonly old man here and the story has a distinctly contemporary feel—was the last he was to write for fifteen years. This was not, however, because he was disillusioned. Rather, he was now more determinedly focused on the novel.

He returned the page proofs of *Games of Choice* promptly in mid-October: a short novel again, but which had taken him four difficult and distracted years to write. He had finally sent it away 'not happy with it',[15] but feeling that there was nothing more he could do with it save put it in a drawer. He was pleased with it now, though. The provincial town setting is Hardinge again, in its topographical detail undisguisedly Napier (Gee's fictional town is named, like Napier and nearby Hastings, after a British army officer and Indian viceroy); the house lived in by its unhappy Pratt family is Maurice and Margaretha's in France Road. Kingsley Pratt is a bookseller in middle age and a disappointed marriage which, by the end of the three days of the novel's present time, will be over. He loses his wife, Alison, to her lover, Bart, a pompous local historian whom Kingsley regards with superior and largely deserved contempt—he affects a faux English style, with 'toothbrush moustache, corduroy jacket, paisley cravat'. ('Perhaps the one misfortune', he observes in his address to the local historical society on 'The Street Names of Hardinge', 'was that the city's pattern of growth had made Emerson the main street rather than Browning or Tennyson or Thackeray.')[16] In marrying Kingsley, Alison has married beneath herself—her father was a surgeon, his a carpenter—attracted by his articulate talk and the romantic allure of his literary aspirations. Disillusionment has turned her, to Kingsley's eye, into 'this cool private malicious person' who wears the scar sustained in a car accident while he was driving as a badge of honour or revenge.[17]

Their son Malcolm, a blithely confident but limited and cruel-minded seventeen-year-old, announces on Christmas morning, to his parents' dismay, that he has decided to join the army. On Boxing Day—in the novel's most memorably shocking but also comic scene—he casually stabs his mother's beloved cat Yehudi to death with a garden fork. Their lovely daughter Miranda, in her first year at university, is having a relationship with her older, physically unattractive (and slightly preposterously named) history tutor Philip Armbruster, whose superior, academic earnestness, like Bart Somers' amateur version, also attracts Kingsley's disdain. (The son and daughter, and the novel's opening scene, resemble those in the Takapuna novel Gee had begun and abandoned in Dunedin in 1964.) Kingsley's father Harry lives resentfully in a converted shed at the bottom of the garden ('Journey's End', Alison has thoughtlessly—or perhaps not—named it), from which he makes furtive, mischievous forays into the house when there is no one around, leaving tell-tale signs of his presence in the bathroom. He smells 'of clothes worn too long, and tobacco, and something unidentifiable that had an odour of mutton fat': a 'tough and limited old man', part Harry Gee, a Crassin-like character, but not a wholly unlikeable one (his disoriented stumble down the hill into town after he witnesses Miranda and Armbruster's lovemaking, losing all sense of himself and who he has been—'He could not remember the name of anyone he knew'—is the novel's most affecting scene).[18]

There are other Gee and Chapple stories here too: Kingsley's sentimental, Labour-voting, literary-inclined mother Dora (she writes Lyndahl's 'Tiger Town'); Dora and Harry's 'moonlight flit'[19] from a smoky tin shack during the Depression; Harry's brother Lennie's boxing career, bridge-building in Katikati, diving for sunken jarrah; and Kingsley's—and his author's—terror of large dogs. (Invited to dinner by a local bookseller not long after he arrived in Napier, Gee had sat rigid with fear when he was left alone in the living room for half an hour with his hosts' Doberman Pinscher.)

'Kingsley Pratt is not me, though he gets close in a number of ways I'm not going to think too closely about', Gee told his editors at Faber; not his circumstances, nor his family life 'thank God. But his backward-looking stance is mine'.[20] Kingsley is intensely self-aware, like Paul Prior observing and alternately congratulating or—more often—criticising himself, as he looks back at a life he sees marked by guilt, 'cruelty and shame'. (Like, later, Jack Skeat: 'I've always had myself watching me.')[21] He is by nature solitary: 'Relationships seemed to set him on edge or disappoint him. He was happier alone, a meandering consciousness—a green thought.' But Kingsley's mind is his trouble: he has, he knows, 'a shallow tricky mind', and his mastery at evasion and at drifting about in the alternate possibilities of his past (this is the 'game of choices') leaves him with no solidity or sense of identity, 'a shifting centre. He wished his mind would be still.' In his both self-awareness and lack of awareness, he finds himself 'disturbed by a sense of having no role, of being, almost, outside common nature' (sounding now like the twenty-something-year-old Moss Gee).

'You're a weird person, Kingsley', remarks one character. 'I can't seem to focus on you.'[22]

For all Kingsley's brooding introspection, *Games of Choice* was a brittle, acerbic, and often funny novel, a black suburban comedy; 'Whose hideous invention was the family?' he asks, encapsulating both its subject and tone. But in losing his (though that, he reflects, 'was unremarkable, the common experience. But how had he got this far without a friend?'), he seems to have reached by the novel's end an understanding with himself and of his past, and a *modus vivendi* with his father.[23] It bothered Gee that most reviewers would find the novel pessimistic, pleased him that at least one found it funny. '[A]ll sorts of grim and dreadful happen', that was true, but surely it was optimistic, he told an interviewer after it came out, 'that at the age of forty-five someone can begin to see himself for what he is, that the things which happen to him now are likely to be of *his* choosing, rather than . . . He's out of his trap'.[24]

Gee could call himself now 'an established but moderate selling author'.[25] He had written four 'well-made small novels' and received one or two awards. His short stories had been collected and were beginning to be anthologised; not only 'The Losers', although it was this one that had been chosen for an anthology of New Zealand short stories in German published by Horst Erdmann Verlag in 1972—the volume's reviewer in *Islands* (University of Otago German professor E.W. Herd) finding especially good examples here of the difficulties of translation ('No translator can hope to catch the full flavour of "you miserable cow" or even to find an equivalent expression for "I'm getting the bum's rush"', though 'Maurice Gee's translator should have guessed that "Song and Dance" was one horse, not two').[26] 'A Retired Life' and 'Right-hand Man' were included by Vincent O'Sullivan in the third volume in the Oxford *New Zealand Short Stories* series which came out in 1975, and 'Eleventh Holiday' and 'A Glorious Morning, Comrade' by his old boss Phoebe Meikle for a Longman Paul anthology for secondary school students (about which she had first approached him in 1974 although the volume was not to appear until two years later). 'The Losers', meanwhile, continuing its vigorous independent life had been adapted for radio broadcast for a New Zealand short story series (six by Katherine Mansfield, the rest by Gee, Shadbolt, Janet Frame, James Courage and A.P. Gaskell) which ran on the National Programme in September–October 1974.

But he knew, despite what he had told his mother, that he was capable of more; and he knew what that was going to be.

A falling-out between Margaretha and a neighbour resulted in the five-year plan becoming midway through 1975 a three-year plan: by the end of May they had decided that they would leave Auckland for Nelson at the end of the year. Hence, when he was approached that month about joining the international writing programme at the

University of Iowa for four months from September (the offer was for a return airfare, $US600 a month and no obligation other than to write) he declined to be nominated.[27] He handed in his resignation at the teachers' college in mid-September, immediately they had signed an agreement for the sale of their house.

It was a brave thing to do, to give up work and try to live by writing, and a rare thing to do. 'I envy his courage', McEldowney recorded in his diary (after having taken copies of *A Glorious Morning, Comrade* straight off the press and round to him at the teachers' college one afternoon).[28] But he was not doing it recklessly: he made preparations. Over the previous spring and summer he had written a children's novel, and had it finished by the end of May. There were mixed motives behind this. He had young children himself—Emily was just reaching reading age—and he wanted to write something for them. He was also broadening his range, and children's books as a rule sold better than adult ones. He had been asked by the editor of School Publications in October 1974 to contribute a piece on his own childhood reading for *Education* magazine, as one of a series in which writers discussed favourite or formative books or authors: he wrote about Zane Grey.[29] It was not Zane Grey, however, he took as his model for his own but Alan Garner's *The Weirdstone of Brisingamen*, which a colleague at the teachers' college library had recommended to him. He liked the mix of the familiar, natural world and the supernatural, and of a children's story in which bad things might happen—as they did in children's actual lives—and not everything necessarily turned out well, in which there was challenge and danger and real risk. He liked the idea of setting such a story in Auckland (as Garner's was set among the places of his native Cheshire).

Walking to work one grey morning and looking up to see Mount Eden loom into view from behind a bank of thick misty rain, then sink down behind the houses again as he drew closer, gave him the start of his own, which featured red-headed twins—Rachel and Theo—with telepathic powers. His twins' weirdstones are river pebbles, given to them by a mysterious, kindly stranger, Mr Jones, which bestow on them the power, which they must learn how to access (Rachel proves better at this than Theo), to defeat the forces of evil, giant worm-like creatures, the Smiths, who live deep underneath Auckland's volcanic cones and are preparing to destroy the world. He had great fun writing it.

He sent 'The War of the Smiths and the Joneses' (a poor title for a children's book, he knew) to Faber in May but the response (from several readers) was not encouraging. The setting was vivid and the story 'ingenious and exciting', but not entirely credible and the ending bleak, the children's editor reported.[30] (That the twins who would save the world must have red hair was also a little whimsical, she thought; but of course they had to because Emily and Abigail did.) They suggested he try Gollancz, who had an interest in children's science fiction, or Collins. He sent it instead to Hodder and Stoughton, whose New Zealand editor was more enthusiastic ('I never did like Lake Pupuke', he divulged, 'and I must confess to feeling quite different about the harbour bridge going home that night!'), but the advice from London was that it was much too long and the dialogue unconvincing, and it would need major rewriting.[31]

He may have found a children's fantasy story quicker and easier to write than an adult novel, but he would not find it easy to get it published.

A more lucrative and reliable source of potential writing income was television. This was new territory not only for Gee. Locally made television drama had scarcely existed in the 1960s, when he had had his first set in the Rossmore Crescent bedsit for Nigel, and was just beginning to appear in the early 70s, notably with the gritty timber-town drama *Pukemanu*. The advent now of two channels—the existing single channel restyled as Television One in April 1975, and Television Two (soon to be renamed South Pacific Television) launched in July—was about to usher in what would come to be recognised as its golden age. The country's first soap opera, *Close to Home*—*Coronation Street* in Seatoun—began screening in May, written by Michael Noonan. Gee had heard, from Noonan among others, that they were looking to recruit a team of scriptwriters. (Alex Guyan, another old Dunedin friend, was among those who were already signed up.) They sent him a scene breakdown for a trial script, for three scenes, for a fee of $50 in May. It would mean that he would have to watch the series, about which he was not enthusiastic (the Gees had bought a TV set only in November, mainly to give Margaretha something to do in the evenings while Gee was writing), but if he could bear that, and if he was good enough to get a regular commission, it would keep them at least in food in Nelson.

It was not his first approach from or to television, in fact. In 1974 a young Christchurch director, Peter Muxlow, had contacted him, interested in making a film of 'The Losers', having inquired from Robin Dudding about the rights late the previous year. In May 1975, the same month he received his brief for *Close to Home*, Gee also signed a contract with TV One for 'The Losers', accepting a fee of $250—which was small, he had found out from other writers, and he queried it only, he explained apologetically to Muxlow, because '[w]e're on the point of burning our bridges . . . so cash becomes very important.'[32] It was still several times as much as a publisher would pay for a story.

He sent his trial *Close to Home* script back in June, 'very very anxious' that they liked it[33] because by this time he had become determined that he was going to give up 'proper' work altogether and support his family with his pen.

He also applied for the Literary Fund Scholarship in Letters. When he had first inquired about doing so in May this had been worth $4000. By the time applications were due in September it was worth $6000, with a rumoured possibility of an extension for a second year, thanks to a large increase in the Fund's annual grant allocation from a new, Labour government (the same government that had also established in 1973 the public lending right scheme for which PEN had been campaigning). His intention, he explained in his application, was to write a novel based on his grandfather.

They left Auckland at the beginning of November, a week after the house sale went through. Gee drove down, stopping for a night in Taupō and another in Picton after a late-night ferry. It was a noisy, nerve-racking trip. They had bought a new car five weeks earlier (selling the VW Variant, purchased from art collector Warwick Brown, that had replaced the Austin), a 1962 Datsun Bluebird. It was another in a succession of troublesome vehicles: the starter motor gave up in Picton and he had to call the AA. '[C]ars and I don't seem to be on the same wave-length', he remarked to his mother.[34] (In truth he hated cars, and hated driving.) Margaretha and the girls flew down. They had been collecting house-for-sale advertisements all year, for properties in Nelson and Golden Bay, but decided to leave looking properly until they got there. For the time being they had a place to stay at the home of Margaretha's friend Ivy Brett in Māpua while Mrs Brett was away for two weeks visiting her daughter overseas. When she returned they moved into apple pickers' accommodation on the orchard next door.

They started Emily at tiny Māpua School, and with three-year-old Abigail (unhappily) in tow went house-hunting. Prices were comparable with Auckland's but there was plenty on the market: they found something after two weeks, the asking price $21,500, of which they paid $17,000 in cash, taking out a three-year mortgage (guaranteed by Len) for the rest. 'Money tight', Gee wrote to Dudding (sending him a copy of the children's novel for his opinion). 'I may have to pick apples. Everything now depends on the Lit. Fund'; to which Dudding replied with a discreet offer of help: 'if you ever get really stuck financially—can always manage a quiet (very quiet) advance payment on the next couple of years' Gee stories in ISLANDS. Seriously.' (He sent, meanwhile, what Gee worried was an 'excessively generous' cheque for his last one—some of which Gee spent on a gift subscription to *Islands* for Lyndahl.)[35] They were to move in at the end of the month.

'Well ma,' he wrote to his mother, 'we're happy & settled and now it remains only to write novels.'[36]

17

Nelson

And so it was to Nelson he went to put into practice his 'secret scheme': a small town with orchards and a creek. Or rather, a river. Nelson's waterways were not deep, green, slow-moving tidal creeks through which eels slid invisibly, but clear, fast-flowing mountain rivers and streams. Nelson had appealed for a number of reasons, not only Margaretha's connection there. It had beaches handy, hills and mountains. It was small and quiet and slow, but not stuffy like Napier. They had been thinking for a year or two that this was where they would like eventually to end up—of buying some land in Nelson, Golden Bay or perhaps Marlborough to which they would retire. It was where Paul Prior had retreated to write the story of Celia Inverarity, 'in a house by the sea in Nelson Province'.[1]

It was the kind of place where one might go to set up a commune, as Robin Dudding's friend Michael Beveridge had been planning to do, hoping to persuade Dudding and family to join him (instead, however, he opened a second-hand book and record shop). It attracted 'arty-crafty' people:[2] potteries abounded. The Gees thought of themselves not as having moved down the social ladder (although of the economic one that was true) but as taking a step sideways, to the margin of the mainstream. This did not, however, mean that they were going 'alternative': Maurice was 'a city person', Margaretha would observe a few years later, 'and dislikes most do-it-yourself tasks'.[3] They did both vote Values at the 'disastrous'[4] election of November 1975, at which the Robert Muldoon-led National Party decisively ousted the third Labour government after the campaign remembered for its Hanna-Barbera 'Dancing Cossacks' television advertisement—in the first election held after the introducton of colour TV. (The dog that bites Kingsley Pratt in *Games of Choice*—an Alsatian 'as large as a Shetland pony'[5]—is called Muldoon.) They joined the Values Party—leftist and environmentalist—in Nelson, although attending party barbecues would be the extent of Maurice's active involvement.

When Margaretha roasted and ground up barley to make 'coffee' in these early Nelson years, though, this was not a lifestyle choice but because they could not afford the real thing. One could also live more cheaply in Nelson than in Auckland or Wellington.

The house they bought—home for the next thirteen years—was not at all the 'old style place' on a good-sized flat section they had been hoping to find. Those they couldn't afford. It was a three-bedroomed, 1950s, tile-roofed, stucco-clad bungalow—'stucco stodge', they called it[6]—in Cleveland Terrace on the south-east side of the city. It was solid (built by the builder-husband of the vendor), and comfortable enough inside 'if a bit cramped',[7] but with a large basement space underneath where they could put in another room or two: a guest bedroom or playroom, a study for Maurice. Its attraction was its spectacular site and view. Cleveland Terrace wound steeply up from Nile Street at the start of the Maitai Valley. The house (number 125) sat on a plateau halfway down a largish—3/8-acre—but mostly very steep section which dropped away precipitously to the Maitai River below. Standing on the front lawn, one could lob a stone all the way down into the river (a feat Gee slightly exaggerated when he wrote to a friend in Auckland, Simon Cauchi, that if he threw anything out the front window it would end up in the Maitai; 'but what sort of things do you throw out of the window?', Cauchi wrote back).[8] It looked out over the glasshouses of the Italian tomato growers in The Wood, over the city and across Tasman Bay to the mountains beyond; behind to the grass-covered hills above the Maitai Valley. They became enthusiastic hill-walkers (the girls at first less so), over time climbing most of the skyline from Mt Duppa to the Richmond Range—hills with names which sounded as if they came from a children's book: Gun Mountain, Saddle Hill, Little Twin, The Doubles, Wooded Peak, Fringed Hill. They became connoisseurs of the region's rivers—the Maitai, the Roding, the Wairoa, the Lee—and their picnic spots and swimming holes: Girlie's Hole, Buck's Hole, Sunday Hole, and the Moki right below the house. They invented a family game of river-walking: wading and boulder-hopping as far upstream as you could go.

The section was overgrown with trees: three plums, a nectarine, a peach, apple, two lemon trees, two loquats, plus a grape vine and 'non-fruit trees of every description'.[9] Nigel and a friend, down for a week in December just after he had sat (and failed) his School Certificate exams, helped Gee top the macrocarpas that were obscuring the view.

There were birds in abundance: a family of quails; tui and bellbirds in the flax flowers; wood pigeons that ate all their plums, 'huge fat birds that sound like threshing machines when they fly'—Gee counted seventeen one day.[10] They acquired two kittens, despite Gee's misgivings: he did not love cats, possibly because he was fond of birds and lizards (spiders too). They were named Eustace and Amaryllis after the fairies that lived on the Maitai in the stories he told the girls (but were usually known as Boy and Girl). (Some time later they also acquired a dog, Peppy—a corgi-dachshund cross.)

The whole family had fallen sick before the end of the year—colds, mumps, back trouble (Margaretha's), while 'your protege', she told Dudding, 'has been jumpy, tense, irritated, has had constant hay fever'[11]—but they were happy to be there. He would admit to Dudding six months later that 'I . . . sometimes feel a hell of a long way from everything'. He looked forward to each new *Islands* turning up in the letterbox: 'these things are important out here in the provinces'.[12] And leaving Auckland when he did he had missed seeing Kevin Ireland, who was over for six weeks in the new year (and talking of moving back for good), 'one of half a dozen old friends I'd go a long way to see'.[13] (For the *Listener* later this year Ireland wrote a nostalgic and romantic account of the Wellington literary-bohemian 1950s days.)[14] But he had no regrets. 'I feel very settled here', he had written to his mother in December, 'and feel that I've got a very good chance of establishing some sort of style & view of life that will see me through the next 30 years.'[15]

While he waited for news from the Literary Fund he set about building a study under the house. It took him several weeks, and advice from Len, to lay the floor, frame and gib the walls and hang a sliding door. This used up the $400 he had budgeted for the job and converting the rest of the space—a much larger project—would wait another year. It was not much more than two metres square, with the base of the chimney forming one wall. He placed a desk under the one small window in the outside wall. 'Tell dad', he wrote to Lyndahl with satisfaction when he had almost finished, 'a good deal of the knack of carpentry must have rubbed off on me.'[16] (His brother Aynsley would have disagreed.) They developed a 'stamp chart', pinned to the kitchen wall, by which Margaretha could communicate with him when he was working. One stamp meant he had a phone call, two a visitor, three she had made him a cup of tea, four there was important mail; five meant an emergency, running on the spot that she was going out. (It didn't work so well in reverse: when Yvonne du Fresne was visiting once he had managed to lock himself in and was 'beating steadily on the floor under our unheeding feet' as she and Margaretha talked upstairs.)[17]

A less happy DIY task faced early on was digging out the blocked and impacted septic tank (the second septic tank story of his life, and not the last): a foul experience.

The Literary Fund committee made its decision on the scholarship on 8 December, but did not announce it until six weeks later. Gee was surprised not to have heard anything by Christmas, but had 'a good feeling about it', he told his mother, and 'somehow will be surprised if I don't get it this time'.[18] He rang them a couple of weeks later, worried by now, and was told confidentially that the scholarship was his. He told his mother of course (and Margaretha hers) straight away: 'good news of course'. It meant they could relax financially for a year; he wouldn't have to pick apples after all.[19] When he and Margaretha began working part-time in February in Mike Beveridge's Everyman book and record shop, which had opened just before Christmas (Gee helped move in the stock), sharing a two-hour shift two afternoons a week, it was more to meet people than because they needed the money.

They would have been able to relax, that is, if the Department of Internal Affairs had been a little more efficient about actually paying him the money. When he wrote to the Literary Fund in February asking after the first instalment (they had agreed to split the scholarship across two tax years) he was told that it had been delayed in the accounts branch. He didn't get the second cheque until the middle of May, after two letters, a telegram, a visit to their offices when he was in Wellington in April to do research for the novel, and a toll call. ('Speedier payment would help', he commented in his response to an Internal Affairs survey of writers about the Fund the following year.)[20]

He was planning, in fact, to write not one novel but three (the first only, needless to say, in the scholarship year): 'three linked novels covering the years 1880 to 1970', he had explained in his scholarship application. It was a plan he had been 'turning . . . over in my mind for several years'. The first novel would be based on the life of James Chapple, of whose career and achievements he had given the Literary Fund a brief précis: 'member of the Salvation Army, a Methodist minister, a Unitarian minister, and an evangelizing communist', pacifist and heretic, 'gifted orator', author, 'cricketer and the father of fifteen'. It was not, he emphasised, to be 'a fictional portrait of my grandfather but a novel . . . about a man in similar circumstances making a similar political and religious journey'. The second novel would take up the story of two of his daughters; the third 'a grandson who comes to manhood in the years after the second war'. The first, he further elaborated, 'might be described (loosely) as religious and political, the second as political, social and domestic. In the third the characters will interest themselves in commercial and financial matters, though not exclusively.'[21]

'Mr Gee's projected novel chronicle', Wellington's *Dominion* newspaper observed in an editorial commenting on his 'well deserved' scholarship win, 'should stimulate discussion and interest in what constitutes the New Zealand ethic'—which was probably a little more than he would have claimed to be aspiring to.[22]

This was what he had come to Nelson to do: the 'big novel' he had been waiting to write. He had been carrying the germ of it around with him for perhaps as many as twenty years: 'it was kind of a lump that existed at the back of my skull' (or as his fictional grandfather will put it more elegantly, 'an extra chamber in his mind').[23] His rich Chapple family history, he had long known, was a gift, an opportunity (as well as, in more private ways, a burden). And he knew that if he didn't do it now it might be too late: he might miss his chance, the material and motivation would fade. Orwell, he read later this year, had said that in most writers 'the creative impulse seems to last for about 15 years', which for the novelist would 'probably be between the ages of 30 and 45' (an observation he found 'very depressing').[24]

The Irish novelist Joyce Cary's 1940s trilogy—the final volume of which, *The Horse's Mouth*, he had first come across on the English syllabus at Auckland University College—was what he had in mind when he devised the work as a trilogy rather than the more conventional, unwieldy one-volume lump of a family saga, which he feared might become 'sloppy and shapeless' (not his style at all).[25]

He started work in mid-February, 'nervous as hell', he told Dudding, beginning by reading again his grandmother Florence's diaries and the reminiscences of her life as a home missionary's wife on the West Coast which she had written for him a few years before she died—in her eighties and feeling 'a bit out of plumb with age' like the bird bath outside the window at Lincoln Road.[26] He read again his mother's pieces of memoir and fictionalised memoir; he had her Chapple stories in his head. He asked her to send down his grandfather's two published books and his funeral service (written by himself). He already had his heavily annotated Bible, the unpublished manuscript of a third book, and his dozen or so small notebooks which he 'raided frequently' as he went along for 'quotes and little ideas and thoughts' (the published works by contrast he found were rather boring);[27] also a family scrapbook compiled by his aunt Bernice, whom he had asked about family history and memories back in 1969.

The novel would be set largely at Peacehaven in 1947, with 'raids on the past'; but he was 'not', he insisted to his mother, and would repeatedly insist, 'writing a novel about Grandpa. . . . I want to let this man develop in his own way & just use Grandpa's career etc as a kind of convenient reference and grab-bag.' His political and religious life would be very similar, but he would not, for example, have fifteen children, only twelve, and there would be 'no Dora figure . . . no King, no real Joyce or Flo, or for that matter Lyndahl or Aynsley', although characters with 'superficial similarities', and characters quite a lot more like 'Len and Dick and Holl'.[28] There would be a Bluey Morrow figure too, about whom he asked his mother now: the worried lapsed Catholic who used to come regularly for Sunday dinner when Moss and his brothers were small, and had made an appearance already in Gee's fiction in his first published story (as had James Chapple too): 'a good and generous man', Lyndahl remembered him, 'albeit a rather grubby man in a spotty blue suit', 'a lonely man seeking comfort from a family set up—he was very generous with you boys, and seemed to encourage you to be yourselves, as if he was still trying to escape the frustrations of his own childhood'.[29]

The family character he felt he wanted to draw closest to life, however, was Florence. Reading her reminiscences and diaries had left him 'in quite an emotional state . . . it brought her back so strongly'.[30] He was calling his central characters George and Edith Plumb, he told his mother: 'That's no pointer at Chapple although it may seem like it.' It was the 'fruit connection': Chapple–apple–plum; and a name he meant to suggest depth and straightness.[31]

He wanted to see again as well the memoir his aunt Dora Hagemeyer, still living in Carmel, had written, but she wouldn't send it. This novel would be 'rather different' from his previous ones, he had explained to her, written in the voice of Chapple's generation rather than his own. He was right to think that Dora would be 'fairly much out of sympathy' with his novels and stories: 'They're written in a rather grim manner, with what you would I think regard as an undue emphasis on behaviour of a squalid sort.'[32] And yet when she wrote to thank him for the copy of *A Glorious Morning, Comrade* he had sent her she complimented him: 'I now realize that you can really write Moss. You have a keen and almost uncanny perception of underlying motives and an ability and beauty of description', although there 'are times when your writing descends to the ordinary, the shocking and the vulgar'.[33] She withheld the memoir, even after Lyndahl asked on Maurice's behalf, because, although essentially a hagiographic portrait of her father, it had upset both her parents, with its frankness about the hardships of Florence's life as a young wife with a large family and a husband so singlemindedly devoted to his mission. It was for this reason she had never tried to get it published.

He had also written to Muriel Parker, Lyndahl's Jungian friend and her father's 'pupil', as she called herself. She replied to him at length about his grandfather's spiritual beliefs: how 'Religion to him was cognition; cognition of oneself, one's inner self.' 'He always used to tell me', she went on, 'that of Lyndahl's three sons, you were the one most likely to end up with a modern version of his ideas. He considered you the most intense, the most likely to have difficulty in finding yourself, the most likely to be at odds with your own self-nature. The direction your writing has taken'—its 'sordidness' (his word)—'would not surprise him at all.'[34]

Early in March when he went to Wellington to see the television people—at the new studios out at Avalon in Lower Hutt—to consult on the production of 'The Losers', he spent a few days in the Turnbull Library looking at newspaper reports of Chapple's sedition and heresy trials and researching doctrinal matters. At home, in his 'cell'[35] under the house, he wrote for four or five hours a day, in the morning (after Emily had gone to school) and sometimes part of the afternoon, with a discipline and routine his writing had not had before. Going downstairs each morning, across the dirt floor of the basement and up a step into his writing room, was going to work. It took hard thinking, this novel, but once he got into the flow of it it came well. 'And I felt great. I felt that I had come home, in a sense. I felt that at last I was doing what I was meant to be doing'.[36]

By the end of March he had written close to 40,000 words. 'It's coming out very dense, perhaps too much so,' he told Dudding, 'but

I've had the stuff so long it's like dipping into a barrel.' By mid-May he had done 70,000 words and he estimated was about two-thirds the way through.[37] Now, however, he found himself 'a bit stuck',[38] so put it aside for a while to do some carpentry around the house and some work in the garden—planting citrus, feijoa and a bougainvillea.

'Did I tell you', he had written to his mother the week before he started (he had), 'we like it here very much. I feel relaxed & at home—in touch with the town, on top of my work, pleased with my house & section, delighted with my family.'[39]

Games of Choice came out in London on 17 May (in New Zealand in July), with a 'lousy' cover, Gee once again thought.[40] So it was: inky blue with his name in red and the title, surrounded by a geometric pattern resembling a children's string game, in white edged with electric blue—it seemed to read 'Cakes of Choice'. The abstract design, his Faber editor had explained, was meant to represent 'the lines of conflict between the members of the family' and 'can also be seen as a distorted Christmas star'.[41] (He would always prefer figurative cover design.) Faber sent two short but 'splendid' reviews the next day, from the *Sunday Times* and the *Observer*—'two really influential London reviewing papers', Gee informed his mother—and more followed, although the *Times Literary Supplement* had reservations about his pared-back style ('interpretation follows observation so quickly that a sense of what it is that is being interpreted is often drowned out'), and Auberon Waugh in the *Evening Standard* was typically arch: 'Although the smelly, muddled old grandfather strikes me as a magnificent character,' he wrote in a review titled 'Poor old dad', 'I was not quite so happy with Kingsley. Perhaps it was just his name. One does *not*, even in New Zealand, call one's son Kingsley' (unless, that is, one is a Chapple). First week sales in Britain were around 600. Everyone liked Harry: Susannah Clapp in the *TLS* pictured him and Kingsley in domestic accommodation at the novel's end as 'a sort of Antipodean Steptoe and son'.[42]

In New Zealand too it was reviewed on the whole favourably, if with less verbal gusto, with Gee, as before, praised for the authenticity of setting ('a bland and brutish suburbia'), his precision of style and character ('A careful book, with a highly concentrated focus—all microcosm') and his craftsman's 'sureness of touch'. The *Otago Daily Times* reviewer thought it stopped 'just a little short of being a classic'.[43] The cat assassination, though, caused disquiet—not the first cat killing in New Zealand literature, as one reviewer noted, citing Barry Mitcalfe's recent 'Black Cat' and a Katherine Mansfield story ('Ole Underwood'); but curiously forgetting Sargeson's (very brutal) 'Sale Day'.[44] The discordant note came from Gordon McLauchlan in the *New Zealand Herald*, who, under the heading 'All in the dull Kiwi family', complained that the novel lacked 'significant events', that Kingsley was 'an introverted, ineffectual little guy', his children 'kinky', and that the characters spent most of the time boringly 'contemplating their own inertia, scrutinising their own anguish'. He regretted that Gee had gone back to 'the heavy introspection characteristic of much of New Zealand fiction'; he had preferred *In My Father's Den*.[45]

Gee was not one of those authors who professed not to read their reviews: favourable critical response mattered to him (at the least, he told the *Evening Post*, because it encouraged publishers and sold books).[46] More so, however, did the opinion of friends and of fellow writers whose literary judgement he respected. His letter was 'worth any dozen others I could get', he replied to Frank Sargeson, who told him he thought it 'a splendid affair! . . . your remarkablest of all achievements'.[47] His mother, however, to his regret but probably not surprise, found the characters—Miranda especially—and their 1970s ways 'a little shocking'. 'As for the old man being like Grandpa Gee', he acknowledged to her that there was a likeness but it was not intentional: 'I don't go about things in that way.' The bits of family story she found in his novels 'are just picked up and put in like bits of coloured glass'.[48]

He may have moved to a quiet provincial backwater town, and still regarded himself as 'a pretty anonymous figure in New Zealand writing' with 'no real following', but Gee's literary and, to a lesser extent, public profile was starting to rise. He made that modest comment late this year in an interview for the Nelson College creative writing magazine, in which he also commented on the change in his style—its increasing concision, for which the *Times Literary Supplement* had faulted him but was intended: 'What I'm going for these days', he explained, 'is closer and closer precision to make each word do as much as it can possibly do—to have no extraneous matter or padding'. (Hence his novels were short, he added, and his attraction 'I suppose, to the short story form'.)[49]

In June the whole family travelled to Wellington for the New

Zealand Book Awards, held at Harry Seresin's Settlement restaurant in Willis Street on the 22nd, the awards (his for *A Glorious Morning, Comrade*)—and cheques—presented by the minister for the arts. He 'hoped "never to work again"', he half-joked to a *Dominion* journalist afterwards.[50] Later that month he appeared on Fiona Kidman's 'Writing' programme on 1YC, the two-minute interview followed by a reading from *Games of Choice*. 'Unfortunately', he had warned his mother, it competes with *M*A*S*H* on TV 'so not many people will hear it'. Robin Dudding did and wrote to reassure him: 'I thought you said you were no good at that sort of thing. Bollocks. You weren't even nervous!'[51] In July the *Nelson Evening Mail* did a profile on him under the headline 'Writer finds solace over Nelson harbour', setting him in cosy and creative domestic harmony with 'a house with a view, an unhurried lifestyle and time to write'. He was working at the moment, he said, on 'something special'.[52] The following month he spoke at the Nelson Institute's 'Coffee and Books' coffee morning.

Games of Choice also earned Gee his first book launch; in fact two. There had been a kind of launch for *In My Father's Den* in 1972, when guests were invited to a combined Christmas party and to 'meet and greet Maurice Gee' at the Minerva Bookshop at the Auckland Art Gallery, jointly hosted with Oxford University Press (Faber's local agent). *Games of Choice* was launched at OUP's Wellington office in Ghuznee Street in August (again the whole family went up). Interviewed afterwards by the *Evening Post*, he explained that he was not in the business of writing bestsellers—formulaic constructions of violence, sex and romance—because 'I'm trying to make some explanation of life in New Zealand'; 'the softly-spoken, greying Gee', the reporter described him.[53] There was another launch three weeks later in Nelson at the ABC Bookshop, to which a hundred people came and which he found a 'trying affair' of 'stilted conversations' (though Margaretha, Emily and Abigail, more socially talented than he, enjoyed themselves).[54]

The following Saturday he did a long interview with Ian Wedde for the occasional arts magazine *Spleen*, which was published by experimental theatre group Red Mole. 'The interviewer was tired and spaced', Wedde's write-up began; 'Maurice Gee was obviously nervous and reticent: he frequently apologised for being either inarticulate or for not "having ideas"'; but on a hot September morning they both soon relaxed 'into a pleasant intensity'. Wedde recorded the interview on cassette tapes which already contained music—'The Mothers, The Poynter Sisters, other stuff'—and as he later played it back

> the music erupted from time to time through the spaces between Maurice Gee's quiet and sometimes almost inaudible talk. The effect wasn't a bad metaphor for the impression you got of the way this man works: on a thin crust below which Chaos enters its contenders in the Cosmic Lists: a sense of Evil Abroad, a sense of humour that accepts people as falling well short of Ideals they are not responsible for setting up anyway . . . a kind of music muffled sometimes by apprehension that the crust might cave in . . . **Spleen** had decided to adopt a somewhat circular line of enquiry: hoping eventually to spiral down (to play Dante to Gee's Virgil): **facilis est decensus avernus** [easy is the descent to the underworld] . . .

It was an ambling, wide-ranging interview in which Gee answered questions about what he wrote, why he wrote, and how. The family tried to live on $50 a week, he said, after mortgage repayments—enough to 'run a small car, have enough to eat, heat the house, enough warm clothes'—and were happy with their modest means of living. Occasional awards, fellowships and payments from the Authors' Fund ($700 this year) helped. But '[t]his is the way I see my life going on from now. I'm fairly determined not to get a job', at least a full-time one. 'I feel that these are the crucial years for me . . . certainly I'm more in control of the things I'm writing than I ever have been, and I don't want to waste any of this'. (He did quite like, he added, the idea of 'some kind of pension for writers'.)[55] Yes, it did bother—'sadden'—him that his new novel from Faber at $10.40 was expensive. But he was resigned to the fact that it was unlikely his readers would be the kinds of people who appeared in his books, and was grateful for '"the passionate few" who care about fiction'. He himself 'read fiction obsessively, all the time' (from the library: he could not afford to buy books anymore), including crime fiction (Chandler, Macdonald) and science fiction of the 'space fiction and bugeyed monsters' variety, and was an avid watcher of any science fiction on TV. Also and increasingly he read biographies.

Of his own writing, he agreed with Wedde that 'the old person seems to be a kind of King Charles' Head to me', but that was not because he had any special concern for the old: it was about aloneness, or alienation, his 'belief that we are all essentially lonely'. When asked further about obsession, and would he suffer if he didn't write, he replied that what obsessed him more and more was 'pain and cruelty, violent acts, and so on . . . to the point where . . . if it were unrelieved in the first instance by family life and the degree of communication that's there, and secondly by writing, I could see a situation in which I could possibly go over the edge'. Writing was 'a way of holding onto sanity'. About his current novel, he would not 'give too much of it away' except to explain that it was about his heretic, Presbyterian parson grandfather—a 'fictional creation' of, he stressed.

Were there areas that were *tabu* in his writing? 'Certainly in my experience a long and tortured relationship that I went through is something I can't look at', Gee replied. 'My adolescent agonies likewise . . .'. When Wedde then asked about *In My Father's Den* he was coy. 'To some extent . . . you see there are two brothers in the book, both of whom have problems which point in a certain direction—problems which were very real for me . . .'. It was as much as he was to say publicly on these subjects (other than surreptitiously, in his fiction) for a long time. Of the physical territory of that novel, however, as opposed to the psychological and emotional territory—moving the interview onto safer ground—'the magical territory . . . Henderson . . . that I think I probably will return to again': it 'has a life in a way no other place I've ever lived has'.

After the interview they had lunch, '*Then **Spleen**, the Gees and their two children drove down to the Old Folks' Hall*' to see a performance by Red Mole's White Rabbit Puppet Theatre (in which Wedde's wife was the lead).[56]

Accompanying the interview in *Spleen* was a review of *Games of Choice* by poet Russell Haley, a review which pleased Gee despite being a critical one. Its theme was Haley's impatience with the naturalism and unconscious restraint that remained the dominant mode of New Zealand fiction (Janet Frame being a notable and brilliant exception), and the limited, but important, extent to which Gee's transcended it: 'If I had not been able to detect a kind of dismay, a sort of bulging of the surface of Gee's tailored prose, I would not be writing this review.' In Sargeson, for another example—another of 'the best of our writers'—that disruptive bulging came from 'a hidden sexual charge'; 'in Gee it is an overwhelming sense that he can reach something numinous and atavistic when he deals imaginatively with place'. What interests Haley in Gee is his 'obsessive interest in a private place from which one can view, voyeuristically, the world': his work is full of dens, rooms (from which characters look outwards, like Cliff Poulson in 'A Retired Life'), thickets and groves, which lift it out of its tidiness. It 'is in this secret place that there is the tightest sexual tension in Gee's work. This is where the real imagination is functioning', here '[t]here is a more interesting, more powerful (because organic) imagination working in Gee below the level of the action, event, and characterisation.' 'I hope he does not raze *his* secret groves', he concluded. 'The pan-goat-man will have no place to hide and watch in a defoliated suburbia.'

Haley and Wedde were of a different generation from Gee. As poets they were part of a group—of sorts—influenced by the American Black Mountain school in particular (Robert Creeley, Charles Olsen). Their writing was experimental, international, interested in language as content as much as for what it had to say. In prose too there was a loosening of style and form, and a reaction to and expansion outwards from the earnest nationalist realism of a previous generation. The succession of *Landfall* by *Islands* had demonstrated the shift in the literary landscape, from the Brasch/Sargeson era at the tail end of which Gee had started writing and publishing to this postmodernish 1970s. Dudding had carried on *Landfall*, faithfully, much in the Brasch style, but *Islands* looked and felt different: more relaxed, casual, almost messy sometimes in its design, and Dudding was a more inclusive editor than his mentor. *Islands* though was still a place in which Gee's realist but threatening short fiction was at home; just as his carefully crafted, naturalist but disturbing fictions, and his aim to 'make some explanation of life in New Zealand', still interested the editors of *Freed* and *Spleen*. Thus Bill Manhire, when he was approached by James Bertram late in 1976 about doing a volume for the Oxford University Press 'New Zealand Writers and their Work' series, chose for his subject Gee. (By the time that was written and published, though, Gee was three more novels along.)

He had sent a progress report to the Literary Fund committee in July, informing them that he had written 90,000 words and expected to have a complete draft of around 110,000 done by mid-August—which he did, finishing it a few days before his 45th birthday. This was in addition to writing a script for *Close to Home*: TV One had found his trial script 'a bit academic' but had finally commissioned one from him in June.[57] After the launch of *Games of Choice* on the 23rd he went on to Auckland for a week with Emily, while Margaretha and Abigail stayed with her mother in Thorndon. They both experienced flying back into Nelson, above snow-capped mountains beneath cloudless skies, as a return to paradise; and Gee, he wrote to his mother, was now ready to 'make the big final push with the novel'. 'It is fiction', he had continued to assure her: 'I'm emphasising this now because I'm sure I'll be accused of writing about the family' (of which he already knew the dangers).[58] Perhaps he reiterated this because he felt his characters were becoming more like Chapples as he went along rather than less as he had expected ('the more I brood on it', he had written at the outset, 'the further the central figure gets away from [Grandpa]').[59]

He consulted Ray Grover on some Presbyterian details (Grover being not only the deputy Turnbull librarian but the son of a session clerk in the Presbyterian church): would a Presbyterian in private prayer go down on his knees, for example, and do they kneel in church? (probably, 50 years ago; and no, Ray replied); can a minister take a dying man who is not a Presbyterian into a church for repentence? (this for 'the deathbed conversion bit. The subject is a murderer': he can but he wouldn't); would it be heretical, or doctrinally unsound, for a Presbyterian to believe that he can achieve salvation by strength of faith and by works rather than by divine grace? (definitely half a century ago, and still to some extent); do Presbyterians rent pews?[60] Such little matters cleared up, he started typing his draft in October—on his mother's old typewriter which she had sent down to him (he had been shocked when he had investigated replacing his own at how expensive even second-hand ones were)—experiencing the usual final-draft 'ups and downs about it—thinking it's junk one day & a masterpiece the next. Whatever it is, it's different from my usual'. 'As usual', though, the title was 'likely to be a problem': he was thinking of calling it simply 'Plumb', he told her, although he knew she didn't like short titles (Margaretha didn't like it either).[61]

He finished the typing on 25 November. After a read-through and revisions he declared it finally finished a fortnight later, and put it away until after Christmas.

18

Making a Living

While 'Plumb' rested Gee got on with other things, not all of them literary. After Christmas (a picnic in the Wairoa Gorge) he installed a pool for the girls, a more pleasurable excavation task than last summer's septic tank; and on 12 January opened his first batch (six dozen bottles) of home brew, fearing the worst but it turned out to be 'very good—very light and dry'.[1]

Back in July he had responded with a tentative yes to a request from Robin Dudding for a contribution to a new series of 'Beginnings', of which his would be the first: 'small chapters of autobiography' in which writers told how they began writing.[2] It was a follow-up to the series Brasch had commissioned for *Landfall* between 1964 and 1966. Back then (in 1966) Gee had either 'refused or failed' Brasch's invitation.[3] He wrote his piece for Dudding in the weeks before Christmas after he had put the novel away, a task he had expected to be 'painful' proving to be quite fun, and asked his mother to read it before he sent it to Dudding in January, with typical hesitancy: 'I don't know whether this is the sort of thing you had in mind. It's not particularly well done and I'll have no objection if you don't want to use it'; 'Marvellous . . . they'll do me nicely', Dudding replied.[4]

He had woven his childhood and his family into his stories and novels but this was his first piece of straight autobiography—kind of. It was a fond, evocative, and carefully suggestive account of his Henderson boyhood—'the magical territory'—nicely described by Yvonne du Fresne: 'directly written & hilarious . . . I loved the sentence structure—like nice little arrows'.[5] 'Henderson Creek began at the dam and ended at Falls Park', it began.

> We walked on its ferny banks, red mats of willow hair gave under our feet. A naked man washed himself in a pool. His eyes did not blink. My mother turned us back, we felt her fear and asked over and over, 'Why Mum, why are we going?' We knew there was something we had not understood. That was up by the dam.

> The dam was half a dozen logs held together with rusty spikes. A tumble-down shed stood at the far side, with an iron wheel bedded in concrete. Someone had once made heel and toe plates there. It was a spooky place. Huge eels lived in pools on its lower side. On the far bank was a pit we could not see the bottom of. The man was a part of the place. He had black eyebrows and a black unshaven chin. My mother said perhaps he was a swagger. We knew what swaggers were. She had written a story about one. He had eaten scones in the kitchen, butter ran down his chin. He had threatened the cook (our mother) and Jim the foreman had punched him on the jaw.[6]

He wrote about Newington Road and school and neighbours; about Peacehaven; of the literary example of his mother and aunt and grandfather, and about the other kinds of stories: those his parents told about their early married years in the Depression, through which '[t]heir struggles and triumphs became a part of my history. . . . Some of it may not have happened. It all happened to me'; and his mother's about his grandfather, through which '[o]ver a period of ten or fifteen years his history became a part of my own.' And the moment his mother's exalted version of her father became tarnished for him, when he beat him for the first time at draughts and his grandfather told him that he had let him win: 'He tumbled a long way that day.' He wrote too of how a boy named Clyde, 'bounc[ing] up and down in his seat' ('Practising') at the desk next to him at Henderson School, 'discovered what I carried with me like a handicap of lead', his disgust at and denial, under the influence of his mother, of sex. And of the time he 'glimpsed sex and death' at Falls Park when he saw a drunken man dive into the creek and break his neck—in what would be the first of several tellings of this story.[7]

Dudding made some minor editorial suggestions, and asked for one or two clarifications: shouldn't that read his 'head and back floating' on the water rather than his 'head and chest', if the man appeared to be searching the bottom? (Gee had this right, though.) And 'he did die did he?' he asked (just out of curiosity), of the 'dying man' whose 'eyes were open, he stared at the sky. I knew that was not what he saw.' 'He died in the ambulance but no need to say so, I think', Gee replied. He knew the story carried more power told that way.[8]

'Memory', George Plumb writes, 'is an active thing'.[9]

Searching for photographs to illustrate the piece, and perhaps 'an evocative pix of Henderson' for the cover, Dudding came across one of Henderson creek (probably taken in the 1920s) which he sent to Gee: in fact, Gee told him, a photograph of the Falls Park pool, 'a real genuine lump of my past'; taken a bit later and '[o]ne of those kids swimming could be me'. He tacked it to the wall of his study.[10] It 'read okay—in its simple way', he remarked of the essay when *Islands* came out in April. (He hadn't read the stories in this issue yet, he added, 'but I see another cat gets killed. Someone will do a thesis one day on the killing of cats in NZ fiction.')[11]

After 'Beginnings' he had spent two weeks working on an adaptation of 'Right-hand Man'—which he didn't think was very good either[12]—and submitted it to both Television One and South Pacific Television, without success. Next he started a story for Emily, about a little girl called Caroline who wears glasses and in a junk shop finds a magic pair which allow her to see into another (endangered) world. Possibly he had no intention of getting it published at this stage. The girl was Caroline because Emily had been so taken with Margaretha's old school friend Caroline Brett who been visiting recently that she had decided she was going to change her name to Emily Caroline Gee.

Nelson came alive at Christmas, he found, with people on summer holidays and passing through, including some old friends of his own. Among them, Carl Freeman, who like Gee had at last found a settled life and was working in Geneva, stayed for three nights at New Year with his young Sicilian wife, Franca Rosati; and Ray Grover for a weekend the next month. Gee had already been over to see Ian Middleton, who, now totally blind, was living in the chosen remoteness of Parapara in Golden Bay. Towards the end of January Maurice Shadbolt and a friend passed through. 'Moss Gee is industrious', Shadbolt reported to Kevin Ireland, '—another novel finished—but seems on a financial razor edge . . . Otherwise I suspect he's in full flow, and we can expect something major . . . But above all, he's happy: and God knows Moss has hard earned a little happiness.'[13] 'I feel as if my batteries have been re-charged', Gee wrote to Shadbolt after his visit. 'Although it's an unequal pairing, you having done so much more than me, I think of us as running in harness.'[14]

When he had been asked at the Nelson Institute 'Coffee and Books' morning the previous August if he had been influenced by any other writers, he had replied: not stylistically, but his friendship with

Shadbolt had influenced him 'in some way, although not consciously. "He was at school with me and always seemed to be ahead of me. In some ways I think some of my books have been written to keep up with him."'[15] Numerically, it was true; although it was also true that *A Glorious Morning, Comrade* had beaten Shadbolt's latest novel (the second part of a planned trilogy) at the New Zealand Book Awards. Along with a handful of non-fiction and collaborative books and his journalism, Shadbolt had published nine works of fiction by now, including his own 'big novel', *Strangers and Journeys*. This was the 'long novel' he had embarked on at Te Marua in 1960 and abandoned in Dunedin three years later: in its final version a 600-page historical and generational saga and work of large, ambitious and earnest themes. It had won the Sir James Wattie Book of the Year award in 1973 but a mixed critical reception. To Ireland Shadbolt now wrote about Gee, with candour: 'He's the one New Zealand novelist I have envied, and always shall, for his exact eye; and for efficient craftsmanship. I've never written anything, by comparison, which hasn't been flawed by some perverse need to build hurdles over which I'm bound to tumble. I've been—until now—the professional in theory; he's the professional in the practice of our craft. He makes me feel like a dilettante.'[16]

When they saw each other Shadbolt also told Gee that he must 'come out of my ivory tower', advice Gee thought he should take.[17] Still, he would leave it to the last minute (until he thought it might be too late) to agree to go to the inaugural SPACLALS—South Pacific Association of Commonwealth Literature and Language Studies—conference at the University of Queensland in Brisbane in May, with Witi Ihimaera and Patricia Grace the other New Zealand writers invited. He enjoyed himself despite having to participate in a panel discussion.

He had already agreed to be nominated as PEN's second representative on the Literary Fund's Authors' Fund committee. When he flew up to Wellington for the day for his first meeting in February he also went out to Avalon for a screening of Peter Muxlow's just-completed film of 'The Losers'—'complete with dead horse' from Massey University. It was 'not bad', he thought, 'terribly grim though . . . & very sleazy'.[18] While there he also asked about *Close to Home*. Having heard nothing since doing the one script last June he had written to TV One at the end of the year, expressing his keenness also to try his hand at adaptations of his short stories: he had seen Martyn Sanderson's of 'The Losers' by this time and he thought he could do this kind of thing quite well. He had watched as well the 'Winners and Losers' series (made by independent production company Aardvark) which screened in 1976, half-hour adaptations of stories by Katherine Mansfield, Frank Sargeson, Maurice Shadbolt, Maurice Duggan, John A. Lee, Barry Crump and Witi Ihimaera, directed by Ian Mune and Roger Donaldson; and Mune's film of *The God Boy*. The personal approach worked and between February and June this year he did five scripts for *Close to Home*, in the year in which the programme attracted its peak audience of nearly a million viewers. They earned him $225 each and took three intensive days' work, but he found it easy and 'even a bit of fun'.[19] A few months later he was contracted to write one of six episodes of *Rachel*, a moody, psychological rural drama starring expatriate actress Barbara Ewing which screened the following year (foreshadowing the rural Gothic that would become a strong vein in New Zealand film). This was a more interesting and lucrative ($1200) commission, involving not just writing dialogue but creating the story outline for the 50-minute episode as well.

Yet writing for television he still regarded 'as a way of selling part of my time to be able to do what I want to do'. It was 'a hammer and tacks sort of job', he told an audience at the Nelson Institute when he spoke there again the following year, employing a favourite metaphor, compared to the writing of a novel which was 'the living of a piece of one's life'. He had been asked to speak on this occasion about writing for television, but he preferred to talk about his novels, starting out with another metaphor which was to become a favourite when he described what he did as both social and psychological realism. Social realism he likened to open-cast mining, where one's territory was society, the world. As a psychological realist the writer went down into a mine shaft: 'you look into yourself, you come to terms with the things that made you by turning them to imaginative use', although not necessarily consciously: 'very often a writer doesn't know he's made it'—that psychic descent—until he's finished and 'then he's able to see—perhaps he doesn't see till years later—that his work illustrates his most private obsessions'. This was the part that interested him, 'the things that break up from underground whether he wants them to or not'.[20]

*

He had sent his novel away to Faber on 25 March—still with the title 'Plumb', he apologised to his mother, but 'one of the best American novels of recent years was called simply Burr' (and, interestingly, was a novel written as part narrative, part fictional memoir): 'One year of hard concentrated work', in marked contrast to *Games of Choice*. 'Now I have to forget about it for a month or two while they make up their minds. Surprising how easily one can do that.'[21] In fact Faber would not receive the manuscript until three months later.

The screening of *The Losers* on 12 April provided one distraction. Perhaps unfortunately it was scheduled against the Academy Awards on South Pacific Television, but previewed by a full-page feature in that week's *Listener* which described the story as 'still one of the best-known pieces of New Zealand writing. Three novels and many more short stories later "The Losers" is still so strongly identified with Gee's reputation that "some people think it's the only story I ever wrote"'. Because she knew the ending well, he added, 'his wife won't be watching the television version'.[22] Sanderson's dialogue stayed very close to Gee's but he moved the focus of the story away from Mrs Betham to Connie and Stan, with, in Gee's words, 'a lot of sympathy generated for the poor little jockey',[23] who was handsome, quietly spoken, brooding, and drove a canary yellow and pale blue DeSoto. The film's tone was subdued and intense (accentuated by its slow pace and absence of background music), the art direction gritty. Reviews were mixed, with the acting variously described as 'meaty', 'indifferent' and 'atrocious', but all acknowledged that it was powerful, and the 'retching shock' of the final scene. '[E]agle-eyed racing folk had plenty of niggles to take to the stipes', the *Christchurch Star* couldn't help observing: 'The starring horse, for instance, started off as a chestnut and ended up as a bay and really there shouldn't have been a runner carrying No.24 while parading in the birdcage for what looked like an eight-horse race', while the *Manawatu Evening Standard* was equally disparaging of the director's ignorance of racing form.[24] It had been filmed at the Feilding race course.

In *Comment* later in the year James Bertram, comparing the film unfavourably with *The God Boy* (which had just been re-screened), wondered how anyone who hadn't read the story could have followed what was going on, and lamented that with the shift in focus '[a]ll the neat balance of Gee's story was tilted' and 'the *social* patterns—so important in all Gee's work—just didn't register'.[25]

Gee busied himself for the next three months revising his children's novel 'The War of the Smiths and the Joneses', which had finally found a publisher in Oxford University Press. He had offered it at the beginning of 1976 to Christine Cole Catley, who ran a small publishing house, Cape Catley, from her home at Whatamangō Bay in Queen Charlotte Sound. It was 'earthside s.f., no intergalactic stuff', he described it to her, written for ten-to-fifteen-year-olds, 'but adults should find it entertaining too'. Despite Faber and Hodder and Stoughton's responses, he still thought it was 'an exciting and competent piece of juvenile fiction in its present form'.[26] He remained undeterred too by Robin Dudding's reaction. Dudding read it to his six children, who were enthusiastic in varying degrees, but he (and his wife Lois) hated it: 'it's grey, slimy, nasty given in all the good competent story-telling things. Excrescence rather than inspiration; effective local colour but attached to nought.' He couldn't see its point: 'Every good writer has to write a bummer—even if only marginally it reaches this point. I think this is your bummer'. (Jokingly he added, of the story's climax which saw the destruction of Lake Pupuke and Takapuna: 'I'm sure you realize that you've finally knocked off your poor old mum: is this the climax of M. Gee's literary pilgrimage'.) He was not at all upset, Gee assured him when Dudding subsequently apologised for his frankness (though not for his opinion). 'I'm keen to get into this sort of writing, if only to be able to give up writing Close to Home scripts'; but 'I can't buy your Freudian analogies, even though it's probably correct as comment—not as criticism though'.[27]

Chris Catley liked it, however, and was keen to publish it if he agreed to some revision, and if she could overcome her pressing, and perennial, problem of capital: sales of her last book had been 'pitifully slow'. She was looking into the possibility of 'imprint schemes with selected British publishers', and would be in London for the purpose later in the year. 'Cape Catley/Faber' perhaps, Gee suggested.[28] A few months later, however, he wrote to warn her that she was unlikely to have success there: Tony Read, Oxford's New Zealand manager—whom Gee had met for the first time after the New Zealand Book Awards in June—was currently in London trying to arrange joint publication of future New Zealand titles with Faber. The upshot of this was that Oxford would bring out paperback editions of *Games of Choice* and *In My Father's Den* in July 1977, the contractual details of which were finalised when Read visited Gee in Nelson in April that year. (Gee's Napier bookseller friend Graham Beattie, now in Auckland and Penguin's newly appointed New Zealand marketing manager, happened to turn up too and they both stayed for dinner.)

Read had also expressed interest in seeing his children's novel, Gee told Catley. When at the end of 1976 she negotiated her own distribution arrangement with OUP she proposed to them that they co-publish it with Cape Catley. Oxford, however, preferred to do it on their own (subject to approval from their Australian and London offices), looking at a print run of 3–5000 in time for Christmas 1977, and Catley graciously relinquished her option. All of which left Gee a little embarrassed but it did not prevent he and Catley becoming good friends over the coming years. He sent his revised manuscript to Oxford at the end of July. It would be another eight months though before they got the go-ahead from London and the book would not come out until 1979. (Nothing, it seemed, happened quickly at OUP.)

The Gees 'cheerfully admit to having dropped their standard of living since Maurice became a full-time author', *New Zealand Bookworld* reported in October. '"We were having wine with every meal and now we simply don't go out"'.[29] They were not always so sanguine. Although they were by no means desperate they had started to worry at the end of 1976, with the scholarship money now used up. The Arts Council had declined the Literary Fund's application for funding to extend the scholarship beyond a year, about which Gee had inquired when he submitted his progress report. A royalty cheque from Faber for *Games of Choice* in November was timely: it meant that 'we are in food for a good part of next year', supplemented by the fruit trees and a thriving vegetable garden.[30] The novel missed out, though, on the New Zealand Book Award in 1977 (prompting Frank Sargeson to write to the Department of Internal Affairs in protest; it went to Ian Wedde's short novel *Dick Seddon's Great Dive*, which Dudding had published as a special issue of *Islands*), while James Bertram's Oxford volume on Brasch won the $2000 Wattie Book of the Year. *Close to Home* scripts became critical this year in keeping them afloat financially, so long as they kept coming. Their mortgage repayments, thankfully, were 'so low as to be embarrassing if we mention them to people'.[31]

Possibly as an immediate response to Maurie Shadbolt's ivory tower advice, but also to earn some money, Gee had offered at the beginning of this year to take a fiction-writing course for the Community Education Service at the Nelson Polytechnic. He was probably alarmed when they accepted. 'What do I do? All suggestions welcome', he wrote to Dudding—who advised him that the first thing 'of course is to get all students to subscribe to ISLANDS'.[32] The ten-week course ran on Wednesday evenings through the second term. It was, he wrote to a friend, a 'fiasco'.[33] Although he had also sought advice from Chris Catley he was largely unprepared and expected to be able to wing it; numbers were down by half by the second week. He made it to the end, was paid $150 and swore never to do it again. He was happier, however, to participate—along with historian Michael King—in one of the more intimate weekend residential writing workshops Catley ran at Whatamangō Bay, and this he did again the following year.

Margaretha's ability to take on more than casual or part-time work remained constrained as long as they had a child at home. Abigail, whom Gee described to his mother as 'a pagan', had decided after a few weeks' attendance that she wasn't going to go to kindergarten, and she seemed so happy on her own at home with the kittens for company, a solitary child with 'quite a private life that we know nothing about', they didn't insist.[34] They were not to enrol her at school until she was nearly six, and shared the childminding: Margaretha keeping an eye on her in the mornings while Gee wrote, he in the afternoons. The book reviews Margaretha did for the *Nelson Evening Mail* earned only pocket money. She applied without success for them both to be live-in managers of the Nelson Youth Hostel over Christmas–New Year of 1976–77, for a job at the Nelson Polytechnic library, and another with Heylen Research. A possible, lucrative commission to write the history of Transport (Nelson) Ltd (later Newmans) which promised $3–5000 fell through. In mid-1977, however, she landed a 'very odd job' as 'casual technical secretary' at the Cawthron Institute, a privately endowed scientific research institute, for which she was to work on and off for several years 'for an exorbitant wage'.[35] The work was research rather than secretarial, varied and interesting—and would prove creatively useful for the novelist. He, however, missed out on the wood chip-testing job at the Cawthron for which he had applied at the same time.

In late September he heard from Faber that they 'should very much like to publish' his novel.[36] For some reason, though, the formal offer they posted a few days later never arrived and he did not receive the offer until November. The advance was £350, a considerable increase on the £200 for *Games of Choice*, and they hoped to publish in the following (UK) autumn. Faber's new arrangement with Oxford

University Press meant that Oxford would also do a paperback edition 'in association with Faber' for the New Zealand market, details of which were discussed when Faber managing director Matthew Evans visited New Zealand in November, taking the opportunity to meet Gee—who hoped this meant he would get two advances. But there were stronger reasons than this, Gee was aware, and the risk of lost mail, for having one's publisher close at hand. For all the kudos of being published by Faber, and their generous advances, Faber did not have a good reputation as energetic marketers of their titles, even in Britain let alone elsewhere. (And then too, one might also be able to have an input into cover design.)

With *Plumb* enthusiastically received, he applied to the Literary Fund for $3000, and was granted $2000, to write the second of what he was now thinking of as not three novels but four, which he hoped to begin work on in March.

He did not get on with *Plumb* 2 in 1978. Instead he spent some months working with Margaretha on a history of Nelson Central School—the school Emily attended just down the hill—which was celebrating its centenary this year. Margaretha did most of the research; he did the writing. They had accepted the joint commission in September, initially intending to do the job gratis, but when it became clear after a few months how much research was required they asked to charge $2 an hour (for the research only, not the writing). In response the centennial committee voted to pay them $500, and later an additional $100 when the first draft was done. (They would return, however, another $100 the committee sent when it was wound up in 1979.) The bulk of the text was with the printer by mid-September 1978, except for a postscript chapter describing the centennial celebrations which were held over a wet Labour weekend in October, when orders were taken for the 100-page booklet 'edited by M. Gee, a professional author': the curtailed festivities (the parade, plaque-unveiling and tree-planting had to be called off) culminated in a banquet for 600 in the Trafalgar Centre and after-dinner speech by old boy and law professor Geoffrey Palmer.[37] As school histories go, *Nelson Central School* was distinguished by its engaging style and focus on social history and personalities, notably inspirational early headmaster F.G. Gibbs. (More typically, it was cheaply and disappointingly produced.) It was an extracurricular project which would, again, be fruitful for future work.

This had been a formal collaboration (although the authorship was attributed to Gee alone). But to an extent his novels had been a shared enterprise, and would continue to be, ever since he had read to Margaretha his morning's work on *In My Father's Den* each night in Oban Street. She became his first reader, did bits of research, helped check final page proofs, and to find titles (or not: 'The Stones are Bare' was her suggestion for *Plumb*). The whole family, meanwhile, enthusiastically discussed ideas for children's stories: a trip to Harwood's Hole one Easter, for example, might suggest a plot involving alien spirits that flit from sinkholes down to underground rivers. In a broader sense, too, a settled and fulfilling family life, at last, along with Margaretha's willingness to accept financial insecurity and sometimes hardship, were a vital support for Gee's writing. Important too—indeed crucial—was her financial contribution to the family income. '[H]ow I envy you a wife-secretary-housekeeper-gardener-shopper all rolled into somebody marvellously attractive to roll up to', Sargeson wrote to him in 1979.[38]

He had no desire, however, Gee had told Ian Wedde, 'to write about this relationship'.[39]

He did not go up to Frank Sargeson's 75th birthday celebration on 25 March this year, to which Dudding had sent him an invitation. Nor did he contribute to the special Sargeson birthday issue of *Islands*, although (of course) asked (and for which he subsequently apologised to Sargeson—'a kind of paralysis struck me at the thought of trying to put on paper anything that would come up to the subject. This note is my private tribute': he had just read Sargeson's third volume of memoir, he told him, *Never Enough!*: 'what can I say except that I read it with real delight, taking it like a kind of food—a nourishment. It's full of <u>mind</u> and <u>feeling</u> . . . With the other two <u>Enoughs</u> it makes a great work—unique. We should all shout it out').[40] But he continued to make his effort to do the right thing by the literary community, albeit often with reluctance. In March 1978 he took part in a literary symposium at the Christchurch Arts Festival, and in August a weekend short story seminar at Victoria University, where he gave a memorable reading of 'A Glorious Morning, Comrade'. On behalf of PEN he judged the Air New Zealand *Jetaway* short story award this year, and the PEN young writers' award; the Katherine Mansfield Memorial Award in 1979. Judging he found almost as hateful as book reviewing and manuscript assessing. Faced with the 283 entries for the Mansfield award, he would write in his report, 'a reader can only be thrown into panic and despair'. He was quite frank about not enjoying the experience: he had found only a dozen superior stories amongst an 'undifferentiated mass' and was struck by how conventional the vast majority were—social and psychological realism using traditional methods of narration. There was little experimentation; dominant themes were childhood, old age, marriages turning sour: 'The picture one gets of New Zealand from these [stories] is of a solid middle-class lump disturbed now and then by minor eruptions of social discontent or private distress.'[41] Did he notice that he was giving a gentle description of his own stories? The winner, by Vincent O'Sullivan, was about a lonely old man.

When Shadbolt saw Gee in Auckland in mid-October he found him this time less than happy. 'His isolation in Nelson seems to be draining him rather than helping', he told Ireland: 'he's written little all this year, has been harassed by financial worries', though his new novel, he added, 'out in the UK this week, sounds potentially marvellous'.[42] The Gees were feeling the financial stress. Gee's writing income in the 1977–78 tax year had been $1500 less than the previous year. The absence of the $4500 (as taxed) Literary Fund scholarship was balanced to some extent by higher royalties and income from television: his royalties were four times greater (nearly $1600, including the advance for *Plumb*), income from scriptwriting (just over $2000) nearly three times. But he had had no television work now since September 1977. Their joint family income in 1977–78 was $7300; next year they expected it to be around $6000, which included Gee's $2000 grant from the Literary Fund and the $500 for *Nelson Central School*.

When Abigail started school in May he placed a newspaper advertisement: 'WRITER requires regular afternoon job, active rather than sedentary, anything considered, light-delivery, semi-skilled, reliable.'[43] Over the coming summer he worked part time at Noeli's Book Nook for several weeks. For a time in their Nelson years he and Margaretha shared a community newspaper delivery round, taking half the city each. They also took on in 1978 proofreading the collected poems of James K. Baxter for Oxford University Press, but this proved more complicated than they expected and they didn't finished the job. Still, they went ahead with house alterations, for which they had had plans drawn up in 1977 but then shelved. Margaretha, ever restless, but also frustrated by a too-small house, had begun looking at others only a year after they moved to Nelson, half-heartedly then but more seriously in 1977. Now, instead, they refinanced their mortgage to have the living/dining space extended and add a family room (this one not a DIY job).

Earning a living by writing was always going to be precarious. Next year, however, things were going to get easier.

19

Plumb

Gee had hardly been then the 'literary celebrity' he was described as on the invitation to the Nelson launch of *Games of Choice* in 1976.[1] *Plumb* made him something close to one. The novel was announced in the London trade paper the *Bookseller* in August 1978 as '[l]eading Faber's fiction list' with Lawrence Durrell's *Livia*,[2] and released there in October, in a dust jacket with which, for once, he was pleased: a collage design in dark purply-red (plum) tones featuring a church, a tree, and the superimposed figure of a bespectacled man in a fedora who looked rather a lot like (but was not) James Chapple.[3] It was the work of Wellington designer Lindsay Missen, Faber having agreed to Gee's suggestion that they use the cover being commissioned by Oxford University Press. When OUP editor Bridget Williams had asked him if he had any particular ideas he had replied, 'just a determination not to allow anything as bad as that for Faber's edition of Games of Choice', and that it be pictorial not abstract or simply lettered: 'I see figures, perhaps in or against a landscape', perhaps a collage, or else a painting—Don Binney's *Colonial Garden Bird*, for example (the bird as spiritual messenger), or Illingworth's *What Lies Beneath these Fragments of Reference*. (The cost of multi-colour printing, however, ruled out a painting, which was a pity because the Illingworth (aside perhaps that it was too modern) would have been ideal.)[4]

Plumb was launched in New Zealand at the end of November at Melrose, a grand historic house in Nelson, at the suggestion of John Griffin—who had replaced Tony Read as head of the New Zealand branch of OUP—by another New Zealand Presbyterian heretic, Lloyd Geering, who had been tried by the church for 'doctrinal error' in 1967. The whole Gee family had a horrible flu and had to go straight home to bed afterwards, so Gee could not join Griffin and Geering for dinner, but he had had the chance to ask Geering if he had found any mistakes: he had only been puzzled, Geering said, by references to the 'Blue Book', which Gee had assumed was an official church volume rather than, in fact, just the blue-bound notebook his grandfather happened to use to keep a record of parish affairs.

The first British review was a 'somewhat puddingy effort' in the *Observer* by Hermione Lee which made the novel sound very dull. (Hermione Lee is a new name to us, Rosemary Goad, Gee's new editor at Faber, added, and 'our spies haven't yet reported who she is'.)[5] But it was the exception, both there and in New Zealand. Sargeson sent Gee a not only admiring but slightly awed letter before he had finished a first reading: 'Is this to be perhaps the first book of quality (expect I mean quality fiction) to get to the big public without any doubts in the matter whatsoever? I very much hope it may be.' Even if not (if the 'big public' found it 'too "difficult"'), 'nothing can alter the fact that here we have a most wonderful contribution to the great Literary House we are (for me, have been) so busy building. I kiss your hand if you will let me'.[6]

What Sargeson did not say to Gee (as he did to someone else) was that being 'under the disadvantage of knowing a good deal about the old man from some of his suffering daughters' he did not think Gee 'had in sum succeeded in beyond all doubt <u>creating</u> his character . . . quite'.[7]

In a short afterword Gee described the novel's provenance—how far event and character were based in fact. 'Much of George and Edith Plumb's early history is Chapple history', their later and their domestic life not.[8] The novel tells George and Edie's life from their first meeting at a cricket match (an unconscious borrowing from Sargeson's *Memoirs of a Peon* for which Gee, embarrassed, apologised; Sargeson assured him he had read it as 'well, a compliment'),[9] their courtship and their joint decision to enter the Presbyterian church, through their time in Kūmara, Emslie (Eltham), Thorpe (Timaru), California and Christchurch, until they move to Peacehaven—a house with an orchard and a slow-moving stream in 'a little town out by the ranges'—in 1919 (earlier than the Chapples).[10] It recounts Plumb's tussles with the church, his conversion to socialism and pacifism, the trials for heresy and sedition. From his grandmother's memoir Gee took Edie's description of the long muddy walk to visit an old couple in a tumble-down house where they are offered bread that 'looked dark in places' (dirt, she suspected); the texture of life on the weather-beaten nineteenth-century West Coast.[11] They are Florence's stories of the local ministers' ecumenical wood-chopping expeditions, the lady parishioner who was offended by the minister preaching in tan boots (they were just coming into fashion; Chapple had bought them in Christchurch on the way to Kūmara). Edie's 'another shake of the kaleidoscope' was one of her favourite sayings. They are James and Florence in appearance (he 'short in stature, red of hair, small in hand and foot', and increasingly deaf: Chapple's bakelite ear trumpet provided a ready symbol, for Plumb's both chosen and unknowing remoteness, that might otherwise perhaps have seemed contrived) and in character (Edith's gentleness and her 'gentility', learnt from her very English mother, as her daughter learns it from her in turn).[12] Little details as well as larger stories from Chapple life are threaded through *Plumb*. It is true that Bluey Morrow sent the Chapples a parcel of corned beef in the mail.

The story told early in the novel about the curate who flees town on his bicycle, abandoning his calling and his fiancée—Edith's sister Florence—never to be seen again after he is observed answering a call of nature by a party of ladies out picking raspberries, was the experience Florence told of her sister Edith (who remained heartbroken and never married). The episode is characteristic of what Bill Manhire would term the novel's 'pared richness', of character and incident, economically told, and humour—the young man riding off on his 'bone-shaker' down the country road, Manhire aptly noted, 'whimsically reminiscent of Zane Grey's outlaw heroes, riding off into the badlands'.[13] It prefigures too some of the novel's central themes: the contingent nature of truth (three versions are told), and the opposition between belief and nature, principle and human behaviour (which had so tormented Gee's long adolescence): they are both there in the name Plumb, which suggests fruitfulness and abundance as well as the straight line.

Gee took from Joyce Cary not only the trilogy form but from the second volume of Cary's trilogy, *To Be a Pilgrim*, the particular form of *Plumb*: an old man looking back on his life, narrating his own story, and the interweaving of past and present in short, numbered chapters. Plumb makes two journeys: in the present time from Peacehaven to Wellington to visit those of his children who live there; and a journey through memory, 'a searching of my past', as he recounts his spiritual and intellectual journey into and beyond Presbyterianism in search of what he comes to recognise as 'cosmic consciousness', or Love (he has a penchant for capitalising big concepts). It is also an account of his marriage, and his 'disappointment in my children'.[14] What he learns, though, is how he has disappointed them.

'The twelve Plumb children are not the fourteen Chapple children', Gee stated in his afterword. 'My uncles and aunts are not to accuse me of putting them in a novel.'[15] But some would have recognised themselves in more than the 'passing historical likenesses' referred to in an interview.[16] Not so much in Felicity, the eldest daughter (although there are aspects in her of both Bernice and Dora)[17]—Felicity who has 'passion, fire, and the prophetic mind' and becomes her father's acolyte and comrade in his political crusade, until her conversion, to his enduring mystification and disappointment, to Roman Catholicism. He will be a second time disillusioned by Felicity when she tells him that she was never the true believer in his spiritual quest he had thought her to be: 'All that Unitarian stuff. . . . It meant nothing to me.' Oliver, the eldest, cleverest but 'most limited' of the Plumb sons, draws directly on Leonard, the eldest Chapple son, who similarly defied his parents by enlisting for the First World War and remained distanced from his father ever after. Oliver, lawyer and Supreme Court judge, to Plumb is a 'scrubbed and Lysolled man', with a 'narrow pricking mind' and mean nature; who as a child—in a perfect vignette—had eaten his porridge each morning as if embarked on a military campaign: 'spooned his way round it clockwise; made an island of it with scalloped cliffs; then eaten round it again, and again, keeping it perfect all the way. He kept milk and porridge in exact proportion so that the last of each came together in his final spoonful.' (This is so well captured one suspects the author, who remained devoted to porridge for breakfast all his life, had done the same.) Yet it is Oliver, the child he least understands and respects, who eventually and bitterly informs Plumb about 'the miserable life you led mother', about the extent of the sacrifices she (albeit willingly) bore: that while he ate meat and potatoes in his study (which he names Journey's End, the name he would have preferred for Edie's Peacehaven), in the kitchen the children had 'porridge, even for tea' sometimes and Edie 'the scrapings out of the pot'. Felicity will tell him more, about the petty cruelties they suffered from small-minded townspeople while he was in prison.[18]

Willis, womaniser and adventurer, as his name suggests owes much to Hollis, Gee's likeable, wayward uncle, who had also been a sailor and traveller (though whether he had brought back the incense-burning brass Buddha in his grandfather's study Gee did not know) and lived on a small orchard along Millbrook Road: 'a happy man, always laughing'.[19] His wife Connie chasing him around the orchard with a carving knife, as Mirth will do, is one of the stories Lyndahl told about Hollis (in his case, an axe), as was her spying him canoodling in the cinema stalls one night with another woman as the town's mayor sees Willis with Mirth. (Gee gives the cuckolded mayor the name of his Napier nemesis, Richards. Hollis, however, was not burdened with the second name that Plumb has given Willis of Theophrastus—the given name of Paracelsus, the medieval alchemist and physician (Gee had read the poem in his grandfather's Browning); nor with a wooden leg.)[20] Gee's favourite, fun-loving aunt, Joyce, already met in 'The Widow', who 'drank port and cherry brandy and *crème de menthe* by the tumbler full, pulling a face as though they were vinegar' and told vulgar jokes, is present in Esther.[21] Her younger sister Meg by contrast is a much fuller portrait of Lyndahl. She is her father's favourite: 'the most vulnerable of my girls', with an 'affectionate nature and sentimental habit of mind', whose 'soul sparkled like water', but whose '[s]entimentality was her vice' (as gentility was Edith's). She reads Mary Webb not Wordsworth, and enrols at teachers' college not university as he had hoped. It saddens him that she 'grew up to marry a plumber'—handsome, stolid Fergus Sole—'and smoke cigarettes and worry about the colour of her lipstick'. Gee gives them, newly married, his parents' Depression-time experiences, and depicts Fergus after the war as Len, 'a good and useful man, enjoying his first taste of success, and dying a little to his wife and children daily'.[22]

Lyndahl's favourite brother, Dick, here becomes Meg's favourite, Robert, to his father the 'bravest of my sons, but the simplest too, not understanding his way but taking it from instinct', the antithesis of his own cerebral, high-minded way. Robert leaves school against Plumb's wishes and runs Peacehaven during the lean slump years as a small farm, keeping a flock of sheep and a house cow, tending the orchard and vegetable garden in which as a child he had run 'like a pagan', and building the tea-tree summer house as Dick did.[23] Though he doesn't quite follow his parents in their pacifism, he is brave enough to refuse to go to the war. Dick Chapple wasn't and, reluctantly, went when he was called up; Robert spends the Second World War in detention camps as a military defaulter, from which he escapes, damaged and, in the novel's present, has retreated to a commune in the Wairarapa lead by an evangelical Christian who believes him to be the second messiah. (This was not Dick's experience. The commune Gee had in mind here was Beeville, a pioneering pacifist, proto-hippie community established in the 1930s near Morrinsville in Waikato.)

Emerson, however, the daredevil aviator son, is not a Chapple except in the parental aspirations of his name: he has the career of Oscar Garden, the Sundowner of the Skies. (The newspaper report of his departure from Croydon airfield in the *Kia Ora* is quoted almost word for word.)

As Meg is her father's favourite, Alfred, the youngest, is his mother's: the bookish, beautiful boy who at fourteen looks like Shelley and reads and writes poetry perched in the branches of the Peacehaven trees, the son of whom Plumb has the highest hopes but is also afraid because '[h]e kept a part of himself hidden from me'.[24] Alfred resembles in some part the youngest Chapple, Aynsley, who was homosexual too, and of whom Florence was especially fond. Aynsley, however, was never banished from the family.

It is Plumb's reaction when he finds Alfred in the arms of John Willis in the Peacehaven garden that is his greatest failure, and the novel's fulcrum. He has aspired to live by the Wordsworthian ideal of 'plain living and high thinking', believes he has plucked all 'evil passions . . . lust or rage or envy or greed' from his heart, and now in his disgust and incomprehension and an outpouring of 'Old Testament bloodiness', calling down death and brimstone and fire 'I smote them . . . I killed him; and killed him again'. He not only banishes Alfred from Peacehaven but gives him money to change his name. In one of many precisely crafted structural ironies in the novel, this happens when he has been out walking and thinking about his moment of revelation, in the same garden on the day of Esther and Fred's wedding—also the day Alfred first met John Willis—when he had his 'vision splendid' and 'passed into the room of my own soul', and a 'great light, a bliss, a splendour, a white radiance, streamed through me'; now as he chances upon John and Alfred under the quince tree he has been contemplating the clear path he has at last seen towards his final goal, to Love. What he fails at is love. Even after Edie's death and knowing that she would have wanted him to make his peace with Alfred, he cannot. He will learn that she continued to see Alfred, meeting him in secret in the Peacehaven garden: 'She had perfect love', he comes to understand, 'And I did not.'[25]

But it is Robert, finally, whom he had ordered back then to cut the quince tree down, who cures Plumb, literally he believes by healing with his touch his burnt hand, and by example by teaching him acceptance. And Whitman too, naturally, plays a part in this process: it is in reading his 'Song of Myself' (Chapple's favourite Whitman poem) that he 'understood for the first time that in the mystical state all was not joy, that dark and light were complementary parts'.[26]

'Of course nobody yet (so far as I know) has mentioned your remarkable way with "time"', Sargeson wrote to Gee. 'Something quite new so far as I know.' The old man putting his hand on the stove element, for example: 'To me a most memorable kind of literary discovery—just another way of making time pass in the pages of one's story. Very high compliments'.[27] In the opening scene, Plumb, asked to admire Meg's new electric stove, lays his hand on the element after she turns it off, expecting to find it cold. 'I explained my belief that electric stoves cooked with electricity not with heat'. The incident instantly bridges the gap between the 1940s present and the past in which Plumb's two journeys take place. Similarly, and slightly differently, 'Fred Meggett hums like an electric motor', beginning a later chapter, in a sentence changes time and pace, jumping the reader four decades forwards from Kūmara.[28] The novel's complex, contrapuntal time scheme, as it moves forwards and backwards between the long past and short present, works in several ways: by abrupt juxtapositions, and across large passages of time and text via repeated metaphors and symbols. The hand Plumb burns on the stove—the hand Robert heals—is also the hand that touches evil when Plumb hears the confession of the murderer Joseph Sullivan in a shack in the West Coast bush. (Gee's historical reference here is the Maungatapu murders in 1860s Nelson.) Such echoes and ironies create a fugue-like narrative flow.

Perhaps, Bill Manhire thought (reviewing *Plumb* in *Islands*), there were 'rather too many plum trees and plum cakes', and also eels, with which Gee agreed ('I was happily putting [eels] into the second novel too, now I'll have to think again'); and perhaps the significance of Robert healing his hand is made too explicit (again Gee agreed: 'I was wondering if anyone would pick it up').[29] He might have countered though that Plumb as a literary and religious man has a metaphoric habit of mind. Plumb's short sentences and wry humour are characteristic of Gee, but the language of this novel has a precise and epigrammatic quality that is also Plumb's own. A key part of Gee's achievement and the novel's power is the convincing singularity of the narrating voice—to an extent apparently lost on his editor at

Faber, Rosemary Goad, when she queried his shyness about 'strong language', suggesting that the asterisks (as printed, dashes) in the swear words ('b-----', 'a---holes', 'F--- F---') be filled in. 'I quite take your point that they're in character as they are', she subsequently agreed.[30]

Plumb was indubitably, as Gee knew, a step up in his writing, but was not entirely a departure. He had already been writing 'backward-looking' novels, stories in which a middle-aged or elderly, and not wholly likeable, protagonist reviewing his or her life finds things they didn't expect, and reaches some point of acceptance and self-knowledge (the central theme of *Plumb* as Gee saw it); he had already been mining personal history. He had played with time before, though not so cleverly. His themes—'obsessions'—were already the damage inflicted within families, the loneliness inside them, the existence of evil. Still, this was on another level. Local reviewers recognised *Plumb* as something special: 'a splendid novel', 'of genuine importance'. Just as after 'The Losers' 'horsefloats never seem quite the same', journalist David Young concluded a two-page profile of Gee in the *Listener*, 'after *Plumb* . . . New Zealand writing will never be quite the same.'[31] It had a craftsmanship, wrote Roger Robinson, professor of English at Victoria, 'which in subtlety and poise goes far beyond Gee's earlier novels', and transcended its small flaws (as in, he concurred with Manhire, some too pointed dramatic moments) to build towards an 'almost mythic import'. 'If Maurice Gee is able to complete the next two books of his proposed trilogy, and they come anywhere near this one,' Manhire concluded his review, 'then New Zealand will have its most remarkable and intelligent piece of extended fiction. But *Plumb* is a magnificent achievement in its own right; and George Plumb is the most considerable character to have found a home in our literature.'[32]

Of the more substantial reviews it was Manhire's Gee most appreciated: his reading, he told him, was 'pretty much what I would have wanted from "ideal reader"—close to what I hope my own would have been'. He had appropriated some phrases from it for the next book, he added, hoping the reviewer didn't mind; Manhire on the contrary was flattered and only wanted to know what they were (but Gee didn't say). 'The really fascinating thing', he remarked in reply, 'is the number of people who've read the novel & make it a subject of conversation—which is really what I felt most strongly about it, that whatever you "think" of Plumb himself, the bugger steps right out of the book & takes root somewhere in your imagination. There aren't many novels where that happens—the portrait living beyond the frame.'[33]

Gee received many personal expressions of appreciation, a number from other writers, and was perhaps most chuffed to get a letter from Dan Davin in Oxford: 'your good opinion of Plumb bowls me over', he thanked him. (Among his other comments, 'It really is a man's book', Davin wrote: 'your handling of the homosexual is excellent, much better than Frank S. has been able to manage'.)[34]

Aunt Dora thought it was 'splendid'. And Muriel Parker too was impressed: 'No, it may not be the novel I wanted, but it is so good, that that becomes superfluous.' He knew that she would recognise aspects of herself and what he had drawn from her letters to him about his grandfather.[35] It was Muriel and her brother Jack—who had lived together at Peacehaven after the Chapples left—whom Gee had in mind when he created Merle and Graydon Butters, Plumb's Peacehaven neighbours and most fervent devotees, of whose serial enthusiasms he is privately disparaging: 'cultists', he calls them, who embrace in turn Rosicrucianism, the Oxford Group, Radiant Living, anthroposophy and theosophy; 'Lately they profess themselves socialists, and pacifists to boot, and believers in the Higher Consciousness, and some extraordinary *mélange* of these, some politico/mystical porridge, they have the impertinence to call Plumbism.'[36] The Parkers, however, did not share the Butterses' silliness, but they had the same emotional closeness that allowed them to complete each other's sentences as the Butterses do; he would use this relationship again. Muriel was also a model for Wendy Philson, who aspires to be not only Plumb's pupil but also his wife and bearer of his child. (The strange tenant in the Peacehaven cottage, though, who covered its interior surfaces—'walls, floors, table tops . . . chairs sideboards, pots and pans'—with brown paper stuck on with condensed milk and flour-and-water paste, as Wendy does when she loses her mind after Plumb sends Alfred away, was not Muriel Parker.)[37]

Muriel subsequently sent Gee her poems, on which he declined to comment (they were not really his thing, he demurred). 'Don't let Muriel Parker "latch" onto you Moss', his mother warned him when he told her this; 'I remember her from the past . . . a brilliant type in some ways, but also very boring and persistant.'[38] Lyndahl's own response to *Plumb* is not recorded, further than that she was 'pleased and proud' on his account. But she had told him not to be worried about what she would think—'I see my family without putting on "rose coloured glasses" as I used to in my sentimental past'.[39]

Faber printed 3000 of the hardback of *Plumb*. They had intended to do more (5500), but OUP took fewer for the New Zealand market than they expected. Those 1000 sold out within two months of release and another 650 were ordered from London. At the beginning of March it had been on the New Zealand fiction bestseller list for eleven weeks and was at number one. In Britain sales were around 1000 by the end of the 1978, including 200 pre-sales to the recently established New Fiction Society, which had made it a monthly choice. The hardback *Plumb* was out of print in both countries in little more than a year. The Faber/OUP paperback came out in October 1979 (with the biblical typo to which Gee had alerted a '[h]orrified' Rosemary Goad when his Faber author copies arrived corrected: 'bowels of compassion'—from 1 John 3:17—had been amended in misguided tastefulness to 'bowls').[40] The over 3000 pre-sales to the book trade was 'far more than we usually presell for other good New Zealand writers, like Frank Sargeson, Janet Frame, or even Gee's past books', the *Dominion* quoted John Griffin, who wrote to Gee, Sargeson and Frame to apologise ('pretty vulgar, and certainly not what I said').[41] A second printing was ordered before the first was in the shops.

It won four awards. In April Gee learned that it had won the James Tait Black Memorial Award for fiction, given annually by the University of Edinburgh, news which was widely reported in the local press before he had cabled his formal acceptance and the university put out its press release: 'the first time a major international award has gone to a New Zealand author', the *Auckland Star* observed.[42] It was a prestigious award, the oldest established in the United Kingdom, its previous winners including E.M. Forster, Arnold Bennett, Graham Greene and Joyce Cary; the previous year's was John Le Carré. Happily for Gee, the prize money had been increased this year, for the first time since the award was first given in 1919, from £500 to £1000. At home, the next month he won the more modest ($500) Jessie M. Buckland Award. In July he went to Wellington to collect the New Zealand Book Award for fiction at Turnbull House (while Kevin Ireland, back in the country for the occasion, took the poetry prize). 'Maurice Gee's <u>Plumb</u> is an obvious winner for 1979', the judge's report had commented.[43]

It was not so obvious perhaps that it would also win the Wattie, if only because, as Griffin had told Gee when he entered it, '[t]he rules appeared plainly to exclude it (an overseas, not N.Z., publisher's imprint [the paperback was not yet out]) but the Committee appears prepared to take a lenient view of the matter'; or else perhaps the judges would feel that it had won enough prizes already.[44] The Wattie awards were held in September at Trillos nightclub in Auckland's Westhaven, a glamorous affair which the *Listener*'s Bookmarks columnist described as 'rather like a very formal, and very large, wedding breakfast'. It was the first year since they had begun (in 1968) that they had been presented at a dinner and the guest list extended beyond the book trade to include 'civic dignitaries', politicians and academics; the invitation had billed it as 'THE LITERARY EVENT OF THE YEAR'.[45] Gee took along Nigel (who had just turned twenty and had a job driving a baker's delivery van, and still lived with his grandparents in Takapuna).

'[T]his novel has given me a gigantic bloody ego-trip,' Gee had admitted to Manhire in May; 'but I'm coming down now', he added.[46] The critical praise, financial reward and personal achievement he enjoyed; the 'kerfuffle' too at first, until it became 'all a bit heady for a while'.[47] But he would never feel comfortable with glamour, and would not come to enjoy attention, and especially talking about his writing. The homeliness, ordinariness and quiet lack of pretension David Young portrayed in the scene-setting opening of his *Listener* profile would remain Gee's enduring, and largely true, public persona:

> The day is overcast as Maurice Gee comes back down the path in his dressing gown, carrying the milk. He goes inside, returns with a bucket of chlorine solution which he up-ends into the children's pool and checks the laden loquat tree for pigeons. Inside the house the family are getting up.
>
> It could be a scene from one of his novels of domestic turmoil, except that peace seems to grow at the heart of this home. After three years here Gee finds Nelson fits him like a familiar sandal.

'Nelson-haven', the journalist calls it. 'In his setting', he continued, 'it is tempting to take Gee at his word when he says he is a middle-class writer. His achievement is to live within many of the conventions of middle New Zealand while remaining mentally detached.'[48]

Most likely Arthur Richards or Vincent Brown would not have read *Plumb*. It could probably be said though that it had reached Sargeson's 'big public' in the terms that he meant—not the numbers who read Barry Crump's good keen yarns, maybe, but more than the 'passionate few'. OUP paperback sales totalled 12,000 to 1985 and were then steady at around 1450 a year; as Griffin had told the *Dominion*, 'It won't be a book that sells a million today and none tomorrow. Gee's book will be a steady seller for the indefinite future.'[49] It is worth asking why readers responded to it as they did. It was a dense and, as Sargeson said, difficult novel; 'a book that explores or at least makes contact with Evangelicalism, Darwinism, agnosticism, socialism, communism, pacifism, patriotism, migration, materialism and human rights, public and private justice', Roger Robinson commented, and for an English professor a welcome addition to a literature lacking in novels 'of ideas' but not of obvious appeal to the 'ordinary' reader.[50] It is partly to do with the power of Plumb's voice, his compellingness as a character one both can and cannot admire, for what a British reviewer called his 'appalling and yet appealing rigidity'.[51] Plumb is likeable for his liveliness and humour, admirable for his courage and purity of belief; considerably more than an earnest, ageing Presbyterian parson.

It is partly too to do with the novel's amplitude, its rich variety of life, event and character. It offers, Manhire observed, 'a curious sense of life at the edges, of a great variety of events taking place beyond its two hundred and seventy pages'.[52] This was something Gee had hoped to achieve. In the course of writing *Plumb* he had copied down a passage from an essay by British writer Angus Wilson, in reference to his own novel *Anglo-Saxon Attitudes*: 'I was . . . able for the first time to expand the canvas of the novel, to give it a setting of an imaginary world broad enough in social scale to make [his central character] Middleton's personal problem seem no abstraction but the centre of "life" which expands beyond the novel, beyond the reader's view into "reality". It is this, I believe, that prevents a moral theme from seeming a "set piece" or a formal pattern.' By creating, the essay continues, 'that sense of being fully made alive, of disseminating the moral proposition so completely in a mass of living experience that it is never directly sensed as you read but only apprehended at the end as a result of the life you have shared in the book.'[53] Gee was echoing Wilson when he told his audience at the Nelson Institute in March 1978—just before he sent it off to Faber—'I think the novel achieves what I was after—that is, a sense of a life which expands beyond the novel.'[54]

There are other ways too in which Wilson's commentary on his novels in this essay echoes what Gee was doing in *Plumb*: his central characters' 'concealment from themselves of their ignorance of the shape of their own lives, a concealment which has to be subtle because it must deceive a habit of rigorous self-inquiry and a trained observation of the shape of the lives of other people'; 'the existence side by side of constant intellectual self-inquiry and emotional blindness'; the 'technique of flashbacks and word echoes'; 'the hell of the human failure to communicate' (and 'the opposed hell of the maze of self-pity and neurosis').[55]

And there is mystery in *Plumb*, too. We learn in the first few pages that there is something—something dark—we must discover about Alfred, 'the one I do not name. Who died to me on that morning long ago.'[56] It is divulged 200 pages later.

Plumb brought Gee as well as fame and fortune—that is, readers and royalties appreciably greater than he had enjoyed before—academic critical attention. This he did not enjoy. In August he was approached by a postdoctoral fellow at Auckland University, Brian Boyd, fresh back from completing a PhD on Vladimir Nabokov at the University of Toronto. His fellowship was in New Zealand literature, and when he had arrived back in New Zealand everyone had recommended he read *Plumb*. He proposed coming to Nelson to find out 'how <u>The Plumb–Sole Line</u> (as I've dubbed your trilogy) is developing', perhaps do an interview for *Islands*.[57] Gee declined, politely, but Boyd went ahead and made him the subject of his study anyway. It was published in *Islands* over two issues, with the weighty title 'Maurice Gee: ironies of growth and judgement', in 1980 and 1981. Dudding had not at first been keen, finding it too academic ('I've just finished struggling through Boyd', he told Gee—'so <u>impersonal</u> & <u>serious</u>') and sharing Gee's resistance to the whole enterprise: 'In a way I wish you hadn't seen it . . . how the hell can you expect to write while people insist on telling you that you write what they think you're writing'. But, he eventually decided, 'it seemed to intelligently lead the reader back to the Master's work. Which is all one should ask.'[58] In the first part Boyd discussed Gee's earlier fiction, identifying the consistent themes—in broad statement 'human growth, its desirability and difficulty and cost', and the human habit of judging others—which in the second he explored in *Plumb*, a work of 'vigour and amplitude and a real moral complexity far beyond anything he has written earlier' (there was no question he was a fan). In the slightly schematic way of the academic he teased out in detail the echoes and ironies, laying out the novel's intricate narrative and thematic structure. 'What is lucid and compelling on a first reading', he concluded, 'discloses on repeated examination a richness and craftsmanship and a complex humane ironic vision any literature could be proud of.'[59]

Gee responded generously when Boyd sent him the 58-page article in November 1979. He read it 'with fascination', he told him. 'No one has had such a close look at my work before. I'm astonished to find how much is in it.' He didn't disagree with his identification of 'my themes/subjects/obsessions', but 'I'm more instinctive and less calculating than you suggest, perhaps less clever than you seem to suggest': 'There's a point at which a piece of writing begins to generate its own complexities and throw things up from sources the writer is not aware of'. The writer's mind, he is saying, works not so differently from the reader's, finding patterns, making unconscious connections, simultaneously recognising and creating. *Plumb* 'was rich ground and things grew out of it without a great deal of help, without any help at times, from me.'[60]

He was finding the next one, though, much harder to write.

20

Mortimer's Patch

It was coincidental that the name Gee gave to the Lyndahl character in *Plumb*, Meg, who became the central character and narrator of the second novel, was the name of the eponymous heroine of Angus Wilson's next novel after *Anglo-Saxon Attitudes*, *The Middle Age of Mrs Eliot* (which had won Wilson the 1958 James Tait Black prize). Gee had not read *Mrs Eliot.* Meg was simply a name he had always liked; the more so after he met and fell for Meg Anderson. He had thought for a while of doing a quartet not a trilogy, with one novel for Meg and another for Esther, until deciding there was not enough substance, or complexity, in Esther for her to carry a novel on her own, and that she would be an unlikely narrator. An early note, made while he was still working on *Plumb*, suggests that he also had in mind at one point a larger role in novel two for Felicity than for Esther: the narrator was to be 'the quiet sister who marries a plumber', main character number two 'the political sister who works in a leftist bookshop and knows politicians' (others 'the wild sister: the homosexual brother').[1]

He struggled with *Plumb* 2 in 1979, mentioning writer's block to his mother early on, having difficulty with finding the female voice and point of view. Nevertheless he had a first draft completed by late in the year. It would 'please people less than Plumb', he thought, '—the high points are fewer and less dramatic'.[2] He now regretted having said publicly that he was planning a trilogy, as he told David Hill when answering questions for him for a short critical reader on his work Longman Paul were publishing (as the first in a series for secondary school students)—not wanting, he explained, either to feel constrained (by expectation) or be reproached (if he changed his mind), so 'If parts two and three could be quietly forgotten until they appear I'd be grateful'. (And would Hill also, he added, please keep it 'fairly quiet' that he was answering his questions: he had turned down two other people lately 'and I don't want them any more offended than they are at the moment'.)[3]

Along with the buzz and kerfuffle of the success of *Plumb*, and getting on with the next one, there was a lot more happening in this busy, fruitful year. His children's science fiction fantasy, after yet one more rewrite and now with the title *Under the Mountain*, was launched at Dorothy Butler's children's bookshop in Auckland in August, for which Gee went up, four weeks before the Wattie awards. For a while, after he changed the name of the evil worm-like creatures in their human form from Smith to Wilberforce, the title had become 'Alias Wilberforce and Jones': perhaps the 1970s television series *Alias Smith and Jones* had caught in his mind, while Robin Dudding had already alerted him to Monsarrat's (Victor Brown's favourite) 1963 espionage novel *Smith and Jones*.[4] Whether the Alias or the Wilberforce came first, it was an inspired choice: Wilberforce was a much more evocative name. Among her suggestions for revisions Bridget Williams had saved Gee from a major children's literature faux pas by pointing out that he could not have eleven-year-old Rachel and Theo in the opening chapter meeting the mysterious Mr Jones in the street and going back with him to his house: as a parent he surely should know that children did not go home with strangers. Hence the novel's prologue establishing Mr Jones as a benign figure.

With the significant dissent of children's literature specialist Betty Gilderdale, who thought the characterisation was thin, the Wilberforces 'either unrealistic or frighteningly macabre' and the whole thus lacking credibility,[5] *Under the Mountain* received almost unanimously glowing reviews, and a devoted readership. Whereas for one generation of New Zealand readers *Plumb* would be the first book they would for ever associate with Maurice Gee, for another it was to be *Under the Mountain*. It became by far his biggest-selling title: he had been right that writing (well) for children was more lucrative than writing serious fiction for their parents. Fantasy and science fiction were not new in New Zealand children's fiction (there had been his mother's own underworld fantasy *Mihi*, for one), but were only beginning to become a significant genre for this age group. The comparisons made were not with local but with overseas authors: Alan Garner, Susan Cooper and Madeleine L'Engle. The novel clearly had a compelling appeal, and genuinely frightened, through its mix of fantasy and reality and its grounding in the local setting. Children's author Joy Cowley wrote of the ability of a writer to permanently alter one's experience of something ordinary, mentioning Hitchcock and shower curtains; Stanley Kubrick, *The Blue Danube* and Beethoven's Ninth; and here Rangitoto: 'Never again will I look at that sacred cow of a mountain without a feeling of unease.' Dudding had told Gee of taking his children up Mt Eden one day not long after he'd read the manuscript to them and 'the kids recit[ing] Jones-type incantations before galloping down the crater'. (He also informed him that a freshwater lake had just been discovered under Rangitoto, which 'obviously explains why the Smiths could move so easily from Rangitoto to Pupuke to Mt Eden'.)[6]

In April Gee had meanwhile sent Oxford University Press the 'Caroline' story he had written for Emily. It came out the following year with the title *The World Around the Corner* and drawings by Gary Hebley (the illustrator's first commission). This was a smaller, charming rather than frightening book written for a younger age group (eight- to eleven-year-olds)—'a gentler tale', as he described it[7]—also set close to home, this time in Gee's Nelson neighbourhood; and also well received, though not in the way *Under the Mountain* was.

Interviewed on the television arts programme *Kaleidoscope* a few years later, he stated frankly that he found writing for children easier than writing for adults, because the important things were pace and story not character and thematic depth. It was an opinion that did not go down well with the growing children's literature community and which he learned to keep to himself.

That other lucrative and easier genre, television, also kept Gee busy in 1979, although he was no longer receiving commissions from *Close to Home*. In February he had been approached by Tom Finlayson at South Pacific Television about writing for a new series they had in development, a 'small-town cop series' to be called *Mortimer's Patch*. It was to be set in a fictional semi-rural town named Cobham, to which a 'seasoned and somewhat scarred' detective has been sent down from the big city after antagonising his superiors in a controversial case.[8] Finlayson already had in mind to play Doug Mortimer Irish-born actor Terence Cooper, best known for his role in the 1967 James Bond spoof *Casino Royale* (he had also been a candidate to play Bond in the official film series) before he moved to New Zealand in 1976—where his career besides acting was to include running a restaurant, Trouper Cooper's Curry House, in Auckland and writing two cookbooks.[9] The series was filmed on location in Helensville just north of Auckland, with the Helensville Plunket Rooms standing in for the Cobham police station.

Irish lead aside, *Mortimer's Patch* was New Zealand's first home-grown police drama, the originating concept being a uniquely New Zealand take on the genre, distinct from the urban 'high paced, cops and robbers' British and American version of the likes of *The Sweeney* and *The Professionals*: something 'distinctively, and essentially, our own'.[10] It proved a highly successful one and the series ran for three seasons, winning both ratings and awards. On its debut in August 1980 it attracted 20 per cent of viewers, despite being scheduled opposite *Fawlty Towers* (by the end of the season *To the Manor Born*); by the end of the second season it was being watched by over 40 per cent of the viewing audience and was out-rating the likes of *The Professionals*, *Minder* and *Mork and Mindy*.[11]

During 1979 Gee wrote four of the six episodes of the first season and two for the second, which screened in March and April 1981, earning between $1800 and $2000 for each. The success of *Plumb* appreciably increased the family's income, certainly, but it was *Mortimer's Patch*, he would later remark, that 'finally got us out of our poverty'.[12] In the 1979–80 tax year he earned $6000 from his books (including a $1100 payment from the Authors' Fund) and $7750 from South Pacific Television. And it was fun: writing for *Mortimer's Patch* was much more satisfying than the light drudgery of turning out *Close to Home*s. Developing and scripting a *Mortimer* episode was much like writing a short story, and indeed he considered turning his scripts into stories and publishing them as a collection; also, he told the *Listener* in an interview before the first episode went to air, of using the main characters in a novel: he had been thinking for a while of writing a police procedural thriller, he said.[13]

He found story ideas in local events and items in the news, and the whole family participated enthusiastically in plot-inventing sessions. 'Strictly for the Birds', the final episode in the first season (and in the opinion of television critic Barry Shaw probably the best), took its cue from a newspaper story about international bird-smuggling and featured both bird- and drug-smuggling through Cobham's nearby fishing port and seaside resort, Tahuna. 'The Pleasure Ground', about protest against 245-T spraying and over the Cobham council planting a forestry plantation on land gifted to the town for a reserve (with other plot elements including sabotage and marijuana-growing), was inspired by the Maitai campaign of 1977 when the Nelson City

Council decided to plant a commercial pine plantation on the grass-covered Maitai hills, land it had purchased in 1971 and designated the Maitai Recreational Reserve. The Gees had joined the Friends of the Maitai who campaigned (unsuccessfully) against the project, with Margaretha serving as media organiser and meetings frequently held at their house. In a rare demonstration of political activism on Maurice's part, when out walking on the hills one day they bent down every few steps to pull out the seedlings—as do the lead protestors in Cobham, 'a little straight ferocious lady in middle-age and her husband, a slow-moving quiet determined man'.[14]

For his first script he went back to his Paeroa experience and Heysham House for a plot involving the robberies of Cobham's TAB and two pubs, for which keen young constable Gilchrist ('Dimp') immediately suspects a former professional safe-breaker ('tank-buster') now going straight after a long stretch; whom Mortimer, however, put away the last time and knows is too good for these amateur jobs. A Henderson bookmaking story—a police raid on one of his father's bookie mates—was the starting point for another.

His best script went further back. 'Fighting Johnny Fuller' was a reworking of a radio play, 'Fighting Johnny French', which Gee had submitted unsuccessfully to Radio New Zealand's drama department in January 1978. It was the story of an old boxer. When Dimp and his girlfriend stop to get fruit from an overgrown pick-your-own orchard (plums when first scripted, apples when filmed) one Sunday afternoon they find the old man living in failing health and squalid conditions in the tumbling-down orchard cottage. There are boxing trophies on the sideboard and framed photographs of a fighter posed in his boxing trunks and gloves on the wall. When told of this, Mortimer realises that he is the famous Fighting Johnny Fuller, a 1920s champion and once contender for the world lightweight title, and goes to visit him. There is some mystery, it seems, surrounding the sudden disappearance of Fuller's wife 30 years ago—rumour has it she ran away with one of the orchard workers—and his hermit-like existence ever since. Mort discovers that he murdered them, and finds their remains buried under the 'special' tree whose fruit Fuller had never allowed anyone to pick.

'Fighting Johnny Fuller' was not your typical crime show script. Finlayson at first rejected it as too difficult to realise as police drama, with no victim and no clear antagonist and much of the story taking place in memory, but rereading it a few months later came to agree with Gee that 'there is room for a retrospective mood piece such as this in our series'. It was a 'beautiful script', he told Gee of his final version, 'The dialogue sings and the atmosphere it evokes is sometimes quite stunning', and after seeing the rushes: 'I think it will go down as the outstanding piece of television drama here for many years. The number of people who have volunteered comment about your script has been extraordinary.'[15] 'Fighting Johnny Fuller' achieved the rare feat for a local drama of making number one in the weekly ratings when it screened in April 1981, pushing TV One's 6.30pm news into second and third positions, and won the best drama award at the Feltex Television Awards the next year.

Mortimer's Patch was the most successful local drama of the early 1980s. The critics were astounded, then, when what was now Television New Zealand announced midway through the second season that it was cancelling the third: 'crazy', remarked a columnist in the *Auckland Star*, when this was 'the first local production with a touch of relaxed professionalism to it'. Finlayson announced that he was leaving Television New Zealand.[16] Public outcry saw a change of mind a month later, but an apparently final decision to axe the show was made in July. The reasons were primarily a climate of escalating television production costs along with a stubborn wage dispute with one of the actors (although personnel changes involved in the restructuring into the new Television New Zealand also played a part). *Mortimer's Patch* had always been 'something of a luxury programme',[17] 30 per cent more expensive to make than a one-off drama of the same duration, and five or six times as much per minute as *Close to Home*. But even *Close to Home* was reportedly under threat. The series intended to replace *Mortimer*, an 'agricultural and pastoral saga' then titled 'Stock and Station', for which Gee wrote two scripts in the first part of 1981, was already the subject of sceptical reports while it was still in pre-production. 'My pessimism for the show lifted considerably when you agreed to write for it', the script editor told Gee.[18] It screened, now titled *Both Sides of the Fence*, in 1983, and was as predicted a critical and ratings failure.

By this time, meanwhile, *Mortimer's Patch* had been revived, within tighter budget constraints: writers were instructed to avoid season- or weather-dependent plots and anything involving animals. Gee wrote two episodes for season three which went to air in June 1984, but was less successful than the first two. 'Scratch Cat' (there was no actual cat) was about the murder of a young female hitchhiker whose deranged killer attempts to strangle his invalid wife when she suspects and accuses him, picking up a topical subject of the 1970s, but also suggestive of an unhappy married couple in an early Gee short story. 'Intrusions' was a quieter, sparingly scripted episode which focused on the issue of assisted suicide (the Gees had both joined the Voluntary Euthanasia Society), while also taking some elements from the story 'A Retired Life' and including a reference to the Yelash/Fussell cheque-forging scandal of the 1950s.

He would devise two storylines as well for a fourth season, before this was aborted midway through 1984.

While the first season of *Mortimer's Patch* was in production in 1979, Tom Finlayson had been putting in motion the prospect of a television adaptation of *Plumb*. It was *Mortimer* script editor Christine McCourt who first mentioned this possibility to Gee, referring by example to a recent British serial, *Holding On*, a low-key period drama about a London stevedoring family spanning several decades which had 'managed to be very simple without being boring'.[19] With Gee's and Broadcasting Corporation director general Ian Cross's approval, Finlayson approached Faber in October 1979 seeking the rights for a six-part, one-hour serial to be made some time in the next seven years. In response to their concern about such a long option period (and for world not just New Zealand rights), he explained to them 'the chaotic state of the industry at the moment' and there being no permanent head of drama, which, along with budgetary constraints, meant that they could make only one costume drama at a time.[20] Faber also expressed qualms about simultaneously negotiating with South Pacific Television and with the Broadcasting Corporation for rights for a radio serialisation of the novel. The latter negotiation was successfully concluded the following year, with Faber accepting the corporation's 'absolute maximum offer' of a little more than half what they considered a normal rate,[21] and an eighteen-part adaptation, by Robin Fry, was broadcast in 1981. This followed serialisations in 1980 of *Games of Choice* and *In My Father's Den*, as the success of *Plumb* created renewed interest in Gee's earlier work. 'The Losers' and 'Eleventh Holiday' featured in a ten-part New Zealand Short Story Theatre season in 1981, while there had already been a reading of *Under the Mountain*. There would be numerous radio adaptations of Gee's work over the coming years, a modest but helpful income contribution. Getting things onto the screen was more expensive and more complicated.

Plumb was not the first 'big' New Zealand novel to be considered for television as local drama flourished in the 1970s. There had been the successful 1976 'telemovie' of *The God Boy. The Losers'* Peter Muxlow and Michael Scott-Smith at TV One began working on a series adaptation of Bill Pearson's *Coal Flat* in 1975, with Michael Noonan as the writer and Sam Neill in mind for the lead. In 1977 South Pacific Television bought the rights to Shadbolt's *Strangers and Journeys* with plans for a thirteen-part serial to be filmed the following year. Both these projects, however, fell over in 1979, largely for economic reasons. The second oil shock hit that year; while already the hugely and controversially over-budget (if very successful) historical series *The Governor* (1977) had made everyone nervous about large-scale historical dramas.

With the go-ahead at last to start working on a *Plumb* series for production late the following year, Finlayson finalised the purchase of the rights from Faber in mid-1981, although, as he warned Gee, still not full of confidence that the series would ever get made. Jonathan Hardy was writing the screenplay (Gee having declined to do it himself), a director was booked, and New Zealand-born, British-based actor Denis Lill—recently seen on New Zealand screens in the post-apocalyptic BBC series *Survivors*—offered the role of Plumb. But Finlayson's pessimism was not misplaced: although TVNZ retained its option for seven years—and the scope of the project would change as Gee's trilogy progressed—the *Plumb* series was never made. The stumbling blocks were not solely economic: senior script editor Chris Hampson remarked in 1983 that he thought the novel 'intractable' for television adaptation because its success owed so much to George Plumb's memory and point of view.[22]

Film projects even more than television ones happen in a never-never land of ambitious ideas and funding difficulties. Patrick Cox acquired the film rights to *In My Father's Den* in 1980 and obtained development money from the New Zealand Film Commission. Stuart Devenie worked on a script (again Gee had declined, saying he was too busy) and Sam Pillsbury, then finishing off Ronald Hugh Morrieson's *The Scarecrow*—which was to become, the following year, the first New Zealand feature film to be invited to Cannes—was to direct. Cox was planning to shoot around Henderson or Nelson in the autumn of 1982 for release later that year, but 'after many unsuccessful scripts' he relinquished his option in July (though he remained interested, he told Gee, if Gee would write it himself).[23]

Back at Avalon, Television New Zealand purchased a twelve-month option on *Games of Choice* in 1982, with plans for a one-hour film, but abandoned the project (already scripted) the following year: it was, said Hampson, too much 'a novel of its time'.[24] A more modest project which did come to fruition, however, was a half-hour adaptation of 'A Glorious Morning, Comrade' by independent filmmaker John McKay. He had contacted Auckland University Press in the first instance and already written a script himself before he consulted Gee. Starring British actor John McKelvey as Charles Pitt-Rimmer (and missing out the punchline), it screened in September 1983 (following a première screening at Nelson's Suter Gallery, to which the Gees were invited, a month earlier).

Before it was published Gee had been aware that there was good television potential in *Under the Mountain*. His daughters had told him so, as had Robin Dudding's children him, and Chris Catley optimistically suggested that it was 'not beyond possibility that TV2 would do a co-production with the BBC on it': both were looking for good children's scripts.[25] Tom Finlayson knew it too as soon as he read the novel, after his eleven-year-old son had in one sitting, and gave it to his director general to read at the same time that he was first pursuing the *Plumb* option with Faber. Children's drama was a more likely prospect, being already a conspicuous strength of the emergent local drama industry. The screenwriter Finlayson chose for *Under the Mountain*, Ken Catran, had worked among other things on the pioneering and very successful historical children's drama series *Hunter's Gold*. (Once again Gee had turned down the offer to script his novel himself, being too busy, although it would have been worth $7500 to him.)

Feasibility studies for the design work on what was New Zealand television's first attempt at science fiction began in June 1980. 'It is a designer's dream (or nightmare)', Finlayson had told Gee when he first put the proposal to him; later he described the financial and creative challenges as 'horrendous'.[26] The total budget for the eight-episode series was $25,000, less than 1 per cent of the $9 million cited for the special effects alone for the second *Star Wars* film, which had just been released. This was to be a 'steady, resourceful Kiwi' job. 'We did some tests this week with a variety of disgusting materials, including gelatine, liver, various plastics and so forth'—for the shape-changing Wilberforces and their subterranean terrain—Finlayson reported, while the costume designer worked out concepts using a mould made from cabbage and spinach leaves.[27] (The production designer was Robert Gillies, a former, founding member of the avant-garde pop band Split Enz, working under head of design, Gee's old friend Tony Stones.)

In the end they used fibreglass and old tractor tyres for the Wilberforce costumes (which were so heavy the actors could wear them for only 15 minutes at a time) and fine clear plastic and wallpaper paste for their slime trails. A Takapuna dental technician and facial prosthetist assisted with the masks. The entire Shortland Street studio space was taken to build the six different subterranean sets through which Rachel and Theo travelled. For their cousin Ricky's beach buggy, a standard buggy was modified with a reconditioned 1600cc Volkswagon engine and gearbox (to give the required throaty sound and enough power to tow a boat), customised pale blue lambskin seat covers and black carpet, a glossy red body (for the 'snazzy' look) and chrome extras (for luxurious effect).[28]

They auditioned 1200 Auckland schoolchildren to find their Rachel and Theo—both natural redheads, although Finlayson would not have insisted on this. (Nine-year-old Emily had written to him several months earlier about auditioning, but was told they were some time away from casting yet.) 'I haven't been as excited about anything in my entire career', Finlayson told the *Auckland Star* two months before shooting started in February 1981.[29] He splashed out on booking the New Zealand Symphony Orchestra for the score: 'a bit of an indulgence,' he told Gee, 'but hell, why not?!!!'.[30]

The series went to air in October 1981, with much advance publicity and a parental advisory that they should watch it with their children. It had been made with a weekday 7pm time slot and ten- to twelve-year-old audience in mind. TVNZ screened it on Sunday at 6pm, when younger children were likely to be watching and parents less able to. Finlayson was 'dismayed and bitter', he told the press, and that if he had not resigned already over the axing of *Mortimer's Patch* 'I would have done so over this'. The final episode in particular, he warned, would be 'fairly gruelling' for younger viewers.[31] In the final, desperate struggle to save the world from the Wilberforces, Rachel and Theo's likeable, fun-loving older cousin Ricky is drowned (and Rachel's mind, Gee had written, 'held one picture only—of

Ricky floating face down in a sea as black as oil').[32] Gee originally wrote the tough ending, he told the *Listener*, 'out of concern that the young heroes in children's literature always seemed to score very easy victories'; here the victory was achieved at great cost. But many children who had written to him about the book had told him they were upset by it: 'At the time I thought it was the right thing to do, but now I'm not so sure.'[33]

It didn't seem to hurt the series' reception. Finlayson had been confident it would do well but was 'amazed' by the response, even from adults.[34] By the third episode it was attracting the same adult viewership as *Close to Home* at the same time on TV One, while topping the ratings for children aged up to nine; by later episodes it was coming second among teenagers after pop show *Ready to Roll*. Auckland teachers testified to its 'tremendous impact' and that the book was currently 'a big reading and talking point in Auckland primary and intermediate schools'. Whitcoulls' city branch quickly sold out of the last 50 copies they had. The novel had come out in paperback this year, from Puffin in the United Kingdom and Ashton Scholastic in Australia and New Zealand. When their paperback stock ran out OUP brought in 500 from Australia, where sales were slower (and reviews had been less enthusiastic), but these were almost gone by the beginning of December, meaning the loss of some pre-Christmas sales. By mid-1982, Wendy Harrex at OUP informed Gee, Ashton Scholastic had sold 'a stunning 24,855 copies'; while the series that year won the Feltex best drama award.[35]

Down in Nelson, meanwhile, Gee had 'become the talk of the town': 'all the town seemed to be watching'.[36]

21

Meg

The downside of the growing film and television interest in his work was the number of offers to think about and complicated contracts he didn't understand. He needed, Gee realised, an agent. At the end of 1980 he signed up with Ray Richards, who, with his wife Barbara, had set up the country's first literary agency four years earlier after a long career in publishing at Reeds. Richards was the son of a Presbyterian minister, which had given *Plumb* a special resonance for him, he told Gee; though he had not yet read the novel when he first wrote to him in May 1979 to congratulate him on the James Tait Black award—assuring him however that he was 'not touting for work when I enclose a copy of my latest agency leaflet'.[1]

When he approached Gee on the subject the following February—by which time they had met at the Wattie awards—it was in response to an article Margaretha had written for the *Nelson Evening Mail* in which she described the family's continuing financial struggle ('On the rocky road to success', it was titled),[2] which made him 'very sad', Richards wrote; and in the larger context of the shaky position of the New Zealand branch of OUP. It concerned him that Gee had given the *Plumb* paperback to Oxford, when Penguin was a much stronger and more energetic publisher internationally, especially in the paperback market, than either Faber or Oxford. Graham Beattie had told him that Gee had done so largely out of loyalty to John Griffin, who, as well as being an old friend, he regarded as his de facto agent: 'but did you calculate what that decision might cost you in dollars and reputation?' This can only have made Gee uncomfortable, just as he had felt bad about letting Chris Catley down over *Under the Mountain*—as Richards evidently realised, writing again two days later to apologise and assure Gee that he did 'not want to interfere in a good working relationship between author and publisher' and 'was certainly not offering myself as your agent'.[3] But Gee had Dudding too bemoaning to him later this year about how 'shabbily' he had been treated by Oxford in the production of his books, with the exception of *Under the Mountain*: 'paper, inking, type, lay-out . . . Shameful. (Bugger Oxford generally . . .'.[4]

In the end it was Gee who approached Richards, late in 1980, just before news was out of the impending retrenchment of OUP (New Zealand), which was more severe than people had been anticipating, with the Wellington office closed and Auckland staff reduced to two, and distribution to be through Whitcoulls. (Griffin left at the end of March; the Wellington office closed two months later.) With this development, Faber decided to publish the second novel of Gee's trilogy, which it now had on its autumn 1981 list, in association with Penguin; while Richards, as Gee's agent, looked forward to getting all of his titles, past and future, with Penguin/Faber—in the first instance and most importantly a uniform series of the *Plumb* three. (Penguin had needed no persuading: 'I would give my eye teeth, as the saying goes, to publish Maurice', Beattie had said to Richards.)[5]

Penguin would be Gee's main publisher, and Richards remain his literary agent, for the rest of his writing career. Wresting the lucrative *Plumb* paperback rights from Oxford, however, was not to be easy.

Faber had received the manuscript of 'Getting Acquainted'—*Plumb* 2—from John Griffin in August 1980 and responded to Gee with an offer within two weeks (the advance offered this time £500). They did not, however, nor did anyone else it seemed other than Gee and Griffin, like the title. It was Griffin who suggested—if it had to change—simply 'Meg'. A potentially trickier problem over naming arose when Griffin sent the manuscript to legal firm Bell Gully, concerning Esther's husband, Fred Meggett, and his property development company Meggett Enterprises, which is being investigated for (and Meggett eventually charged with) fraud. There was a Meggett involved in real estate in Wellington, Griffin informed Gee, who was 'quite excitable and litigiously inclined', so he might like to think about renaming his character, which of course was not that simple as Meggett had already been introduced in *Plumb*. 'Maybe the real Meggett can be bribed?', Faber's copy editor offered.[6] Neither, though, proved necessary. A legal opinion delivered by Bell Gully in December also cleared the book over Meggett's similarities to two other real-life figures: a G.T. Gillies who, as does Fred, made a large amount of money from undervalued US army surplus trucks being sold off by the government after the war (a royal commission had been held into the scandal); and Jim Jeffs, the Auckland company director imprisoned for fraud over the massive and high-profile JBL collapse in 1972.[7]

The third area of concern, where some changes (but minor ones only) were required, were passages describing Alfred Plumb's death and the ensuing trial, which Gee had based closely on the 1964 Hagley Park murder that had long ago partly inspired his shipboard story 'Holding Hands'.

'Mine has been a tale of deaths', writes Meg towards its end.[8] It opens with the death of Sutton, Bluey Considine's club-footed, hump-backed friend, who has stayed on in the Peacehaven cottage he shared with him after Bluey died. It ends with the death of Robert, Meg's favourite brother, whom, in the novel's present—it is the late 1960s—she moves into the cottage and nurses through the last painful stages of emphysema. As she looks back over her life, as Plumb did over his, we learn again of Rebecca's death, drowned at New Brighton beach at thirteen, the daughter her father barely knew but the sister to whom Meg was closest ('She saw things I was able to see. Like me she drew wizards and witches, magical doors and sleeping princesses. I loved her next to Robert').[9] We learn of Plumb's, less than a year after the close of his story—a gentle event, 'not a time of battle but, for most of it, a tranquil running-down', his face in death 'faintly querulous' and 'more friendly than stern'.[10] *Meg* gives us a softer, more benign portrait of Plumb than his own (when Felicity remarks, for example, on Emerson flying his Gypsy Moth too low over the Peacehaven garden and Meg reminds her that he can't hear it: 'The story of his life. He just looks up and sees a great white bird'; when Meg learns, and is jealous, that as a boy Robert had been allowed to play with their father's ear trumpet, polish the brass Buddha and light the incense), as well as a stronger, sadder sense of the aftermath and cost of his failure: when he 'locked himself away. He was like a man in sickness', and in their last years together 'darkness lay between Mother and Dad'.[11] We learn of Alfred's brutal death—30 years after Plumb metaphorically killed him, four years after Plumb—kicked to death by four queer-hating boys in Loomis's Moa Park (Henderson's Tui Glen); as with his expulsion from Peacehaven in the first novel, the details of this focal event withheld from us for most of this one.

Robert's dying brings the siblings we met in the first novel together again, Felicity and Oliver travelling to Auckland (in a reverse of Plumb's journey to Wellington). Oliver has remained the brother no one had bothered to know, now a retired and knighted chief justice (about to head a royal commission on property development), and still so Calvinist he has to go off to his room when the others pour themselves a drink. (He has not, in fact, come to Auckland to see Robert but to look though his father's papers to assist him with writing his memoirs.) Esther is a heavier drinker than ever, carrying her port wine everywhere with her in a brown paper bag. It was her lonely marriage, we learn, as Fred became consumed by his business affairs that first drove her to drink, and (like Alice Matthews in 'A Sleeping Face') into an obsessive love for her only son; then, taking her deeper, her belief that she is responsible for the death of Alfred—the brother to whom she was as close as Meg to Robert—by sending him from her house (a second banishment) on the night he later died out of fear that he would 'corrupt' her son.

Willis, his wooden leg now replaced by a pink plastic one, remains joyfully married to Mirth on his little orchard (their five feral children now grown and gone); while Emerson still has the career of Oscar Garden: he has given up flying for TEAL to grow tomatoes. Along Millbrook Road the Peacehaven orchard has been cleared and developed by Fred and Fergus Sole into a subdivision—a 'little tongue of suburbia' which Meg observes from across the creek at Peacehaven. Merle Butters lives there, channelling George Plumb in the séances she holds (she has now embraced spiritualism; Graydon has died) and leaving notes for Meg, who does her best to avoid her ('*Your father came through last night, Meg dear. He and Alfred are the best of friends now. He says beware of electric stoves and bottles without labels*'). Wendy Philson, now dropsical and diabetic, is writing Plumb's 'spiritual biography', working her way through his letters and 71 notebooks.[12] (The book was already at the printers when Rosemary Goad noticed, just in time, that Gee had diabetic Wendy offering sweets to Meg and sugaring her tea.)[13] Meg has agreed to this project even though she has never liked Wendy, for her loopy high-minded devotion to her father, and especially her wanting to marry him and have his children—about which Plumb, frightened, goes to Meg for advice. In reality—or as Muriel Parker, Wendy's original, told it to Gee—it was Chapple who wanted Muriel to have his child, in the belief 'that we were close to each other in the inner evolutionary scale' (the phrase becomes Wendy's) and that such a child would carry on his work. When he confided their feelings for each other in Lyndahl—where Plumb confides a mix of confusion and concern: he looks on Wendy as a daughter—Lyndahl warned Muriel off.[14]

Meg's retrospective journey is not so much one of self-discovery as Plumb's—she is not so unknowing at its start—than it is (or is also) one of self-preservation. She aims to take a clear-eyed and unsentimental view of herself, her family and her past in order to hold on to the self she has already gone a long way towards remaking. 'If I am to hold myself steady in my shape . . . I must look at the person I came from. There was a girl, a sister, a wife, sentimental, tender, green, open, painfully open, closed, darkly closed. I was that woman; brought surely, unknowing, to my doom—which was to see. See life, understand circumstance, know death—to get an eyeful, as my sons would say.'[15] She must demythologise her life in order to understand it; as Plumb had done the reverse. So the Plumbs will no longer be seen as the Chosen Ones (like her father, the young Meg had a liking for capital letters); Peacehaven is no longer 'the magical home I had once made of it . . . outside the laws of this place': the orchard that 'had been elf country once' is now, like her family, 'nothing special'.[16]

In her writing as well as her seeing she will avoid 'fancies' and sentimentality: as her son Raymond tells her, she 'must be plain'. ('I have a weakness for the airy-fairy poetic phrase', Gee had long ago said to Maurice Shadbolt.)[17] In the retelling in this novel of key episodes recounted in *Plumb*, Meg's pared-back version of her father coming across Alfred and John Willis under the quince tree is this: 'One Saturday morning Dad found Alfred and John Willis in the orchard. Doing something unspeakable? Making love? Both are true. Dad cursed Alfred and drove him out from Peacehaven'; though the event still holds its significance—'[b]etween them . . . grieving and hatred and pain'—and the place, where the quince tree stump rotted, had for many years been one she 'approached with a shiver, half-expecting to find something hideous there'. (Alfred's sardonic description of the moment contrasts just as strongly with Plumb's: '"You should have seen Jehovah when he found us. His eyes went red. Literally. He nearly fell over. And his hat fell off . . . He ran away like this, like a chimpanzee."') When Meg recounts how, at Alfred's funeral, Robert rested his hand on her shoulder and restored her—'in the space of a second [I] remade myself and accepted life'—just as his touch had healed Plumb, she will not 'play the moment up', as Plumb (perhaps Gee) had: 'It was quick. It was, I suppose, ordinary.'[18]

Like *Plumb* this is also the story of a marriage, and its failures.

Fergus Sole is not wholly, but is in essential ways, Len Gee, with his widow's peak and eyes the 'blue of water and sky', his sense of honesty and honour: 'a simple man' who 'believes in goodness', and who saw himself 'above all as a man—tough, decisive, a person who gets things done', and 'lived so much in the regard of men, and so much in his own private regard that took in notions of manliness and honesty and courage, inexpressible though they were by him, that little room was left for a third place in his life, a place for me'. But '[h]e has pockets in his mind where corrupting influences work' (he is not uncomplicated).[19] Much but not all of this is Len. Her parents saw clearly what Meg, when she was courting, did not: her mother that she was romanticising Fergus, her father that they 'were not suited'.[20]

Meg and Fergus's marriage is not Lyndahl and Len's, but not unlike it. Meg begins to withdraw from Fergus—from the 'man-light in his eye', his sexual want—after the birth of her third child. From that time '[w]e got along, we gave each other a good deal of honest kindness, but where we had come together once in love we came now only in duty on my part, and in a dumb rage and resentment and greed—and sometimes in guilt—on his', and 'lived together and grew apart'.[21] Fergus finds happiness in business success, firstly as a plumber when Fred Meggett, after making himself rich through his 'fishy' dealing in war surplus, goes into construction 'putting up blocks of shops on the Great North Road between the Loomis bridges'[22] (as Len Gee did working for Steve Ozich) and he wins the contract for the plumbing work; then as a builder when he sets up Sole Construction as a division of Meggett Enterprises after he and Fred have persuaded Meg to sell the Peacehaven orchard. In the course of the novel he also has an affair (in which he does not find happiness) and leaves Meg (rather, she insists that he go); at the end of it he will perhaps come back.

When David Hill was preparing his Longman book—and Gee was finishing the first draft of *Meg*—and asked him why many of the marriages in his books were 'unhappy, strained, or involve one character hiding something from the other', Gee had replied: 'I think that's the way many marriages are. People see coming together in this way as a means of escaping from their aloneness, and that can never be escaped from.'[23]

For Meg, the disillusionment of her marriage is part of the larger 'withering away of my romantic and sentimental view', which began—in another narrative parallel with *Plumb*—when she comes across Esther masturbating Fred by the creek at Peacehaven—'stepped into the dreaming ground of my childhood, but advanced on another level into a place where adult things might happen'—and culminates in her six-month breakdown. Again she 'will not exaggerate the moment—the moment I caught sight of an enemy' in Fred's swollen, red, grinning face 'and was slain by him. . . . I laugh at it now.' That defeat 'lasted only the space of a heartbeat or two'. Twenty years later, it is Fred bringing ugliness to Peacehaven in a different guise that precipitates her emotional collapse, from which she will not 'get better' but recovers enough to gather 'up the pieces I could find of myself' and go on, but 'less than I had been'.[24] Gee's characters find small victories, not, as Plumb wished to believe, large ones.

Meg was also Lyndahl's story in a more intimate way than just likeness of character and experience. 'I can go quite a long way towards understanding how, as you put it, "getting her right was a job that nearly broke you"', Ray Copland, emeritus professor of English at the University of Canterbury, wrote to Gee after having interviewed him when the novel was in its final stages: 'after all, in these cases, the whole novel becomes a sort of huge amplification, not only in action but in language too, of the narrating personage; so it's no wonder the good lady nearly did for you.'[25] It helped, of course, that Gee knew his mother so well. And Joyce Cary, again, had provided an example, of 'going inside a woman's mind' for his narrator in the first volume of his trilogy (*Herself Surprised*).[26] He also had his mother's stories, both stories told and stories written—these he drew on extensively (with her blessing), not only taking much of the detail of childhood memory and incident but sometimes sentences and phrases ('your feeling for words is a long way better than mine', he had told her, and would continue to believe).[27] There is by consequence of this, perhaps, a variation in tone in *Meg* that there is not in *Plumb*: Meg's childhood experience is narrated in her child-Meg voice, one distinct from her adult one.

Lyndahl's memoirs and stories provided little details as well as larger stories: Meg being told she has 'a face like a cow', and leaving her blue tea-set in the macrocarpa hedge when the family goes to California, where snakes slithered under the dry leaves in the gutters and she 'wasted away . . . a tree that would not transplant'; the homesick poem she writes here, 'A Mother's Love', is Lyndahl's.[28] The sackman too, from whom Meg hides in the roadside ditch and Robert saves her, comes from the autobiographical 'The Change', in which Lyndahl is Lynda and Dick/Robert is Dickie; as does Meg finding a grave in the sandhills at New Brighton beach with 'a jam jar with red geraniums at each end', and being unable to find it the next day: her brothers tell her she was dreaming it because 'I am so romantic'.[29] Lynda dreams about her and Dickie—like Meg and Robert—hiding from the Germans 'under the trellis with the scarlet runner beans on it and . . . the German boots marching past us'; from here comes too Meg's Land of Missing, 'grey and blind, deaf and tongueless', where the 'missing' soldiers are and missing family and dead people go.[30]

Her account of Esther's 21st-birthday party draws from the earlier, more fictional 'The Meek', where it is Margot's sister Rae's 18th. Alfred (and Aynsley) in this story is named Emerson, 'the youngest and handsomest of Mrs Calthorpe's children and the most complex in character, emotional and inclined to morbid introspection', and with 'a flair for details in dress and hair arrangement': as he watches her dress for her party '[a]s a last touch Rae tucked a poinsettia flower' (Esther tucks a hibiscus) 'into the dark waves of her hair [and] pinned it securely with a diamante clasp', and then follows his advice to remove them both ('girls always overdo things'). Their older brother, meanwhile (there are only four children, not fourteen, in the Calthorpe family), who leaves school early wanting to get some land and go farming, is a version of Robert and Dick: 'Brer's dream was happiness through simplification.'[31]

From 'The Change' came also Meg's recurring dream, her California dream in which she is 'standing on the banks of a dark river, while my dead family floated by, Mother first, and then my brother and sisters, one by one—I reached out my hands to catch them until I found myself in the water too and sinking down'. She has it again when Rebecca drowns, and sees it then as a premonition—'The Plumbs were floating by on the Black River. One by one they were sinking. Rebecca was first'; it comes again when Alfred is cast out. In 'The Change' Lynda recounts this nightmare: 'I thought I was standing on the bank of the Avon River and as I looked at the water my Mother floated past dead drowning and then one by one the rest of my family'.[32]

'Imagination or memory?' wondered Alice Matthews: 'She couldn't tell', when the Piha cutty grass reminds her of 'a game that would end with bleeding fingers'.[33] Lyndahl's drowning dream, and then Meg's, echo in Gee's accounts of his own near-drowning in Henderson creek when he was two or three, which his mother told him of: when 'you fell into the creek . . . I saw you go floating past under the water, and ran along the bank until I could pull you out.'[34] He thought he remembered it, he once said, 'I think I can remember lying under the water and watching the other world, the real world, go by. Perhaps I've invented it but it seems like a memory'; elsewhere he is surer that he doesn't. This drowning becomes Donald Pinnock's near-drowning in *A Special Flower*: when Donald's sister Jean 'saw him below her, floating below the surface of the water. He was on his back, with his fists tightly clenched on his chest. His mouth was pinched shut, and his eyes were staring up with a grave expression'; and then becomes again Gee's own: 'My mother saw me go floating by under the water, with my hands folded on my chest and my eyes wide open, staring up at I don't know what.'[35] Memory flows into fiction and fiction into memory; remembered experience, dream and story echo and overlap. 'I'm pretty sure I'm not inventing', Gee will say to his biographer many years later, 'but can't be absolutely sure that those memories that went into the fiction are not flowing back in an altered form and pushing out the true ones.'[36]

There will be many more drownings in Gee's stories. And those stories will continue to explore and betray the creative interplay of experience, memory and telling; the 'folding together of now with memory' (in Jack Skeat's words).[37]

His mother would never read *Meg*.

Three distressing events occurred in February 1981. Emily (now ten), in a fall on the Gees' treacherously steep Cleveland Terrace section suffered a serious eye injury from which it would take her sight several months to fully recover. A huge fire swept down the Maitai Valley, destroying houses; the Gees' house was not threatened but they could see the flames licking over the tops of the hills behind them, and friends further up the valley lost theirs. And Lyndahl died, on 16 February (her wedding anniversary). Len was away at the time and it was Nigel who rang his father to tell him—it was early in the evening—that she had had a stroke and was in hospital. Gee made arrangements to go up the next morning, but she died later that night. He could only be there for her funeral (a secular one, the eulogy given by her nephew and friend—and a long-time member of the Communist Party—Rex Hollis).[38] Her death had come sooner than anyone expected, although it had been clear for the last few years how much her mind was diminished, as well as her physical health damaged, by her drinking and smoking. Len, despite their troubles, and still a 'man's man', at home at the races or with his mates down at his club, had cared for her lovingly.

It saddened Gee immensely that she had not had the chance to read *Meg*. 'I had very much wanted her to read it, and I had very much wanted her to say that she approved of it and liked it.'[39]

Gee would last have seen his mother late the previous year when—*Meg* now safely in the hands of Faber—the family took a month-long road trip through the North Island. While in Auckland he also called in to the TVNZ studios, where set-building was under way for *Under the Mountain* (an opportunity too to catch up with Tony Stones); and to see Ray Richards to ask him to take over his business. The trip left the Gees exhausted rather than refreshed—Abigail did not travel well, they discovered—and rethinking the idea of an overseas one any time in the next three or four years. For now, Gee was 'so relieved to be home I just want to vegetate here a while'.[40]

Rather than launch straight into *Plumb* 3 (and while turning out two scripts for 'Stock and Station') he wrote another children's book, this one dedicated to Abigail. *The Halfmen of O* went to OUP in May: Oxford already held an option on Gee's next children's book, but Richards was happy to let them have it in any case because of their success with overseas sales of *The World Around the Corner*—6500 in the UK and United States (earning Gee a nice $3000), while Wendy Harrex (about to take over at OUP from John Griffin) had secured Scandinavian and Japanese first options at the Bologna Children's Book Fair for both this and *Under the Mountain*.

The Halfmen of O has strong similarities to *Under the Mountain*: with two cousins, a girl and a boy, embarked on a dangerous and frightening mission to vanquish the forces of evil which threaten the world, a mission which again involves subterranean journeys. But Gee wanted this time 'to move entirely into fantasy and invent a world of my own',[41] and almost the entire story takes place in this other world, the land of O, a world in which, for its human inhabitants, there is no colour, taste or smell (it is Meg's Land of Missing—where 'it would be grey and if you went to it you would not be able to taste anything or hear anything or see any colours'):[42] a grey land with a moon the colour of pewter and a black sun. Susan, to whom the task of saving the once beautiful planet of O—and the cousins' own—is entrusted, wears a strange mark on her wrist, placed there by the mysterious old man who appeared at her cot-side the night she was born (a stormy night, of course). She is an odd, dreamy girl; 'weird', thinks her more practical and impatient cousin, Nick; 'a funny kid, all right', agree both his parents and hers: even as a baby 'she'd be looking away, way out over the horizon, as though there was something there only she could see'.[43] By her mark, she now learns—it is the faint impression of the Taoist yin and yang sign—Susan has been chosen to retrieve the sundered halves of the original Mark of O which once rested on the Motherstone, holding good and evil in that world in balance. Ever since the halves were torn apart by corrupt and power-hungry Otis Claw the people of O have been Halfmen, containing only evil and no good, and Humanhome has been known as the Darklands.

On their quest Susan and Nick are helped by the assorted creatures, the Woodlanders, Birdfolk, Stonefolk and Seafolk, who inhabit the various other realms of O: there is a little here, perhaps, of Lyndahl's *Mihi*, especially in Gee's anthropomorphised birds. But if this was influence, it was this time an unconscious one. And Gee had, as well, a special fondness for birds: 'I have no favourite word, favourite colour, favourite animal, but I like birds very much. I'd like to be a shag on a sandbar', he said a few years later (as, in a later novel, will Noel Papps).[44] Tolkien was the obvious literary reference made by reviewers, with the cousins' journey to the Darklands, aided and escorted by a motley band of unearthly beings, likened to Frodo's to Mordor. The struggle of good against evil is of course familiar fare in children's fantasy literature. Gee's particular exploration of this here—the theme of their necessary co-existence: that people are by nature both and '[g]ood must be won daily in the battle that never ends'; the Halfmen have 'lost their natures'—is also what Plumb learns (that 'dark and light were complementary parts', even in the mystical state, even in himself), and for Gee an enduring preoccupation.[45]

The best things in O are not otherworldly. A trip to Golden Bay had provided the two plot mechanisms Gee needed to get his story started. An abandoned mine shaft cutting into the side of the hill with a sign at its entrance reading 'Enter at your own risk' suggested the portal through which Susan and Nick would get to the planet O. The day before he had come across an old gold prospector up a narrow creek, ragged and snub-nosed, using a small suction dredge consisting of a two-stroke motor on a tiny raft: here was Jimmy Jaspers, who sends Susan on her way to O, an ugly, 'dirty, evil-natured, evil-spoken'[46] old man (another of Gee's Crassins) who becomes, however, an ally. Here Gee learned again the lesson he had with *Under the Mountain*. When he read the first draft of chapter 9 to Emily and Abigail—as he did each chapter of the book as he finished it—they loudly protested when Jaspers went over Sheercliff with Odo Cling. Despite Gee's intention to move wholly into fantasy, it is Jaspers' familiar earthiness and gruff, vernacular humour that gives the novel its liveliness, and a sense of humour otherwise almost entirely lacking. It is no wonder children loved him. For Gee, Jaspers was merely a plot device who could be dispensed with once he had served his purpose; for Emily and Abigail, and many young readers, he was the best thing in the book.

The Halfmen of O came out midway through 1982: Abigail (who also had a birthmark on her wrist) was the model for Susan in the cover drawing, again by Gary Hebley—as Emily had been for Caroline on *The World Around the Corner*. Reviews were highly enthusiastic (although not in Britain, while Betty Gilderdale was once again Gee's sternest local critic). The readers were too: like *Under the Mountain* it was to become an enduring New Zealand children's favourite. Within a few months (if not already) he had decided that he would write two sequels, to make an O trilogy.

By mid-1981 Gee was deep into part three of his Plumb–Sole trilogy. He found this one even harder to write than *Meg* (which had been, in his own words, 'harder than anything I've done').[47] That, meanwhile, was out in September, launched at Nelson's Suter Gallery (Gee attended reluctantly), while in London Rosemary Goad celebrated its publication date the following month with Bill Manhire and his wife, Marion, and New Zealand musicologist John Mansfield Thomson (editor of *Early Music* and formerly music editor at Faber) over lunch at the Venus Kebab.

Meg did not make the impact *Plumb* had, as Gee had anticipated—Meg's voice was quieter, her storytelling (though not story) gentler—but the reviews were mostly good ones, with an especially virulent exception in the British *Listener* (which drew an equally strongly worded letter to the editor from Manhire). By contrast, in the first review to come out in Britain Martin Seymour-Smith in the *Financial Times* described the novel's first paragraph as 'one of the best . . . of any novel I have read', and was informed enough to refer back to *The Big Season*: there, he wrote, Gee 'was actually puritanical in his attack on puritanism', but 'he has outgrown all that' and this novel, like *Plumb*, 'teems with life at the expense of "moral propriety"'; in concentrating on story 'he eschews close analysis in the interests of an almost Joyce-Cary-like humanist gusto'.[48] In the *New Zealand Listener*, John (J.E.P.) Thomson found it typically 'incisive and often very funny', and, although sad, not unhappy: as in *Plumb* '[t]here is always the sense of a possible goodness in life . . . one is borne up on a wholly credible conviction of human potential. Other New Zealand fiction for a moment seems heartless.'[49] These were both reviews which would have pleased the author greatly.

Some thought it better than *Plumb*. Manhire was one: 'It's excellent', he remarked to Gee a few years later, when he was working (finally) on his critical study for Oxford, '—and I think there is something in it that's finally stronger than *Plumb*. (I'm not sure quite what it is, though.)'[50] Dan Davin was another, and knew why, congratulating Gee on having managed 'the difficult job of becoming a woman' as successfully as Cary.[51]

There was no letter of appreciation this time, however, from Frank Sargeson. When *Meg* came out Sargeson was ill with the prostate cancer from which he would die the following March. It is unlikely he read it. His was a loss Gee felt, for although they had not been personal friends they had been professional ones in an important way. After Brasch's death, Gee would later remark, it was Sargeson who had (though to a lesser extent) taken his place 'in my head' as his critical touchstone, his internal-external reader; while '[a]mong New Zealand novels', he told David Hill in 1979, 'none have given me more pleasure than . . . Joy of the Worm and Memoirs of a Peon'.[52]

Sales of *Meg* totalled 1800 in the first month, which, Ray Richards told Gee, was 'remarkable' for a New Zealand novel.[53] They were 'on the slow side' in Britain,[54] despite the almost unanimously positive reviews: around 500 by the end of the year (half those of *Plumb* in its first three months), still only 600 by April. In New Zealand, though, Penguin had sold 1500 of the 2500 they had taken by mid-November; the remaining 1000, which they had then expected to last another twelve months, were gone by February, with an extra 400 ordered from Faber's stock not due to arrive until April.

More excitingly, it had been picked up in the United States, by St Martin's Press—'a good, middle-of-the-road American publisher' with a strong fiction list, Goad told Gee.[55] Faber had so far failed to interest American publishers in *Plumb* (Knopf, and George

Braziller, Janet Frame's American publisher, were among those who had turned it down). It would be 'quite ridiculous' now, Richards assured him, if St Martin's did not also take *Plumb*—especially with the television prospect (he thought) so encouraging—and after that *Plumb* 3. 'Nelson author achieves U.S. breakthrough', he headed the press release he sent out in May.[56] 'It's all movement and activity with Maurice,' he wrote ebulliently to Faber managing director Matthew Evans that month, what with the St Martin's signing, *Mortimer's Patch* on TV (the second series had just screened), *Under the Mountain* just filmed and a *Plumb* series in pre-production, film contracts signed for *In My Father's Den* and 'A Glorious Morning, Comrade'; he was confident too of the television prospects of *The Halfmen of O* . . . 'these are exciting days', he wrote to Gee the same day, 'I hope the flow of dollars steps up as well.'[57]

At home *Meg* won Gee the New Zealand Book Award for fiction (jointly with Vincent O'Sullivan), as well as the Buckland award. At the book awards ceremony in July 1982, Graham Beattie accepted on his behalf; Gee was then on holiday in Stockholm.

22

Sole Survivor

In May 1982 the Gees left for a six-month trip to Europe and Britain. The original plan had been to spend most of it in the south of France; that is, if Gee had been awarded the Katherine Mansfield Memorial Fellowship, for which he had applied in August. He had had this in mind for a while, though was not sure if they could afford it. The fellowship, established in 1970, provided an airfare, $4000 and the use of a room in the Villa Isola Bella in the Côte d'Azur town of Menton where Katherine Mansfield had lived and worked towards the end of her life. Living costs there, though, were 'very high', he had been warned by the secretary of the Literary Fund when he inquired a year earlier, and no, there was no provision made for families.[1] He was confident enough, regardless, of his chances of getting it that he felt 'very sour' when he found out that he hadn't, as he told Maurice Shadbolt, who had applied and missed out too: 'Surely I'm not being pig-headed if I say one of us should have had it', with which Shadbolt agreed (and on Gee's behalf especially: 'The whole bloody thing mystifies and appals', he wrote to Anton Vogt).[2]

They decided to go anyway, with their travel plans 'drastically altered'.[3] Money would be tight, but their finances had been helped by Margaretha having had a full-time job at the Nelson Provincial Museum for the last year or more. The trip was timed so they would be back before Emily turned twelve in November (and became for airline purposes an adult).

Before they left Gee had managed to finish—just—*Plumb* 3, its working title 'Sole Survivor'. (It had not been hard to pick, as several reviewers of *Meg* had, that the narrating character of novel three would be Meg's son Raymond.)[4] When he had applied for Menton he had expected to have only a first draft finished by March (completing this book was to be his first Menton project). In late November three months later he was hoping to have a typescript done by the end of April; but it was 'full of difficulties'—'a raw lump at present and needs a lot of hard work', he told Dan Davin.[5] In the first week of April he decided to 'put it in a drawer for six months' and come back to it later; after a final read-through over Easter he changed his mind.[6]

'R. SOLE or ARSEHOLE is just my joke title', Gee had assured Ray Richards in October. (The joke was originally Esther's—'The way R goes with Sole'—when she observes after Raymond is born that all three of Meg's children have the same initial; Meg in her innocence doesn't get it for more than 30 years.)[7]

Over that time, as well as wrestling with the novel he had written a film script. This was a spin-off from *Mortimer's Patch*, a proposal Tom Finlayson put to him midway through 1981, shortly after the (first) cancellation of the series. Gee responded enthusiastically and produced a story outline and treatment within a month, and the second draft of a script by February, working on it over the Christmas holiday. The brief Finlayson gave him was tailor-made for Gee: the film he had in mind would 'have much of the feeling for small community of Games of Choice and In My Father's Den', revealing its 'vanities and conceits . . . the secrets, the unspoken attitudes, the gossip and, above all, the threat that the fabric of this little society can so easily be rent'. It should also have 'wry humour, even whimsy'; and it should have violence, of the kind Gee did so well: 'I like violence which is sudden, short-lived and shocking', Finlayson told him (citing the cat death in *Games of Choice*).[8]

The story Gee came up with involved an obsessive, emotionally repressed, fundamentalist lay preacher, a widower; his nineteen-year-old daughter of whom he is pathologically protective; a pseudo-spiritual hippie commune to which she flees, and from which she flees in turn; a rape, a suicide and murder: *Plumb* meets *Mortimer's Patch*; or as Tony Stones put it to Kevin Ireland, 'very Moss'.[9] In December Finlayson's request for development money was flatly turned down by the New Zealand Film Commission, the two script assessors critical (caustically) of its sexual politics, gratuitous violence, obsessive and conservative characters and unfocused plot. Undeterred, Finlayson went looking for the $1.4 million he needed, hoping to secure both local and overseas investors.

Gee received $2000 for the treatment. When he sent the revised script Finlayson was promising the rest of his fee—or half of it at least—by the end of April. This was, Gee confirmed to Ray Richards early in April, money they were relying on to enable their trip to go ahead. It would not come through until September. A week or so before they left they sold their car; but perhaps they had already intended to.

The family flew from Auckland on 4 May, with Eurail passes, Youth Hostel Association membership cards, and a list of names and contact details of people Richards wanted Gee to see en route (most of whom he didn't), bound for Athens via four nights at the Hotel Equatorial in Singapore. A few paragraphs' description of the flight (Gee's first long-haul one: 'not so tiring as expected', but nor a bit romantic) and of Singapore was as far as he got with keeping a travel diary.[10] (The girls were more assiduous, being required to by their school.) They had two weeks in Greece, where they were dismayed by the smog ('Maurice immediately developed near-asthma', Margaretha reported to her mother),[11] dirtiness and litter. From Athens they visited Cape Sounion and Aegina, and took a bus tour of the Peloponnese. Leaving Athens to head north to Kalambaka and the Meteora monasteries, they nearly lost Emily: getting a taxi outside their hotel to take them to the station, as they turned around to pick up the rest of their packs to load into the boot Emily hopped into the cab with hers and the driver drove off. While her parents stood helplessly on the footpath imagining her being sold into child slavery, she had the presence of mind to ask to be let out at a small suburban station she recognised on the other side of the Plaka and make her way back. Her parents were still so distressed by the time they got to the central station they got on the train going south rather than north (pulling the emergency stop cord 300 metres out). The girls, they found, stood up to the rigours of travel better than they did, Emily 'master[ing] currencies and undergrounds like a computer', while 'Abigail sort of wanders round not knowing whether she's north-south-east or west, and not caring': contrary to their expectations she absolutely loved it.[12]

The itinerary became a work in progress. After Greece, Yugoslavia was refreshingly 'clean and bright';[13] here travelling by public transport was the challenge. All the signs seemed to be wrong. Heading north from Dubrovnik for the Plitvice National Park, they lost their bus at Split when the driver held up his hand twice to indicate (they thought) ten minutes and left after five (twice had been for emphasis), with their luggage, necessitating an unscheduled overnight stay in Zadar when they finally caught up with it. They had had four or five very happy days in Dubrovnik, renting spacious rooms from a lovely old woman who met them off the train (they had booked nothing in advance) and her retired sea-captain and English-speaking husband, who took them out in his boat and showed them around the city. Dubrovnik remained their European highlight.

Blundering (Margaretha's word) north through Yugoslavia, they went on to Austria (Vienna, Salzburg and Innsbruck, and when the weather improved a few days in the Tyrol), then Switzerland: Zurich for Gee to meet with an agent to discuss German translation of *Plumb*, and Geneva, where they spent five nights with Carl Freeman and Franca. This was a mistake. The last thing a family of exhausted travellers needed, observed Margaretha with characteristic frankness to their house-minders back in Nelson, was sleeping for several nights on the living-room floor of a small apartment, with 'not even a table to put gear, or place for clothes'. But 'we are loving it', she assured them, and assured her mother; and, despite mistakes and mishaps, they were.[14]

In Geneva mail was waiting, including news from Rosemary Goad that Faber had received and were 'most enthusiastic' about *Sole Survivor*.[15]

Their stay in Paris, next, was about as successful as Gee's last, despite the useful discovery that he could speak passable traveller's French. It was July now, and Paris too hot, 'too big, too dirty, too noisy' and too crowded.[16] They had been directed to a seedy hotel in Montmartre, an area quite unsuitable for children. Margaretha was ill, which meant Gee spent much of the time traipsing about with the girls on his own. They went up the Eiffel Tower, and visited the Louvre, where they failed to see the Mona Lisa (obscured by a crowd fifteen deep). At Versailles they took fright at the length of the queue; but on their way back to Paris spent an engrossed hour watching a film crew they chanced upon setting up a guillotine scene. After two days they fled, skipping Germany (to the great sorrow of Emily and Abigail who were dearly looking forward to the Romantic Road, the Rhine and Hamelin), and took quiet refuge for ten days on a Danish pig farm, before the six-day bicycling tour they had booked around Djursland (it had been too late to find a cottage in the Dordogne, as they'd earlier fancied). It was disappointing that the pigs were kept inside and that the whole place was infested with flies, but the girls enjoyed themselves.

The Scandinavian leg took them next to Sweden and Norway (Finland also falling off the list). Almost all of their seven weeks in Sweden they spent in Stockholm, where they were generously welcomed by Margaretha's relatives: it was the first time she had been back (indeed out of New Zealand) since leaving the country with her mother as a baby in 1941. They were blessedly spared, moreover, from sleeping on anyone's living-room floor. On their arrival in Stockholm they were met by a young Swede and his girlfriend—friends of friends who had once camped for a few days on the lawn at Cleveland Terrace: Broren and Inger lent them their apartment while they moved out to his mother's for a while. Then they had several idyllic days on a small island owned by Margaretha's cousin (also Margareta), one of the thousands of tiny, low stone islands that make up the Stockholm Archipelago—five or six acres covered with pines, silver birches and wild strawberries.

In Stockholm Gee also spent some of his time checking the first proofs of *Sole Survivor*, which Goad had posted to him there. The news that *Meg* had won the New Zealand Book Award had been waiting for them when they arrived.

In Norway they had three or four days in Oslo; travelled as far north as Narvik, inside the Arctic Circle (just to say they had); and took a ferry trip through the fjords from Flåm. He was hoping, Gee had told the press before they left Nelson, to develop ideas for a children's fantasy set in a Norwegian fjord, but this was a book he never wrote. Apart from one paragraph on a page of his abandoned travel diary—the sketchiest novel or story idea, perhaps—none of the foreign places or landscapes he encountered on this trip would leave a literary imprint.

Crossing by ferry from Norway to Newcastle, they hired a car and drove north through 'drab & dreary North England and Scotland' on another pilgrimage—via castles and ruins, dramatic coastlines and eccentric B&Bs—to Tongue on the north Highland coast where Oscar Garden had been born, and they found his initials carved into the church pew where he had told them they would. There had been a plan to go from here to Iceland, but this was abandoned and they headed instead straight back south via the western coast and the Lake District to London, where they stayed with a Turnbull librarian friend, Diana Pope, and her lawyer husband, Jeremy, in comfortable Kensington: another uncomfortable experience, however (feeling crowded in the Popes' one-room-wide, four-level, typical London row-house), which only reinforced what they had learned in Geneva, that it was not the best idea to stay with friends.

Money was waiting for them in London, forwarded by their Nelson accountant: royalty cheques from Ray Richards, the book award prize money, and the first half of Gee's film script payment, finally, from Tom Finlayson, along with some cashed-up investment savings. Faber at Gee's request were already holding for him the television rights payment for *Plumb* they had received from TVNZ the previous year. He now met Rosemary Goad, his editor at Faber for three books now, one day for lunch (one of only two business meetings he managed). They had already established a friendly rapport in their correspondence, although this was never extensive (Gee's books never needing much editorial work). Goad had a New Zealand family connection, and more importantly a huge admiration for his work, and was to remain his enthusiastic and sympathetic editor at Faber until she retired.

There were older friends to catch up with. He met up with Neil Perrett in a pub with several of Perrett's friends, and couldn't keep up with the drinking: when time was called he still had four or five untouched pints lined up in front of him. After five or so days in London they travelled out through Devon and down to Cornwall where they stayed for a night in Truro with Tony Perrett (pausing on the way down the Cornish coast at Tintagel to see King Arthur's castle). From here they went up to Oxford—where Janet Wilson (writer Phillip Wilson's daughter), who was then studying at Oxford and arranged their accommodation, found them seeming 'harassed by travelling & . . . looking forward to returning to N.Z.'.[17] In Oxford Gee met Dan Davin briefly (in another pub) and visited Oxford University Press, before they embarked on the narrowboat trip they had booked, starting from Aynho on the Oxford Canal.

On board, Gee went back to revising his film script, which he had spent two or three days on already in a quiet hotel they had stayed at in off-season Ilfracombe on the Devon coast. Having finally secured the funding, Finlayson needed a final script from him by the third week of November. From Oxfordshire they went by train back to Cumbria and the Lake District, where Emily and Abigail were booked into an Outward Bound school at Ullswater for a week, while the parents did some walking and literary touring; and in a hotel in Penrith Gee read his revised script to Finlayson and the film's director, Peter Sharp, who had come over to London to cast for the lead role of Katie, the escapee daughter of Gee's tormented puritan, Fred Wells. Back in London for a few more days before they started the journey home (in a hotel this time, found for them by Finlayson), Gee met the young actress Sharp and Finlayson had chosen: 28-year-old Emma Piper ('a cross between Katie Hepburn and Glenda Jackson', Finlayson would describe her in the film's pre-publicity).[18] To play her father they had already lined up Patrick McGoohan, of television series *The Prisoner* fame: he had been out to New Zealand for secret discussions in June and was still keen.

The Gees flew out from Heathrow on 29 October, via Los Angeles and a promised trip to Disneyland, and arrived home on 3 November—four days short of Emily's birthday—exhausted, broke, carless, but happy. For all the vicissitudes of travel, and the things not done and places not seen, it had been, as Gee would later put it, 'a nice big sort of island of pleasure in the middle of our staid, sedate lives'.[19]

A first priority was a new car: they successfully tendered for a second-hand station wagon being sold off by the Nelson Hospital Board. Margaretha finding a new job would take longer. Gee didn't expect to be in a frame of mind for work—to start a new book—for a while; until the new year, that is. Checking the final proofs of *Sole Survivor*, though, which came before Christmas, was not demanding.

In December Finlayson flew him up to Auckland for discussions about the film, shooting of which was scheduled to start in January (when he went up again to see a day's filming). In a hotel up there he had a prickly meeting with Patrick McGoohan. He was expecting a cordial chat, but McGoohan was not happy with his character and wanted Gee to change him from a brooding, tormented Calvinist into a raving Roman Catholic, which would have been more fun to play, undoubtedly, but entirely wrong. Gee did nothing, although McGoohan had insisted, he would recall, 'quite belligerently'.[20] As it was, McGoohan's twitchy, tortured performance as the increasingly deranged Wells (all twitching facial muscles and tight-lipped Old Testament pronouncements) was, as the *Listener* film reviewer wrote, 'definitely the weirdest and best thing about this movie'.[21]

The script had undergone many and significant changes since Gee's original version, particularly in that holiday rewrite, with enough input from Finlayson for Gee to insist they share the writing credit. The role of the Cobham police was much reduced and the story focused more firmly on the disturbed relationship between Katie and her father, which Finlayson had recognised from the outset as more interesting and a stronger subject than small-town Cobham and its cops: a study of obsessive love and emotional repression. (As Gee remarked to Finlayson when he sent him the first story outline: 'I feel fairly much at home with obsessive characters'.)[22] But the essential story remained the same. There was no suicide, but still a murder. Since the death of her mother when she was a child Katie has been protected—virtually imprisoned—from the outside world by her grieving father, until she one day meets 'happy-go-lucky young farm worker'[23] Albie (a tousle-haired Andy Anderson) and runs away to the commune he has joined, Still River (in the original version Xanadu)—evidently modelled on the Esalen-inspired Centrepoint commune at Albany founded by former pest exterminator Bert Potter a few years earlier (and already attracting notoriety). There she is raped by the commune's Potter-like guru, Stan Gubbins (a convincingly creepy Frank Whitten in a kaftan), and escapes, and in the earlier version of the story makes her way to Auckland where she ends up in a seedy boarding house and takes an overdose; the autopsy reveals that she was pregnant. As revised, the ride she hitches when she flees the commune takes her up north to a rugged sheep farm, where she gets work as a shearer's rousie and thrives in the rustic setting and 'the rich and easy friendship of the farming family',[24] until, discovering she is pregnant, she decides to return home to her father. Shifting the action from Auckland and Mortimer's search for the missing Katie there (the film's working title was 'Finding Katie') to a Northland sheep farm was Finlayson's idea (as, in fact, had been the Auckland section in the first place, intended to beef up the Mortimer role), partly for the visual appeal, and 'not least because it could provide humour and optimism'.[25] And it didn't require Katie's suicide to prompt the sudden, brutal murder of Gubbins and Wells' final mental disintegration.

'Finding Katie' was shot at Bethell's Beach, Muriwai and Anawhata on Auckland's west coast, at Silverdale, and for the commune on a Hare Krishna farm at Waimauku. By the time it was released in March 1984 the title had become *Trespasses* (Finlayson's suggestion). It was not a success, attracting poor audiences and unexcited reviews, although new 'lifestyle' magazine *Metro* would rate it fifth of the 'five most underrated/misunderstood movies' of 1984.[26] It did get some overseas sales, but not enough to earn Gee the $15,000 from his 1.5 per cent profit share (on top of his $8000 writing fee) that Finlayson had suggested it would if successful. Its major weakness, which reviewers saw, was the uncomfortable fit between psychological drama and detective story: that it seemed to be trying to be two films at once. (He had managed the mix better with *In My Father's Den*.) The film looked good though. The cinematography was by Leon Narbey.

Of his involvement with the project, Gee told a reporter on the local paper after he had been up to watch the filming that it had been fun but 'only a harmless flirtation . . . It was all extremely interesting but he'd really rather write a good book.' The film's familiar theme, he also said, 'the violence that stems from puritanism and repression', was 'a preoccupation that he has largely "gone past" in his fiction'. Just as Raymond Sole, cub reporter in Gerritson, a small town 'on the edge of the Hauraki plains', thinks he has 'grown out of' his family and Peacehaven now.[27]

Sole Survivor was published in June 1983, with a launch at Book House in Wellington—a 'modest affair', at Gee's request[28]—and two–three months later in London, delayed by an unfathomable error on the part of the Hong Kong printer who had pasted the final page onto the inside back cover, as Rosemary Goad was 'appalled' to discover when she returned from her Easter holiday in April.[29] Faber returned their stock to be [rebound], but Penguin went ahead and released theirs anyway. Reviewers (a few at least) did not fail to notice: 'Ordinary buyers of books will be annoyed', wrote one. 'Librarians will be furious.'[30]

The narrative present this time is the early 1980s, and Golden Bay, where Raymond Sole, 50, has retreated to his daughter Sharon's to lie in the sun and take stock of his life. While it had been fairly obvious that this would be Raymond's story, not so was the prominent role of his cousin Duggie, son of Willis and Mirth; although it had been a clue, perhaps, that he had been born in the adjacent maternity-hospital bed. As Raymond's story, it is also the story of the complicated, symbiotic relationship between him and his cousin. Meg, describing and dismissing the adult Duggie, when he is the upstart 32-year-old National member of parliament for Epsom with ambition to become prime minister—'Raymond . . . seems to detest him, although I'm not sure . . . But enough of Duggie. He's not worth anyone's time'—had been both right and very wrong.[31]

The opening scene of the novel resonates with both *Plumb* and *Meg*. When Raymond comes across his niece Jilly and her boyfriend and second cousin, Hank (son of one of the Plumb daughters who stayed in America), making love in the Aorere River he reacts as 'an old ex-puritan and ex-family-freak. I caught a brimstone whiff and mounted on my toes to thunderbolt them', then sees that 'what they made was beautiful' and lingers to watch, until '[m]y vision, if I can call it that, was over.'[32] But while *Sole Survivor* is very much of the trilogy, it also feels different. There is less, or seems to be less, overlap of time and story than between the previous two, although structurally and through language, symbol and metaphor it works in a similar way; and, like *Meg* did of *Plumb*, it revises and enriches our reading of those two.

Our picture of Willis and Mirth is one of the corrections, or re-seeings, *Sole Survivor* gives us. Both Meg's and her father's respective myths of their happy, good marriage and orchard Eden are contradicted by Ray's account of them as 'flamboyant and tricky', 'life-lovers' who devour what they desire,[33] and his understanding that it is his chaotic and frequently violent home life that has damaged his cousin: that from here come Duggie's capacity for cruelty, need to control and ruthless pursuit of power. Duggie will not become prime minister but he will destroy many people in his ambition to. That rise, and sudden fall, more than the less dramatic story of Raymond Sole provides the novel's narrative shape and its momentum.

We get too a different, and very slight, version of Robert: to Ray '[s]low and adenoidal. Shirt tucked into his underpants. It astonished me that Mum had romanticized him' (though he thinks, fleetingly, that he also perceives some 'cleverness').[34] Also a lesser, smaller Plumb. To the young Duggie his grandfather is merely a figure of ridicule and easy victim of cruel-spirited pranks (our first sign of Duggie's nastiness). To the Sole children his random pronouncements at the Sunday dinner table, before he goes off to his study 'to scribble something down', leave them 'sniggering; confused; or in a state of wonder'.[35] As a teenager Ray will come to share his mother's veneration of her father, in answer to his own needs: 'I overlooked his confusions and saw him as a kind of monolith, an Easter Island god frowning at the horizon. He took me out there with him and for a time I was safe. . . . I came to believe I was descended from a special line. It helped explain my loneliness and helped me fix my superior smile.' But this is only after the death of his Grandpa Sole. The younger Ray venerates his railway-blacksmith grandfather, with 'his grimy head and porous cheeks and granite chin. His hairy ears. His body clothed in railway black' and 'little clear blue eyes': 'a great block of a man [who] stands at one side of my childhood like a wall I could lean against', whom he helps in his vegetable garden and to bottle his home-brew; while Grandma Sole's front room, where the curtains are always drawn and the light never on, and which he is allowed in for five minutes during his weekly visits, not Plumb's study is his cave of treasures.[36]

'Getting a proper distance from it is the problem', Gee told Ray Richards when he was struggling with *Sole Survivor* in 1981.[37] It was not autobiographical, but of course it contained 'a lot of stuff that connects with my life'.[38] Gerritson, where Ray spends two years as a proofreader and junior reporter, is Gee's Paeroa; Primrose Hall, its cabbagey smell and porridge, its 'dodgy' residents, Mrs Fitz and Friday night fish and chips, is a composite of Heysham House and the boarding house he stayed in in Waihī, with the 'genteel' dining room with 'bubbly' wallpaper, its Maxfield Parrish and *Soldiers of the Queen*. Here 'I felt I was away from home at last.'[39] Ray spends some bohemian years in Wellington, living in the Ghuznee Street bach, reading Kierkegaard and Camus, and struggling with a 'melancholy' which 'was a result of breathing air thick with disappointments and defeats. . . . No girls—at least none of the sort I wanted—and not much money.' The writer types we meet at a party in a flat just off The Terrace (Angela Sears') bear assorted resemblances to those of Gee's 1950s Wellington: poets wearing berets and red cravats, one a 'renegade Catholic', whose work is published in *Image* and *Numbers* (some Yelash in one, a bit of Baxter in another); John Jolly who writes stories and gets a job on *Truth* (Brian Bell); girls finishing BAs and going on to teachers' college in Auckland. When Ray marries Glenda they buy a house in Wadestown with a harbour view: from their bed they watch the Orongorongos on the eastern skyline 'browse like herds of elephants'. Wellington will always retain its magic in Gee's literary imagination. It 'lifted me and blew me about', Raymond Sole writes. On his first visit there (a weekend jaunt with Duggie which turns to disaster) 'I promised I would live in Wellington.'[40]

'Creepy' is the word women find to describe Ray. It is a word that is suggestive of both his lack of substance, which he recognises in himself ('there was little to me'; 'I wasn't there'),[41] and a voyeuristic, vicarious quality about his life (the opposite of Duggie, who is all ego and will), and of his sexual preoccupations. At university he was 'filled with envy of those easy boys who sat in the cafeteria, who walked in the cloisters and the park, holding girls by the hand. I had an image of myself wrapped in a sticky membrane' (a creepy image).[42] '[T]he darkness that surrounds sex in my mind would take some explaining', he writes towards the novel's end. Yet there has been some: in his humiliation at the hands of Myra in the back of a van on the side of a road in Wadestown on that trip with Duggie; and in his adolescent pain, when he had been 'eaten with sexual guilt. Guilt was the big thing in my life', and humiliated by his 'trouble', and only in his uncle Alf finds someone in whom he can confide 'about the thing that worried me—tortured me': it is Alfred whose understanding and advice 'put me back in the human race'.[43] (The 'admiration' Gee would have for himself for 'getting through' his own tormented adolescence gives another meaning, perhaps, to the novel's title.)[44]

The childhood experience of watching a man dive into the tidal pool at Moa Park and break his neck is the fulcrum of this novel, in much the way Alfred's casting out and death were in *Plumb* and *Meg*—another involving sex and death and evil—although here the event is narrated in the early chapters. In fictionalising this experience Gee moves it on a few years from his own and makes the man an American marine, and conflates the story with another powerful boyhood memory: Ray, Duggie and their friend Beak Wyatt have paddled down Loomis creek that day 'in canoes made from roofing iron and sealed with pitch'. (Beak, however, 'a stringy boy with a blade of a nose', is not Minnie from Falls Park but is drawn from another boyhood friend: Lofty Blomfield when he and Moss—Ken Kenneth—wrestled in the Henderson school playground.) As in the first story, Ray is left alone with the man beside the pool and the girl who won't let him leave, collecting 'a series of images: his eyes staring up with a faraway look; the wound in his head, oozing like a boil; and the lump on his neck, white and shiny as an egg', and his fingers broken and nails bleeding except for the little finger on one hand which 'was bent back at an angle and the nail there was a lady's, white as milk and beautifully clean' (Gee's own collected memory). The event will stay inside Ray, and Beak too, for the rest of their lives—'I see him still . . . I can feel the day break apart. Something broke in me, like snapping rubber'; it will cause Beak to take his own life; Duggie will use it as political capital (it made a good story).[45] The evil is there at the beginning in Duggie's knowledge, as they watched the man bouncing on his toes at the end of the board, showing off to his friends, that he really is going to dive.

More than Meg's, Ray's is a tale of deaths. There is Glenda's suicide, by drowning off Wellington's south coast on the day of the *Wahine* storm, having never got over her father's, by shotgun when she was a teenager after a torrid, very public divorce (the case presided over by Oliver Plumb). Beak Wyatt drowns himself in Loomis creek, in grief and loneliness after his wife's death, and still carrying the guilt-laden memory of that day at Moa Park (he saw that Duggie knew and could have yelled out in time, he believes, to save the man): this death too Duggie watches, knowing. Wendy Philson had tried to—Ray's mother told him—lovesick for and rejected by Reverend Plumb. Ray only fantasises about it, that night of his humiliation by Myra—of 'tumbling off like a shot man, sinking into the clean cold, not coming up'—plays it as a scene until he sees himself being self-indulgent.[46]

The catalogue of off-stage deaths includes Fergus's, Merle Butters', lost Helen Plumb's. We witness Meg's, by fire when she accidentally pours petrol instead of kerosene onto the wood range and the Peacehaven cottage burns down—an echo across two books and 30 years of her father burning his hand on her new electric stove (and making sense of the mysterious message Merle passed on to Meg after his death, to '*beware of . . . bottles without labels*').[47]

First and last there is Duggie's, the fact of which we learn in the first pages of the novel, the reason for at the end: a revenge killing by the improbably named Alaric Gibbs (a name which seems to belong in *Plumb* rather than this novel; but the allusion is deliberate), whose 'pure but *corruptible*' nineteen-year-old daughter never recovered from her callous treatment by Duggie and has spent the rest of her life in a psychiatric hospital. As Ray tells Duggie (as Gee's novels are always telling us): 'Things have got a way of coming back.'[48]

'It's a book that could have been much longer, perhaps should have been longer', Gee told Bill Manhire, '—but length was predetermined by its being part of the trilogy.'[49] In truth he had rushed the ending, and the book suffered from it, he recognised himself,[50] wanting to get it finished before they went away. And perhaps, too, because he was 'getting tired of the Plumbs now'.[51] The last third of the novel does feel rushed: compressed and in a hurry. To Manhire, who thought so, the earlier parts, however, contained some of Gee's best writing: 'His sense of the way in which childhood experiences give rise to adolescence, and adolescence to adulthood, is remarkable'.[52] Gee saw too 'a kind of thinning out, perhaps a loss of solidity in the social background . . . as I get up towards the present day', oddly, perhaps, because this was more recently lived experience; but he would always find writing about the past more satisfying (if not easier) than writing about the present.[53]

There was criticism also that there were too many plot contrivances, betrayals of character to advance story, with which he did not agree, notably from academic critics Brian Boyd, in the *Listener*, and Lawrence Jones in a more extended assessment in *Landfall*. It was Boyd's letter to Gee enclosing a copy of his (otherwise positive) review and elaborating at some length on the point ('I'm sure you can eradicate all these convenient eyewitnessings and handy confessions motivated evidently by you rather than the characters' own nature and circumstances. It would take careful and probably very gruelling foreplanning, but . . . to put it another way: if you have to choose whether to leave out or persist with a scene you're sure you must have but have to rig up precariously then I'd say leave it out') that prompted a comment to Manhire that he 'seems to have made it his mission to instruct me how to write', and Gee's continuing wariness of Boyd's critical interest in him—'I have the feeling that I'm becoming a bit of his property.' (He continued to turn down his requests for interviews.)[54]

He had Boyd to thank for one thing in the book, though: Ray reading that Edward Carpenter had been Whitman's '"friend"'—'Would Grandpa have banished them like Alf if someone had forced him to know?' When Boyd had noted in his essay on *Plumb* in *Islands* the irony of Plumb invoking Edward Carpenter, 'the prophet of . . . high-minded homosexuality', when he is musing on his 'vision splendid' on the morning of the day he banishes Alfred, Gee told him that he had known once but had forgotten that about Carpenter (though was aware of Whitman's sexual nature); 'I agree that it provides a splendid irony.'[55]

If *Sole Survivor* was not as well liked as *Plumb* and *Meg*, it had more to do, though, with its bleakness of vision and its narrative tone. In part this lies in the depth of Duggie's depravity, and in Duggie as a study of the corruption of power: yes, 'an ugly picture of N.Z. Perhaps things aren't as bad as I picture them—a bit of colour taken from my own temperament I think', Gee responded to Davin's appreciation ('A most powerful work; grim, even. . . . What a poisonous bastard your Duggie is'); 'I hope to lighten things next time'.[56] It is also to do with Raymond himself. He is less admirable and (by Gee's admission) 'much less likeable' than Plumb and Meg; he doesn't even much like himself. Ray's concerns, as his author comments, are 'shallower' than theirs.[57] The adult Ray has no faith in his grandfather's big concepts, in Love and Man. The vision he has, looking down on Wellington city from above Wadestown on his first night there, is no transcendent 'vision splendid' but a smaller, prosaic (but disturbing) one: 'people showing glow-worm lights on the edge of nothing. I thought it was a good one—it would do me.'[58] He doesn't have political convictions: in the brief youthful period when he did, during 1951, when he paints anti-Sid Holland slogans on the Gerritson water tower (making up for Gee's studious non-engagement in the year of the waterfront dispute) he gets his swastika the wrong way round.

He lacks too Meg's sustaining (if battered) belief in love and family. Ray does not only fail at love, and fail Glenda; he does not believe that love can save her. His cynicism develops early, and he doesn't lose it. 'I do not believe in right woman. Or right anything much', he writes after his brother Bobby has asked him—early in the novel's pages, late in its narrative time—if he thinks he'll get married again, 'Right beginnings, right ends. Even right circumstances.'[59] He learns less than Plumb, and his hopes are smaller than Meg's. The position he has reached by the novel's end—sitting on a rock at the confluence of two 'rivers, creeks', looking out for an eel—his accommodation with his past and a way to go forwards, is a blander, accepting stoicism.[60]

Ray's narrative voice, also, is both less compelling and singular than Plumb's and less engaging than Meg's. The style is a mixture of laconic and the journalist's glib slickness and flourish (described by Lawrence Jones as 'the Shadbolt shoddy of the Sunday papers'), which he doesn't admire himself: he would rather strip away the adjectives, adverbs, even verbs—'The truth is in nouns and pronouns'—as Meg wished to rid hers of the sentimental.[61] As a journalist he is especially good at satire. He too is a failed writer: his projected biography of Michael Joseph Savage remains a collection of research notes in a suitcase, while his uncle Emerson won't let him write his. Appropriately for a man who knows himself that he lacks substance, and observes rather than does, the books he does write are ghost-written biographies of the unimportantly famous: footballers and film stars. Another writer who observes himself writing, it is telling, too, that 'meanwhile' is a favourite word—one suggestive of a habit of absence, indirection or evasion.[62]

Britain's *Financial Times*, in an admiring review, captured *Sole Survivor*'s discomforting tone: 'deadpan and staccato; the eye steady, rather chill; the sense of uncosiness powerful'.[63] Reviewers there liked the novel better than (for the most part) those in New Zealand, and more than *Meg*: 'brilliant . . . Gee is surely one of the richest writers around. His strength, like Cleopatra's, is his infinite variety, and he, too, makes hungry where he most satisfies' (the *New Statesman*); his 'vigorous writing style'—his 'short jerky sentences'—were 'reminiscent at first of Ed McBain' but it 'soon reveals a depth and sensitivity that place him in the forefront of Commonwealth novelists' (*Oxford Times*); in the *Scotsman* it was praised as 'a subtle and mature achievement by a masterly novelist'.[64] There were equally enthusiastic reviews in the *Observer*, the *Standard* (excerpted in the *Auckland Star* under the heading 'UK critics acclaim new Gee novel'), the *London Review of Books* and the *TLS* (by Fleur Adcock).[65] Only the title came in for negative comment. 'The British publicity seems to be booming though Maurice is morose about it', Margaretha told Bill and Marion Manhire: 'Hates words like "best" or whatever was used & is sure a Gee backlash is developing.'[66]

Again, as with *Meg*, this critical enthusiasm was not matched by sales: 'respectable' rather than 'spectacular', Rosemary Goad reported in February.[67] In New Zealand the reviews were more mixed than for *Meg*, but conversely this did not stop it selling just as well, the initial, hardback run at least; paperback sales over the following three or four years would be only half *Meg*'s. In America, where it was published by St Martin's—theirs 'a much nicer book than Faber's', Gee thought—it sold poorly, although they had done reasonably well with *Meg* (2500), and the reviews, as of *Meg*, were mostly admiring.[68] It can't have helped that still no one would take *Plumb* (however confident Richards might be): that one was considered too strongly rooted in New Zealand political and religious history for parochial American readers. And for some there, *Sole Survivor* was just all too sordid: 'lurid and perverse', said the *New York Times Book Review*; 'the reader is inundated with suicide, assassination, deviant sexuality and depression' (*Tulsa World*): 'Macabre and eccentric, it will win awards for fiction, but will justifiably fail to win an audience.'[69]

23

Life After Plumb

Sole Survivor did not win any awards; it was not even shortlisted for the New Zealand Book Awards. The fiction winner for that year was Keri Hulme's soon-to-be Booker Prize-winning *the bone people*. That itself, and the shortlist overall, were a marker of two dominant trends in New Zealand fiction since the 1970s: all but one of the titles were by women and/or Māori writers (along with Hulme, Janet Frame, Fiona Kidman and J.C. Sturm); the exception was a conservationist- and Māori-themed novel for children. Gee might be seen in these literary times as unfashionable. 'Old-fashioned' was a term he himself used of his novels, but placing them in the context of another trend of the times: the rise of the self-reflexive, postmodern novel—linguistically self-conscious and playing with its form. 'I have an old fashioned interest in character, a belief in consequences, especially moral consequences, . . . and I believe that the world that presents itself to my senses is a real world', he told a PEN audience in November 1984. And while he admired the cleverness of the playful postmodernists he didn't particularly enjoy reading their novels.[1] (His literary discovery of the year, he told the *New Zealand Listener* for its 'best of the year' round-up in 1983, was Alice Munro, a small writer with a narrow range who 'simply tells stories', but in which 'one instantly recognises particular truth, and truth of another sort behind it'.)[2]

'Literary survivor', the *Listener* (a little unflatteringly, perhaps) introduced the *Kaleidoscope* segment on Gee which screened on television in June 1983, on the eve of the publication of *Sole Survivor*, although in reference apparently to the seven years he had spent writing the *Plumb* trilogy, and to the 'long apprenticeship' he had put himself through before it.[3] Or perhaps it meant surviving financially as a full-time writer. Filmed at Cleveland Terrace, the piece projected his ordinary, slightly old-fashioned persona: 'a shy man living quietly in Nelson', as the *Listener* described him. Realising that a shy writer sitting at his desk with an exercise book and a ballpoint pen would not make riveting television, the director was challenged to find something to show him actually doing: hence the shot of him mowing the lawn. His next novel, though, was to push at the edges of that uncosy mainstream realism, even if Gee might not think of himself as consciously engaging with the postmodern idea.

He had felt a huge sense of 'completion and relief' on finishing *Sole Survivor*, and with it the *Plumb* trilogy, the 'big novel' he had waited so long to write, relief at the achievement rather (or more) than from fatigue. 'I can remember thinking, well gosh, even if I die now I've done it . . . I could relax.'[4] His next one was to be his most enjoyable writing experience. But it was a while coming. The next half-dozen years were productive but frustrating ones. The Gees were making 'a moderately good living'[5] in the 1980s, but it was neither a regular nor a secure one. Twice he put aside an adult novel when the money ran out.

He went back, firstly, to O and was well on the way with book two of the trilogy, *The Priests of Ferris*, when the first won the recently inaugurated New Zealand children's book award in May 1983. He sent the manuscript away in July, slightly delayed, he had advised OUP, by his financial situation (they offered to send an advance on his advance to pay for a typist to get it finished). Richards was helping him out from time to time too, but more substantially—advancing him $1000 that May, for example, and at the same time hassling OUP for speedy payment of his royalties because he was 'genuinely short of funds'.[6]

'I'm still grinding out TV scripts', he told Bill Manhire later in July, but he hoped to be done with them in a month or so: two episodes for the revived third season of *Mortimer's Patch*, and one for a new, post-war rural medical drama, *Country GP*.[7] He had accepted a commission as well for a one-hour television play (one of a projected series), titled 'Titles are My Weakness' in his contract and eventually 'A Public Life, or a Hiding Place'. He had written this firstly as a short story which he entered for the Katherine Mansfield award this year. It was to be neither produced nor published (nor was it placed in the awards), but its main character was to reappear. Florence Norton ('Florrie' of the story's title) is a once Labour cabinet minister and mayor—she went into politics in the 30s, was voted out in '69—knocking back the sherry in her retirement but staunch and straight-talking still. She is being interviewed by the journalist-boyfriend of her niece, who won't, her son tells her, adamantly, be interested in hearing about her private life and in lifting any lids on the past; these are things she has never spoken about. But unlike her son she is ready now to acknowledge the moment of self-knowledge—'almost a vision of evil'[8]—that her whole political career has been a running away from: on that day when she was told that her fifteen- and thirteen-year-old sons, swimming in the creek ('one of those khaki ones, smelling of mud and eels and decay') had become entangled in submerged barbed wire and only one had been saved, and as she ran to the swimming hole she 'asked for it to be one drowned and not the other'. That she had made a choice—'offered one for the other'—is the terrible realisation she has spent the rest of her life trying 'not to see'. (Yet the further, more unsettling revelation is that the choice she made is not the one her surviving son, ever since that day he 'came up from the creek and found that a huge mistake was made', has thought.)[9]

He had been hoping to be getting started on a new novel in October. In October he was digging out—again—a blocked septic tank: 'an appropriate job'.[10] Then it was back to scriptwriting, and a film treatment he had begun working on the previous month. He had been approached to write a film about the Erebus disaster, the crash of Air New Zealand sightseeing flight 901 into the side of Mt Erebus in Antarctica in November 1979, killing all 257 people on board, and the ensuing investigations, based on the just-published book *Impact Erebus* by crusading Air New Zealand pilot Gordon Vette—a story of 'human tragedy and triumph', Ray Richards pitched it to him.[11] The commission came from an American company who were looking to make a 90-minute feature film, hopefully a New Zealand–US co-production, possibly with a New Zealand director. Their projected budget was $US6.5 million: this was a bigger deal than *Trespasses*. With input from Vette, Gee produced a preliminary treatment by the end of September, and another, longer one by November, fictionalising it this time (for both legal and dramatic reasons). LA had also advised him to keep the story simple, its focus on the theme of 'one man battling for the truth to be discovered and to be told'—'CHARACTER: Think of Steve McQueen in BULLITT or some such film; think of Paul Newman in Hud'; and to add a little humour. They liked his second version, in which he also added at their suggestion a romance between Vette (now Strid, a Henderson name)[12] and the attractive young lawyer who assists him ('[t]he lone hero can have no wife'; thus Vette was no longer married but instead widowed).[13] It failed, however, to attract development funding and by the end of the year they had taken the project away from him to give to two American writers. Gee was philosophical. 'I dreamed of big money for a while,' he told Richards, but was not surprised at what had happened. He was only aggrieved about the meagre $US500 he had been paid: that time spent on a *Mortimer's Patch* episode would have earned him $3600. (Vette, meanwhile, upset by the developments, paid him $500 out of his own pocket.)[14]

'[H]ints of prosperity from movie and television scriptwriting; hard booze in the cupboard now instead of home brew', Maurice Shadbolt reported to Kevin Ireland after seeing Gee in Nelson at Christmas; 'but on to a new novel nonetheless'.[15] This was still not, however, the new adult novel, which Gee was now hoping to get started on in June or July. In January he had begun the third O book, *Motherstone*, and finished it in October, a month after *The Priests of Ferris* came out, after a few interruptions along the way.

In *The Priests of Ferris* Susan and Nick had returned to O a year, or a hundred O years, later to find that evil had once again taken hold and the people of O were held in sadistic subjection through the power of a sham religion; also, happily for Gee's young readers as well as for Susan and Nick, that Jimmy Jaspers, who had stayed behind last time, is not long since dead but has been in hibernation with his bear-friend Ben, a Varg, a race of great blue-white bears who cannot speak but communicate through telepathic power. Susan's flight from Deven's Leap in an improvised hang glider (handily built by Nick) at the end of the last book has become the founding Miracle of the cult of Ferris, whose sinister priests in their skin-tight white leather suits and white-painted faces resemble skeletons (or *Star Wars* Stormtroopers); around their necks on leather cords they wear human bones—the bones of heretics who have been thrown to their deaths from Deven's Leap—which click together as they move (reminiscent, perhaps, of the beads and crosses that 'jigged heavily' on the chests of the Holy Cross nuns—'sinister, dangerous'—of Gee's childhood).[16] Susan's mission is to destroy this corrupt religion that has been created in her name before the Chosen One, Soona (a girl her age), is sacrificed in the upcoming centennial ceremony. But Susan's plan to persuade the High Priest—who turns out, disappointingly, to be a mousy, 'roly-poly', bespectacled little man who looks more like a retired judge or a headmaster[17]—by words and truth that his religion is a lie is thwarted because he knows that: it is merely a means by which the people of O are kept under control. (It is the Varg, finally, who comes to everyone's rescue, by wielding his silent power of persuasion over the High Priest's tame Bloodcat.)

Susan and Nick have not even left O when, as *Motherstone* opens, they are seized just as they reach their cave-portal by Osro, a renegade priest of the High Priest's inner circle who now aspires to rule over O. While Nick manages to escape, Osro takes Susan to the northern Hotlands—thermal country which, as Jimmy Jaspers puts it, 'makes Rotorua look like a Turkish bath'—where he is building a secret Weapon, one which will 'shrivel men to ashes', 'sear down buildings', 'burn trees and melt stone': something between an atomic bomb and a laser.[18] Hearing this, the ruling council of the Freemen of O set about building their own, believing that this is the only way to defeat Osro and his Hotlander army. The allusion to a nuclear arms race, at the time of United States president Ronald Reagan's Strategic Defense Initiative, is very clear. He was writing exciting adventure stories in the first instance, Gee always insisted, but there were 'lessons' in them if children wanted to find them. In *The Priests of Ferris* it is the danger of totalitarianism and abuse of political power: 'It's an attempt to describe for children a kind of police state', he told the *Listener*, in which the priests are 'simply secret police', like the Stasi, used to control the people through 'threat, terror and superstition'. In *The Halfmen of O* (though less overtly) it was the degradation of the natural environment.[19]

Susan's task this time, a harder one, is to replace the two halves on the Motherstone with two new stones, at which point the humankind of O will be returned to a primordial state from which it can start again: she must destroy civilisation in order to save it. Taken together, the O trilogy is a bleak vision, in its cyclical pattern of fall and redemption. Each time, the two cousins find that the lessons of the past have not been learned and evil has again taken hold, and the promise of another future at the end seems a precarious one. But Gee's audience didn't seem to mind. Unlike the *Plumb* trilogy, the response to which was progressively less enthusiastic, for this one it remained undiminished—even though Gee's young readers, it seems, did not much like Susan Ferris. When a *Listener* writer asked a group of primary school children to review *The Priests of Ferris* 'our critics,' she reported, 'with a few exceptions, disliked the heroine with varying degrees of intensity': 'a goody-goody', said one; conversely, 'moody, inconsiderate and determined to get her own way and to do everything by herself', thought another, though they admired her bravery and initiative. It was still Jimmy Jaspers—'funny and yet serious and fantastically brave'—who stole the show.[20]

Those interruptions as Gee worked on *Motherstone* in 1984 had included more work for television. He had been invited by Television New Zealand at the end of the last year to submit an idea for a 'major' production, the subject and setting of his choosing: 'It is I suppose obvious', head of drama Stephen McElrea told him, 'that TVNZ look on your skills with the highest regard'.[21] He came up with a series about a middle-aged couple running a boarding house in a town 'like Collingwood, but bigger': the husband has been made redundant by the local cheese factory; she is the slightly snobby daughter of the founding family of the town. The major theme would be 'marital harmony'—and some disharmony—'amidst the pressure of constant invasion by the outside world and under the handicap of wide diversities of character and outlook . . . It's a marriage that works, in spite of its being a joining of opposites.' The boarding house guests would provide the storyline for each episode.[22] He submitted a script for a pilot episode of 'Winchip House' mid-year—one of three they were commissioning for the projected 44-episode series—then heard nothing from them for over a year. Winchip was another programme that was never made.

He also wrote another short story, which he sent in June along with his last *Islands* story, 'Buried Treasure, Old Bones', to Penguin for a proposed collected stories. With *A Glorious Morning, Comrade* now nearly out of stock, Auckland University Press, at the prompting of Robin Dudding, had made plans to reprint, with additional stories if there were any (Dudding had suggested there might be), before relinquishing their rights to Penguin—as according to Richards' plan. If 'Joker and Wife' was a new story, though, there was not much new about it. It was set in a Henderson-like town called Beavis, and described the relationship between a couple strongly resembling Lyndahl and Len, and their son's (the narrator's) shifting allegiance. From his father he learned practical things, and admired quickness and cruelty; with his mother he learned to venerate beauty and the spiritual plane: 'We were a little mad, my mother and I, engaged in a form of *folie à deux*'; alone with her 'I believed myself special', stepping outside 'I . . . behaved in a proper way'.[23]

While Penguin's publication plans for the volume remained uncertain he entered 'Joker and Wife' for the Katherine Mansfield award in 1985 (it came second). Two new stories in two years did not, however, signal a return to the form; he was not to write another for another sixteen years.

A distraction rather than an interruption, meanwhile, had been a fight with the Inland Revenue Department, who had just noticed that Gee had not declared his prize monies for *Plumb* in his 1979/80 tax return and were now demanding that he pay up. Gee had assumed, not unreasonably, that literary prizes were not taxable. He won this fight, with the support of PEN who had decided to treat it as a test case (but were careful to note that the IRD's decision that 'the prizes in question' were not liable for tax did not necessarily make it a general ruling). 'It is difficult to see', PEN's Fiona Kidman had written in the *Listener* in an article on authors and their incomes, 'how the few thousand dollars involved will greatly affect the country's economy. But it may make it difficult for Gee to commence a new novel next month.'[24]

That was several months away still, during which he wrote another television script, a five-part 'kidult' series he had been approached about by TVNZ in June. They preferred something historical, they had said ('period material is more saleable'),[25] and he found the beginnings of his story in the research for his history of Nelson Central School, setting it in Nelson during the First World War: a story about a serial arsonist whose identity is discovered by 'a Blyton four'[26] of twelve-year-olds. He sent in his script of what was provisionally titled 'Mr Hedges' School' in September and they were 'delighted' with it. This was a series that would be made. As these things work, though, filming and broadcast were well over a year away.[27]

When Gee spoke as guest of honour at PEN's 50th jubilee dinner in Dunedin in November 1984 he revealed some anxiety about getting on with that new novel. 'Life after Plumb isn't easy', he said. It was three years since he had written adult fiction and while that was partly because he had been busy writing for money, it was also 'that I've felt used up'. Recently though 'the clouds have started to lift away from something else', although he was 'not sure what it is' yet.

He had been asked to speak about how he came to write the

Plumb novels, and he talked about his two youthful, failed novels, about his Henderson and Chapple inheritance—the weight of place and family—and about the construction of the trilogy; but not about the novels themselves (that he would leave to others). Among other things he also talked about the vagaries of reviews and the fascination of critical essays, and about the labour of writing, with which he struggled at the most basic level: 'I'm not a natural writer,' he said, 'and I'll never be a stylist'; he could construct a novel, write chapters and paragraphs, find words and make phrases 'but with sentences I just can't seem to get on' (hence he liked to keep them short). And, not for the last time, he addressed that annoyingly frequent accusation of 'being gloomy, of putting in too much death and suicide. I can only reply', he said here, 'that in my fifty years I've known five people who committed suicide, two who were later murdered, and I've seen a person die in an accident.' And he had grown up by a creek in which people did drown and where bodies were hidden, not only by him: where a family of four children drowned during the time he lived there, and later a body was disposed of in 'a murder too horrible to describe here' (both recorded though, passingly, in 'Joker and Wife').[28]

Still, he had told a journalist this year, 'I'd love to write a good comic novel. Change my standpoint, look through another prism. But that's a dream more than a hope.'[29]

He started the new novel, finally, in February, calling it 'Papps' after its main character, a curmudgeonly retired soil scientist. He put it aside at the end of August, with a rough draft done and needing nine months to complete it, but out of money, and sent off an application for the Literary Fund Scholarship in Letters (turning down a few weeks later another big television contract, which, he commented to Bill Manhire, 'felt good, but risky').[30]

While he waited on the outcome of this he went back to his kidult drama, now called *The Fire-Raiser*, for which TVNZ were about to start casting. Before he signed his contract he had made sure that he would retain the rights to reuse the material for a novel (a 'very common publishing idea these days', Tom Finlayson had remarked to him a few years earlier, 'seems to be to develop a novel from the screenplay. The Americans have a word for it . . . Novelisation!!! Ych').[31] He had a manuscript written in a couple of months and sent it to Ray Richards in November. At this point, however, things became complicated. Although Oxford had published all three of the O books now, Richards offered *The Fire-Raiser* to Penguin, with 'a twinge, but not much more, of conscience about OUP', he told Gee. It was a matter of timing, in part. The plan was for publication of the novel to coincide with the screening of the series on TV—currently scheduled for July or August the next year—and Richards had no confidence that OUP would be able to get it out that fast. It was also important, he told them, that it come out in paperback in order for Gee to get maximum royalties: he was 'going through a period of serious financial deprivation', he explained. *The Fire-Raiser* was 'a quickie, out of the mainstream of Maurice's other junior novels'.[32]

This was not all of it, of course, and somewhat disingenuous. Richards had already suggested to Gee more than once over the last eighteen months that he should consider moving his children's fiction from Oxford to Penguin, partly in the interests of tidiness, and of Gee's economic returns, partly because he was finding OUP since its retrenchment more and more difficult to deal with ('something of a Mickey Mouse outfit these days', as he put it to Faber, and—more bluntly to Gee—'a pain in the neck').[33] Gee signed a contract for *The Fire-Raiser* with Penguin in December (for a hardback, in fact, under Penguin's Viking Kestrel junior hardback imprint, to be followed by a Puffin paperback). Oxford's response was to seek legal advice and threaten to begin injunction proceedings on the grounds of breach of contract (as Gee's *Motherstone* contract had an option clause).

The situation was resolved soon and apparently amicably enough, with no further legal action, with *The Fire-Raiser* published (in paperback and on time—in August 1986) under the imprint 'Puffin Books in association with Oxford University Press'; and Gee telling Oxford that he was not signing any more contracts which contained option clauses. But it marked a further souring of relations with OUP, the real bone of contention in which was *Plumb*.

'Woe is you and woe is me, in contractual dealings with OUP', Richards quipped in a rhyming couplet to Faber vice-chairman Tony Pocock the following year. Along with *Plumb*, Oxford also held Australasian paperback rights for *In My Father's Den* and *Games of Choice*, which Richards hoped to secure for Penguin when the recent 'well-intentioned but low-selling' Oxford New Zealand Classics editions had 'done their dash'.[34] (*In My Father's Den*, along with John Mulgan's *Report on Experience*, had launched this series in 1984; *Games of Choice* had come out in 1985.) 'I must say', Pocock had replied in February 1985 to a letter from Richards about both these and *Plumb*, 'that the whole of the Gee rights situation, already overgrown before you and I came on the scene, is still a most awful jungle': 'Tiresomely' Oxford's paperback licenses for the two earlier novels were on the same contract, 'something that should always be avoided' (while the original rights for *In My Father's Den* had long since reverted to the now-defunct Winant, Towers). And it was 'extremely embarrassing' that they could find no contract for the license for *Plumb*. Further hunting turned up not only a Faber/OUP contract which was open-ended (thus technically giving OUP the *Plumb* paperback rights in perpetuity), but a second one between Faber and Gee—a 'strange second contract, for which I know of no precedent', and which locked him in with OUP even more firmly: 'Who was advising Maurice in those days?' Richards described OUP's attitude towards *Plumb* to Pocock as 'somewhat obsessively parental'.[35] But Oxford, as they both knew, were hardly going to voluntarily relinquish the lucrative *Plumb* rights when the book was still selling a steady 1450 copies a year and made (as they put it to Gee) 'a significant contribution to our revenue'. Accepting this, Richards instead advised that he would seek a reversion of rights when the current paperback (only recently reprinted) 'reaches the end of its natural life'—which was, Gee had told him, what John Griffin had agreed (verbally) when the deal was first done.[36] But Oxford were remaining coy.

It was in the middle of this conversation that the matter of *The Fire-Raiser* had arisen. In June 1986 Oxford managing director Anne French went down to Nelson for 'a sort of rebuilding of bridges visit. Pleasant enough', Gee reported to Richards, but '[a]s for Plumb, they won't give it up'.[37] That stand-off was to go on for several more years (and become more acrimonious) yet.

The two catalysts for *The Fire-Raiser* were the charismatic, polymathic headmaster of Nelson Central School, Frederick Gibbs, who is closely drawn as Jessop's 'Clippy' Hedges (the story's setting is Nelson in everything but its name), and a local arsonist, a German immigrant bricklayer named Johann Blecher who burned down several Nelson buildings in the 1890s—including the nearly completed Nelson Central School, having seriously damaged the original building two years earlier—claiming in court to have done so in order to make work for the town's unemployed. Gee's arsonist,

Edgar Marwick (a Dickensianly suggestive name), would have a very less noble and much darker motivation. The gang of clever and brave (and entirely fictional) children who unmask him are a disparate foursome brought together by both the mystery and adventure, and a recognisable complex of pre-adolescent like and dislike: Noel and his sister Kitty Wix are the children of the town baker; pretty Irene Chalmers the daughter of Jessop's prosperous mayor and his stuck-up wife; Phil—'Fleabites'—Miller a working-class boy, a 'Port Rat' who has been left to fend for himself after his drunken and unemployed father abandons him.

Updating the fire-raiser story from the 1890s to 1915 (to the displeasure of the TVNZ drama department) allowed Gee to build in a theme of jingoism and xenophobia—unrelated, however, to Blecher's German background—and to utilise another fortuitous library discovery. Gibbs, like Hedges a liberal-minded and tolerant man, had controversially befriended and defended a German music teacher (Jessop's Frau Stauffel) during the First World War. The script of the 'patriotic pageant' the Jessop schoolchildren put on was one Gee had found in the Auckland Teachers' College library in the 1970s and kept a copy of (just in case he might want to use it one day): its performance whips up the less-tolerant Jessop townspeople into an ugly xenophobic fury and a mob, at the incitement of Marwick, attack Lotte Stauffel's house, drag her 'Hun' piano out onto the lawn and set it alight.[38]

Gee's Hedges is Gibbs in not only his liberal-humanist views, the Renaissance breadth of his interests—especially science, music and astronomy—and his imaginative teaching methods but also in quirkish detail: the folding magnifying glass and tuning fork he carried in his pocket; the articulated skeleton he kept locked in a cupboard and brought out for anatomy lessons. Not, though, in his exaggerated ugliness: his 'nose like plasticine dented by a thumb, eyes that went one this way, one that', his 'mouth like a leather purse, full of crooked teeth', skin pitted from childhood illness and 'one of his ears mauled as though by a cat. Children had been known to cry at the sight of him';[39] but it is Edgar Marwick who is truly scary.

The Fire-Raiser is a wholly realist novel but with a Gothic overlay. Marwick is a macabre and genuinely terrifying figure, in flapping black coat and crimson balaclava, stealing by night along Jessop's 'secret ways' in a 'long, wolfish, loping stride', emitting horse-like whinnies and owlish screeches as he watches flames take hold. Batty

Mrs Marwick is a Miss Havisham figure, like a 'witch or spider', Hedges thinks. Mother and son live together in a decaying mansion (the Marwicks had once been rich and respected) whose bow windows look 'like bulbous eyes watching'. Lighting fires gives Edgar Marwick a visceral (almost sexual) charge: 'Flame filled the inside of his head. It ran along his arteries. It licked around his bones', it 'bathed him like water and made him newborn'.[40] But he is shown in the end to be a pathetic as much as a psychotic figure—as the actor who played him in the series put it, 'a frightened man and a bit nasty. Repressed everything—you name it.'[41] Marwick's fire fetish, we learn, arises out of a damaged psyche and his twisted, toxic relationship with his mother, ever since she locked him in a cupboard as punishment after his eight-year-old sister Lucy drowned in Girlie's Hole while he was supposed to be watching her. The terrified Edgar had vanquished the darkness and his mother's power by lighting fires in his head; now he lights real ones.

Lucy's drowning, we also understand, is why Mrs Marwick is so incensed at the schoolchildren swimming. Here are Gibbs stories too: the swimming lessons in the Maitai (the girls in Girlie's Hole, the boys in Buck's); his battle over riparian rights with a local landowner (a Mrs Richardson), who once stole the boys' clothes while they were swimming, and the boys' naked dance around her house (most of the boys at the television auditions were too embarrassed to take off their clothes). It was Gibbs who sabotaged the hydraulic ram. In the penultimate, not so comic scene Mrs Marwick, thinking Kitty is her lost Lucy, almost drowns in Girlie's Hole too.

In an inspired piece of casting, Royal New Zealand Ballet principal Jon Trimmer played Edgar Marwick, in his first straight dramatic role and doing all his own stunts. (It was not through one of these, however, but from an overenthusiastic punch thrown by Peter Hayden as Hedges, that his jaw was broken in rehearsals and had to be wired for three months.) The series was filmed in Whiteman's Valley in Upper Hutt (after an unsuccessful location search in the South Island and Wairarapa) on the reconstructed 'Mason's Valley' set of *Country GP* in February 1986: Maurice and Margaretha went up for the final read-through (followed by cast and crew barbecue) the day before shooting started. It began screening on TV One in late August, in the same week the book went out to the shops, which did not, contrary to the fears of producer Ginette McDonald, seem to do it any harm. The scripts, she told Gee, were 'the best we've ever worked on', reviews glowing ('a beauty', wrote Barry Shaw, 'the sort of children's venture that made Mark Twain so beloved . . . a jolly good story stunningly told') and ratings 'outstanding': by week three it was attracting almost as many viewers as *Happy Days*.[42] It won four awards at the GOFTAs (previously the Feltex awards) the following year—for best drama, best director, best children's programme and best writer (for episode one)—and also an award in Australia (to that industry's surprise and disappointment).[43]

The novel had sold out of the warehouse and a second printing was ordered before the first was in the shops—as *The Fire-Raiser* not the preferred *The Fire-raiser*, TVNZ having 'decided, in its distinctly ungrammatical wisdom, to cap Raiser, so we must follow suit', Penguin's new senior editor, Geoff Walker, grumbled to Gee.[44] By the time of its fourth printing two years later it had sold an 'extraordinary' 10,618 copies (excluding the 5000 to Ashton Scholastic for Australia). In Britain, Penguin waited until a television screening there was confirmed before committing itself, and were to sell 9000 of their 1987 UK Puffin edition (though, disappointingly, would have more than 3000 returns); the series screened on BBC in October that year. A re-edited telemovie version (with the title *Undercover Gang*) was shown on American cable television; it won an award there too. Within three years it had sold to a total of nine overseas countries.[45]

Nineteen eighty-six, as Richards remarked in October in the *Australian Bookseller and Publisher*, was turning out to be a 'vintage year' for Gee (if a grim one for the New Zealand publishing industry in general).[46] As well as the success of *The Fire-Raiser*, and *Motherstone* which had won the Library Association's Esther Glen Award, and by now having completed and had accepted a new novel, his *Collected Stories* had been published in July. For cost reasons Penguin had chosen to offset this from the AUP original (even though that 'wasn't much to shout about') rather than start again, and encountered 'frightful problems' trying the match the original typeface for the two new stories.[47] It was as well that Gee had decided to make only minimal changes and not revise the earlier ones. Although he hadn't wanted it, the back cover blurb contained the explanation that these were 'all I want to republish, the ones that seem to me still worth reading'—'Thirteen stories to show for thirty years' work isn't much, but I don't feel like explaining it', he had told Penguin.[48] The front cover had a photograph of the author looking pensive (even a little sad) in a windbreaker and grey sweatshirt against a rustic backdrop down by the Maitai. But the new edition was a success. Pre-publication sales, Geoff Walker told him as it was about to go to print, were 'a stunning 7000 copies', of which over half were export sales: 'It really has been quite a triumph for us all.' Of those, 1500 were to Viking Penguin (New York). 'At last,' enthused Richards, 'a U.S. paperback!' (albeit the 'quantity is small').[49] This proved not, however, to be the big break into the sought-after US market he, and of course Gee, hoped for. Viking a few months later rejected *The Halfmen of O* ('a bit bizarre and a little too strange' for their list, they said).[50] The next success there would be Houghton Mifflin taking *The Fire-Raiser* in 1992. Another adult novel in America continued to elude them.

24

Prowlers

With the Literary Fund Scholarship in Letters in hand—he had had the good news formally in January—Gee had gone back to 'Papps' at the beginning of the year. 'I like my new novel,' he had told Manhire after he put it aside the previous August, and he was happy enough with it still to read from it at the 1986 Adelaide Writers' Week in March. Typically, it had taken him some time to decide to accept his invitation to this, Australia's premier literary festival, and he did not particularly enjoy it, not the formal sessions at least and the 'faking and posturing [that] goes on' when writers talk about themselves.[1] Of his own he gave a deadpan report to Kevin Ireland: 'did my reading well enough, a chapter from my new novel, untried stuff that might have been juvenile nonsense for all I knew. People clapped, old ladies came up afterwards.' He enjoyed most the two-day 'writers' retreat' beforehand at The Estate winery and first-class hotel in the Southern Vales (the plentiful fine food and alcohol especially, he told Kevin), and the weather: 'It was bloody hot'.[2] The high-powered line-up of international writers that year included Ian McEwan, Ken Kesey, Mario Vargas-Llosa and Alain Robbe-Grillet. A young Tim Winton later wrote to Gee appreciatively: 'I enjoyed your company and was grateful to meet someone still serious about the craft of fiction. Writers' Week makes me depressed too.'[3]

'It seems quite funny in parts', he had described the novel to Ireland, the manuscript draft just finished. 'Very little sex. Lots of excitement in the mind. Anyway, I've proved to myself I can still do an adult book. After three children's books in a row I needed to know that.' When he sent it to Ray Richards in July he told him he intended to drop children's fiction and concentrate on adult novels from now on. He had 'enjoyed writing it more than any of my other novels and still feel very involved with it', he said to Rosemary Goad four months later.[4] He was calling it finally *Prowlers*—a little too thematically obvious, he thought, and perhaps melodramatic, but a title he was pleased with. As well as to Penguin and Faber, Richards sent it to St Martin's, who would turn it down, as would Viking New York (too 'idiosyncratic', the American agent Richards then approached advised),[5] and to TVNZ with an outline by Gee of its television possibilities. Faber scheduled it for their autumn 1987 list, Penguin for the Christmas market, having initially and ambitiously thought to do it in time for Father's Day—to the puzzlement of Faber: 'I don't know of this mysterious festival and you will have to explain to me why it's so important to publish the book then', Pocock wrote to Walker, advising him, however, that they would be unlikely to be able to ship the book that early.[6] As it was the schedule would be nervously tight.

Gee's own father died in October, of lung cancer, with his sons at his bedside. It was six months after he had celebrated his 80th birthday with a party at the North Shore Club, another just for family and a week of whisky evenings with his mates in between. He had been a young and fit 80-year-old then, holding his own with his drinking companions, most of them ten or twenty years his junior. In his eulogy Gee described his father as 'I think, the most generous man I've ever known, and the kindest'.[7] His club named a Len Gee Annex after him.

Len's illness had brought Nigel back from Europe, where he was working in a ski-field restaurant in Switzerland (three years into his 'OE'). It also brought Margaretha back—in its final stages—early from Wellington, where she had been working since June at the General Assembly Library, taking what they called 'a marriage sabbatical . . . Did us all good', Gee remarked to his friend Ian Middleton.[8] It was something she had admired a friend for doing, going off somewhere on her own. She had thought first of Sweden, but that proved too expensive, or an overseas trekking holiday until a health scare ruled that out. (A quiet library job in Wellington was also an opportunity to recuperate fully, away from the responsibilities of family, from major surgery.) It expressed too some restlessness on both their parts, not with each other so much as where they were. 'I'll be here—I'll peg out here, I think,' Gee had written to Ireland in April (Kevin was on his way to Christchurch to take up the University of Canterbury writers' residency and Gee hoped he might call in en route), 'because it's too expensive to move. I'd like a year or two somewhere else at this stage. . . . What I need is a tonic, or a prize, or a fellowship.'[9] The previous year Margaretha had been investigating the DAAD artists-in-Berlin programme, with the thought of the whole family going. To a *New Zealand Woman's Weekly* journalist writing an article on him in August, he 'seem[ed] inappropriately in sole charge of two adolescent daughters while his wife, Margaretha, is away in Wellington. Too vulnerable for teenage family life.'[10] She was wrong. This was to be the first of three such 'sabbaticals' on Margaretha's part: the next year she would spend four months trekking in the Himalayas.

An added bonus for Gee of her library sabbatical was the de-accessioned 1902 Webster's International Dictionary she brought back for him: a battered, re-bound, 2000-plus page, six-kilogram volume he would go to from now on whenever he was lost for a new word or an idea.

After an anxious few months for Penguin—the advance copies arrived with the wrong jacket (a Faber not a Viking one; reprinted ones had to be air freighted); the bulk of the stock was not shipped until the beginning of August, a month later than Faber had intended—*Prowlers* came out in November, only incidentally on Armistice Day, though that was thematically more appropriate than Father's Day: it was not a novel about war, but wars and the psychological damage they inflict are strongly present. As *Nelson Central School* had been the starting point for *The Fire-Raiser*, so that book was the catalyst for *Prowlers*; though not the only one, nor the first. Gee had found himself wondering about the four children's adult lives, and how the experiences related there would have affected them. And it would be an interesting exercise, he thought, to see how much of a children's novel he could transpose directly into an adult one: not much, he discovered (richness of writing and variety of pace were lacking, the children were 'too impossibly heroic').[11] But he kept the characters and their first connection, in a novel which charted their evolving relationships through the retrospective gaze of the cleverest, Noel Papps: the 'territory . . . a kind of quadrature' that his scientist's mind seeks to make of it.[12]

Keeping their Christian names and changing their surnames was an indication that they had started as the same characters, but were different (a licence, in other words, for the author to do with them what he wanted). Noel—Sir Noel by the time he is writing his memoir—his clever boy's curiosity and intelligence nurtured by their gifted teacher, has had a prestigious career as a soil scientist, winning a scholarship to study overseas and on returning home becoming director of Jessop's Lomax Institute (a version of Nelson's Cawthron: an oral history project Margaretha had done for the Cawthron, and the institute's library and archives she put in order for them, were Gee's research sources for the novel). His sister Kitty has Florence Norton's political career, and a private life no one knows about. Irene (Lomax: her father founded the institute) is a gifted amateur pianist whose talent has been constrained by a small town and by a family bond that is her own private, hidden knowledge. Phil (Dockery, an obvious name), in whom Hedges had seen another kind of intelligence than Noel's, is a grasping property developer and womaniser: the relationship between the two unlikely boyhood friends (brothers for a while when Phil lives for several months with the Pappses) is quite a lot like Duggie Plumb and Raymond Sole's.

'Clippy' Hedges is now 'Tup' Ogier (unhappily married to the music teacher, Lotte Reinbold), whose more obscure nickname derives from his habit of muttering 'tup, tup' as he walks around the school: not a Gibbs idiosyncrasy, this one, but that of another Nelson Central School teacher, 'Boop' Worley (as Tup's enthusiasm for blowpipe analysis was too). Even the articulated skeleton, Miss Perez (Gibbs called her 'the French lady'), changes her name, becoming Miss Montez.

Irene's brother, Royce, Gee would later say, 'just suddenly arrived in the book', unplanned; 'I had no knowledge that he was coming, or would be a painter. He just presented himself to me.'[13] This was not entirely true. It was before he wrote *The Fire-Raiser*—in February 1984—that Jack Parker wrote to Gee after his sister Muriel's death: Jack and Muriel Parker who had partly inspired Graydon and Merle Butters, and Muriel Wendy Philson. 'You knew how close Muriel & I were to each other', Jack wrote, '& I wonder whether you have perhaps thought (as others have I'm sure) that ours was also an incestuous relationship. No it wasn't, although we were often tempted that way', held back not by any sanctions but by fear, 'the knowledge that this would introduce an element that we both wondered whether we could handle'. 'I never thought that', Gee replied, 'I don't think it ever crossed my mind', although it would not have shocked him. But '[y]ou are right in thinking that a relationship of this sort interests me as a writer'—Jack had told him that he did not 'mind in the least if anything I've written sets you off along a train of thought'—'and in fact a brother/sister relationship of the close sort may form a part of a novel I hope to begin about mid-year.'[14] In an exchange of letters over the following few months Parker told Gee more about his and Muriel's lives. It was not only their close brother/sister relationship that interested Gee at this stage (and '[p]lease warn me off Jack if I am trespassing', he told him) but Muriel herself: 'the idea of Muriel . . . her way of engaging herself with things, her English, or European, sensibility, trapped in the antipodean setting—all this sets up a kind of simmering in my imagination and I want to do something with it.'[15] To the extent that he did in *Prowlers* it was less in the character of Irene than, to a degree, in Ruth Verryt (the rapacious Dutchwoman and historian who becomes Papps' lover); but characters of this kind—Europeans, or European sensibilities, displaced in New Zealand—will appear in several later novels. The relationship between Irene and Royce, however—the novel's shadowy centre—had its origins in the Parkers.

As a novel about an old man looking back at and coming to terms with his past, and told in the first person, *Prowlers* was familiar territory: the novel 'localised in a mind . . . a kind of perturbation, held within the pages', as Gee expressed it,[16] and in which richness, unsettling and understanding are generated by the interplay of past and present, and of the minds of author, narrator and reader. The first-person narrative held another attraction for Gee as well, he had explained to his PEN audience in 1984, in his struggle with those pesky sentences, which '[t]oo often in my writing . . . come flying in your face like bits of gravel' or 'tend to dislocate and head off in unintended directions': the first-person narrative allowed him to 'stand aside and let a proper relationship develop between character and syntax'.[17] The triangulation of author, narrator and reader is extended here, however, with the character of Papps' grandniece—Kitty's granddaughter—Kate. As the novel opens she is bothering Papps with her research for an archival project for the Lomax Institute (a post-degree summer holiday job). She plans then to begin work on a biography, and it is the realisation that this is to be about Kitty not himself that prompts Papps to start writing his own. While Kate—moving in with him when he falls sick—asks him questions about Kitty, she also begins to read the pages he is writing, surreptitiously but to his knowledge. She becomes an intermediate reader in this novel's more complex narrative layering; on occasion he is provoked to address her directly. (They have a tetchy relationship. 'I do not like her', is the novel's first sentence; she calls him in private

'The Chimp'.) This is again a novel in which writing is implicated, and with a narrator who is closely attentive to the act of it and to language. 'Questing is a good word', he writes in its opening pages, 'Confusion is a good word. Extraordinary to be confused after a life so full of magnifications and clarity. And mysteries penetrated. And governing principles understood'; 'To know the name of things is my desire; our only proper knowing is through names. Circles are completed in the noun, margins and boundaries are clear, and we are free from vagueness, free from fear, with every object known from the other.' Yet as a chemist (and unlike Raymond Sole) he knows that verbs are needed too, that it is verbs that 'bring activity and change', and so '[n]oun and verb unite in my craft or science.'[18] (He is not the only character in the novel who controls his world by naming: Les Dockery, Phil's father, whose mind has been damaged by the war, keeps hold of his life by remembering and compulsively reciting the names of the people and places he has known.)

While the form of the novel was a comfortable one Gee had deliberately set himself a challenge in making his narrator a scientist: someone who understands and describes the world through language entirely different from his own (or any of the Plumbs). This was partly why he grew to like Papps so much: 'I liked his mind . . . I liked the fact that he was dragging me into strange places, that he had a vocabulary that I had to struggle to keep up with.'[19] He was curious to see what metaphors science would throw up. He also liked him for his crankiness and forthrightness, his irascible temper and sharp, sometimes nasty tongue (and for knowing his own 'darkness and . . . malice'): 'an admirable gentleman', although 'he'd be impossible to live with'. 'I think I'm fonder of him than of anyone else in my fiction', he said three novels later.[20] He had great fun writing Noel Papps.

Although Papps is a soil scientist, the dominant metaphor is astronomy, one of Tup's enthusiasms: he had seen Halley's comet (as had Hedges and Phil Miller) in 1910. (Gee didn't in 1986, when it made its next apparition: 'I've given up on the comet', he told Ireland. 'I've climbed up on the roof several times with binoculars. That's enough. There's not going to be any second coming, and my gloomy view of things is shown to be right.')[21] Cosmology conjures spinning and circling, fear and void, the limits of understanding. 'The world I find back there', writes Papps of his past, is 'atom and void, a multitude of bodies rolling about and damaging each other when they come close'; 'I've flown apart. There are bits of me floating off as I spin and spin. Can I persuade them back by being still? Here they come, the asteroids, the basalt moons.'[22]

'Nasty things lie under surfaces', the 80-year-old Papps knows. 'That's the sum of my wisdom learned through lenses—my lifetime of squinting through bits of glass.' Where once he had believed, with Tup, that 'magnification banished fear', now he knows 'it shows empty places, endless recession, and how can we hope to travel there?' Sight, or seeing, is a related motif: microscope, telescope, Tup's wall eye, things observed through windows, Papps' desire 'to look *straight* at the *single* thing. Obliquity makes me dizzy, multiplicity smothers me'[23]—his voice, its language and cadence, is as singular and compelling as Plumb's. Papps' examination of—his prowling about in—his past brings him to the realisation and acceptance of the limits of his scientist's understanding: that there is another kind of knowledge 'where rational enquiry does not hold . . . There are no names we can agree on.'[24]

His mysteries—in a novel full of mysteries, secrets—are Rhona and Irene. Home from England with his Cambridge degree, he marries Rhona for wrong, selfish reasons: because he thought Dr Papps needed a wife; because she cried on the first night he met her ('I was, you must remember, still eighteen, although thirty-one'); to increase himself; and because he cannot have Irene. He not only fails her in love, he cannot (or doesn't try to) comprehend her; even now she is 'weightless, featureless'. The comparisons with Raymond and Glenda are strong. Rhona has been damaged by Phil, he will learn (here she recalls Jennifer Gibbs); but she was doomed from the start, he believes, 'to failure in the self, a kind of cognitive failure to find oneself as object': she was unequipped for life and 'I couldn't save her.'[25] Five years after their marriage she goes to Soddy's Point, Jessop's mental hospital (one of three people in the novel who lose their minds), where she stays for the short rest of her life. Her drowning death, of the many in Gee's novels, is surely the most horrible: wandering out of the hospital one day, to the end of the peninsula and out across the mudflats, she walks until the sand becomes soft and she becomes trapped, and sinks in to her thighs, her hips, her chest, then the tide comes in. It takes Papps 30 pages of evasion before he can set this down.

The death Papps wishes for himself is Mr Krook's, by spontaneous combustion (he is reading *Bleak House*; as a boy he had been captivated by Dickens, 'that magnified inner life, those monstrous obsessions.

My small deceits and guilty fantasies stopped hurting me'): a quick one, neither slow nor watery.[26] Or perhaps by falling, he muses when he is standing at the rim of Harkin's Hole, 'fall and dark and oblivion; terror, peace'.[27] Fire too recurs and carries meaning and imaginative force. The culminating moment of Papps' adolescent fall in love with science is the oxidising flame (Tup's blowpipe demonstration), which trembles and bends and dances at his command, within it a cone of transparent blue; and the flame which then turns 'green and red and black. He told me why. The why was as beautiful as the colour.' At the very beginning there was fire, and the fire-raiser, Edgar Le Grice, 'red and black'—'I think of him now as pleochromatic, but . . . it leaves out black. And as the piano crackles and the flames turn crystalline, it's black I see: Le Grice spinning at me, basalt moon.' These are the images the novel closes on: comet, fire, consummating flame: 'I know it's just a cloud of cold gases in the sky but how marvellous if it should lean to me and burn me in a blue or yellow fire.'[28]

The deeper mystery is Irene; the unknown quantity in Papps' equation is Royce. Irene is the thing he 'cannot name' but will never be free of: she 'strikes me with her fingers and makes me sound' (music is Irene's defence against pain and 'the aching void').[29] He is eighteen when he sees her through the window of an empty, tumble-down house at Long Tom's beach cradling four-year-old Royce in her arms, and in that moment 'I knew she was never mine'. Twelve years later, just arrived back in Jessop, he watches her at the piano (another 'prowling at the window, in the dark') while Royce stands behind her, his hand on the nape of her neck, caressing the back of her head, and understands that Royce 'had possession of her'; this is the scene he is fleeing when he meets Rhona. Royce's paintings (for which he becomes famous) are disturbing to him: strange, threatening landscapes, 'slitted caves and phallic trees, the hills wrenched askew'. Noel doesn't like them because he can't figure them out. 'Where does the darkness come from? What are these shapes? What is that light? Who is he? . . . He has always been good at things lying underneath; shapes within; shadows under surfaces.' Royce tells him: 'I spent most of my life painting Irene.'[30]

He also tells him, of what they knew all of Jessop believed: 'it's not true. We should have done it. We talked about it sometimes and we did it in our heads. But we kept on stepping back'. When Jack Parker read *Prowlers* he recognised himself and Muriel, but reassured Gee: apart from their 'rather cloistered, enclosed' sibling lives (and yet it was more than this) 'they are as unlike Muriel & me as all people are unlike. I certainly do not think that you have trespassed at all.'[31]

Incest, madness and drowning aside, Gee was not protesting too much when he pointed out that 'there's a lot of fun in the novel':[32] Phil Dockery's drunken fall through a first-storey landing window onto the cactus plants below (one of Len Gee's feats); Ruth Verryt peering over the fence in a Kilroy-like cartoon drawing—'rosy frog face' beaming, eyes 'huge behind her glasses', her '[e]ight white fingers with pink nails gripp[ing] the top of the fence'[33] (Gee did the drawing himself); Noel cowering in a tree with the crotch bitten out of his trousers after Irene sets her German shepherd Queenie on him (after he has broached with her Phil's claim of an incestuous relationship between her and her philandering father), a brilliantly comic dog-phobia scene. 'I find myself more and more able to focus on something that is darkly comic in a situation', he said in an interview on the eve of the novel's release.[34]

He was disappointed that others did not like *Prowlers* as much as he did. It did not fare badly, but not as well as anticipated, especially after 'dramatic' early pre-publication sales (only to be expected, however, for Gee's first adult novel since the *Plumb* trilogy), and sales, initially strong, fell off sharply after a month. The first reviews were superlative: 'Prowlers is wonderful', declared the *Dominion*'s; Kevin Ireland in the *Sunday Star* called it a 'work of stunning brilliance' and 'a magical return to form . . . a marvellous narrative maze worthy of Dickens'.[35] But most were, as Gee put it, 'lukewarm', including two by Brian Boyd, a full page in the *Listener* and a shorter one in *Landfall*. Like several reviewers Boyd was not taken with the novel's present-time narrative, Papps' interaction with Kate and her buff, mullet-haired boyfriend Shane, and he thought there was too much going on: 'a spider's nest of spindly legged little stories scampering away in different directions at every sentence' but no one of them 'powerful enough to draw us on'.[36] Thanking Ireland for his review, a few months later, Gee told him that '[i]t came when other people were clobbering the book or giving it a patronising pat or two on the head'.[37] As one reviewer commented, it would be churlish to measure all of Gee's novels against *Plumb*, but they did (this one included).[38] Gee must have sighed. He can only have shrugged at another's opinion that the novel consisted mostly of a boring (by implication) 'Proustian barrage of detail and events', and the *Nelson Evening*

Mail's that 'save in the choice of half a dozen magnificently esoteric words . . . there is not a great deal in the book to betray [Papps'] scientific mind'. Mostly—once again—the most admiring reviews were the British ones: 'surprising, clever and lingering—a book which gives literary satisfaction'; to the *Literary Review* 'Maurice Gee's astonishing technical skill' recalled 'the equally scientific spirit of Virginia Woolf's *The Waves*'.[39]

'Obsession of a quiet man', was the heading of a substantial profile which appeared in the *Dominion Sunday Times* in October, a few weeks before the novel came out, employing a word Gee and journalists were fond of; as were journalists of their customary portrayal of Gee as 'a comfortable presence in battered corduroys and sweatshirt' surrounded by the orderly clutter of family life. 'The novelist has thinning grey hair,' Anthony Hubbard here continued, deep crow's feet and 'a wide mouth with teeth like small headstones leaning haphazardly against one another' (paraphrasing, unconsciously or not, Gee's description of Tup Ogier's which 'jutted or lay back like head-stones in an old cemetery'). 'His voice is flutey and precise', and 'outside those discreetly hidden places . . . [h]e is willing to discuss ideas about his work with interest and a certain detachment.' His obsession, he readily acknowledged, was violence, and cruelty and loss ('I'm very simple in my obsession', he said elsewhere, '—I can't understand how human beings can be evil'). Those discreetly hidden places where he would not go he said only were 'episodes in my youth that I can only look at in fictional terms'—that part of his life he remained, indeed was increasingly, reticent about. Asked about having compared himself to Noel Papps in 'still making adolescent mistakes in his 30s . . . He "grew up slowly"', he said: 'no, he does not want to elaborate'. (Like Donald Pinnock's, the story he told still 'stopped short of the time of his adolescence'.)[40]

Obsession was his own word. Quiet he was happy with too, in so far as '[m]y voice is quiet and I'm not screamingly self-assertive', he had told the *Nelson Evening Mail* a few months earlier, '—but modest?', as journalists also always wrote: there he disagreed.[41]

'He believes he has now written his way past the early Henderson memories', that article reported, his 'Henderson and family past, where', he had said to Jack Parker just a few years before, 'most of my imaginative living still takes place'.[42] He might not have been fictionalising it—like *Prowlers*, his next novel, which he was already well on with, was a Nelson one—but he was still writing about it, and still making it story, in another way. In September 1986 he participated in the New Zealand Book Council's annual Winter Lectures series, giving a lunchtime lecture in Wellington and repeating it in Nelson a few weeks later (they hoped 'the giving of your first public lecture was not too much of a strain for you', they wrote to him after the first; clearly it wasn't)[43] and editing it for publication in the *Listener*. Calling it 'Where I am, how I got here' (for the *Listener* 'The way of a writer'), he described his earliest attempts at writing and surveyed his novels to date, but began back further:

> First things. Kitchen with wood range. Zwieback in the oven. Stew with doughboy bubbling in a pot. Work socks drying on the wire rack and the chimney roaring. . . . Remembering these things makes me want to write stories. They're no sooner in my mind than I want to put them into lives and demonstrate their continuity and the primal quality they have.

A primal charge carried by words, by the single word: 'kitchen' is always that kitchen, street is Newington Road; and creek is that creek, 'with deep slow-flowing dark-green pools' where 'I seem to have spent half my boyhood'. The creek marked the division and also a tension between dark and light, unknown and familiar, 'never clear, never defined, and pleasure/pain, and allowed/forbidden'. (And yet, if creek was both pleasure and pain, adventure and danger, was kitchen also?) Evoking the generative power of the word, by making it allegory, he mythologised it here—his Henderson, his creek—beyond the fond recalling of his earlier *Islands* essay, 'Beginnings':

> the weight, the significance, of this thing can't be escaped. It extends itself, even when it's physically absent, into all parts of my work. Light and dark, happiness and terror, getting and finding knowledge in the face of darkness. I won't try to measure how much comes from creek. There are other things, many things, some more important, but there's potency in that remembered place and I know it will never leave me alone.[44]

In 1988 he contributed (after his habitual initial reluctance) a shorter piece to an anthology of childhood recollections of twenty 'prominent New Zealanders', in the company of a politician, an All Black and a millionaire businessman but mostly of other writers. 'Creek and kitchen', he called his, a more crafted version of 'Beginnings' overlaid with the stronger mythologising impulse of

'Where I am'/'The way of a writer'. It was a theme and a text he would return to again and again.[45]

Although the response to *Prowlers* had been disappointing—and it missed out at both the national book awards this year, though shortlisted for the Wattie (and judged 'unfashionable', in Ray Richards' assessment, while Gee's philosophical expectation had been 'I don't think it's my year')[46]—he gained attention and recognition of various kinds in these years. Manhire's short volume in the Oxford New Zealand Writers and their Work series appeared finally in 1986. Gee was one of 21 writers featured in *Moments of Invention* (1988), by Gregory O'Brien and Robert Cross, a collection of text and photographic portraits aiming to capture how they lived and how they worked: Gee for four hours a day in his underground study ('a mess of books, overflowing shelves and pieces of paper'). 'Making sentences work', the piece was titled. There was no mystique for Gee about the act of writing, which 'is what matters to me most', he said. 'The finished text' on the other hand 'can seem a strange object, and the way people react to it can be even stranger.'[47] In April 1987 he accepted an honorary degree from Victoria University, wearing the late playwright Bruce Mason's DLitt gown, for which Mason's widow, Diana, had been looking for some time for a suitable recipient, she told him. He had declined, however, a year or two earlier to be nominated for a New Year or Queen's Birthday honour. His reasons were political, nothing to do with modesty: were it for a purely New Zealand honour it would have been different.

No such complications arose of course (nor were any duties involved, he had made sure) in accepting the honorary presidency of PEN for 1988. He also agreed, against his instincts, to appear at the Writers and Readers Week in Wellington in March that year, part of the city's second annual International Festival of the Arts. He read at length from *Plumb* during his 'An hour with' session, chaired by Bill Manhire, and more briefly from *Prowlers* at an evening reading. He had been grateful for the offer to stay with the Manhires: 'a safe haven, I know, during a week that could be fairly harrowing'.[48] (The most harrowing part may have been being expected to sing at the marae welcome given for the writers the evening before: he couldn't possibly sing a song, he had protested.)[49] But while he could be persuaded to take part in these events, occasionally, he remained sceptical about their point: it was not his job to talk critically (or even at all) about his writing; and '[a]s Maurice Gee quietly pointed out during his session',

British novelist Margaret Drabble said during hers, 'in a context like this, to the great, general questions of life writers can only answer with their own variations of everyone else's cliches. It's when they put pen to paper that something deeper, something more significant may emerge.'[50]

It was to become increasingly difficult, though, to keep one's head down and writing life private in the more and more public literary culture which such festivals and anthologies represented, without seeming churlish.

It was a mark of recognition too to be awarded the Literary Fund's special 40th anniversary scholarship, offered in addition to the regular Scholarship in Letters for 1987. When he put an application in for the latter he had just finished *Prowlers*, and planned to spend the remainder of the year—and he hoped the next—on a new novel, already forming in his mind: 'one that marks a change of method and direction for me'.[51] This too would be an interrupted one. He had a first draft down by spring; he would not go back to it for over a year. He was putting it aside to 'mature', he told Greg O'Brien who was interviewing him then for *Moments of Invention*; but also (and perhaps more) because he had had an offer from Television New Zealand he could not afford to refuse. This was to write another kidult series, the subject again of his choosing. Something that would repeat the success of *The Fire-Raiser*, though not 'attempt too strenuously to reproduce the unique ingredients' of that one, was what they wanted.[52]

This time he went back to Henderson (still) and his wartime boy's memories: firing BB guns, bayoneting Japs, trading gum and candy and empty packets of Camels and Lucky Strikes. The story took place in the summer of 1943 and saw a trio of twelve-year-olds drawn together in unlikely, sometimes uncomfortable friendship (its early working title was 'Summer Friends') when Jackson Coop, a black American soldier, comes to convalesce with the Pascoe family of Kettle Creek. 'I am confident that your own rich imagination will overcome any tendencies to "Blytonism"', producer Ginette McDonald remarked in response to his initial outline.[53] There was to be less adventure and mystery in this one (although some), a quieter study of prejudice and a boy's coming to terms with the disillusionment of his ideals of heroism. It took longer—and more negotiation—to script than *The Fire-Raiser* and considerably longer and harder work to turn into a novel, which he was not sure he would until he had the script finished (by the early months of 1988), partly, he thought, because the material was personal. The town of Kettle Creek is 'a farming and orcharding community, with vineyards just being established' and a tidal creek: 'I can't imagine growing up without those two things—three things', the narrator, Rex Pascoe, writes, '—mud, mangroves, warm brown tidal water'. The Pascoes' house in Barrington Road is the Gees', with its kitchen with 'match-lined walls and brown lino curling at the edges like stale bread, and a black wood-burning stove in an alcove with a wire drying rack above'; a rose-patterned stained-glass window which casts 'a lovely sunset glow' of light into the living room from the sunporch.[54]

Rex avidly reads his weekly *Champion* (the series' title by the script's first draft) and idolises Rockfist Rogan. He is devastated when the American soldier his mother has invited to stay with them turns out not only to be black, and a private, but frightened of war and killing: 'I wanted a hero and Jack would not take that shape.' It takes Rex some time to realise that everyone else likes Jack except him, and 'I was left out'—everyone being his parents, his grandparents and his almost-friends Leo and Dawn. They are all, like Jackson Coop, in some way outsiders. His 'poetry-writing mum, who never stopped hoping' (the Kettle Creek poem is Lyndahl's) is often dreamy, or else a whirl of 'mad activity that left you giddy and not knowing where you were'; 'a woman with a questing mind and currently . . . gone on Krishnamurti', in everyday things 'slightly off centre', Gee described her in his notes. His 'gabby tricky dad', who has a barber shop with a billiard room out the back, is also a bookie and trades in black-market war-shortage good (to his almost obsessively tidy and serious-minded son's embarrassment).[55] Leo Yukich is a Dally—a 'squarehead'—whose winemaker father refuses the sugar Alf Pascoe offers to sell him for sweetening the sherry that (to his disgust) is the only wine New Zealanders will drink. Dawn Stewart is half-Māori and has been abandoned by her mother to live with her sad, bitter grandmother, who everyone in town knows is watering down the milk she supplies from her struggling dairy farm.

'There will be a few larger than life characters, some fairly sinister stuff, a fair bit of bucolic comedy and small town intrigue', Gee's first outline had promised. Prospective characters he discarded included a Willis and Mirth-like couple on an orchard (she 'a kind of aging rural nymph and yea-sayer' who has 'married down'), and her parents, a

Butters-like pair who hold séances and 'are trying to establish world peace by psychic force', but there is eccentricity enough in Rex's grandparents.[56] Grandma rides into town on a Harley Davidson, its sidecar full of the vegetables she sells from her organic garden; in the summer she gardens naked. Grandpa is a backyard inventor whose failed or abandoned inventions include Harry Gee's concrete block-making machine, and who is currently building an amphibious vehicle which he intends will help win the war: it plays a role in the story's finale.

That final scene plays out on the creek, and involves two drownings, probably: of Dawn's grandmother (to an adult reader perhaps the sadder of the two) and of Jackson Coop. In the television series the latter is made more explicit than in the novel, where Gee decided to leave his young readers, and Rex, 'some little hope that it didn't happen; but very little' ('He's in Chicago now, living happily', Rex likes to imagine). Yes, 'it's a pity he dies', Gee replied to Geoff Walker who had queried how definite it was meant to be: he had at one point found a way of saving him, he said, but when he suggested it to the producer and script editor 'they were horrified and rejected it outright'. He was not worried about his intended audience and readers (a bit older than for *The Fire-Raiser*) being able to handle it. 'It's a bit tough though, this death thing.'[57]

He was two chapters into the novel by July and he had it finished in November—a harder book to write but, he would later say, 'deeply satisfying'.[58] 'Ouch!' had been Walker's response when told that TVNZ planned to screen the series the following winter, but printing in Australia rather than Hong Kong, while economically risky, would make it possible to get the book out to coincide: his first original mass-market (A-format) paperback, Richards noted to Gee, 'to catch the full tide of TV-induced buying fervour'.[59] In fact the novel got there first. The seven-part series began screening in October 1989. An American actor (Michael James) played Jack; future musician Milan Borich Rex; and a customised Suzuki jeep Grandpa Crombie's amphibian. '[A] little ripper,' Peter Calder in the *New Zealand Herald* called it, with class and depth.[60] Yet it did not make the same impact as *The Fire-Raiser* or *Under the Mountain*. Its director, Peter Sharp, later remembered *The Champion* as the best of the kidult dramas of the 1980s, of which he and McDonald collaborated on several (including *The Fire-Raiser*), but that it 'slipped into obscurity through bad timing', lack of publicity and with the film and television awards in abeyance that year.[61] It was the last in-house drama made by Television New Zealand (following the free-market-driven restructuring of broadcasting and introduction of contestable funding).

Gee had anticipated that the novel too would be less popular than *The Fire-Raiser*, being 'more of a novel, less an adventure story', and Walker agreed;[62] still, Penguin sold 8500 in New Zealand and Australia by the end of the year, and it was enthusiastically taken by Puffin in the UK, despite their disappointing sales of *The Fire-Raiser*. It was rejected by Houghton Mifflin, however (who thought it was 'a terrific read' but were puzzled that Gee had chosen to transplant 'an American situation onto a New Zealand stage' rather than focus on racial prejudice there).[63]

When he was in Auckland for the pre-production launch of the series in February Gee had said that he had something else 'up my sleeve', a contemporary, three- or four-part adult series, 'something I would very much like to do' if he could find the time and the commissioning, which he evidently didn't.[64] *The Champion*, though, had not been his only writing for the screen while the novel was set aside. For the National Film Unit he wrote a half-hour kidult drama (one of a series of six), *A Small War on the Edge of Town*: a story about the rekindling of the relationship between a boy and his estranged father when their house truck breaks down on the outskirts of town (also featuring a pet turtle and a neighbourhood feud—the small war of the title). He worked on this in the second half of 1988 and it was made in 1989, but apparently never screened. He also devised, at the invitation of former TVNZ head of drama Ross Jennings, a story outline for a telemovie-length episode of the popular Scottish detective series *Taggart* set in New Zealand, a project which, to his regret, did not progress.

It was early 1989 when he got back to his new novel.

25

The Burning Boy

Gee finished his second Nelson novel in Wellington, as Victoria University's 1989 literary fellow. When he had applied for this in September he was unsure if it was to be a permanent move, but it 'more likely than not' would be.[1] He had thought of the Burns fellowship for this year too, but Victoria's was better: no, 'nothing other than writing' was expected of him, he was told, 'you are not even expected to use the room in the Department unless you want to'; but they welcomed his offer to meet informally with students who were interested in writing ('I wouldn't like to be too isolated').[2] And it was in Wellington, one of the magic places.

Perhaps it was partly that Nelson had outgrown its small-city charm. But the main reason for wanting to move away now, however, was Margaretha's mother, who had been living in Nelson for the last ten years. In her deepening dementia she had decided that Maurice was the devil. It made being in the same city difficult.[3]

Of course, there was also the money. The fellowship provided $27,000 for the nine months of the academic year, and a room probably for twelve. Bill Manhire offered Gee his while he had the year off with the Literary Fund Scholarship in Letters. The English Department occupied the eighth floor of the Von Zedlitz building, a newish, ugly, poorly designed ten-storey tower which rose controversially amidst the old wooden houses occupied by the university on one side of Kelburn Parade, the building and the four 50-foot ventilation chimneys atop the services block behind it forever to blight the harbour views of the wealthy residents of nearby Central Terrace. But Manhire's room had one, ideally: 'I'm sorry about the windows', he apologised. 'They haven't been cleaned since 1986.' He was leaving up the Hotere and Jeffrey Harris paintings, he added, but would take them away if Gee preferred.[4]

The uncertainty about whether or not the move was permanent was about the prospects of buying and selling. Either way the whole family was going, including the dog (although Emily would be spending her last school year in Sweden on an international student exchange). Even finding something temporary in Wellington was difficult, the market tight and rents 'huge',[5] and they considered house-sitting or caretaking. Leaving Cleveland Terrace in the hands of tenants, they rented a house for nine months from the end of January from Hugh Price—publisher, socialist and unlikely landlord, who mostly let the several Kelburn properties he owned to visiting academics—in Central Terrace, five minutes' walk from the English Department: number 48, far enough up still to enjoy an unspoilt view. This cost $250 a week; for their Nelson house with a view they were getting $150.

By the end of the year, Gee had told Manhire, 'we should know if we're staying' and if so 'will look around' then for a house to buy.[6] In fact they had made that decision and found one (after looking at dozens) within a few months, taking possession of an unexceptional, three-bedroomed, 1950s wooden house in the western suburb of Ngaio in May. It was not what they wanted, which was something more central, and with a harbour and Orongorongo view—the one Raymond and Glenda Sole had. 41 Chelmsford Street looked out to Wellington's low, scrub-covered, bleak western hills. But it would do: it was big enough (if a little cold) and affordable. They converted a large conservatory into a second living room. One of two small rooms over the garage became Maurice's writing room: he placed his desk under the north-west facing windows, which gave a bushy suburban outlook through a sprawling pōhutukawa tree to the hills and Mt Kaukau. They would stay there for fifteen years.

In every way this university fellowship year was a happier one than Gee's last. He enjoyed working in the English Department and the company of his colleagues. And he was more active than he had indicated he was prepared to be, in the first part of the year at least, doing readings, and even on occasion speaking to New Zealand literature classes—somewhat to the annoyance of the department chair, Kathryn Walls, who had studiously refrained from asking him, then to discover that other staff members had been able to twist his arm; he did, subsequently, a 'wonderful' session with her Margaret Mahy/Maurice Gee honours class.[7] Hesitant he might still be, but he was not terrified any more, as he had been in 1964.

Bible scholar and lecturer David Norton tutored him in Microsoft

Word. Gee had experimented with the new world of the word processor when he was writing *Prowlers*—borrowing the Richards Literary Agency copy of *The Writer and the Word Processor* by Ray Hammond (the first book of its kind)—but found himself in the 'Luddite' camp, in the good company, he would have read there, of Iris Murdoch. '[T]oo many things got in the way of me and the words', he said,[8] and he continued to write his first drafts in 1B5 school exercise books (this novel took fifteen) and blue ballpoint pen. But from now on he would do his later drafts and final editing on a word processor instead of his old pale-blue Olympia.

The writing year did not go exactly as planned. He had intended to spend the first few months of it finishing off the novel-in-progress, then start another one, for which he had a 'so far shadowy' idea.[9] But finishing *The Burning Boy* took three months longer and was harder work than he had expected. After four novels written in the same—retrospective, interior—narrative mode, and 'wondering if there's another way I ought to try', he was writing this one in the third person, with the action set almost entirely in the present, over the space of four or five months, and 'found great difficulty in arriving at an authorial standpoint'.[10] His novels, since *A Special Flower* at least, had had very little editorial intervention. Unusually (but not to his surprise), this time Rosemary Goad asked for some revision.

Goad had retired now from Faber, but was still working for them from her home in Dorset, deep in Hardy country. With her leaving, it occurred to Geoff Walker's 'slightly devious editorial mind'—in his own words to Ray Richards—that it was an opportune time for Gee to shift his primary publishing relationship (for his adult novels) from Faber to Penguin: that is, for them to be published firstly in New Zealand by Viking Penguin, with Faber taking stock for the UK, a proposition he discussed with Faber's editorial director, Robert McCrum, in London midway through 1989.[11] Gee, however, was not ready for this yet, and *The Burning Boy* went (at the end of July) firstly to Faber. The publication process was to be no less anxious at the Penguin end than last time, bedevilled by 'some bizarre breakdowns in communication',[12] for which Faber apologised, and a hold-up in the UK warehouse which meant that 1000 copies had to be air freighted to reach New Zealand in time (for publication in November 1990). For the first time, though, Penguin paid Gee a royalty advance on their edition, at the suggestion of Richards as 'Maurice is obviously a virtually guaranteed seller in his New Zealand hardback edition';[13]

which is not something the author would ever feel so sanguine about, but Walker obviously agreed: he had accepted the novel and started talking to Faber before he had read it.

Walker also asked this time for jacket approval, or for an input at least, having so disliked the *Prowlers* one—which, 'although an excellent piece of design', he had told them, 'was rather too dark and gloomy for New Zealanders used to the harsh South Pacific light'.[14] Nor was he, and nor was Gee, at all happy with their first go for *The Burning Boy*: 'all that red, the wide open spaces. . . . And the trees, the trees'; it looked (as he had also complained of *Prowlers*) like 'something Australian'. It didn't look anything like the Maitai.[15]

The Burning Boy had its beginning in a newspaper report about a teenage boy badly burned in a petrol-sniffing accident, and in the 1981 Maitai fire, which Gee had been 'itching' to put in a novel ever since he had witnessed it. Its narrative mode might be different but the novel shares the same colour palette as *Prowlers*, a brightness and a sharpness in the texture of the language: a Nelson tone, perhaps, the colour of a place where the streams are glass-clear not murky. 'He enjoyed the brightness about those words, the little space around them, like a coloured cloak', says the burned boy.[16] There is fire again too, of course; and astronomy.

Gee's burning boy is fifteen-year-old Duncan Round, burned when his friend Wayne Birtles flicks a cigarette lighter while the two of them are sniffing petrol in the Rounds' garage. Noel Papps at the end of *Prowlers* had imagined a blue and yellow flame leaning in, gently, benignly, and consuming him; this flame rears up like a python. Wayne dies; Duncan is horribly scarred. Shunning school and becoming more self-contained (to others strange, dull or just stupid) than his nature already made him, Duncan spends his time filling his mind with information—watching intently, reading compulsively and randomly, not to learn but to fill up the space emptied out in his mind by the fire, the 'huge emptiness he saw in the burning moment', with 'accumulated sentences', with 'seconds, hours, days, with smells and sights and movements', until he reaches the 'black wall' at the end of it. This is Duncan's void, this 'plain of light' and the black wall which both compels and terrifies him.[17]

Duncan's intense, intent, busy mind is not the primary point of view of the novel, however, one Gee intended to be 'more socially inclusive and "panoramic" than the stories I've told so far'.[18] This is Norma Sangster, 45-year-old principal of Saxton College for Girls.

(The Nelson of this novel had been Jessop again in the first draft before he it changed it to Saxton, to extend the creative room, and point of difference between the novels, that playing with names allowed. It puzzled Gee that some people were bothered by his giving fictional names to obviously real places (a complaint made of both *The Burning Boy* and *Prowlers*). Sense of place is a powerful quality in Gee's fiction, but geography had to obey the needs of the story (and, as he once also remarked, of the author: the protection of memory). Nelson has no Soddy's Point with a psychiatric hospital on it but the 'story wanted something from the invented place that the real place could not provide'; needed mudflats which 'gleamed like polished stone' where Rhona would drown.)[19]

Norma is a local girl (though she has spent time away); her position as both school principal and a friend of Duncan's mother places her both at a distance from and close to the events told, outside and inside. Widowed after a brief, and in hindsight unfulfilling, marriage, she is not entirely comfortable with her decision to remain alone, and constantly interrogates herself about the varieties of her need still for others (especially men), is constantly checking herself ('Oh do stop it Norma, she told herself'):[20] another of Gee's watchful, self-reflective, self-critical characters (if happier than most). Varieties of connecting, or not; love or lack of it; degrees of self-knowledge and deception: these too are again Gee's concerns in *The Burning Boy*.

Though we learn Norma's history, the stories which shape the novel are not hers; nor only Duncan's. The Birtleses and the Rounds—two broken, sad families—bound Gee's social canvas (to the extent that he meant the novel to be one). The Rounds 'have their dinner later than the Birtleses', he tells us, acute to the small, quotidian manifestations of class difference. The Birtleses have flounder, brought home from the fish factory where Ken Birtles and older daughter Shelley work, with boiled potatoes and frozen peas, tinned peaches and ice cream for dessert. The Rounds are having 'millet and tofu patties' (the youngest daughter, Belinda, has turned vegetarian) with 'vegetables marinaded in lemon juice, honey and ginger and stir-fried in oil', and steak for Tom Round, then ice cream with lychees.[21] The Birtleses live on the semi-industrial outskirts of Saxton, past the car yards and wreckers' yards and the paint factory. They are broken by Wayne's death, his mother losing her mind, Shelley mixed up with a delinquent boyfriend and going to jail; Norma holds hope for her stronger, more sensible, younger sister Hayley.

The Rounds live two kilometres up Coppermine Valley in a house which 'looks like a series of white pill-boxes dropping down the hillside'—and is clearly modelled by the author on iconoclastic Wellington architect Ian Athfield's in Khandallah. The similarities stop there, however. Tom Round, architect, is a study of supreme and appalling egotism, another Duggie Plumb. Handsome and openly a philanderer (tough good looks, blue eyes), he is a man who needs, he believes, 'no attention but his own', for whom others exist only to his purpose: if he turns his back they will 'have no existence any more'. As an architect he is the archetype (or caricature) of the Romantic artist: he 'knows he is a great man and no one understands . . . the thing that happens in his mind, in his *being*, when . . . all the preliminaries are done and creative functions take over'. Friends who don't like him call him behind his back Home Beautiful. His wife calls him 'a selfish man, nasty person, inadequate individual, utter bastard, poor weak sod, people-eater'; all of which is true. There was a comic element, albeit a ghastly one, in Malcolm Pratt's running Yehudi through with a garden fork in *Games of Choice*; there is no comedy in Tom Round's drowning the family dog (it's a dachshund-corgi cross) in their swimming pool.[22]

Tom Round is also a west Auckland boy (Henderson gets in after all), his father a brickie from whom he 'gets his gift for putting things together', while from his mother he had 'that extra thing . . . whatever it is—synthesizing skill', the artist thing; he remembers her 'reading, explaining, thinking, laughing, in the little kitchen, and a light shining out of her, love and ambition for *him*'.[23] But Tom has nothing for his own son, neither love nor need; and a dangerous love for his attractive, clever daughters. This Duncan knows (for he is cleverer than people think), 'has known from early in his life that his mother loves him too much, and not properly or all the time, and his father doesn't love him at all'.[24] Of both he is wary. Josie Round has the measure of her husband but not of herself, unable to untangle her love from her pity for Duncan, and her pity for Duncan from her pity for herself: 'a consummate self-deceiver who tries for self-definition through the fashionable worlds of others', in the words of one reviewer.[25] (Her trendy and crafty pursuits—weaving, Wimmins Werk, rebirthing—Tom regards with sardonic disdain, Norma with a more sympathetic scepticism.)

'The interior of a family can be a pretty murky place', Gee had said in an interview several years earlier.[26] The place where Tom Round is brought finally to recognise his own nature—and the murky heart of this novel—is his incestuous abuse of his daughters. In this moment of knowing he loses his sense of order and thus of self; 'There's a flying about of fragments and he'll never draw them in and make shape.' We are in the figurative territory here of Noel Papps. He also recalls Brian Hughes in response to a similar (if less explicit) realisation in 'Eleventh Holiday', who wanted to 'hide in the darkest place he could find': Tom finds 'no place where he can turn and hide. He draws up his legs. He tries to be tiny in the chair.'[27]

In this novel and the Rounds, wrote one reviewer, 'I think [Gee] has come closer to "naming" evil, in a sustained sense, . . . than ever before'.[28]

When Gee started writing *The Burning Boy* Duncan was going to die at the end. Symmetry demanded it: the novel began with fire, which Duncan survives; it would end with a fire—the Saxton forest fire—in which he would die. Three quarters of the way through the first draft he realised that it would not be Duncan who died; 'Living, scarred or not, was what the boy was all about.'[29] Duncan does more too than just survive the first burning. His story is the distance he travels from the boy counting ants when the novel opens, guarding his secret. His path is astronomy. Norma, in the hope of drawing out the potential of his mind, introduces him to her orchardist friend John Toft—one of Gee's lost Europeans, although this one has chosen to lose himself. Toft is a Norwegian-Swede who has fled as far as possible from his experience in the war and chooses 'to be alone and have no past', to withdraw from the world. 'There is no step along a human path for me to take', he tells Norma (it is not a strategy of which she approves). But John Toft's telescope is what brings Duncan back to it, impelling him beyond merely filling up 'the length and breadth' of his mind to a desire to know and understand.[30]

It is Lex who dies: Lex Clearwater, teacher gone feral. Introduced to us by Norma 'in his red utility with the rust-eaten panels, looking like Heathcliff escaping to the moors', Lex has been abandoned by his wife and their baby; abandoning teaching, he retreats to his ten scrubby acres, decaying house and his small tribe of goats. While Duncan has been intent on filling his mind, Lex tries to empty his. He discovered goats when he followed the distressed bleats of a baby one one day, finding it cruelly tied by its legs (as Maurice and Margaretha did one time in the Maitai, but their goat got away). Compelled by their 'yellow hard unblinking eye[s]' with their coffin-shaped pupils, and increasingly obsessed by the goat's 'perpetual now', Lex seeks his own 'goat consciousness': he 'wants no comprehension of his own subtleties . . . wants, complete, a self that's co-extensive with what his senses find. He wants to be his own single point, always now.'[31] He goes further than John Toft, seeking to remove himself not just from the world but from self-consciousness, and he goes too far to come back. When the fire comes Lex goes to ground with his goats and with them is burned.[32]

We have met goats before, the goats at the end of *Sole Survivor* who observe Raymond Sole: whose 'yellow eyes watched without curiosity. There seemed to be millions of years between us', and 'the bush too seemed to watch me with an uncaring eye and want all my memories and obsessions out of it'.[33] Russell Haley earlier (in his *Spleen* review of *Games of Choice*) had drawn on another association of goat when he invoked the 'pan-goat-man' hiding in Gee's secret places, disrupting the naturalistic surface of his fiction.

The draft of the novel Gee sent to Faber had included an epilogue, which he removed at Rosemary Goad's request. It followed Norma Sangster out and about on a school holiday morning some time after the fire, and shifted between the third-person and authorial first-person voice. From them one learns that the Birtleses are moving to Australia; the Rounds have divorced and Tom has moved to Wellington; Sandra Duff as well as John Toft leaves Saxton; Duncan enrols at Correspondence School. In what now became the final, short section of the novel ('Fire') he had initially toyed with having Duncan 'teleport' himself out of the way of the fire ('You should have teleported yourself away', Belinda had said to him in hospital the first time)—'go over and not die', to where 'that's himself on the other side, that is all of him opened up . . . Just by saying, Go'—but stepped back from this beyond-realist, science-fictionish note, leaving just the idea in the final version (but weakened from its first drafting).[34]

The other deletions Goad requested were of italicised passages of direct authorial comment, the two remaining of a number more in the earlier drafts. These read less like postmodernist playing than the author 'thinking aloud' about his characters and process, and working through his difficulties with fixing the point of view—as indeed he was. 'This is Norma Sangster, bit by bit', began the first, in the opening pages: 'She's almost as new to me as she is to you. I have the advantage of knowing where she's from, and I can guess where she's going to. There's enough of her to point this way and that, and she'll become determined page by page. The free time's now and I'm troubled by what I'm not going to find.' Further on, in the longer first draft of this: 'I'm going to keep to the conventions soon, but may want to chip in now and then with this sort of thing. You'll notice some unevenness, mistakes—and I may have to say a word or two by way of correction'.[35] It worried him, he explained in an interview the following year, to have introduced this person for the purpose having someone watching the burning boy and then to have to decide who and what she was. 'I realised she could go off in any one of a number of directions and who was I to choose? It worried me. It seemed to bring into question the whole business of novel writing.'[36]

He had been troubled too, in an earlier-deleted aside, by Wayne 'and the insufficient gravity with which I'm letting him go. I can save him if I choose. Do I have sufficient grounds to write the words that see the end of him? . . . My trouble is, he's more now than simply an invention. But the act is done, in my head, and I don't seem to have the right to interfere.' 'There are other people waiting to come in', he chips in a few chapters on, 'I've held them to one side and will not need them if they don't come now. For need read want. There's no necessity in any of them although one or two seem to hold a place.' Stella Round, he remarked later, 'doesn't have a large role in the story. She helps out with the plot, as far as we have one.' He pondered aloud too about where characters came from as well as where they were going: John Toft, he explains, 'was a Dutchman, Bill Tiedeman, in the beginning, but has been changing all the time, and now is a Norwegian-Swede or Swedish-Norwegian, Lars-John Toft, John Toft. There are no unarguable reasons for the change. I know more Swedes than Dutch people, that is all, and have been as far north as Narvik in Norway and Kiruna in Sweden. The northern land and seascapes are a reason. I wanted to write about a man who knows them.'[37]

One learns too that Hayley interests Gee more than Duncan. 'I'm sorry to be leaving Hayley Birtles. I like her better than the Rounds; her predicament engages me. I'm "dangerously touched" by the girl (to borrow from another novelist). Inclined to be a little sentimental. Suspicious of some of the things I've put in her.'[38]

The vestiges of this authorial voice-over (the beginning of chapter five, in particular: 'I'm inclined to get rid of the man I've called Clive Schwass; and Daphne, his wife') were noted by reviewers, who found it variously 'irritating', 'disconcerting' and 'awkward', 'intrusive' and 'unnecessary'.[39] The general consensus though was that Gee had succeeded with, even mastered, the unfamiliar third person. John Thomson in the *Listener* was an exception—the 'demands of omniscience', he felt, were 'still . . . not altogether satisfactorily met'—while he described Gee's authorial interventions as 'more like Thackeray than a postmodernist'.[40] The instability of the authorial stance—not only that 'I' but the shifts in tense and more frequent collective 'our' and 'we'—Colleen Reilly argued was not a weakness but a strength, unsettling not the author's but the reader's position in relation to the text (although Gee himself didn't see it that way).[41]

British reviewers remarked instead on how un-postmodern the novel was: 'so resolutely uncontemporary that you want to blush for it', wrote Nick Hornby in the UK *Listener*: 'no experimentation of any kind (although at one point Gee does interrupt the text in an endearingly tentative fashion, like an uncle dancing at a wedding disco)'. He meant this as a compliment. In this literary context, Gee's 'unashamed clarity' of style and gaze was evidently refreshing. Hornby's was the most entertaining of a raft of highly complimentary notices there ('three times as good as he [Gee] expected', Robin Dudding reported in the *New Zealand Listener*'s 'Bookmarks' column, excerpting from three). 'It has been written with a breathtaking patience', admired Hornby: 'would that all humans were favoured with the love and care and understanding that the author lavishes on his characters.' His Duncan Round and Norma Sangster were 'writing-class three-dimensional perfection. The quality of Gee's insights and observations are such that you recall why, in your youth, you thought writers had a monopoly on humanity; his attention to detail makes you smile with pleasure. How many New Zealanders know that Hartlepool play in blue and white? (How many Hartlepudlians? Has Gee just made it up?)' (He hadn't.)[42]

Faber sold out of their hardback within a year (and had a paperback edition already well under way) when Penguin still had 700 in stock. 'The London sales . . . are certainly mysterious', Richards remarked (evidently wondering if Faber had got their figures wrong). But the strong sales were presumably not to Faber, who had anticipated (Walker reported to Gee) that this novel 'could be the one which propels you once more to Plumb heights in terms of your readers'.[43] The New Zealand sales of *The Burning Boy* were barely better than those of *Prowlers*, to Gee's surprise, but the critical response was measurably stronger. Gee's take on the first crop of local reviews was that they 'have been generally good, if a little wishy-washy' (the UK reviews 'have been much better, more perceptive and informed').[44] One he had not yet seen was Roger Robinson's in the first issue of a new critical quarterly, *New Zealand Books*. Gee, Robinson considered, had always been weakest in 'the big moments' but not here: in the Rounds' New Year's Eve party, the Saxton fire, the brutal burglary of Norma Sangster's elderly parents (there was 'a new power, even for Gee's long line of funny/sad old Alzheimer victims, in the comic brutality' of this scene, as Ken Sangster tries to defend himself and his wife with his walking stick). Perhaps, he surmised, 'he has gained from writing so well for children'. And while there were familiar types and motifs and preoccupations, these were not stereotypes: he cited particularly the late and quiet sketching in of the springs of Tom Round's character in his 'working-class origins and mother-driven compulsion'. ('I don't like Tom, but don't dislike him altogether', Gee had written in a deleted aside.) But his main point was the quality of Gee's realism: a 'realism so intensely particularised that, under pressure, it becomes imbued with deeper, almost surrealist meanings, especially through the imagery of fire'. It was a realism, too, 'which is entirely, unrepentantly, painstakingly local', he wrote, contrasting Gee's with the fiction of Dickens, which was 'megalopolitan in every glittering fibre'. This for New Zealand fiction 'is an important task': that *The Burning Boy* was 'never trivial, never mean, and never parochial is a measure of its craft and intelligence. It is a small-town novel of a high order (which would also fit *Middlemarch*).'[45] There is a common theme in this and Hornby's review of Gee's generosity.

The *Times Literary Supplement*'s Tom Aitken was reminded of Hardy, describing the novel's setting (and conflating, apparently, Gee's Saxton/Jessop and Loomis, and perhaps also Hardinge) as 'a city which, under different names in successive novels, he is steadily making into his equivalent of Hardy's Wessex. Hardy comes quite often to mind', he went on, in Gee's 'feeling for landscape, for storms and other natural events, and his liking for large set-pieces', in his 'profound sympathy for his female characters', and 'a Hardyish near-villain in Tom Round'.[46] (By contrast, the one negative New Zealand review invoked Jackie Collins, Wilbur Smith and Colleen McCullough.)[47]

At the 1991 New Zealand Book Awards Gee found himself up against Alan Duff's *Once Were Warriors* and Bill Manhire's *The New*

Land (Manhire's second work of fiction, which Gee had launched at Writers and Readers Week in March 1990, striking perhaps not quite the right note when he observed that '[p]oetry is usually looked on as the higher art, so making the move across can be seen as a fall from grace, or as a decision to consort with a homelier muse', and 'can sometimes make established fiction writers feel a bit sour, because they're not able to make the journey the other way'): 'A right old battle indeed', observed Geoff Walker.[48] It surprised both Walker (who was picking Manhire) and Gee that *The Burning Boy* won. It was Duff's huge-selling, widely discussed and critically contested novel about the urban Māori underclass, though—which Gee had awarded PEN's Hubert Church Award for best first book of fiction—that took the Wattie.

Gee had barely got started on his 'shadowy' next novel in 1989, no further than note-taking, before he put it down when his application for a Literary Fund grant was turned down. There was little point in starting serious work on a new novel in the few months he had left of his university fellowship, as he told them, and he would go on instead to other things—television, maybe a children's novel next year. He was also kept busy for longer than he would have liked reading the 62 longlisted entries for the American Express short story award, which he had agreed to judge only because he had understood that he and Margaretha would be flown to Auckland for the awards dinner, which was in fact held in Wellington. The $5 per story offered, he also let them know, working out at seven dollars an hour was 'hardly professional rates').[49] He was similarly frank about his dislike of judging literary awards—although he still sometimes agreed to do so—when he spoke at a PEN panel discussion on the subject in December: not only was it hard work with little reward, he still did not trust his own judgement. (Also, he advised, avoid co-judging. When he had judged a short story award jointly with Keri Hulme in 1985 they had come up with completely different shortlists and awarded two prizes.)

Presenting prizes as guest of honour at the Avondale College senior prize-giving, though, was different (and a paid trip to Auckland after all; Emily went with him and presented the junior prizes). Like Norma Sangster, he referenced James K. Baxter's 'Prize-giving speech'.

Promising television assignments included concept development for a family drama series for British TV (for Tom Finlayson's UK partner: something to 'appeal to a sixteen year old on the dole in Liverpool'), and one at least with Pat Cox—a 'Marlborough Sounds' project for which he was writing a pilot script.[50] These things had all fallen through by late summer, which had Richards worrying about his financial outlook: his currently anticipated income for next year, from royalties and advance royalties (and residuals), 'may not be sufficient to put marmalade on your toast'.[51]

Gee returned, regardless, to the novel, which he had started 'almost without thought' beyond the idea of it he had had in 1988: an Antipodean 'tale of two cities . . . pagan sub-tropical Auckland and platonic Wellington, enclosed by hills and swept by Antarctic gales'. He was at this stage not planning it but 'letting possible characters float in and out of my mind' and between those places.[52] He had moved back to Wellington in more ways than one. He was also backing away from the third person: *The Burning Boy* had taught him that he was uncomfortable there, 'hard up against the story' with no one 'standing between me and the page'.[53] But not entirely. He had two short chapters written when he was interviewed in February by Colleen Reilly, one in the first person and one in the third, but the same character: it was 'too early to say if it's working'. (He was not even sure, he said, he was going to finish this novel.)[54]

That interview was destined for a Canadian academic journal, but appeared first, along with an extract from the forthcoming *Burning Boy*, in local literary magazine *Sport*—a relative newcomer on the local scene, established in part to fill the gap left by the demise of *Islands*, which Dudding appeared to have wound up, and in emulation of Dudding's editorial style (its facetious title a nod back to *Mate*). Gee here was typically reluctant to discourse on meanings and larger questions, such as evil ('I regard all my speculation in these areas as banal . . . the furniture of a writer's mind isn't necessarily interesting, it's the way he arranges it that has the interest'); happier to talk about method and process, and pleasure. The best of it was the putting together (working the carpentry metaphor he was so fond of: 'I don't know how much of this is a genetic gift from my father'), 'the close and exact fitting of part with part—especially when time gets into it'. Language *per se*, yes was '[e]normously important'. He had to be sure of and comfortable with his words, the smallest unit, before 'I can move on to the point where they quiver and shimmer, reverberate a little'. (This could be Noel Papps speaking.) But his prose was not 'poetic', just as his novels were not experimental: clarity, 'prosaicness' was what he sought and took pleasure from. 'I like to think of myself as saying exactly what I mean, but having some ability to make it mean a little more.'[55]

A flaw in his writing, he said, might be that he was too much of a 'leaver-out' as opposed to a putter-in: 'I feel that I might have written a little more richly if things had—well, if I'd been a different writer . . . I sometimes feel a thinness, I have a feeling that I've left some of my novels a little too soon, there's something else that wants to come out.'[56] It was something Bill Manhire had observed: 'Sometimes it is possible to wish Gee's novels a little more garrulous.'[57]

26

Going West

The next novel would be, Gee thought, 'long' by his standards. He had 50,000 words written by the middle of the year when he put in an application for the Katherine Mansfield fellowship, and was expecting it to come to 150,000: he hoped to write another 50–60,000 this year, and would finish it off, if he got there, in Menton. Not only was it long, he explained, it was 'a difficult and ambitious piece of fiction', 'a step forward in the complicating of my fictional ground'. 'I cannot claim that six months (I would hope to stretch it to eight or nine) in Menton are absolutely necessary to the completion of the novel', he added conscientiously. 'They will though free me from financial worries and put me in a congenial and interesting locality.'[1]

He subsequently withdrew this application, explaining that family circumstances had caused him to 'reassess my priorities'.[2] Abi was not well at this time, and they had just moved (or were about to move) Greta Garden into a rest home in Wellington. Going away no longer seemed such a good idea. Instead he applied for, and was awarded, the Literary Fund's 1991 Scholarship in Letters.

Not Menton then, but he got out of town a few times nevertheless while he worked on 'Two Cities', and was a more than usually active presence in the literary scene in these years. Just being in Wellington, rather than the comparative isolation of Nelson, enabled this: even if he was no longer in the English Department, it was a city where writers were around. He attended the local PEN meetings, and allowed himself to be elected one of the two vice-presidents on the national executive at the 1990 AGM, even though he was not there.

It was an uncomfortable time, at least for someone of Gee's temperament, to become active in PEN. This was the year in which the literary community was thrown into a vituperative uproar over the Bloomsbury flat affair, when the government purchased a flat in London to be a visiting writers' residence: on the face of it a benign and generous act. The purchase was a sesquicentennial gesture; in

1990 New Zealand marked, uneasily, the 150th anniversary of the signing of the Treaty of Waitangi. It had originated, though, in a suggestion from Fiona Kidman to minister of arts and culture Michael Bassett that the government buy a property a friend of hers was selling on a harbour island in the Bay of Plenty for a writers' retreat. The minister was receptive to the idea, but an informal canvass of the PEN executive and Auckland members by C.K. Stead revealed that people would prefer somewhere more urban, and, perhaps more importantly, further offshore. Thus Stead was despatched, firstly to Sydney and then to London, and with instructions to keep his mission secret, and purchased the flat in Bloomsbury's Ridgmount Gardens in December 1989. When the news of this was announced PEN's management committee wrote to thank the minister, whereupon 26 writers, including Gee, signed a public letter dissociating themselves from that sentiment and in protest at the secrecy and lack of consultation with which the whole business had been conducted—the start of what Stead would later call a 'ferocious, politically ill-judged and sustained attack',[3] which was mainly about the argument that the choice of a flat in London was an anachronism (smacking of a time when London was the centre of everything and England Home).

Gee, an executive member by now, was one of three PEN representatives on the committee set up to oversee the residency—there to keep a watching brief, as they saw it—and found himself chairing it. Not everyone took the dissenters' high-minded position and more than twenty writers applied. But no one in the end got to use the Bloomsbury flat: amidst further controversy and recrimination it was sold by the incoming National government, with difficulty and at a substantial financial loss. Gee, meanwhile, had very quickly regretted being persuaded to ally himself with the anti faction, and he resigned from the PEN executive as soon as he could.

Most literary engagements were not so fraught. In July 1990 he had spoken at the Federation of Country Women's Institutes' biennial national conference—held that year, being International Literacy Year, on the theme of the 'Power of Words'—and given a version of 'Creek and kitchen' to an evidently appreciative audience: 'I am sure your personal anecdotes brought back many happy memories to our members', the secretary wrote to thank him afterwards, 'particularly the reference to kitchens and creeks—a comfortable scene.'[4] In April 1991 he took part in Dunedin's New Zealand Writers' Week (having declined to for the inaugural one two years earlier), doing an 'hour with' session, a panel for school students and readings. In his solo session he read from *Prowlers* not *The Burning Boy* (Noel Papps' ill-tempered opening salvo went down well with audiences, he found) and spoke about creeks and violence and looking backwards—all of which there was plenty of in his novel in progress. *Metro* writer Stephen Stratford, in a seven-page write-up of the week titled 'Pissed poets' society', described Gee's, by contrast, 'all very clear, unpretentious craftsman talk' and the generosity, tact and care with which he answered questions. Meeting Gee for the first time, at Cargill's for a drink with Kevin Ireland and Elizabeth Smither, 'I feel, foolishly, like a teenage girl on a date with Jon Bon Jovi'.[5]

He did a solo session again at the Maungawhau/Mt Eden Writers' and Readers' Festival (everyone was holding them now) in early October, chaired by Brian Boyd. Two weeks later he was in Toronto at the longer-established and considerably larger Harbourfront International Festival of Authors, with 80 other writers. (He went over there alone, however, Margaretha having not long come back from her own tripping about on her third 'sabbatical', a ten-week Swedish language course in Uppsala and a three-week camping tour of Lapland.) Toronto was in all ways a more enjoyable experience than Gee usually found these things, involving only reading—from *Prowlers* again, and in his memory 'the best I've ever done' (afterwards he was asked if he had had drama lessons; his nervously trembling voice, he concluded, was just right for Papps).[6] There was a trip to Niagara Falls too, and a hotel hospitality room offering 'every sort of booze you can imagine'—for all of which 'you're asked to read for half an hour'.[7]

His invitation had come about through Boyd, who was there too, but Gee was not previously unknown in Canada, even if his name was: 'Pronounced, unfortunately, like the car', he had pointed out to a Canadian interviewer a few years earlier.[8] *Australian and New Zealand Studies in Canada* had devoted most of its Spring 1990 issue to Gee (the interview with Colleen Reilly appeared here). In Toronto he talked to Thomas Tautsky of the University of Western Ontario (this interview published in the same journal a few years later).[9] He also did an interview with Boyd for a collection of 'conversations with New Zealand writers' being published by Auckland University Press, *In the Same Room*. In Auckland Boyd had given Gee a list of questions to which Gee responded in writing, and he had intended 'that they might be modified by voice and tape in Toronto'. Here, however, 'Gee talked happily enough, and sadly enough, about his life, but only with the tape switched off' and the published interview was almost entirely the written conversation. And yet he had acquiesced to having the English Department tape recorder in the same room when he talked to Colleen Reilly. That interview, though, had been very focused on writing and craft. This one Boyd clearly wished to be more wide-ranging, but Gee did not stray far beyond familiar territory where the personal was concerned. Henderson, Chapples and creeks: 'People must be tired of hearing about them.'[10]

Boyd's first question had been about autobiography, Gee having 'reach[ed] an age and a status', he suggested, where such a thing might 'seem natural' or be expected. But Gee was not there yet: he was still in the middle of his writing life. And '[b]esides, there's a lot I don't want to tell.'[11] Biography too was not something he wanted to contemplate.

A less usual literary request Gee agreed to this busy year was to read from *Plumb* at the Anzac Day commemorations in Wellington—not at the dawn service, thankfully, but in an afternoon programme of readings, chamber music and contemporary dance at the National War Memorial (an attempt to popularise both the occasion and the place).

It was in July 1991 that a Penguin *Plumb* paperback finally came out, to the relief of university teachers who had been finding the novel's lack of availability a problem. The ceasefire reached in 1987, when Anne French made her bridge-building visit to Nelson, had lasted a year before Richards had raised the *Plumb* question again, and the conversation quickly deteriorated into more acrimony. Gee looked on from the sidelines (but as keen to rescue *Plumb* from Oxford as Geoff Walker and Richards were). Oxford's commitment was to release the paperback rights once theirs went, or was about to go, out of print. Their intransigence in refusing to do so before now, argued Richards, writing to French and Jeff Olssen in June 1988, had been 'putting a considerable sales restraint on a major New Zealand work for nearly a decade', especially by 'denying the book to overseas readers' (it was hardly available at all in the United Kingdom; had sold poorly in Australia, in an Angus and Robertson paperback under licence from OUP): 'a visible and quotable aberration in New Zealand publishing history'. The implied threat was intentional. 'This is about as gentle as I can be with OUP', he annotated this letter for Gee. 'If they reject this request I suggest we use the episode publicly?'[12]

Two months later, and on the basis of a misunderstood exchange at the Wattie awards, Walker informed Gee and also Penguin (UK) that he was at last buying the paperback rights from Oxford. Not so, said Anne French; and in any case July 1989, when Walker was looking to release a Penguin paperback, was likely to be 'a bit soon' in terms of the stock they had remaining.[13] He was planning for not just a new paperback but a 'series package'—a box set, Richards suggested, to get around the problem that they had only recently re-jacketed *Meg* and *Sole Survivor* in printings of 2000. This especially pleased Gee: 'I'll be delighted', he told Walker, 'to see the trilogy sold as a unit at last, the way I always intended it.'[14] In April 1989 OUP advised that they had about a year's worth of stock (a little under 500) in the warehouse. In the belief that they would therefore be relinquishing the rights the following February, Walker now looked to putting out a paperback in March 1990, and a 'monster' omnibus edition—*The Plumb Trilogy*—for Christmas. (This, rather than a slip-case set, had been Robert McCrum's suggestion, noting Faber's success with Lawrence Durrell's *Alexandria Quartet*.) But when Richards asked OUP for a formal reversion letter from Faber, French again stalled: they were still not out of stock, and would 'let you and Fabers know when we want to terminate the contract. But that time has not yet arrived.' Richards fumed about 'word-games and delaying tactics'; McCrum wrote a polite and conciliatory letter suggesting that OUP revert the rights in mid-1990, by which time, very clearly, the edition would be out of print.[15]

She gave them the word in April 1990. It would take five more years, however, to sort out the *Plumb* omnibus;[16] though in the meantime Gee was to give his 'bemused approval' to a continuous reading of the trilogy—a '*Plumb*athon'—at the 1993 Writers' Week in Dunedin.[17]

It was getting to be 'a little annoying' to him by now that people continued to measure everything he wrote against *Plumb*, even if in praise.[18] A novel 'to easily rival his best-known book, *Plumb*', the *Evening Standard* said of *The Burning Boy*; his 'best since *Plumb*', reviewers wrote of *Going West* ('Two Cities'). '*Plumb* doesn't really have anything to say about *Going West* that I can see', Gee said.[19] And yet there are the similarities of territory and technique. It was, he supposed, because he started the novel without much thought that he found himself in chapter one back in Henderson, or Loomis as it had been and was to remain since *Meg*—a name he wished he had found sooner; Wadesville had been just a lame derivative of Wadestown. Both the narrator and his subject are almost exact contemporaries of Gee and of Raymond Sole. He didn't 'really want to go into' the ways 'in which Jack resembles me and in which Rex resembles me', Gee told an interviewer, other than to concede the obvious ones.[20]

In *Going West* Gee plays with biography and autobiography and narrative voice: 'turn[ing] postmodern tricks with the best of them', critic Mark Williams observed,[21] or, as Gee preferred to put it, 'complicating . . . my fictional ground'. His narrator, Jack Skeat, is a failed poet (hence Skeat, from Keats), once librarian and now retired national archivist; 'a wordy individual—and not my favourite among my characters'.[22] He is writing a memoir of his lifelong friend Rex Petley, the real poet, prompted by the pestering of Petley's official biographer, the diminutive, self-important, 'pouter-pigeon chest[ed]' John ('the Elf') Dobbie (once an aspiring poet himself), and by his need to understand the meaning of Rex's death. As in all Gee novels there is a mystery to uncover. Skeat writes in 'a tiny windowless hole under the stairs', while his wife Harry, a botanical illustrator, works in the sunny sitting room above him, shining 'my torch back into the dark'—employing a metaphor Gee does of his *Plumb/Prowlers* type of novel, flashlights shining back and forth between the narrated past and the narrating present, compounding and creating meaning—but knowing (as Plumb did not) that danger lies there. Of course the life he is exploring is not only Rex's but also his own.[23]

He is writing two narratives, in two sets of books: in Olympic 1B5 exercise books and black biro in the first person, in Warwick 1B5s in blue in the third. 'Blue seems to flow more easily. On the other hand, he prefers the back cover of the Olympic, where cartoons and text teach water survival'—not an innocent detail. ('On the back of the Warwick there are only measurement tables.')

Jack is of 'middle height' and 'an undistinguished face', eyes 'green, uncertain, innocent. Surprised, uncomprehending, even though Jack Skeat believes that all the crimes and cruelties we can imagine have somewhere been committed, or will be'. Evil confounds him. He possesses a guiding 'moral intelligence' which makes him 'insufferable and vulgar at times' and which he tries, at times, to turn off—that urge 'to make sense; control by means of finding significance . . . to make moral assessments'. Thus he found his trade in archives, a safe, ordering career. 'Arrangement and description has been my work'; '[p]reservation became an absolute and put me in a moral workday universe.' He keeps himself too under observation and control: always 'I sat on my shoulder watching me'. But 'Jack is not the self-doubting person this account begins to make him seem. He has a strong sense of his own worth . . .'. Yes, Gee will agree, Jack Skeat is 'a little bit like me'.[24]

Jack is also a man 'elated by the inevitability of death'[25] and preoccupied with the ways of it. Like Papps he has his own already worked out: on the top of Mt Duppa, west of Nelson, or Mt Kaukau in Wellington's western hills.

The 'two cities'—Auckland and Wellington—and their topographies are themselves characters, tangible presences in the novel. Gee's two-page account of the three-way journey from Loomis to Auckland (by bus, train or tram) with which the novel opens is a tour-de-force of memory and evocation. The journey Jack makes from Auckland to Wellington on the Limited, in a few sentences, 'was falling down a chute'. Auckland spreads and bends and curves, is 'pulpy and greasy and comfortable'. West is (was) Loomis: mud and mangroves, 'Black lands. Navy-blue. Earth-brown. Clay-yellow. Ochrous. Brackenish. Brackish. Creek-green'; westwards further the coast which 'crushes language flat'. Wellington is precipitous, vertiginous, 'swoop and dive and exhilaration'; 'crazy steps and zigzags' and 'crooked roads with treasure at the end', hills that 'push you in the harbour' and have you walking on a slant. Jack will never be at home there, but he stays for 40 years. Wellington suits him, Rex tells him: 'a town for clean bones and moral certitudes'.[26]

Both Rex and Jack inhabit Gee's childhood, but especially Rex. Loomis—'Petley', as Jack knows it, place and family—remains 'the template of his moral and emotional world', the creek a stock symbol in his poetry—'deep, dark, mysterious, exact' (although it 'stops working in his later poems. It is just a number he paints in'). His father was a brickie (like Tom Round's), for whom '[p]utting things together was his passion', a boxer and a racing man, but in his rages (and his backyard inventions: another failed concrete-block machine) more Harry Gee than Len. Lila Petley, '[c]lever, sad, graceful, beautiful', 'preternatural', weeps by the creek at midnight for a life that might have been; her aspiration for her favoured son was 'a soft relentless pressure'. Jack, by contrast, is an only child (the Petleys were many) of a loveless and claustrophobic marriage, like one in an early Gee story (though the house they live in is a composite of Peacehaven and Newington Road). His mother is monstrous in her stern, cold remoteness; until a stroke turns her into 'a sweet old lady' singing 'Danny Boy' in her rest home bed, someone he can no more reconcile with the unloving mother of his childhood than he can with the Mrs Skeat who previously, in her paranoid dementia, had thought he was the devil and trying to poison her. (The rest home scene is another Pitt-Rimmer-like comic vignette.) His father, a solicitor, is a diffident, private (secretive) man, drawing on his pipe through dry lips as he imparts moral precepts to his son in his study (do's and don't's that 'knot his son at the wrists and ankles'), a contained man who 'did not like anything that broke out of bounds. Metaphors. Apostrophes. Statements of intention. Disliked storms. Hated sunsets when the sky went bloody.'[27]

Jack too dislikes metaphor, and will have 'things neatly in their place'. In this novel again characters are defined by their use of language, by parts of speech. As poets Rex liked nouns, Jack 'fell prey to adjectives'; Rex's poems describe, Jack's explain.[28]

It is Jack—going to Wellington to go to library school—who rents a bedsit at the back of a house in Tinakori Road; Rex who gets a job as a postie and a hospital porter: his hospital poems, first published in *Landfall* in 1954, are regarded as his best. (His most loved poem for children, meanwhile, is 'Porridge', a recipe in disguise.) Gee chose to make his writer a poet in order to make things harder for himself. Too hard, and there are no Petley poems in *Going West*, not even a line. ('He should follow Shadbolt's example. Shadbolt got Kevin Ireland to write the verse', Alistair Campbell noted after Gee had told him he was having difficulty writing convincingly good enough examples.)[29] Some reviewers were disappointed; others saw it as a clever feint. In person as well as name Petley bears a resemblance to Rex Fairburn, in his height, his physiognomy ('a bold nose, perhaps too fleshy, and an angular forehead, heavy-boned. Fortress head') and his physical prowess (he is a formidable swimmer), his 'exaggerated hatreds', and his premature death. He had seemed to the youthful Jack 'to have no mess in his head, none of the human mess simmering and stewing in me. Large plain movements Rex had, a tilting and intersecting of planes.'[30] ('Petley' though was a random choice, although 'p' seems a good letter for Gee: we have had Pinnock, Prior, Platt, Plumb, Papps; a previous, walk-on Petley too.)[31]

Gee populates Jack and Rex's 1950s Wellington with types bearing various degrees of relation to the real. He had no one in particular in mind among the people at Rita Bullen's party:

> Laurie Sefton, Rita's protégé, whose first poems had just appeared in *Serpent*; the Training College poets and the coffee shop hobohemians . . . ; Len Mooney, the short short-story writer, wearing his Marxist armour and looking for a fight; tall private-schooled Ray Candy, the abstract painter, who gave him one out in the garden (and married Mooney's girlfriend before long, that was what it was really about); a woman I thought was Ngaio Marsh, but who turned out to be the next door neighbour; some students selling copies of their poetry magazine.

James K. Baxter didn't come.[32]

'Watch the way he invokes all the cliches of the novel of literary New Zealand, then sends them up when James K. Baxter *doesn't* come to the Wellington literary party', wrote Mark Williams admiringly (while a British reviewer saw in Gee's New Zealand boho-literati 'a satirist's portrait of the cannibalism perpetrated by mediocrity').[33] Nor was Andra, the troubled Estonian girl who commits suicide, real, although there had been 'a number of sad young women floating about' Wellington, Gee remembered, when he was there.[34]

Euan Brightmore, the 'clean white gentleman with a rosy face and hair as light and soft as a baby's' who recruits Skeat to organise his papers (precipitating his conversion from librarian into archivist), is an amalgam of an older generation: the journalists and litterateurs of the teens and 20s and 30s, the likes of Alan Mulgan and Pat Lawlor, a chapter of New Zealand literary history precisely but sympathetically drawn in three paragraphs: Euan Brightmore, author of letters and journals, novels and verse and a 'huge and still unpublished autobiography', had 'intended to be "great" . . . and was on his way until a "clique", a "coterie", sometimes even a "congeries", of "avant-gardiste poseurs" betrayed him. He could not see it was the times, the age, it was New Zealand.'[35] Mervyn Soper, editor of the *Serpent*, is a more particular and affectionate portrait of *Arena* editor Noel Hoggard: a civil servant 'with a passion for good verse' and a handset printing machine in his shed, 'diffident, provincial, amateur' and widely liked.[36] Hoggard too once fell down steps after a party and was not found until several hours later, but not fatally.

Auckland has death by drowning. Rex's sister Joy drowns in Loomis creek, tangled in barbed wire like Florence Norton's son; Jo Bellringer drives her car off the road into the creek, like Donald Pinnock. There is Rex's own, out in the Hauraki Gulf, his clinker-built dinghy found empty and out of fuel (Phil Dockery too died while out with his boat, and mysteriously); and the drowning that somehow precipitates it, by his nephew Tod—the Tod we first meet as the silent boy at the creek shadowing Rex and Jack on their latter-day reprise of the tin-canoe journey they had made as boys—of his wife and daughters. (Williams read 'a hint of pastiche of Sargeson's splendidly macabre *A Great Day* in the boats and drownings that crowd the narrative' towards the novel's end.)[37]

Wellington has death by falling: Merv Soper's, down the steps from Upland Road to Glenmore Street on the night of Rita Bullen's party; the predatory Sidgy's—Jack's landlady's unsavoury boyfriend—from the steps at the back of the house on Tinakori Road. Soper's is sad; Sidgy's is dangerous, threatening. The exception is Walter Skeat's, in a fall while stepping from the train before it had stopped at Loomis station one Friday afternoon when his son was sixteen or seventeen. Jack had set out to uncover the meaning of Rex's out-of-character death. In that carefree leap—Mr Skeat stepped down from the train early every Friday, the stationmaster tells his wife and son—lies a bigger discovery. Jack's first clues to the secret it contains are his father's books: the two John Buchans and a Sapper still in his Gladstone bag, inscribed with someone else's name; and his 1907 Webster's International Dictionary with random words (adjectives all) annotated in a private code ('light-footed, +5', 'lightsome, +3', 'liliaceous, +5', 'like-minded, –5 +3').[38] Walter Skeat was not what he had seemed.

Gee described *Going West* at the time he sent it to his publisher as being 'about a friendship between two men over fifty years'.[39] It was also a novel about a marriage. Jack meets Harry by falling, staging a fall on the Allenby Terrace steps to attract the attention of the two young women sunbathing on their lean-to kitchen roof: a 'cute meet' in the parlance of the romance novel. It was the lovely one with the long legs who had caught his eye but her 'plump and plain and sharp-eyed' flatmate who was interesting. Harry too is an Aucklander (from the North Shore), and they will move back there: Skeat writes under the stairs of the Castor Bay house they buy five months after his retirement (a house that isn't what they wanted but 'will do'). But theirs is a Wellington marriage. He was living in a bedsit on Upland Road (close to where Merv Soper fell) when they met; their relationship is consummated in the rain and southerly on a winter's night in the Botanic Garden. They rent a villa in Ngaio before buying a house on the wrong side of the hill in Kelburn, then one in Central

Terrace with a view ('a risky thing' but a necessary one).[40]

'Marriages are more interesting than affairs', writes Jack Skeat. And are more difficult and rewarding for the novelist. Marriages take time and constant, small calibrations of intimacy and distance; 'produce marvellous long-term slow-paced privacies' and 'silences'.[41] 'I, she, we, in a thousand ways. Married people know all about it. There's a lazy gravity at work between these two that don't escape but never touch.' Harry starts loving Jack less when he starts knotting his shoelaces double, and turning their children timid; when he tries to turn their marriage into 'the Land of Steady Habits' (one of his father's instructional phrases, which, he later discovers, comes from the Webster's).[42] She began going off on her own—taking 'sabbaticals'—tramping, camping, for a few weeks, sometimes for just a few days and unannounced. Suddenness is one of Harry's defining qualities, as is a 'willed aggressiveness, a willed projecting of herself' he recognises when they first meet. She remains to him 'a mystery', and this is what saves them: 'her escapes became a part of our status quo and her strangeness to me one of the things that kept us together'. He learns that '[o]ne can take pleasure, even delight, from knowing that the person one loves is free'.[43]

He learns also that '[y]ou can love your friend who has made love to your wife' (a key sentence nearly lost by the typesetter). It is after Jack discovers the connection between Rex and Harry that for 'the first time in my life I didn't need Rex': pertinently, Rex drowns on the day Jack and Harry leave for a trip (Maurice and Margaretha's 1982 trip) overseas. It is in finally arriving at the mystery of Rex's death that his two narratives come together and he discards the third-person Jack Skeat: 'That has been a curious evasion.'[44]

Gee had written *Going West* 'very easily', and sent it away in November 1991, telling Walker that he didn't 'think it will be popular'.[45] Walker was not sure he agreed. Faber put it on their list right away for spring 1993, Penguin on theirs, a little optimistically, for late 1992 (Faber happy to let them go first).

He already had then the title and starting idea of his next novel, and he had been told, back in September, that he had been awarded the Katherine Mansfield fellowship for 1992. He gave this news to Margareta (no longer Margaretha: she had finally decided to drop the 'h', since New Zealanders always did anyway) when he met her off the plane from Sweden. The fellowship was worth considerably more now than when he had first applied ten years ago: $36,000 ($4000 back then), including airfares and a month's rent on the apartment provided. The apartment was available for six months or more, except August when the owner returned from London for her summer season. They planned to stay 'until the money runs out', which they hoped would not be until November. He had been only to Paris and only for a few days before, so 'for him the prize was also the gift of France itself'.[46] He would not feel this way when he got there.

They left New Zealand in early March, getting to Nice, after a two-day stopover in Amsterdam, on the 8th, and were met at the airport by William Rubinstein, the fellowship's Nice-resident trustee, conspicuously holding a copy of Gee's *Collected Stories*. Gee had been fretting about how they would recognise him, and 'didn't see it of course'.[47] Earlier fellows had had to find their own accommodation but the previous year the lease had been arranged on a second-floor apartment in the Palais Lutetia, one of the many grand residences built in Menton during the Belle Epoque when the town became fashionable with English and Russian émigrés. The apartment was large and shabby in an old European way which some might find 'charming', but the Gees did not: 'It's big and dark and old and wobbly and coming apart', Gee wrote to Emily and Abi.[48] All the furniture except the beds was uncomfortable. There was no washing machine, so they had one installed, which meant moving the fridge into the living room; nor a vacuum cleaner so they bought one (at their own expense), which blew all the fuses the first time they plugged it in. There was no radio or television, nor a phone: it was a mistake, they later realised, not getting one put on. But the balcony was good, with its view out to a sea which seemed to have no horizon, in the foreground the town's marina 'full of launches that look like they belong to arms dealers & chocolate millionaires, but here & there among them a little chugger that wouldn't be too much out of place on a mangrove creek'.[49]

Gee hated the conspicuous, lazy wealth of the Côte d'Azur: 'All those useless people with all that money.' Even more he hated the dog mess that fouled the footpaths of Menton, 'the dog-shit capital of the world', as he described it to the girls (and others): 'They squat in the street and drop what Clive James calls "rancid coils" when they see me coming.' In the cafés the 'tiny toy' dogs responsible (how 'the French love their poodles') sat on the tables with ribbons in their hair.[50]

In France, he discovered, one could not buy lined exercise books or paper, only graph. More annoyingly, one could not buy rolled oats. Emily and Abi sent food parcels: porridge oats for him, muesli for Margareta. French food was a generally disappointing experience. At dinner at William Rubinstein's the weekend after they arrived they found the lamb undercooked to their taste and breaking up baguettes on the tablecloth (with no side plates) 'strange'. The following Sunday they were taken by local members of the New Zealand–France Association to a village two hours from Menton where they had a 'peculiar dinner—from noonish to 4.30—rough country food, costing 160 francs a head' they both thought 'frightful'. (They enjoyed the people they met, though, and were to find William Rubinstein in particular a very supportive friend.) Because they couldn't afford to and couldn't read the menus they seldom ate out on their own. They enjoyed the wine, though, especially Côte du Rhone: how were they going to get on back in New Zealand where you couldn't buy decent table wine for $3–$5 a bottle?[51]

They found their lack of language a major handicap. Gee could manage the most basic questions with his 40-year-old, level-two university French; Margareta could sometimes understand the answers. This meant wearying daily cross-cultural misunderstandings; and exacerbated Gee's battle with the Menton police department over his required *carte de séjour*, which they seemed to be maliciously (Gee's word) determined to withhold. (Margareta had a European passport and didn't need one.) The process should have taken eight days. Each time he went in, however, there seemed to be another document he didn't have. 'I come out dazed. The man behind the counter is dazed too, & he holds his head in his hands & then stands up & addresses the room & the only words I understand are "Nouvelle Zélande" and "impossible". The whole room looks at me with sympathy as I gather up my papers and go out'. After a month he was ready to pack up everything and go home, at which point Margareta rang William Rubinstein, who rang the town clerk, who rang the police chief, and the document was expedited the same afternoon. It was only after this, and after the second half of the fellowship money, which should have been waiting for him, arrived that his mood began to lift; and the sun began to come out (March and April are still cold months on the Côte d'Azur) that he 'start[ed] to see the point of Menton'.[52] But they both had a very strong sense of being displaced, which lessened but did not go away.

Gee at least had the writing room and his novel. Each weekday morning he walked 40 minutes to the Villa Isola Bella in Garavan and the little basement room beneath the house in which Katherine Mansfield wrote some of her finest stories. The room was 'clean & cool & bright' (once he had cleaned the mould off the walls), with a desk, a bed, hundreds of dead spiders on the window sills when he first arrived, and a handful of books left by the previous fellow, Nigel Cox, to be the beginnings of a library. Outside, he had to crawl past an overgrown palm with 'vicious thorns' to get to the toilet, until municipal gardeners appeared one day and cut it back. There was a lock on the gate to keep the 'KM worshippers' out.[53] He had come to Menton with the first chapters of two novels written, an adult one and a children's one (the children's one he'd written first), on Cox's advice that he have something already started and in case the first didn't work out. Once in the room, and unbothered by the trains that passed close by every twenty minutes on the line to and from Italy, he had no trouble 'teleporting' himself back to Wellington, and a gritty contemporary story of petty and white-collar crime and family dysfunction. 'That room was like a little cell labelled New Zealand.'[54] By the time they left he was within one chapter of finishing it. The only trace in it of Menton would be a reference in the opening pages to dog turds.

After his morning's writing he would eat his lunch outside the room, watching the lizards, then walk down to meet Margareta outside the Codec *marché*. Afternoons were spent shopping, walking, exploring, struggling with the mysteries of the French postal system, or going to Nice to see films at the Acropolis (including Krzysztof Kieślowski's *Dekalog*, in Polish with French subtitles which Gee could follow but Margareta not).

Walking saved them. At least one day each weekend, and sometimes more, they took a bus up into the grey limestone hills that rose steeply behind Menton and set off from some village or other on one of the hiking trails—*sentiers de grande randonnées*—'in sneakers and sun hats and dark glasses, with little Swedish day-packs on our backs' like Jack and Harry Skeat (like they themselves) on Wellington's hills, covering the skyline between Mont Agel and Roc d'Ormea on the Italian border. They frequently got lost, missed buses; once, departing from Gorbio, found themselves in the middle of a car rally. They went to La Brigue 'on the crazy railway round and through the mountains while lightning flashed and the thunder roared', the journey as well as the fifteenth-century frescoes of Notre Dame des Fontaines 'something I'll never forget'; to Tende and its tiny chapel built a thousand feet above the town by 'crazy monks' in the thirteenth century.[55]

Modern art, though, of which the towns of the Alpes-Maritimes hold some notable collections, left them unmoved. In Saint Paul de Vence at the Fondation Maeght they discovered 'basically that we are not interested in being tourists or in modern art . . . What is wrong with us? There should have been thrills to see Arp in the stone, Giacomettis striding or standing around.'[56] When they had tried early on to go to the Musée d'Art Moderne in Nice they found it closed until May, and did not go back.

They went further afield in June on a pre-booked two-week walking and camping tour of Tuscany. It rained almost constantly and they returned vowing never to go camping again, but enjoyed the walking (and their walking companions), and Florence and Siena and San Gimignano, and dinner in Pisa with a student at the university there who was doing a thesis on Gee's novels, along with her professor, Anna Grazia Mattei, 'who kept on calling me a great writer until I wanted to get under the table'. A month later they would 'look back on Tuscany with enormous pleasure' and hoped that Menton would 'assume the same aura' in retrospect.[57]

Around Easter they had been to Paris—the French government gave the Mansfield fellows a courtesy trip—and once again the city of light failed to enchant. They stayed for a few days in a tiny sixth-floor apartment (belonging to the brother of someone they had met through the New Zealand–France Association) in a 'rather seedy district' and a building with no lift, before moving to the disconcertingly plush guest quarters at the New Zealand embassy at the invitation of the ambassador, Chris Beeby, whom Gee had known in Wellington in the 1950s. They had three disappointing restaurant dinners; went to the Jeu de Paume and found the Impressionists were no longer there ('we gave up the chase for art at that point'); picnicked at Versailles but baulked again at the length of the queue and did not go inside ('something goes wrong with nearly everything . . . It's extraordinary').[58] Back in Menton they felt more disoriented that ever.

On the way they had stopped in Geneva for a night with Carl Freeman and Franca (who shouted them an underwhelming 600F meal).[59] In Menton they themselves had only a few visitors, to their quiet relief. It puzzled them when people wrote thanking them for memorable or fun evenings: 'We don't have fun evenings', Margareta wrote to the girls. 'We're wimpish and slowish and bumbling and I would have thought irritating.'[60] Gee's cousin Geoff Chapple (of 'Schooldays') visited en route to the Seville Expo in May. Brian Boyd, who was attending a Nabokov conference in Nice, came for an evening. He was looking for the pension Nabokov had stayed in in 1937–38: Nigel Cox had found it but not written down the address, only given him vague directions. (It was Margareta who found it for him, not very far from the Palais Lutetia.) And Tony Perrett—of Cheyne Gardens days, whom Gee had last seen in Truro in 1982—and his two teenage sons stayed for a week in July, a visit which left them both, but Maurice especially, exhausted.

By then they were drinking beer instead of red wine. It was too hot now for walking; the mountains were hidden in a gauzy haze, the beaches and streets were overflowing and Menton 'looks like one of the Circles of Hell'.[61] The sea looked inviting but they wouldn't swim because of the pollution. In the comparative cool of the Palais Lutetia Gee corrected the proofs of *Going West*, which had arrived from London at the beginning that month—full of mistakes, including that grievous omission of 'one of my best sentences—one I'm very proud of!'[62] He remained nervous about whether it would get back in, Faber having failed to make the requested corrections for the paperback of *The Burning Boy* (his copies of which had arrived in Menton in May, as did news that that novel had won the Buckland award). Robert McCrum had asked Rosemary Goad, although retired, to be his editor once more, knowing how Gee liked working with her and she his work. She was not 'totally knocked sideways' by *Going West* as she had been by *The Burning Boy*, she'd told him, but still loved it: '*No* one interweaves character and language as skilfully as you do. In these days of proliferating magic realism it's wonderful to sink into what I think of as a <u>real</u> novel'.

'Let me know if you're serious about a cottage over here in the autumn', she added, offering to look out for one if he was.[63]

He had been sustained too these last five months by the prospect of escaping in August when Madame Lilley, the apartment's owner, returned. But where to? There was Margareta's family they could stay with in Stockholm; invitations to Poland and Helsinki; Gee hankered for a country cottage in England. Margareta was keen to get to Morocco as well, but this proved impossible. They left Menton on 2 August—unsure if they were going to return—and spent four days in Dijon at the invitation of Jean-Pierre and Carole Durix who taught Commonwealth literature at the University of Burgundy. The Durixs had learned Gee was in Menton from fellow academic Jacqueline Bardolphe, for whom he had given a talk at the University of Nice (which had gone well, although there were only eight people there). Passing through Paris, Gee left a copy of his novel draft with Chris Beeby to send back to New Zealand in the diplomatic bag: he had been terrified of taking it with him, and, after an abortive start by Margareta at typing it for him (as he read it to her), had photocopied it at William Rubinstein's international language school in Nice. From Paris they took a couchette to Berlin for a three-day reconnaissance, with the thought of Gee one day applying for a DAAD fellowship—'a perfectly bearable city', they found—and on from there to northern Poland.[64]

'Poland was strange, almost like stepping out and back.'[65] They had been invited there by John Borrell, an expatriate New Zealand journalist and an admirer who had written to Gee in late 1991 after he had read that Gee had been awarded the fellowship. He and his Polish, artist wife, Ania, spent their summers and autumns in Sytna Góra, a tiny village 30 kilometres from Gdansk, where they had seven acres of forested and meadow land (family land) bordering a freezing but beautiful lake, and were living in a caravan while they built a fishing lodge. Maurice and Margareta stayed for two weeks in the summer cottage of one of Ania's uncles. It was a relaxing, though 'quite a peculiar', time,[66] walking and cycling around the flat sandy country, and Gee did a lot of writing. From Gdynia they then made a twenty-something hour ferry trip to Helsinki, where friends of Brian Boyd who taught at the university had invited them to visit, although they did not stay with them but in a student hostel. Margareta had been keen to go back, having spent a few days in Helsinki the previous year; Gee to see some nineteenth-century Nordic art—his novel having a Swedish character 'marooned' in New Zealand and obsessed by it—and was thrilled by a Gallen-Kellela exhibition. They took a bus next through the 'endless rolling'[67] Finnish countryside to Turku, and from there a ferry cruise through the Finland archipelago and on down to Stockholm.

Stockholm was lovely, Gee told the girls, 'my favourite foreign city',[68] but their two weeks there were not. After two nights in the same youth hostel they had stayed in ten years before, they moved

At home at Cleveland Terrace, Nelson, 1987
Robert Cross photograph

Charles Brasch at home, Heriot Row, Dunedin
Zelda Louise Robertson photograph. Hocken Collections, University of Otago S09-188g

Kevin Jowsey (Ireland), Tony Stones and Robin Dudding, Auckland, about 1953
Adam Dudding

Moss Gee and Jim Baxter at a party at Ron Polson's flat, Terrace Gardens, Wellington, 1957
Brian Bell photograph

Moss Gee, Maurie Shadbolt, Dave Walsh and Kevin Jowsey, at Brian Bell's, Gladstone Road, Ponsonby, 1956
Brian Bell photograph. Brian Bell Collection, Alexander Turnbull Library PAColl-9389

Nigel Cook, Queen Street, Auckland, 1954
Nigel Cook

Julie Cook in the mid-1960s
Marti Friedlander photograph. Nigel Cook

Moss at Nigel and Julie's

Opposite:
Smiling for Marti Friedlander, 1959
Marti Friedlander photograph

Hera Smith
Marti Friedlander photograph

With Hera and Nigel just before leaving for London, January 1961

Len and Nigel

'MAURICE GEE, 1964 Robert Burns Fellow, revises his latest novel.' *Otago Daily Times*, 15 October 1964

Otago Daily Times

With Margaretha Hickman, Wellington Railway Station photo booth, 1969

The new Napier city librarian, first day on the job, February 1970

New home owners and parents-to-be: at France Road, Napier, 1970

THE BIG SEASON
MAURICE GEE

A SPECIAL FLOWER
maurice gee
A New Zealand critic wrote of THE BIG SEASON, Maurice Gee's first novel:
"Confirms the opinion I expressed when reviewing Gee's work in NEW AUTHORS SHORT STORY ONE that he showed more promise than any other young New Zealand prose writer. This book lives up to that promise."

P·L·U·M·B
MAURICE GEE

MEG
MAURICE GEE

The first two books:
The Big Season (Hutchinson, 1962);
A Special Flower (Hutchinson, 1965)

Covers designed in New Zealand by Lindsay Missen:
Plumb (Faber and Faber and Oxford University Press (NZ), 1978);
Meg (Faber and Faber in association with Penguin (NZ), 1981)

Under the Mountain (Oxford University Press (NZ), 1979); cover illustration by Roger Hart

Going West (Faber and Faber and Viking (NZ), 1992); the Faber cover format was used for a number of New Zealand editions

The Scornful Moon (Penguin New Zealand, 2003); this series design by Nik Andrew was introduced in 1996 for *Loving Ways* and used thereafter for new books and reissues

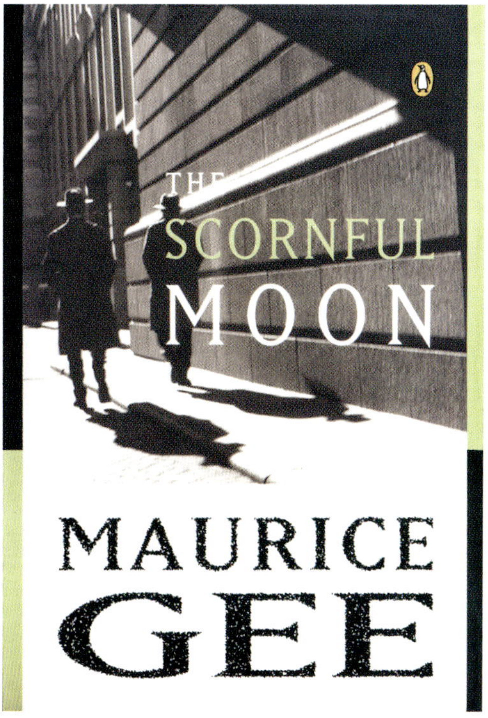

Family portrait, Cleveland Terrace, 1979: Abigail left, Emily with glasses
R. Milligan photograph for the *New Zealand Listener*

At the Tomb of Agamemnon, Mycenae, Greece, May 1982

Digging out the septic tank, Cleveland Terrace, 1983

Writing, Cleveland Terrace, 1983
Photographer unknown. George Griffiths collection P99-054, Hocken Collections, University of Otago

Three photographs from Greg O'Brien and Robert Cross's visit to Gee in Nelson in 1987 to interview and photograph him for *Moments of Invention*
Robert Cross photographs

Emily, Nigel, Abi (wearing *Under the Mountain* T-shirt) and Maurice, 1980s

Menton-bound: the newly selected Katherine Mansfield Memorial Fellow, late 1991/ early 1992, posing with Bill Manhire's *Zoetropes*, the manuscript of *Going West* and his 1902 Webster's International Dictionary

Escaping from Menton: at San Gimignano, Tuscany, June 1992

With Larry Parr on the set of *Fracture*, 2002

On stage as the inaugural Honoured New Zealand Writer, Auckland Writers and Readers Festival, May 2012
Steven McNicholl photograph. New Zealand Herald

to Margareta's cousin's tiny apartment (while she went to her archipelago island). Each morning Gee walked across town to the equally tiny flat of Alan O'Donnell, a New Zealander who had lived in Stockholm since his twenties and had been the student counsellor at Emily's school there in 1989, and worked there on his novel; and did his back in and thereafter had to spend much of his time lying down. In Stockholm he was also afflicted by a severe and debilitating allergy and extreme lethargy. Margareta began to worry that he had some terminal illness and might not make it home. He suspected mercury poisoning from the tooth he had broken in Berlin; or perhaps it was the mosquito that bit him in Dijon. Or perhaps, and more likely, it was just chronic fatigue and homesickness. On their next stop, Göteborg, they gave up and, skipping Lund as well as Skagen and stopping for only two hours in Copenhagen, took the train back to Menton; where the tourists were largely gone but the mountains still there, and 'slippers and lolly papers land on our balcony from five floors up and the rubbish wakes us at 4 a.m. and the mad dog barks—lovely to be back.'[69]

They spent another month in Menton, where Gee's health improved immediately though not completely. The mould, he found, had grown back over the walls of the writing room, the smell becoming so bad that for the last two weeks he could no longer write there. With lingering concerns on Margareta's part about his stamina, they kept to their planned homeward itinerary, via New York and Vancouver. They left France in mid-October, Gee leaving behind 100 francs in the Menton bank account he had opened and forgot to close, and his marked proof copy of *Going West* in the writing room (Owen Marshall sent it back to him in 1996). In New York they stayed for a week with a friend Margareta had made at the Uppsala language school and her partner, a painter, in their loft apartment on West 26th Street, and had two days at their hosts' upstate country house, the New York fall at its most spectacular. Gee made a half-hearted effort to see his two editors at Simon and Schuster (who were publishing *The Champion*), calling unannounced and finding them out at lunch. In Vancouver they stayed with Margareta's old Nelson friend Caroline Brett who lived on a houseboat on the Fraser River. Gee's mysterious illness returned here. It was Margareta, though, who arrived back in New Zealand (on 1 November) in a wheelchair, with a sprained ankle suffered in Menton and a collapsed arch in the other foot. 'We walked too hard, I guess', Gee remarked to Ray Richards.[70]

27

The Fat Man

The Menton year had tested not only their physical stamina. The strangeness and difficulty of France had made them dependent on each other to an unaccustomed degree. 'This is not to say that we didn't have a working partnership before', Margareta afterwards wrote, 'but this was real, the daily grind of partnership in NZ was chickenfeed by comparison.'[1] Menton had strained and broken up relationships before, as they knew; Nigel Cox's had been one. This was never going to happen to the Gees, but it was a 'fairly gruelling' eight months in a number of ways.[2] 'I look at Gee and I boxing along in such a mismatched union', Margareta confided to her New York friend from Menton, as they were preparing to leave. Perhaps, she mused—had in fact suggested—they could live in adjacent townhouses: 'On my side I am "allowed" a cat and a dog [it would be an Alsatian] and to be untidy. We haven't decided who does the cooking. Will he come to my side to eat? Watch TV? Will we sleep in the middle? I bags the stereo.'[3]

Yet, a journalist doing a profile on Gee observed three years later, '[b]oth give the impression of being deeply content with the other', despite being, Margareta explained, 'quite different creatures in many ways: "He's a rugby, sports-watching sort of person, while I'm a tramper. I'm a talker, he's a good listener"'—although, she observed, strangely unintuitive except in his writing ('He doesn't pick up clues. Things have to be spelt out.'). 'He reads biographies, I read autobiographies.'[4] Writing was an intense and solitary activity. She had a different kind of energy, a restlessness and abruptness of manner (a bit like Harry's). It was Margareta who went to Sweden and Lapland and the Himalayas; Maurice who preferred being at home.

The reception of *Going West* boosted Gee's reputation and his profile to an extent he had not experienced since *Plumb*. It also gave a welcome boost to his income; as in 1982 they had arrived home cash-strapped. (An application Gee had sent from Menton for the 1993 Auckland University literary fellowship had been unsuccessful.) Gee, wrote Nigel Cox in literary magazine *Quote Unquote* in July, 'is one of a tiny cluster of our writers for whom greatness seems possible and he appears to be on the brink of international recognition. His recent novel, *Going West*, had the English reviewers juggling superlatives.' 'It has become a near-certain pleasure to read a new book by the New Zealand writer Maurice Gee', began the *Times Literary Supplement*'s; the *Sunday Times* described him as 'one of the finest writers at work . . . in the English-speaking world'. 'Yes, there have been one or two good reviews', Gee was quoted in Air New Zealand magazine *Pacific Way*, the press as always enjoying his quiet, unassuming manner.[5]

Going West was released there in January, in New Zealand in March, brought forward from May to qualify for the Wattie awards. (Walker had long since realised that publication in 1992 was not feasible; it was pity, then, that Penguin neglected to amend the imprint page.) The 'novel of the year', Michael King was prepared to declare it in *Metro* in May, complaining only that 'it will make other fiction seem contrived, unwieldy and unauthentic by comparison'.[6] The *New Zealand Listener* review—another rave by Kevin Ireland—was accompanied by a full-page photograph of Gee and followed in the next issue by an excerpt from the novel. (By coincidence or clever editing, the previous issue had carried an extract from Maurice Shadbolt's just-published memoir *One of Ben*'s, describing the 1950s writers, prominently Baxter.) Jack Skeat, wrote Ireland, was 'one of Gee's finest creations', 'a connoisseur of moments of disappointment'. In a similar appreciation Colleen Reilly captured the novel's tone, and in her view most rewarding quality: 'a unique combination of resigned sadness and modest rage'.[7] ('[T]hat bitter carping tone of a man who feels that he has failed', Gee described the voice he found for Skeat in the novel's first few pages.)[8]

It was usual by now to praise Gee's care and control and intricacy of plotting. With Gee, a British reviewer observed, 'fussiness is a virtue'.[9] Writing to him directly, Dennis McEldowney remarked especially on the 'richness of detail, of reference, of what you might call harmonics, . . . as well as the right language. And thanks', he added, 'for the tip about Johnson's Baby Shampoo [which Jack uses on his fine, thinning hair]. I'll try it.' Toss Woollaston had advice in turn for Gee as well as admiration, noting Skeat 'striking a match after using the lavatory': 'It is even better to burn a dried blue gum-leaf or sprig of Rosemary'.[10] In Gee's words, 'the writing of novels is such a particularizing business: it's small things all the way'.[11]

Where several reviewers did have reservations, however—and this was becoming a familiar one—was with the ending (a 'hasty (if orgasmic) finale', in the *TLS*'s words).[12]

Gee had been wrong to think *Going West* would not be popular. 'I have never seen a novel sell quite like this!', Walker told him in January 1994 as paperback sales were approaching 8000, 'including an astonishing 1554 copies in the month of December'.[13] Penguin's promotional brief for the book trade had described Gee's market as 'modest but strong. His followers buy each book.'[14] Of *The Burning Boy*, which had outsold *Prowlers*, they still had 400 of their initial 2500 print run in stock after a year and a half (with a paperback a few months away). In December 1994 New Zealand paperback sales of *Going West*, now into its fifth reprint, passed 10,000, bringing total sales (with the hardback) to 11,800, making it 'one of the biggest selling New Zealand novels in recent years, perhaps up in the top three or four in the 1990s'.[15]

The paperback had been rushed out when the novel was shortlisted for the Wattie, which it won, Gee having told the press that he would probably spend the $20,000 if it did on replacing the car (a rusting Toyota), doing up the bathroom and paying off the mortgage—said 'with quiet deliberation—Maurice Gee the householder, taking inventory. Checking wear and tear.'[16] It also won him for the fourth time the Buckland award. He was not too disappointed, however, to miss out on a fifth New Zealand Book Award: feeling that he'd 'had more than his fair share', he wouldn't mind, he had said a few days earlier, if *The Miserables*, Damien Wilkins' first novel ('marvellous') won it, which it did.[17]

He had described himself in 1979, Nigel Cox reminded him, as 'the least known of the New Zealand novelists', and still had, he felt, 'a very low profile, compared with someone like say Alan Duff, or Janet Frame'.[18] Not so low, however, that a letter addressed simply to 'Maurice Gee, Famous Author, Nelson' would not find its way to 41 Chelmsford Street, Ngaio. The offer of a knighthood in 1992 (for the 1993 New Year honours; he turned it down, of course) was another measure of recognition.[19]

Going West was Gee's tenth adult novel and his twentieth book. 'I'd like to still produce three or four novels if I can', he told Cox. 'If I get to 70'—he was 61 now—'with my mind alive enough to continue writing fiction, I'll be happy.'[20]

He had two novels published in 1994. He had his Menton one, *Crime Story*, to Richards and Walker by mid-1993, and it slipped through the production process just as efficiently. Title aside, *Crime Story* was not a crime novel, a genre novel, less so (and less intentionally so) than *In My Father's Den*. He had had a go at writing one of those, after *The Burning Boy*: a 'blockbuster' which would make him the kind of money his '"literary" sort of novel[s]' never did.[21] He got to chapter three before he gave up, finding he didn't have the enthusiasm for it, nor it the necessary creative spark. Also, it bothered him that such novels almost invariably centred on violence done to women. His own, as far as it got, involved a disappeared (murdered) American hitchhiker and a mysterious note, exotic locations (Vienna, Lokrum, Piraeus, and the West Coast), a Greek hitman and a sinister Yugoslav. He found writing it boring. Still, he retained the ambition to one day write a real crime novel, a Chandleresque detective *noir*.

Crime Story told of many crimes, not only the one or perhaps two he had in mind when he applied for Menton: 'possibly something violent, a house theft gone wrong for example; although I'm more inclined to go into the white-collar area and have something clever and corrupt . . . Perhaps there will be two crimes, that approach each other and join and won't let go.'[22] Rather than a crime novel, *Crime Story* is Gee's political novel, in that it was prompted by political anger, his 'gut anger' at what had been done to the country by its political leaders and the greedy and vain in the past six years: at the betrayal of its principals by a Labour government fallen sway to free-market liberalism, or 'Rogernomics' (so called after finance minister Roger Douglas), at profiteering by financiers and property speculators, at 'rampant materialism and commercialism and greed' and the growing disparity between rich and poor.[23] One could call it, he supposed 'a state of the nation novel'. 'Some bad things have happened since 1987 and while I'm not actively political I wanted to explore them in fictional terms', 'to have a look at the way we are now, & perhaps identify, in a small way, what E.M. Forster called "the inner darkness of the commercial age"'.[24] It had been in the background of *Going West*, where Tod kills his family after losing his money and his job in the 1987 sharemarket crash.

Being a Gee novel, the crimes in *Crime Story* are not only crimes of violence and greed but also (and as well) of failure of empathy and love.

It begins with steps and a fall. The botched burglary from which the story unfolds happens in Central Terrace. Brent Rosser, our burglar, is disturbed by the house's returning owner, panics and pushes her as he escapes down the stairs; the fall breaks her neck. He flees down the steep flight of steps from Central Terrace to Glasgow Street, down through the university and into the city. 'Wellington was perfect for dropping out of sight. You came out on a new road, on a different level of the world.'[25] Both Auckland and Wellington feature again here but *Crime Story* is strongly a Wellington novel; it is a tale of two cities in a different way.

Ulla Peet is left a paraplegic. She is the marooned Swede Gee was thinking about when he visited art galleries in Helsinki: trapped inside her stricken body, she travels back in her mind to the landscapes of her childhood, to which she has not returned since she came to New Zealand and married at nineteen (just as Greta Garden never did,[26] but in her case Oscar forbade her; Ulla's estranged husband, Athol, has told her he wouldn't mind, she could take the children and go back if she wanted). Athol Peet, it turns out, is Brent Rosser's landlord (the levels of the city are not so far apart as he thinks). Next door to Ulla lives her mother-in-law, Gwen: when the burglary happens she is out walking her granddaughter's dog (a dachshund-pug cross which she regards with as much affection as Gee did the dogs of Menton: 'Smelly, overfed, useless'),[27] passing Rosser on the street as she goes out, coming home via the steps which lead from Central Terrace over to Upland Road (a few houses along from the one where David Minnitt shot his wife Leigh in the back of the head in their bedroom in May 1980).[28] The bond between the two women, strengthened now as Gwen cares for and seeks to understand Ulla, is an exception to the empty, acidic relationships which define the two families in the novel, the Rossers and Peets. 'They circled like a family of planets, never touched—she, Athol, Damon, Olivia', Gwen writes of hers, echoing Noel Papps.[29]

'All her men were greedy . . . grabbers and getters', Gwen reflects.[30] Athol owns 46 houses as well as commercial properties through his rental company Athco, and has a past involvement with a shady land deal that won't leave him alone. Up in Auckland, his brother Gordon is facing trial for his part in the dealings of fallen finance company

Lupercal (the company Tod had lost his money in; it is Gwen who mischievously suggested its name). Their father, Gwen's ex-husband, Howie, is a high-flying property developer, close to closing a deal to put up a tower block on Lambton Quay. He lives with his new, young wife Darlene in a cliff-top mansion in Auckland's East Coast Bays, jetting to Wellington to conduct his business deals. Gwen feels pity for Gordon, who has been greedy and stupid rather than corrupt (a 'poor dumb softy', Howie calls him: a minion in the Lupercal business, Gordon will get off lightly with eighteen months); anger and dislike for Athol, for his emptiness and his selfishness; for Howie admiration alongside contempt. Against her better judgement she still likes Howie, because 'he dreamed . . . he had a vision of beauty. Athol did not have one. Gordy had some poor lopped-off thing.' Howie blames Gwen for making his sons small and weak (she 'had sewn their seams up tight').[31]

'And she, Gwen? What she saw would not hold its shape; what she desired was multifarious.' She has something of Meg about her, in her post-divorce self-reflection, and her appreciation of liking over love: 'It was nourishing and steady, while love was always too much or too little and made one overcertain or uncertain, never sure.' (That had been Kingsley Pratt's realisation too: that '[l]ove isn't enough. Liking's much more important.')[32] Narratively, Gwen's is the novel's predominant and most sympathetic point of view.

When Gee first conceived of *Crime Story* he knew nothing about financial speculation and property development or the ways of white-collar crime. He mentioned this to a neighbour who introduced him to Tor Klevstul, the managing director of property development company Norseman Pacific, and, Gee was to find, one of the most interesting people he had ever met. Klevstul was a Norwegian who had trained in England as an architect and worked in the North Sea oil and gas industries before coming to New Zealand to work for Fletchers in 1978, and establishing Norseman Pacific in 1984. He was, like Howie, a passionate believer in free enterprise. He also (unlike Howie) read philosophy and Greek mythology and Camus and wrote poetry, and later a novel: 'I was very lucky to meet you', he told Gee when he was halfway through reading his way through his, 'You have really been a great inspiration for me to pursue my long held ambition to write.' He 'had just a sort of an excess of energy . . . he was a sort of incursion if you like into our lives'.[33] (Margareta and Abi didn't care for him much: he was also like Howie in his attitudes towards women.)

Klevstul lived in Auckland in Mairangi Bay but kept a permanent room in the Parkroyal Hotel—*Crime Story*'s 'bronzed and sheathed' Glencoul—which had been Norseman Pacific's first major (and award-winning) Wellington project and had carried it through the 1987 crash. Gee would meet him there for dinner and research. To Menton he sent Gee an account of the rise and fall of investment company the Kupe Group, one of the big casualties of the '87 crash, and updates on his own development-in-progress. Howie Peet's Kitchener project—his mirror-glass 'diamond in the sky', the negotiations with a divided city council over resource consents and the trade-off underground carpark, opposition from heritage advocates and environmentalists ('the greenies and their mates, the sandal-wearers and lentil-eaters, and the usual claque of old-building freaks and car-haters')[34]—closely resembles Norseman Pacific's controversial Midland development on the site of the former Wellington central police station on Waring Taylor Street and Lambton Quay, which was ongoing through 1992–93. 'Is this getting too close?', Gee asked Klevstul, seeking his permission, 'I'll stop if you say. Or I can make the building a hotel' (Klevstul on the contrary was flattered).[35] In any case, Howie, Gee assured him, was very different from him in age, background and other ways: Howie is a Henderson boy (son of a brickie), who has brought himself up from nothing; but feels no sense of distance travelled from that place and time, '[t]he creek, his mother's kitchen'. ('Henderson creek has got in too', Gee admitted to Emily and Abi, '—can't keep it out.')[36] At Gee's request Klevstul outlined for him a typical day of meetings Howie might have, close to closing a deal: who the people are (his own and the council's), what their roles are and what they discuss, how it all works; '& when they stop for lunch & where they go & what they eat; and how it ends; the jokes; the likes & dislikes etc . . . I can't have too much detail, hard fact, quotation, common word & special word.' Gee enjoyed finding out and writing about the mundane and particular details of people's work, its special language. 'What I feel is,' he continued to Klevstul, 'there's part of life, Kiwi working life, that hasn't got into fiction yet, and I'd like to try it, even if it turns out to be just a couple of pages.'[37]

Tor Klevstul was not a crook, though he had 'always quite liked the mafia image we gained in Wellington' in the early 90s, he later told Gee, and he knew how the crooks worked. (A 'straight shooter', but 'he can be tricky', Gee described Howie to Klevstul.)[38] The example for Lupercal's criminal dealings was the Equiticorp scandal, then (and still) New Zealand's most notorious white-collar crime, whose principals were on trial in 1991. On a smaller scale, the Shearwater land deal in which Athol is almost implicated he based on a 1986 case he remembered—in which, similarly, an engineering and surveying company had bought up large tracts of marginal land in Porirua while advising the city council on a flood protection scheme that would open up the land for subdivision. (In adding a politician to the mix—*Crime Story*'s Gilbert Fox—he also had in mind the Long Gully Marginal Loans Board affair in 1980.)

He sent Klevstul a copy of his final draft, Klevstul responding with a few suggestions ('"Fucking good work, Tony. Good stuff, Howie." (I don't think Howie would say "nice work")'; he would like to see some mention of put and call options and pyramid selling) and approbation. He was pleased with Howie, who was basically, he thought, incapable of real compassion '[b]ut I know him well and I quite like him'. It was 'the first of your novels that I was unable to put down, and I don't think that was all vanity on my part. Your ability to see into people's souls is becoming a bit frightening though.'[39]

Peet, like Petley, was a recycled name (again from *Meg*: the medium whom Meg recognises as Merle Butters). Rosser was a found one, in a 1992 newspaper report about a sickness beneficiary who robbed a New Plymouth bank out of desperation.[40] Here Gee was in equally unfamiliar territory. He consulted a criminal lawyer about the ways of petty thieves and fences. He went to Abi (to whom he would dedicate the novel) for a description of a pub gig (from a school essay she had written) and suggestions for a band name. 'There's an Australian group called "I Spit in Your Gravy". Wish I'd thought of that. . . . something like "The Greasy Feet" or "The Big Square Toes"—believable'. She gave him detailed and informed advice (there was, she noted, an 'increasing trend towards childish & naive names & words', techno talk, industrial references, and celestial and spiritual words (The Jesus and Mary Chain, Faith No More, Nirvana); also irony (calling a thrash metal band The Happy Flowers, for example)), and eight or nine suggestions, from which he chose Killing Bambi. (He rejected, among others, The Steaming Faeces (though he was tempted), The Halitosis Kids and Making Rorschach Read Jackie Collins: 'Really, some bands go in for names like this. Someone's already got The Freudian Slips'.)[41]

Brent is a serial burglar with a perverted sense of pride and code of ethics (he leaves his houses tidy, doesn't do drugs or touch pornography); a loner. His tough and likeable sister, Leanne, is a solo mother of a half-Samoan baby boy and lives in a flat in Newtown or Te Aro which even Brent thinks is a slum. The abusive, tattooed, foul-mouthed Danny with whom she is forced to share it and her favours is where the novel perhaps comes closest to caricature. Here is where Gee was least comfortable. Originally Danny was Māori, until Walker queried whether this was wise. Gee had been wondering so himself: 'I'll gladly talk about changing Danny the Bad Maori to Danny the Bad Pakeha', he replied. 'I've done a bit of soul-searching about it . . . and . . . I can't get the right and wrongs clear in my head'.[42]

Out in Wainuiomata, Brent and Leanne's father, Clyde, has been made redundant from his job as a storeman and lovingly tends his state-house vegetable garden, while his wife has abandoned her Presbyterianism for a fundamentalist church in the Hutt whose followers speak in tongues and await the Last Days. Wainuiomata is presented here—through Leanne—not as a working-class dead end and object of middle-class derision (the infamous *Heartland* television documentary episode featuring Chloe of Wainuiomata screened the same month *Crime Story* came out), but as a childhood Eden; another Henderson. In this tale of two broken families, the relationship between Leanne and her father is the exception as Gwen and Ulla's is in the Peets. Mrs Rosser (we do not learn her name) is another of Gee's mothers who loves too little (Leanne) or too much. Brent is not only a convincing portrait of a petty burglar but a powerful portrayal of psychosis and paranoia. Rejecting his own, in his increasing delusion and desperation he seeks a surrogate mother in his fence, Mrs Ponder, who rejects him in turn; sanctuary in the smallest place he can find in her Cuba Street yard, a chest freezer: 'wrapped . . . round with kitchen and his mother'.[43] ('Everything', said Paul Prior, 'took its tone from Mother.')[44] 'Gee's delineation of his descent into madness', critic Mark Williams wrote, 'is as compelling as anything of the kind in Lowry or Frame.'[45] It is a gruesome and sad ending to a novel in which the usual Gee humour is hard to find.

While not a crime novel, nor aspiring to be one, *Crime Story* is a taut and pacy read: 'a fairly simple, linear novel, [which] lacks some of the complexities of the others', Gee described it.[46] 'You'd mentioned that Crime Story would be something a little different', Walker remarked after he read the manuscript. 'I hadn't realised that you were going to write something quite so different to previous work.'[47] *Crime Story* also marked a change in Gee's publishing relationships, for which Walker had been angling for some time. His frustration at publishing second to Faber, and with Faber themselves, had been exacerbated once again by their cover design for *Going West*: 'a single brooding male figure against a dark and ominous landscape is not what this book is about', he informed them snippily, though he would go along with it. And Gee in any case disagreed and liked it: yes, it was 'a bit Man alonish', but after all, as he said to Robert McCrum, 'Jack Skeat dreams of dying alone on a mountain'.[48]

Well before they knew anything about the new novel other than its title Richards had approached Bloomsbury and Hodder Headline, and Walker Viking Penguin (London) and Hamish Hamilton inviting their interest in publishing Gee in the UK. This was not only about design and editorial control: Penguin were finding Faber's 'expensive hardbacks', with which they had done 'moderately well', increasingly uneconomic in the New Zealand market.[49] Not until Viking and Hamish Hamilton had turned *Crime Story* down ('too relentlessly dark and unsympathetic', said the latter, though they liked it 'very much') did they offer it to Faber.[50] The agreement eventually reached was not all that Walker wanted, which was for Faber to purchase their edition from Penguin (NZ). Faber was not prepared, after eight novels and 21 years, 'to surrender our central role in his publishing in English', but they were happy to separate out the New Zealand and Australian rights, and (after some hesitation) to collaborate on editing and typesetting.[51]

In the event editing was done in Auckland; Faber printed their edition themselves and designed their own cover. This was all fine with Gee, who was pleased to be staying with Faber as his London publisher, and told them so. While he sympathised with Walker, he had wondered if he could do better in England than Faber and their loyalty and 'amazingly generous' advances.[52] (It didn't seem to matter to them that of eight novels only two, *Plumb* and *Going West*, had so far earned back their advances.)

As for covers, he confided to Richards, he had not thought much of recent Penguin ones. Somewhat ironically, Walker's brief to his designer was for something 'a little like the Faber crime covers', 'quite flashy' but with 'a literary feel'.[53] It was certainly flashy: a cartoonish collage in bright yellow, blue and red. Gee, with his taste for 'simple and figurative', preferred Faber's, a graceful watercolour sketch of Wellington rooftops, harbour and hills (by the same artist who had done *The Burning Boy* and *Going West*), making no reference to crime at all.[54] The shift to local editing, however, began a long and happy author–editor relationship between Gee and Jane Parkin: the book was 'such a pleasure to edit', she told him, while the proofs, Gee told Walker, were 'the cleanest . . . I've ever handled'.[55]

The reception of *Crime Story*—which appeared in New Zealand (simultaneously in hardback and paperback) in August 1994 and in England the following March—was a familiar one. His publishers loved it; the reviews were mostly excellent; it sold 'only moderately well'.[56] As with *Prowlers*, very strong initial book trade orders made Walker overly optimistic. (It was sold out before publication and he ordered an immediate reprint of 4000, matching the original paperback run.) 'What we need is a scandal of some sort', Gee remarked two months later, '—I had hoped the mayor of Wellington might become upset by it.'[57] Still, just over 4700 by March 1995 was 'pretty good', Walker let him know.[58] When sales passed the 5000 mark the following January he had Penguin managing director Tony Harkins send Gee a bottle of bubbly. It was a disappointment, though, after *Going West*.

It was a disappointment too that they could not place it in America, despite Richards trying it with eight publishers there, including Bantam Doubleday's crime division whom he warned that it was 'a work of serious social fiction' not crime fiction as customarily understood: unfortunately, they replied, it 'falls directly into that hard-boiled abyss in which nothing except name-brand authors are selling successfully . . . But I will certainly keep this in mind when the era of the Lady Sleuth is over'.[59]

At home it was reviewed not as a failed cross-over into genre but as a chilling portrait of the ugliness and moral bankruptcy of post-Rogernomics New Zealand, and familiar Gee: 'a New Zealand—no, Wellington—version of Crime and Punishment'; his 'bleakest and blackest' novel so far (or, the *Levin Chronicle* understatedly put it, 'a somewhat dim view of life in New Zealand'); a 'rich, wise and wonderful novel . . . in the traditions of the great 19-century novelists excoriating the gospels of greed, self-interest and efficiency, and their devastating consequences on what Gwen calls "Roger's children"'; 'Its familiarity is startling and disturbing.'[60]

In the *New Zealand Herald* retired professor of English Ian

Gordon also welcomed the novel not as any kind of departure but as Gee reassuringly doing what he did best: his writing is 'so limpid and clear it is easy to miss the skill with which it is crafted: no purple passages, no brooding soliloquies, no contrived flashbacks, no streams of consciousness, no adjectival rhapsodies on landscape or atmosphere. The narrative moves onwards with a clean athletic grace, every word carefully targeted at its central core of meaning. This is writing of a very high order', delineating New Zealand urban and small-town life 'with the fidelity of a Balzac'.[61]

'Dickensian, without the prolixity', Dennis McEldowney called it: 'Brent Rosser's demoralisation and the horror of his further crime brings to mind the last days of any number of dark Dickensian characters—Jonas Chuzzlewitt, James Carker, Bill Sykes; though Brent is a more ambiguous villain than any of these'. But he also found 'a touch of Dickensian—I won't say sentimentality—softness'.[62]

Crime Story would be the first of Gee's novels to be made into a feature film. That was ten years away, however. For now, as soon as he had sent away the manuscript he got to work on a treatment for an eight-part television version for Chris Hampson, head of development at TVNZ's production house South Pacific Pictures. On the basis of a three-page outline they were offering him $200,000 for a treatment and script and film and television rights—'as much as I'd get from a dozen novels'.[63] Hampson loved the treatment ('wonderful, great, superb, fascinating'), but after he lost his development role a few months later interest lapsed. This was 'disappointing and disturbing', Gee told Richards: he was only a few weeks away from finishing the children's novel he had taken a chapter of to Menton and needed to know what he would be doing next, *Crime Story* scripts 'or the new adult novel that is waiting to start'.[64]

It had taken him three or four months to write *The Fat Man*, the children's novel, which came out two months after *Crime Story*. Speaking about it in public he remained unashamed about children's fiction being easier for him than writing for adults, perhaps not always choosing his words wisely—'[a]dmitting that children's books, while an enjoyable diversion, do not stretch him as novels can'; 'When I'm writing for children I know I'm writing for human beings of smaller understanding than the adults I also write for. I go and look out of another window.'[65] The controversy that surrounded *The Fat Man*, however, was over another issue: whether the book was too nasty.

The genesis of *The Fat Man* was an experience he had recalled in his 'Beginnings' essay, of walking by the creek one day with his mother and brothers when they came across a naked man, probably a swagger, waist-deep in a pool washing himself, and his mother hurrying them back the way they had come. The memory came to him again unbidden—the visceral memory of the man's 'deep-pitted eyes that fixed on us and never moved', the '[a]bsolute stillness' of the place and moment. 'They are like old belongings in a suitcase at the back of the wardrobe', he remarked in a 1994 interview about the experiences and incidents that become or get into novels. 'You don't know you have got them but when you need them you will suddenly remember that they are there.'[66] To that incident and its fear and mystery he added another discomfiting childhood memory to make the plot of *The Fat Man*: his complicity in the bullying of Fatty Walker at Henderson school, which still brought back feelings of shame 50 years later (a memory that also surfaces in *Crime Story*).

The swagger 'had black eyebrows and a black unshaven chin'.[67] The fat man is pink and white and bald, and has, at odds with the repulsion he inspires and the evil he harbours, an obsession with cleanliness (alike to Brent Rosser's tidiness fetish, an early sign of that character's disturbance of mind). But it was the eyes that Gee remembered most, the unblinking stare of eyes 'small and deep and blacker than sheep pellets' that fix on his eleven-year-old protagonist, Colin Potter.[68] There is a scar on the fat man's cheek which curls like a worm when he grins. He is the most terrifying person Colin Potter has ever seen.

The setting is Loomis, 1933; the story about cruelty and revenge and shattered illusions. It is a gripping, dark and powerful one. The Depression Gee invokes is the one his parents told him of: of pride and shame; of his father's boxing trophies being sold to a passing second-hand goods dealer; his father riding off on his bicycle every morning after the timber mill truck in hope of a day's work, as Colin's father does. Colin's grandparents run the Bellevue boarding house, once the Great Western Hotel before Loomis went dry—Henderson's Central (later Falls) Hotel. (The paintings on its walls, though, are the ones that hung in the boarding houses in Paeroa and Waihī.) It was 'a pretty tough story with elements of gothic and melodramatic', Gee described it,[69] in this way akin to *The Fire-Raiser*, and there are more direct echoes of *The Fire-Raiser*. The Muskie family—the fat man's—had been an important family in Loomis once. Now only old Mrs Muskie lives, Miss Havisham-like—Mrs Marwick-like—in the once grand, now falling-down two-storey house (Loomis's only one) on Millbrook Road. Every afternoon she walks into town to the shops, and on the way home rests for ten minutes at the station as the 2.30 train from Auckland comes in, waiting for the favourite son who left Loomis thirteen years ago and has never returned: this, Gee freely admits, is 'a straight steal' from Frank Sargeson's story 'An Affair of the Heart'.[70] There, however, Mrs Crawley's son never comes. Herbert Muskie does return, with an evil purpose. In the course of the novel he insinuates himself into the Potter family with sinister cunning, 'as if he knew every secret, as if he had some power over them'; Colin, watching, knew that '[s]omething adult was going on and the fat man was tying his father by the thumbs'. He is seeking revenge for the bullying he endured at Loomis school—the names, the spit sandwiches, being nearly drowned one day in the creek—of which, Colin learns, his father had been the lead perpetrator ('He felt his father shrink to something small and dark inside him' in that moment). He steals his mother's fortune—the gold sovereigns she keeps hidden in a chamber pot—a crime which he forces Colin to be a party to, and drowns her in the creek because, although he loves her, '[s]he couldn't save him' back then.[71] At the heart of this story, like *The Fire-Raiser*, is a twisted relationship between a mother and son.

Herbert Muskie is physically Edgar Marwick's opposite, except in his speed ('How could a fat man move so fast?'). He is mercurial in another, more terrifying way: 'He was mad and clever, mad and sane; he slipped in and out.'[72] Muskie is more really—rather than theatrically—frightening than the fire-raiser; *The Fat Man* a much darker, more complex, more disturbingly suspenseful tale. For its child protagonist, there is much more at stake.

Gee has described *The Champion*'s Rex Pascoe as the first fully rounded child character in his junior fiction.[73] *The Fat Man* was a step up to another level again from *The Champion*. In part the difference lies in, or is allowed by, the third-person narration (mediated occasionally by an unidentified author-narrator), whereby the reader understands or intuits things Colin cannot—in particular, the suggestion of Muskie's incestuous interest in his stepdaughter, Verna (and a similar, less explicit inference regarding his relationship with his mother). This is a depth of evil eleven-year-old Colin—or an eleven-year-old reader—is unable to comprehend. Margaret Mahy—

contributing to a March 2000 *Landfall* symposium, 'Bookmarking the century', for which contributors were asked to identify one 'key event' in their field—chose *The Fat Man*, as 'both a single event and the exemplification of a twentieth century process which allows children's books to be taken seriously as literature': as the point at which 'Gee's writing for young readers becomes one with his most central adult writing. One feels the author is engaged in a primary way'—it 'draws on complex and sometimes dark themes, but he writes with truth, including truths that children's writers are generally expected to avoid or symbolise'.[74]

That Colin understands less than we do doesn't lessen the fat man's power: 'When people like Herbert Muskie take up residence in your mind there's nothing you can do to get them out.' For Colin, 'Everything had changed' that day the fat man appeared: 'He had changed. His mother and father had changed. It was like an open door and the fat man had come through from the dark place where he lived.'[75] Through the course of the novel Colin and the fat man travel opposite psychological trajectories. As in Gee's adult novels (and to an extent *The Champion*), hard-won self-knowledge is a key theme. Colin grows though his discovery of his parents' fallibility, his developing affection for Verna (he 'liked the way she was tough and pretty at the same time'), above all in achieving a measure of sympathy and compassion for Muskie and in the part he plays in bringing about Muskie's end. Muskie, meanwhile, has regressed to a childlike state, first glimpsed when we see him clinging, distraught and weeping, to his drowned mother's body. In the final scene, fleeing Loomis with Colin and Verna as his hostages, he is panicked and helpless as the pursuing police close in, and Colin sees that '[s]omething in him shifted and gave way. Herbert Muskie turned into the fat boy again, running from the playground gang at Loomis school.' Our final image of him is satisfying, comical and sad: crammed 'squatt[ing] like a child' in the cage of a rotting-away flying fox, which Colin lets go, on a wire which 'looked as thin as a cotton thread', out over the river into which he falls—back into the element from which he came, a neat narrative symmetry.[76] ('I never seem to be able to get away from some kind of waterway where something nasty happens.')[77]

Complaints about the novel—that it was too tough, too dark, too frightening for young readers—came after it won the AIM Book of the Year Award and junior fiction award in April 1995, presented at a lunchtime function at Government House. It also received the New Zealand Library Association's Esther Glen Medal, in this award's 50th anniversary year (along with a recently established and privately endowed Claire Pollard Children's Book Award). The criticism was led by a letter to the *New Zealand Listener* from respected children's author Dorothy Butler, lamenting the 'current passion for depriving children of their childhood', which, she felt, *The Fat Man* epitomised—a 'bleak, spellbinding tale' of 'unrelieved hopelessness' in which evil 'reach[es] depths of depravity that will embrace—as well as the milder forms of criminality—the cruel and repeated humiliation of the man's stepdaughter, the physical abuse of his wife and, ultimately, the murder of his deranged, pathetic mother'. The last, short chapter, which 'will, we know, haunt [Colin] for life . . . reinforces the desolate truth of it all: even mildly happy endings are strictly for fairy tales'. Writing in agreement a few weeks later (and managing to work in an argument about state-sponsored, communist-style propaganda), Nelson children's author Agnes-Mary Brooke was offended even by the title ('crudely upfront' and 'almost aggressive').[78]

Such responses left Gee at first puzzled, and then angry, which he was prepared to let show. There were some 'thick-headed and coarse-minded readings of the book around', he told the *Evening Post*.[79] 'Depriving children of their childhood? That's a hanging offence isn't it? It's like calling me a pornographer. It is quite bewildering to me. What do they expect children to read?' There were far more disturbing children's books on the market. Crucially, he pointed out, Colin's relationship with his parents is not destroyed, and instead is deepened. Look at Bambi, he suggested, or Babar, 'whose parents get killed off in the first scene'.[80] He also objected to it being read as a novel about bullying, as an issues novel. It was 'quite deliberately a genre book, I suppose it could be described as a psychological thriller for children', which had 'a lot of menace and gothic overtones and melodrama, all of which I think children enjoy immensely'; and, he believed, a satisfying resolution.[81]

As for describing the fat man's 'black hair on his chest pasted down like slime' and creek water squirting from his mouth 'like a draught horse peeing', to which one particularly squeamish reader took offence, he knew whereof he wrote: he had seen that man; 'I used to see draught horses peeing every day'.[82]

The controversy might not have arisen at all had the book not been judged in the junior fiction category (fiction for readers aged eight to around thirteen) at the AIM awards, which had surprised Gee. The decision to do so 'was not taken lightly' by the publisher or by the judges, who responded to Butler's 'forceful attack' at length in the *Listener.* (It needed to be taken seriously, they said, because she was 'an international commentator with many decades of accumulated wisdom, experience and generosity'.) The judges had voted two to one to agree with Penguin in placing *The Fat Man* in the junior section, dependent on a statement being included in the AIM resource kit for schools and libraries that it contained 'some issues and concepts which may not be suitable for younger readers'. Yet it was 'clearly written *to* children and is therefore *for* them', they argued.[83] The problem was with the category: they agreed that the book was more suitable for intermediate-age children than younger, as did Gee who saw it as being for ages eleven (Colin's age) and over—including, he hoped, adults.

The controversy did the sales no harm, and more likely the opposite. They were approaching 8000 eighteen months after publication; 14,000 at March 1998, including over 3600 to Penguin Australia. And it sold in America, though only after being turned down seven times[84] before being picked up by Simon and Schuster (considering it for the second time). Simon and Schuster had published *The Champion* in 1993, and it had been well-received—even getting a mention in the *New York Times Book Review*, which for a children's book was, they told Gee, 'quite a coup'—and was listed by the American Library Association and the New York Public Library, but they had subsequently declined Gee's other children's titles (considering them 'far below the caliber of THE CHAMPION, or dated').[85] They loved *The Fat Man*, describing it to Gee as 'on par with "Cape Fear" in its portrayal of psychological terror' and Muskie as 'a wonderfully evil character'—before sending the usual list of queries about unrecognisable New Zealand idioms: 'I must say I scratch my head a bit over the American anxiety to protect US children from words they've not come across before', Gee replied. 'NZ children are not protected from US terms in their reading . . . I remember as a boy tracking down "hominy grits" and "collard greens" and being pleased to find out what they were. But I won't labour the point'.[86] It received spectacular reviews there—'a fascinating mixture of Saki and Alfred Hitchcock at their most artfully disturbing', *Booklist* wrote—and was chosen as best children's book of 1997 by

Publishers' Weekly and the *School Library Journal*, and nominated as an Honor Book by the venerable *Horn Book Magazine*: 'yet more fantastic news', Simon and Schuster advised Gee, 'for one of the best reviewed books of the year'.[87]

The success of *The Fat Man* prompted Ray Richards, ever opportunistic on Gee's behalf, after it went into a second printing in America to suggest that he write another—a prequel perhaps: 'When the Fat Man was a Boy', 'Fat Herbie'—which Gee, however, had no interest in pursuing. He had already said the same (sounding a little baffled) to the editor at Penguin who had asked when they first read the manuscript if he had given any thought to a sequel. 'I don't think there's a sequel to be written', he replied. 'The fat man is dead and I couldn't put those kids through another adventure with some new character equally evil. Enough's enough, I think.'[88]

28

Loving Ways

Nigel Cox had put the question of repetition to Gee directly when he interviewed him for *Quote Unquote* in 1993. He had 'written a number of books in which elderly narrators look back over their lives', Cox observed, and it was a model that had 'produced wonderful results for you, but I can't help wondering if what is yielded by this kind of book might have become over-familiar to your readers'. 'I think that's fair comment', Gee replied.[1] Yet when he sent in an application at the end of the Menton year for a DAAD fellowship to write his next novel in Berlin (he would do so again, and again unsuccessfully, the following year) he had described something very familiar. He had barely given this novel any thought, he explained, being still immersed in his current one, but 'I have been turning over the idea of a man (or it might be a woman) setting out to write an autobiography that will throw a favourable light on his or her life. . . . an artist, a politician, a policeman, a businessman, or perhaps someone unknown and obscure? . . . In the writing, my fictional character will be ambushed by various truths and will become both lost in his times and disoriented by the changing shapes of people and events he had thought he knew, and by his own changing shape. . . . There will be a parallel text, so to speak, of present times that will throw a clarifying, perhaps a distorting, often an ironic light into the past.'[2]

The novel he wrote in 1994–95 was nothing like this. Nor was it anything altogether new. 'There's usually a murder in my novels', he said apropos of this one as he was finishing it. 'I can't get away from it.'[3]

'I've just begun the next one—two pages written', he told Geoff Walker in July 1994 when Walker sent him an advance copy of *Crime Story*; 'You can expect it in two years.'[4] He had it done in one. Instead of a DAAD he wrote it with the support of a $9000 grant from the Arts Council (having applied for the Scholarship in

Letters), his application hinting at some anxiety over Cox's charge in stating that he intended 'writing the story in the third person to keep it strong in present incident and avoid too much backward looking'.[5] Its location was Nelson and Golden Bay, where he and Margareta had had a recent summer holiday. He had not thought he would go back to Nelson again fictionally; since they had moved to Wellington the colours had faded. But now he 'found whole landscapes establishing themselves in my mind', the river valleys and pools, the 'beaches, the orchards, the forests, the hills . . .—all alive again'—so he told a Nelson audience. He had wanted, besides, a rural setting and this was one he knew. They visited old friends in Nelson and Parapara; stopped at an orchard above the Tasman bluffs where Margareta and Emily had once worked; went to Gee's favourite beach, wild Wharariki at the top of the West Coast. The novel was 'very much a landscape book', he would tell *Quote Unquote* when it came out, 'but I don't do landscape. I just let it happen—I don't try to describe it.'[6] He evoked it, nonetheless, with the briefest sketches: 'the punctuation, stops and dashes, of Farewell Spit. Some days you could not see it, others it drew a pencil line'; the drive along the valley towards Takaka which felt 'like climbing up to the sea instead of going down'.[7]

Retaining the real name of Nelson this time—it is not Saxton or Jessop—he saw as an act of homage, and little risk as little of the action in the novel took place in the city. The only place name he interfered with was Parapara, giving the town a fictional twin. The only geographical liberty he took was with the configuration of the Tasman bluffs. He was surprised to find how little constraint the real landscape placed on the story: 'I did not find the story and place moving apart' (was a little disappointed, in fact, that the challenge of geography did not 'lead to interesting ways of escape').[8]

The story was prompted by a murder that had taken place in Nelson a few years earlier, the victim of which (whom he had met) was an old friend of Margareta's, and which had continued to haunt his memory. James Dahlberg, a former policeman, had been convicted and given a life sentence in 1992 for the murder of his estranged wife, Ann Urquhart, who had gone missing after a bridge evening in October the previous year; neither her body nor a murder weapon were ever found.[9] Gee's fictional murder comes at the end of a novel that is not a murder mystery but a novel about, in his own words, 'love, in its many forms'.[10] *Loving Ways* tells the story of the bitterly alienated MacPherson family, using a shifting third-person narration. At its distant centre is Robert MacPherson, 91 and dying, and being cared for by his granddaughter Heather (a situation, and to some extent relationship—a mix of wariness and affection—a little like Noel Papps' and Kate's in *Prowlers*) on the orchard she manages for him. MacPherson was initially, when Gee was first planning the novel, to have once been a pioneer aviator like Oscar Garden; instead he has been a tugboat captain, before resigning in anger after being passed over for the harbourmaster's job (reminiscent of Garden's unhappy departure from TEAL) and buying the orchard above Ruby Bay: MacPhersons, he calls it simply, later renaming it (as a marketing strategy) Ben Alder Orchard, from Robert Louis Stevenson's *Kidnapped* from which his sons also have their names.

Robert MacPherson is a hard, violent man who does 'not believe in love' ('That's a woman's word') or its physical expression, and would not allow in others 'the existence of feelings he did not have'. His three children, each with a different mother, have fashioned ways of living (and loving) in escape from an abusive, lonely childhood in which love was absent, but carry his imprint. 'There's no softness in this family,' thinks May, 'not an ounce . . . Natural affections turn to stone, we bang against each other and make sparks.'[11] The narrative shifts between their three stories as Alan, the eldest, returns to Golden Bay for the first time in 35 years, summoned by Robert who plans to leave the orchard to Heather, but needs to be assured first that her mother, May, is indeed his daughter. May's mother had been MacPherson's housekeeper, whom he paid off and sent away when she became pregnant. She sent the child back alone five years later with a note stating just her name (Clare then, not May) and birthdate. May fled the orchard at seventeen with one of the pickers and went to live on a commune. Now she runs Inlet Arts at Woods Inlet—'Parapara's twin'—with her partner Evan. Having 'repeatedly declared that she was happy with her own company thank you', finding and loving Evan took her by surprise. She is fiercely protective of what they have made, wanting most of all 'Evan and May left alone in all the world', potting and painting, keeping complication—'Guilt. Susceptibilities. Desire'—at bay, her protectiveness the remnant of habits of 'distrust . . . withdrawal. Sullenness. Submissiveness. Ferocity. Self-loathing' she had learnt as a child.[12]

Gee based Inlet Arts loosely on friends Rosie Little and Bruce Hamlin's Estuary Arts at Parapara. For the character of Alan he had no original, and was not only inventing but experimenting: he wanted to try to write 'a thoroughly good man', and someone with strong Christian beliefs whom he would 'try and treat . . . with sympathy, rather than the usual sort of veiled derision that I usually treat them with'.[13] Alan escaped the orchard and his father for Duntroon and a career in the army—a life of order and control—before taking early retirement and a job as office manager for an accountancy firm. He keeps his feelings under control too. Love had eluded him until he met Phoebe; and then Phoebe showed him a capacity for evil he had not until then conceived of: this is what sends him back to the church he had joined only because he had to at Duntroon. Since Phoebe, women find him absent, lacking substance, and don't stay.

The phone call from the half-sister he has not seen or spoken to for 35 years turns Alan about in a way and in language Gee characters and readers are familiar with. 'It had been like someone taking him by the shoulders and jerking him round from the window he was looking out to an entirely different view. The configuration of the world was changed'; 'The past comes spinning up and holds him hard.' He travels back there from Auckland—'going deep down'—and nothing would be 'familiar or ordered. The years had turned things on their base and made his orientation wrong.'[14] David, the younger son, has had his world set out of kilter (so that he 'could not find himself') by his wife Freda (friend of May) leaving and taking out a non-molestation order against him. 'Before Freda had left him he had been spread wide and she had been small, at the centre, where he had come to at the end of the day. Now he was shrunken, and wrinkled, and dry, and she was out there filling all that space and he could not put his hand on her.'[15] He had been a policeman for twelve years until he broke a teenager's arm while apprehending him. Violence is part of his inheritance. When he was a boy his father had made him shoot May's cat; Alan, leaving the orchard the next day, had noted his pleasure in the act, the 'gleaming in his eye' (whether from pride or pleasure he couldn't tell).[16] A 'kind of distillate of family violence', one critic described him,[17] in David loving is manifested as control. His determination to get Freda back, then to take vengeance provides the novel's narrative momentum.

Gee punctuated the third-person narrative with an 'Interlude' in the form of an interior monologue, following the disjointed memory-thoughts of bedridden Robert: he was reading *Ulysses* at the time and thought, 'I've never tried that', why not do an interior monologue? It softens Robert (a little) as we see that in his own way he had loved one of his women (Alan's mother). It also served to slow the story down: Gee had 'found that the narrative was running along in a very headlong way, and this was a way of stopping it running too headlong'.[18] *Loving Ways* is a taut novel, tightly focused in time, place and action. It has a claustrophobic feel despite its Nelson and Golden Bay landscapes, which, Gee felt, broke it free of precisely that; a grimness that is of a different quality from *Crime Story*'s. The few secondary characters hardly relieve the tone. There is a glimmer of black comedy in May and Evan's neighbours, retired Wellington accountant George and his tranquillized wife Daphne who pines to go home to Khandallah: she has already stabbed George with a pair of scissors and tried to poison him by putting dioxin in his porridge. Junior Mott, Evan's friend, is a sad, ugly character, an embittered old hippie who makes misshapen, unsellable pots, a man 'muddy brown in his perceptions', with '[e]yes like wrap-around glasses' and 'a widow's peak that wanted to grow down the ridge of his nose . . . like a pick-axe'.[19] The destruction Junior Mott wreaks in the Inlet Arts showroom one night is, however, only the prelude to the larger act of violence. Here Gee's alternating third-person narrative 'throws the time scheme out a little bit', as the sequence of events is told from different points of view: he hoped it 'hasn't made it too confusing'.[20] Instead it contributes to the narrative tension: one reviewer described the novel's final scenes as Hitchcockian. The murder to which its second half builds quickly and intensely is a chilling, calculated one, in contrast to the frenzied, gruesome killing of Mrs Ponder at the end of *Crime Story.*

Gee might have found this novel easy to write but the title was a struggle. It was 'Magpies' (referring to May once saving her young daughter from a pair of aggressive birds) when he sent the manuscript off, but Ray Richards didn't like this and asked him to 'wind it up a bit, to catch the eyes of passersby in Lambton Quay', offering a dozen (uninspired) suggestions. Gee made a list of 30-odd alternative titles (which Richards forwarded to Geoff Walker along with 40 more of his own). 'Shooting Season' was his favourite, except that it pointed too openly to the conclusion; he also liked 'BLOOD RELATIONS (but it's much used) and SORRY, DEAR, which is nicely creepy'. It was Margareta who came up with *Loving Ways*, which Walker and Richards both thought soft but could appreciate for its irony (the latter, however, was still coming up with suggestions four months later: 'I hope you do not think I am fussing', he said to Gee). For Gee, '[m]ore importantly, it points to the story being about love as much as murder and death'—even if one of those loving ways is murder.[21]

Tor Klevstul after he read *Loving Ways* thanked Gee 'for writing an optimistic book': he was pleased that Alan survived. It had bothered him, he had told Gee earlier, that 'you keep killing them off with booze, bullits [sic], drownings and strokes' (referring to the stroke which finally brings Howie Peet down). 'I think the next time you should let the male main character live on, not as a ball of frustrated anger . . . but as a balanced mature man noble in his strengths and weaknesses—sins and good deeds.' It was not quite Gee's style. But he too saw *Loving Ways* as 'a fairly optimistic novel', in the various 'small victories' that are won and that '[e]verybody loves somebody . . . and only one of the relationships turns bad.'[22]

For the cover of *Loving Ways* Penguin came up with a design they meant to use as a series design for Gee novels from now on: a simple and tidy, rectilinear collage format in muted colours (entirely unlike the loud, messy style of the *Crime Story* cover, which Gee expressly said he did not want), here featuring a woman against a backdrop of a Nelson beachscape, and a magpie. Gee seemed pleased with it, though his own first thought had been something rather like his recent Faber covers: 'pictorial and relatively simple . . . Perhaps a beach, seen from high up and back, small figures on it, the islands [the Archway Islands at Wharariki beach, where the novel goes in the short epilogue] off shore, and maybe a magpie in the sky, like a Don Binney bird, to suggest threat and spoil the idyll.'[23]

It came out, in June 1996, in a paperback edition only (which Walker had been wanting to do with the previous few novels). The sales were stronger than those of *Crime Story*: it was 'striking a real chord with buyers and readers', Walker told him as they approached 4000 after a month; a reprint was ordered in August.[24] But this would not be one of Gee's most loved and remembered novels. The critical response was mixed. This one was not described as 'Gee at his best' (or, if it was, it was Gee 'at his chilling best'); rather, in Lawrence Jones' words, as 'a worthy if not particularly unexpected addition to' his oeuvre.[25] There was high praise for the novel's construction and pacing (as always) and few reviewers baulked at the violence; nor this time did the ending disappoint. But opinion was divided on the characters. For Owen Marshall the novel was let down by the weak characterisation (usually one of Gee's strengths, he observed) of David: 'It's not that David is too brutish, but that the brutishness reduces him to a cipher. I remain baffled as to any but stereotypic links in personality and motivation between his experience and his actions.' Others found David 'horrifyingly convincing': he 'fairly leaps off the page. His interior voice is dead on. He's the hurting hating self-centred male whom Gee does so often', and 'a compelling portrait of a killer'. 'In getting inside the criminal mind', and his description of David's 'psychopathic obsession', Louise Alley wrote in the *Listener*, 'Gee is as expert here as he was with his portrayal of Brent Rosser'; Andrew Johnston, reviewing the novel in *London Magazine*: 'Each of the Macphersons is painted in with astonishing psychological veracity . . . This superbly rich, layered characterisation is where the novel's rewards lie'.[26]

One of the harsher assessments of the novel, by contrast, came from critic and academic John Newton, who (writing in *Landfall*) thought the characterisation overall 'routine', and described Alan as '[d]ecent but fatally ineffectual', (like Kingsley Pratt in *Games of Choice*) 'a chronic apologiser'; another found Alan 'dull' and his Christianity only sketched in. Gee felt himself that he had not entirely succeeded here, in writing a thoroughly good character, or at least that Alan was not 'treated in any depth'. ('I don't believe in exemplary characters in any case', he had said ten years earlier, in reference to Noel Papps. 'All my characters are of the grey colouration—no saints and no one utterly evil.')[27] Newton too was not the only one to observe—though he did so with more critical acuity than others—that this was more of the same. 'Haven't Gee's novels done all this before, and with more conviction?', he asked, quoting Kingsley Pratt ('Whose hideous invention was the family?'). Compared to the *Plumb* trilogy, and in a different literary-historical time (when the concept of a national narrative was no longer relevant or tenable), '(and without Plumb himself) this latest family saga seems perfunctory and etiolated; familiar echoes and preoccupations (violence under the genteel crust, voyeurism, corruption of the paradisal orchard, decades-long estrangements and futile reparations) serve only to emphasise this sense of fatigue'.[28]

For his part Gee would agree that *Loving Ways* was not 'one of my better novels', and while he had enjoyed writing about Nelson and Golden Bay he would later describe it as 'more of an exercise, it was just a novel I happened to be writing at the time';[29] there had not been the engagement he had felt with *Prowlers* and *Going West*.

*

The post-Menton fatigue had worn off enough by October 1994 for Gee to raise with Faber the possibility of an invitation to the 1995 Hay Festival, the ten-day literary festival held in the booky town of Hay-on-Wye in Wales in May/June, to coincide with the UK publication of *Crime Story*; or perhaps (even better) the following year. Faber sought an invitation for 1995 and approached the New Zealand Arts Council for funding (neither they nor Hay being in a position to bring him over on their own). By that time, however, Gee was already worrying that he had been presumptuous (he had only raised it, he said, because he had met Hay director Peter Florence in Toronto in 1991 and Florence had suggested he consider going) and told them it was too late to get himself organised anyway. He didn't make it to Hay with *Loving Ways* either. This time when a formal invitation finally arrived—in December 1996 for 1997—the timing of the Arts Council's newly restructured funding round meant that he would have to pay for his plane ticket upfront himself, which, he told them, he could not afford to do. Faber then offered (between him and them) to reimburse his airfare if he applied to the Arts Council and was turned down, but by now he had gone off the idea: 'It all got too complicated and doubtful and my enthusiasm for a UK visit is gone.'[30]

But he was not (yet) entirely put off literary travel. In 1995 he accepted an invitation from the Singapore national arts' council to a writers' week at the end of August. His 'tentative' schedule involved only reading, but when he was rung three days before he was due to leave, at 11.30pm, and told that the programme had been changed and he would be expected to do something quite different he angrily withdrew. His irritation was all the more because he had turned down an invitation to Canberra (a New Zealand literature week at the University of Canberra) in October because of his Singapore commitment, followed by the Storylines children's literature festival (which involved a bus tour around Auckland schools) in September: he didn't think he could cope with a third the next month.

The following year it was his health that caused him to cancel an invitation to the Melbourne Writers' Festival in October (an honour, Walker told him: 'Not many New Zealand authors get invited'). Early in the year, getting up from the bed after putting on his shoes one day he collapsed in agony with what turned out to be a prolapsed disc. It was not until two hours later that Emily came home and found him and called an ambulance. He spent most of the next two or three months lying down. He felt optimistic enough at the end of May, however, when approached by the organisers of the Sydney Writers' Festival to agree to appear (back permitting) at their next in late January 1997. They had wanted him to come the previous year but the timing didn't suit then, he had told them. He agreed now keenly, with the proviso—or rather preference—that he come as an adult writer and not a children's one (or at least as both). It was as the latter that Melbourne had invited him. His profile in Australia had been significantly raised by *The Fat Man*, but he had already been much better known there as a writer of children's fiction. Of his adult novels, only *Crime Story* and *Loving Ways* were available; he fielded 'a large number of complaints' in Sydney, he informed Walker, that the *Plumb* trilogy, *Going West* and *Prowlers* (from which he read) were not.[31]

He made it plain when he accepted the Sydney invitation what he saw as his limitations, 'so that you may withdraw your invitation if you find me unattractive': that he could 'talk about my work', that was all and preferably not about 'significance and meaning', and definitely not about 'large themes' (such as the state of literature or the New Zealand cultural scene); was hopeless in panel discussions because 'I'm a slow thinker'; would take audience questions as long as he was protected from 'the silly and pretentious ones'. For all this reluctance, he did four appearances over the five days, including in a panel on 'Good, Evil and Morality: the big issues' (the title when they sent him the programme had made him nervous) and in a solo session with festival organiser and children's author Libby Gleeson. She had told him earlier, no doubt to his relief, that she wanted to have 'a *writer's* conversation' about 'process and practice' (it began, though, biographically with creek and kitchen).[32]

The festival package included three days afterwards at the Varuna Writers' Centre in Katoomba in the Blue Mountains, where—as it is liable to do in the Blue Mountains—'it rained steadily and the fog stayed down' and they (Margareta had gone too) saw 'not even one of the Three Sisters'. As always, 'Wellington was wonderful to come back to.'[33]

29

Live Bodies

A reviewer of *Loving Ways* had remarked on Gee's 'remarkable output in the 90s of four novels (not including *The Fat Man*)'.[1] He was to keep up the pace: there were ten more novels over the next fourteen years. Fugue-like, familiar themes, motifs and locations, stories and memories continue to echo and repeat. There is a matching rhythm in his preferred short, two- or three-word or syllable titles; with one exception.

His slipped disc meant that he wrote much of the next novel, *Live Bodies*, lying on his back on his bed. The title this time came easily. 'Live body' was a military term meaning human cargo, in this case the nearly 200 Germans, Austrians, Italians, assorted other suspicious-seeming Europeans, German Samoans and Japanese interned as 'enemy aliens' on Somes Island in Wellington harbour during the Second World War. 'Employing a technique he ruefully claims to have used in "all those other 'old man' novels that I've written"' (as Gee was quoted in the *Nelson Mail*),[2] *Live Bodies* is the memoir of Viennese Josef Mandl, interned because of a map of Auckland harbour he innocently drew to send to his sixteen-year-old sister Susi in Paris (marking him as a spy), and for his Jewish 'shiftiness and . . . free way with the truth', in the anti-semitic eyes of the Aliens Tribunal, low morals and political associations. He had arrived in New Zealand in 1938, not as a refugee, as many did, except from his family, having been banished by his father because of his involvement in Vienna's communist underground opposing the rise of national socialism. From Vienna he had gone to New York, and run from that city's oppressive verticality, 'across America, and let gravity tumble me down the oceans' as far as he could go: in Auckland 'held myself still and looked around'.[3]

Here the physical world is stranger to him still. 'I was not used to moving waters, not on this scale, or to such intimacies between elements', where 'the sea and land lapped at each other or they contested'; to the mangrove swamps like a 'khaki garden rooted in the mud'; at Muriwai the waves 'as high as houses rolled in half a mile apart. . . . turned their shoulders into their laps and made the coastline tremble. . . . A beach, they called it. I felt it suck the breath out of me and weaken my blood.' With a handful of precise evocations of place and feeling Gee maps Mandl's experience of dislocation, loss and acceptance. In the New Lynn garden of Karl and Rosina Weiser on the banks of the Whau, where Auckland's Austrian refugees come on Sundays for food and wine, music and conversation, he climbs up from the river and looks across at the green oval of the Avondale racecourse, enclosed by its white fence, and understands at that moment that he has no home to go back to: it was 'a hole in nature', 'It was—how can I say it?—it was the emptiness Vienna left. It was Vienna stolen from my life and never to be mine again.' Three years later, from Somes Island he looks across at Wellington, 'the ragged hills and the flimsy houses', and 'thought, There's an emptiness here I'll come to like . . . If they'll let me off this island I might stay in their town.' In this place 'bleakness and simplicity might be endured and a way found to a life in spite of them'.[4]

Live Bodies is Gee's most researched novel. Almost too much so: he found himself having to pull back from the wealth and interest of the material. A remark made by Margareta when she was reading the recently published autobiography of Czech refugee, businessman and philanthropist Fred Turnovsky, about how difficult life here must have been for the central and eastern European refugees who came to New Zealand in the late 1930s and the war, had been its initial inspiration. Margareta also put him on to rich sources in the Turnbull Library, where she started a full-time job in the manuscripts section in 1995. She had left her previous job at Turnbull, which she had started in 1989, when they had gone to Menton and not got it back, and since then had only part-time work (as an insurance clerk and a proofreader). She loved it at Turnbull manuscripts, but working full-time was not entirely a matter of choice. They had not been so hard up, she told friends, for a long time: 'G has simply stopped earning money', as deals and projects (television and film) fell through.[5] Moreover, he had not applied for an Arts Council grant for this novel. He had been hurt by remarks made about him by newspaper columnist Rosemary McLeod in June 1995, commenting in her *Dominion* column on the renaming of the council and a substantial increase in its funding. 'As for me, I plan to join the arts gravy train, now that I see Creative

New Zealand will be given even more millions than its predecessor', she had written. 'I like overseas travel, I'd like guaranteed publishing for books I'd write that nobody need ever read . . . Take Maurice Gee. He's just won two major literary awards for his latest novel *The Fat Man*. Already this country's leading novelist, winner of copious other awards, and in paid employment, he's been on the arts council payroll for years, on a semi-wage, to write novels.'[6] It was a mean and unwarranted barb and it caused Gee to stop applying to Creative New Zealand for writing grants from now on.

The Turnbull had just acquired the papers of librarian and labour historian Bert Roth following his death in 1994, and these included autobiographical notes on his early life and activities as a member of the socialist and communist underground in Vienna in the 1930s, of which Gee had known nothing when he worked for Roth in Auckland in the 1970s, and which gave him the details of Mandl's. (Giving Roth's name to an incidental character was both an acknowledgement and to make it clear that Mandl was, however, fictional.) Margareta also alerted him to a memoir by Somes Island internee J.C. Klingenstein (a New Zealand-born German) which had been loaned to the library for copying—not realising that the manuscript was under access restriction and he should not have been reading it. Happily, Klingenstein (a sprightly 87-year-old retired in Sumner)—whose permission was not sought until Gee had finished his first draft—was quite happy with (indeed was chuffed by) Gee's use of his memories. There would be others who felt differently.

For the Somes Island chapters Gee also spent many fascinated hours at National Archives looking through Aliens Tribunal files and others relating to the Somes internment camp and its prisoners (and the bleaker Pahiatua camp where they were relocated in 1943–44 as the Japanese advanced down the Pacific). One of the fifteen or twenty personal files he read was that of Odo Strewe, who appears in the novel as Willi Gauss, the wily and charismatic German whose story and relationship with Mandl are one of the novel's central and structuring narratives. Like Gauss, Strewe had been one of the first internees, declared an enemy alien in December 1939 on suspicion of being a Nazi. He had talked freely about his time on the island, including his briefly successful escape (one of three attempts) by dinghy, when Gee knew him in Auckland in the 1950s at the Queen's Ferry and around. Willi Gauss on Somes is very closely based on Strewe, as is his political and journalist background in 1930s Berlin.

Their later histories diverge, but Gauss is also recognisably Strewe in character. Willi is charming and magnetic, elusive and tricky; 'It pleased him to deceive, it was his nature', writes Mandl (while of himself, 'memory is in my nature').[7] Odo, Gee commented privately, '[a]lthough he was gifted in many ways' was also 'malicious and devious'.[8] In Gauss's post-war embracing of free love and composting and 'Bacchanalianism' there is perhaps a little of Strewe too.

Gauss will eventually return to Berlin. Mandl makes his material way in New Zealand as a baker, making real bread—dark, heavy bread made with wholemeal flour and cracked wheat and honey—for the European immigrants and refugees who can't stand the 'white pap' New Zealanders call bread. Later he branches out into importing continental foods and prospers. His start in bread is based on that of Max Reizenstein, the German-Jewish refugee who introduced the first German-style—barley, oat and rye—bread to the New Zealand market from a small bakery in Ponsonby in the 1940s. Here Margareta had an input too. She had been childhood friends with Maria Collins (the wife of Erebus pilot Jim Collins), whose parents, Josef and Annemarie Tretter, had known Reizenstein well back then. From Annemarie Tretter and from friends of Reizenstein's family he made contact with Gee learned about the practical details of his early bread-making business: the kneading at first by hand, then in a cast-iron washing machine; making deliveries by bicycle. She told him too about living in Vienna during the war and lent him books on the city's history, and about the everyday challenges the refugees faced in a conservative, small-minded culture, the small embarrassments and hurts: from her came the story about being shooed peremptorily out of a grocer's shop when she asked for sour cream.

In Gee's hands, bread for Mandl is about more than making his way; it is a way back. 'Colour of crust and firmness of bread-flesh, grain and texture of crumb . . . it is almost synaesthesia, magical. Time and place slide across their natural boundaries and become a function of consciousness. For a heartbeat. For a breath.'[9]

In his research for *Live Bodies* Gee also learned to play bowls, playing weekly at the Thorndon Bowling Club with old friend Michael Noonan, as Mandl does with Denis and Clive, retired Catholic priest and socialist returned soldier respectively. (Gee's description of the three on the green is at once a fine character study and sports cameo, one of several in his fiction.) On his release from Somes, Mandl lives at first in a room at the back of a house in Tinakori Road ('one of a pair in a lean-to shed beside a vegetable garden', with a bathroom and washhouse separate). By the mid-1950s he had become successful enough in his business to buy the house up the hill in Wadestown he had coveted since he first saw it back then: the one in Wadestown Road Maurice and Margareta fancied living in but could never have afforded. From there, writing his memoir, he looks out at the island, and '[m]y third eye, the island, watches me', a conduit of memory. Like *Loving Ways*, *Live Bodies* begins with escape. 'May MacPherson made one of her escapes', opens the former; Mandl as this novel opens desires to escape consciousness, 'to be forever, with fear and resentment put aside, and longing, gratitude, disappointment, love . . . The social existence, affective existence, put aside and lids placed on the trashcans and honey pots of the past'. The narrative segues from here to Somes in the 1940s and he and Willi digging a tunnel under their barracks. They are discovered before it is finished, but in that tunnel 'I altered my shape . . . passed from one life into another, changed hemispheres, and would have to pass through a similar wormhole to go back'.[10]

Consciousness, too, 'has been digging a tunnel'. In the novel's present-time narrative the knowledge Mandl cannot avoid, the 'thing that must be understood, or at least held in the light', is his son Kenny's 'betrayal of all I have done'. In a rare touch for a Gee novel, Josef Mandl has a contented marriage, though it is made at the cost of his wife, Nancy, severing all ties with her family, the appallingly bigoted, xenophobic Brisboises (pronounced 'Brisboy, none of that fancy stuff': the unusual, and somehow entirely fitting, name Brisbois Gee had found on the letterhead of an American legal firm writing to him about film rights to *The Fat Man*). He regrets, however, his relationship with his children. Like Jack Skeat, 'I was too insistent on pointing moral standards . . . I generalised too much, I see it now; gave too many lessons, and pushed my children off' (while Nancy burdened them with expectation). Kenny especially disappoints him. Timid as a boy, when Kenny marries he readily acquiesces to his in-laws' insistence that he anglicise his name. That is one betrayal. He goes to work for and eventually takes over his father-in-law's finance company; 'a greedy man, of limited interests and poor intelligence', his father sums him up, much as Gwen Peet did Athol. 'He has no curiosity. Kenny cannot wonder.'[11] He is, Gee admits, 'perhaps a slightly over-the-top', 'rather caricatured, personification' of the free market philosophy prevailing still, and (in his father's words) a 'common or garden fascist'.[12]

When he adds reverse annuity mortgages to his portfolio Gee had in mind Wellington investment brokers Gene and Eugene Thomas, who had been shot dead in their office on The Terrace by businessman John Barlow in February 1994. Murder might be taking it a bit far though, he thought; instead Kenny has his hand sliced open by an enraged client (who is not quite coincidentally Willi Gauss's daughter) wielding a kitchen paring knife, in a classic Gee gruesome-comic scene.

The other, more difficult family knowledge Mandl must confront is the sexual abuse of his granddaughter, Kenny's daughter, Julie: it wouldn't be a Gee novel without some 'twisted or frustrated sexuality', and an answer to find.[13] For Julie this is an exercise in memory (Gee references here the topical and controversial subject of repressed or false memory syndrome), for Mandl of comprehension. In Mandl and his granddaughter Gee sets up another relationship alike to (though less developed than) Noel Papps and Kate's, to Robert MacPherson and Heather's, in which a troubled, younger female relative becomes in some way a catalyst for an old man's remembering.

Like other Gee narrators Mandl aims to look plainly—'I have no taste for retrospective prophecy or for the elegiac mood but am happier remembering matter-of-factly, thinking flat'—and is alert to his use of words. A new language ('It was not the easy language I'd once thought') 'helped put me together after I'd been broken apart'. (He becomes a master of the local idiom, relishing 'good as gold', 'off my rocker', 'strewth'.)[14] But Mandl's voice, and the novel's tone, is gentler and more generous than Papps' and Plumb's: he is one of Gee's most sympathetic narrators. Perhaps Gee needed this after *Loving Ways*. Keatsian, the *Times Literary Supplement*'s reviewer described Mandl, 'in the freshness of his descriptive prose', his 'sense of the sublimity of the detail and of the sufficiency of the everyday'.[15]

When the manuscript went to Walker, Gee specifically requested as light as possible an edit. He had worked very closely on and given the text more readings than he normally did and was 'satisfied that it's as right as I can make it—the text I mean, in the way things are expressed and the way the sentences and close meanings go'. (He would be more than usually nervous at page proof stage too, making a number of small adjustments, and 'having made them I've come to regard them as enormously important—a curious psychological condition'.) He had worried that readers would lose interest in the latter third of the book—the difficult 'long stretch of the marriage and kids', with 'no island, no Vienna, no refugee days, no Tribunal—the things that are the real meat in the story'.[16] But he had high expectations of this novel (which was not always the case), as did Walker who sent a contract on the strength of an outline alone, 'Maurice being Maurice', and planned to publish it in a new, larger format than his last one (following Penguin Australia's lead): 'Making it big and bold like this signals, I think, that the publisher has special faith in it.'[17]

It was launched in Wellington during Writers and Readers Week at the 1998 International Festival of the Arts in March. It was the first launch Gee had assented to since *Sole Survivor*: perhaps the fact that it was a combined launch (with two Victoria University Press titles, Elizabeth Knox's third memoir-novella, *Tawa*, and Catherine Chidgey's debut novel, *In a Fishbone Church*) and the collegial party-like atmosphere of Writers and Readers Week made it easier to agree this time. (The venue was fun too: the travelling, circular wooden Dans Paleis, temporarily in town for the festival.) He read from it only reluctantly two months later at the Burns Fellowship 40th anniversary celebrations (taking place on 22 May as part of Wordstruck!, as Dunedin Writers' Week had decided to rename itself).

His confidence in the novel was not misplaced. In July it won the inaugural Deutz Medal (previously more humbly known as the award for fiction) at the Montana New Zealand Book Awards. (Since his double win in 1993 the Wattie award had become the Montanas under the new sponsorship of Montana Wines, and in 1996 these had merged with the New Zealand Book Awards—meaning, to the consternation of writers and publishers, that there was now only one national book awards.) The ceremony at the Auckland Art Gallery left him 'a little dazed and disorientated' and disappointed that afterwards he could not be sure 'who I met or what I said': evidently a good night.[18] By the end of the year Penguin had sold 7500 copies (the initial print run of 4000 had been followed by a B-format paperback in advance of the awards), earning Gee another bottle of bubbly from Penguin. There would be another when sales passed 10,000 ten months later.

If not every reviewer expressly agreed with the verdict of the *Listener*'s Ian Richards, quoted on the book's cover, that 'This may be Maurice Gee's best ever', the overwhelming view was that it was one of them; though 'in a body of such fine work,' added Simon Garrett in the *Dominion*, 'why quibble?'[19] '[R]ich, fluent, exact, humane', Mark Williams described it, and one which confirmed Gee's status as 'our major fiction writer, aside from Janet Frame'; although he also posed the tougher critique, continuing his examination of the transmutations of Gee's 'complex and textured' realism. Was Gee's focus on New Zealand as a place of 'small decencies and betrayals', our recognition of Mandl as 'someone on our own scale, like ourselves ordinary and unheroic' ('The island was my war. It's nothing special', Mandl writes), enough when he took in the larger canvas of modern history, and in the contemporary literary context of writers such as Salman Rushdie, Gabriel García Marquéz and Peter Carey and their 'more extravagant renditions of the various nightmares of twentieth-century history'? But he was pleased to find still 'depths and darknesses swirling just below the surface of the narrative . . . as though the anarchic and fantastic world of his children's fiction is occasionally allowed to tweak the curtains of familiar Gee restraint, exactness, clarity'; that his 'calm, orderly worlds contain apocalypses', as well as 'the bizarre' and 'almost Gothic' (in, for example, *Crime Story* and *The Burning Boy*); that occasionally his prose breaks almost into expressionism, and '[a]ll the energies of the children's fiction are present . . .; they float just under the surface'.[20]

Ray Richards was not too far overstating the case when he remarked to Gee after he read the novel outline that it was 'entirely new in coverage, from any other work of fiction I know'.[21] The World War Two history of Somes Island was not widely known; nor perhaps (though here to a lesser degree) the reality of life in New Zealand for the newly arrived European immigrants and refugees, 'enemy aliens' and not. (At least one reviewer thought the small-town bigotry of the Masterton Brisboises was overdrawn.) Of those who knew the history, a few were outraged by Gee's fictional version, and let him know. Alongside several letters from grateful readers who had learned from the novel about an episode of their family history they had not or had little known, he received two, in particular, extremely angry ones. One came from a woman who recognised—she thought—her father in Hoch, the leader of the Nazi-sympathising German internees. She was wrong: Hoch was an invented character, although his attitudes and activities were not. He was, Gee agreed, 'a hideous character' but '[i]t is a matter of record that <u>some</u> of the Germans and Austrians interned on Somes Island had strong Nazi sympathies' and that 'they did many of the things described in my novel—celebrated Hitler's birthday, wore swastikas when they could, sang the Horst Wessel song, behaved aggressively towards the Jewish internees . . . I did not invent these things.' Hoch himself, however, he had made up: 'That is what novelists do.'[22] The only real name and character he used—apart from the extent to which Willi Gauss was Odo Strewe—was the melancholy Russian, Sargoff.

The other was from Gregor Riethmaier, the man whose photograph appeared, ironically, on the novel's cover. Riethmaier had come to New Zealand as the radio operator on Felix von Luckner's *Seeteufel* in 1938 and had been one of the pro-Nazi German group on Somes (though he might not have termed it that himself). Geoff Walker had tracked him and his photographs down, and sent him a complimentary copy of the novel. He had 'had many a sleepless night since reading it,' Riethmaier wrote to Gee a few months later, 'being so upset and dismayed at the devastating and inaccurate portrayal of the Somes Island camp, especially the description and characterisation of the German internees'; the novel was filled with 'so much hate and misinformation and bad language' and 'ugly, horrible misrepresentations', especially of 'our camp leader, a fine, cultured, sensible and sensitive married man of the very best qualities.'[23] Gee replied to both at length, detailing his research and responding to their objections point by point. (Her accusations against him of 'malice and cruelty', he said to the former, 'are serious. I am not guilty of these sins, even in the smallest degree.')[24] He did not hear from either of them again.[25]

Faber's acceptance of *Live Bodies* was conditional on Gee making a promotional visit to the UK. This was no reflection on their appreciation of the novel—'an extremely well written and skilful book—head and shoulders above the more overtly ambitious New Zealand novels I've come across recently', his editor said—but rather of the fact that his sales there had 'started to tail off recently', and the reality that author visibility had now become a necessary part of the book business.[26] Their publication date in October would coincide with the Cheltenham literary festival. (They hoped Creative New Zealand would fund Gee's travel, which it did.) Gee was pleased to accept, and to build in a trip to France he and Margareta had been thinking of for the last two years—investigations had been made of a walking tour in the Dordogne and cycling in Bordeaux.

They were away for five weeks, leaving Wellington on 20 September.

After a few days in Paris (which began with a classic mishap: taking the Metro from the airport, Gee got on the train when the doors opened and Margareta didn't; they arrived at their hotel separately some hours later), they travelled to Avignon and then St-Rémy-de-Provence where they embarked on a four-day cycling tour with Susi Madron's Cycling Holidays—cycling from hotel to hotel where meals and their gear awaited them. 'Cycling for Softies', the business styled itself. They found it hard work. They had not done enough training—and only on exercycles—and the season was wrong, too hot and too dry. But they enjoyed the walking and the sites (though failed to get as far as the Pont du Gard as intended) and some of the food. The rest of France was gentler: two days looking around Marseille, a day in Carcassonne, and three in the Loire Valley staying with Philip Mann and Nonnita Rees in their converted barn in the village of Choussy, before travelling with them by rental car and ferry to England. (They did not know the couple well but Mann had extended an invitation when he heard the Gees were going to be in France.)

The Cheltenham Literature Festival, the oldest and one of the world's most prestigious, ran for ten days in the Gloucestershire spa town on the edge of the Cotswolds. They went up just for Gee to do his session (on 12 October) and stayed overnight. Faber might have been starting to worry about his sales, but he met 'some real fans'.[27] One who would stay in touch was Michael Estorick, an enthusiastic reviewer as well as reader of Gee's novels (and a novelist himself). Back in London he was a generous host to the Gees for a day, including showing them around the newly opened Estorick Collection of Modern Italian Art in Islington, which housed his father Eric Estorick's significant collection. Faber put them up in a hotel just off Russell Square, and Gee had an 'exhausting' four days of interviews, newspaper and one radio, and met, among other Faber people, his new editor there, Emma Platt. 'I worked very hard to promote the book', he told Richards, but 'I got the impression that beyond that they really didn't know what to do with me'.[28] One of his and Margareta's pleasanter engagements was dinner with Rosemary Goad and Robert McCrum (who had now also left Faber).

In a profile in *Scotland on Sunday* Tom Adair, who had chaired Gee's session at Cheltenham (and had reviewed him before), described him as 'smiling, crinkle-eyed, avuncular', a man from whose laid-back demeanour '[y]ou'd never suspect the laser-sharpness of his work'—the familiar (curious) observation of the disjunction between the character of the man and his work. He seemed at ease but his were not easy novels, '[t]heir unfolding is criss-crossed by tremors, emotional undertow, currents of quiet, malign suspense, by the flotsam and jetsam of fractured lives, washed-up relationships, the murmur of distant trauma, closing in.' Mention of him having been compared with Ibsen and Shakespeare, wrote Adair, 'makes him laugh with amused self-detachment'.[29] He had never had a big breakthrough, Gee said. 'Back home, I guess I'm a pretty big frog in a fairly small pond. Over here, of course, they can hardly hear me croak.'[30]

Once again he was turned down in America, despite Richards' feeling that the Jewish background would increase *Live Bodies*' chances there. Simon and Schuster found it 'lovely, quaint, occasionally powerful' but unlikely to be a commercial proposition, they replied ruefully (bemoaning 'commercial publishing's version of political correctness' which 'we can't wait . . . to be overthrown').[31] It did, however, find a German publisher, thanks to the efforts of New Zealand-based translator Anita Goetthans. *Lebende Fracht* came out in Germany in 2002 from the small, young publishing house Black Ink, to the delight of Gee who 'had begun to think that my books just did not suit the European taste'.[32] Yet this and *Plumb*—in a Japanese edition from Simul Press in 1987—would remain his only adult novels to be published in translation until a 2007 Italian *Crime Story*.

It had not been the trip they had been looking forward to. Their extended stay in France in the Loire had put paid to Margareta's hopes to get to Scotland or St Ives. London they had found 'too big and crowded', and the flight home, a direct one, was 'a nightmare, took years of[f] our lives'. It would be the last such trip that they would make: the UK, for all its attractions, after this seemed to lie 'on the other side of a dangerous chasm'.[33]

30

Hostel Girl

A month after they got back from Cheltenham Gee was in Auckland to receive a Distinguished Alumni award from the University of Auckland. He was not going to treat this 'as an exclamation mark', he said in his acceptance speech, 'even though distinguished alumnus has a lovely sound. Rather, it's a dash in the sentence, a resting place—because I'm not finished yet, I've got plenty still to do.'[1]

It was a long time since he had made any categorical statements about giving up children's fiction and concentrating on adults'. Gee followed *Live Bodies* with two teen—or, as this expanding genre was increasingly known, young adult—novels. *Orchard Street* was written in the second half of 1997, with Penguin (after some revising) by February, and published in October, making 1998 another two-novel year. After his return from Sydney and the rainy Blue Mountains early in 1997, and finalising *Live Bodies* (which went to Richards and Walker in late April), he had spent a month or so revising a film script of *The Fat Man*, the first draft of which he had written the year before. The novel had been optioned in 1995 by Ginette McDonald and Settlement Films, initially with television in mind, with Larry Parr (with his new production company Kahukura Productions) joining the project as executive producer when the New Zealand Film Commission granted development funding. Gee had been commissioned in January 1996 to write a script for a 90-minute feature film ('Better I do it than anyone else', he told Ray Richards, though he regretted interrupting work on *Loving Ways*), of which he delivered a first draft in June (while Richards was negotiating a fee in the range of $50–60,000).[2]

Working on this script again, along with the continuing success of *The Fat Man*—local sales of which passed 10,000 in December 1997 (with another 3000-odd in Australia)—may have prompted him to write another children's novel, and another one set in Loomis. He had just been back there, too, to take part in the Going West literary festival in June. The small and friendly Titirangi festival, in its second year in 1997, had taken its name and its inspiration from Gee's novel and the train journey described in its opening pages. This year Gee was 'guest of honour' on the steam train excursion from Auckland to Helensville and back, with '[s]tops at historic locations for food, wine and entertainment', which became a feature of the festival each year, reading from *Going West* at Henderson station and again at Swanson—after lunch at Waimauku and dessert at the Grand Hotel in Helensville—on the return. 'I don't think I've ever had a better time while on book business', he told Murray Gray, the festival organiser, later.[3]

Orchard Street was not another *Fat Man*, to the disappointment (at least initially) of his publisher and agent. It was 'a nice little story', in Gee's words when he sent them the outline, with 'a bit of off-stage sex, some politics, and some strongly expressed anti-religious opinions' but nothing 'over the top';[4] with suspense but not menace. The setting is 1951, the year of the waterfront lockout, but that is only part of the story: 'Orchard Street was a busy place in 1951,' its narrator tells us, 'but a lot of what happened there went on in the dark'; after it 'our lives could never be the same'.[5] The story is told by fourteen-year-old Austin (Ossie) Dye (some of his friends call him 'Morris eight'), whose father, a printer and ardent trade unionist, is illegally printing pro-wharfie leaflets in his job-printing workshop under the house. His older brother Les, a junior at the Loomis bank, distributes them around the town after dark—as, one eventful night, does Ossie—and paints slogans; his favourite, like Raymond Sole's, is $id 卐olland. Their mother is one of Gee's portraits (in part) of his own: 'she believed in "things of the mind". Polite behaviour, nice thoughts. Elevated thoughts, she sometimes said'; the topic of religion, though, arouses an 'excitement and . . . vehemence' that terrifies her husband and sons.[6]

Orchard Street is, of course, undisguisedly Newington Road, its inhabitants versions (and combinations) of Gee's childhood neighbours, their stories and idiosyncrasies. Over the road, old, widowed Mr Worley feeds apples from his two remaining Gravenstein trees—the orchard he long ago sold lies abandoned and overgrown—to the draught horses in the next-door paddock. He beats Ossie at draughts and lends him Zane Grey novels (he is not ready yet for Dickens), and dies of grief not long after his beloved dog Jimpy (once Ossie's) is run over by a car (as, Gee recalled, did Ben Hart, whose

Jimpy—a dachshund-corgi cross—had been Gus's).[7] There is Mr Raffils who beats his sons with tomato stakes; next door to them the Pikes, she a follower of Radiant Living, he a railway signalman who in his spare time grows flowers in a glasshouse, keeps budgies in an aviary and builds kites. Their son Bike—tall and thin and awkward (*Sole Survivor*'s Beak Wyatt again)—works in the bank with Les Dye.

In the Redknapps, Lionel and Winifred (Mr Worley's daughter), Gee portrays the Pinckneys, though he gives them perhaps a sadder story: her snobbishness, but also depression since the stillbirth 30 years ago which has left her childless; he having been gassed in the war; their business sewing canvas goods. There is more to Mr Redknapp, however, than Ossie had thought. Unlikely discoveries, and friendships, is one of the novel's gratifying themes. Lionel Redknapp is an amateur astronomer, setting up his telescope on clear nights in the Flynns' paddock: 'He gave me my first lesson in astronomy'—thrills Ossie with Jupiter, 'huge and impossible up there . . . hanging silent out among the stars'—'on a night that changed my life'. On another night Mr Redknapp comes to tea and he and Ossie's mother talk animatedly about religion, and poetry, 'then art and music and Nature (big N)', and he 'had never seen her sparkle like this before'. To Ossie she seemed at first to be flirting, but then 'opening a lid and letting out things she hadn't known she still possessed. I saw her give a little start of wonder now and then'; while 'Mr Redknapp, free from his wife, was also turning into someone he had once been. . . . The world seemed to have made a lurch, then settled down', but Ossie wonders 'about those things Mum kept in her head' and 'what use she would make' of them now.[8] All of the adults were behaving strangely that year.

At the blind end of Orchard Street the Catholic Collymores live. Frank Collymore is the town's bookie and Eddie Dye's best mate. Les takes out his daughter Eileen (theirs is the offstage sex). Ossie is sweet on her younger sister Teresa, both of them on the cusp of first love. After walking home with her after the pictures, he 'went home, humming like a fridge, like a radio. . . . Holding hands with her was the best thing I had ever done.'[9] This is a story of, amongst other things, young romance. The novel's penultimate climax comes when the police raid the Collymores' house and Teresa flees with her father's book hidden down the front of her blouse (a true story, one of Len's bookie mates'), inadvertently leading them to the discovery of Eddie Dye's printing press. At the pictures with Teresa again that night, 'It seemed impossible to me—and sometimes wrong—that I should be sitting in the pictures, eating chocboms, holding hands with my girl, on the same day that our fathers had been arrested.' This time Ossie kisses her goodnight: 'She tasted of chocolate and ice-cream, and of Eileen's lipstick, which she'd pinched. . . . It had been a Saturday full of happiness and fright. July 7, 1951. That should have been the end of it.'[10] The final act, which plays out later the same night, involves Bike Pike, his obsessive, unrequited love for Eileen Collymore, and the bank revolver; and another surprising turn from Mr Redknapp.

It was, as Gee said, a nice little story, though not without its share of difficult and sad things. Some of its subjects would receive a darker treatment in his next. The opening, a chance encounter between Ossie and Bike 40 years on, making the story a reconstructed one, while this was a familiar Gee mode he added at his publishers' suggestion. But he was not prepared to change the ending. He had reread the manuscript in the light of their suggestions but no, he told them, 'I can't see my way to killing Eileen, or anyone else'. It was not and he had never intended it to be 'that sort of story', and the ending was, he felt, 'as close to perfect as I can get it', in tone 'bitter-sweet, not tragic'.[11]

He had not expected *Orchard Street* to do as well as *The Fat Man*, but sales of nearly 5000 after ten months was nothing to be disappointed about. Nor was it picked up in America, again as Gee anticipated—the left-leaning politics and anti-religious sentiments would not find favour there, he assumed, though the stated reasons were simpler ones, the distant setting and lack of the suspense of *The Fat Man* (which had just gone into a second printing there, and would be out in paperback the following year), that it was not 'exceptional enough'. Houghton Mifflin's *The Fire-Raiser*, though, continued to do well for them, they noted as they turned *Orchard Street* down, as did *The Champion* for Simon and Schuster until they let it go out of print, after two printings, in 2000.[12]

At home, notwithstanding growing competition from *The Fat Man*, the fantasy novels remained the most enduringly popular of Gee's children's fiction.[13] In April 1998 Penguin flew him up to Auckland for the launch party in the Old Town Hall of their Penguin 25 Club, marking the 25th anniversary of Penguin publishing in New Zealand. The eight members were authors of Penguin books that had sold over 25,000,[14] in Gee's case *Under the Mountain*, of which they were about to print another 2000 to meet a surge in demand following its inclusion in a Whitcoulls list of 100 favourite children's books. *The Halfmen of O*, meanwhile, had reached its own milestone of 20,000 sales the previous year.

Gee had the next one underway by midway through 1998 and with Penguin before he left for Cheltenham in September. Richards was still hoping for another *Fat Man*, if not a prequel or sequel at least 'a new strong junior novel' featuring a 'single stand-out character': perhaps 'a marijuana villain or an Asian gang protagonist, a boy whose father is an undercover cop and/or a helicopter pilot with a record . . .', he suggested, ever helpful (the 'potential horror of the Endeavour inlet abduction'—of 21- and 17-year-olds Ben Smart and Olivia Hope in the Marlborough Sounds on New Year's Day 1998—was, he acknowledged, 'too close for comfort at present').[15] *Hostel Girl* was not that, but its tone, of sinister threat and danger, places it closer to *The Fat Man* than to the more benign *Orchard Street*. Its story, of obsessive love, and its 1950s setting connect it with the latter.

For this novel Gee drew not on his own experience but on Margareta's. Two of its major plot elements had already been in his mind when he was first making notes for *Live Bodies*: the 1947 polio epidemic (which had delayed the start of his lower-sixth-form year) and the YWCA hostels in Lower Hutt. For two years when she was fourteen and fifteen Margareta had lived in the Woburn hostels, where her mother was matron of hostel 4 for trainee dental nurses: 'House 4' was the novel's working title, which he held out for until Richards (who thought it was too cryptic, while Penguin thought it too flat) came up with an alternative he liked. It was 'a bit cheeky' of him perhaps (he told to an interviewer for his local paper)[16] to write a novel about and from the point of view of a teenage girl—sassy, self-possessed fourteen-year-old Ailsa McGowan—but Margareta had allowed him to read her teenage diaries, about friends, books, boys and movies and the daily life of the hostel. Ailsa's mother, a war widow, like Greta Garden is matron of house 4 while also working as a cashier at the Griffin's biscuit factory in Lower Hutt. It is 1955 and her mother has withdrawn Ailsa the previous term from Hutt Valley High School and sent her to all-girls, church-run Willowbank—standing in for the real Chilton Saint James—following the publication of the Mazengarb report on juvenile delinquency. The findings of a government-appointed committee of inquiry into reports aired in

Truth of 'immoral conduct'—'sex parties, nudity, illegitimate babies': 'the sex scandal year', Ailsa calls it[17]—among Hutt Valley teenagers, the Mazengarb report, and its moralistic castigating of parents and call for a return to traditional Christian values, had been distributed to every household in the country. Gee sets his novel in a moment of cultural awakening and fear that belies a commonly held conception of the 1950s in New Zealand as a dull and conformist place (that had been his experience of it no more than it is Ailsa's). Yet it is not bodgies and widgies who pose the threat in *Hostel Girl*.

It opens with Ailsa standing on the footbridge over the railway line at Woburn station, above the silver rails which cut the valley, 'and in a way cut her life', in half: on one side the hostels, state houses, and 'delinquent' Naenae teens who congregate at Elbe's milk bar; on the other Willowbank, bigger houses on tree-filled sections and cars parked in garages not on lawns. 'Sometimes she imagined that it existed outside the world. She went down from it, one way or the other, into places where her life was tangled, where too much trying was asked of her.' A prospective friendship with new classmate Helen introduces her to the Page family, and their posh house full of 'fat frilly chairs' and '[t]hingy things'. Mrs Page, tall and elegant (her neck 'looked as if it had been stretched'), specialises in quick, 'almost non-existent smile[s]', while Mr Page—partner in Page Endacott, lawyers—potters in the garden cheerfully rueing his marriage. It is Helen's polio-crippled brother, Calum, however, who interests Ailsa, as she does him: 'a strange-looking boy . . . bent in his face, which made him ugly and good-looking at once: a sinister look', his manner a confusing mix of aggressive and sardonic and hurting (his mother has distanced herself from him—withdrawn her love even—after he contracted the disease: 'People like us don't get polio, it's working class', Calum flatly comments).[18] He and Ailsa become boyfriend and girlfriend; Helen and Ailsa do not become friends.

The other relationship at the centre of the story is Ailsa's with her new roommate Gloria, one of the dental nurse students, nineteen (Ailsa guesses), pretty and sophisticated. To Ailsa she looks like Ann Blyth in *Mildred Pierce*, with 'a profile that was pretty and pointy at the same time, small nose, pink ears, floppy hair—runny hair, like toffee—and lips that were pouty and discontented', but she also has a concealed vulnerability and (we discover) unhappy past which make Ailsa feel '[s]ad and curious, protective in a way'.[19]

His intention, Gee has said, was to write another frightening character who is terrorising people. This one, as he turned out, did not have 'the weight . . . the darkness' of Herbert Muskie,[20] but he is sinister enough—in a more subtly drawn way—from the first encounter, when Ailsa goes to retrieve the tennis ball she has lobbed over the back wall of the Pages' tennis court. From the top of the creosoted timber wall she looks down on their neighbour's lawn where '[t]he tennis ball lay in the centre, a tiny moon in a green sky; making her, for a moment, feel strange, as though things went wrong on the far side of the wall.' She climbs down into an unnatural quietness, stillness; a large Alsatian appears, baring teeth that 'shone at the tips like a circular saw'. It is not the dog, however (incongruously named Bruce), who truly terrifies her but its owner, who has been silently watching her from a wicker chair partially obscured in the garden, 'a plain man trying to be handsome . . . big-nosed, fat-mouthed' and horsey-toothed, wearing clothes too elegant for his 'fattish body'—a silk shirt with a green cravat and a tropical hat that 'was wrong for his pale thinning hair'—and holding an affected movie-star pose. (He had, Ailsa will learn, once played the romantic lead opposite Mrs Page in amateur theatre.) Film is an important reference in the novel, as it was in the teenage world of the 1950s which *Hostel Girl* evocatively recreates. But it was not Errol Flynn Gee had in mind (though he came to Ailsa's) in naming his character Errol Parkinson but Errol the tax-dodger at Heysham House in Paeroa, in Gee's own 1950s (a nasty and frightening man, he remembered him still, though in a very different way from Errol Parkinson).

The man's creepiness frightens her. He 'stayed in her mind no matter how hard she tried to push him out'—like Herbert Muskie—'and grew more sinister the way Calum got better-looking'. He may or may not be the peeping Tom who is stalking Gloria at night, the mysterious figure on a bicycle wearing a long coat which 'flapped like vulture wings when he mounted his bike and rode away', whistling Maizy Doats. Or the person who is sending Gloria at first cryptic, then increasingly threatening anonymous letters.[21]

Ailsa is the same age as Austin Dye (and Gloria as Eileen), but Gee saw this novel as written for an older age group than *Orchard Street.* In this story of obsessive love (which *Orchard Street* is only in part) the stakes are higher. From that first moment of uneasiness, a subtle menace, the novel builds with a tension that is not as visceral as *The Fat Man*'s but which has its own compelling quality, as Ailsa, abetted by an initially sceptical Calum, sets out to prove her suspicions and protect her friend. There is a frightening night-time bike pursuit; when Ailsa breaks into Errol Parkinson's house, full of Maxfield Parrishes, she finds in a darkened closed-off room an eerie shrine to Gloria. It culminates in an abduction at knifepoint, a car crash, and villain and rescuer wrestling on the train tracks as the unit from Waterloo, 'invisible behind its swelling light',[22] bears down: this story, like *The Fat Man*, ends with a death.

Again, *Hostel Girl* did not make the same impact as *The Fat Man*: sales were slower than those of *Orchard Street*, and no one was surprised that it was not taken overseas. ('[N]ot a world-beater', had been Richards' first response to the manuscript.)[23] But it left an imprint in another way. When it came out in July 1999 Gee had his next novel already in progress. With this novel, which he was 'feeling my way into' in November 1998, only a month after finishing *Hostel Girl*, he decided to repeat the experiment of *Prowlers*, of taking the protagonists of a junior novel into an adult one. He had considered doing so with *Orchard Street*, but, fond as he was of Ossie as he was of Ailsa, there 'I would be writing my own life again'.[24] This did not mean, of course, that he would not put various bits of it into *Ellie and the Shadow Man*, including a wry caricature of his writer self.

As before he changed his characters' names (with the exception of Ailsa/Ellie's communist social studies teacher Mrs Nimmo): the heroine becomes Ellie Crowther; Gloria Dolores; Calum Page the more memorably named Hollis Prime (the Chapple family name here recalling wooden-legged Willis Plumb). This time the original novel provides more than backstory. The opening scenes of *Ellie* closely reprise those of *Hostel Girl*, with Ellie standing on the railway overbridge that 'marked a transition from a state of easiness into unease',[25] and going to a tennis party at the Primes'. Some lines of dialogue are directly repeated. (He wondered if readers who had read *Hostel Girl* would feel short-changed.)[26] Difference lies in texture. On the tennis court side are '[l]awns mown so close they looked in pain. Blinds that made the windows seem like pages in a notebook, unwritten on'. Adult novels, Gee observed, are 'more language-oriented' than children's ones (his at least), where the focus is on action and event.[27] In this version he dispensed with the thriller aspect of the story, with Errol and the stalker/peeping Tom, and set it a few years' later, making Hollis significantly older than Calum: 22 to Ellie's 14 or 15. He is more complex, more mysterious, too: 'sneering, bad tempered, crooked, cruel' to Ellie on first impression, with 'a widow's peak as sharp as a pen nib', but interesting—'utterly strange'. The quick shifts of his character, and her responses to him, confuse her. It is Dolores, however—'so beautiful, so sulky, so extreme'—with whom he has a romantic, and here sexual, relationship. We last see Dolores as Ellie sees her off on the *Wanganella* for Sydney, where she has no intention of having the abortion the Primes have paid her off to have.[28]

By now, as the first section of the novel closes, Ellie and her mother have moved in with her mother's new husband in his house in Brooklyn, a 'small and dark' house in a gully, not the 'little house in Wellington, halfway up a hill, with the city shining below' that Ailsa and Mrs McGowan had dreamed of.[29]

'Do you think we'll get to 300 pages with ELLIE?', Gee asked Penguin when he sent them a floppy disk of the manuscript. 'This would fulfill one of my ambitions. The closest I've been before is 296.'[30] It came to 348. Its length—including of its title—is not the only thing that sets *Ellie and the Shadow Man* apart among Gee's novels. It tells the story of Ellie's life in a linear, third-person narrative, with no playing around with time or point of view. Where he did experiment was with the rhythm. The novel focuses on five times in Ellie's life, each of about a year; short, interspersed Between Times chapters briskly recount the intervening decades in the present tense: 'bridges of notes', a reviewer referred to these.[31] It was not something he had seen done before, just an idea he had, and which 'worked very well indeed', his publisher thought, though having been initially suspicious.[32] Critics had reservations. Unnecessary, Lydia Wevers thought them, reviewing the novel in the *Evening Post*. C.K. Stead, in an extended review-essay in *Landfall*, went further to suggest that they had the effect of undermining the rest in begging the question, 'Why not give it all in summary and be done with it?' (Missing the complex time scheme and its representation of memory, which was, for him, a distinguishing feature of Gee's fiction, the episodic structure of the novel, Stead continued—while acknowledging that he was 'overstating the negative case here'—which this device emphasised made its narrative mode feel like 'the eye of a god who is making it up as he goes along'.)[33]

Gee borrowed from Margareta again for the first Between Times, in which Ellie does a library school course, becomes a tramper and takes a job as a borough librarian in Taumarunui, works as a fleeco in a shearing gang and a waitress at the Tongariro Chateau. During a month in the UK and Europe she is arrested at a demonstration in London, and discovers ('stunned, with her skin stripped off') Goya at the Prado. In the second extended section of the novel which follows, Good Life, it is 1969 and she picks apples on an orchard in Māpua, and meets painter Fan Anerdi and her weaver friend Audrey who live in the 'witchy villa' (Ivy Brett's house, where the Gees had first stayed when they moved to Nelson in 1975) next door. (Fan Anerdi, formerly Frances Clark, has no model in real life, but her French-Italian husband's name was that of the owner of the Villa Isola Bella when the Gees were in Menton.) With her apple-picking boyfriend Mike she goes to live on a commune in the Aorere valley in Golden Bay, whose self-appointed guru reads Carlos Castaneda and partner Glenys calls herself Rain. The landscape, not the hippie believing, seduces her. It is here Ellie does the first work that suggests she might become an artist: three lines drawn with tar on the malthoid roof of the converted railway carriage she shares with Mike—'a rounded hill, a broken one, the gorge jagging down'.[34] Later she will return to Māpua and ask Fan to teach her how to paint.

Good Life is the first of two communes in the novel, and was not drawn from personal experience: for the details he had gone to the Whole Earth catalogues published by Alister Taylor in the 1970s. By 1990 and part four of Ellie's story the Good Life land has become home to an Anabaptist religious community calling itself Gethsemane, where her half-brother Derek is living. This Gee modelled closely on the Gloriavale Christian Community at Haupiri, 60 kilometres inland from Greymouth, which he and Margareta had visited while on a trip to the West Coast and Canterbury in March 1999. Friends of theirs who lived at Blackball had been invited to visit the remote, normally closed community and asked the Gees if they wanted to come along. They were given an hour-long talk about and then a tour of Gloriavale by its leader Hopeful Christian—or Neville Cooper, the Australian Pentecostal-style preacher who had founded the community, originally at Cust in Canterbury, in 1969. Gee found it both fascinating and very creepy, as Ellie does Gethsemane and its charismatic Cooper-like leader Robert Early: 'A pleasant strain of normalcy ran over something deeply abnormal and possibly dangerous.' (The fictional version was, Gee has said, 'if anything . . . toned . . . down'.)[35]

He told Ray Richards after they got back that he hoped the trip, and in particular the visit to Gloriavale, would help 'kick start' a novel he was then finding it difficult getting underway.[36]

Before Gethsemane, and before her return to Māpua and apprenticeship with Fan Anerdi—who on her death will bequeath to Ellie her house and land and her paintings, her own and her McCahons and Woollastons—Ellie has spent eighteen months in a relationship with writer Neil Higgs, whom she meets at a Coffee and Books reading in Nelson. He is about to publish his fourth novel, *The Dark Before the Light*, about a brave and unlikeable clergyman with a patient wife and many children; his previous one (which she finds disappointing) features a hero who is 'meant to be deep and sensitive but is shifty and hysterical'.[37] Gee based his writer on himself, he told interviewers, to protect himself against accusations that he was writing about his friends. He liked to think, though, that he was 'a much nicer person' than Neil.[38] He has 'a way of crinkling his eyes that's perhaps over-sweet', Ellie thinks, eyeing him up at that first meeting, but is all the same masculine, his mind 'a nice mix—sensitive and tough'. She moves in with him in his house in Glenmore Street, where he writes in 'a cave' at the bottom of the house and is precious about interruptions (unlike Gee): a sign on the door directs visitors upstairs; Ellie is allowed to communicate with him when he's working by the Gees' stamp chart system. She discovers 'almost straight away' that he 'had an ordinary mind' (to go with his plain and old-fashioned tastes: 'Steak and wine was his idea of high living'), which only makes him 'mysterious. Where did his books come from?' To make money he writes for television, a police show called *Paget's Casebook*, 'all with a dark edge and plenty of suspense'; he 'was clever with twisted motives—surprising, really, considering how much he needed to have explained in real life'. [39]

Her love for and interest in him survives 'later discoveries: his selfishness, obtuseness, snobbery, silliness'; his way of driving the car ('impatient and dreamy by turns'), his dislike of climbing hills for the view. She starts doing research for him (his new novel is about a soil scientist), and comes to see, finally, that he will only use her more and more, and understand how much of him is invested in his writing: if his novel was no good 'he would be too small to see'. For the strong-minded and self-possessed character we know Ellie to be, it seems to take her a long time to decide she must leave, and leave him to 'go on splashing around in the deep end of his life, where he belonged, where perhaps he made the only sense he would ever make'.[40]

'It's sort of about a person understanding herself', Gee replied to the question what was the novel about, which she does through her art: 'in her brushstrokes, in her palette. She reached a kind of deep acquaintance with herself' (in the words Meg had used).[41] Ellie Crowther is another of Gee's self-reflective protagonists, but hers is a calm, measured consideration; she has a sureness of self and none of the angst and self-criticism of Paul Prior or Kingsley Pratt, or even Raymond Sole (nor the happy irascibility of Noel Papps). She knows herself and is pleased to be 'clever and sharp', 'sudden and eager' (like Harry Skeat), loud and bossy. Unusually too for a Gee protagonist she 'had always been comfortable with people . . . Being alone was no more than a story she wrote for herself now and then.' A 'down to earth, practical, sweaty in some places' book, Gee described the novel to Geoff Walker.[42] There is a matter-of-factness about Ellie and her gaze, as she 'wonder[s] if other moments could be recaptured like this; if she could make her life and carry it, study it whenever she chose', package experience up and take it with her, in a way which seems to mirror the structure of the novel with its focused episodes and elided stretches of time. Leaving Mike and the commune, she thinks to herself, 'It's not running away, it's finishing. . . . Good Life was bundled up; it was property, which she took away as well as left behind.'[43]

Language too is matter-of-fact. As a visual artist rather than a writer Ellie lacks the attentiveness to language that other of Gee's self-regarding protagonist-narrators have. (Humour is lacking too: Mrs Nimmo having a cat named Beria—a stray that moved in with her after killing all the sparrows in her garden—is the only joke in the novel.)

Missing also in the uncomplicated episodic narrative is mystery, the early intimation that for both reader and character there is something to find out—the nature of Kenny's betrayal, and what has made Julie this way; 'I must believe that it connects with things that came before', thinks Mandl; what happened 'on that morning long ago' that Plumb cannot speak Alfred's name—the Gee-ish atmosphere of threat; in Tom Adair's words the 'currents of quiet, malign suspense'.[44] Who is Ellie's shadow man—the mysterious male figure, a dark vertical stroke, scratched at the edges, 'scarcely defined, only suggested', who appears suddenly in her landscapes—is a question that does not need an answer.[45] Death, fear, fate, mused Iain Sharp in the *Sunday Star Times*; 'a metaphor for self-discovery if ever I've seen one', said another reviewer; Ellie's muse, her myth, her stalker, or it 'might be Gee', suggested Adair.[46] Perhaps her father, Ellie for a moment wonders, who died falling under a train (an echo of Walter Skeat's death) when she was two years old. Or perhaps, more simply, Hollis Prime, whose reappearance in her life, and of the strange hold they have on each other, brings the novel full circle.

For the practical details of the artist's life—brushes and canvases, dealers and exhibitions, the creative process of painting—Gee questioned Glenda Randerson when she painted his portrait in 1999 (one of a series of 24 portraits of New Zealand writers Randerson produced between 1996 and 2001. He declined to buy the finished work, which was later purchased by Brian Corban of the Henderson wine-making family and donated to the new Henderson Public Library). For Ellie's paintings he had in mind the work of Sydney-based artist Euan Macleod, whose *Anniversary (five years)* (1998) appeared on the novel's cover, after considerable persuasion. Gee had first come across Macleod's 'crepuscular paintings'—'marvellous rough landscapes with shadowy unformed figures haunting them', as he described them to Geoff Walker[47]—in the early 1990s (and yet, curiously, Royce Lomax's in *Prowlers* might almost seem to prefigure them), and he and Margareta bought one from an exhibition at Wellington's Bowen Galleries, the artist's New Zealand dealer, in May 1995 (a small work, *Figures 1*, for $300). Macleod's remark to Gee when they met at the opening that he would love to do a jacket for one of his novels, having related so strongly to *Going West*, had prompted Gee to suggest to Walker using one of his paintings for the cover of *Loving Ways*.

The sense of an affinity between their work was mutual. In subsequent correspondence with Macleod, Gee described the powerful effect Macleod's paintings had on him as a 'feeling . . . of disturbance and satisfaction at the same time'.[48] Before *Ellie* he had included a Macleod painting in his contribution to *Writing Wellington*, an anthology marking twenty years of the Victoria University Writing Fellowship, edited by Roger Robinson and published in 1999: a descriptive sketch entitled 'Waterfront', tracing a man's journey across the city and his thoughts about his dead wife, a love letter to both the city and her. (The painting, *Geoff and Patrick hidden* (1990), had been purchased for the university art collection in 1992 and hung in the library, where Gee, like his character, liked to look at it whenever he was up there. It was, he apologised later to Macleod, an 'inaccurate' reference 'I discovered when I looked at it again a few days ago, but never mind; it was meant as a compliment'.)[49] The same year, by way of thanks for his support and inspiration Macleod gave the Gees a small painting (*Lyttelton landscape/figures (1)*), which had, he felt, 'a sense of "Going West" & "Live Bodies"'.[50]

Walker was sceptical when Gee proposed a Macleod painting for the cover of *Ellie and the Shadow Man*, which was before he had seen even a summary of the novel. He remained so after he had read the manuscript: it was too 'elusive', he felt, and besides did not fit 'our Maurice Gee cover series design', for which they had been using only photographic images. Only after further persuasion—in the form of a barrage of emails from Margareta—did he agree to commission a design using the Macleod painting, along with another, photographic one (showing 'an illusive shape among trees') which 'is obviously our preference'. The result, Gee told Macleod, was 'no contest' (though only after Walker had surveyed his marketing people and sales reps). 'For years I've been dissatisfied with the jackets of my books,' he told Macleod, 'but at last I'm getting one I can be wholeheartedly proud of.'[51]

Ellie and the Shadow Man was favourably received, on the whole, but not unreservedly. Not everybody loved Ellie, though it was agreed that she was 'admirable' and convincing: 'invariably believable, not always likeable but certainly sympathetic', the *Times Literary Supplement* review put it, though that paper's Australasian editor, Nicola Walker, writing in the *Guardian* was unconvinced by the 'almost unreasonable calmness' with which she left the ghastly Neil, in a review which summed the novel up as 'flawed but thoughtful'.[52] (Gee himself was, he admitted, 'not enamoured of her' but became as he wrote 'deeply involved and deeply admiring'.)[53] And while one could not disagree with the essential qualities Gee delineated—'truth, courage, independence'—Lydia Wevers wrote, 'I would have liked a bit more trashy pleasure in Ellie's life'. Some reviewers were let down by a too-tidy ending, the late arrival in the novel of Hollis and Dolores's daughter Debbie and the frantic search for her bipolar son Dion on the remote West Coast, which seemed 'rushed and melodramatic', 'contrived'; 'at times he seems busy just tidying up his story'.[54] Endings were proving still difficult.

A second printing ordered and only 500 in the warehouse on publication day was 'quite amazing', Walker told Gee and Richards, a reflection both of the quality of the book and also of 'Maurice's huge reputation among New Zealand book lovers these days': 'one of our grand old literary stars', he had described Gee to Faber two years before.[55] Faber loved the novel, but were again frank when they replied that, while they had 'enormous respect for [Gee's] work . . . we have always found it difficult to sell and the current climate in the market here is making things doubly difficult', and offered an advance of £2000, less than the £3000 for *Live Bodies* and less than half what Richards was anticipating.[56] It was accepted nevertheless. Richards had earlier raised with Gee the Faber question once again, of whether to forgo the likely considerable upfront payment 'against the possible difficulty of getting an equally good contract or any contract from Bloomsbury or Headline—and a much smaller advance' (while Walker too, with more intent, put to Gee the suggestion of submitting the manuscript to Penguin (UK) ahead of Faber). The answer was no, although Gee remained frustrated that Faber did not sell his books 'with more energy'. He had been reminded too of their less than efficient ways when he had visited their offices when he was in London in 1998, and the children's editor, expressing an interest in seeing *Orchard Street* and 'House 4', told him they had never received *The Fat Man*: he was hardly surprised, Gee reported to Richards, that the manuscript 'went astray—the Faber offices are chaotic'.[57] As Richards put it, though, inefficient and unenergetic publishers though Faber might be, '[t]he result is an elegant trade paperback, some prestigious reviews, the same sales pattern—mainly to libraries one guesses. For which you get a handsome advance.'

Gee wrote himself to Faber's Jon Riley thanking them for a 'generous' offer, especially considering how little his novels had ever earned for them.[58] He would calculate a year later that they had paid him more than $25,000 that they had not got back. In 2003, only five of his eleven novels published by Faber—*Plumb*, *Meg*, *Prowlers*, *Going West* and *Loving Ways*—had yet earned back their royalty advance. 'As you say,' he told Richards, 'Faber are a phenomenon.'[59]

31

The Scornful Moon

Ellie and the Shadow Man—which Gee dedicated, anonymously, to Margareta[1]—was launched at the Auckland Writers' Festival in May 2001, at which he also participated in two panel sessions. This was, he told Wellington Writers and Readers Week organiser Chris Price two months later, 'much against my will, the result of arm-twisting that I submitted to because I had a novel being launched there'.[2] He decided he wasn't doing it again. He had taken part in the inaugural Auckland festival two years earlier, in two reading sessions that time, and when Price sounded him out the same year about the next Wellington one had gently turned her down: he wasn't agreeing to any more panel discussions, he told her then, at which he had 'had bad experiences'; 'I'm willing to read, of course, but I think people have heard enough from me.' Now when they invited him to give the New Zealand Book Council lecture at the 2002 Writers and Readers Week he was adamant: after Auckland he had 'made up my mind "no more festivals, no more panels, no more talking"'.[3] He thought of it as a 70th birthday present to himself.

While he let his draft of *Ellie and the Shadow Man* rest (and before leaving with Margareta for a week's holiday in Brisbane), in July 2000 he had written a short story, his first for sixteen years. It was for a collection Gordon McLauchlan was editing as a fundraiser for the New Zealand Society of Authors (formerly PEN) in collaboration with Tandem Press. Thirteen writers—Gee was the first—had been invited to contribute a story set in a 'humble twelve-unit' motel in a 'semi-mythical South Taranaki town' over a weekend in March: 'three days of drama, romance, sex and mystery', as the introduction had it. *Morrieson's Motel*, the establishment and the collection's name, was a homage to Ronald Hugh Morrieson. The idea was not an original one but came from a 1997 Irish collection, *Finbar's Hotel*, edited by Dermot Bolger. In the published volume the authors were named but not identified with their stories. (It was Gee's idea to have a competition inviting readers to match them, for which a book token prize was offered of $250.)[4]

Gee's, entitled 'Tact', is a gentle story about a man dying of cancer, and a moving portrait of a marriage, its third-person point of view shifting between Tom and his considerably younger wife Vera Gregg as they return to the home town he has not been back to for many years. He is of an age when the 'small disappointments of life no longer threw him out of step' ('This motel was a disappointment too', its cheap furniture and even cheaper pictures and 'those insulting hangers that let you steal only part of them, made you feel accused'); 'He passed them on to her because they seemed to give her pleasure.' She is 'bright and tactful, beautiful and sharp, soft-tongued, enigmatic, always at a distance yet always in this room or the next'. Through their marriage they have 'learned how much they could be together and how much they must stay apart'. It is a more generous story than its recognisably Gee-ish opening sentence ('He was sorrier for the car than for his wife') suggests.[5] In an otherwise unimpressed review, *Listener* books editor Denis Welch in *New Zealand Books* singled out only two stories for praise: 'whoever wrote "Tact"'—he suspected it was Gee—'has to be someone blessed with the greatest gift a writer can have—that of knowing exactly how much to leave out'.[6] The story's title applies also to the implicit, off-page suicide with which it ends.

'Tact' was the last story Gee published, but not the last he wrote, or tried to. In 2002 Euan Macleod asked him if he would write something for the catalogue of his forthcoming exhibition (a small retrospective at the Bathurst Regional Art Gallery). He didn't want the usual critical essay—'another "art talk" contextualizing'—ascribing meanings to his paintings, which were 'intentionally ambiguous'; but perhaps Gee could write something that captured a personal and emotional response, as his novels provoked in Macleod. Gee spent two days drafting a short story, 'Father, Child and Euan Macleod', about a young girl's visit to a gallery with her father, before deciding that it was 'puerile and embarrassing' and giving it up. 'If I could have arrived at something more by accident, integrating it into an interesting fictional happening, instead of going after that thing, it might have been different', he apologised; 'I can only conclude that good stories aren't generated in that way.'[7] But that was something he knew already.

*

A collaborative novel was the catalyst for Gee's next, which he was mulling over the idea of in the early months of 2001: a novel very different from *Ellie and the Shadow Man.* Margareta had shown him the manuscript in the Turnbull Library of 'Murder by Twelve', a composite detective novel written in 1936–37 under the initiative of journalist Pat Lawlor; his fellow contributors were a variously talented assembly of newspaper- and literary men and old friends, among them Alan Mulgan and Charles Marris, historian James Cowan, poet, journalist and anthologist O.N. Gillespie, theatre producer Victor Lloyd—the literary fraternity of *Going West*'s Euan Brightmore. It was 'marvellously handy', Gee remarked to an interviewer, having a wife who worked at the Turnbull.[8] Through Margareta he also found the strange story of poet D'Arcy Cresswell and the homosexual mayor of Wanganui C.E. Mackay, in which Cresswell had been shot in the chest by Mackay during an apparent blackmail attempt in 1920. These were two of the handful of historical elements from which Gee crafted *The Scornful Moon* (a different way of working from his usual, he observed: normally a novel followed from a single idea). 'There's a group of literary gents writing a composite detective story,' he described to Carl Freeman the novel he was 'working a bit half-heartedly on' in August, 'an ousted politician using devious (worse than devious) means to get back, a woman painter struggling to get free, a moon scientist, a couple of homosexuals, one of them involved in a nasty plot like the one Darcy Cresswell was in in the 1920s', its setting 1935, 'the year of the Labour victory . . .—quite a mix'.[9] It was not until three months into the writing that he felt it was coming together.

The title was taken from a line of Robin Hyde's ('the scornful crystal moons' in *Journalese*).[10] Its subtitle, *a moralist's tale*, was a nod to C.K. Stead, whose review essay in *Landfall* (republished in his 2002 collection *Kin of Place*) had been titled 'Maurice Gee, moralist'. Gee's 'mode of characterisation is that of the inveterate moralist', Stead had observed. 'His characters are not just portrayed; they are judged', and when his 'writing falls a notch or two below its best it is usually because moralism has triumphed at the expense of representation', his urge to judge character leading him to compromise story.[11] There was some truth in that, Gee agreed; and his appropriating it for his title was not out of pique. He didn't mind being called a moralist.[12] His narrator, Sam Holloway, retired journalist and novelist *manqué*, is a moralist of the old-fashioned kind—prudish and proper (about language as well as behaviour: 'Note: "decimated" used in its proper sense', he tells us as an aside; 'I'm too fond of "ish" as a qualifier', he checks himself')[13]—and an inveterate judge of others. In his professional as well as his moral life he is loosely based on Lawlor: like Lawlor he has been a member of the parliamentary press gallery and is a connoisseur of beer (the Frothblowers' Club he once convened takes its name from the home-brewing manual Lawlor wrote). The tale he tells, circuitously and a little squeamishly, six months to a year on, is one of political wrong-doing—ambition, intrigue, villainy and betrayal—entangled with a family web of secrets and disappointment. The detective story he and his 'fellow scribblers' set out to write quickly falls by the wayside.[14]

Sam is one of three men married to three sisters. Eric Clifton, married to the youngest, May, is the novel's moon scientist, another of Gee's cast of likeable astronomers, internationally known for his theory explaining the circular craters on the moon, and a popular public lecturer. (His science and his talent as a populariser of it, and his renown, Gee took from Wellington College science master and astronomer A.C. Gifford.) He is also one of Sam's novel-writing collaborators. They get along despite being utterly different. Eric is a man large in appetite and curiosity, 'heavy, water-logged in appearance, yet light and airy in his mind', with a 'ploughman's face and thick-fingered hands and hairy forearms . . . untutored voice and wide-open laugh'. Sam disapproves of his friendship with brothel-owner Lily Maxey, as he does his taste for Shelley, and finds his tolerance crucially tested when her house is raided by the police. (Newspaper coverage of a raid on an Upland Road 'house of ill-fame' in 1918 and the subsequent court case was Gee's source here.)[15] Their brother-in-law James Tinling is something else again: cold and imperious, his youthful handsomeness now stripped down to deathly angularity; 'bared and antiseptic—too white in his skin and fine in his hands and clean in his face. His ears sat close to his skull and seemed all cartilage. His nostrils were slashes in a barely fleshed nose.'[16] Appearance is character. A lawyer-turned-politician—a cabinet minister in the Reform government before losing his seat in 1928—he is planning to put himself forward again in the coming election, to the dismay of all who see that he doesn't stand a chance, especially after the unexpected challenge for the nomination from the younger and energetic Oliver Joll. Tinling had married the beautiful and doomed Vi, eldest of the Barr sisters, 'ethereal and docile

. . . and frantic', now wasting away in bitter disappointment and mental distress—'one of [Gee's] most unsettling female characters', a reviewer accurately described her. Her drowning in the creek on the dark and stormy night that is the narrative centre—'I see it as a crossing', Sam writes—of the novel takes us back to Mrs Muskie and Mrs Marwick.[17] But this is a story about the men, not their wives.

The struggling painter is only daughter Charlotte (Charlie), summonsed home by Tinling to nurse her ailing mother after nine years away in London and Paris and St Ives. In the studio she is allowed to fashion from the toolshed at the back of the garage she keeps up her art: modernist paintings that Sam cannot like or understand. Charlie's career Gee based in part on that of Edith Collier, who likewise returned to New Zealand (in 1921) at the behest of her family, where the expectations of her as the unmarried daughter—as well as a hostile public reception—constrained her career, and whose father was so shocked by her female nudes that he burned them, as Tinling does Charlie's paintings, though out of muddier and more complex motivations than merely aesthetic affront.

In his devotion to truth and beauty and rectitude Sam Holloway is a man out of step with the mood of his time. '"Is there any need . . . any need . . . ?"', he asks when Charlie exhibits her nude studies, 'I meant for this sort of thing, in a world where knowledge was plain and beauty never more than a head's turn away, and truth somehow—wasn't it proven?—the product of those two and the sum of art; and what could a half-woman in a muddy pond contribute to this hallowed stepping forth?', referring to the painting his wife, Rose, has decided to buy. ('Don't gabble, Sam. Don't talk nonsense', Rose tells him.) Literature too should be clean and proper. '"You cannot," I cried, "you cannot use gutters in poetry"—and "smell of steak in passageways" and "yellow soles of feet"' (T.S. Eliot), in one of his normally friendly literary arguments with Eric, '"it's unlovely, and worst of all it's unmusical'", offending him just as the art of 'Charlie and her kind' does his 'strong sense of morphological rightness'. He will have no truck with 'the new men—Glover and his kind', who, he knows, would snort with derision if they knew about the detective novel.[18]

For this,

> I wanted a neat bullet hole and no more than a trickle of blood. It fitted with my notions of politeness if not with my understanding of death. There would be no pain of a physical kind, and as for mental

> anguish and dark ways where the beast might lurk, we would discover those as we went along and shine on them the healthy light of reason, I said. Let's keep it clean, a nice quick murder, or two, or three—there's no harm in multiplication. As for plot: a twist and a double twist incorporating that dark place if we light on it (laughter), but nothing Viennese, we'll keep away from sex, there's altogether too much of that sort of thing.
>
> My collaborators nodded and quaffed their ale . . .[19]

—so *The Scornful Moon* opens. The introduction of Owen Moody, upstart young poet and friend of Sam's motorcycle-riding nephew Taylor Barr, to the venture spells its demise. A mix of knowing deference and arrogance, Moody both intrigues and irritates Sam, but he turns out to be 'the goods', turning in a chapter written with 'sinew and blood' and bringing their faltering story alive. Defeated or offended, one by one the other contributors begin to fall away (Marcus Waller the librarian; Sam's 'dear friend' Roy Kember, 'sunk almost overnight into a slough of despond and feebleness . . . lost ambition, wasted chances'; pompous Euan Poynter in protest over the 'cult of violence' and 'proliferating of psychology'; young, ambitious and talentless Tom Gow).[20] There are nine chapters written when Sam shuts it away in his bottom drawer: 'the misconceived thing', which provides a teasing 'ironic shadow' of the real-life melodrama which engulfs Sam's family and his moral certainties.[21] Moody is the D'Arcy Cresswell character, instrumental in (though not the instigator of) the plot which brings down Oliver Joll, Tinling and the weaselly duplicitous ex-relief worker Len Ferrabee, and exposes the family secrets around sexuality and paternity towards which Gee has left a trail of quiet hints along the way. ('She's my daughter, can't you see?', says Eric of Charlie 160 pages before the truth of this is revealed; 'Nonsense too, I thought, to talk of James opening a dark room in his head and letting out some creature prisoned there', opines Sam.)[22]

Sam Holloway was 'a masterful creation', critic David Larsen wrote, commenting on Gee's audacity in choosing to tell his complex tale—'which, as presented, doesn't quite make sense'—via 'a narrator who doesn't know how to tell a story'. Gee found his voice easy to capture (compared to some other of his narrators: Meg, for example, and Noel Papps) and Sam 'a decent man . . . I like him'. His tone is both conversational and stuffy—'combining the short punchy sentences of the newsroom with the over-ambitious imagery and self-conscious wordplay of someone who's spent decades resenting the subeditor's blue pencil', in Larsen's words—and coy, as he sidles up to and circles around the things he would rather not know.[23]

In his research for the novel Gee read through the Turnbull Library's newspaper holdings for 1935 for historical detail and texture. The police breaking up a game of two up outside Joll's office on the waterfront he found there, for example, and the women heckling from the public gallery in parliament, and the oil spill in Oriental Bay which leaves a 'grey-brown halo'[24]—a found phrase—on a swimmer's head. He left in one historical error deliberately because it worked so well: the Harry Holland statue Sam and Eric walk past in the Bolton Street cemetery, 'gleaming white and showing too much buttock for my taste', was not in fact erected until 1937. By the end of his tale, however, Sam is less of a moralist than he was. 'I'm stupid to have held the belief that good writing, of whatever sort, rests on virtue', he reflects as he puts away Moody's chapter for, he hopes, the last time. Of character, he has also come to realise, 'I'm not competent to say. Not really competent for judging at all.'[25] (Also, in the election he votes Labour.)

It was a novel Gee intended to be entertaining '[i]n a Graham Greene sort of sense',[26] and while he may have got started 'half-heartedly', as he claimed, his enjoyment in writing it is palpable in the reading. He needn't have been concerned that, as he suggested to Ray Richards, the 1935 setting would mean it probably would not be popular. Published in October 2003 (he had had it finished in August 2002, but Penguin delayed it for the Christmas market), there was already a reprint in the shops in early December; in January it was at number one on the New Zealand fiction bestseller list. (Faber, meanwhile, took 3000, as they would of the next novel—the extent of their active involvement with the publication process now.) For all Sam's squeamishness and superiority, the reader can't help but like him too. A 'terrifically entertaining fiction of villainy and betrayal, wry social history and deft political analysis', novelist Emily Perkins described it in the *Guardian*; 'Pulp fiction, from Maurice Gee. Unforgettable', John McCrystal in *North and South*.[27]

The Scornful Moon missed out on the Deutz Medal at the 2004 Montana awards, coming runner-up to another historical novel (and one also concerned with the price of homosexuality), Annemarie

Jagose's *Slow Water* about missionary William Yate. It was a small disappointment in what was otherwise very much Gee's year. In October he received a Prime Minister's Award for Literary Achievement at a ceremony in parliament's Grand Hall, along with Anne Salmond and his old friend Kevin Ireland. Janet Frame had been the inaugural fiction winner when these awards, administered by Creative New Zealand, were first made in 2003, recognising 'significant achievement' in fiction, non-fiction and poetry with $60,000. 'This makes me feel that I made a good career choice', he began his acceptance speech.[28] For the one-and-a-half minute reading requested he chose the opening of *The Scornful Moon*, at the mischievous suggestion of Emily and Margareta, over a passage from *Plumb*. (Sam Holloway's detective story starts with the murder of the prime minister.)

This award followed his receipt of an Icon award the previous year from the privately endowed Arts Foundation of New Zealand. Gee was one of eight inaugural Icons, along with Frame and Hone Tuwhare, artists Ralph Hotere and Milan Mrkusich, potter Len Castle, architect Miles Warren and choreographer Russell Kerr, honoured at a function at the St James Theatre in June—for which he hired a suit, a rare occurrence. This award did not come with a cheque; just the slightly bemusing (to Gee) recognition as a 'cultural icon', along with a bronze and pounamu medallion and a silver and pounamu lapel pin.

His children's fiction received further accolades in these years, with *Under the Mountain* winning the Storylines Gaelyn Gordon award for an enduring children's classic in 2004, two years after he had been awarded Storylines' Margaret Mahy Medal (for which his award lecture was a new version of 'Creek and kitchen'). And in June 2004 he accepted an honorary doctorate from the University of Auckland, at a private ceremony in the English Department to which the university had reluctantly consented: he had agreed to receive the degree only on the condition that he did not have to have it conferred at the public graduation ceremony. 'Maybe it's about time you just started to accept a little of the hoo haa that goes along with being good at what you do', his son Nigel commented in a congratulatory email.[29] Still he was not accepting any state honours, despite these now being ostensibly New Zealand (not British) honours and the discontinuation in 2000 of titles: they still, he would point out, had to be formally approved by the Queen. He declined to have his name put forward for Principal Companion of the New Zealand Order of Merit (a knighthood as it had been) in the 2005 New Year honours round.

The year 2004 also saw the release of two feature films based on Gee novels. Larry Parr's *Fracture*, an adaptation of *Crime Story*, premiered in Wellington at the New Zealand International Film Festival's autumn mini-festival, the World Cinema Showcase, on 1 April, Gee seeing it for the fourth time and amidst 'a real buzz in the theatre, lots of goodwill etc. and even I got a good clap when I was (briefly) introduced'.[30] Part of the warmth and goodwill surrounded the mere fact that the film had made it to the screen. It had had a difficult history. The South Pacific Pictures project for which Gee had written a treatment in 1993 had been revived a year later, Gee reworking his treatment for a four- instead of an eight-part television series, before being shelved again, this time for good. Parr—already with *The Fat Man* signed up—optioned the novel in 1998 with plans to make a low-budget ($1 million) film which he would script himself. It would be his second stint at feature film directing (after *A Soldier's Tale* (1988), based on the M.K. Joseph novel). Four years, five drafts and intermittent grumblings of frustration from Ray Richards later, and funding of $2.6 million in place, the film was shot on location in Wellington over seven weeks in March–April 2002—the Gees having great fun visiting the set several times and cast as extras in one scene (as disgruntled investors attending Gordon Peet's court sentencing).

Six weeks later Kahukura Productions went into liquidation owing creditors half a million dollars, over half of it to the Film Unit (the former National Film Unit) owned by Peter Jackson, who had instigated the proceedings. In the industry Kahukura's financial troubles had been known for a few months. The New Zealand Film Commission, with $2.2 million invested in *Crime Story* (as it was then titled), had already, controversially, paid nearly $160,000 (and New Zealand on Air and TV3 smaller sums) to try to rescue the film, one of four in production that were under threat. It was the last to be released to the commission by the liquidators, in March 2003.[31] (While the film made it out safely, however, the business had severely shaken the industry and was the start of a long-running antagonism between Jackson (then working on the second part of his *Lord of the Rings* trilogy) and the Film Commission.)

Gee liked *Fracture*. It stayed close to the novel while shifting the 'moral weight' of the story, as he put it, onto Leanne. The script, he told the *Dominion Post*, he thought was 'skilful, balanced and intelligent', the film 'sharp, hard'.[32] Parr had initially intended to focus his film entirely on the story of Leanne and Brent, but it was 'very dark' and his final screenplay drew in most of the threads and characters of the novel (omitting Damon, and also Danny's rape of Leanne which had loomed large in the first version; though he also added a gruesome scene of Brent acting out his paranoia).[33] The film received some respectful, and some very positive, reviews; others less so. Russell Baillie in the *New Zealand Herald* described it as 'a mildly captivating saga . . . overburdened by its vast cast, labyrinthine plotting, and need to resolve the plights of all its characters'; 'you need to go into this movie with a flow chart and a family tree', said *Listener* critic Philip Matthews in a much harsher review which called it 'muddy and incoherent' (not at all sharp and hard), 'sluggish' and 'suspenseless . . . in one word—*boring*'.[34] Parr had been attracted to the novel by Gee's 'beautifully drawn characters', and the film was most admired for its strong performances and its evocation, both socially and geographically, of Wellington.

Fracture suffered from its entanglement in the Kahukura collapse. It had a limited release—three prints in three centres (Auckland, Wellington and Christchurch)—in September, and it did disappointingly at the box office. It also suffered from opening a few weeks before Brad McGann's far better received *In My Father's Den*, which had had its New Zealand première at the film festival proper in Auckland in July, after opening the Sydney Film Festival—a first for a New Zealand film—the month before. This film had followed a much smoother path. Producer Trevor Haysom took a three-year option on the novel in 1999, after enlisting the interest of writer-director Brad McGann whose award-winning short film *Possum* (1997) he had produced. They had a script ready in May 2002, a UK co-producer and finance in place by June 2003—for a $7.1 million production, double what Haysom had initially envisaged—and it was filmed in September–October.

Gee had approached *Fracture* with 'no trepidation whatsoever, just a great curiosity': once he had signed it over it was no business of his what a filmmaker made of his work.[35] That was easy to say. McGann had rejected the idea of adapting *In My Father's Den* when Haysom first approached him, wanting to do 'something contemporary and a little more edgy' for his first feature.[36] His screenplay updated the story to the present day and relocated it from west Auckland to Central Otago. His Paul Prior—Gee's English teacher—is a Pulitzer-nominated war photographer with a guilty secret, returning home for his father's funeral. Celia is revealed, finally, to be the daughter of his first girlfriend and not her husband (as in Gee's novel) but Paul's father: the discovery of the illicit affair between Jackie (the novel's Joyce) and Jeff Prior, we learn, had led his religious and manic-depressive mother to kill herself (witnessed by Paul) and Paul to leave. McGann also changed the 'whodunnit'. In his version Celia is not murdered by Paul's brother Andrew (here an ostrich farmer rather than a furniture manufacturer) but killed accidentally by spookily uptight wife Penny, the two of them then disposing of the body—a resolution Gee thought was 'a cop-out'.[37] Writing subsequently about the process of adapting the novel—and turning Gee's story into his own—McGann explained that he needed to find 'some damage, something psychological . . . of a significant magnitude', a past trauma, to make sense of Paul's emotional isolation which Gee had located in the crippling influence of his mother's puritanism.[38]

Gee responded positively and encouragingly to the first draft of the script McGann (a little nervously) sent him, which, despite the change in time and place, stayed 'very true' (in McGann's words) to the novel. When he read the revised version two years later he was less happy, though philosophical. Updating the story had 'uglified' it, which he recognised was inevitable (his 'rather quiet studious' Celia, for example, had become 'a rebellious teenager into booze and sex'). His concern, expressed to Richards, was whether the film should be presented as an adaptation of his novel at all when it had moved so far away from it: it was a very good script and he was keen to see the film made, but 'he has lost the book on the way. I can just make out the skeleton of it in his story.' Writing to Haysom, he congratulated McGann on a 'brilliantly written script' but admitted frankly that he had been 'resentful at first' at the 'huge changes'—'almost a reconceiving in fact'—and 'found the increase in ugliness disturbing'. But he accepted that he had made it 'a "now" story and I can't complain at the loss of my more sedate world'.[39]

In My Father's Den received superlative reviews (save for some reservations about a jarringly melodramatic denouement to what was a restrained, brooding, tone and theme rather than plot-oriented film), and won ten of the twelve categories at the 2005 New Zealand Screen Awards (the others, for original music and costume design, went to *Fracture*), along with a handful of awards overseas. A film tie-in edition of the novel—the first since the Oxford New Zealand Classics edition of 1984—was reprinted five times over the next eighteen months. (A new *Crime Story* was less successful.)

'[T]he first real pay day of my life', Gee remarked after Richards invoiced the Film Commission in September 2003 for $160,000 (his contracted fee of 2% of the film's budget plus GST).[40] It more than quadrupled his writing income for that year over the previous year's. *Fracture*, by contrast, paid out in 2001–02, had been a smaller deal, bringing him just under $30,000 gross, which was half what South Pacific Pictures had paid for their option and his treatment in 1993.

Film and television option payments had been making a more modest contribution to Gee's income, and raising tantalising hopes of much more, for many years. Through the 1990s and 2000s, along with *Crime Story* and *In My Father's Den* three other of his adult novels were at various times under option—*The Burning Boy*, *Live Bodies* and *Loving Ways* (*Loving Ways* coming closest of those to a film being made)—and six or seven more novels being looked at, including *Prowlers*, *Going West*, *Ellie and the Shadow Man* and (once more) *Plumb* (by Owen Hughes of Frame Up Films). The children's novels gave the most exciting prospects. *The Halfmen of O* had a steady option/proposal history going back to the early 1980s, in the immediate wake of the success of the television series of *Under the Mountain*. Before the novel was published Television New Zealand had Ken Catran writing a treatment for a six-part series, while Michael Scott-Smith and *The Losers* director Peter Muxlow within a month were developing plans for a television film. A feature film became a serious prospect for a while in 1986–87: a US/New Zealand co-production between Marie Hoy of Cori International (the LA producer behind the stillborn Erebus film) and Grant Bradley in Auckland, using a Catran script. In the 1990s a young Sydney producer held an option for a number of years, but struggled to find a writer and good enough script.

In 2002 the O trilogy was suddenly 'a hot prospect',[41] in part no doubt due to the success of Peter Jackson's *Lord of the Rings* and the associated development and reputation of local digital special effects craft (though Jackson himself declined to consider it). One of the several reservations Gee had had about Catran's script was that the Bloodcat had become a blood-dog (which 'I can't agree to . . .

Children will lynch us if we make it a dog'), he guessed because this would make things easier for the animal handler.[42] CGI (computer-generated imagery) took the film potential of O into another realm. Three proposals were being pitched in the early months of 2002, from South Pacific Pictures, Philippa Campbell (former TVNZ script editor-turned-producer) and Larry Parr. Richards was negotiating contract details with Parr—for two thirteen-part TV series—when Kahukura went into liquidation. A few years later *The Halfmen of O* was optioned by a starting-out Auckland producer, Steve Adams, and his LA-based partner Keshama Jane, calling themselves Shy Films: they wrote their own script, enlisted the enthusiastic interest of Richard Taylor at Weta Workshop and a third production partner; there was talk for a while of three films and Gee earning in the vicinity of $6 million. This all went nowhere—as, Gee well knew by now, film projects more often than not did.[43]

The Fat Man, meanwhile, and Gee's screenplay had been taken off Larry Parr in 2000, after five years and mounting impatience on Richards' and eventually even Gee's part. There had been a competing expression of interest too, from Tom Manning, a Wellington businessman looking to diversify into film production, and American actor-producer Michael Lerner (who had first made inquiries in 1996, anonymously through the usefully named law firm of Lewis, D'Amato, Brisbois and Bisgaard). Lerner, who had seen himself playing the title as well as a producing role, now dropped out after a year and another American producer, (then) New York-based Cielo Cerezo, was brought on board by Richards in 2002. It surprised Gee that she was keen to use his script. When that failed to attract production funding, however, she commissioned a new one from a local writer (her husband, Humphrey Gyde). Gee was not too bothered by this development, and the inevitable 'Americanisation' of the story he knew it would entail: he just wanted the film to be made. Some film prospects he felt more strongly about than others and *The Fat Man* was one. Still, when he read the final script he could not help feeling some disappointment that the story had been relocated to Louisiana. In other changes Gyde added new material filling in Herbert Muskie's gangster backstory (running bootleg liquor over the border from Canada during the prohibition), which Gee approved: 'I . . . like the way things are hardened up, the way an already black story is made even blacker and turned towards adult viewers.'[44]

By this point—2006—the film's projected budget was $US10 million (making it a small- to medium-sized one by American standards) and they were looking to cast a major international actor in the title role. Those approached and who turned it down included Russell Crowe (Gee's first choice), Eric Bana, Philip Seymour Hoffman (who was interested, Manning reported, until he was offered the *Capote* role), Keifer Sutherland and James Gandolfini. Five or six years later, though, the project had shrunk somewhat, with its projected budget now $4.5 million, filming to be in either New Zealand or North America and New Zealand director Toa Fraser signed on, and the fat man still to be cast.

Through all of this Gee left the complicated business of options and contract negotiations and the hustling and hassling—mostly—to Richards. To date the only other film project to have been realised is the 2009 feature film version of *Under the Mountain*, directed and co-written by Jonathan King. King had come in late to this project, which was one in which Gee had minimal involvement. Chris Bailey, who had directed the 1981 television series, had taken out an option to remake it as a film initially in 1996, and again in 2000 in partnership with Chris Hampson and writer Greg McGee, with whom he had formed production company ScreenWorks. The script they commissioned (from Matthew Grainger) had reached a second draft by late 2003—and was, Gee thought when Bailey sought his opinion, 'a bit flat'.[45] While the script struggled, the project stalled for three more years as ScreenWorks struggled with financial crises and a partnership change.

Bailey had up to this point intended to direct himself; the project was revived by his decision to hand over to King, who, like Grainger, was 'after all exactly the same age as I was when I first made the original series'. King would be good, Gee agreed: he had 'a dark imagination'.[46] His first feature, *Black Sheep* (2006) (another collaboration with Grainger), was a comedy horror about genetically modified mutant sheep running amok. The new *Under the Mountain* was shot in September–October 2008 on the North Shore and Mt Eden, with the original house (Uncle Clarry and Aunt Noeline's; here Uncle Cliff and Aunt Kay) on the shore of Lake Pupuke given a fleeting cameo. The creature make-up and special effects were done by Weta Workshop. It was a good-looking film, but nothing like the success of the original, in, it must be said, a very different media and cultural context, missing its market: too scary for younger children and not scary or complex enough for present-day teens; while the

DVD release of the original series in 2008 was probably of more interest to the original audience. It did indifferently at the box office (though rather well for Gee: his gross fee was just over $300,000).

This time, the significant change made to the story was one Gee requested himself, redressing a long-held regret: in the film *Under the Mountain*, cousin Ricky doesn't die.

32

Ghuznee Street

At the Auckland Writers' Festival in 2001 Gee had spoken about place: childhood places where primal connections are made, but 'must be made again, if you're to make use of them, not through passive memory but by acts of imagination'; mid-life places which, if you stay long enough, enter the imagination 'by a process like osmosis'. He described an organic, dynamic relationship between place and action and people: place had to be more than backdrop, landscape not just scenery.[1] Of Alan and David in *Loving Ways*, reviewer Louise Alley had written, '[t]heir minds are mapped like their routes; cartographic details determine or confuse further action. Identifiable locations are signposts to more than they appear to be.' The locations and landscapes of *Ellie and the Shadow Man*, Stead observed, 'figure so strongly that they are like a parallel set of characters', each 'is not just a physical place but the location of a particular range of feelings, only some of which are directly expressed or consciously entertained by the characters. In this as much as in anything, one feels the New Zealandness—New Zealanderness—of Gee's writing.'[2]

The places conspicuously absent from Gee's writing (albeit ones where he spent less time) are those where he was unhappy. London and Spain in 1961–62 and the overseas trips of 1982 and 1992 feature, at least in passing, in the lives of several of his characters: Paul Prior, Ellie Crowther, Jack and Harry Skeat (there is also a Cosy Caf in Mortimer's Cobham); Rex Petley too, though '[t]here's no documentation of his London year' (only a postcard sent from Madrid: Goya's 'The Execution of the Defenders').[3] But he never returned fictionally to Dunedin or Rotorua.

Gee's last two adult novels go back to his two most important places: 112a Ghuznee Street and Newington Road.

He had 'managed to start something new', he told Michael Estorick in February 2003, 'but it goes along sentence by sentence, unlike my palmy days when it was page by page. The mind's joints grow creaky.'[4] These days a morning's work was two hours, not four or five. (Indeed, Estorick, when he had seen Gee in Wellington while on a visit to New Zealand the previous month, had gained the impression that Gee 'might have (involuntarily) hung up your pen'.)[5] He had been wanting to make some more use of the research Margareta had done for the Cawthron Institute, which had given him *Prowlers* and Noel Papps. The narrator of this novel, 73-year-old Alice Ferry, is a retired mycologist, a specialist in fungi. 'Strange that so many mycologists are women', Papps had mused. 'Is it those curled-in heads, embryonic shapes, and growth in warmth and darkness, that attracts them? Someone should look into this.'[6] Alice Ferry is attracted to fungi because they grow 'in secret places, in the dark', and are parasites, living not by photosynthesis but 'by breaking down other living things, making them decay and feeding on the dead'.[7] Her secondary field is limnology, the study of inland water: lakes, creeks.

'My brother and I circle each other like binary stars', Alice writes (Pappsishly).[8] *Blindsight* also arose from Margareta's suggestion that she and Maurice attend the funeral of homeless man Robert Jones, popularly known as 'the bucket man', who had been a familiar sight on his regular route through Wellington city for several years until his death, by the side of the road in Thorndon, at the end of June 2003. She thought it might be interesting, she told a sceptical Gee. At the packed service at St Andrew's on the Terrace (several hundred people were there) Gee was struck particularly by the comment made by one of Jones's fellow homeless that it was wrong to assume that he had been unhappy or a failure, that instead he had chosen to live that way (refusing any form of welfare or state aid). It set him to imagining what might cause someone to do so. As he wrote, though, he became more and more interested in Alice and less in her damaged brother, Gordon.

A 'nice, tight, controlled, exact sort of book', Gee described it, and 'fairly bleak'.[9] The essence of the story is contained in the characteristically abrupt sentence with which it begins, and ends: 'Father taught us how not to love.' We do not have to wait until the end, however, to understand what this means—not an absence of but 'too much closeness, too much love'[10]—only where it leads. Father is Earl Ferry, the Loomis chemist, his shop opposite the railway yards 'between Hudson the Butcher and the billiard saloon': Gee gives Alice and Gordon a happy Orchard Street childhood, with a 'kitcheny mother' and 'a father who completed us, coming home from work', and a sense—Alice's at least—of the Ferrys as special ('our Ferry-ness', she calls it). Gordon, a sensitive child, 'stepped out into the world with such innocence and goodwill', and 'served himself by feeling good about serving other people'; Alice self-focused and with a strong sense of self-worth, confident in her 'gifts . . . Intelligence, energy, persistence, intuition.'[11] From the outset she is hard to like.

In Gordon Gee also revisits his own adolescent suffering (at secondary school he 'became disconnected from the practical. . . . I suppose it had to do with puberty, with things already fixed in him—gentility, notions of purity—uniting to divorce him from the new part of himself that made itself known. . . . All he has ever told me was that it took ten years to get himself right'), as well as his sportiness, including the dislocated elbow that ends his promising rugby career. Mary and Earl Ferry's marriage, too, is one more version of Gee's parents' own. She has a long, difficult menopause, when there 'were times . . . when husband, children, house and all possessions slid into a fog of unbeing', partly the effect of the phenobarbital her doctor prescribes. It is during this time that Earl succumbs, once (as Len apparently did not) to the advances of Josephine Imrie, wife of Loomis property developer Jock. Through Gordon's unobtrusive ministrations the marriage survives—'that afternoon was the making of him'—but altered, her trust 'damaged beyond repair', while 'Father no longer trusted himself . . . to be honest, manly, honourable': 'they stayed together. They were always kind. They tried to make each other happy. There's no way of measuring what they achieved.'[12] (Earl loses too his chance of a space in the new block of shops Jock Imrie is putting up on the Great North Road; his business fails.)

From an apprenticeship in her father's shop Alice goes on to a job with the DSIR, then two years' study in England, and joins the Harvey Institute in Nelson—where she has a flat in Nile Street where the Maitai runs at the bottom of the garden. Gordon goes teaching, at which he fails, moves to Wellington and works for Commercial Cleaners—'polishing linoleum floors in department stores, cleaning windows in Lambton Quay on mornings when southerlies carried sleet and hail, and the water in his bucket grew a film of ice and his cleaning rags, torn from old pyjama tops and underpants, wrapped themselves around his hands like eels from Loomis creek'—before getting a job as a hospital porter. (He tries to write poetry too.) He has just moved into the Ghuznee Street bach, early in 1959, when Alice makes the fateful intervention in his life on which the novel hinges. She has come to Wellington wanting Gordon to rescue her from the 'deep black hole' (in her doctor's diagnosis a 'nervous prostration') into which she has fallen in the wake of a failed love affair; instead she tries, misguidedly, to 'save' Gordon. Alice can recognise the 'seedy charm' of his Ghuznee Street place (though not refrain from tidying it) and that his lowly job as a hospital porter 'was where he really found himself'; but cannot approve of his relationship with fragile, 'unstable' Marlene Wilkinson (whom he met in the psychiatric ward) or his befriending and helping out down-and-outs like alcoholic Cyril Handy (introduced to him by a Baxter-like friend).[13]

Alice's retrospective examination of her life and Gordon's has been prompted by the arrival on her Wadestown doorstep one day of a young man claiming to be her great-nephew, the grandson of Gordon and Marlene. With the form of the novel Gee is back on his familiar and favourite ground. Adrian (barista, jazz student, double bass player) is searching for his grandfather. Alice 'want[s] to know how Gordon came to be and where he has travelled and where his memory has gone': to understand how he has become this person she passes on Molesworth Street, eyes cast down meeting nobody's as he makes his slow, deliberate way between a makeshift camp on the side of Tinakori hill and a boarding house in Te Aro, where he goes by the name of his murdered friend Cyril Handy. She comes to interpret it as a wilful stepping away: 'It was as if he had shifted half a second outside time . . . and that the fragment of time, Gordon's step aside, made an unbreakable wall between him and all that went on commonly: between him and me, Gordon and Alice.'[14]

But Alice Ferry is not an unreliable but a disingenuous narrator; she lies not only to Adrian (telling him at first that his grandfather is dead). She has known all along what happened that night in Ghuznee Street in 1959, the night '[h]e change[d] from Gordon then into Gordon now'. When she explains of herself and that night, 'the Willis Street corner and Gordon's face. Always, that is where I go. There are pits of forgetting on either side. Some protective force is responsible. I don't believe I dug them by myself'—that hers, in other words, has not been a wilful evasion—she is being false. She knows all along that Gordon knows too. ('*I know it was you, Alice. When are you going to say?*', reads the two-sentence letter he sent her, which she divulges in her 'confession' in the novel's final pages.)[15]

Alice Ferry, as David Larsen wrote, 'is neither likeable nor easy to keep up with. She tosses off troubling observations and dense metaphors as though she were telling you the obvious, which she very much is not.' Her narrative is condensed, frequently obscure, cryptic, not least in the hints she leaves towards what she will finally reveal: 'I was in Gordon's "place" only twice. There's another room for the second time. I won't go there'; 'I did that' (a quick, sly admission).[16] *Blindsight* contains murder, suicide and mental illness, but the real bleakness lies in the character of Alice Ferry.

For Gordon's hospital portering job Gee went back to the notes he had made in 1957 as well as memory. In recreating the bach he also had help from Nigel Cook, who did some sketches for him (as far as he could: he was shocked at how hazy his recall was and wary of the danger of inventing) in the course of a nostalgic exchange of memories. Gee had received an email out of the blue in late 2003 from Cook, whom he had not seen for many years and was now living on Waiheke Island: he was re-establishing contact with old friends, Cook said. 'I've been lazy in friendships', Gee confessed in reply, 'and let a lot of them go and so deservedly find myself pretty isolated now', a combination of inclination and neglect. He was in yearly contact with Carl Freeman (who was still in Geneva) and had regular phone talks with Ian Middleton (in an Auckland rest home), and spoke occasionally on the phone with Angela Sears (now in Martinborough). Three or four times a season he watched rugby on Sky Television (he and Margareta did not subscribe) with Ray Grover in his apartment in Oriental Bay—enjoying as much as ever the 'aesthetic experience' of the game. 'These are all people from the 50s', he remarked to Cook. 'Strange isn't it? The later friendships didn't seem to take in the same way. It sometimes seems that the only people I'm still easy with are the ones who call me Moss.'[17]

The 2005 Going West festival provided an opportunity to catch up with some other old friends from Ghuznee Street days, Alistair and Meg Campbell. This was the third time Gee had taken part in the festival (the second was in 2000), its tenth year and the last for Off the Rails, the steam train excursion, on which Meg and Alistair Campbell read their love poems at the Little Chapel of Faith at Waikumete cemetery, and Gee once again from *Going West* in the New Lynn community hall.

Maurice Shadbolt he had last seen in 2001 (en route to Auckland for Ray Richards' 80th birthday) when he visited him in the Taumarunui nursing home to which Shadbolt had moved after developing dementia in the late 1990s: Maurie didn't recognise him. 'It was sad and terrifying and made me feel fragile, lucky, in danger, barely hanging on—all that, centred on me, when I should have been more concerned with his tragedy', he wrote candidly to Carl Freeman; but also that 'I get quite choked up about it sometimes, even though Maurie and I had moved pretty far apart.'[18]

Family now was both bigger and smaller. There were grandchildren: Nigel's two sons Nicholas and Lewis, now in their teens, to whom Gee had dedicated *The Fat Man*. Nigel—now separated from their mother and living in Wānaka—had gone back to school after coming home from Europe when Len was dying in order to train as a helicopter pilot, and had been flying professionally for fifteen years, doing mainly fire and rescue flying, in Asia, Australia, Papua New Guinea and around Wānaka and Mount Cook, which made Gee both proud (of what he had achieved 'in spite of his mad squabbling parents')[19] and anxious.

At home it was just Maurice and Margareta. Abi was in Auckland after living for some time in Sydney and working in film animation, at which she had started out doing cel painting (pre-digital hand-colouring) in her first job out of school. Emily was the restless one. After a degree in geology and geophysics, working briefly for an Australian mineral company, travelling extensively overseas, then a postgraduate diploma at Massey University in visual impairment rehabilitation, she had moved at the end of 2003 to Blenheim to work on a vineyard and study viticulture and oenology. She was also writing—novels, but not like her father's: romantic fantasy novels and Regency romances. She had three completed manuscripts when she signed with an agent in 2004. Newly established UK imprint Solaris, specialising in fantasy and science fiction, would publish her debut *Thief with No Shadow* in 2007, followed by *The Laurentine Spy* (2009) and *The Sentinel Mage* (2010); she would also publish historical romances under the pseudonyms Emily May and Emily Larkin.[20]

'A writer's writer seems a fair description,' Gee wrote to Michael Estorick, who had used the phrase in a review of *Blindsight*, 'although I've wanted to be more than that. Popularity eluded me. I've scratched my head, wondering why. I mean my novels to be entertaining.

They entertain me.'[21] At the 2006 Montana awards two months later *Blindsight* made a clean sweep, winning the fiction category, the Deutz Medal and, most surprising and pleasingly for Gee, the readers' choice award (jointly with Fiona Kidman's *The Captive Wife*). 'My first feeling was one of bewilderment', he told the press the following day. 'I thought I was there to make up the numbers and drink some wine.'[22] The fiction category adviser had described is as 'a small but perfectly formed masterpiece'; judges' convenor, and long-time Gee scholar, Lawrence Jones praised its 'moral and psychological complexity', and its ending (Alice's 'confession' at the bedside of the dying and insensible Gordon) as 'a narrative *tour de force*'. Afterwards Gee and Margareta had 'broke[n] one of our golden rules' and back in their hotel room opened one of the bottles of whisky from the mini-bar.[23]

His success was overshadowed, however, by some sadness. Many people, he expected, had been hoping that Nigel Cox would win the fiction award (for *Responsibility*, his fifth novel, which followed the brilliantly conceived (and later controversial) *Tarzan Presley* (2004)); 'even I was hoping it', he told Ray Richards.[24] Cox, terminally ill with cancer, received a standing ovation after his runner-up speech; he died four days later.

There was a feeling in some quarters too that this was the year for poetry to take the Deutz Medal. *Blindsight* won over Bill Manhire's *Lifted* only by 'a slight edge' on the 'community impact' criterion.[25] In part, no doubt, the popular response to *Blindsight* drew on a sentimental interest in the figure of Robert Jones, a representation of whom appeared on the novel's cover. In the paper's four years, *Dominion Post* editor Tim Pankhurst told Gee, no local story had attracted as much interest as the bucket man's. In the wake of the Montanas Penguin ordered a third reprint, and another in November, with sales to that date at '14,441 with no sign of flagging'.[26]

When he finished and sent away *Blindsight* Gee had had no idea what he was going to do next. 'My mind is completely blank', he said to a journalist after the prime minister's awards a month later. It was not a good feeling; 'I'm a bit afraid of drying up.'[27] During that next year he wrote, and abandoned, a children's novel. '[I] seem to have come to an end, which I'm doing my best to regard as natural', he told Nigel Cook after he had posted him a copy of *Blindsight*, in October 2005: it's 'maybe my last. The first one was started in the bach in Ghuznee St—that's quite a neat circle to draw.' After a year of writing nothing, and feeling 'no confidence that I'll write again', he picked up the discarded children's novel again in the early months of 2006, and sent a completed manuscript off to Richards in September, a month before he and Margareta packed up their house and moved to Nelson.[28]

It had been their plan for several years to move back to Nelson after Margareta retired from the Turnbull. Their house sold at the end of September and they went in the third week of October, not without some ambivalence still. Margareta was going to open homes in Wadestown and Khandallah up to the weekend before they left; they had never stopped 'quietly longing for the harbour view that lack of money keeps out of our reach'.[29] And there were other things they knew they would miss about Wellington. Music—which Margareta had brought into Maurice's life—was one: they had been regularly to orchestra and, especially, chamber music concerts, to lunchtime recitals at St Andrews on the Terrace and Old St Paul's, jazz concerts at the university music school. They had gone regularly to the theatre too, and the dealer galleries, buying work when they could afford to.

Like the last time they waited until they got there to look for a house to buy, and found something relatively quickly, on the flat this time, in Nile Street just a few blocks up from the cathedral and the centre of town. Within a few weeks they decided they had made a dreadful mistake and would sell it and start again. But they stayed, and came to enjoy Nelson again, while continuing to miss Wellington. Intermittently over the next eight years they decided they would put the house on the market. They had not known when they bought it about the major construction project about to get underway on the corner opposite; nor that Nile Street would become a popular street for 'boy racers'. It was a small house, as well, necessitating an arduous culling of books.

Nelson is a popular place to retire to. But writers—this one at least—don't retire. 'Without my writing I would probably just curl up and die', he had told a journalist ten years before. By the new year, with reading, gardening, walking by the river, feeding ducks and eels, he was feeling that 'I was just frittering away my time not doing anything'.[30] By May he was nearing the end of the first draft of another children's book, a sequel to the one he had sent away the previous September, *Salt*, a dystopian fantasy which Penguin brought out in June.

Salt was Gee's first foray into fantasy since the O trilogy, and he reported on its progress to Ray Richards with more than his usual doubts and disclaimers: 'I've probably gone over the top a bit and that, combined with laziness creeping into my writing habits, might mean this one doesn't make the grade'; 'I'm not being modest, just realistic, when I say that it doesn't seem as good as my previous children's books', he wrote when he sent off the manuscript. Also, 'it's fairly dark and cruel and won't make me any friends but that's the way it goes'.[31]

In the O trilogy an old mine shaft was the portal between Susan and Nick's, and their readers', world and the imagined world of O. *Salt* takes place within an entirely self-contained invented world. Familiarly, though, the story takes two teen protagonists (not cousins, however, this time) on a perilous mission to save the world from evil and destruction—a journey across the 'dry lands', through forests and over mountain passes. That world is a grim dystopian vision of industrial capitalism; the allusion is not subtly drawn. In the ruined city of Belong the people of the burrows live a brutal, survival existence. Long ago, Company came to Belong and over the years, with nobody understanding how or even that it was happening, the Belongers had become slaves, the men sent to work for Company—in Ship, Coal, Farm, Factory, Granary and Salt—with the promise of happy retirement in a Golden Village afterwards. Company rules from its citadel called Cebeedee; the Company Families live in mansions in the walled Compound on the hill.

Our two heroes come from the opposite poles of this world. Hari of Blood Burrow, schooled by ancient Lo, the sole survivor of a failed rebellion against Company, is unusually adept at making his way through the swamps and alleyways, the rubble and rotting foundations of the ruined city. He also possesses a telepathic ability to communicate with animals. When his father, Tarl, is sent to Deep Salt, Hari sets out with his dog companion to rescue him: no one comes back from Deep Salt, the furthest reaches of the deepest tunnels of the mine; rumours abound about what is down there. Pearl is a daughter of one of the Families and is fleeing the city, with her maid Tealeaf, to escape an arranged marriage to Ottmar, head of the house of Salt. Pearl too has nascent telepathic powers, as her maid had at once recognised: Tealeaf is one of the Dwellers, a three-fingered, cats'-eyed, peaceable people who live beyond the mountains north of Belong. The Dwellers are 'speakers', endowed with a mind-power that enables them to not only enter into the minds of and silently speak with others, but also control them. On their journey Pearl and Hari come into and master their own.

Rescuing Tarl is only their first task. From the Dwellers, when they reach Tealeaf's seaside village of Stone Creek, they learn more about Deep Salt, about the poisonous substance buried deep within a barren grey hill which sickens and kills the men sent to bring it out: 'turns their skin white. Their skin will tear like paper. It makes them bleed, with blood like water—so thin, once it starts it never stops. Their bones burst through their skin and break like rotten branches on a tree.' The nuclear reference is more explicitly and fully developed here than it was in *Motherstone*. From Tarl they learn of Ottmar's plans. Since they left the city, Company has fallen and civil war and chaos rage, and Ottmar has declared himself king. In his quest for absolute power he is using the lethal, luminous green salt to make a weapon that 'burns men into dust'.[32] Pearl and Hari's task is to steal it back, return it to the dead hill and seal it up forever.

The character dynamic between Pearl and Hari is also familiar, and a traditionally gendered one: between impulsive, headstrong Hari and pacifically minded Pearl, like that between Rachel and Theo, Susan and Nick; as is the broader theme of peaceful versus violent means of confronting evil. (It is an internal conflict too: Hari's 'conflicting dreams, of peace and slaughter', confuse him.)[33] But this story is also a love story. Over the course of their quest Pearl and Hari's relationship develops beyond initial, typically teenage wariness to trust, affection and, eventually, consummation (narrated so briefly, however, as to feel coy).

The novel ends happily, with Hari and Pearl—who is pregnant—leaving Stone Creek to make a home for themselves and a family by the shore of the Inland Sea. But *Salt* is a serious, harsh story, as Gee warned; there is no Jimmy Jaspers to lighten the tone.

In the next one—which came out in June 2008, the same month *Salt* won the young adult section of the children's book awards—it is sixteen years on and Hari and Pearl and their children, Xantee, Lo and twins Blossom and Hubert, are living in a peaceful arcadia 'in a timber house above a white-sand beach, with fields and gardens running back to the forest and a village growing beside them'; other children, orphaned or displaced, have been brought into their care by the Dwellers. But the world beyond the Inland Sea is once again in turmoil, and there are 'rumours of a creeping darkness in the jungle':

some 'creature from outside nature' which is feeding on the world, 'suck[ing] it dry of all its life'. It was the forest-dwelling, and never seen, 'people with no name' who first discovered this thing, and called it gool, meaning 'unbelonger': tiny jellyfish-like creatures 'no bigger than slugs, oozing from damp crevices low on seamed hillsides, or surfacing in the red water of swamps', hiding 'in the roots of drowned trees', and now growing bigger and stronger—and rather reminiscent of the slug-like Wilberforces of *Under the Mountain*.[34] In the novel's opening scene, Hari is nearly taken by one and a cold, grey, foul-smelling residue is left on his skin, a fragment of gool, circling his neck and slowly killing him.

Meanwhile, back in the city of Belong new despots have arisen: Keech of Keech Burrow (first met in *Salt*) and Clerk of Cebeedee feud and scheme—their 'hatred drifting back and forth like a mist'—and there is 'no peace, always rebellion—and murder and starvation and slavery'. Hari's despondent vision at the end of *Salt*—'someone else would rule, but everything would stay the same'—has proven true.[35]

The narrative is more intense and fast-paced still than *Salt*, as Lo and Xantee and their friend Duro set forth to save Hari and destroy the gool. There is much trekking: they cross two mountain passes and walk through three jungles—guided by the people with no name—to find Tarl (now Tarl the Dog King: since *Salt* he has gone feral and is barely recognisable anymore as human, except by his eyes). Tarl can lead them to what remains of the ancient library of Belong, where they hope to discover the meaning of an old Dweller legend that will tell them where to find and how to defeat the mother gool.

'It's pretty far-fetched', Gee described *Gool* when he was nearing the end of the first draft, 'and I'm going to have to write something real when it's finished'; 'some parts call for a very large suspension of disbelief'.[36] The mother gool lives in the basement of the ruined Ottmar mansion, feeding on the greed and malice and cruelty of Clerk and Keech from which it was born, and emanating hatred in turn: an undulating, translucent, sticky gourd-shaped blob with multiple eyes that 'floated inside her, white cloudy discs, deep one moment, shallow the next'. Unlike her children she has no smell, 'but thickened every indrawn breath so that it slid into the lungs like an eel'; the sound she made 'was a sound no one was meant to hear, from a darkness no one was meant to see'.[37] In the novel's climax, Xantee's attempt to reason with Clerk and Keech—like Susan with the High Priest of Ferris—and persuade them to renounce the gool is a spectacular failure, and in the ensuing bloodbath Tarl along with Keech and Clerk are killed. It proves impossible, however, to physically kill the gool. Pity—Xantee's for this creature which has no feelings other than hatred and greed—is what finally succeeds.

Gee had no more intention of writing a third episode in the story of Belong than he had had at the outset of writing a sequel. The ending of *Gool* feels conclusive. Hari lives; Lo, wounded early on and cared for by the people with no name, stays with them; Xantee and Duro—this novel's romantic story—are married. 'The seasons went on. There were children. There was much happiness. No new gool has found its way into their world.'[38] *The Limping Man* (2010) came about after Text Publishing in Australia made an offer for *Salt* and *Gool* conditional on him writing a third: trilogies, according to publisher wisdom, fare better in the young adult/fantasy market than duets.

There is little variation on the pattern and theme. It is another sixteen years on and the world once again needs saving from a short man with a lust for absolute power. Like the High Priest of Ferris, Clerk and Keech (a short, thick-chested, bandy-legged man with 'a blind milky eye and a lopsided face': it is tempting to think Gee had in mind Robert Muldoon), beneath his ceremonial robes the Limping Man is disappointingly ordinary, a 'round-faced little man with soft cheeks and weak eyes', 'watery and red-rimmed and pale'.[39] But he rules by a mysterious combination of awe and mental compulsion, casting a kind of psychic force-field which causes everyone who comes within it to worship him slavishly, even speakers. The small band who, separately and together, set forth to discover the source of this power and destroy him are thirteen-year-old Hana of Bawdhouse Burrow, whose special gift is an ability to communicate telepathically with birds (her companion Hawk plays a decisive role in the story's resolution), and one-handed Ben, the son of Lo; Lo himself (because he too limps); and the twins Hubert and Blossom, whose mental power is second only to the Limping Man's.

Over the course of the *Salt* trilogy the stories become simpler and darker. *The Limping Man* opens with Hana fleeing Belong after her mother commits suicide by swallowing the poisonous frogweed to escape being burned as a witch. They are not really witches, her mother has told her, the women the Limping Man ritually burns alive in People's Square (while their husbands are drowned), only women who seek lost knowledge, 'to learn all the things that have been forgotten'. When he has dealt with them he plans to exterminate everyone else who poses a threat: the Dwellers and other speakers. His bounty hunters—who kill 'everything they find. They call it cleansing. Everyone different from them'—cut off the thumbs of their victims to take back to him.[40]

The Limping Man, we learn, was once a swamp boy named Vosper who was crippled in a beating by his father, whom he later drowns. He keeps his mother, Queenie, half-mad and half-starved, imprisoned on an island in the middle of the swamp (she is an extreme version of Mrs Marwick and Mrs Muskie), and has her killed before she can reveal his secret. In a particularly ghoulish scene, after he has failed in his attempt to kill Vosper, Ben escapes capture by concealing himself beneath her floating dead body—'Blood had drawn eels like perfume. They twisted round the body, wrapping Queenie in their arms'[41]—and swimming unseen across the swamp.

That secret, it is finally revealed, is the toads Vosper keeps as pets and on which he feeds, drawing from them his hatred and greed: on his shoulders, concealed beneath his scarlet robes and headdress, a large toad squats (somewhat outlandishly) with its mouth fixed to his neck. He derives his power from the swamp in which he was raised. (Freed from his power when Hawk swoops down and detaches the toad, the people turn on and drown him.)

Salt and its sequels express a bleak vision similar to the O trilogy's, of a cyclical rise and fall of tyranny and evil, articulated in *The Limping Man* by the Dweller Danatok: 'The humans in the city went on much as before', he recounts to Hana, '—fought and starved, made little armies, murderous gangs, in the place known as Cebeedee and in the burrows, and some grew rich for a while, then they starved while others prospered. "Nothing changed"'.[42] But there is a counterpoint here—a softer note—in the conception of a semi-spiritual oneness with nature—an extension of the ecological concern of *The Halfmen of O*—represented by the people with no name, and by the simple rural life at Stone Creek and the village by the Inland Sea. The gifted speakers, first Hari and Pearl, experience it as a harmony they distantly hear in the forest, a 'pitch of sound' made by these invisible people, keeping them safe; then as a silent 'great voice . . . saying their names, joining them to the spirit animating the world. Xantee had heard it'—'the wind and sea and forests and mountains breathe her name silently inside her diminished self one morning . . . just Xantee, yet those two syllables united her with the thing that spoke—took everything from her, gave everything back, increased in all its cells by its oneness with the voice'—'Blossom and Hubert too', and Hana. 'She seemed to hear a whisper, an edge of sound. Taste it too. It tasted like honey.'[43] There is a mellowness of vision here that we are not used to. Perhaps it was to do with age.

33

Newington Road

The 'something real' Gee was anticipating when he was writing *Gool* became *Access Road*, his 'end of the road novel', as he called it in the dedication. Only a writer of such 'perverse semantic wit' as Gee, Roger Robinson observed, would give such a title, suggestive of opening, to a novel he intended to be his last.[1] He started it within two months of finishing *Gool* and had it completed within a year. Its working title was 'Loomis Novel'. *Access Road* weaves the events and textures of Gee's childhood, one more time, into a story of murder, guilt and fear—a creeky story, a Newington Road story.

He had not thought he had another novel in him; didn't think he had the stamina anymore, and *Access Road* is a short one. Its genesis was a visit he and Margareta made out to Henderson when he was in Auckland for Going West in September 2005. As Abi drove them along Newington Road he saw an old man in his dressing gown sitting on the front steps of number 52: it was Gordon Greenough, who had lived in the house since his parents bought it when the Gees moved to Tirimoana Road. He would not invite Gee inside but was happy for him to look around the section. The dunny was still there, dilapidated and long disused; the remains of a greenhouse were submerged by creeper; the lean-to at the back of the house was half-collapsed. It was a shock to see the house painted turquoise green. It had always been white: 'The Beach house is white, eternally.'[2]

How easily memory takes hold, and 'I become retrogressive, deeply retrogressive . . . A muddy street, a clay bank, a little weatherboard house with a leadlight window in the front wall. The evening sun strikes through a rose with blood-red petals and pea-green leaves and makes opposing handprints on my bedroom door.'[3] The narrator is 78-year-old Rowan Pinker, once Rowan Beach, sister of Lionel and Roly. She lives now with her husband Dickie in a two-storey house a street back from the beach in Takapuna: the novel opens, comically, with a retelling of Len's (and Phil Dockery's) drunken fall through the stair landing window into the cactus garden below. *Access Road* is in part a homage to Gee's parents and their marriage. Rowan and Dickie first met at a dance at the Loomis RSA hall when she was nineteen; she is attracted by both his 'simplicity' and his 'glamour'. He is a star rugby player until an injury ends his career, and 'Dickie was over, the Dickie I knew. He never came back, the footballer or the rowdy, gentle boy.' After a troubled, often distant marriage—the 'wasteland of our middle years'—they are back together, in the novel's present time, in care and tenderness and tolerance—a moving portrait of late-marriage: 'It's love of a sort, our invention, behind which no anxiety lurks . . . putting-up-with, at my time of life, is only a nudge away from love'.[4]

There is Len and Lyndahl in the Beach parents too: Fred, a bootmaker, a kind, moderate, chivalrous man ('what is known these days as a softie'), and Isobel, who came from a 'good Christchurch family' and was 'pure in thought and deed, and . . . superior', which, to her children, 'was a plain state although mysterious'. They met on the beach when Isobel was staying in Auckland with an aunt after rejecting a Christchurch suitor. The attraction was sensual (he was 'quietly showing off his muscles and his tan'); 'She took his difference from her as an opportunity for adventure'. Lionel was born several months too soon.[5]

Rowan Pinker is also a would-be writer—Gee quotes in full as hers Lyndahl's *Woman To-day* story 'Mother's Holiday'—and another self-aware narrator, her narrative punctuated with hesitations and questioning and self-conscious regard, enriched by 'the sense of writing as creation'[6] as well as a self-reflective mind. We have been here before. But the relationship between author, narrator and reader, and between the narrative past and present is more straightforward in this novel. There is no deception, intentional or otherwise; though there is mystery.

In the old house in Access Road the two brothers live, 'silent, gruff and dirty'. Roly, recently moved back in, has reclaimed the garden from jungly ruin and supplements his pension selling his produce at the Loomis Saturday market. Inside, Lionel 'rules by negative influence', surrounded by squalor: the place is 'creased and clogged, it's hairy with dust', 'archaeological'; the kitchen and living room 'little better than corridors through junk'. (In reimagining the house Gee was not only relying on his memory. Photographs of the interior he saw when he was writing *Access Road* showed it little changed from when the Gees had lived there; the state of neglect and decay he described was not an exaggeration.) He had bought the house twenty years back (the Beach family had sold it and moved to Te Atatū Road in 1948), 'moved in and scarcely came into the open air again'. In his bedroom, which he seldom leaves, there is a smell 'of things that don't have smell: eyes that don't see, skin that doesn't feel. The smell, too, of a mind closed in on itself'. How had Lionel come to be like this?, Rowan asks Roly.[7]

There are two mysteries here. There is a crime novel plot involving rape and murder (and a body disposed of in the creek), and Clyde Buckley, the creepy, sadistic boy who cut the heads off baby birds, and held, and still holds, a strange power over Lionel. And there is something deeper. As a boy Lionel ran wild; 'He was bold and mysterious and he *knew*'. He made the territory of Access Road—creek, culvert, orchard—his own, and 'came in from his outside world bursting with self . . . [t]here was a glow on him, a glow *in* him'. Until an afternoon when '[t]he sky was full of black clouds and dark was coming early' and he came in sobbing, terrified by something 'dark down there' which he cannot name or describe. ('Was it Clyde?', Roly had asked.)

> Something stirred in the trees that night, something floated up from deep in the water. A cold hand touched him on the neck.
>
> I'll have no truck with animism or forest gods but will go along with imagination peopling the dark. Lionel took a step too far. Perhaps with the aid of a movement or a sound, and with a movement of his head, the opening of a door that might have led him nowhere at another time, he created a presence—that's my amateur view. If we had been churchy, he might have glimpsed Satan.

He was nine years old. After that day he began suffering from night terrors (as Gee had himself).[8]

This is Gee's creek: dark and light; danger and threat as well as excitement, mystery and adventure; sex and death.

Access Road can be seen as a companion novel to *The Fat Man*. Clyde Buckley, reappearing in Loomis and the Beach lives with unfinished business, is Herbert Muskie, and similarly sinister. A boy from the other side of the creek—his father a linesman, his mother 'a hump-shouldered woman with ankles always bandaged because of a skin disease'—he had latched on to Lionel—an out-of-school friend—and not let him go. A 'large-bodied boy, thick rather than fat', he 'was short in his limbs, as though they had stopped growing while his body kept on, but large in his face, where his skin was at the full stretch of its elasticity'; 'His eyes shone as though coated with oil, but seemed not to see, unless it was something going on in his head.' 'He's like a swamp', Rowan thinks later. (Swamp, swampy; the word recurs.) Of the adult she writes, his body and features do not hold together. 'Clyde Buckley was never finished. Some infection got in and stopped the bonding of his parts and stopped his bonding with the rest of us.' And there are his eyes: 'Small, blue, bright, amused and human. That is a terrible thing about Clyde Buckley.'[9]

Buckley does not only recall Herbert Muskie. He is based on—is a slightly grotesque fictional version of—a boy from Gee's own Access Road, a Newington Road neighbour who had 'a kind of thick aggressiveness in his behaviour', was 'wheedling' and needy and 'indefinably creepy'. Even 70 years later '[a] shadow falls on my childhood' at the memory of him; he 'spoiled things for us—or perhaps just for me'.[10]

Roly had left school and Loomis at fifteen to get as far from him as he could. Lionel became a dentist: 'clean and arid, a germ-free life', Rowan observes.[11]

The language of *Access Road* is typically spare, at once precise and allusive. In his review of *Blindsight*, and again of *Access Road*, Roger Robinson described the 'characteristic Gee texture of cadenced, metaphoric, musically structured prose'; 'Its movement always matters'. It is writing which gains resonance, he argued, from recognition, through the familiarity of images and metaphors, place and story. '[T]he poetry of memory', he described it.[12]

The novel's climactic scene is a piece of very Gee-ish black humour (intended to be more comedic than black): three septuagenarians, Rowan, Dickie and Clyde (who has just smothered Lionel in his bed, the novel's third murder), grappling on the living-room floor. It ends with a subdued coda: Rowan and Dickie walk hand in hand on Takapuna beach. 'It's too cold for bare feet. Thin waves edge up the sand and melt away. I hunt for rhymes. Wave, cave. Sky, belie. Find, end. That's a half-rhyme. At my age I think I'm allowed.'[13]

It was an 'end of the road' novel in another way too. Faber declined to publish *Access Road*.

In 2012 Maurice and Margareta decided to sell their house and move into a retirement village, a pre-emptive move against age and debility. They thought about going to Auckland, which would take them close to family—Abi and her partner and their two children (grandchildren three and four), Aynsley and Margaret, and Gary and Ngaire at Waiwera—or Wellington. They investigated Auckland options in May when they were up there for the Auckland Writers and Readers Festival, where Gee had agreed to do a session as the inaugural Honoured New Zealand Writer: he gave his favourite reading, from *Prowlers*, and took questions from Geoff Walker, to a full auditorium and a standing ovation. This was emphatically, he said, the last such public appearance he would make.

Instead they stayed in Nelson, buying a self-contained villa in the Stillwater Gardens Retirement Village at Richmond, moving in at the end of October. Within a very short time they realised they had made a dreadful mistake, again: they hated it. It was their luck that the couple who had bought their Nile Street house were nervous about having overcommitted themselves and that they were able to buy it back. They moved home again, somewhat poorer, enormously relieved and not a little embarrassed, three months later. They intended to never move again.

It was more than 40 years since Margareta had bounded up the stairs and into his office at the Turnbull Library in 1966 and introduced herself. That was a meeting which changed his life. It was a time when he was, he would later say, 'sliding and going under. I had no belief in myself or what I was doing'; Margareta 'saved' him, and their relationship he would come to see as the firm foundation of his writing life.[14]

Of course, with *Access Road* Gee had not in fact stopped writing. He wrote three chapters of another novel, before abandoning it when 'it just died on me'.[15] There was a memoir about his parents (entitled 'Double Unit' after his mother's story), written for the family. And there was a memoir of his childhood—'Blind Road'—not for publication but to keep his mind active, and because he could not stop going back there, to Henderson, to Newington Road, to the creek.

Notes and References

Abbreviations

ATL: Alexander Turnbull Library
MG: Maurice Gee

A Life in Writing; A Writing Life

1 *Sole Survivor*, London: Faber and Faber in association with Penguin, 1983, p.197.
2 P. Rolfe, 'Kiwi characters come to life', *Bulletin*, 18 Feb. 1997, p.72.
3 C.K. Stead, 'Maurice Gee, moralist', *Landfall*, 202, Nov. 2001, p.101; I. Gordon, *New Zealand Herald*, 30 July 1994, section 3, p.7.
4 Patrick White to Ben Huebsch, 17 Feb. 1963, in D. Marr (ed.), *Patrick White: letters*, Sydney: Random House, 1994, p.219.
5 M. Hewitson, 'The man in the grey cardy', *Weekend Herald*, 29 July 2006.
6 *Going West*, Auckland: Viking, 1992, p.241; *Meg*, London: Faber and Faber in association with Penguin, 1981, p.28.

1. Beginnings

1 Talk for PEN, Dunedin, 20 Nov. 1984, MS-Papers-8732-140, ATL; *Going West*, Auckland: Penguin, 1992, p.245.
2 *Bay of Plenty Times*, 22 May 1926.
3 *Auckland Star*, 14 July 1924, p.9; *New Zealand Herald*, 15 July 1924, p.9.
4 *New Zealand Herald*, 27 July 1927, p.16; *Auckland Star*, 14 July 1925, p.13.
5 *Daily Telegraph* (Napier), 27 Aug. 1926, p.3.
6 *New Zealand Herald*, 25 July 1928, p.16; *Auckland Star*, 25 July 1928, p.15.
7 Lyndahl Gee to Joanne [Hollis], 12 Feb. 1973, MS-Papers-4678-029, ATL; manuscript fragments, 1972–73, in the possession of MG.
8 Lyndahl Gee to Joanne [Hollis], 12 Feb. 1973.
9 *War Cry*, 13 Sept. 1890, p.2.
10 Florence Chapple reminiscences, 4678-024.
11 *Timaru Herald*, 14 Sept. 1910, p.2; James Chapple to Rev. William Jellie, 14 Sept. 1910, 4678-030.
12 Lyndahl Gee, 'The Change', 1954–55, in the possession of MG.
13 Lyndahl Gee, memories, 1975, in the possession of Gary Gee; Lyndahl Gee to MG, n.d., 4678-040.
14 *San Francisco Chronicle*, 18 July 1915.

15 Lyndahl Gee, 'The Change'.
16 Unsourced clipping, 27 Nov. 1916, Chapple family scrapbook, fMS-Papers-4678-01.
17 *Lyttelton Times*, 11 May 1918, p.9; 18 May 1918, p.10. The offending lectures were entitled 'Julius Caesar or Jesus Christ' (at which particular offence was taken at his comment that he told his children not to sing the National Anthem at school) and 'The glorious Bolsheviks of Russia'.
18 Lyndahl Chapple to Joanne [Hollis], 12 Feb. 1973; manuscript fragments.
19 Lyndahl Gee, 'My narrow escape from a Reverend', in the possession of MG; MG, 'Creek and kitchen', in M. Gifkins (ed.), *Through the Looking Glass*, Auckland: Century Hutchinson, 1988, p.86.
20 Lyndahl Gee, 'Those dunners', 5 Feb. 1973, in the possession of MG.
21 Aynsley Gee, interview with the author, 15 May 2008.

2. Creek and Kitchen

1 J.T. Diamond, *Once . . . the Wilderness*, 2nd edn, New Lynn: V.H. Wilkinson, 1966, pp.9–10.
2 Sale notice, quoted in ibid., pp.43–4.
3 Quoted in ibid., p.47.
4 The number came later; there were no street numbers in Newington Road when the Gees lived there.
5 *Crime Story*, Auckland: Penguin, 1994, p.40.
6 MG, 'Creek and kitchen', in M. Gifkins (ed.), *Through the Looking Glass*, Auckland: Century Hutchinson, 1988, p.82.
7 MG, 'Blind Road', unpublished memoir, p.8.
8 MG, 'A letter to my family', funeral eulogy, in the possession of MG.
9 MG, 'Place', New Zealand Book Council talk, 28 March 1995, MS-Papers-8732-140, ATL; 'The way of a writer', *New Zealand Listener*, 17 Jan. 1987, p.40.
10 *In My Father's Den*, London: Faber and Faber, 1972, p.22.
11 Land Sales Court file, Auckland Registry, BBAE 5632, 125af, 1944/6579, Archives New Zealand, Auckland Regional Office.
12 James Chapple to Rev. William Jellie, 12 July 1929, MS-Papers-4678-030, ATL.
13 Florence Chapple, 'Memories 1954', p.62 verso (21 March 1955), MSX-3603, ATL.
14 *Plumb*, London: Faber and Faber, 1978, p.212.
15 A.G. Flude, *Henderson's Mill: a history of Henderson 1849–1939*, Auckland: Henderson Borough Council, 1977, p.51; D. Scott, *Fire on the Clay*, Auckland: Southern Cross Books, 1979, p.175.
16 MG, eulogy for Len Gee, 7 Oct. 1986, 4678-298.
17 *Access Road*, Auckland: Penguin, 2009, p.41.
18 Ibid, p.44.
19 *The Champion*, Auckland: Puffin, 1989, p.33.
20 Advertisement reproduced in Flude, p.130.
21 MG, 'Beginnings', *Islands*, 17, March 1977, p.288.
22 MG, email to the author, 15 Feb. 2008.
23 Advertisement reproduced in Flude, p.112; Flude, p.82.

24 Lyndahl Gee, '(A few) potato peelings', p.16, in the possession of MG.
25 Aynsley Gee, interview with the author, 15 May 2008.
26 MG, eulogy for Len Gee.
27 'Double Unit: the lives of Lyndahl and Len Gee', unpublished memoir, p.64.
28 MG, 'Beginnings', p.286; eulogy for Len Gee.
29 '(A few) potato peelings'.
30 Dora Hagemeyer to Lyndahl Gee (typescript copy), n.d., 4678-029.
31 Florence Chapple, diary, 23 April 1956, MSX-3604.
32 'Memories 1954', p.81 verso.
33 '(A few) potato peelings'.
34 MG, interview with Kim Hill, Saturday Morning, Radio New Zealand National, 9 Oct. 2004.
35 '(A few) potato peelings'.
36 Ibid.
37 Florence Chapple, 'Memories 1954', p.83; MG, email to the author, 22 March 2009.
38 Henderson School committee minute book, 1938–45, 4 May 1942, BBOX 10064, 1b, Archives New Zealand, Auckland Regional Office.

3. Swamp

1 *Taikaka*, 1945, p.19.
2 Ibid., p.6.
3 Avondale College speech, 8 Nov. 1989, MS-Papers-4678-061, 216, ATL.
4 MG, interview with the author, 1 June 2006.
5 Ibid.
6 MG, interview with Kim Hill, Saturday Morning, Radio New Zealand National, 9 Oct. 2004; K. Coughlan, 'A reluctant successor to Sargeson', *New Zealand Times*, 18 Sept. 1983, p.9; 'Where I am, how I got here', New Zealand Book Council winter lecture, 24 Sept. 1986, 4678-188.
7 MG, interview with the author, 1 June 2006; *Orchard Street*, Auckland: Viking, 1998, p.34.
8 MG, interview with Kim Hill.
9 Lyndahl Gee, '(A few) potato peelings', p.10, in the possession of MG.
10 Lyndahl Gee, 'The Meek', in the possession of MG.
11 MG, interview with the author, 1 June 2006.
12 Ibid.
13 *Plumb*, London: Faber and Faber, 1978, p.71; *Ellie and the Shadow Man*, Auckland: Penguin, 2001, p.14; *Sole Survivor*, London: Faber and Faber in association with Penguin, 1983, pp.45, 60.
14 *Crime Story*, Auckland: Penguin, 1994, p.259.
15 Interview with Kim Hill; 'Creeks and kitchens', Margaret Mahy lecture, 23 March 2002, in *The Inside Story*, Auckland: Children's Literature Foundation, 2003, p.15.
16 'Early reading: Maurice Gee on *Zane Grey*', *Education*, 24 (8), 1975, p.25; 'Creeks and kitchens', p.15.
17 'Early reading'.
18 'Creeks and kitchens', p.17; 'Beginnings', *Islands*, 17, March 1977, p.292.

19 Draft talk notes, n.d., 4678-189.
20 'Creeks and kitchens', p.17; MG, interviewed by Brian Boyd, in E. Alley and M. Williams (eds), *In the Same Room*, Auckland: Auckland University Press, 1992, p.160.
21 MG, 'Blind Road', unpublished memoir, p.79.
22 Florence Chapple, 'Memories 1954', p.13, MSX-3063, ATL.
23 After the death of her first husband, Dutch businessman Hendrik Hagemeyer, in 1926 she married Hurd Comstock, a retired Chicago banker, in 1931, and after his death the sculptor (and close friend of Albert Schweitzer) Louis Meyer in 1957.
24 *Auckland Star*, n.d. [1940], in Chapple family scrapbook, fMS-Papers-4678-01.
25 Unsourced review of Dora Hagemeyer, *Swords of the Grass* (c.1927), ibid.
26 Lyndahl Gee, '(A few) potato peelings'.
27 Lyndahl Chapple-Gee, 'Mother's Holiday', *Woman To-day*, April 1939, pp.2–3; 'Mother Callahan', *Mirror*, Sept. 1941, p.66; 'The Parting of the Ways', *Mirror*, July 1941, p.66.
28 Lyndahl Gee, 'Tiger Town', in the possession of MG.
29 '(A few) potato peelings'.
30 Unsourced radio review, Chapple family scrapbook.
31 She received £82 in royalties for *Mihi* (4p per copy on a first print run of 5000); and in 1940 £5-5 from the National Commercial Broadcasting Service for the broadcast rights.
32 *New Zealand Herald*, 11 Dec. 1943, p.4.
33 *New Zealand Listener*, 25 Feb. 1944, p.15.
34 A.W. Reed to Lyndahl Chapple Gee, 26 April 1946, 4678-041.
35 Lyndahl Chapple Gee, 'Double Unit', in F. Sargeson (ed.), *Speaking for Ourselves*, Christchurch: Caxton Press, 1945, pp.23–6.
36 Sargeson to Lyndahl Gee, n.d., 4678-185.
37 Sargeson to Lyndahl Gee, 13 March, 27 July 1947, 4678-185. The 'novelette', as she described it—'a long short story (or very short novel)'—which has not survived, was entitled 'The Million but One'.
38 Charles Brasch to Lyndahl Gee, 7 March 1949, MS-0996-002/144, Hocken Collections.
39 Frank Sargeson to Lyndahl Gee, 27 July 1947.
40 MG, interview with the author, 1 June 2006.
41 Lyndahl Gee, 'The Change', in the possession of MG.
42 MG, interview with Hugo Manson, 21 Aug., 8 Sept. 2008, Arts Foundation of New Zealand Heritage Oral History Project, OH Coll-0926, ATL.
43 'The Change'.
44 Florence Chapple, 'Memories 1954', p.15 (29 March); 'Essay: personality', MSX-3063.
45 MG, talk for PEN, Dunedin, 20 Nov. 1984, p.1, MS-Papers-8732-140.
46 *Taikaka*, 1949, p.52.
47 Ibid., p.13.

4. Albert Park

1 C.K. Stead, 'Eric McCormick – the scholar ambulant', in *The Writer at Work*, Dunedin: Otago University Press, 2000, p.66.
2 *Going West*, Auckland: Viking, 1992, p.69.
3 MG, speech at Auckland University Distinguished Alumni awards, 21 Nov. 1998, MS-Papers-8732-141, ATL; S. Braunias, 'Our man in Loomis', *New Zealand Listener*, 24 July 2004, pp.50–4.
4 MG, 'The way of a writer', *New Zealand Listener*, 17 Jan. 1987, p.41; 'Creek and kitchen', in M. Gifkins (ed.), *Through the Looking Glass*, Auckland: Century Hutchinson, 1988, p.91.
5 MG, 'Beginnings', *Islands*, 17, March 1977, p.292; 'The way of a writer', p.41.
6 Florence Chapple, diary, 1 June 1953, MS-Papers-4678-024, ATL.
7 Ibid., 14 June 1953.
8 Florence Chapple, 'Memories 1954', p.15 (29 March), MSX-3603, ATL.
9 Florence Chapple, diary, 25 Sept. 1955; 'Memories 1954', p.61 (9 July).
10 *Sole Survivor*, London: Faber and Faber in association with Penguin, 1983, p.71.
11 Lyndahl Gee to Len and Delanie, n.d., 4678-074.
12 They were Terry Sturm and Les Holborow, whose father ran the Henderson butcher's.
13 'While the Flag was Up', *Arena*, 50, Summer 1958–59, p.14.
14 Charles Brasch to MG (annotated copy), 11 March 1954, MS-0996-002/144, Hocken Collections.
15 MG, interview with the author, 1 June 2006; *Sole Survivor*, p.76.
16 Brasch to MG (annotated copy), 4 Aug. 1954.
17 Brasch to MG, 1 Nov. 1954.
18 'Facade', *Mate*, 4, Feb. 1960, pp.29, 30, 32.
19 Ibid., pp.29–30.
20 MG, email to the author, 14 May 2009.

5. Paeroa

1 MG, interview with the author, 7 June 2006.
2 Bruce Seaton, interview with the author, 16 May 2008.
3 MG to Maurice Shadbolt, 3 April 1956, 91-047-16/03, ATL.
4 'In at the Death', *Kiwi*, 1955, p.22.
5 Notes for writers workshop? [1978], MS-Papers-4678-212, ATL.
6 'In at the Death', pp.21, 22, 23–4.
7 'The Widow', *Landfall*, 35, Sept. 1955, pp.196, 197, 200, 201, 204.
8 MG to Charles Brasch, 11 April 1955, MS-0996-002/144, Hocken Collections.
9 MG, interview with the author, 7 June 2006.
10 'Character sketches of the senior school', *The Ohinemuri*, 1955, p.9.
11 M. Shadbolt, 'Annual Holiday', *New Zealand Listener*, 10 June 1955, pp.8-9.
12 Kevin Jowsey to Shadbolt, 14 March 1956, 94-180-5/18, ATL; *Here & Now*, 49, April 1956, p.29.
13 Jowsey to Shadbolt, 15 May 1956.
14 MG to Shadbolt, 3 April 1956.

15 'Editorial: we launch ourselves', *Numbers*, 1, July 1954, pp.32, 31; J.K. Baxter, 'The critic as schoolmaster', 4, Oct. 1955, pp.2–3.
16 MG to Shadbolt, 8 Oct. 1956.
17 Brasch to MG, 11 Feb., 22 April 1956, MS-0996-002/144.
18 MG to Shadbolt, 3 April 1956.
19 MG to Shadbolt, 30 July [1956].
20 *New Zealand Truth*, 18 March 1958, p.14; MG, speech at the launch of Ian Middleton's *Pet Shop*, Nelson, 11 March 1980, MS-Papers-6901-02, ATL.
21 MG to Lyndahl Gee, 7 Jan. 1957, MS-Papers-8732-050, ATL.
22 *Here & Now*, 49, April 1956, p.29; *Arena*, 44, 1956, p.7.
23 Jowsey to Shadbolt, 12, 9 July 1956.
24 Jowsey to Shadbolt, 19 Sept. 1956.
25 Chosen, Jowsey explained to Brasch when the first issue was finally out, 'as the most unlikely title we could think of—and the amount of criticism this has brought us has been its own reward'. Jowsey to Brasch, 10 Nov. 1957, MS-0996-003/109.
26 MG to Shadbolt, 8 Oct. 1956.
27 'Evening at Home', *Arena*, 45, 1956, pp.22–4.
28 MG to Shadbolt, 8 Oct., 10 Dec. 1956.
29 'The Quarry', *Arena*, 46, March 1957, pp.7, 13.
30 MG to Shadbolt, 10 Dec. 1956. The editor and judge, Noel Hoggard—who had already noticed Gee's story in *Kiwi*—praised 'The Quarry' as a 'powerfully written story with a strong dramatic element and showing an acute insight into the thoughts and emotions of the principal characters' (*Arena*, 43, March 1956, p.23; 46, March 1957, p.5). In a newspaper notice of the win it was described as 'a competent little story of a small-town "character" and her relationship with the truck driver who boards with her' ('Auckland writer wins "Arena" literary prize', unsourced clipping, n.d., MG scrapbook, MSY-3432, ATL).
31 Insert in *Landfall*, 36, Dec. 1955; 'A prose award', *Landfall*, 37, March 1956, pp.3–4.
32 MG to Shadbolt, 19 Dec. 1956, 91-047-16/02; Brasch to MG, annotated copy, 30 Sept. 1956.
33 'In a Sleeping Face', *Landfall*, 43, Sept. 1957, p.200.
34 MG to Shadbolt, 19 Dec. 1956.
35 'In a Sleeping Face', p.195.
36 Ibid., pp.205, 196, 202.
37 Ibid., p.211.
38 Ibid., pp.206, 207, 198. Hilda's abortion was a late revision to the story; in an earlier version there was an illegitimate child.
39 MG to Shadbolt, 10 Dec. 1956.
40 'Notes', *Landfall*, 41, March 1957, p.3.
41 M. Shadbolt, 'Sing Again Tomorrow', *Landfall*, 36, Dec. 1955, pp.288–92.
42 MG to Shadbolt, 10 Dec. 1956; MG to Maurice and Gill Shadbolt, 26 Nov. 1956, 91-047-16/04.

6. Wellington

1 M. Shadbolt, *One of Ben's*, Auckland: David Ling, 1993 (revised edn, 1994), pp.207–8.
2 *Going West*, Auckland: Viking, 1992, p.91.
3 MG, interview with the author, 7 June 2006.
4 The relationship between Sargeson and the Cook family is described in M. King, *Frank Sargeson: a life*, Auckland: Viking, 1995, pp.105–6. Nigel had spent school holidays working on the Okahukura farm of Sargeson's uncle Oakley Sargeson when Sargeson—then still Norris Davey—was living there, and remained a friend.
5 MG to Maurice Shadbolt, 31 March [1958], 91-047-16/02, ATL.
6 MG to Lyndahl Gee, 7 Jan. 1957, MS-Papers-8372-050, ATL.
7 I. Wedde, 'The Splinterview 6: Maurice Gee . . .', *Spleen*, 6, Dec. 1976 (unpaginated).
8 *Going West*, p.90.
9 Shadbolt to Frank Sargeson, 21 Feb. 1957, MS-Papers-0432-112, ATL.
10 MG to Lyndahl Gee, 7 Jan. 1957.
11 Meg Campbell, 'Arlin', unpublished autobiography, 1999, pp.3–4, MS-Papers-11519-64, ATL; MG, interview with the author, 7 June 2006; Alistair Campbell via Sarah Gaitanos, personal communication.
12 MG, speech at Louis Johnson book launch, 8 Dec. 1998, 8732-141.
13 MG, interview with the author, 7 June 2006.
14 Ibid.
15 MG notebook, MS-Papers-4678-212, ATL.
16 *Going West*, p.111.
17 MG to Nigel Cook, 13 Dec. 2003, 8732-007.
18 He had a volume published with Pegasus, *Prince of the Plague Country*, in 1964.
19 *Blindsight*, Auckland: Penguin, 2005, p.86; MG notebook.
20 'Jazz at the coffee club', *New Zealand Listener*, 28 March 1958, p.6; 'Found: a new pleasure', 12 July 1957, p.8.
21 J. Watson, *Stand in the Rain*, Christchurch: Pegasus Press, 1965, p.28.
22 Wellington Telephone Directory, 1959, pink pages.
23 MG to Shadbolt, 31 March [1958].
24 MG to Shadbolt, 30 Dec. 1957; email, 31 Aug. 2007.
25 Bruce and Mary Seaton, interview with the author, 16 May 2008; MG, interview with the author, 7 June 2006.
26 *New Zealand Truth*, 25 March 1958, p.16; MG to Shadbolt, 12 Oct. [1958].
27 MG to Shadbolt, 31 March [1958].
28 MG notebook; interview with the author, 7 June 2006.
29 A. Hayes, *In Love*, London: Victor Gollancz, 1954, pp.2–4.
30 MG to Shadbolt, 31 March [1958].
31 MG to Lyndahl Gee, Saturday, n.d. [late Oct.] 1959.
32 *Going West*, p.8.
33 MG to Lyndahl Gee, 7 Jan. 1957.
34 MG to Shadbolt, 30 Dec. 1957.
35 MG to Shadbolt, 31 March [1958], 30 Dec. 1957; MG notebook.

36 MG to Shadbolt, 31 March [1958].
37 Kevin Ireland to Sargeson, 14 Jan. 1959, 0432-170. The novel, he told Sargeson, was not intended for publication. It was to be called 'Like a Crusade' and involved 'house burnings, crazy hitch-hike trips, lonely love-making and lovely orgies of organised sex and booze, general iconoclasm and destruction etc.'
38 MG to Shadbolt, 31 March [1958].
39 Ibid.
40 MG, email to the author, 4 March 2007.
41 *Stand in the Rain*, p.33.
42 Ibid., pp.28–9.
43 MG, interview with the author, 7 June 2006.
44 Ray Grover, interview with the author, 21 Aug. 2007.
45 MG to Shadbolt, 12 Oct. [1958].
46 Robin Dudding to Charles Brasch, 17 Nov. 1958, MS-0996-003/109, Hocken Collections.
47 MG to David Walsh, 4 Sept. 1958, MS-Papers-8988-261, ATL.
48 *Here & Now*, 61, Oct. 1957, p.10.
49 'A Girl in Blue', *Mate*, 2, Nov. 1958, pp.12, 11.
50 Brasch, journal, 7 June 1958, MS-0996-009/026.
51 MG to Brasch, 24 July 1958, MS-0996-002/144.
52 MG to Shadbolt, 12 Oct. [1958].
53 *Landfall*, 4, June 1958, 'Notes', p.101.
54 MG to Shadbolt, 12 Oct. [1958].
55 MG to Brasch, [Dec. 1958]; Brasch to MG, 30 Dec. 1958.
56 Sargeson to Ireland, 23 July 1959, MS-Papers-3920, ATL.
57 'The Losers', *Landfall*, 50, June 1959, p.121.
58 Brasch to MG, 3 Jan. 1959.
59 MG to Shadbolt, 25 Oct. 1959, 91-047-16/05; Alan Horsman to MG, 12 Aug. 1959, 4678-180.
60 MG to Shadbolt, 25 Oct. 1959.

7. Nigel

1 Gee's passing comment in a letter to Charles Brasch in December 1958 that he might be having a spell in Christchurch or Dunedin next year suggests that this was something she had worked out well in advance. MG to Charles Brasch, [Dec.] 1958, MS-0996-002/144, Hocken Collections.
2 Brasch, journal, 6 July, 16 June, 26 July 1959, MS-0996-009/026.
3 MG to Maurice Shadbolt, 5 July 1959, 91-047-16/05, ATL.
4 MG to Lyndahl Gee, [27 July] 1959, MS-Papers-8732-050, ATL.
5 MG to Robin Dudding, 15 July [1959], MS-Papers-8988-261, ATL.
6 MG to Dudding, n.d.; Dudding to MG, n.d.; MG to Dudding, 15 July [1959].
7 MG to Gill Shadbolt, 20 Sept. 1959, 91-047-16/05.
8 Alan Horsman to Brasch et al., 6 May 1960, 00-156, box 52, Hocken Collections.
9 MG to Lyndahl Gee, [27 July] 1959.
10 MG to Maurice Shadbolt, 5 July 1959.
11 MG to Gill and Maurice Shadbolt, 18 Aug. 1959.

12 MG to Maurice Shadbolt, 5 July 1959.
13 Maurice Shadbolt to Brasch, 24 Dec. 1958, MS-0996-002/355.
14 MG to Gill and Maurice Shadbolt, 18 Aug. 1959.
15 Ian Cross, 'Writers in conference', *Landfall*, 52, Dec. 1959, p.308.
16 Brasch to Harry Scott, 13 Sept. 1959, MS-Group-1579, 85-114-2, ATL.
17 MG to Gill and Maurice Shadbolt, 18 Aug.; MG to Maurice Shadbolt, 5 July 1959.
18 MG to Lyndahl Gee, [26] Aug., 13 Sept. 1959.
19 MG to Lindahl Gee, 13 Sept., n.d., [late Oct.] 1959. The written record here is not complete: not all of the letters Gee wrote to his mother at this time have survived, and none of hers to him have.
20 MG to Gill Shadbolt, 20 Sept. 1959.
21 MG to Maurice Shadbolt, 30 Aug.; to Gill and Maurice Shadbolt, 18 Aug. 1959.
22 MG to Maurice Shadbolt, 25 Oct. 1959; to Brasch, 9 Dec. 1959; to Lyndahl Gee, n.d. [late Oct.] 1959.
23 MG to Maurice Shadbolt, 25 Oct. 1959.
24 MG to Lyndahl Gee, [23 Nov.], [Nov.] 1959.
25 MG to Lyndahl Gee, Saturday [late Oct.], [1 Nov.] 1959.
26 MG to Gill Shadbolt, 25 Oct. 1959.
27 MG to Lyndahl Gee, [Nov.] 1959.
28 Ibid.
29 MG to Maurice Shadbolt, 18 Nov. 1959.
30 MG to Lyndahl Gee, [23] Nov. 1959.
31 *Evening Post*, 7 Nov. 1959, p.20; *Auckland Star*, 8 Dec. 1959, p.19.
32 In her memoir, *Self-Portrait*, Friedlander recalls asking Gee if she could photograph him because 'I thought he was gorgeous'. M. Friedlander (with H. Manson), *Self-Portrait*, Auckland: Auckland University Press, 2013, p.147.
33 MG to Brasch, 9 Dec. 1959.
34 Ibid.
35 MG to Maurice Shadbolt, 18 Nov. 1959.
36 Hilary Rubinstein to Gill Shadbolt, 26 Oct. 1959, 91-047-17/10.
37 Brasch to MG, 14 Dec. 1959.
38 Florence James to Maurice Shadbolt, 18 Nov. 1959, 91-047-16/05.
39 MG to Brasch, 24 Dec. 1959; James to Shadbolt, 21 March 1960.
40 Maurice Shadbolt to Dudding, 25 Nov. [1959], MS-Papers-8988-045; Victor Gollancz to Shadbolt, 18 Jan. 1960, 91-047-17/10; Carl Freeman to Shadbolt, 14 Nov. 1959, 91-047-16/05.
41 MG to Lyndahl Gee, 16 Nov., [23] Nov. 1959.
42 Brasch to Dudding, 9 Apr. 1960, MS-0996-003/109; Brasch to Maurice Shadbolt, 22 March 1960, 91-047-16/05; Brasch to Frank Sargeson, 10 May 1960, MS-Papers-0432-148, ATL.
43 Shadbolt to Dudding, 24 Sept. 1959. Shadbolt had had in mind a collection of essays entitled *Declaration* published by MacGibbon and Kee in 1957. His own essay was titled 'Sing All Things Sweet and Harsh'—and 'I think already I can say with confidence that it's the best piece of prose, outside my creative work, that I've written', he told Dudding when he sent the first draft: 'It is a rough attempt to define the position of my generation and myself'. Shadbolt to

Dudding, 25 Nov., 10 Dec. 1959.
44 Dudding to Shadbolt, 27 Feb. 1960 (draft), MS-Papers-8988-045.
45 MG to Lyndahl Gee, [Jan.] 1960.
46 The A-frame had been built by Schwimmer, the Dutch-born editor of the Māori Affairs Department quarterly *Te Ao Hou*, with the help of a bunch of his literary friends, among them poets Alistair Campbell and Gordon Orr and poet-historian W.H. Oliver—as recorded in Campbell's *Poets in Our Youth*, Wellington: Pemmican Press, 2002 ('Letter to Pat Wilson').
47 Maurice Shadbolt to Kevin Ireland, 1 Mar. 1960, 91-047-17/08.
48 MG to Maurice Shadbolt, 5 July 1959.
49 'N.Z. Literary Fund. Grants to authors', unsourced newspaper clipping, n.d., MSY-3432, ATL; State Literary Fund committee, minute book, 31 May 1960, IA 81, Archives New Zealand.
50 MG to Maurice Shadbolt, 6 June 1960.
51 Brasch to Shadbolt, 21 July 1960, 91-047-16/05; Shadbolt to Brasch, 11 July, 20 Oct. 1960, MS-0996-002/395.
52 MG to Brasch, 13 Sept. 1960.
53 'Burns Fellowship 1961' list of applicants, Burns Fellowship file, 00-56 box 52, Hocken Collections.
54 MG to Brasch, 2 Oct., 13 Sept.; Brasch to MG, 24 Sept. 1960.
55 Brasch to MG, 4 Jan. 1961.
56 'Schooldays', *Mate*, 6, Dec. 1960, pp.3, 8.
57 MG to Lyndahl Gee, [Oct./Nov.] 1959; Brasch to MG, 4 Jan. 1961; Dudding to Brasch, 13 Oct. 1960, MS-0996-003/109.
58 Brasch to MG, 4 Jan. 1961.

8. London

1 MG to Lyndahl Gee, 1 Feb. 1961, MS-Papers-8732-051, ATL.
2 Florence James to Maurice Shadbolt, 27 July 1960, 91-047-16/05, ATL.
3 MG to Lyndahl Gee, Jan., 13 Jan. 1961.
4 MG to Lyndahl Gee, 20 Jan. 1961.
5 MG to Lyndahl Gee, [Feb.] 1961.
6 MG to Shadbolt, 12 Oct. [1958], 91-047-16/02.
7 MG to Lyndahl Gee, 28 April; to Charles Brasch, [19] April 1961, MS-0996-002/144, Hocken Collections.
8 MG to Lyndahl Gee, 28 Feb. 1961.
9 Kevin Ireland to Frank Sargeson, 4 March 1961, MS-Papers-0432-170, ATL; MG to Lyndahl Gee, [Feb.] 1961.
10 MG to Lyndahl Gee, [Feb.] 1961.
11 Ireland to Shadbolt, 16 Jan. 1961, 94-180-5/18, ATL.
12 Ireland to Sargeson, 21 Aug. 1959, 16 Sept. 1960; Ireland to Robin Dudding, 10 Aug. 1959, MS-Papers-8988-016, ATL.
13 See S. de Montalk, *Unquiet World: the life of Count Geoffrey Potocki de Montalk*, Wellington: Victoria University Press, 2001.
14 L. Tickner, 'The Kasmin gallery', *Oxford Art Journal*, 30 (2), June 2007, pp.233–68. The interior's plain white walls were as innovative as the Pirelli industrial rubber floor.

15 MG to Lyndahl Gee, 28 [Feb.] 1961.
16 MG to Lyndahl Gee, 26 March 1961.
17 MG to Shadbolt, 5 July 1959, 31 March 1958, 91-047-16/05, 16/02.
18 Ireland to Shadbolt, 7 March, 16 April 1962; MG to Lyndahl Gee, 6 Nov. 1961.
19 C. Driver, *The Disarmers: a study in protest*, London: Hodder and Stoughton, 1964, p.121.
20 MG to Lyndahl Gee, 8 May 1961; *New Zealand Herald*, 1 May 1961, p.1.
21 Bob Brockie diary entry, 17 Sept. 1961, 8732-005; MG to Lyndahl Gee, 27 Sept. 1961; M. Randle, 'Non-violent direct action in the 1950s and 1960s', in R. Taylor and N. Young (eds), *Campaigns for Peace*, Manchester: Manchester University Press, 1987.
22 MG to Brasch, 21 Feb. 1961.
23 For a time this year he studied under Oskar Kokoschka in Salzburg. Perrett's grandfather, J. Douglas Perrett, had been a prominent watercolour artist in Auckland in the 1890s. Ireland to Dudding, 14 Aug. 1961, MS-Papers-8988-015; D. Lloyd Jenkins, 'Pursuing John Douglas Perrett', *Décor Extremis*, www.decorextremis.wordpress.dom, 18 Apr. 2011.
24 MG, interview with the author, 15 June 2006.
25 Ireland to Sargeson, 7 Oct. 1961.
26 MG to Lyndahl Gee, 28 Feb. 1961.
27 Ibid.
28 'A note on New Authors Limited', *New Authors Short Story 1*, London: New Authors Ltd, 1961.
29 Brasch to Sargeson, 28 Sept., 1960, MS-Papers-0432-148.
30 MG to Lyndahl Gee, 28 Feb. 1961.
31 MG to Lyndahl Gee, 12 March 1961.
32 MG to Lyndahl Gee, 26 March 1961.
33 District superintendent of education, Department of Education, Auckland to the secretary, Ministry of Education, London, 11 Jan. 1961; Ministry of Education (Teachers Branch) to MG, 24 April 1961, MS-Papers-4678-300, ATL.
34 MG to Lyndahl Gee, 17 April 1961.
35 'The Eleventh Holiday', *New Authors Short Story 1*, pp.168, 170, 181, 177
36 Ibid., p.195.
37 MG to Lyndahl Gee, 26 March 1961.
38 MG to Lyndahl Gee, 3 July 1961.
39 MG to Lyndahl Gee, 15 July, 23 Oct. 1961.
40 MG to Lyndahl Gee, 15 July 1961.
41 MG to Lyndahl Gee, 30 July 1961.
42 MG to Lyndahl Gee, 30 July, postcard (n.d.), 20 Aug. 1961.
43 MG to Lyndahl Gee, 11 Sept., 27 Aug. 1961.
44 Ireland to Shadbolt, 20 Oct. 1961.
45 MG to Lyndahl Gee, 11 Sept., 27 Sept. 1961.
46 Ireland to Sargeson, 7 Oct. 1961.
47 MG to Lyndahl Gee, 11 Sept., 9 Oct. 1961.
48 'Three New Zealanders in the first four', *New Zealand Herald*, n.d., clipping in 4678-430; *Landfall*, 61, March 1962, pp.80–1.

49 Shadbolt to Ireland, 5 Apr. 1961, 91-047-17/08.
50 MG to Lyndahl Gee, 9 Oct. 1961.
51 Ibid.
52 MG to Brasch, 19 April, 8 Dec. [1961].
53 MG to Lyndahl Gee, 1 Dec. 1961.
54 MG to Dudding, 14 Dec. 1961, MS-Papers-8988-261.
55 MG to Lyndahl Gee, n.d.
56 MG to Brasch, 8 Dec. [1961].
57 MG to Lyndahl Gee, 6 Nov. 1961.
58 Ireland, quoted in C. Brett, 'The Gee genius', *North and South*, Sept. 1995, p.96; Ireland, interview with the author, 7 Nov. 2007.
59 Used to treat erectile dysfuntion.
60 MG to Lyndahl Gee, 1 Dec., 11 Dec. 1961.
61 MG to Lyndahl Gee, 1 Jan., 22 Jan. 1962.
62 MG to Lyndahl Gee, 1 Jan. 1962.
63 MG to Lyndahl Gee, 22 Jan. 1962.
64 Ibid.
65 *New Zealand Truth*, 23 Jan. 1962, p.32.
66 Shadbolt to Ireland, 27 July 1961.
67 MG to Lyndahl Gee, 10 June 1961; Ireland to Dudding, 2 June 1961, MS-Papers-8988-015.
68 Ireland, interview with the author. The letter he wrote to Gee has not survived.
69 Ireland to Shadbolt, 7 March, 16 April 1962.
70 B. Boyd, 'Maurice Gee, interviewed by Brian Boyd', in E. Alley and M. Williams (eds), *In the Same Room*, Auckland: Auckland University Press, 1992, p.161.

9. The Big Season

1 MG to Lyndahl Gee, 13 March 1962, MS-Papers-8732-051, ATL.
2 Ibid.
3 'Great Britain: you can walk across it on the grass', *Time*, 15 April 1966.
4 'Ship Story', 'The Lights of Panama City', 'Holding Hands', MS-Papers-4678-074, 075, 077, ATL.
5 Maurice Shadbolt to Kevin Ireland, 2 April (postscript dated 8 April) 1962, 91-047-17/08, ATL.
6 Ray Grover, interview with the author, 21 Aug. 2007.
7 Shadbolt to Ireland, 2 April (postscript), 19 July 1962.
8 Ibid.
9 'Burns Fellow to finish book', *Otago Daily Times*, 16 Jan. 1964, p.5.
10 MG to Shadbolt, 14 Sept. [1962], MS-Papers-8044-044, ATL.
11 Unsourced review, 4678-224.
12 Ibid.; 'N.Z. author's first novel', *Otago Daily Times*, undated clipping; 'Small-town boy', *Evening Star*, 18 Aug. 1962; L.McD.V., 'Author's skilful portrayal of conflicting characters', *Bay of Plenty Times*, 18 Aug. 1962; F.K., 'Splash of colour on NZ scene', *Rotorua Daily Post*, undated clipping, 4678-224.
13 *The Big Season*, London: Hutchinson, 1962, p.58.
14 Ibid., p.16.
15 Ibid., pp.16, 36.

16 MG notebook, 4678-212; MG, 'The way of a writer', *New Zealand Listener*, 17 Jan. 1987, p.42.
17 *The Big Season*, p.130.
18 Ibid, pp.26, 105.
19 MG interviewed by Greg O'Brien, 'Maurice Gee: making sentences work', in G. O'Brien and R. Cross, *Moments of Invention*, Auckland: Heinemann Reed, 1988, p.115; 'The way of a writer', p.42.
20 *The Big Season*, pp.148, 152.
21 Ibid, p.177.
22 'Depends on crudeness', *Southland Times*, undated clipping; A.R. Dunlop, 'Maurice Gee's *The Big Season* will likely prove disappointing book', *Southland Daily News*, 18 Aug. 1962, 4678-224.
23 N.M., 'Outspoken study of N.Z. youth', *New Zealand Herald*, 21 July 1962, section 3, p.2; Shadbolt to Ireland, 6 Sept. 1962.
24 'Novelist with something to say', *Auckland Star*, 21 July 1962, p.12.
25 'Saison d'enfer', *New Zealand Listener*, 24 Aug. 1962, p.35; 'The Big Season, and some stories', *Comment*, 15, April 1963, p.48; *Landfall*, 64, Dec. 1962, pp.392–4.
26 Draft letter to the editor, n.d., 91-047-16/07 and MS-0996-2/356, Hocken Collections; Shadbolt to Robin Dudding, 16 Nov. 1966, 91-047-16/08; Shadbolt to Ireland, 3 July 1961.
27 Shadbolt to Ireland, 19 July 1962.
28 MG to Charles Brasch, 21 March 1963, Brasch to MG, 26 Feb. 1963, MS-0996-002/144.
29 MG to Lyndahl Gee, 20 Dec. 1962, 8732-052.
30 MG to Lyndahl Gee, n.d.
31 MG to Shadbolt, 1 Oct. 1963, 91-047-16/07.
32 MG, interview with the author, 15 June 2006.
33 MG to Lyndahl Gee, 4 June 1963.
34 MG to Lyndahl Gee, n.d. [early Sept.] 1963; MG to Shadbolt, 16 July 1963.
35 Ireland to MG, 31 July 1963, 4678-181.
36 Ireland to Dudding, 8 Jan. 1962, MS-Papers-8988-015, ATL.
37 Dudding did subsequently do some publishing under the imprint Mate Books: Peter Bland, *My Side of the Story: poems, 1960–64*, in 1964 was his first title.
38 Shadbolt to Ireland, 12 June 1963.
39 'New Zealand books—the end of a drought?', *Auckland Star*, 5 Oct. 1963.
40 'Notes', *Landfall*, 30, June 1964, pp.112–3; Brasch to Frank Sargeson, 19 Jan. 1964, MS-Papers-0432-148, ATL.
41 Brasch to Dan Davin, 15 April 1963, quoted in J. Geraets, '"Landfall" under Brasch: the humanizing journey', PhD thesis, University of Auckland, 1982, p.187.
42 MG to Lyndahl Gee, 4 June 1963.
43 MG to Shadbolt, 16 July 1963.
44 Shadbolt to Ireland, 27 June 1963.
45 MG to Shadbolt, 16 July 1963.
46 W.A. Lishman to MG, 20 Aug. 1963 (replying to letter of 14 Aug.), 4678-299.
47 Affidavit of Eric Bridgman, 1967, 8732-066; MG to Lyndahl Gee, n.d.
48 MG to Lyndahl Gee, 28 Aug. 1963.

49 MG to Shadbolt, 28 Aug. 1963.
50 MG to Lyndahl, n.d., [early Sept.] 1963; MG to Shadbolt, 28 Aug. 1963.
51 MG to Shadbolt, 1 Oct. 1963.
52 MG to Lyndahl Gee, n.d.; 'Chance for ambitious novel', unsourced clipping, MG scrapbook, MSY-3432, ATL.
53 MG to Shadbolt, 1 Oct. 1963. There had been only five applicants this year, and Gee was a clear choice, ahead of Alex Guyan, Phillip Wilson, Brian Fisher and Colin Kane Bell. Brasch, journal, 25 Sept. 1963, MS-0996-009/033.
54 MG to Lyndahl Gee, n.d., 1963.
55 MG to Shadbolt, 16 July 1963.
56 MG to Lyndahl Gee, n.d. [early Sept.] 1963.
57 The *Reynolds News* was a Labour Party Sunday tabloid, founded in 1850 with a *New Zealand Truth*-like 'radical working class approach combined with sensationalism' (University of Bradford library website). Gee kept no clippings of any British reviews of the novel, and never mentioned any in his correspondence with his mother, or Shadbolt or Brasch.
58 MG to Shadbolt, 16 July 1963.
59 MG to Shadbolt, 28 Aug. 1963.
60 Ibid.
61 MG to Lyndahl Gee, n.d., 28 Aug. 1963; Brasch to Margaret Scott, 11 March 1962, 85-114-3, ATL.

10. Burns Fellow

1 MG, interview with the author, 20 June 2006.
2 Judith Binney, conversation with the author, 27 Nov. 2006.
3 The fellowship paid at least £1200 (the starting salary of a full-time lecturer). Gee was getting £1275, a little less than he had expected—perhaps, he speculated to Shadbolt, because he had not mentioned having a family in his application.
4 MG to Lyndahl Gee, [10] Jan. 1964, MS-Papers-8732-053, ATL.
5 L. Jones (ed.), *Nurse to the Imagination*, Dunedin: Otago University Press, 2008, p.8.
6 MG to Maurice Shadbolt, 16 July, 1 Oct. 1963, 91-047-16/07, ATL.
7 MG to Shadbolt, 21 April 1964, 91-047-16/08.
8 MG to Lyndahl Gee, [10] Jan. 1964.
9 *Otago Daily Times*, 1 Oct. 1963, p.6.
10 *Otago Daily Times*, 16 Jan. 1964, p.5.
11 'Burns Fellowship '64', draft, MS-Papers-4678-075, ATL.
12 'N.Z. his subject', *Critic*, 4 March 1964, p.5.
13 D. McEldowney, *Full of the Warm South*, Dunedin: John McIndoe, 1983, p.82 (entry for 1 Oct.).
14 'Burns Fellowship '64'; 'The Burns Fellowship', *Landfall*, 87, Sept. 1968, pp.242–3.
15 MG to Lyndahl Gee, 13 April 1964.
16 Charles Brasch to Frank Sargeson, 19 Jan. 1964, MS-Papers-0432-148, ATL.
17 Brasch, journal, 8 March, 3 May 1964, MS-0996-009/033, Hocken Collections.
18 Michael Noonan, interview with the author, 15 May 2008.

19 Brasch, appointment diary, 28 April 1964, MS-0996-009/067.
20 MG to Lyndahl Gee, 5 Feb., 1 March 1964.
21 MG to Lyndahl Gee, 28 April 1964.
22 MG to Lyndahl Gee, 17 Oct. 1964.
23 Hera Smith to Len and Lyndahl Gee, Tuesday, n.d. [17 March 1964], 8732-073.
24 Brasch, journal, 8 March.
25 MG to Lyndahl Gee, 28 April 1964.
26 MG to Lyndahl Gee, 16 July, 3 July 1964; MG to Shadbolt, 29 July 1964. That Noonan did nothing with the play was in part because he left Dunedin at the end of the year.
27 MG to Lyndahl Gee, 12 June, 16 July 1964.
28 MG to Lyndahl Gee, 12 June 1964.
29 MG to Lyndahl Gee, 16, 29 July 1964.
30 4678-213, pp.8, 17. Perhaps too from a racecourse scene deleted from an early draft of *The Big Season*.
31 Muriel Parker to MG, 19 Dec. 1963, 4678-183.
32 MG to Lyndahl Gee, 6 [Oct.] 1964.
33 MG to Lyndahl Gee, 12 June, 3 July 1964.
34 MG to Lyndahl Gee, 29 July 1964; to Shadbolt, 29 July 1964.
35 I. Cross, *Such Absolute Beginners*, Auckland: David Ling, 2007, pp.90–6; interview with the author, 28 Jan. 2008.
36 *Otago Daily Times*, 13 April 1963, p.9, 7 Sept. 1962, p.6; 'The Burns Fellowship', *Landfall*, 87, Sept. 1968, pp.239–41; F. McKay, *The Life of James K. Baxter*, Auckland: Oxford University Press, 1990, pp.195–6. The pictorial volume was *Gift from the Sea* with Brian Brake. The big novel was what later emerged as *Strangers and Journeys*, at this point entitled 'The Sleeping Breeze'.
37 MG, interview with the author, 20 June 2006; 'Robert Burns Fellowship', talk for Burns 50th anniversary, 2008; MG to Dan Davin, 31 Jan. 1984, MS-Papers-5079-083, ATL; Brasch, journal, 18 Sept. 1964.
38 He had intended to go to Rotorua and Auckland in the first week of August (among other things, to see a play Michael Noonan had in the Auckland Festival): it is not clear if he made this trip, or postponed it. He was evidently just back from there when he next wrote to his mother in mid-September.
39 MG to Lyndahl Gee, 14 Sept.; to Shadbolt, 1 Oct. 1964.
40 MG to Lyndahl Gee, 23 [Sept.] 1964; Brasch, journal, 18 Sept. 1964.
41 MG to Shadbolt, 1 Oct.; to Lyndahl Gee, 6, 17 Oct. 1964.
42 MG to Lyndahl Gee, 27 Oct. 1964.
43 'Extract from a novel', Otago University *Review*, 1964, pp.6–16. 'It was half-baked and should have been rejected', he wrote in his draft *Landfall* Burns contribution a few years later, though in fact very close to the published version.
44 MG to Shadbolt, 1 Oct.; to Lyndahl Gee, 17 Oct. 1964.
45 MG to Lyndahl Gee, Nov. 1964.
46 'Burns Fellowship '64', draft.
47 *A Special Flower*, London: Hutchinson, 1965, pp.12, 13.
48 Ibid., p.89.
49 MG, talk to Nelson Institute, 16 March 1978, 8732-140.
50 *A Special Flower*, pp.20, 21, 23.

51 Ibid., p.33.
52 Ibid., p.61.
53 Ibid., pp.43, 44, 45–6, 74.
54 Ibid., pp.74, 63.
55 'Burns Fellowship '64'.
56 *A Special Flower*, p.62.
57 *Otago Daily Times*, 15 Oct. 1964, p.5.
58 MG to Lyndahl Gee, 6 Oct. 1964.
59 MG to Shadbolt, 1 Oct. 1964; to Robin Dudding, 16 Oct. 1964, MS-Papers-8988-261, ATL.
60 MG to Lyndahl Gee, 6, 17 Oct. 1964.
61 By the recently established Old Tote Theatre Company (later the Sydney Theatre Company), who performed the Edward Albee play at the Theatre Royal in Christchurch in November after seasons in Auckland and Wellington the previous month.
62 Brasch, journal, 24 Dec. 1964. Brasch was overseas in November and the first half of December.
63 MG, interview with Hugo Manson, 21 Aug., 8 Sept. 2008, Arts Foundation of New Zealand Heritage Oral History Project, OH Coll-0926, ATL.

11. Ballsed Up

1 MG to Charles Brasch, 7 Oct. 1965, MS-0996-002/144, Hocken Collections.
2 MG, interview with the author, 15 June 2006.
3 MG to Brasch, 7 Oct. 1965; interview with the author, 15 June 2006.
4 Brasch, journal, 8 March 1964, MS-0996-009/033.
5 Maurice Shadbolt to Kevin Ireland, 12 Feb. 1965, 91-047-17/08, ATL.
6 MG to Lyndahl Gee, Monday, n.d., MS-Papers-8732-054, ATL.
7 Ibid.
8 Shadbolt to Ireland, 20 July 1965.
9 Ross O'Rourke, interview with the author, 19 Aug. 2009; Ray Grover, interview with the author, 21 Aug. 2007.
10 MG, interview with Hugo Manson, 21 Aug., 8 Sept. 2008, Arts Foundation of New Zealand Heritage Oral History Project, OH Coll-0926, ATL.
11 Obituary, *New Zealand Medical Journal*, 94 (690), 26 Aug. 1981, pp.153–4; *Rotorua Daily Post*, 25 Nov. 1987; *New Zealand Herald*, 15 Aug. 1969.
12 Eric Bridgman, affidavit for Supreme Court, 1967, 8732-066.
13 Bridgman was made a Chevalier de la Légion d'honneur by the French government in 1956 for his work in the Society Islands, particularly with the establishment of a leper hospital at Orofara.
14 M. Shadbolt, *From the Edge of the Sky*, Auckland: David Ling, 1999, p.120.
15 MG to Lyndahl Gee, Friday, n.d., 14 Oct. 1965.
16 MG, interview with the author, 15 June 2006; interview with Hugo Manson.
17 MG, draft letter, 17 Nov. 1965, MS-Papers-4678-075, ATL.
18 MG to Lyndahl Gee, Monday [1] Nov. 1965.
19 MG to Brasch, 7 Oct. 1965.
20 Ibid.
21 MG, draft letter to Graham [Nicol], n.d., 4678-075.

22 MG in 'Bought any good (NZ-written) books lately?', *Auckland Star*, 23 Aug. 1969, p.11. Hutchinson still had 1000 in stock two years after publication.
23 'Style and squalor', *Dispute*, 1 (9), Nov.–Dec. 1965, pp.11–12.
24 'Official rose', *New Zealand Listener*, 11 Feb. 1966, p.14.
25 Brasch to MG, 10 Feb. 1966; MG to Brasch, 1 Feb. 1966.
26 Brasch to Margaret Scott, Christmas Day 1965, 85-114-4, ATL.
27 *Landfall*, 78, June 1966, p.197.
28 Scott to Brasch, 16 Jan. 1966, MS-0996-003/185; Brasch to Scott, 24 Jan. 1966.
29 *Landfall*, 78, June 1966, pp.198, 197, 199.
30 D. McEldowney, *Full of the Warm South*, Dunedin: John McIndoe, 1982, p.154 (entry for 24 Jan. 1966).
31 *Landfall*, 78, June 1966, pp.197–8, 199.
32 *A Special Flower*, London: Hutchinson, 1965, pp.69, 61.
33 J. Frame, 'Notes on Maurice Gee's *A Special Flower*', in D. Harold and P. Gordon (eds), *Janet Frame: in her own words*, Auckland: Penguin, 2011, p.223.
34 Frank Sargeson to H. Winston Rhodes, 15 May 1965, MS-Papers-0432-141, ATL.
35 'The Burns Fellowship', *Landfall*, 87, Sept. 1968, p.240.
36 M. Shadbolt, *Among the Cinders*, Christchurch: Whitcombe and Tombs, 1965, p.259; R.P.L. Jackson, *Landfall*, 77, March 1966, p.95. Joan Stevens in the *Listener* recognised the broader literary references but not the author's stated tone and found the novel clichéd and contrived, as did most critics (*New Zealand Listener*, 9 July 1965, p.18).
37 Ireland to Sargeson, 31 Aug. 1965, MS-Papers-0432-170.
38 C.K. Stead, *The Secret History of Modernism*, London: Harvill, 2001, pp.124–7, 178–81. The genesis of this enmity was a letter to the editor of the *New Zealand Listener*, written under the pseudonym K. of Henderson, criticising Shadbolt's story 'An Annual Holiday', and which Shadbolt deduced to have been written by Stead with the collusion or encouragement (he later discovered) of Sargeson. It was a petty squabble, although the criticisms of the story were sound. In fact, Stead would like Shadbolt 'enormously' when he finally met him in London in 1958, but continued to have little regard for his writing. (M. King, *Frank Sargeson: a life*, Auckland: Viking, 1995, pp.337–9; C.K. Stead to Sargeson, 1 Jan. 1959, MS-Papers-0432-179.)
39 MG to Brasch, 1 Feb. 1966.
40 MG to Robin Dudding, 16 Oct. [1964], MS-Papers-8988-261, ATL; to Lyndahl Gee, 1 March 1964.
41 'Holding Hands', typescript, p.11, 4678-077.
42 Brasch to MG, 10 Feb. 1966.
43 'The Champion', *Landfall*, 78, June 1966, pp.114–5, 119, 125. Earlier titles for the story were 'Triple Peel' (a croquet term), 'Left Hook' (although it is with his right that Wilbraham floors his son-in-law Harry) and 'A Classic Style'.
44 Brasch to MG, 10 Feb., 10 March 1966.

12. Library School

1 MG to Lyndahl Gee, Tuesday, n.d. [Feb. 1966], MS-Papers-8732-055, ATL.
2 MG to Lyndahl Gee, n.d. [Feb. 1966].
3 MG to Lyndahl Gee, 14 Oct. 1965; Monday, n.d., 1966, 8732-054, 055.
4 Charles Brasch to Margaret Scott, 9 Nov. [1965], 85-114-4, ATL.
5 Scott to Brasch, 2 March, 18 Dec. 1966, MS-0996-003/185, Hocken Collections.
6 Scott to Brasch, 2 March 1966.
7 Scott to Brasch, 16 April 1966.
8 Brasch to Gee, 10 March 1966, MS-0996-002/144.
9 Brasch to Gee, 10 Feb. 1966.
10 MG to Lyndahl Gee, Tuesday, n.d.
11 Scott to Brasch, 2 March 1966.
12 Scott to Brasch, Wednesday, n.d., 16 April 1966.
13 Margaret Scott, affidavit, 3 Dec. 1967, 8732-066.
14 MG to Lyndahl Gee, Monday, n.d.
15 MG to Lyndahl Gee, Monday, n.d.
16 MG to Lyndahl Gee, Wednesday, n.d.
17 MG to Lyndahl Gee, Tuesday, n.d.
18 MG to Lyndahl Gee, Sunday, n.d, Sunday, n.d.
19 MG to Lyndahl Gee, Sunday, n.d.
20 MG to Lyndahl Gee, Tuesday, n.d., Sunday, n.d.
21 MG to Lyndahl Gee, Sunday, n.d.
22 Robin Dudding to MG, 25 June 1966, MS-Papers-8988-261, ATL.
23 MG to Lyndahl Gee, Sunday, n.d.
24 Katherine Mansfield Memorial Award 1967 judge's report, MS-Papers-4678-281, ATL.
25 'Down in the World', *Landfall*, 83, Sept. 1967, pp.97, 296.
26 MG to Lyndahl Gee, Sunday, n.d.; Thursday, n.d. She was helping Ray Grover with either research or acquisitions for the Turnbull Library as well, although precisely what at this time is unclear. Its photographic archive, though, contains a collection of snapshots of wharf construction at Mt Maunganui and road workers on the job at Aongatete in the Bay of Plenty in the mid- and late 1920s, presumably acquired—and possibly taken—by either Harry or Len, and given to the library by Lyndahl and Len in 1968.
27 Dora Hagemeyer to Lyndahl Gee, 4 Aug. 1966, 8732-071.
28 MG to Lyndahl Gee, Tuesday, n.d., Thursday, n.d.
29 MG to Lyndahl Gee, n.d. [6 Dec.].
30 Scott to Brasch, 18 Dec. 1966.
31 MG to Lyndahl Gee, Tuesday, n.d. [1967].
32 MG to Lyndahl Gee, n.d. [30 Jan.].
33 Scott to Brasch, 18 Dec. 1966.
34 MG, interview with the author, 20 June 2006.
35 MG to Lyndahl Gee, Tuesday, n.d.
36 MG to Lyndahl Gee, Friday, n.d., Wednesday, n.d.
37 Scott to Brasch, 4 April 1967.
38 Ibid.; Scott, affidavit, 3 Dec. 1967, 8732-066.

39 Scott to Brasch, 4 April 1967.
40 Hera to Nigel, n.d., 8732-066.
41 MG to Lyndahl Gee, Wednesday, n.d.
42 MG to Brasch, 8 Aug. 1967, MS-0996-003/132.
43 Brasch to MG, 19 Aug. 1967, 8732-066.
44 Angela Sears, interview with the author, 13 Sept. 2007.
45 Scott, affidavit, 1967.
46 Dr Anne Hall, consultant psychiatrist, to Shirley Smith, 11 Dec. 1967, 8732-066.
47 Affidavit of Eric Bridgman, [Nov.] 1967, 8732-066.
48 Shirley Smith to MG, 29 Nov. 1967.
49 MG, interview with the author, 20 June 2006.

13. The Lost Child

1 MG, interview with the author, 20 June 2006.
2 Ibid.
3 Jennifer Perkins, Winant, Towers to MG, 30 Nov. 1967, MS-Papers-4678-280, ATL.
4 MG to Ursula Winant, draft, n.d., in notebook headed 'Story', 4678-075.
5 Ursula Winant to MG, 16 Oct. 1968.
6 Michael Dempsey to Ursula Winant, 4 Dec. 1968; Winant to MG, 28 Jan. 1969.
7 Joan Beard to Lyndahl Gee, 12 Dec., MS-Papers-8732-066, ATL.
8 MG to Margaretha Hickman, Thursday, n.d., 26 Feb. 1969, in the possession of Maurice and Margareta Gee.
9 MG to Margaretha Hickman, Thursday, n.d..
10 MG to Margaretha Hickman, Tuesday [18 March] 1969.
11 MG to Margaretha Hickman, Friday [21 March].
12 Ibid.
13 Ibid.
14 MG to Margaretha Hickman, Wednesday [26 March].
15 MG to Margaretha Hickman, Tuesday [18 March], Thursday, n.d.
16 MG to Margaretha Hickman, Thursday, n.d., Wednesday [26 March].
17 MG to Margaretha Hickman, Wednesday [26 March].

14. In My Father's Den

1 *Auckland Star*, 4 Feb. 1941. On Oscar Garden's career see S. Berry and MG, 'Garden, Oscar 1903–1997', from *The Dictionary of New Zealand Biography*, Te Ara—the Encyclopedia of New Zealand, http://www.TeAra.govt.nz/en/biographies; M. Garden, 'Oscar for a Bay aviator', *Bay of Plenty Times*, 11 Jan. 2006, p.13.
2 MG to Margaretha Hickman, n.d., Thursday [1969], in the possession of Maurice and Margareta Gee.
3 MG to Margaretha Hickman, n.d., Thursday [1969].
4 *In My Father's Den*, London: Faber and Faber, 1972, p.113; 'Where I am, how I got here', New Zealand Book Council winter lecture, 24 Sept. 1986, typescript, p.8, MS-Papers-4678-188, ATL.

5 Robin Dudding to MG, 9 April 1969, 4678-178.
6 MG to Margaretha Hickman, 26 Feb. 1969.
7 MG to Margaretha Hickman, n.d., Thursday [1969].
8 'A Retired Life', *Landfall*, 90, June 1969, pp.101, 103.
9 Frank Sargeson to MG, 13 Aug. 1969, 4678-185; Gee to Sargeson, n.d., MS-Papers-0432-056, ATL. *Joy of the Worm* was dedicated to Nigel and Julie Cook. Nigel had designed an extension to Sargeson's house in 1967; the novel's story was based on parts of the Cook family's (M. King, *Frank Sargeson: a life*, Auckland: Viking, 1995, pp.371–2).
10 Sargeson to MG, 22 Nov. 1969.
11 Dudding to MG, 9 April 1969.
12 Dudding to MG, 20 Nov. 1969.
13 MG, 'Double Unit', unpublished memoir, p.110.
14 Shirley Smith to MG, 6 Feb. 1970, MS-Papers-8732-066, ATL.
15 'Puts human beings before N.Z. novel', unsourced clipping, MSY-3432, ATL.
16 *Games of Choice*, London: Faber and Faber, 1976, p.154.
17 MG, interview with the author, 26 June 2006.
18 Margaretha Gee to Greta Garden, 7 Nov., n.d. 1970, in the possession of Margareta Gee.
19 Ibid., 12 Jan. 1971.
20 Peter Crisp to MG, 8 Jan. 1970, 4678-178.
21 Margaretha Gee to Greta Garden, 6 May 1971, 25 Jan. 1973.
22 'A new home for the Napier Public Library', *New Zealand Libraries*, 35 (1), Feb. 1972, pp.25–9.
23 'The value of the library in the community', talk to the National Council of Women Napier branch AGM, 23 May 1972, 4678-188.
24 'A new home for the Napier Public Library'; Napier Public Library annual report, 1971/72, pp.1-2.
25 'The Hole in the Window', *Landfall*, 100, Dec. 1971, p.425.
26 I. Wedde, 'The Splinterview 6: Maurice Gee . . .', *Spleen*, 6, Dec. 1976, unpaginated.
27 'The Hole in the Window', pp.431, 432, 434.
28 MG, interview with the author, 26 June 2006; J. Millen, *Ronald Hugh Morrieson*, Auckland: David Ling, 1996, p.221; O.E. Middleton, 'Fiction writers confer', *Landfall*, 100, Dec. 1971, pp.445–8.
29 Dudding to MG, 18 Oct. 1971. The Mansfield award had recently been restricted to unpublished stories.
30 Roy Hope, Rothmans of Pall Mall, to MG, 9 Dec. 1971, 4768-281.
31 Charles Brasch to MG, 7 Jan. 1972, 4678-176; to Sargeson, 2 Jan. 1972, MS-Papers-4261-024, ATL.
32 Sargeson to MG, 23 Jan., 27 Feb. 1972, 4678-185; MG to Sargeson, 21 Feb. [1972], MS-Papers-4261-064.
33 Sargeson to MG, 27 Feb. 1972; MG to Sargeson, 21 Feb. [1972].
34 Dudding to MG, 2 June 1972.
35 Unsourced clipping, MSY-3432.
36 *In My Father's Den*, pp.101, 44, 108.
37 *Auckland Star*, 7 Oct. 1972, p.18.
38 *In My Father's Den*, pp.45–6.

39 Ibid., pp.14, 19.
40 Ibid., p.164.
41 Ibid., pp.13, 47, 55, 101.
42 Ibid., pp.68, 144.
43 Ibid., pp.147, 131.
44 Ibid., p.78.
45 'In My Father's Den', talk at Auckland University, 1989?, 8732-140.
46 Wedde, 'The Splinterview 6: Maurice Gee . . .'.
47 *Daily Telegraph* (Napier), 27 July 1972, p.5.
48 *Sunday Herald*, 15 Aug., 17 Sept. 1972; *Auckland Star*, 7 Oct. 1972, p.18; Maurice Shadbolt to MG, 13 Nov. 1972, 91-047-16/13, ATL.
49 Dudding to Sargeson, 10 April 1972, MS-Papers-4261-043.
50 Brasch to Margaret Scott, 26 April 1972, 85-114-7, ATL; to Sargeson, 17 May 1972, MS-Papers-4261-024.
51 Dudding to MG, 11 July, 2 June 1972.
52 J. Williamson, 'The potent beast', *Islands*, 1, Spring 1972, p.79.
53 MG to Dudding, 10 Oct. 1972, MS-Papers-8988-082, ATL.

15. A Glorious Morning, Comrade

1 Napier *Daily Telegraph*, 13 Dec. 1971, 4 March, 1 April 1972.
2 MG to Lyndahl Gee, [3 Feb. 1972], MS-Papers-8732-056, ATL.
3 Margaretha Gee to Lyndahl Gee, 15 June 1972.
4 MG to Charles Brasch, 21 Feb. 1972, MS-0996-003/063, Hocken Collections.
5 'The value of the library in the community', talk to the National Council of Women Napier branch AGM, 23 May 1972, MS-Papers-4678-188, ATL.
6 MG to the town clerk, 'Napier Public Library proposed staff changes', 31 July 1972, 4678-314.
7 MG to Lyndahl Gee, [2 Aug. 1972]; MG to the secretary, New Zealand Library Association, 6 Aug. 1972; MG, interview the author, 26 June 2006.
8 MG to Robin Dudding, n.d., MS-Papers-8988-082, ATL.
9 *Daily Telegraph*, 10 Aug. 1972; MG, interview with the author, 26 June 2006; obituary, *Daily Telegraph*, 23 March 1998, p.1.
10 'Library row ends abruptly', *Dominion*, 2 Aug. 1972; 'Library sackings are investigated', Napier *Daily Telegraph*, 2 Aug. 1972
11 *Daily Telegraph*, 2 Aug., 'A public library is not a book club', 5 Aug. 1972. The submission, calling for an investigation by the council, regular meetings between the library committee and librarian and that committee members 'should understand the purpose of the library', and suggesting the formation of a Friends of the Public Library Society, was swiftly dismissed by the council (*Daily Telegraph*, 17 Aug., 29 Sept. 1972; submission dated 14 Aug., MS-Papers-0995, ATL). Richards stepped down from the library committee chairmanship early the following year 'to devote more of his time to social services'; the former children's librarian became acting librarian in August 1972 and was appointed librarian in March 1973.
12 MG to Brasch, 19 Nov. 1972, MS-0996-007/014.
13 'Right-hand Man', *Islands*, 3, Autumn 1973, pp.47, 48, 50.
14 Ibid., p.61.

15 MG to Lyndahl Gee, 2 Sept.; Margaretha Gee to Greta Garden, 24 Aug. 1972, in the possession of Margareta Gee.
16 Margaretha Gee to Greta Garden, 12 Sept. 1972.
17 MG, interview with the author, 26 June 2006.
18 MG to Dudding, 28 Oct[?] 1972.
19 Ibid.; MG to Brasch, 19 Nov. 1972.
20 MG to Lyndahl Gee, [June 1972].
21 MG to Dudding, 28 Oct.[?], 20 Nov. 1972.
22 Brasch to Frank Sargeson, 28 June 1971, MS-Papers-4261-024, ATL.
23 Brasch, journal, 26 Sept. 1971, MS-0996-009/036.
24 Brasch to Janet Paul, 20 Oct. 1972, MS-Papers-5640-036, ATL; to MG, 31 Oct. 1972, 678-176.
25 MG to Brasch, 19 Nov. 1972; Brasch to MG, 2 Dec. 1972.
26 MG to Brasch, 21 Jan. 1973.
27 Brasch to MG, 2 Feb. 1973; Paul to Brasch, n.d., MS-0996-007/014.
28 MG to Brasch, 21 Jan. 1973.
29 MG, interview with the author, 20 June 2006; MG to Margaretha Gee, Thursday, n.d.
30 Brasch to MG, 7 Feb.; MG to Brasch, 28 Feb., 4 March; Brasch to Paul, 28 Jan. 1973.
31 Margaretha Gee to Greta Garden, 9 Oct., 28 Sept., 5 Nov. 1972.
32 Ibid., 28 March. 1973.
33 MG to Dudding, 30 Jan. 1973.
34 Nick Nobilo to M. and M. Gee, 10 Aug. 1973, 4678-305.
35 Margaretha Gee to Greta Garden, 24 July 1974.
36 Sargeson to Lyndahl Gee, 8 April 1973, 4678-185.
37 'Demolished', 1973; 'Memo of a day ill-spent', 17 March 1974, in the possession of Gary Gee.
38 Nigel Gee, interview with the author, 27 April 2010.
39 MG to Dudding, 20 May 1973. 'Don't envy you the Sargeson/Pearson/Shadbolt tightrope—that trio will just about prematurely retire me in one way or another—or perhaps not prematurely', Dudding had replied (Dudding to MG, 26 May 1973).
40 MG, interview with the author, 26 June 2006.
41 Brasch to MG, 8 May 1973.
42 MG to Dudding, 20/21 May; MG to Paul, 26 May 1973, MS-Papers-5640-037; talk to PEN, Dunedin, 20 Nov. 1984, 8732-140, p.4.
43 Dudding to MG, 26 May; to Kevin Ireland, 28 May, 94-180-2/04, ATL.
44 MG to Paul, 26 May 1973.
45 Brasch to MG, 27 Feb., 8 May; MG to Brasch, 15 April; MG to Paul, 26 May, 27 Oct.; Dudding to MG, 26 May 1973.
46 'A Glorious Morning, Comrade', *New Zealand Listener*, 22 Dec. 1973, p.45.
47 MG to Dudding, 22 Nov.; Dudding to MG, 20 Dec. 1973, MS-Papers-8988-081.

16. Games of Choice

1 MG to Robin Dudding, 12 Nov. 1973, MS-Papers-8988-081, ATL.
2 Ibid.
3 News clippings, 1973; Margaretha Gee to Ministry of Works and Development, 17 Dec. 1973, MS-Papers-4678-301, ATL
4 Margaretha Gee to Greta Garden, 25 March 1975, in the possession of Margareta Gee.
5 Charles Brasch to MG, 2 Dec. 1972, 4678-176.
6 MG to Peter Muxlow, 6 May 197[5], 4678-248.
7 MG to Dudding, 12 Nov. 1973.
8 Draft response to Faber author's questionnaire [1975], 4678-272.
9 J. Ewan, 'Moved to write', *New Zealand Bookworld*, 40, Oct. 1977, p.34.
10 MG to Dudding, 23 Nov. 1973.
11 C.K. Stead to Janet Paul, 9 April 1974, MS-Papers-5640-031, ATL.
12 D. McEldowney, *Then and There: a 1970s diary*, Auckland: Auckland University Press, 1995, pp.41 (entry for 9 Jan. 1975), 54 (27 March).
13 Ibid., p.67 (7 July).
14 McEldowney to MG, 30 June, 31 Dec. 1976, 4678-271; *Press*, 28 Feb. 1976, p.10.
15 Margaretha Gee to Greta Garden, 24 July 1974.
16 *Games of Choice*, London: Faber and Faber, 1976, p.46.
17 Ibid., p.49.
18 Ibid., pp.15, 78, 152.
19 Ibid., p.70.
20 Draft response to Faber author's questionnaire.
21 *Games of Choice*, p.166; *Going West*, Auckland: Viking, 1992, p.8.
22 *Games of Choice*, pp.66, 24, 156, 98, 161.
23 Ibid., pp.90, 137.
24 I. Wedde, 'The Splinterview 6: Maurice Gee . . .', *Spleen*, 6, Dec. 1976, unpaginated.
25 Ewan, 'Moved to write', p.11.
26 *Islands*, 5, Spring 1973, pp.327, 328.
27 The US embassy in Wellington was to choose a New Zealand writer to go of three nominated, Gee, Ted Middleton and Janet Frame; in the event, however, none did.
28 *Then and There*, p.79 (19 Sept. 1975).
29 'Early reading: Maurice Gee on *Zane Grey*', *Education*, 24 (8), 1975, p.25.
30 Phyllis Hunt to MG, 4 Sept. 1975, 4678-272. Had the children's publishing situation been easier, she added, and Faber looking at expanding rather than cutting back their list they would have considered it.
31 Neil Robinson to MG, 23 Sept., 28 Oct. 1975, 4678-289.
32 MG to Peter Muxlow, 6 May 197[5]; contract dated 1 May and (revised) 30 May 1975, 4678-248.
33 Margaretha Gee to Greta Garden, 13 June 1975.
34 MG to Lyndahl Gee, 4 Nov. 1975, MS-Papers-8732-057, ATL.
35 MG to Dudding, n.d.; Dudding to MG, 27 Nov. 1975; MG to Dudding, 21 Dec. 1975, 4678-178/8988-080.
36 MG to Lyndahl Gee, 25 Nov. 1975.

17. Nelson

1 *In My Father's Den*, London: Faber and Faber, 1972, p.175.
2 R. McL, 'Whodunnit set in N.Z.', unsourced review of *In My Father's Den*, MS-Papers-4678-232, ATL.
3 Margaretha Gee, 'On the rocky road to success', *Nelson Evening Mail*, 7 Feb. 1980.
4 MG to Lyndahl Gee, 1 Dec. 1975, MS-Papers-8732-057, ATL.
5 *Games of Choice*, London: Faber and Faber, 1976, p.50.
6 MG to Lyndahl Gee, 1 Dec. 1975.
7 MG to Robin Dudding, 21 Dec. 1975, MS-Papers-8988-080, ATL.
8 Simon Cauchi to MG, 20 March 1976, 4678-178.
9 MG to Lyndahl Gee, 1 Dec. 1975.
10 MG to Lyndahl Gee, 6 Jan. 1976.
11 Margaretha Gee to Dudding, [Dec. 1975], MS-Papers-8988-080.
12 MG to Dudding, 13 May 1976.
13 MG to Dudding., 1 April 1976.
14 'The literary man looks back', *New Zealand Listener*, 11 Aug. 1976, p.16.
15 MG to Lyndahl Gee, 15 Dec. 1975.
16 MG to Dudding, 9 Feb. 1976.
17 Yvonne du Fresne to MG, 17 March 1977, 4678-178.
18 MG to Lyndahl Gee, 21 Dec. 1975.
19 MG to Dudding, 22 Jan., 2 May 1976.
20 Response to Literary Fund questionnaire, 1976 (via Elizabeth Caffin).
21 MG to Literary Fund, 23 Sept. 1975, 4678-274.
22 *Dominion*, 26 Jan. 1976, p.4.
23 'Oh Gee, the town crier', *New Zealand Herald* Weekend Magazine [1975], undated clipping, 4678-232; MG, interview with the author, 4 July 2006; *Plumb*, London: Faber and Faber, 1978, p.261.
24 MG, talk for the Nelson Institute, 16 March 1978, p.3, 8732-140; Orwell in the *Tribune*, 6 Dec. 1946, reprinted in *The Collected Essays, Journalism and Letters of George Orwell*, London: Secker and Warburg, 1968.
25 MG to Alan Bishop, n.d., 4678-179; interview with the author, 4 July 2006.
26 MG to Dudding, 9 Feb. 1976; Florence Chapple, diary, 1 June 1953, 4678-024.
27 MG, interview with the author, 4 July 2006.
28 MG to Lyndahl Gee, 22 Jan., 22 Feb. 1976.
29 Lyndahl Gee to MG, Monday, n.d. [March 1976], 4678-186.
30 MG to Lyndahl Gee, 22 Feb. 1976.
31 Ibid.; MG, interview with the author, 6 July 2006.
32 MG to Dora Hagemeyer, draft letter, n.d., 4678-179.
33 Dora Hagemeyer to MG, 24 Jan. 1976, 4678-179.
34 Muriel Parker to MG, n.d., 6 Oct. 1975, 4678-183.
35 Draft response to Faber author's questionnaire, 4678-272.
36 MG, interview with the author, 4 July 2006.
37 MG to Dudding, 1 Apr., 13 May 1976.
38 MG to Lyndahl Gee, Wed [19?] May 1976.
39 MG to Lyndahl Gee, 9 Feb. 1976.
40 MG to Dudding, 7 July 1976; to Lyndahl Gee, [June?] 1976.

41 Alison Abel to MG, 8 Dec. 1975, 4678-272.
42 Alison Abel to MG, 18 May 1976; MG to Lyndahl Gee, 17 June 1976; 'Grisly business', *Times Literary Supplement*, 9 July 1976; *Evening Standard*, 18 May 1976.
43 L. Edmond, *New Zealand Listener*, 11 Sept. 1976, p.60; A. Loney, *Landfall*, 120, Dec. 1976, p.340; L. Wevers, *New Zealand Bookworld*, 29, Oct. 1976, p.22; *Otago Daily Times*, 28 July 1976.
44 R. Haley, *Spleen*, 6, Dec. 1976, unpaginated.
45 *New Zealand Herald*, 11 Sept. 1976, section 2, p.5.
46 *Evening Post*, 25 Aug. 1976.
47 MG to Frank Sargeson, 6 Aug. 1976, MS-Papers-4261-064, ATL; Sargeson to MG, 25 July 1976, 4678-185.
48 MG to Lyndahl Gee, 18 July 1976.
49 'Maurice Gee: our unsung comrade', *Growth*, 1976.
50 *Dominion*, 23 June 1976.
51 MG to Lyndahl Gee, 17 June 1976; to Dudding, 24 June.
52 L. McNaughton, *Nelson Evening Mail*, 10 July 1976.
53 J. Callanan, 'Author launches his novel and leaves it to sink—or better, swim', *Evening Post*, 25 Aug. 1976, p.22.
54 Invitation, 4678-286; MG to Lyndahl Gee, 16 Sept. 1976.
55 This was a suggestion he elaborated on in his response to the Department of Internal Affairs survey of writers about the workings of the Literary Fund this year: 'Grants should be made automatically renewable. This is rather like saying writers should have pensions. Why not? There would be problems of course—who qualifies & who doesn't?—and a public outcry. But I think the idea of the state helping to support writers without a break through the productive years of their careers is a good one. I put it forward as a serious proposal.' Response to Literary Fund questionnaire, 1976 (via Elizabeth Caffin).
56 I. Wedde, 'The Splinterview 6: Maurice Gee . . .', *Spleen*, 6, Dec. 1976, unpaginated.
57 Margaretha Gee to Greta Garden, 17 July 1975, in the possession of Margareta Gee.
58 MG to Lyndahl Gee, n.d., 2 May 1976.
59 Ibid., 22 Jan. 1976.
60 MG to Ray Grover, n.d. (draft), 1976, 4678-179; Grover to MG, 8 Nov. 1976, 4678-180.
61 MG to Lyndahl Gee, 10, 25 Nov. 1976.

18. Making a Living

1 MG to Lyndahl Gee, 12 Jan., [9] Feb. 1977, MS-Papers-8732-057, ATL.
2 Robin Dudding to MG, 24 June 1976; MG to Dudding, 7 July 1976, MS-Papers-8988-080, ATL; *Islands*, 17, March 1977, p.284.
3 Charles Brasch to Dudding, 14 June 1966, MS-0966-003-055, Hocken Collections.
4 MG to Dudding, 7 July 1976; MG to Lyndahl Gee, 10 Dec. 1976; MG to Dudding, n.d.; Dudding to MG, 19 Jan. 1977.
5 Yvonne du Fresne to MG, 19 April 1977, MS-Papers-4678-178, ATL.

6 MG, 'Beginnings', *Islands*, 17, March 1977, pp.284–5.
7 Ibid., pp.289–90, 291, 290, 287, 288.
8 Dudding to MG, 19 Jan. 1977; 'Beginnings', p.289; MG to Dudding, 26 Jan. 1977. Gee was wrong here though, and the story more horrible than he knew. The man (a 30-year-old hotel porter about to start training as an observer with the Air Force) died in Auckland Hospital three days later, from his head and spinal injury combined with pneumonia (inquest file, COR 1941/155, Archives New Zealand).
9 *Plumb*, London: Faber and Faber, 1978, p.140.
10 Dudding to MG, 4 April 1977; MG to Dudding, 28 April.
11 MG to Dudding, ibid. The story in question was Rowan Metcalfe's 'The Cat'.
12 MG to Lyndahl Gee, 12 Jan. 1977.
13 Maurice Shadbolt to Kevin Ireland, 10 March 1977, 94-180-2/03, ATL.
14 MG to Shadbolt, 31 Jan. 1977, 91-047-16/15, ATL.
15 *Nelson Evening Mail*, 7 Aug. 1976.
16 Shadbolt to Ireland, 10 March 1977.
17 MG to Christine Cole Catley, 16 March 1977, MS-Papers-11651-136, ATL.
18 MG to Lyndahl Gee, [9] Feb. 1977.
19 MG to Lyndahl Gee, n.d.
20 J. Ewan, 'Moved to write', *New Zealand Bookworld*, 40, Oct. 1977, p.11; talk to Nelson Institute, 16 March 1978, pp.1–2, 4678-189.
21 MG to Lyndahl Gee, 23 March, 5 April 1977.
22 D. Young, 'Winner from way back', *New Zealand Listener*, 16 April 1977, p.21.
23 MG to Lyndahl Gee, [9] Feb. 1977.
24 *New Zealand Listener*, 7 May 1977, p.63; *Manawatu Evening Standard*, 23 April; *Dominion*, 23 April; *Christchurch Star*, 18 April.
25 J. Bertram, 'The God Boy again', *Comment*, Oct. 1977, p.27.
26 MG to Chris Cole Catley, 11 Feb. 1976.
27 Dudding to MG, 16 June; MG to Dudding, 28 April, 7 July 1977.
28 Catley to MG, 14 Feb. 1976; MG to Catley, 19 Feb., 18 March 1976.
29 Ewan, 'Moved to write', p.11.
30 Margaretha Gee to Greta Garden, 17 Nov. 1976, in the possession of Margareta Gee.
31 Margaretha Gee to Greta Garden, 21 Oct. 1977.
32 MG to Dudding, 28 April 1977; Dudding to MG, 31 May 1977.
33 Ray and Elizabeth Worley to MG, 31 Aug. 1977, 4678-185.
34 MG to Lyndahl Gee, 10, 25 Nov. 1976.
35 Margaretha Gee to Greta Garden, 29 April, 23 June 1977.
36 Rosemary Goad, Faber, to MG, 22 Sept., 2 Nov. 1977, 4678-272.
37 Nelson Central School centenary programme, 4678-175.
38 Frank Sargeson to MG, 4 April 1979, 4678-185.
39 I. Wedde, 'The Splinterview 6: Maurice Gee . . .', *Spleen*, 6, Dec. 1976, unpaginated.
40 MG to Sargeson, 2 April 1978, MS-Papers-4261-064, ATL.
41 Katherine Mansfield Memorial Award 1979, judge's report, MS-Papers-2100, ATL.
42 Shadbolt to Ireland, 21 Oct. 1978.
43 Clipping, 27 May 1978, 4678-302.

19. Plumb

1 MS-Papers-4678-286, ATL.
2 *Bookseller*, 5 Aug. 1978.
3 The photograph used was a fortuitous discovery on the designer's part in a box of old photographs in a derelict house on the Himitangi straight. It was taken, Missen ascertained, by a street photographer in Palmerston North, he thought in the 1930s, and could have been of the owner of the house and farm.
4 MG to Bridget Williams, draft, n.d., 4678-276.
5 *Observer*, 22 Oct. 1978; Rosemary Goad to MG, 23 Oct. 1978, 4678-272. A 'New Zealander's solid if rather dogged novel based on his grandparents' lives', Lee described it; 'The nineteenth century, it seems, lingered long in New Zealand.'
6 Frank Sargeson to MG, 7 Jan. 1979, 4678-185.
7 Sargeson to H. Winston Rhodes, 10 July 1979, MS-Papers-4261-221, ATL.
8 Author's note, *Plumb*, London: Faber and Faber, 1978, p.272.
9 MG to Sargeson, 22 March 1979, MS-Papers-4261-064; Sargeson to MG, 4 April 1979, 4678-185.
10 *Plumb*, p.177.
11 Ibid., p.43.
12 Ibid., pp.142, 17, 48.
13 B. Manhire, *Maurice Gee*, Auckland: Oxford University Press, 1986, p.33; *Plumb*, p.15.
14 *Plumb*, pp.9, 213, 11.
15 Ibid., p.272.
16 D. Young, 'Maurice Gee: "non-aligned" novelist', *New Zealand Listener*, 10 Feb. 1979, p.17.
17 Bernice, like Felicity, lived in Wellington in the 1920s, where she knew several of the Labour members of parliament, and had a de facto relationship with a left-wing activist and Unitarian (with the unlikely name of Cyprus Mitchell) which is the basis for Felicity's with Dan Peabody. Her two marriages were also to Labour figures (George Koller and Andrew Kydd). From Dora Felicity has her passion and her devotion to her father.
18 *Plumb*, pp.150, 171, 95, 164, 61, 165–6, 169.
19 MG, 'Beginnings', *Islands*, 17, March 1977, p.285.
20 Where Hollis's own middle names—Miro Blanchard—came from Gee also does not know. It was perhaps potentially confusing to give Plumb's nemesis, John Willis, his son's first name as a surname, but this coincidence came from the family too: Gee's aunt Florence had married Jim Hollis.
21 'Beginnings', p.291.
22 *Plumb*, pp.11, 217, 61, 218, 11.
23 *Plumb*, pp.12, 178.
24 Ibid., p.179.
25 Ibid., pp.11–12, 214–5, 205, 228.
26 Ibid., p.256.
27 Sargeson to MG, 7 Jan. 1979.
28 *Plumb*, pp.10, 56.
29 'Growing points of truth', *Islands*, 25, Spring 1978, p.306; MG to Bill Manhire,

26 May 1979, in the possession of Manhire.
30 Rosemary Goad to MG, 6, 22 Dec. 1977.
31 *New Zealand Listener*, 9 Dec. 1978, p.76; *Otago Daily Times*, 28 Feb. 1979; Young, 'Maurice Gee: "non-aligned" novelist', p.17.
32 *Comment*, 6, Feb. 1979, p.30; *Islands*, 25, Spring 1978, p.307.
33 MG to Manhire, 26 May 1979; Manhire to MG, n.d., 4678-182.
34 MG to Dan Davin, 22 March 1979, MS-Papers-5079-083, ATL; Davin to MG, 31 Jan. 1979, 4678-178. Sargeson tended to sentimentalise his homosexuals, Davin thought.
35 Dora Hagemeyer to MG, 12 Feb. 1979, 4678-179; Muriel Parker to MG, 9 Feb 1979; MG to Muriel Parker, 16 Jan. 1979, 4678-183.
36 *Plumb*, p.30.
37 Ibid., p.255. This woman, a Miss Hibbert, used brown paper and condensed milk can wrappings, and put barbed wire over the verandah as well (Florence Chapple, diary, 13 Feb. 1956, MSX-3604, ATL).
38 Lyndahl Gee to MG, Friday, n.d., 4678-186. Muriel Parker's poems were published as *The Roaring Silence* by the Brookfield Press, 1982.
39 Lyndahl Gee to MG, n.d., 10 Jan. 1978.
40 Rosemary Goad to MG, 9 Oct., 13 Dec. 1978.
41 *Dominion*, 20 Oct. 1979; John Griffin to MG, 29 Oct 1979, 4678-277; Griffin to Sargeson, 10 Nov. 1979, MS-Papers-4261-221.
42 *Auckland Star*, 27 April 1979.
43 Excerpts from judge's report, Jocelyn Harris, 4678-294.
44 Griffin to MG, 13 July 1979.
45 *New Zealand Listener*, 20 Oct. 1979, p.66; Wattie award invitation, MSY-3432, ATL.
46 MG to Manhire, 26 May 1979.
47 G. McLauchlan, 'Perspiration wins rewards', *New Zealand Herald*, 8 Sept. 1979, section 2, p.3.
48 Young, 'Maurice Gee: "non-aligned" novelist', p.16.
49 *Dominion*, 20 Oct. 1979.
50 *Comment*, 6 Feb. 1979, p.28.
51 *Financial Times*, 4 Nov. 1978.
52 'Growing points of truth', p.306.
53 MG, manuscript notes, 4678-030; A. Wilson, *The Wild Garden*, London: Secker and Warburg, 1963, pp.32–3.
54 MG, talk to Nelson Institute, 16 March 1978, 4678-189 and 8732-140.
55 Wilson, *The Wild Garden*, pp.30, 43, 32, 33; *Nelson Evening Mail*, 16 Aug. 1976.
56 *Plumb*, p.13.
57 Brian Boyd to MG, 27 Aug. 1979, 4678-177.
58 Robin Dudding to MG, 7 Nov. 1979, 15 Sept. 1980, 4678-178.
59 B. Boyd, 'Maurice Gee: ironies of growth and judgement, part I: the early fiction', *Islands*, 30, Oct. 1980, p.268; 'Part II: structure and irony in "Plumb"', *Islands*, 31–32, June 1981, p.160.
60 MG to Brian Boyd, 9 Nov. 1979, 4678-177.

20. Mortimer's Patch

1 MG to secretary, Literary Fund, 17 Dec 1977, MS-Papers-4678-274, ATL; notes, Chapple family research folder, 4678-029.
2 MG to Muriel Parker, 27 Nov. 1979, 4678-183.
3 MG to Brian Boyd, 20 Sept. 1979, *Islands*, 31–32, June 1981, p.160; MG to David Hill, written response to questions, 4678-180, and covering letter, 7 Nov. 1979, in the possession of David Hill. *Introducing Maurice Gee*, along with a volume on Sam Hunt, was published in 1981 and launched the series.
4 Robin Dudding to MG, 31 May 1977, 4678-178. 'The Secret Invaders' was another of Gee's tentative titles, but rejected by Bridget Williams and others at OUP as too Enid Blyton.
5 'Ambitious foray into fantasy', *New Zealand Herald*, 15 Sept. 1979, section 2, p.4.
6 *New Zealand Bookworld*, 57, March 1980, p.29; Dudding to MG, 5 April 1977, 4678-178.
7 K. Dermott, 'Writing is his life', *Auckland Star*, 3 June 1986, p.B3; 'Creeks and kitchens', Margaret Mahy lecture, 23 March 2002, in *The Inside Story*, Auckland: Children's Literature Foundation, 2003, p.20.
8 Tom Finlayson to MG, 22 Feb. 1979, 4678-248; *Mortimer's Patch* series three writers notes, 14 Aug. 1983, 4678-132.
9 *The Parnell Cook Book* (1980) and *Trouper Cooper's Curry Cookbook* (1982).
10 Series three writer's kit, 4678-240; series three writers notes.
11 T. Dunleavy, *Ourselves in Primetime*, Auckland: Auckland University Press, 2005, p.136; *New Zealand Listener*, 9 June 1981; *Dominion*, 19 May 1981, p.3.
12 MG, interview with the author, 4 July 2006.
13 MG, email to the author, 6 Aug. 2007; *New Zealand Listener*, 16 Aug. 1980, pp.14–15; *New Zealand Herald*, 20 Jan. 1981.
14 Story outline (working title 'Secret Gardens'), 4678-139.
15 Tom Finlayson to MG, 8 Feb., 16 July, 2 Oct. 1980, 4678-132, 247.
16 *Auckland Star*, 2 May 1981, p.6.
17 Series three writer's kit.
18 *New Zealand Herald*, 22 May 1982, section 2, p.8; Duncan Stuart to MG, 2 Feb. 1981, 4678-128.
19 Christine McCourt to MG, 18 May 1979, 4678-247.
20 Finlayson to MG, 4 Dec. 1979, 4678-247.
21 George Blackburn, senior producer, Concert Programme to MG, 15 Aug., 6 Oct. 1979, 4678-221; Rosemary Goad to MG, 8 Feb. 1980, 4678-272.
22 Chris Hampson to Ray Richards, 8 Feb., 30 May 1983, 4678-198.
23 Patrick Cox to Richards, 19 July 1982, 4678-198.
24 Hampson to Richards, 30 May 1983.
25 Chris Cole Catley to MG, 18 Jan. 1977, 4678-289.
26 Finlayson to MG, 4 Dec. 1979; *New Zealand Herald*, 30 Sept. 1981, section 1, p.14; *New Zealand Listener*, 3 Oct. 1981, pp.22–3.
27 Finlayson to MG, 2 Oct., 16 July 1980.
28 Unsourced clipping, 4678-228. The beach buggy was subsequently put up for sale.

29 *Auckland Star*, 5 Dec. 1980, p.13.
30 Finlayson to MG, 2 Oct. 1980.
31 *New Zealand Herald*, 3 Sept. 1981, section 1, p.19; *New Zealand Listener*, 21 Nov. 1981, p.84.
32 *Under the Mountain*, Wellington: Oxford University Press, 1979, p.148.
33 *New Zealand Listener*, 3 Oct. 1981, p.23.
34 *New Zealand Times*, 8 Nov. 1981.
35 *Auckland Star*, 10 Nov. 1983, p.13; Wendy Harrex to MG, 4 Dec. 1981, 18 June 1982, 4678-276. The television series also sold widely overseas, including to US cable network Nickelodeon and ITV in the UK, screening in over a dozen countries, including Australia, Ireland, Brunei, Kenya, South Africa, the Netherlands, Hungary and Czechoslovakia, Finland and France.
36 *Auckland Star*, 28 Oct. 1981, p.11.

21. Meg

1 Ray Richards to MG, 24 July, 2 May 1979, MS-Papers-4678-197, ATL.
2 'On the rocky road to success: story behind a best seller', *Nelson Evening Mail*, 7 Feb. 1980.
3 Richards to MG, 20, 22 Feb. 1980, 4678-199.
4 Robin Dudding to MG, 15 Sept. 1980, 4678-178.
5 Graham Beattie to Richards, 12 Dec. 1980, 4678-199.
6 John Griffin to MG, 29 Oct. 1980, 4678-277; Elizabeth to Nicole, 18 Nov. 1980, 4678-272.
7 The royal commission was established in 1946 to investigate the sale by tender of US army trucks and parts by the War Assets Realization Board. Gillies was one of several whose purchases were under investigation. It was the conduct of the board, however, with which the commissioners found fault. Profiteering from army surplus (Nissen huts, in this case) also formed a plot element of one of the two scripts Gee wrote, in the first months of 1981, for the television series *Both Sides of the Fence*.
8 *Meg*, London: Faber and Faber in association with Penguin, 1981, p.221.
9 Ibid., pp.47–8.
10 Ibid., pp.176, 180.
11 Ibid., pp.180, 101, 112.
12 Ibid., pp.23, 26.
13 MG to Rosemary Goad, 14 April; Goad to MG, 21 April 1981, 4678-272. The sweets became nuts and the tea was sweetened.
14 Muriel Parker to MG, 19 Dec. 1963; Jack Parker to MG, 27 April 1984, 4678-183; *Plumb*, London: Faber and Faber, 1978, p.254, *Meg*, pp.165–6.
15 *Meg*, p.11.
16 Ibid., pp.11, 15, 197.
17 Ibid., p.9; MG to Maurice Shadbolt, 8 Oct. 1956, 91-047-16/04, ATL.
18 *Meg*, pp.97–8, 205, 197, 98–9, 207.
19 Ibid., pp.104, 19, 21, 216.
20 Ibid., p.110.
21 Ibid., pp.121, 122, 124.
22 *Sole Survivor*, London: Faber and Faber in association with Penguin, 1983,

p.48; *Meg*, p.172.

23 MG to David Hill, written response to questions, Nov. 1979, 4678-180.

24 *Meg*, pp.125, 72–3, 169–70.

25 Ray Copland to MG, 24 June 1980, 4678-178.

26 MG to Dan Davin, 1 Dec. 1981, MS-Papers-5079-083, ATL; and to Cary biographer Alan Bishop, n.d., 4678-179.

27 MG to Lyndahl Gee, 2 May 1976, MS-Papers-8732-057, ATL.

28 *Meg*, pp.35, 34; Lyndahl Gee, 'The Change', in the possession of MG.

29 *Meg*, p.46, 'The Change', p.24.

30 *Meg*, p.33; 'The Change', p.19; *Meg*, p.15.

31 'The Meek', in the possession of MG; *Meg*, pp.82–3.

32 *Meg*, pp.39, 47; 'The Change', p.19.

33 'A Sleeping Face', *A Glorious Morning, Comrade*, Auckland: Auckland University Press, 1975, p.37.

34 Lyndahl Gee to MG, n.d. [late 1978/79], 4678-040.

35 MG, 'The way of a writer', *New Zealand Listener*, 17 Jan. 1987, p.40; *A Special Flower*, London: Hutchinson, 1965, p.89; untitled talk [c.1990]; Sydney Festival 1997 talk, 8732-140.

36 MG, email to the author, 22 March 2009.

37 *Going West*, Auckland: Viking, 1992, p.47.

38 Son of her sister Florence. He had begun training for the Anglican ministry but had left part way through.

39 MG, interview with the author, 6 July 2006.

40 MG to Ian Middleton, n.d., MS-Papers-6381-51, ATL.

41 MG, undated talk on writing for children [c.1980/81], 8732-141.

42 *Meg*, p.33.

43 *The Halfmen of O*, Auckland: Oxford University Press, 1982, pp.10, 22, 19.

44 Draft talk/biographical notes for a writers' festival, undated [1986?]; author profile, unsourced clipping, 4678-313; *Prowlers*, London: Faber and Faber, 1987, p.72.

45 *The Halfmen of O*, pp.77, 63; *Plumb*, p.256.

46 MG, 'Creeks and kitchens', Margaret Mahy lecture, 23 March 2002, in *The Inside Story*, Auckland: Children's Literature Foundation, 2003, p.21.

47 MG to Shadbolt, 31 [sic] Nov. 1981, 91-047-17/03.

48 *Financial Times*, 17 Oct. 1981. Angela Huth in the *Listener* had dismissed it as a 'stifling . . . everyday tale of profoundly dull New Zealand folk' with 'no gusto of any kind'. Manhire described her review in turn as a 'modish blend of condescension and inattention' and 'cheap cultural jibes'; or perhaps these were 'intended to supply anthropologists with an example of the provincial mind labouring to affect a synoptic or cosmopolitan nonchalance. I'm not aware that this condition has a name. But it does seem widespread at the moment' (*Listener*, 12 Nov. 1981, p.584; 16 Nov. 1981, p.650). Goad told Gee that Huth was 'something of a TV and radio personality' whose own novels were 'bitchy modern comedies of manners', and not to be worried about her review (Goad to MG, 13 Nov. 1981, 4678-271).

49 *New Zealand Listener*, 21 Nov. 1981, p.84.

50 Bill Manhire to MG, 9 Sept. 1985, 4678-182.

51 Dan Davin to MG, 26 Oct. 1981, 4678-178.

52 MG, talk to PEN, Dunedin, 20 Nov. 1984, 4678-189 and 8732-140; to David Hill, written response to questions, Nov. 1979.
53 Richards to MG, 28 Oct. 1981, 4678-198.
54 Goad to Richards, 15 Feb. 1982, 4678-198.
55 Goad to MG, 11 May 1981.
56 Richards to MG, 1 May 1981, 4678-197; press release, 4678-199.
57 Richards to Matthew Evans, 22 May 1981, 4687-197; to MG, 22 May 1981, 4678-199.

22. Sole Survivor

1 Secretary, Literary Fund to MG, 16 April 1980, MS-Papers-4678-285, ATL.
2 MG to Maurice Shadbolt, 31 [sic] Nov. 1981; Shadbolt to Tony and Brigitte Vogt, 15 Dec. 1981, 91-047-17/03, ATL.
3 MG to Shadbolt, ibid.
4 The names Raymond and Fergus were more family names: Ray Fergus was the first husband of Gee's aunt Deorwyn (the eleventh of the Chapple children, two years older than Lyndahl).
5 MG to Ray Richards, 25 Nov. 1981, 4678-198; to Dan Davin, 1 Dec. 1981, MS-Papers-5079-083, ATL.
6 MG to Muriel Parker, 6 April 1982, 4678-183.
7 MG to Richards, 29 Oct. 1981; *Meg*, London: Faber and Faber in association with Penguin, 1981, p.120.
8 Tom Finlayson to MG, 22, 31 July 1981, 4678-273.
9 Tony Stones to Kevin Ireland, 19 Jan. 1983, 94-180-1/04, ATL.
10 1982 Collins diary, entry for 4–7 May, MSX-3689, ATL.
11 Margaretha Gee to Greta Garden, 20 May 1982, in the possession of Margareta Gee.
12 Margaretha Gee to Greta Garden, 7 July, 29 May.
13 Margaretha Gee to John and Shirley, 3 June.
14 Margaretha Gee to John and Shirley, 7 July, 3 June.
15 Rosemary Goad to MG, 21 June 1982, 4678-272.
16 MG to Bill Manhire, 18 July 1982, in the possession of Manhire.
17 Janet Wilson to Phillip Wilson, photocopy in MS-Papers-8732-035, ATL.
18 *New Zealand Listener*, 4 Dec. 1982, p.128.
19 MG, interview with the author, 6 July 2006.
20 MG, interview with the author, 11 July 2006.
21 *New Zealand Listener*, 3 March 1984, p.38.
22 MG to Finlayson, 11 Aug. 1981, 4678-273.
23 *Trespasses* press kit, 10 Jan. 1983, 4678-157.
24 Press kit, 4678-153.
25 Finlayson to MG, 1 Sept. 1982, 4678-157.
26 *Metro*, Dec. 1984, p.185. The other four were New Zealand films *Death Warmed Up* and *Constance*, *All the Right Moves* and *The Twilight Zone*.
27 *Nelson Evening Mail*, 2 Feb. 1983, p.13; *Sole Survivor*, London: Faber and Faber in association with Penguin, 1983, pp.78, 81.
28 Graham Beattie to MG, 21 April 1983, 4678-280.
29 Rosemary Goad to MG, 13 April 1983, 4678-272.

30 B. Manhire, *New Zealand Times*, 26 June 1983, p.11.
31 *Meg*, pp.145–6.
32 *Sole Survivor*, pp.9–10.
33 Ibid., p.22.
34 Ibid., pp.147, 148.
35 Ibid., p.50.
36 Ibid., pp.61–2, 36.
37 MG to Richards, 29 Oct. 1981.
38 MG, interview with the author, 11 July 2006.
39 'Facade', *Mate*, 4, 1960, p.32; *Sole Survivor*, p.78.
40 *Sole Survivor*, pp.99, 100, 119, 107, 72.
41 Ibid., pp.71, 78, 155, 212, 157.
42 Ibid., p.76.
43 Ibid., pp.225, 47, 53, 48, 60.
44 MG, interview with the author, 1 June 2006.
45 *Sole Survivor*, pp.27, 30–1, 29.
46 Ibid., p.71.
47 In retropsect Gee would be sorry he gave Meg such a nasty death, when she was a character of whom he was very fond.
48 *Sole Survivor*, pp.228, 145.
49 MG to Manhire, 18 July 1982.
50 MG to Davin, 31 Jan. 1984; 'Maurice Gee interviewed by Brian Boyd', in E. Alley and M. Williams (eds), *In the Same Room*, Auckland: Auckland University Press, 1992, p.162; MG, interview with the author, 11 July 2006.
51 MG to Shadbolt, 31 [sic] Nov. 1981.
52 *New Zealand Times*, 26 June 1983, p.11; Manhire, *Maurice Gee*, Auckland: Oxford University Press, 1986, p.60.
53 MG, interview with the author, 11 June 2006.
54 Brian Boyd to MG, 30 June 1983, 4678-271; MG to Manhire, 14 Oct. 1983.
55 *Sole Survivor*, p.94; Boyd, 'Maurice Gee: structure and irony in *Plumb*', *Islands*, 31–32, June 1981, p.144; MG to Boyd, 9 Nov. 1979, quoted in ibid.
56 MG to Davin, 31 Jan. 1984; Davin to MG, 28 Nov. 1983, 4678-178.
57 MG, interview with the author, 11 July 2006.
58 *Sole Survivor*, p.72.
59 Ibid., p.19.
60 Ibid., p.230.
61 'The Maurice Gee trilogy', *Landfall*, 151, Sept. 1984, p.333; *Sole Survivor*, p.179.
62 *Sole Survivor* p.161.
63 *Financial Times*, 22 Oct. 1983.
64 *New Statesman*, 28 Oct.; *Oxford Times*, 4 Nov.; *Scotsman*, 5 Nov. 1983.
65 *Observer*, 23 Oct.; *Auckland Star*, 5 Dec., p.77; *London Review of Books*, 17–30 Nov.; *Times Literary Supplement*, 11 Nov. 1983.
66 Margaretha Gee to Marion and Bill Manhire, 6 Dec. 1983.
67 Goad to MG, 2 Feb.1984.
68 MG to Manhire, 11 March 1984; Richards to MG, 6 March 1985, 2 April 1984. St Martin's decided to remainder *Sole Survivor* at the end of 1984.
69 M. Leapman, *New York Times Book Review*, 15 Jan. 1984, quoted in Manhire, *Maurice Gee*, p.59; *Tulsa World*, 3 Nov. 1984.

23. Life After Plumb

1 MG, talk for PEN, Dunedin, 20 Nov. 1984, p.9, MS-Papers-4678-189 and 8732-140, ATL; C. Reilly, 'An interview with Maurice Gee', *Sport*, 5, Spring 1990, p.83.
2 *New Zealand Listener*, 10 Dec. 1983, p.99.
3 *New Zealand Listener*, 28 May 1983, p.126.
4 MG, interview with the author, 11 July 2006.
5 J. Westaway, 'Maurice Gee: answers from under the house', *New Zealand Woman's Weekly*, 22 Sept. 1986, p.15.
6 Ray Richards to Anne French, 20 May 1983, 4678-198.
7 MG to Bill Manhire, 19 July 1983, in the possession of Manhire.
8 MG to Chris Hampson, 1 Sept. 1983, 4678-214.
9 'Florrie', by 'Trout', pp.11, 3, 4678-073.
10 MG to Manhire, 14 Oct. 1983.
11 Richards to MG, 10 Sept. 1983, 4678-198.
12 The name of the boy who ran to fetch the police that afternoon at Falls Park in 1940, Noel Strid.
13 Marie Hoy, Cori Films International to MG, 4 Oct. 1983, 4678-130.
14 MG to Richards, 31 Jan. 1984, 4678-197. In fact, Marie Hoy of Cori International explained to Richards, they normally did not pay for treatments but Gee 'had evidently put so much time and thought into it'. Another script was written but the film was never made.
15 Maurice Shadbolt to Kevin Ireland, 9 April 1984, 94-180-2/03, ATL.
16 'Beginnings', *Islands*, 17, March 1977, p.286.
17 *The Priests of Ferris*, Auckland: Oxford University Press, 1984, p.131.
18 *Motherstone*, Auckland: Oxford University Press, 1985, pp.52, 56.
19 'Creeks and kitchens', Margaret Mahy lecture, 23 March 2002, in *The Inside Story*, Auckland: Children's Literature Foundation, 2003, p.20; L. Guerin, 'A balance of good and bad', *New Zealand Listener*, 13 Oct. 1984, p.21.
20 Ibid.
21 Stephen McElrea to MG, 5 Dec. 1983, 4678-248.
22 4678-131.
23 'Joker and Wife', *Collected Stories*, Auckand: Penguin, 1986, p.214.
24 Tony Simpson to MG, 24 April 1984, 4678-261; *PEN Gazette*, 129, Sept. 1984, p.3; F. Kidman, 'Let them eat words', *New Zealand Listener*, 9 June 1984, p.18.
25 McElrea to MG, 11 June 1984.
26 *Prowlers*, London: Faber and Faber, 1987, p.5.
27 McElrea to MG, 11 June; Philippa Campbell to MG, 19 Oct. 1984, 4678-248.
28 Talk for PEN, Dunedin, 20 Nov. 1984, pp.10, 9. The murder 'too horrible to describe here' was of Anne Kievet, a 37-year-old solo mother of three living in Sunnyvale, by her estranged lover in April 1966. After an intensive search involving over 200 police and navy divers, her clothing and body parts were found in the Oratia Stream a few hundred yards downstream from the Sunnyvale station; the rest of her body in a shallow grave a few feet from the edge of the stream.
29 *New Zealand Times*, 18 March 1984, p.8.

30 MG to Manhire, 12 Sept. 1985.
31 Tom Finlayson to MG, 12 May 1983, 4678-273.
32 Richards to MG, 15 Nov. 1985; to Anne French, 3, 12 Dec. 1985, 4678-196.
33 Richards to Mavis Pindard, Faber, 9 Sept. 1983; Richards to David Cunningham, OUP (Melbourne) (copy annotated for MG), 22 Oct. 1982, 4678-198.
34 Richards to Tony Pocock, 3 Feb. 1986, 20 May 1985, 4678-196.
35 Pocock to Richards, 8, 14 Feb. 1985; Richards to Pocock, 4 March 1985.
36 French to MG, 7 July 1985, 4687-275; Richards to French, 4 March 1985.
37 MG to Richards, 9 June 1986.
38 *The Fire-Raiser*, Auckland: Puffin in association with Oxford University Press, 1986, p.20.
39 Ibid., p.21.
40 Ibid., pp.66, 13, 35, 79, 9, 7.
41 *New Zealand Listener*, 23 Aug. 1986, p.19.
42 Ginette McDonald to MG, 18 Aug. 1986, 4687-247; Barry Shaw, unsourced clipping, 4678-230; *Sunday Star*, 24 Aug. 1986, p.C18; Chris Bourn to MG, 22 Sept. [1987], 4678-176.
43 D.J. Monaghan, TVNZ, to McDonald and Peter Sharp, 1 April 1987, 4678-247. This was at the Australian Academy of Broadcast Arts and Sciences awards.
44 Geoff Walker to MG, 11 Feb. 1986, Penguin archives.
45 The American award was at the New York International Film and Television Festival in 1987. The series was also sold over that period to Iceland, Brunei, Spain, Singapore, Czechoslovakia and Kuwait, and the telemovie to Belgium.
46 *Australian Bookseller and Publisher*, Oct. 1986, pp.56–7.
47 Walker to MG, 9 May 1986, 14 Oct. 1985, Penguin archives.
48 MG to John Barnett, 23 April 1985, 4678-280.
49 Walker to MG, 4 Feb. 1986, 4678-280; Richards to MG, 23 Jan. 1986, 4678-196.
50 Penny Morrissey, Viking Penguin (NY) to Richards, 18 June 1986, 4678-196.

24. Prowlers

1 MG to Bill Manhire, 12 Sept. 1985, in the possession of Manhire; MG, email to the author, 22 Feb. 2012; Ray Grover to MG, 14 April 1986, MS-Papers-4678-180, ATL.
2 MG to Kevin Ireland, 11 April 1986, 94-180-1/05, ATL.
3 Tim Winton to MG, 6 July 1986, 4678-185.
4 MG to Rosemary Goad, 16 Oct. 1986, 4678-271.
5 In, she elaborated, 'The first-person narrative, the picaresque structure, the references to Gee's earlier work, Sir Noel's very personal concerns that motivate the novel, even the very particular and, to an American audience, foreign setting.' Diana Finch, Ellen Levine Literary Agency to Ray Richards, 19 April 1988, 4678-195.
6 Tony Pocock to Geoff Walker, 16 Dec. 1986, Penguin archives.
7 4678-298.
8 MG to Ian Middleton, 26 Nov. 1986, 6381-51, ATL; *The Burning Boy*, Auckland: Viking, 1990, p.34; *Going West*, Auckland: Viking, 1992, p.202.

9 MG to Ireland, 11 April 1986.
10 J. Westaway, 'Maurice Gee: answers from under the house', *New Zealand Woman's Weekly*, 22 Aug. 1986, p.14.
11 L. Matthews, 'Gee's quiet struggle with words', *Nelson Evening Mail*, 20 June 1987, p.7.
12 *Prowlers*, London: Faber and Faber, 1987, p.200.
13 T.E. Tautsky, '"I let the story make its own demands": an interview with Maurice Gee', *Australian and New Zealand Studies in Canada*, 12, Dec. 1994, p.163.
14 Jack Parker to MG, 4 Feb.; MG to Parker, 17 Feb. 1984, 4678-183. (Royce is the name of the Butterses' son in *Plumb*.)
15 MG to Parker, 6 April 1984.
16 'Maurice Gee, interviewed by Brian Boyd', in E. Alley and M. Williams (eds), *In the Same Room*, Auckland: Auckland University Press, 1992, p.171.
17 'Maurice Gee: making sentences work', in G. O'Brien and R. Cross, *Moments of Invention*, Auckland: Heinemann Reed, 1988, p.116; A. Hubbard, 'Obsession of a quiet man', *Dominion Sunday Times*, 25 Oct. 1987, section 2, p.17; talk for PEN, Dunedin, 20 Nov. 1984, p.10, 4678-189 and 8732-140.
18 *Prowlers*, pp.1–2, 9.
19 Tautsky, '"I let the story make its own demands"', p.162; 'Maurice Gee, interviewed by Brian Boyd', p.170.
20 *Prowlers*, p.101; Hubbard, 'Obsession of a quiet man'; Tautsky, '"I let the story make its own demands"', p.162.
21 MG to Ireland, 11 April 1986.
22 *Prowlers*, pp.133, 3.
23 Ibid., pp.1, 14.
24 Ibid., p.206.
25 Ibid., pp.96, 101, 108, 116.
26 Ibid., p.56.
27 Ibid., p.205.
28 Ibid., pp.31, 11, 13, 234.
29 Ibid., p.169.
30 Ibid., pp.61, 176, 92, 222–4.
31 Ibid., p.225; Parker to MG, 12 March 1988.
32 Tautsky, '"I let the story make its own demands"', p.162.
33 *Prowlers*, p.171.
34 Hubbard, 'Obsession of a quiet man'.
35 C. Reilly, *Dominion*, 7 Nov. 1987, p.7; *Sunday Star*, 15 Nov. 1987, p.B4.
36 MG to Walker, 22 Feb. 1988; *New Zealand Listener*, 21 Nov. 1987, p.78.
37 MG to Ireland, 21 March 1988, 94-180-1/09.
38 M. Quigley, *Press*, Christchurch, 6 Feb. 1988.
39 *Evening Post*, 12 Dec. 1987, p.35; *Nelson Evening Mail*, Feb. 1988, clipping in 4678-230; *Literary Review*, Oct. 1987.
40 Hubbard, 'Obsession of a quiet man'; C. Reilly, 'An interview with Maurice Gee', *Sport*, 5, Spring 1990, p.85; *Prowlers*, p.5; *A Special Flower*, London: Hutchinson, 1965, p.46.
41 Matthews, 'Gee's quiet struggle with words'.
42 Ibid.; MG to Parker, 17 Feb. 1984.

43 New Zealand Book Council to MG, 25 Sept. 1986, 4678-219.
44 'The way of a writer', *New Zealand Listener*, 17 Jan. 1987, p.40.
45 M. Gifkins (ed.), *Through the Looking Glass*, Auckland: Century Hutchinson, 1988.
46 Richards to MG, 11 Aug. 1988, 4678-197; MG to Walker, 4 July 1988, Penguin archives.
47 'Maurice Gee: making sentences work', pp.114, 116.
48 MG to Manhire, 13 Oct. 1987.
49 A. Mallinson, *Recollections of 5 festivals*, Wellington: Daphne Brasell Associates and Lincoln University Press, 1996, p.19.
50 H. Ricketts, 'Margaret Drabble offers insight at question time', *Dominion*, 18 March 1988, p.9.
51 MG to the secretary, Literary Fund, 28 July 1986, 4678-273.
52 Ginette McDonald, '"1943": Notes for MG', 4678-171.
53 Ibid.
54 MG, 'Story idea for kidult TV serial', 4678-161; *The Champion*, Auckland: Puffin, 1989, pp.18, 7–8.
55 *The Champion*, pp.93, 66, 7, 11; 'Summer Friends: format for a kidult serial', 4678-161.
56 'Story idea for kidult TV serial'.
57 *The Champion*, p.173; MG to Walker, 9 Dec. 1988.
58 MG, 'Creeks and kitchens', Margaret Mahy lecture, 23 March 2002, in *The Inside Story*, Auckland: Children's Literature Foundation, 2003, p.23.
59 Walker to MG, 6 July 1988, Penguin archives; Richards to MG, 21 Oct. 1988, 4678-197.
60 *New Zealand Herald*, 9 Oct. 1989, section 1, p.17.
61 Peter Sharp, quoted on NZ on Screen, www.nzonscreen.com/person/peter-sharp/biography.
62 MG to Walker, 11, 15 Nov. 1988.
63 Mary Lee Donovan, editor, children's trade books, Houghton Mifflin to Walker, 27 Oct. 1989, Penguin archives.
64 B. Shaw, 'Champion writer puts scripts aside for next project', *New Zealand Herald*, undated clipping, 4678-230.

25. The Burning Boy

1 MG to Frasers, 28 Sept. 1988, MS-Papers-4678-179, ATL; MG to Bill Manhire, 25 Sept. 1988, in the possession of Manhire.
2 Katherine Walls to MG, 11 Nov. 1988, 4678-285; MG to Walls, 9 Nov., 4678-179.
3 Margaretha Gee, email to the author, 22 Feb. 2012.
4 Manhire, note for MG, n.d., 4678-061.
5 MG to Manhire, 25 Sept. 1988.
6 Ibid.
7 Kathryn Walls, email to the author, 18 July 2012.
8 R. Hammond, *The Writer and the Word Processor*, London: Coronet, 1984, p.19; 'Maurice Gee: answers from under the house', *New Zealand Woman's Weekly*, 22 Aug. 1986, p.14.

9 Application for Victoria University Writer's Fellowship, 18 Sept. 1988, 4678-285.
10 'The way of a writer', *New Zealand Listener*, 17 Jan. 1987, p.42; *Victoria News*, 1 Nov. 1989, p.1.
11 Geoff Walker to Ray Richards, 23 Nov. 1988, Penguin archives; 13 Feb. 1989, 4678-202.
12 Bernice Beacham, Penguin, to Faber, 19 Sept. 1990, Penguin archives.
13 Richards to Walker, 9 April 1990, Penguin archives.
14 Walker to Faber, 17 Jan. 1990, Penguin archives.
15 Walker to MG, 20 March 1990, 4678-278; Walker to Virginia Bonham-Carter, Faber, 22 March 1990, Penguin archives.
16 *The Burning Boy*, Auckland: Viking, 1990, p.38.
17 Ibid., pp.25, 21.
18 MG to secretary, Literary Fund, 28 July 1986, 4678-273.
19 'Place', New Zealand Book Council talk, 28 March 1995, p.8, MS-Papers-8732-140, ATL; *Prowlers*, London: Faber and Faber, 1987, p.135.
20 *The Burning Boy*, p.243.
21 Ibid., p.112.
22 Ibid., pp.27, 272, 224, 117.
23 Ibid., p.271.
24 Ibid., p.23.
25 C. Reilly, 'Gee's continuing obsession with evil', *Dominion*, 10 Nov. 1990, p.7.
26 D. Jenkin, 'Plumbing the springs of wickedness', *New Zealand Listener*, 27 Sept. 1986, p.33.
27 *Collected Stories*, Auckland: Penguin, 1986, p.122; *The Burning Boy*, pp.275, 273.
28 Reilly, 'Gee's continuing obsession with evil'.
29 'Hour with', talk, [1991], 4678-188. Duncan was not the first of Gee's characters to get a last-minute reprieve. Gee told his audience at the Nelson Institute in 1976 that he had been intending for Kingsley Pratt to die at the end of *Games of Choice* until he was nearing the end of the first draft (*Nelson Evening Mail*, 7 Aug. 1976).
30 *The Burning Boy*, pp.211, 210, 45.
31 Ibid., pp.12, 73, 76, 77.
32 As the Gees' Maitai Valley friends who lost their home, the Wilkies', goats were burned.
33 *Sole Survivor*, London: Faber and Faber in association with Penguin, 1983, p.225.
34 *The Burning Boy*, p.32; revision book p.14, draft manuscript book 14, p.540, 4678-060.
35 Typescript [3], pp.5–6, 4678-063; draft manuscript book 1, pp.8–9, 4678-057.
36 C. Reilly, 'An interview with Maurice Gee', *Sport*, 5, Spring 1990, p.82.
37 Draft manuscript book 2, p.58 (and loose revision sheet); book 3, p.109; book 7, p.240, 4678-057, 058. The name Tiedeman though belonged to Napier friends of the Gees. Clearwater was also a borrowed name, a Henderson one, though the character is an invention.
38 Draft manuscript book 6, p.213, 4678-058.
39 *New Zealand Listener*, 12 Nov. 1990, p.110; *Bay of Plenty Times*, 19 Jan. 1991;

Dominion Sunday Times, 25 Nov. 1990, p.24; *Times Literary Supplement*, 2–8 Nov. 1990, p.1183; *Scotsman*, 1 Dec. 1990.

40 *New Zealand Listener*, 12 Nov. 1990, p.110.

41 'Going West' talk, Christchurch Public Library, 25 May 1993; talk for Bookfest, Christchurch, 16 Oct. 1993, 8732-140.

42 *Listener*, 22 Nov. 1990, p.30; *Times Literary Supplement*, 2–8 Nov. 1990, p.1183; *New Zealand Listener*, 17 Dec. 1990, p.83 (also *Sunday Times*, 4 Nov. 1990; *Evening Standard*, 23 Feb. 1991).

43 Richards to MG, 11 Feb. 1992, 4678-200; Walker to MG, 7 Nov. 1989, 4678-279.

44 MG to Walker, 19 Dec. 1990, Penguin archives.

45 *New Zealand Books*, 1 (1), April 1991, p.7; draft manuscript book 13, p.488, 4678-060.

46 *Times Literary Supplement*, 2–8 Nov. 1990, p.1183.

47 I. Sharp, *Sunday Star*, 2 Dec. 1990, p.C7.

48 Launch speech, 14 March 1990, 4678-188; Walker to MG, 24 May 1990, Penguin archives.

49 MG to Rob Hood, South Pacific Credit Cards, 15 Nov. 1989, 4678-179.

50 Tom Finlayson to MG, 4 Oct. 1989, 4678-217; Richards to MG, 23 Nov., 22 Dec. 1989, 4678-203.

51 Richards to MG, 7 Sept. 1989, 4678-203.

52 Unsourced clipping, 23 Nov. 1988; application for Victoria University Writer's Fellowship, 18 Sept. 1988.

53 'Going West' talk, 25 May 1993.

54 Reilly, 'An interview with Maurice Gee', p.82.

55 Ibid., pp.85, 82, 83.

56 Ibid., p.84.

57 B. Manhire, *Maurice Gee*, Auckland: Oxford University Press, 1986, p.67.

26. Going West

1 Draft application, MS-Papers-4678-312, ATL.

2 Draft letter, n.d., to J. Keats, secretary, Katherine Mansfield Memorial Fellowship.

3 C.K. Stead, *Book Self*, Auckland: Auckland University Press, 2008, p.323.

4 Brenda Harden, national secretary, to MG, 31 July 1990, 4678-219.

5 S. Stratford, 'Pissed poets' society', *Metro*, June 1991, pp.116, 117.

6 MG, email to the author, 8 Oct. 2012.

7 MG quoted in N. Cox, 'Rule of Plumb', *Quote Unquote*, July 1993, p.21.

8 *Aloud*, 1 (1), Sept. 1991, p.15. He had already turned down an invitation to Toronto and one to Guelph in 1983.

9 T.E. Tautsky, '"I let the story make its own demands": an interview with Maurice Gee', *Australian and New Zealand Studies in Canada*, 12, Dec. 1994, pp.155–63.

10 B. Boyd, 'Maurice Gee, interviewed by Brian Boyd', in E. Alley and M. Williams (eds), *In the Same Room*, Auckland: Auckland University Press, 1992, p.159.

11 Ibid.

12 Ray Richards to Jeff Olssen and Anne French, 3 June 1988, 4678-195.

13 French to Geoff Walker and Richards, 8 Sept. 1988.
14 Walker to Penguin Group, fax, 10 Aug. 1988; MG to Walker, 20 Aug. 1988, Penguin archives.
15 French to Richards and Virginia Bonham-Carter, Faber, 12 Sept. 1989; Richards to French, 14 Sept. 1989, 4678-203; French to Robert McCrum and Richards, 11 Apr. 1990, Penguin archives.
16 Untangling the rights situation with *Meg* and *Sole Survivor* was the main reason for the delay. *The Plumb Trilogy* finally came out in March 1995, with the real James Chapple this time on the cover—Gee thanking Walker for having 'humanised my old grandad with a half-smile' (the photograph had been manipulated by the designer) (MG to Walker, 11 Dec. 1994, Penguin archives). It was not a success, as Walker later conceded: 'The exercise of publishing the three books together hasn't really worked in a sales sense, and also as you know there's unhappiness in academia that students studying *Plumb* have to buy the full book. Maybe also the cover design wasn't all that wonderful' (Walker to Gee, 28 Oct. 1999, MS-Papers-8732-102, ATL). A Penguin *Plumb* came out in 2000.
17 'Bookmarks', *New Zealand Listener*, 13 March 1993, p.51.
18 Cox, 'Rule of Plumb', p.23.
19 *Evening Standard*, 23 Feb. 1991, p.8; *Dominion*, 13 March 1993, p.12; Cox, 'Rule of Plumb', p.23.
20 A. Johnston, 'Maurice Gee: our superb storyteller', *Evening Post*, 3 July 1993, p.13.
21 *Sunday Times*, 14 March 1993, p.22.
22 Quoted by Richards to McCrum, 5 Dec. 1991, 4678-201.
23 *Going West*, Auckland: Viking, 1992, pp.81, 16, 5.
24 Ibid., pp.130, 9, 10, 27, 68, 243, 120, 8, 10; MG at Auckland Writers' and Readers' Festival, 13 May 2012.
25 *Going West*, p.14.
26 Ibid., pp.90, 226, 46, 74, 102.
27 Ibid., pp.93, 84, 34, 60, 2, 141, 53, 131, 231, 31, 22.
28 Ibid., pp.22, 23.
29 Alistair Campbell, diary, 6 Feb. 1993 (via Nelson Wattie).
30 *Going West*, pp.28, 71, 2.
31 A Mrs Petley nurses Robert in *Meg*.
32 *Going West*, p.148.
33 *Sunday Times*, 14 March 1993, p.22; *Sunday Times*, 31 Jan. 1993.
34 MG, email to the author, 18 Nov. 2012.
35 *Going West*, pp.118, 119, 120.
36 Ibid., pp.24, 26.
37 *Sunday Times*, 14 March 1993, p.22.
38 *Going West*, p.183.
39 Boyd, 'Maurice Gee, interviewed by Brian Boyd', p.172.
40 *Going West*, pp.114, 113, 194.
41 Ibid., p.81; 'Love in different languages', draft talk for Singapore literary festival, Sept. 1995, 8732-141.
42 *Going West*, pp.243, 180. Connecticut, Gee had read in his own Webster's, was known as the Land of Steady Habits.

43 *Going West*, pp.202, 114, 20, 200, 213.
44 Ibid., pp.218, 222, 253.
45 MG to Craig Steed, 20 Sept. 2001, 8732-031; MG to Walker, 15 Aug. 1991, 4678-280.
46 *North and South*, Jan. 1992, p.12; *Dominion*, 21 Nov. 1991, p.3.
47 Margareta to Emily and Abi, 30 March 1992, in the possession of Maurice and Margareta Gee.
48 MG to Emily and Abi, 11 March 1992.
49 Ibid.
50 MG to Emily and Abi, 26 May, 24 April, 11 March 1992.
51 Margareta Gee to Emily and Abi, 24 March; MG to Emily and Abi, 24 March, n.d. [April] 1992.
52 MG to Emily and Abi, n.d. [April] 1992.
53 MG to Emily and Abi, 11 March 1992.
54 *New Zealand Herald*, 7 Aug. 1993, section 2, p.6.
55 *Going West*, p.242; MG to Emily and Abi, 26 May, 22 Sept. 1992.
56 Margareta Gee to Emily and Abi, 1 May 1992.
57 MG to Emily and Abi, 17 June, Margareta Gee to Emily and Abi, 3 July 1992. 'I don't know where the rumour that we didn't like Menton came from', Gee would subsequently comment to Michael Gifkins; 'We liked it and we didn't like it', and '[w]ouldn't have missed it.' Alistair Campbell, however, recorded in his diary after a party early the next year: 'Had a good yarn with Gee, recently returned from Menton. From what he told me, the links with KM are rather tenuous. Makes more sense, he said, to have the study in London. All there is in Menton is a study connected to a villa that has been condemned. Menton itself is just a city along the Mediterranean. He'd expected a village. Spent much of his leisure time getting out of the city and walking along the hills.' MG to Michael Gifkins, n.d. (draft), 8732-451; Alistair Campbell, diary entry, 6 Feb. 1993.
58 MG to Stephen Bain, 31 Aug. 2000, 8732-038; Margareta Gee to Emily and Abi, 29 April 1992.
59 Margareta Gee to Emily and Abi, 29 April 1992.
60 Margareta Gee to Emily and Abi, 1. Aug. 1992.
61 MG to Emily and Abi, 24 July 1992.
62 Ibid.
63 Rosemary Goad to MG, 8 May 1992, 8732-451.
64 Margareta Gee to Emily and Abi, 26 Sept.–12 Oct. 1992. They had hoped to find accommodation in France and Germany through Servas, an international hosting organisation (established as a peace initiative in Denmark in 1949) they had joined in 1980, but were twice curtly rebuffed. Of the succession of travellers who had stayed with them at Cleveland Terrace over the years, two of the more colourful made cameo appearances in *Prowlers*: the homesick American boy who 'ate us out of ice cream and went into a foetal trance in the shower', and the Hiking Viking, 'a huge Dane' who 'shamble[d] like a bear' (*Prowlers*, London: Faber and Faber, 1987, p.193).
65 MG to Emily and Abi, 22 Sept. 1992.
66 Margareta Gee to Virginia Baron, 30 Sept. 1992.
67 Ibid.

68 MG to Emily and Abi, 22 Sept. 1992.
69 Ibid.
70 MG to Richards, n.d. (draft), 8732-453.

27. The Fat Man

1 Margareta Gee to Jane and Jenny (covering letter with article for *New Zealand Author*), 18 Jan. 1993.
2 Margareta Gee to Rolf Schmelzer, 1 Dec. 1992, MS-Papers-4678-304, ATL.
3 Margareta Gee to Virginia Baron, 30 Sept. 1992; to Alan, 19 Sept. 1992, in the possession of Maurice and Margareta Gee.
4 C. Brett, 'The Gee genius', *North and South*, Sept. 1995, p.101.
5 N. Cox, 'Rule of Plumb', *Quote Unquote*, July 1993, p.21; *Times Literary Supplement*, 8 Jan. 1993, p.18; *Sunday Times*, 31 Jan. 1993; *Pacific Way*, May 1993, p.13.
6 *Metro*, May 1993, p.130.
7 *New Zealand Listener*, 27 March 1993, p.49; *Dominion*, 13 March 1993, p.12.
8 'Going West', talk given at Christchurch Public Library, 25 May 1993; talk for Bookfest, Christchurch, 16 Oct. 1993, MS-Papers-8732-140, ATL.
9 *London Magazine*, Feb/March 1994, p.153.
10 Dennis McEldowney to MG, 9 Aug. 1993, 8732-023; Toss Woollaston to MG, 16 April 1993, 8732-035.
11 T.E. Tautsky, '"I let the story make its own demands": an interview with Maurice Gee', *Australian and New Zealand Studies in Canada*, 12, Dec. 1994, p.161.
12 *Times Literary Supplement*, 8 Jan. 1993, p.18.
13 Geoff Walker to MG, 11 Jan. 1994, 8732-113.
14 Penguin archives.
15 Walker to MG, Ray Richards and Robert McCrum, 15 Dec. 1994, 8732-113.
16 *New Zealand Herald*, 7 Aug. 1993, section 2, p.6; *Dominion*, 3 Aug. 1994.
17 *Norwester*, 11 May 1994.
18 Cox, 'Rule of Plumb', p.21.
19 At the same time his old Napier friend Graham Beattie was canvassing writers' opinions about Gee being put forward for a Nobel Prize; the general feeling, though, was that the first New Zealand writer that should be considered was Frame.
20 Cox, 'Rule of Plumb', p.23.
21 Ibid., pp.21–2; *New Zealand Herald*, 7 Aug. 1993, section 2, p.6; 8732-137, 390–3.
22 Application for Katherine Mansfield Fellowship, [1991], via MG.
23 Brett, 'The Gee genius', p.101; MG, interview with the author, 11 July 2006.
24 Application for Mansfield Fellowship; notes for book awards, 8732-242; *Independent Herald*, 16 May 1995.
25 *Crime Story*, Auckland: Penguin, 1994, p.19.
26 Greta Garden had died when the Gees were in New York on the way home from Menton. Rather than cut their journey short, they delayed the funeral until their return (Emily handling the arrangements with the undertaker for the embalming).

27 *Crime Story*, p.21.
28 Minnitt's conviction for manslaughter instead of murder on the grounds of provocation (his wife's infidelity and drinking and—in his lawyer's words—'verbal abuse') and sentence of just four years (of which he served two and a half) was highly controversial: women protested outside the court and a 900-signature petition was presented to the minister of justice arguing that it had been a miscarriage of justice. F. Walsh, 'No resting in peace', *Grace*, June 2000, pp.58–62; R. McLeod, 'Exile in Westport', *North and South*, May 1986, pp.42–54.
29 *Crime Story*, p.186.
30 Ibid., p.23.
31 Ibid., pp.42, 25, 157.
32 Ibid., pp.25, 21; *Games of Choice*, London: Faber and Faber, 1976, p.134.
33 Tor Klevstul to MG, 24 May 1992, 8732-123; MG, interview with the author, 11 July 2006. Klevstul self-published (under the imprint Rowantree Publications) three books of poetry—*New Millennium*, 1996, *Blessed Be*, 1998, and *Wildflowers*, 1998—and his novel, *Mountain of the Gods*, in 1999.
34 *Crime Story*, p.111, 107.
35 MG to Klevstul, n.d. (draft), 8732-019.
36 *Crime Story*, p.39; MG to Emily and Abi, 5 May 1992, in the possession of Maurice and Margareta Gee.
37 MG to Klevstul, n.d. (draft).
38 Klevstul to MG, 4 Feb. 1994, 8732-019; MG to Klevstul, n.d. (draft).
39 Klevstul to MG, 3 Sept. 1993, 8732-019 (and see *Crime Story*, p.111); 30 Aug. 1993, 4678-123.
40 Also the name of one of Gee's Avondale College teachers.
41 MG to Emily and Abi, 5 May 1992; Abi Gee, notes for MG, 4678-242.
42 Walker, unhelpfully, still wasn't sure either: 'So Danny is to be a Pakeha. That's fine. I suppose I have some ambivalence about it, because as a Maori he was pretty vivid.' Walker to MG, 28 June, 21 July 1993, 8732-112; MG to Walker, 5 July 1993, Penguin archives.
43 *Crime Story*, p.152.
44 *In My Father's Den*, London: Faber and Faber, 1972, p.131.
45 *Landfall*, 189, Autumn 1995, p.116.
46 A. Johnston, 'Maurice Gee: our superb storyteller', *Evening Post*, 3 July 1993, p.13.
47 Walker to MG, 28 June 1993, 8732-112.
48 Walker to Ros Edwards and Robert McCrum, 29 July 1992, Penguin archives; MG to Walker (postcard from Dijon), 6 Aug. 1992, Penguin archives; MG to McCrum, 19 Jan. 1993, 8732-116.
49 Walker to Clare Alexander, Viking (UK) and Andrew Franklin, Hamish Hamilton, 21 April 1993, Penguin archives. Richards had already approached Bloomsbury and Hodder Headline in February.
50 Andrew Franklin to Walker, 20 July 1993; Walker to MG, 6 July 1993, 8732-112.
51 McCrum to Richards, 16, 27 Sept., 13 Oct. 1993, 8732-087.
52 MG to McCrum, 15 Nov. 1993, 8732-116; to Richards, n.d. (draft), 8732-453. Yet he was still bothered that they weren't apparently making much of an effort

to promote his novels: 'What do you make of the Sunday Times reviewer's comment about Faber and Faber not doing enough to make my work well-known in the UK?', he had asked Robert McCrum earlier this year (MG to McCrum, 7 March 1993, 8732-116).

53 Walker to MG, 20 Oct. 1993; to Dexter Fry, 21 Oct. 1993, Penguin archives.

54 MG to Walker, 12 Jan. 1994, 8732-113; to Emma Platt, Faber, 6 June 1994, 8732-116.

55 Jane Parkin to MG, 22 Oct. 1993, 4678-254; MG to Walker, 12 Jan. 1994, 8732-113.

56 Walker to MG, 28 June 1993, 8732-112; MG to McCrum, 7 Feb. 1995, 8732-116.

57 MG to Richards, 4 Oct. 1994, 8732-088.

58 Walker to MG, 6 March 1995, 8732-110.

59 Richards to Kate Burke Miciak, associate publisher, crime, Bantam Doubleday Dell, 15 July 1993; Bantam Doubleday to Richards, 17 Sept. 1993, 8732-087.

60 *Evening Post*, 29 July 1994, p.7; *Dominion*, 30 July 1994, p.16; *Levin Chronicle*, 17 Oct. 1994; *Quote Unquote*, Oct. 1994, pp.26–7.

61 *New Zealand Herald*, 30 July 1994, section 3, p.7.

62 Draft review, with McEldowney to MG, 8 Aug. 1994, 8732-023. The review was for the *Sunday Star Times* (7 Aug.), whose books editor cut it by half, to McEldowney's annoyance and he sent Gee his original version, with the comment: 'It may not be an improvement, but at least it was what I meant.'

63 MG to John and Ania Borrell, 4 July 1993, 8732-002.

64 Richards to MG, n.d., 8732-087; MG to Richards, 21 Jan. 1994, 8732-088.

65 S. Stuart, 'Gentle Gee has grip on all ages', *Sunday Star Times*, 23 April 1995, p.D3; J. Westaway, 'Looking out of another window', *Booknotes*, 110, July 1995, p.3.

66 MG, 'Blind Road', unpublished memoir, p.19; *Nelson Evening Mail*, 29 June 1994, p.11.

67 'Beginnings', *Islands*, 17, March 1977, p.284.

68 *The Fat Man*, Auckland: Viking, 1994, p.14.

69 *Timaru Herald*, 4 Feb. 1994, p.11.

70 MG, interview with Vivian van Rij, 9 Dec. 2003.

71 *The Fat Man*, pp.90, 62, 134, 124.

72 Ibid., pp.17, 120.

73 'Creeks and kitchens', Margaret Mahy lecture, 23 March 2002, in *The Inside Story*, Auckland: Children's Literature Foundation, 2003, pp.22–3.

74 *Landfall*, 199, March 2000, pp.38–9.

75 *The Fat Man*, pp.40, 115.

76 Ibid., pp.92, 138–9.

77 A. Nieuwenhuizen, 'Maurice Gee: creek, kitchen and the art of language', *Magpies New Zealand*, 1, March 1997, quoting Gee at the Sydney Writers' Festival.

78 *New Zealand Listener*, 13 May 1995, p.12; 10 June 1995, p.14.

79 *Evening Post*, 1 Aug. 1995, p.8.

80 M. White, 'A new twist to those old tales', *Next*, Sept. 1995, p.58; Nieuwenhuizen, 'Maurice Gee: creek, kitchen and the art of language'.

81 J. Holloway, 'A fat boy, a creek and personal responsibility', *New Zealand*

Books, Aug. 1995, p.22; Westaway, 'Looking out of another window'.
82 *The Fat Man*, p.11; Nieuwenhuizen, 'Maurice Gee: creek, kitchen and the art of language'.
83 Tessa Duder (convenor), Wayne Mills and Hine Elder, *New Zealand Listener*, 3 June 1995, p.14.
84 By the Wright Publishing Group (who had Joy Cowley on their list), Doubleday, Farrar Strauss Giroux, Random House, Henry Holt, Houghton Mifflin and Putnam's.
85 Joanna Guinther to MG (sent with *New York Times Book Review* clipping, 24 Feb. 1994); Olga Litowinsky, Simon and Schuster to MG, 23 April 1993, 8732-119. *The Champion* was selected as an American Library Association Best Book for Young Adults—'a very impressive honor', Simon and Schuster told him—and was on the New York Public Library's 1994 list of Books for the Teen Age.
86 David Gale, senior editor, children's division to MG, 10 June 1996; MG to Gale, 30 June 1996.
87 *Booklist*, 15 Dec. 1997, p.693; John Rudolph to MG, 5 Jan. 1998, 8732-094.
88 Richards to MG, April 1998, 8732-094; MG to Bernice Beacham, 16 March 1994, 8732-112.

28. Loving Ways

1 N. Cox, 'Rule of Plumb', *Quote Unquote*, July 1993, p.23.
2 DAAD fellowship application, 1 Dec. 1992, MS-Papers-8732-010, ATL.
3 J. Westaway, 'Looking out of another window', *Booknotes*, 110, July 1995, p.3.
4 MG to Geoff Walker, 13 July 1994, Penguin archives.
5 MG to the Arts Council literary committee, 29 June 1994, 8732-001.
6 Nelson talk, 27 Sept. 1996, 8732-140; M. Amery, 'Territorial imperative', *Quote Unquote*, June 1996, pp.12–13.
7 *Loving Ways*, Auckland: Penguin, 1996, pp.13, 37.
8 Nelson talk, 27 Sept. 1996.
9 Dahlberg served twenty years and was released in February 2012, having never admitted his guilt or disclosed the whereabouts of the body and the murder weapon.
10 Nelson talk, 27 Sept. 1996.
11 *Loving Ways*, pp.67, 69, 57.
12 Ibid., pp.38, 16, 18, 49.
13 MG, interview with the author, 18 July 2006.
14 *Loving Ways*, pp.62, 72, 65.
15 Ibid., pp.40–41.
16 Ibid., p.69.
17 J. Newton, *Landfall*, 192, Spring 1996, p.336.
18 Amery, 'Territorial imperative'.
19 *Loving Ways*, p.22.
20 Amery, 'Territorial imperative'.
21 Ray Richards to MG, 10 July 1995, 8732-089; MG to Walker, 13 Aug. 1995, 8732-110; to Richards, 30 Sept. 1995, 8732-089; Richards to MG, 30 Nov. 1995.

22 Tor Klevstul to MG, 18 Aug. 1996, 3 Sept. 1993, 8732-019; Amery, 'Territorial imperative'; MG to Walker, 13 Aug. 1995, 8732-110.
23 MG to Walker, 13 Aug. 1995.
24 Walker to MG, 12 July 1996, 8732-111.
25 *North and South*, 123, June 1996, p.122; *New Zealand Books*, Oct. 1996, p.5.
26 *Dominion*, 22 June 1996, p.18; *Metro*, Aug. 1996, p.110; *Printout*, 12, Autumn 1997, p.84; *New Zealand Listener*, 15 June 1996, p.47; *London Magazine*, Apr./May 1998, p.122.
27 *Landfall*, 192, Sept. 1996, pp.336–7; *Printout*, 12, Autumn 1997, p.84; MG, interview with the author, 18 July 2006; MG quoted in A. Hubbard, 'Obsession of a quiet man', *Dominion Sunday Times*, 15 Oct. 1987, p.17.
28 *Landfall*, 192, Sept. 1996, p.337.
29 MG, interview with the author, 18 July 2006.
30 MG to Faber, 12 Feb. 1997, 8732-117.
31 Walker to MG, 25 March 1996; MG to Walker, 3 Feb. 1997, 8732-111.
32 MG to Libby Gleeson, 25 June 1996, 30 Jan. 199[7]; Gleeson to MG, 10 Jan. 1997, 8731-177.
33 MG to Walker, 3 Feb. 1997.

29. Live Bodies

1 *Printout*, 12, Autumn 1997, p.85.
2 V. Shakespear, 'Island of exiles', *Nelson Mail*, 18 March 1998, p.11.
3 *Live Bodies*, Auckland: Penguin, 1998, pp.93, 49, 65.
4 Ibid., pp.65–6, 87, 13.
5 Margareta Gee to Fiona Farrell and Doug Hood, 26 Sept. 1995, MS-Papers-8732-013, ATL. Among those projects were a script for a 'junior Mobil Masterpiece-type' programme for the Gibson Group in 1993, and an Antarctic thriller for which he wrote a story outline, also for the Gibson Group.
6 *Dominion*, 29 June 1995, p.6.
7 *Live Bodies*, pp.76, 145.
8 MG to Ian Gordon, 24 March 1999, 8732-015.
9 *Live Bodies*, p.50.
10 Ibid., pp.136, 14, 7, 17.
11 Ibid., pp.8, 186, 32, 62.
12 *New Zealand News UK*, 21 Oct. 1998, p.9; *Live Bodies*, p.78.
13 C. Brett, 'The Gee genius', *North and South*, Sept. 1995, p.99.
14 *Live Bodies*, pp.14, 129–30.
15 M. Kerrigan, 'The suburban sublime', *Times Literary Supplement*, 6 Nov. 1998, p.26.
16 MG to Geoff Walker, 19 May, 22 Sept. 1997, 8732-100.
17 Walker to Ray Richards, 27 March 1997, 8732-092; to MG, 9 Oct. 1997, 8732-100.
18 MG to Richards, 29 July 1998, 8732-094.
19 *New Zealand Listener*, 14 March 1998, p.46; *Dominion*, 7 March 1998, p.22.
20 *Landfall*, 196, Spring 1998, pp.312–15; *Live Bodies*, p.14.
21 Richards to MG, 18 March 1997, 8732-092.
22 Heidi Bowick to MG, 16 June 1998; MG to Bowick, 22 June, 8732-021.

23 Gregor Riethmaier to MG, 5 July 1998, 8732-021.
24 MG to Bowick, 22 June 1998.
25 Riethmaier, however, remained incensed enough to write a formal statement, stating that he believed the novel to be based on 'mischieves [sic] statements, deposited in the National archives/Wellgt., by certain members of the Soviet-oriented self-appointed INTERNATIONAL internees', which was to be deposited in the archives along with an extract from his own (unpublished) autobiography after his death. (Statement, 8 Aug. 1998, MS-Papers-8174, ATL.) Riethmaier died in 2004, having worked since the war as a photographer firstly with the National Publicity Studios and later establishing his own studio.)
26 Emma Platt to Ray Richards, 23 July 1997, 8732-092.
27 MG to Walker, 30 Oct. 1998, 8732-101.
28 MG to Richards, 29 Oct. 1998, 8732-094.
29 'Life on the edge', *Scotland on Sunday*, 18 Oct. 1998, p.31.
30 Ibid.
31 Richards to MG, 20 May 1997, 8732-092; Simon and Schuster to Richards, 23 June 1998, 8732-094.
32 MG to Killian Fitzpatrick, Black Ink, 31 Aug. 2002, 8732-118.
33 MG to Judith Hillmore, Faber press officer, 10 Nov. 1998, 8732-117; to Michael Estorick, 4 Dec. 2002, 8732-013.

30. Hostel Girl

1 Speech notes for Distinguished Alumni awards dinner, 21 Nov. 1998, MS-Papers-8732-141, ATL.
2 MG to Ray Richards, 26 Jan. 1996, 8732-091.
3 Going West festival programme; MG to Murray Gray, 9 Feb. 1998, 8732-182.
4 MG to Richards, 8 Jan. 1998, 8732-094.
5 *Orchard Street*, Auckland: Viking, 1998, p.9.
6 Ibid., pp.36, 95, 33–4, 106.
7 'Creeks and kitchens', Margaret Mahy lecture, 23 March 2002, in *The Inside Story*, Auckland: Children's Literature Foundation, 2003, p.23.
8 *Orchard Street*, pp.18–19, 107–9.
9 Ibid., p.61.
10 Ibid., pp.120°1.
11 MG to Bernice Beachman, Penguin, 20 Feb. 1998, 8732-101.
12 David Gale, Simon and Schuster to Richards, 11 May; Margaret Raymo, Houghton Mifflin to Richards, 10 Aug. 1998, 8732-094.
13 It was also the fantasy novels that found publication in translation. There have been Danish editions of *Under the Mountain* and the O trilogy, a Japanese *Halfmen of O*, and French translations of the *Salt* trilogy from a Canadian publisher.
14 The others were Jow Cowley (*The Silent One*), Tessa Duder (*Alex*), Andrew Crowe (*Which Native Tree?*), Stevan Eldred-Grigg (*Oracles and Miracles*), Allyson Gofton (*Food in a Minute*), Gwen Turner (*The New Zealand ABC*) and Patricia Grace (*Potiki*). Five of the eight books, including *Under the Mountain*, were children's or young adult books.
15 Richards to MG, 14 Jan. 1998, 8732-094.

16 *Norwester*, 10 Feb. 1999.
17 *Hostel Girl*, Auckland: Puffin, 1999, p.8.
18 Ibid., pp.6, 9, 31, 11, 50, 13, 51.
19 Ibid., pp.20, 27.
20 MG, interview with the author, 18 July 2006.
21 *Hostel Girl*, pp.35, 37, 40, 45, 50; *The Fat Man*, Auckland: Viking, 1994, p.40.
22 Ibid., p.127.
23 Richards to MG, 12 Oct. 1998, 8732-094.
24 MG to Dick Corballis, 16 Nov. 1998, 8732-008; D. Welch, 'Gee Gee: Maurice Gee's brilliant plagiarisms of Maurice Gee', *New Zealand Listener*, 12 May 2001, p.58.
25 *Ellie and the Shadow Man*, Auckland: Penguin, 2001, p.9.
26 J. McCrystal, 'Maurice major', *Evening Post*, 28 April 2001, p.27.
27 *Ellie*, p.12; Welch, 'Gee Gee', p.59.
28 *Ellie*, pp.28, 16, 51, 23.
29 Ibid., p.56; *Hostel Girl*, p.7.
30 MG to Louise Armstrong (editorial assistant), 10 Nov. 2000, 8732-103. The 296-page novel was *The Burning Boy*.
31 *Press* (Christchurch), 26 May 2001, Weekend, p.22.
32 Geoff Walker to MG, 12 Sept. 2000, 8732-103.
33 C.K. Stead, 'Maurice Gee, moralist', *Landfall*, 202, Nov. 2001, pp.100–1.
34 *Ellie*, pp.89, 106, 144.
35 Ibid., p.277; 'Shadow man: Canta talks to Maurice Gee', *Canta*, 11 July 2001, p.17. Rumours of sexual abuse of children at Gloriavale—as at Gethsemane—had led to Hopeful Christian serving a year in prison on charges of indecent assault in 1994.
36 MG to Richards, 24 March 1999, 8732-096.
37 *Ellie*, p.172.
38 McCrystal, 'Maurice major', p.29.
39 *Ellie*, pp.171, 175, 173, 188, 177.
40 Ibid., pp.181, 234.
41 MG interviewed in *Salient*, 9, 2001, p.24; *Ellie*, pp.269.
42 Ibid., pp.10, 9, 135; MG to Walker, 15 Feb. 2001, 8732-104.
43 *Ellie*, pp.121, 155.
44 *Live Bodies*, Auckland: Penguin, 1998, pp.8, 56; *Plumb*, London: Faber and Faber, 1978, p.13; T. Adair, 'Life on the edge', *Scotland on Sunday*, 18 Oct. 1998, p.31.
45 *Ellie*, p.259.
46 *Sunday Star Times*, 6 May 2001, p.F2; *Sunday Herald* (Glasgow), 17 Dec. 2002, p.10; *Scotland on Sunday*, 17 Feb. 2002, p.13.
47 Welch, 'Gee Gee', p.59; MG to Walker, 13 Aug. 1995, 8732-110.
48 MG to Euan Macleod, 4 July 1999, 8732-024.
49 'Waterfront', in R. Robinson (ed.), *Writing Wellington*, Wellington: Victoria University Press, 1999, pp.56–7; MG to Macleod, 4 July 1999.
50 Macleod to Maurice and Margareta, card, n.d. [1999], 8732-024.
51 Walker to Margareta Gee, email, 4 Oct. 2000; Walker to MG, 5 April, 31 May, 2 Nov. 2000, 8732-103; MG to Macleod, 20 Nov. 2000, 8732-024.
52 R. Williams, *Times Literary Supplement*, 15 March 2002, p.25; *Guardian*, 9

March 2002.

53 MG to Walker, 15 Feb. 2001.

54 *Evening Post*, 4 May 2001, p.5; C. Bourke, *North and South*, May 2001, p.104; L. Jones, *New Zealand Books*, Aug. 2001, p.6; I. Richards, *New Zealand Listener*, 19 May 2001, p.61.

55 Walker to MG and Richards, 20 April 2001, 8732-104; Walker to Jon Riley, Faber, 28 Oct. 1999, 8732-096.

56 Riley to Richards, 13 Dec. 2000, 8732-098.

57 Richards to MG, 9 March 2000, 8732-097; MG to Richards, 24 Oct. 2001, 8732-098; MG to Richards, 29 Oct. 1998, 8732-094.

58 Richards to MG, 9, 21 March 2000, 8732-097; MG to Jon Riley, Faber, 15 Feb. 2001, 8732-117.

59 MG to Richards, 24 Oct. 2001, 8732-098.

31. The Scornful Moon

1 As Nellie, an occasional private nickname.

2 MG to Chris Price, 23 July 2001, MS-Papers-8732-178, ATL.

3 MG to Price, 16 Aug. 1999, 23 July 2001.

4 G. McLauchlan (ed.), *Morrieson's Motel*, Auckland: Tandem Press, 2000, introduction and back cover blurb; McLauchlan, 'A very literary plot at Morrieson's Motel', *New Zealand Herald*, 28 Oct. 2000.

5 *Morrieson's Motel*, pp.181–2, 194.

6 D. Welch, 'Not a hot Friday', *New Zealand Books*, June 2001, p.12. In the competition, more people picked Gee correctly, McLauchlan told him, than any other. (No one got them all; the closest was eight out of the thirteen, and the prize given was a $100 voucher.)

7 Euan Macleod to MG, 12 June; MG to McLeod, 8 July 2002, 8732-024.

8 I. Sharp, 'Morality tales', *Sunday Star Times*, 12 Oct. 2003, p.31.

9 MG to Carl Freeman, 8 Aug. 2001, 8732-014.

10 R. Hyde, 'They want to write', *Journalese*, Auckland: National Printing Company, 1934, p.18.

11 C.K. Stead, 'Maurice Gee, moralist', *Landfall*, 202, Nov. 2001, pp.102, 104.

12 Sharp, 'Morality tales'; *Metro*, Oct. 2003, p.15.

13 *The Scornful Moon*, Auckland: Penguin, 2003, pp.47, 56.

14 Ibid., p.135.

15 Ibid., pp.9, 16. The raid on 48 Upland Road and trial were extensively covered in the *Dominion*, May–July 1918.

16 Ibid., p.19.

17 Ibid., p.10; D. Hill, *Dominion Post*, 4 Oct. 2003, p.E9; *The Scornful Moon*, p.112.

18 Ibid., pp.108, 122, 22, 20, 35.

19 Ibid., p.7.

20 Ibid., pp.98, 100, 8, 96–7, 104.

21 Ibid., p.8; J. Spurling, *Times Literary Supplement*, 13 Feb. 2004, p.22.

22 *The Scornful Moon*, pp.57, 26.

23 D. Larsen, 'Gee whiz: a master at work', *Weekend Herald*, 4–5 Oct. 2003, Canvas, p.28; Sharp, 'Morality tales'.

24 *The Scornful Moon*, p.34.
25 *The Scornful Moon*, pp.78, 212, 221.
26 M. White, 'Interview: Maurice Gee', *Metro*, Oct. 2003, p.105.
27 *Guardian*, 24 Jan. 2004; *North and South*, Oct. 2003, p.96.
28 8732-175.
29 Nigel Gee to MG, 25 June 2004, 8732-067.
30 MG to Emily Gee, Apr. 2004, 8732-060.
31 Of the others, *For Good* and *Kombi Nation* were released into cinemas in 2003; *Aidiko Insane*, a dystopian thriller, was finally completed in 2014.
32 'Writer delighted with Parr's adaptation of Crime Story', *Dominion Post*, 24 March 2004, p.5.
33 'Interview—Larry Parr: fractured crime story', *On Film*, Sept. 2004, p.14.
34 *Weekend Herald*, 4–5 Sept. 2004, Time Out, p.21; *New Zealand Listener*, 11 Sept. 2004, p.50.
35 M. Revington, 'Man found alive in Ngaio', *New Zealand Listener*, 20 April 2002, p.58.
36 B. McGann, 'From book to film', New Zealand International Film Festivals 2004 Souvenir Programme, p.59.
37 MG, interview with the author, 18 July 2006.
38 McGann, 'From book to film'.
39 MG to Richards, 21 May 2002, 8732-081; MG to Trevor Haysom, 25 May 2002.
40 MG to Richards, 23 Sept. 2003.
41 Richards to Larry Parr, 6 March 2002, 8732-080.
42 MG to Richards, 20 Feb. 1986, MS-Papers-4678-196, ATL.
43 The trilogy was subsequently, and remains, under option with another New Zealand director, Ellory Elkayem, whose previous work included comedy horror *Eight Legged Freaks* (2002) and two Romanian-made zombie films.
44 MG to Cielo Cerezo, 18 Feb. 2006.
45 MG to Richards, 12 Dec. 2003.
46 Chris Bailey to MG, 7 July 2007; MG to Richards, 7 July 2007.

32. Ghuznee Street

1 Notes for 'Around the world in one hour', Auckland Writers' Festival, 26 May 2001, MS-Papers-8732-141, ATL.
2 *New Zealand Listener*, 15 June 1996, p.47; C.K. Stead, 'Maurice Gee, moralist', *Landfall*, 202, Nov. 2001, p.101.
3 *Going West*, Auckland: Viking, 1992, p.110.
4 MG to Michael Estorick, 13 Feb. 2003, 8732-013.
5 Estorick to MG, 28 April 2003.
6 *Prowlers*, London: Faber and Faber, 1987, p.106.
7 *Blindsight*, Auckland: Penguin, 2005, p.21.
8 Ibid., p.82.
9 M. Hewitson, 'The man in the grey cardy', *Weekend Herald*, 29 July 2006, p.B5; S. Braunias, 'Our man in Loomis', *New Zealand Listener*, 24 July 2004, p.55.
10 *Blindsight*, pp.5, 6.

11 Ibid., pp.18, 6, 7, 17.
12 Ibid., pp.24, 48, 44, 51.
13 Ibid., pp.84, 188, 118, 87, 85, 71.
14 Ibid., pp.8, 160.
15 Ibid., pp.118–19, 190.
16 *New Zealand Herald*, 8 Oct. 2005, Canvas, p.41; *Blindsight*, pp.74, 170.
17 MG to Nigel Cook, 13 Dec. 2003, 8732-007; to Carl Freeman, 8 Aug. 2001, 8732-014.
18 MG to Freeman, 8 Aug. 2001, 12 Sept. 2000.
19 MG to Carl Freeman, 8 Aug. 2001.
20 *The Earl's Dilemma* (2008), *The Unmasking of a Lady* (2010) and *Beauty and the Scarred Hero* (2010), published by Harlequin, and *The Spinster's Secret* and *The Countess's Groom* as ebooks by Entangled Publishing in 2013.
21 MG to Estorick, 9 May 2006. Estorick had reviewed *Blindsight* in the British monthly the *Oldie*.
22 *Press*, 29 July 2006.
23 Judges' report, p.15, 8732-166; Hewitson, 'The man in the grey cardy'.
24 MG to Ray Richards, 31 July 2006.
25 Judges' report.
26 Geoff Walker to Richards and MG, 16 Nov. 2006.
27 *Dominion Post*, 7 Oct. 2004, p.A4.
28 MG to Cook, 3 Oct. 2005; to Martine Grelle, n.d., 8732-015.
29 MG to Freeman, 29 Sept. 2000.
30 K. McDermott, 'Writing is my life', *Auckland Star*, 3 June 1986, p.B3; D. Larsen, 'So much for retirement', *New Zealand Listener*, 24 May 2008, p.38.
31 MG to Richards, 28 June, 19 Sept., 22 May 2006.
32 *Salt*, Auckland: Puffin, 2007, pp.126, 167.
33 Ibid., p.114.
34 *Gool*, Auckland: Puffin, 2008, pp.23, 11, 25, 39, 38.
35 Ibid., p.37, 36; *Salt*, p.188.
36 MG to Richards, 14 May 2007; email to the author, 23 Oct. 2007.
37 *Gool*, pp.199, 180, 197.
38 Ibid., p.209.
39 *Gool*, p.122; *The Limping Man*, Auckland: Puffin, 2010, pp.17, 18, 14.
40 Ibid., pp.13, 79.
41 Ibid., p.110–1.
42 Ibid., p.31.
43 *Salt*, p.104; *The Limping Man*, p.120; *Gool*, p.85.

33. Newington Road

1 R. Robinson, 'Crimes, creeks, concealment', *New Zealand Books*, 88, Summer 2009, p.3.
2 *Access Road*, Auckland: Penguin, 2009, p.22.
3 Ibid., p.17.
4 Ibid., pp.56, 77, 10, 12.
5 Ibid., pp.40, 36, 37–8.
6 Robinson, 'Crimes, creeks and concealment'.

7 *Access Road*, pp.18, 24, 161, 192, 29, 95, 96.
8 Ibid., pp.42–7.
9 Ibid., pp.57–8, 171, 159.
10 MG, 'Blind Road', unpublished memoir, p.25. The boy was Ernie Lisk.
11 *Access Road*, p.128.
12 Robinson, 'The Gee-spot', *New Zealand Books*, 72, Summer 2005; Robinson, 'Crimes, creeks, concealment', p.5.
13 *Access Road*, p.204.
14 MG, 'A letter to my family', funeral eulogy, in the possession of MG; email to the author, 20 Aug. 2014.
15 G. Smithies, 'Maurice Gee, master storyteller', *Sunday Star Times*, 4 Oct. 2009, p.C3.

Bibliography

Unpublished sources

Research for this biography began with a series of recorded conversations with Maurice Gee in May–July 2006. The bulk of Gee's literary and personal papers are held in the Alexander Turnbull Library, National Library of New Zealand, Wellington, as MS-Group-0193, acquired by the library in two main accessions: in 1993 (MS-Papers-4678) and 2007 (MS-Papers-8732). Some archival material remains in Maurice and Margareta Gee's possession. Other manuscript sources consulted include the papers of Maurice Shadbolt, Kevin Ireland, Frank Sargeson, Robin Dudding, Margaret Scott and Janet Paul in the Alexander Turnbull Library; the Charles Brasch papers in the Hocken Collections, University of Otago Library, Dunedin; and the Gee files of Penguin Books in Auckland.

Works by Maurice Gee

Fiction

The Big Season, London: Hutchinson, 1962
A Special Flower, London: Hutchinson, 1965
In My Father's Den, London: Faber and Faber, 1972
A Glorious Morning, Comrade, Auckland: Auckland University Press; Wellington: Oxford University Press, 1975
Games of Choice, London: Faber and Faber, 1976
Plumb, London: Faber and Faber, 1978
Under the Mountain, Wellington: Oxford University Press, 1979
The World Around the Corner, Wellington: Oxford University Press, 1980
Meg, London; Auckland: Faber and Faber in association with Penguin, 1981
The Halfmen of O, Auckland: Oxford University Press, 1982
Sole Survivor, London; Auckland: Faber and Faber in association with Penguin, 1983
The Priests of Ferris, Auckland: Oxford University Press, 1984
Motherstone, Auckland: Oxford University Press, 1985
The Fire-Raiser, Auckland: Puffin in association with Oxford University Press, 1986
Collected Stories, Auckland: Penguin, 1986
Prowlers, London: Faber and Faber; Auckland: Penguin, 1987
The Champion, Auckland: Puffin, 1989

The Burning Boy, London: Faber and Faber; Auckland: Viking, 1990
Going West, London: Faber and Faber; Auckland: Viking, 1992
Crime Story, Auckland: Penguin, 1994; London: Faber and Faber, 1995
The Fat Man, Auckland: Viking, 1994
Loving Ways, Auckland: Penguin, 1996; London: Faber and Faber, 1997
Live Bodies, Auckland: Penguin; London: Faber and Faber, 1998
Orchard Street, Auckland: Viking, 1998
Hostel Girl, Auckland: Puffin, 1999
Ellie and the Shadow Man, Auckland: Penguin 2001; London: Faber and Faber, 2002
The Scornful Moon: a moralist's tale, Auckland: Penguin; London: Faber and Faber, 2003
Blindsight, Auckland: Penguin; London: Faber and Faber, 2005
Salt, Auckland: Puffin, 2007
Gool, Auckland: Puffin, 2008
Access Road, Auckland: Penguin, 2009
The Limping Man, Auckland: Puffin, 2010

Uncollected stories

'In at the Death', *Kiwi*, 1955
'Evening at Home', *Arena*, 45, March 1956
'The Quarry', *Arena*, 46, March 1957
'A Girl in Blue', *Mate*, 2, November 1958
'While the Flag was Up', *Arena*, 50, Summer 1958–59
'Facade', *Mate*, 4, February 1960
'Waterfront', in R. Robinson (ed.), *Writing Wellington: twenty years of Victoria University writing fellows*, Wellington: Victoria University Press, 1999
'Tact', in Gordon McLauchlan (ed.), *Morrieson's Motel*, Auckland: Tandem Press, 2000

Non-fiction

'A new home for the Napier Public Library', *New Zealand Libraries*, 35 (1), February 1972
Nelson Central School: a history, Nelson: Nelson Central School Centennial Committee, 1978
'On book prizes and writing grants', *On Arts*, 11, November 1998

Memoir

'The Burns Fellowship', *Landfall*, 87, September 1968
'Early reading: Maurice Gee on *Zane Grey*', *Education*, 24 (8), 1975
'Beginnings', *Islands*, 17, March 1977
'Creek and kitchen', in Michael Gifkins (ed.), *Through the Looking Glass: recollections of childhood from 20 prominent New Zealanders*, Auckland: Century Hutchinson, 1988
'The way of a writer', *New Zealand Listener*, 17 January 1987

'Creeks and kitchens', Margaret Mahy lecture, 23 March 2002, in *The Inside Story*, Auckland: Children's Literature Foundation, 2003
'Double Unit: the lives of Lyndahl and Len Gee', 2011, unpublished
'Blind Road', 2012, unpublished

Other published sources: select bibliography

Adair, Tom, 'Life on the edge', *Scotland on Sunday*, 18 October 1998
Alley, Elizabeth and Mark Williams (eds), *In the Same Room: conversations with New Zealand Writers*, Auckland: Auckland University Press, 1992
Amery, Mark, 'Territorial imperative', *Quote Unquote*, June 1996
Barrowman, Rachel, *Mason: the life of R.A.K. Mason*, Wellington: Victoria University Press, 2003
Barrowman, Rachel, *The Turnbull: a library and its world*, Auckland: Auckland University Press, 1995
Berry, Stephen and Margareta Gee, 'Garden, Oscar', from *The Dictionary of New Zealand Biography, Te Ara—the Encyclopedia of New Zealand*, http//www.TeAra.govt.nz/en/biographies
Boyd, Brian, 'Maurice Gee: ironies of growth and judgement, part I: the early fiction', *Islands*, 30, October 1980, p.268; 'Part II: structure and irony in "Plumb"', *Islands*, 31–32, June 1981
Boyd, Brian, 'Maurice Gee, interviewed by Brian Boyd', in Elizabeth Alley and Mark Williams (eds), *In the Same Room: conversations with New Zealand Writers*, Auckland: Auckland University Press, 1992
Braunias, Steve, 'Our man in Loomis', *New Zealand Listener*, 24 July 2004
Brett, Cate, 'The Gee genius', *North and South*, September 1995
Chapple, Geoff, 'Chapple, James Henry Gough', from *The Dictionary of New Zealand Biography, Te Ara—the Encyclopedia of New Zealand*, http//www.TeAra.govt.nz/en/biographies
Clark, Louise, 'Writing vertically and horizontally: the relationship between Maurice Gee's fiction for children and for adults', MPhil thesis, University of Waikato, 2004
Coughlan, Kate, 'A reluctant successor to Sargeson', *New Zealand Times*, 18 September 1983, p.9
Cox, Nigel, 'Rule of Plumb', *Quote Unquote*, July 1993
Cross, Ian, *Such Absolute Beginners: a memoir*, Auckland: David Ling, 2007
Diamond, John T., *Once . . . the Wilderness*, 2nd edn, New Lynn: V.H. Wilkinson, 1966
Duckworth, Marilyn, *A Barbarous Tongue*, London: Hutchinson, 1963
Duckworth, Marilyn, *Camping on the Faultline: a memoir*, Auckland: Vintage, 2000
Dunleavy, Trisha, *Ourselves in Primetime: a history of New Zealand television drama*, Auckland: Auckland University Press, 2005
Edmond, Lauris, 'Definitions of New Zealanders: the stories of Maurice Shadbolt and Maurice Gee', in Cherry Hankin (ed.), *Critical Essays on the New Zealand Short Story*, Auckland: Heinemann, 1982
Ewan, John, 'Moved to write', *New Zealand Bookworld*, 40, October 1977

Flude, Anthony, *Henderson's Mill: a history of Henderson, 1849–1939*, Auckland: Henderson Borough Council, 1977
Friedlander, Marti (with Hugo Manson), *Self-Portrait*, Auckland: Auckland University Press, 2013
Gee, Margareta, 'Exile: the glittering prize', *New Zealand Author*, 171, February 1993
Gee, Margaretha, 'On the rocky road to success', *Nelson Evening Mail*, 7 February 1980
Geraets, John, '"Landfall" under Brasch: the humanizing journey', PhD thesis, University of Auckland, 1982
Gifkins, Michael (ed.), *Through the Looking Glass: recollections of childhood from 20 prominent New Zealanders*, Auckland: Century Hutchison, 1988
Guerin, Louise, 'A balance of good and bad', *New Zealand Listener*, 13 October 1984
Hale, Elizabeth, 'Underworlds down under: Under the Mountain and The Navigator', in Misha Kavka, Jennifer Lawn and Mary Paul (eds), *Gothic NZ: the darker side of Kiwi culture*, Dunedin: Otago University Press, 2006
Harold, Denis and Pamela Gordon (eds), *Janet Frame: in her own words*, Auckland: Penguin, 2011
Hayes, Alfred, *In Love*, London: Victor Gollancz, 1954
Hewitson, Michele, 'The man in the grey cardy', *Weekend Herald*, 29 July 2006
Hill, David, *Introducing Maurice Gee*, Auckland: Longman Paul, 1981
Holloway, Judith, 'A fat boy, a creek and personal responsibility', *New Zealand Books*, August 1995
Hood, Lynley, *Sylvia! The biography of Sylvia Ashton-Warner*, Auckland: Viking, 1988
Hubbard, Anthony, 'Obsession of a quiet man', *Dominion Sunday Times*, 15 October 1987
Ireland, Kevin, *Backwards to Forwards: a memoir*, Auckland: Vintage, 2002
Ireland, Kevin, *Under the Bridge and Over the Moon: a memoir*, Auckland: Vintage, 1998
Jackson, Anna, Geoffrey Miles, Harry Ricketts, Tatjana Schaefer and Kathryn Walls, *A Made-up Place: New Zealand young adult fiction*, Wellington: Victoria University Press, 2011
Johnston, Andrew, 'Maurice Gee: our superb storyteller', *Evening Post*, 3 July 1993
Jones, Lawrence, 'Maurice Gee: three views of the changing scene—the Plumb trilogy', in *Barbed Wire and Mirrors: essays on New Zealand prose*, Dunedin: Otago University Press, 1987
Jones, Lawrence, (ed.), *Nurse to the Imagination: 50 years of the Robert Burns Fellowship*, Dunedin: Otago University Press, 2008
Kidman, Fiona, *At the End of Darwin Road: a memoir*, Auckland: Vintage, 2008
King, Michael, *Frank Sargeson: a life*, Auckland: Viking, 1995
King, Michael, *Wrestling with the Angel: a life of Janet Frame*, Auckland: Viking, 2000
Larsen, David, 'So much for retirement', *New Zealand Listener*, 24 May 2008
Mallinson, Ann, *Recollections of 5 Festivals*, Wellington: Daphne Brasell Associates and Lincoln University Press, 1996

Manhire, Bill, *Maurice Gee*, Auckland: Oxford University Press, 1986
'Maurice Gee: our unsung crusader', *Growth*, 1976
McCrystal, John, 'Maurice Major', *Evening Post*, 28 April 2001
McEldowney, Dennis, *Full of the Warm South*, Dunedin: John McIndoe, 1983
McEldowney, Dennis, 'Maurice Gee's "Plumb"', University of Waikato winter lecture, 1981
McEldowney, Dennis, *Then and There: a 1970s diary*, Auckland: Auckland University Press, 1995
McLauchlan, Gordon, 'Perspiration wins rewards', *New Zealand Herald*, 8 September 1979
McKay, Frank, *The Life of James K. Baxter*, Auckland: Oxford University Press, 1990
Meikle, Phoebe, *Accidental Life*, Auckland: Auckland University Press, 1994
Millar, Paul, *No Fretful Sleeper: a life of Bill Pearson*, Auckland: Auckland University Press, 2010
Millen, Julia, *Ronald Hugh Morrieson*, Auckland: David Ling, 1996
Nieuwenhuizen, Audrey, 'Maurice Gee: creek, kitchen and the art of language', *Magpies New Zealand*, 1, March 1997
Noonan, Michael, 'N.Z. his subject', *Critic*, 4 March 1964
O'Brien, Gregory, *Euan Macleod: the painter in the painting*, Dawes Point: Piper Press, 2010
O'Brien, Gregory and Robert Cross, *Moments of Invention: portraits of 21 New Zealand writers*, Auckland: Heinemann Reed, 1988
Oliver, W.H., *James K. Baxter: a portrait*, Wellington: Port Nicholson Press, 1983
Reilly, Colleen, 'An interview with Maurice Gee', *Sport*, 5, Spring 1990
Richards, Ian, *To Bed at Noon: the life and art of Maurice Duggan*, Auckland: Auckland University Press, 1997
Robinson, Roger (ed.), *Writing Wellington: twenty years of Victoria University writing fellows*, Wellington: Victoria University Press, 1999
Sargeson, Frank, *Speaking for Ourselves*, Christchurch: Caxton Press, 1945
Scott, Dick, *Fire on the Clay: the Pakeha comes to West Auckland*, Auckland: Southern Cross Books, 1979
Shadbolt, Maurice, *Among the Cinders*, Christchurch: Whitcombe and Tombs, 1965
Shadbolt, Maurice, *From the Edge of the Sky*, Auckland: David Ling, 1999
Shadbolt, Maurice, *One of Ben's*, Auckland: David Ling, 1993 (revised edn, 1994)
Shaw, Alistair, 'Gee whiz: Maurice Gee speaks', *Salient*, 2001, issue 9
Sinclair, Keith (with Trudie McNaughton), *A History of the University of Auckland, 1883–1983*, Auckland: Oxford University Press, 1983
Smithies, Grant, 'Maurice Gee, master storyteller', *Sunday Star Times*, 4 Oct. 2009
Stead, C.K., *Book Self: the reader as writer and the writer as critic*, Auckland: Auckland University Press, 2008
Stead, C.K., 'Maurice Gee, moralist', *Landfall*, 202, November 2001
Stead, C.K., *South-west of Eden: a memoir 1932–1956*, Auckland: Auckland University Press, 2010
Stead, C.K., *The Secret History of Modernism*, London: Harvill, 2001
Stead, C.K., *The Writer at Work: essays*, Dunedin: Otago University Press, 2000

Stuart, Sarah, 'Gentle Gee has a grip on all ages', *Sunday Star Times*, 23 April 1995

Tautsky, Thomas E., '"I let the story make its own demands": an interview with Maurice Gee', *Australian and New Zealand Studies in Canada*, 12, December 1994

van Rij, Vivian, 'A (not so) straight steal: Maurice Gee's use and adaptation of Nelson historical material in *The Fire-Raiser*', unpublished essay

van Rij, Vivian, '"A straight steal": "An Affair of the Heart" and Maurice Gee's *The Fat Man*', *Kotare*, 6, 2006

van Rij, Vivian, 'The pursuit of wholeness in Maurice Gee's fiction for children', PhD thesis, Victoria University of Wellington, 2008

Walls, Kathryn, '"My mother was a writer"', *New Zealand Books*, 76, Summer 2006

Walls, Kathryn, '"What I must steer clear of': the influence of his mother's stories on Maurice Gee', in Elizabeth Hale (ed.), *Maurice Gee: a literary companion: the fiction for young readers*, Dunedin: Otago University Press, 2014

Watson, Aaron, 'The spirit of 1935', *Capital Times*, 15 October 2003

Watson, Jean, *Stand in the Rain*, Christchurch: Pegasus Press, 1965

Wedde, Ian, 'The Splinterview 6: Maurice Gee . . .', *Spleen*, 6, December 1976

Welch, Denis, 'Gee Gee: Maurice Gee's brilliant plagiarisms of Maurice Gee', *New Zealand Listener*, 12 May 2001

Westaway, Jane, 'Maurice Gee: answers from under the house', *New Zealand Woman's Weekly*, 22 September 1986

Westaway, Jane, 'Looking out of another window', *Booknotes*, 110, July 1995

Williams, Mark, *Leaving the Highway: six contemporary New Zealand novelists*, Auckland: Auckland University Press, 1990

Wilson, Angus, *The Wild Garden*, London: Secker and Warburg, 1963

Young, David, 'Maurice Gee: "non-aligned" novelist', *New Zealand Listener*, 10 February 1979

Acknowledgements

My first and biggest debt of thanks is, of course, to Maurice Gee, for allowing me to write his biography, and for his openness, honesty and generosity (and patience). Maurice placed no conditions around the writing of this biography, and any revisions I made at his request or suggestion after he read it have been minor. I owe a special thanks too to Margareta Gee, and to other members of the Gee family for accepting this intrusion into their lives.

I am hugely indebted to my brother and publisher, Fergus Barrowman, who, along with Nigel Cook, played an instrumental role in this project getting underway, and whose encouragement and support throughout have been vital; also for his deft editing and elegant book design.

Thank you to all those who spoke to or corresponded with me about Gee, provided material, or in other ways assisted with my research: Judith Binney; Chris Bourke; Elizabeth Caffin; the late Christine Cole Catley; Hera Cook; Nigel Cook; Ian Cross; Adam Dudding; Marilyn Duckworth; Carl Freeman; Marti Friedlander; Sarah Gaitanos; the late Aynsley Gee; Gary and Ngaire Gee; Nigel Gee; Ben Goffman; the late Gordon Greenough; Julie Grenfell (formerly Cook); Ray Grover; David Hill; Richard Hudson; Kevin Ireland; Bill Manhire; Michael Noonan; Ross O'Rourke; Kelly Plummer; the late Ray Richards; Angela Sears; Bruce and Mary Seaton; Gill Shadbolt; C.K. Stead; Vivian van Rij; Sandra Vercoe; Geoff Walker; Kathryn Walls; Barry Waterhouse; Nelson Wattie.

For permission to access and quote from archived correspondence I thank: Graeme Lay for the Frank Sargeson Trust; the Hocken Collections, University of Otago Library, Alan Roddick and the estate of Charles Brasch; Sean Shadbolt and Brigid Magner; Adam Dudding; Barbara Richards; Geoff Walker; Kevin Ireland; Rachel Scott; Elizabeth Caffin; Brian Boyd; Charlotte Paul; Tom Finlayson; Graeme Beattie; C.K. Stead; Jenny Cole and Martin Cole; Delia Davin; Andrew Campbell; Ginette McDonald; Anne French; Helen Sutch; Euan Macleod; Anne Hall; Ingrid Shouler; Janet Wilson.

This book was written with the support of the Michael King Fellowship from Creative New Zealand, and a two-month residency at the Michael King Writers' Centre in Devonport, Auckland, for both of which I am immensely grateful. Thanks also to the Stout Research Centre for New Zealand Studies at Victoria University of Wellington for providing me with a quiet and supportive place to work for the duration of the project, and to director Lydia Wevers and Richard Hill especially.

Thanks to Bill Manhire and Damien Wilkins who read and commented on the manuscript; Ashleigh Young and Kirsten McDougall at Victoria University Press; and to Tordis Flath for the excellent index.

Finally, heartfelt thanks to my family for their love and support through difficult times.

Index

References in *italics* refer to book titles unless otherwise indicated.
I1 denotes photographs in the first insert after page 184
I2 denotes photographs in the second insert after page 368